7 SAINT☆YOUNG MEN

C O N T E N T S

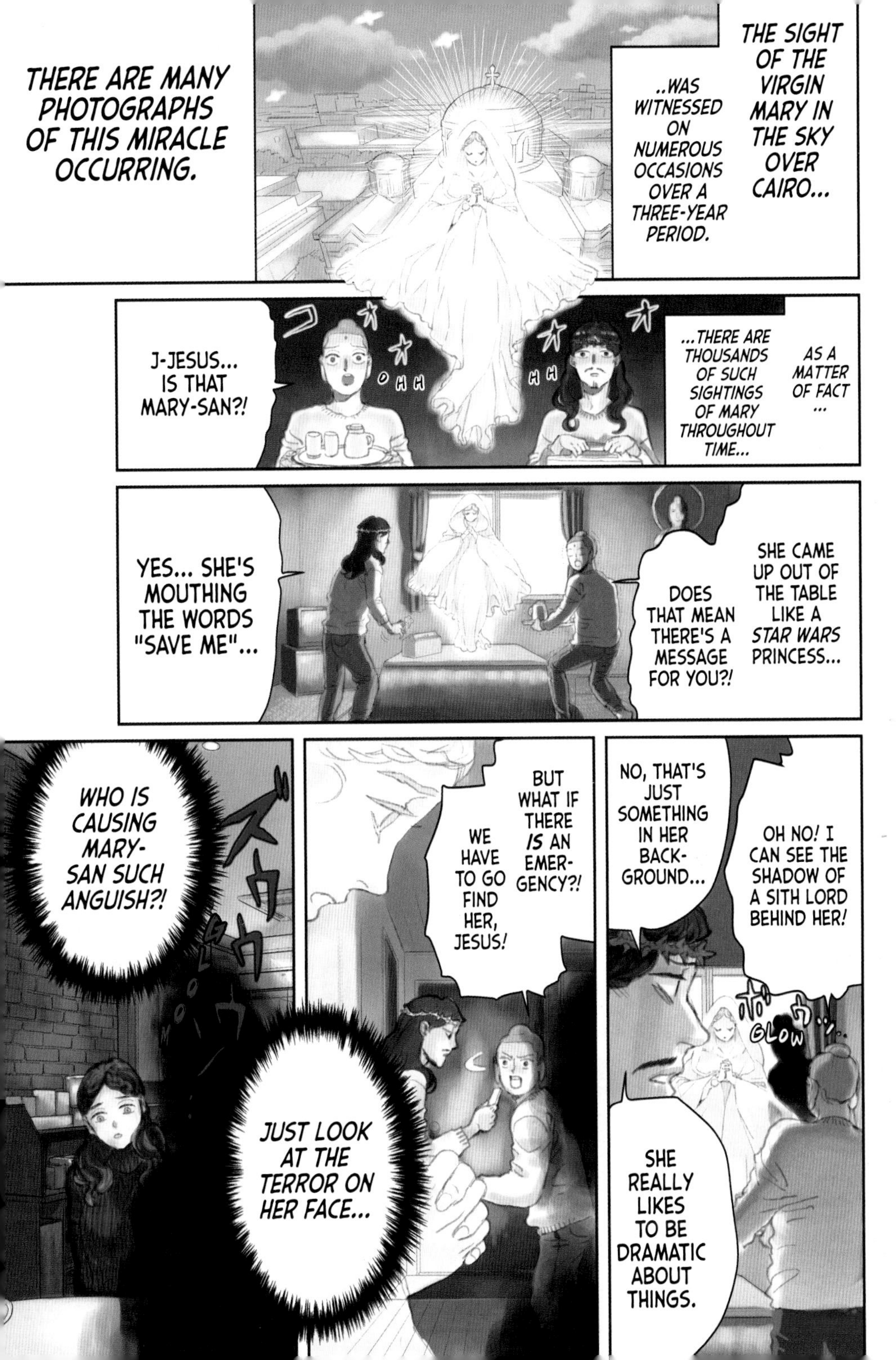
THE SIGHT OF THE VIRGIN MARY IN THE SKY OVER CAIRO...
..WAS WITNESSED ON NUMEROUS OCCASIONS OVER A THREE-YEAR PERIOD.
THERE ARE MANY PHOTOGRAPHS OF THIS MIRACLE OCCURRING.
AS A MATTER OF FACT ...
...THERE ARE THOUSANDS OF SUCH SIGHTINGS OF MARY THROUGHOUT TIME...
HH
OHH
J-JESUS... IS THAT MARY-SAN?!
SHE CAME UP OUT OF THE TABLE LIKE A *STAR WARS* PRINCESS...
DOES THAT MEAN THERE'S A MESSAGE FOR YOU?!
YES... SHE'S MOUTHING THE WORDS "SAVE ME"...
OH NO! I CAN SEE THE SHADOW OF A SITH LORD BEHIND HER!
NO, THAT'S JUST SOMETHING IN HER BACKGROUND...
GLOW
SHE REALLY LIKES TO BE DRAMATIC ABOUT THINGS.
BUT WHAT IF THERE *IS* AN EMERGENCY?!
WE HAVE TO GO FIND HER, JESUS!
JUST LOOK AT THE TERROR ON HER FACE...
WHO IS CAUSING MARY-SAN SUCH ANGUISH?!

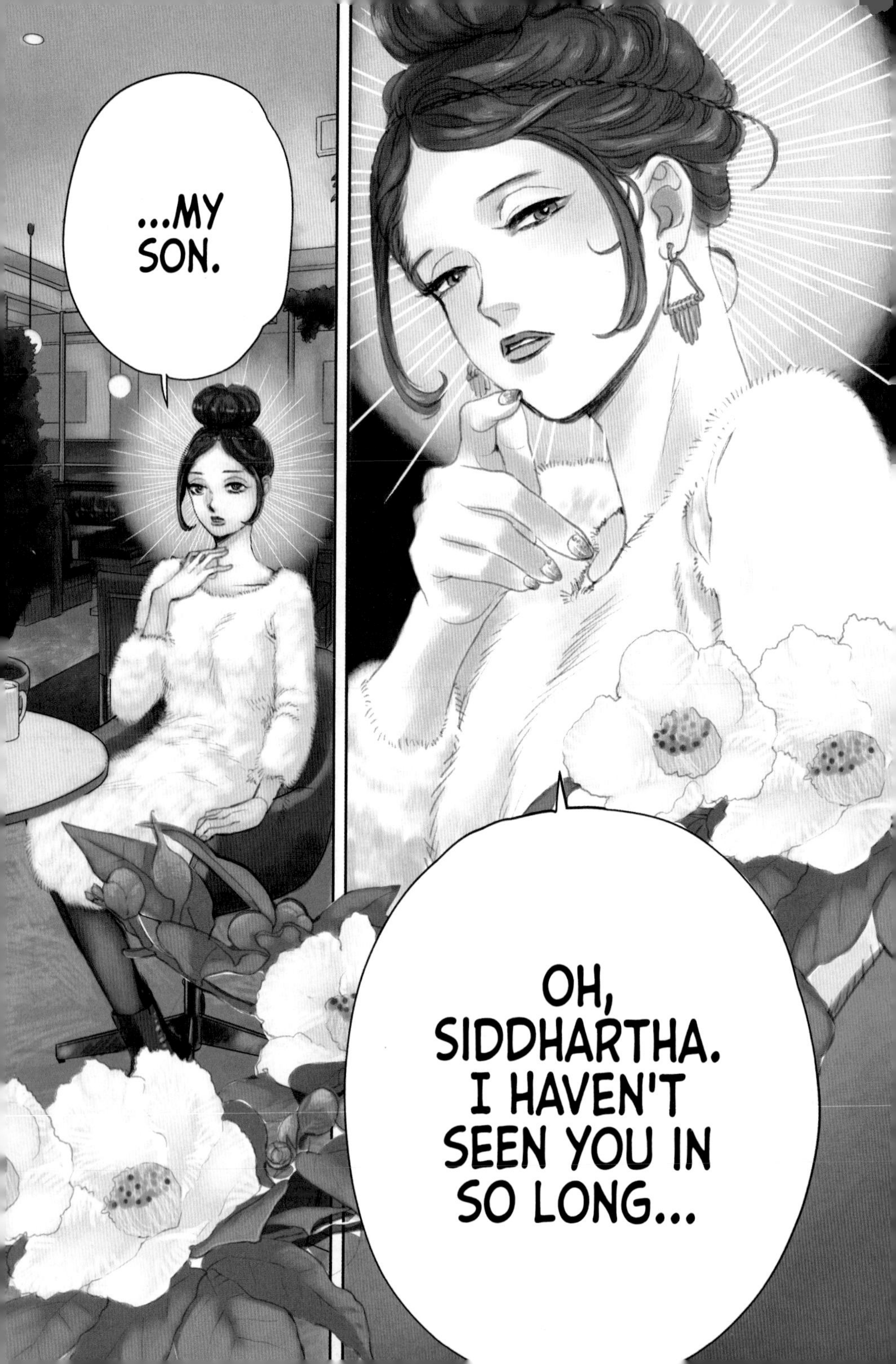
OH, SIDDHARTHA. I HAVEN'T SEEN YOU IN SO LONG...
...MY SON.

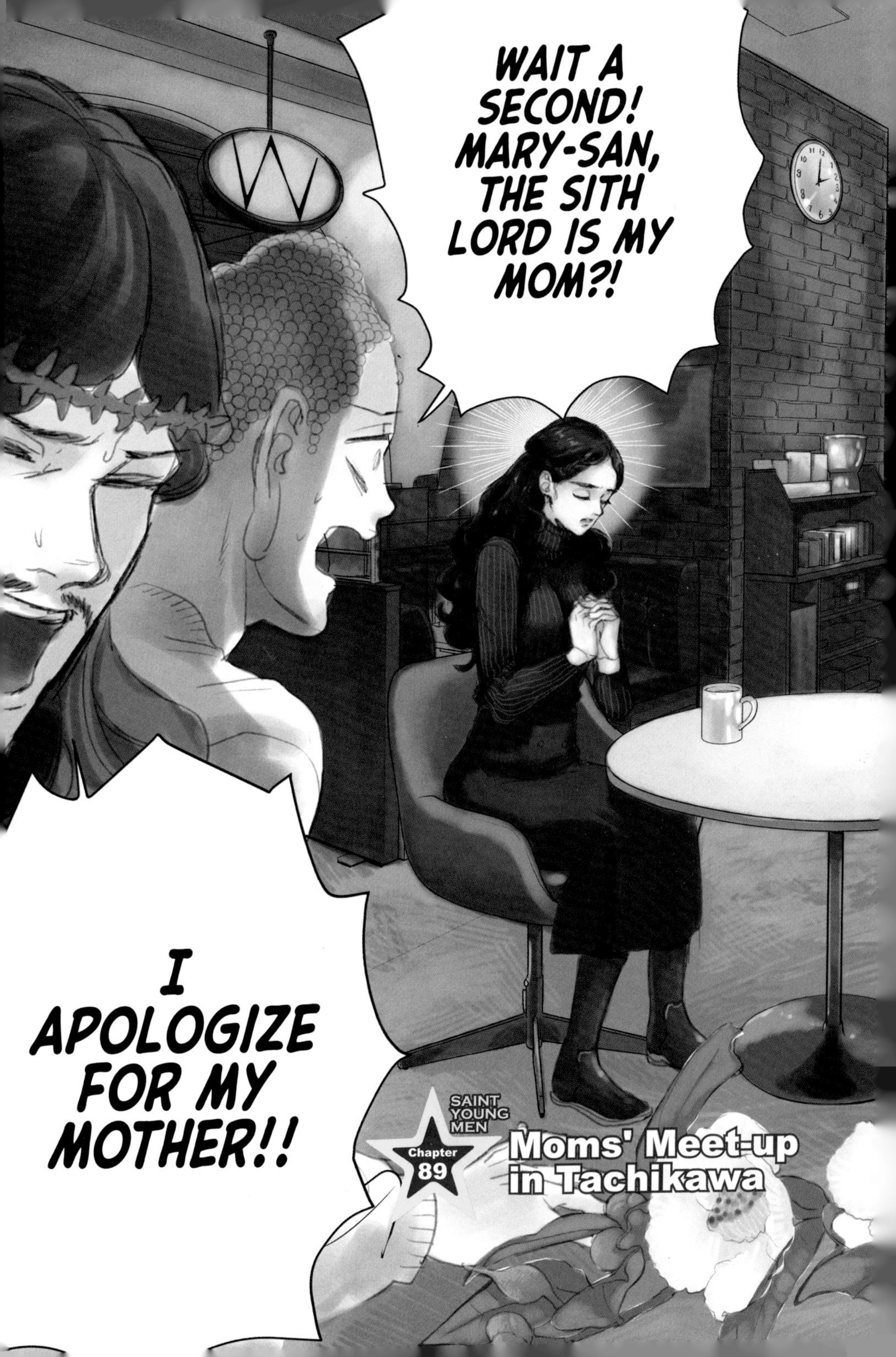
WAIT A SECOND! MARY-SAN, THE SITH LORD IS MY MOM?!
I APOLOGIZE FOR MY MOTHER!!
SAINT YOUNG MEN
Chapter 89
Moms' Meet-up in Tachikawa

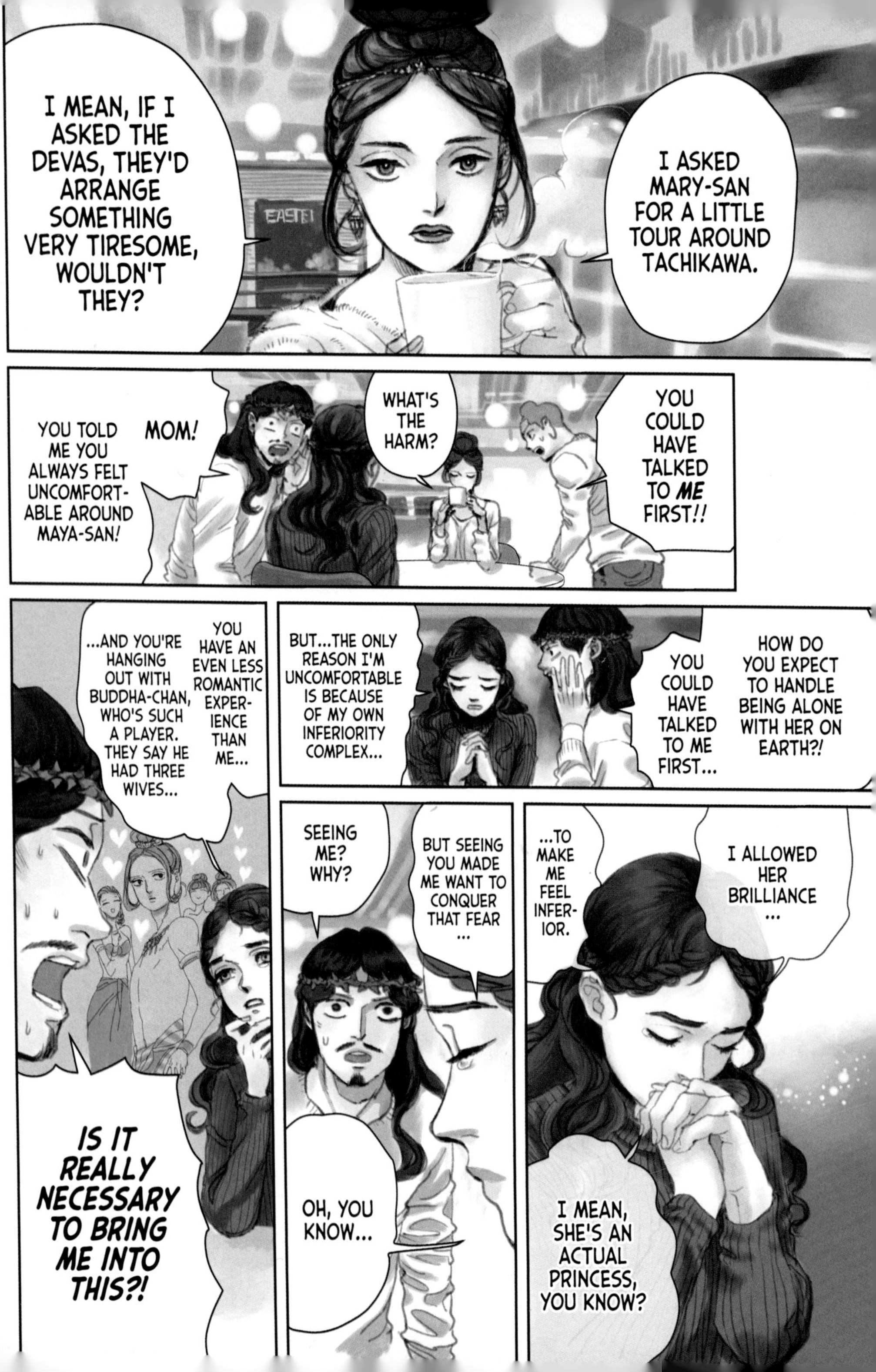
I ASKED MARY-SAN FOR A LITTLE TOUR AROUND TACHIKAWA.
I MEAN, IF I ASKED THE DEVAS, THEY'D ARRANGE SOMETHING VERY TIRESOME, WOULDN'T THEY?
YOU COULD HAVE TALKED TO *ME* FIRST!!
WHAT'S THE HARM?
MOM!
YOU TOLD ME YOU ALWAYS FELT UNCOMFORT-ABLE AROUND MAYA-SAN!
HOW DO YOU EXPECT TO HANDLE BEING ALONE WITH HER ON EARTH?!
YOU COULD HAVE TALKED TO ME FIRST...
BUT...THE ONLY REASON I'M UNCOMFORTABLE IS BECAUSE OF MY OWN INFERIORITY COMPLEX...
I ALLOWED HER BRILLIANCE ...
...TO MAKE ME FEEL INFER-IOR.
I MEAN, SHE'S AN ACTUAL PRINCESS, YOU KNOW?
BUT SEEING YOU MADE ME WANT TO CONQUER THAT FEAR ...
SEEING ME? WHY?
OH, YOU KNOW...
YOU HAVE AN EVEN LESS ROMANTIC EXPER-IENCE THAN ME...
...AND YOU'RE HANGING OUT WITH BUDDHA-CHAN, WHO'S SUCH A PLAYER. THEY SAY HE HAD THREE WIVES...
IS IT REALLY NECESSARY TO BRING ME INTO THIS?!

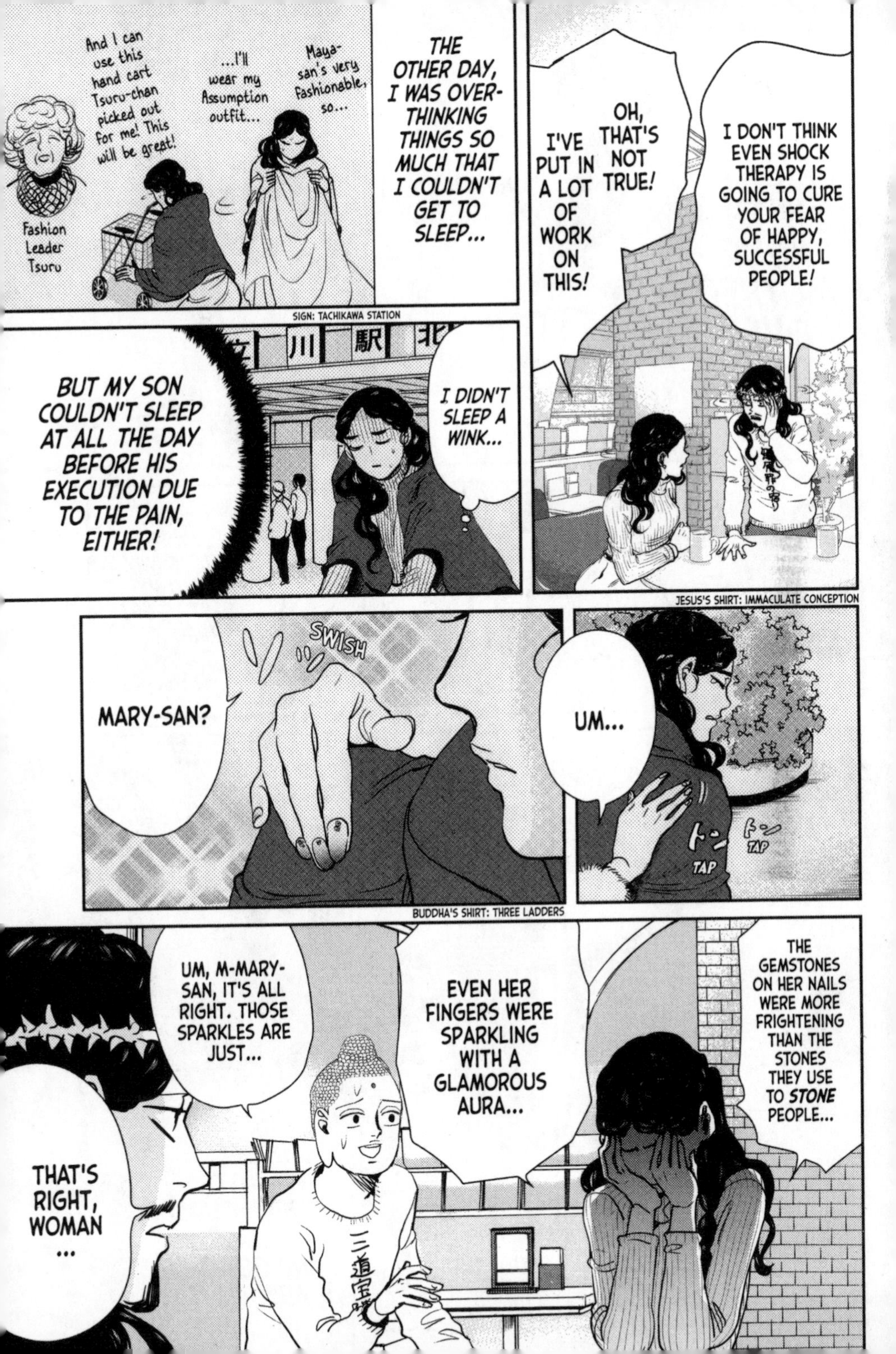
I DON'T THINK EVEN SHOCK THERAPY IS GOING TO CURE YOUR FEAR OF HAPPY, SUCCESSFUL PEOPLE!
OH, THAT'S NOT TRUE!
I'VE PUT IN A LOT OF WORK ON THIS!
JESUS'S SHIRT: IMMACULATE CONCEPTION
THE OTHER DAY, I WAS OVER-THINKING THINGS SO MUCH THAT I COULDN'T GET TO SLEEP...
Maya-san's very Fashionable, so...
...I'll wear my Assumption outfit...
And I can use this hand cart Tsuru-chan picked out for me! This will be great!
Fashion Leader Tsuru
SIGN: TACHIKAWA STATION
I DIDN'T SLEEP A WINK...
BUT MY SON COULDN'T SLEEP AT ALL THE DAY BEFORE HIS EXECUTION DUE TO THE PAIN, EITHER!
UM...
TAP
TAP
SWISH
MARY-SAN?
BUDDHA'S SHIRT: THREE LADDERS
THE GEMSTONES ON HER NAILS WERE MORE FRIGHTENING THAN THE STONES THEY USE TO *STONE* PEOPLE...
EVEN HER FINGERS WERE SPARKLING WITH A GLAMOROUS AURA...
UM, M-MARY-SAN, IT'S ALL RIGHT. THOSE SPARKLES ARE JUST...
THAT'S RIGHT, WOMAN ...

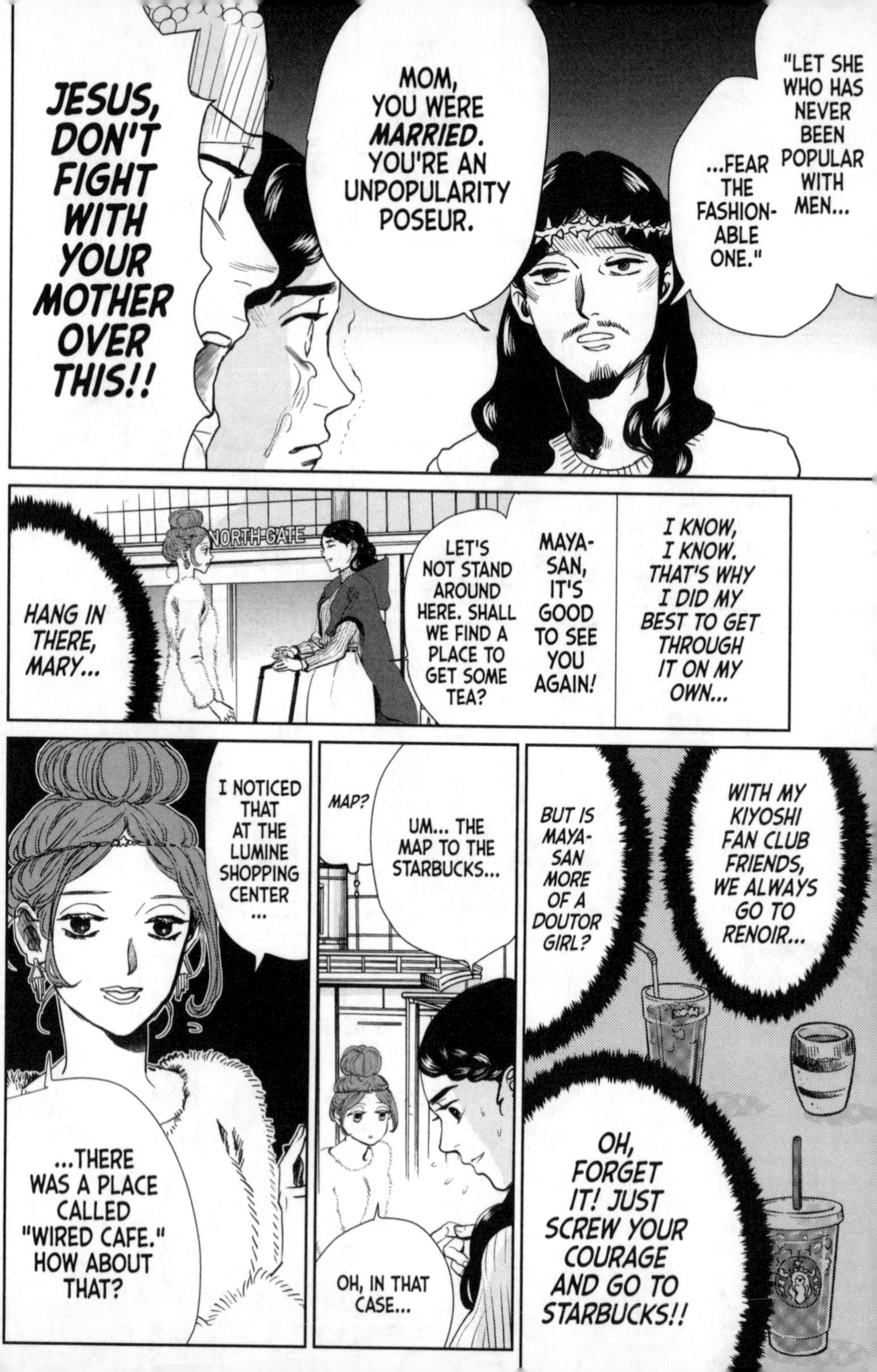
"LET SHE WHO HAS NEVER BEEN POPULAR WITH MEN...
...FEAR THE FASHION-ABLE ONE."
MOM, YOU WERE *MARRIED*. YOU'RE AN UNPOPULARITY POSEUR.
JESUS, DON'T FIGHT WITH YOUR MOTHER OVER THIS!!
I KNOW, I KNOW. THAT'S WHY I DID MY BEST TO GET THROUGH IT ON MY OWN...
NORTH-GATE
MAYA-SAN, IT'S GOOD TO SEE YOU AGAIN!
LET'S NOT STAND AROUND HERE. SHALL WE FIND A PLACE TO GET SOME TEA?
HANG IN THERE, MARY...
WITH MY KIYOSHI FAN CLUB FRIENDS, WE ALWAYS GO TO RENOIR...
BUT IS MAYA-SAN MORE OF A DOUTOR GIRL?
OH, FORGET IT! JUST SCREW YOUR COURAGE AND GO TO STARBUCKS!!
UM... THE MAP TO THE STARBUCKS...
MAP?
OH, IN THAT CASE...
I NOTICED THAT AT THE LUMINE SHOPPING CENTER...
...THERE WAS A PLACE CALLED "WIRED CAFE." HOW ABOUT THAT?

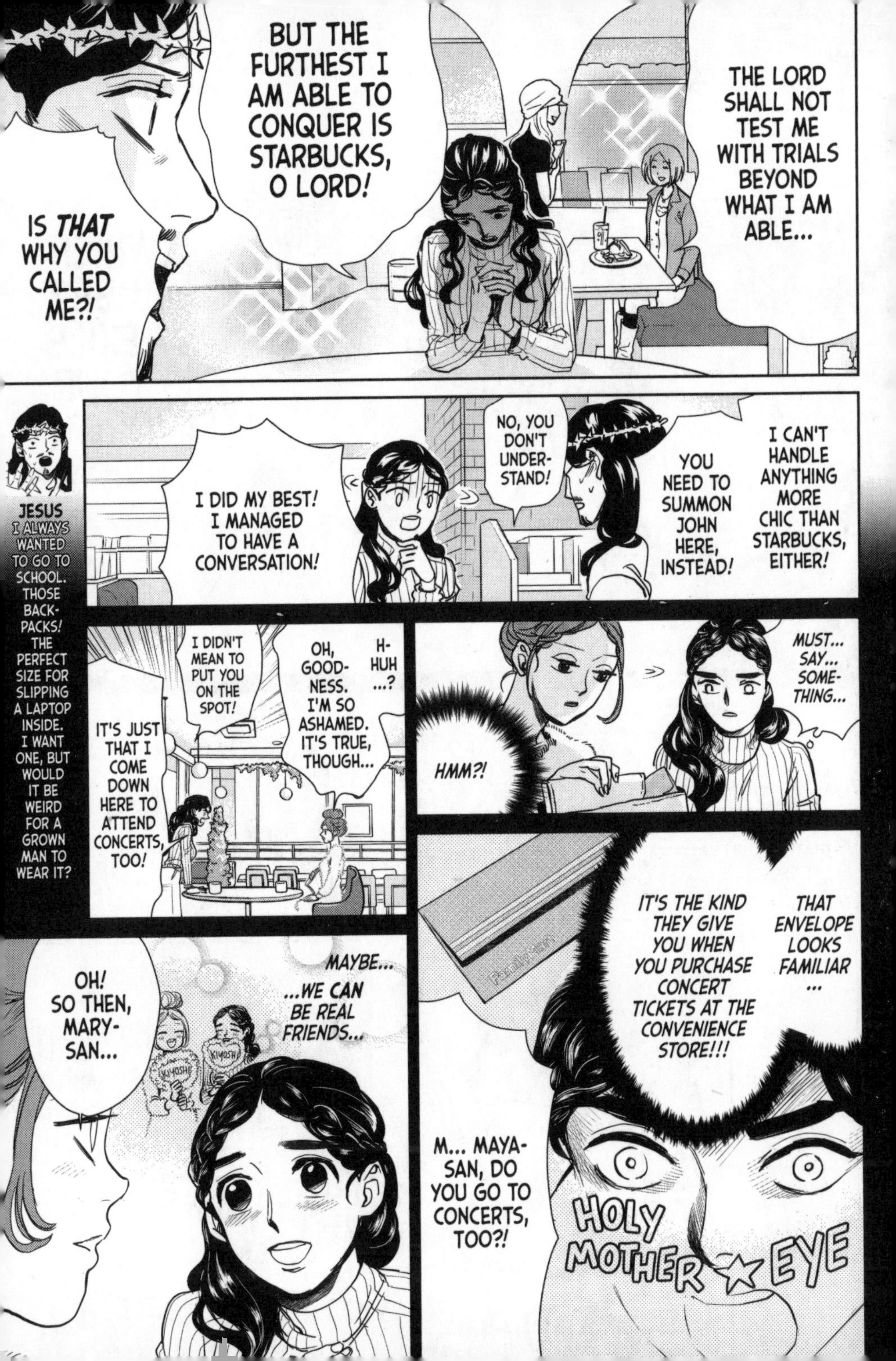

THE LORD SHALL NOT TEST ME WITH TRIALS BEYOND WHAT I AM ABLE...
BUT THE FURTHEST I AM ABLE TO CONQUER IS STARBUCKS, O LORD!
IS *THAT* WHY YOU CALLED ME?!
I CAN'T HANDLE ANYTHING MORE CHIC THAN STARBUCKS, EITHER!
YOU NEED TO SUMMON JOHN HERE, INSTEAD!
NO, YOU DON'T UNDER-STAND!
I DID MY BEST! I MANAGED TO HAVE A CONVERSATION!
MUST... SAY... SOME-THING...
HMM?!
H-HUH...?
OH, GOOD-NESS. I'M SO ASHAMED. IT'S TRUE, THOUGH...
I DIDN'T MEAN TO PUT YOU ON THE SPOT!
IT'S JUST THAT I COME DOWN HERE TO ATTEND CONCERTS, TOO!
THAT ENVELOPE LOOKS FAMILIAR...
IT'S THE KIND THEY GIVE YOU WHEN YOU PURCHASE CONCERT TICKETS AT THE CONVENIENCE STORE!!!
HOLY MOTHER ☆ EYE
M... MAYA-SAN, DO YOU GO TO CONCERTS, TOO?!
MAYBE...
...WE CAN BE REAL FRIENDS...
OH! SO THEN, MARY-SAN...
JESUS
I ALWAYS WANTED TO GO TO SCHOOL. THOSE BACK-PACKS! THE PERFECT SIZE FOR SLIPPING A LAPTOP INSIDE. I WANT ONE, BUT WOULD IT BE WEIRD FOR A GROWN MAN TO WEAR IT?

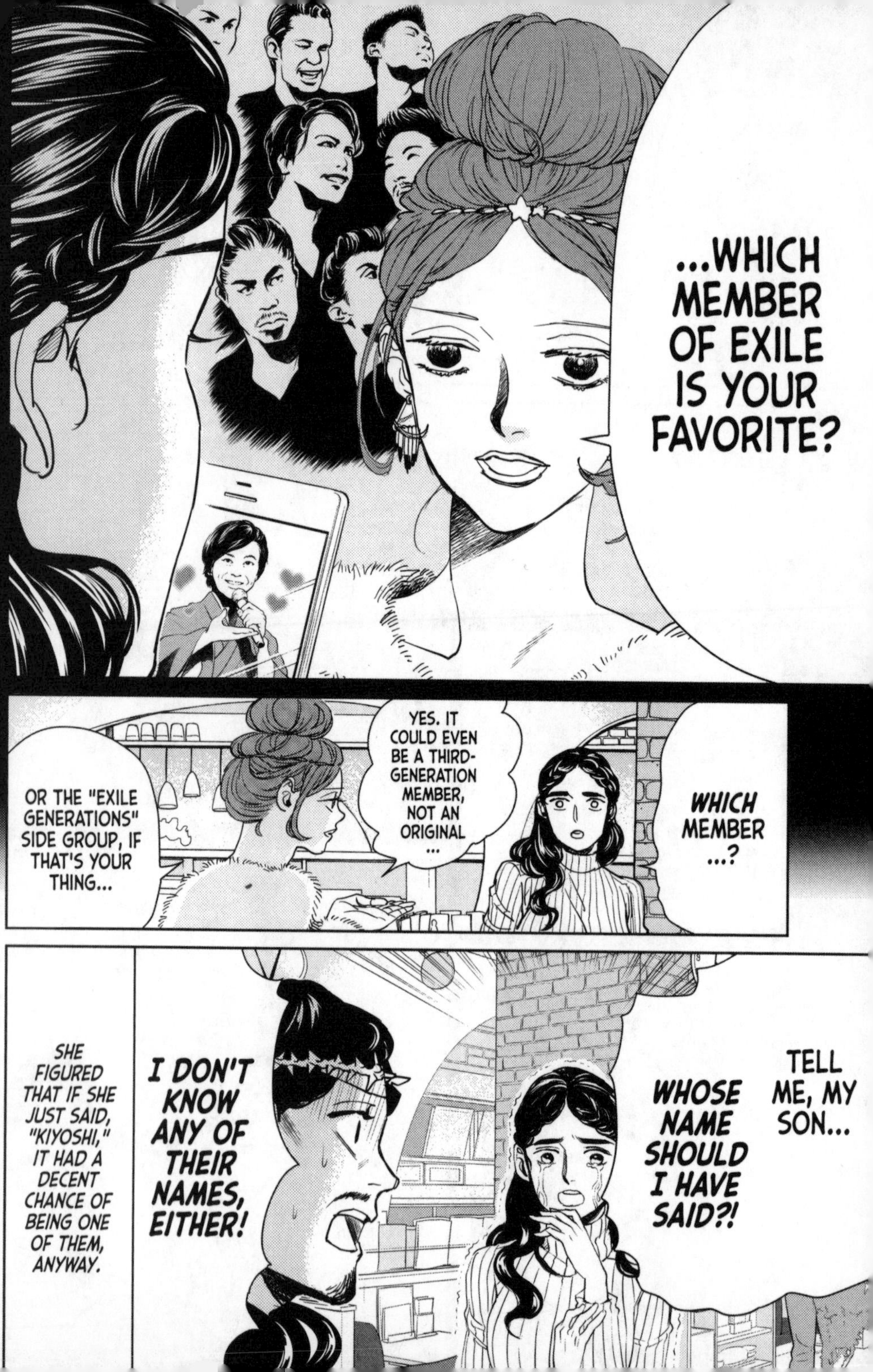
...WHICH MEMBER OF EXILE IS YOUR FAVORITE?
WHICH MEMBER ...?
YES. IT COULD EVEN BE A THIRD-GENERATION MEMBER, NOT AN ORIGINAL ...
OR THE "EXILE GENERATIONS" SIDE GROUP, IF THAT'S YOUR THING...
TELL ME, MY SON...
WHOSE NAME SHOULD I HAVE SAID?!
I DON'T KNOW ANY OF THEIR NAMES, EITHER!
SHE FIGURED THAT IF SHE JUST SAID, "KIYOSHI," IT HAD A DECENT CHANCE OF BEING ONE OF THEM, ANYWAY.

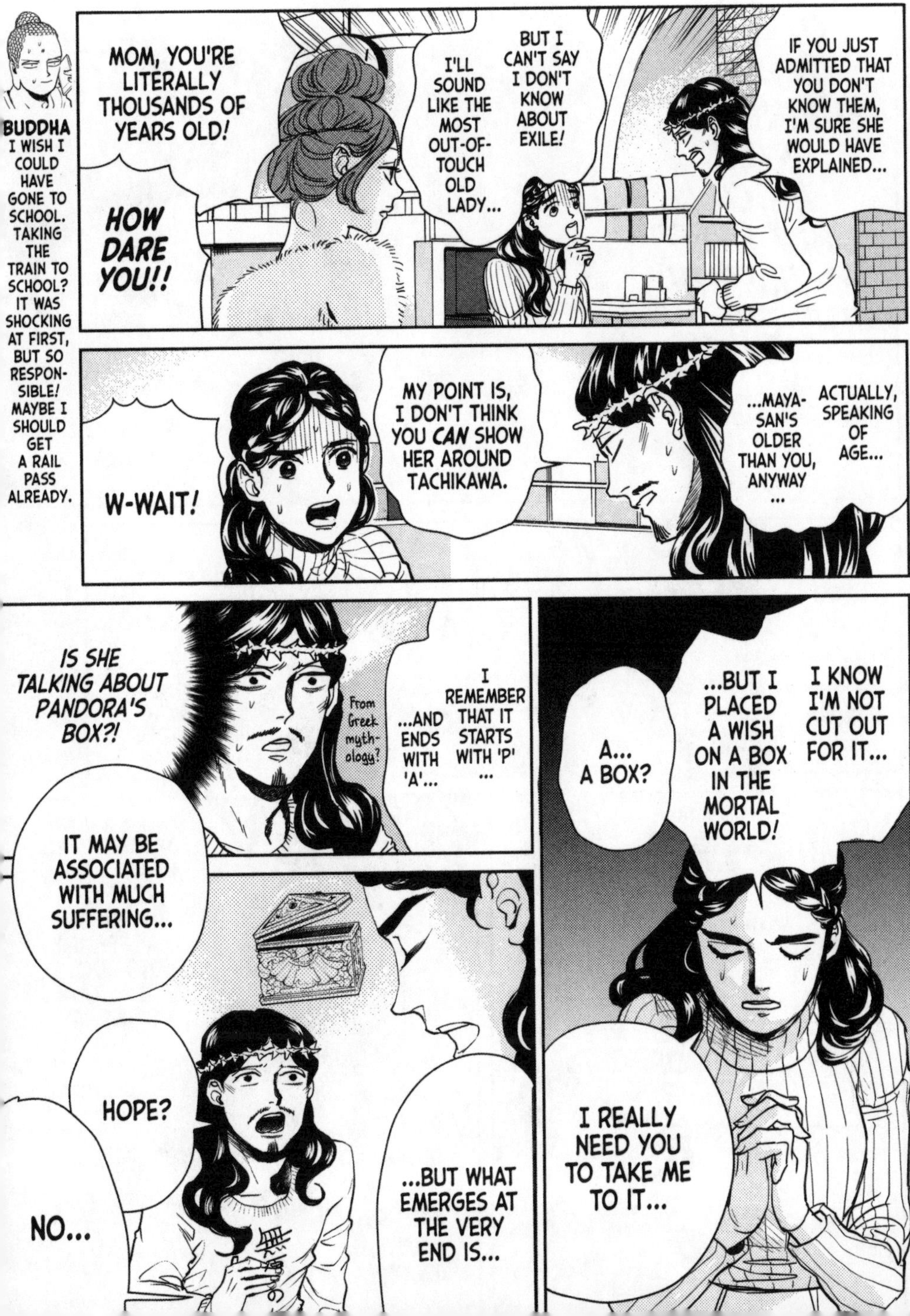
IF YOU JUST ADMITTED THAT YOU DON'T KNOW THEM, I'M SURE SHE WOULD HAVE EXPLAINED...
BUT I CAN'T SAY I DON'T KNOW ABOUT EXILE!
I'LL SOUND LIKE THE MOST OUT-OF-TOUCH OLD LADY...
MOM, YOU'RE LITERALLY THOUSANDS OF YEARS OLD!
HOW DARE YOU!!
ACTUALLY, SPEAKING OF AGE...
...MAYA-SAN'S OLDER THAN YOU, ANYWAY...
MY POINT IS, I DON'T THINK YOU CAN SHOW HER AROUND TACHIKAWA.
W-WAIT!
I KNOW I'M NOT CUT OUT FOR IT...
...BUT I PLACED A WISH ON A BOX IN THE MORTAL WORLD!
A... A BOX?
I REALLY NEED YOU TO TAKE ME TO IT...
I REMEMBER THAT IT STARTS WITH 'P'...
...AND ENDS WITH 'A'...
From Greek mythology?
IS SHE TALKING ABOUT PANDORA'S BOX?!
IT MAY BE ASSOCIATED WITH MUCH SUFFERING...
...BUT WHAT EMERGES AT THE VERY END IS...
HOPE?
NO...
BUDDHA
I WISH I COULD HAVE GONE TO SCHOOL. TAKING THE TRAIN TO SCHOOL? IT WAS SHOCKING AT FIRST, BUT SO RESPONSIBLE! MAYBE I SHOULD GET A RAIL PASS ALREADY.

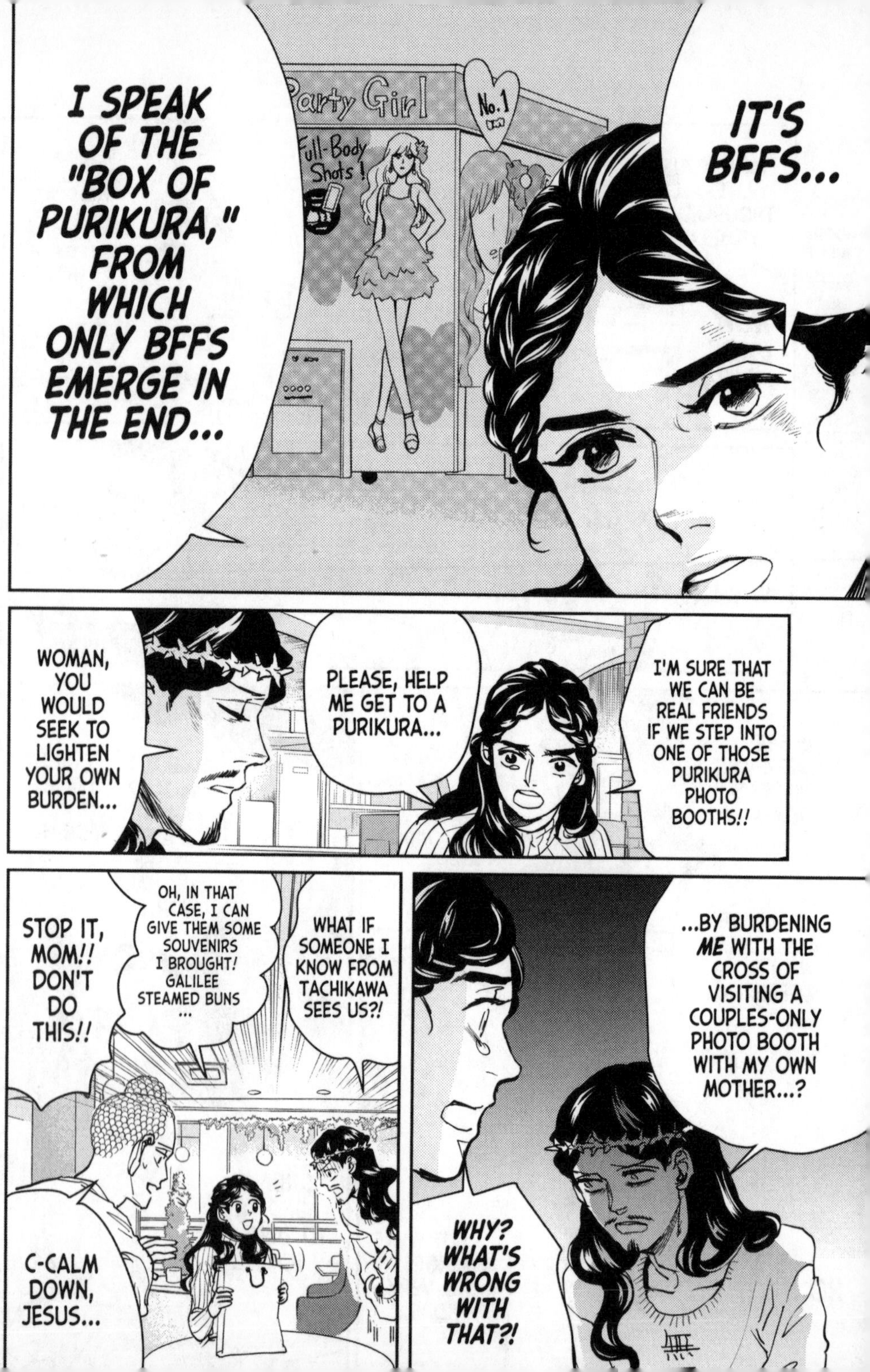
IT'S BFFS...
I SPEAK OF THE "BOX OF PURIKURA," FROM WHICH ONLY BFFS EMERGE IN THE END...
Party Girl
No.1
Full-Body Shots!
I'M SURE THAT WE CAN BE REAL FRIENDS IF WE STEP INTO ONE OF THOSE PURIKURA PHOTO BOOTHS!!
PLEASE, HELP ME GET TO A PURIKURA...
WOMAN, YOU WOULD SEEK TO LIGHTEN YOUR OWN BURDEN...
...BY BURDENING *ME* WITH THE CROSS OF VISITING A COUPLES-ONLY PHOTO BOOTH WITH MY OWN MOTHER...?
WHY? WHAT'S WRONG WITH THAT?!
WHAT IF SOMEONE I KNOW FROM TACHIKAWA SEES US?!
OH, IN THAT CASE, I CAN GIVE THEM SOME SOUVENIRS I BROUGHT! GALILEE STEAMED BUNS ...
STOP IT, MOM!! DON'T DO THIS!!
C-CALM DOWN, JESUS...

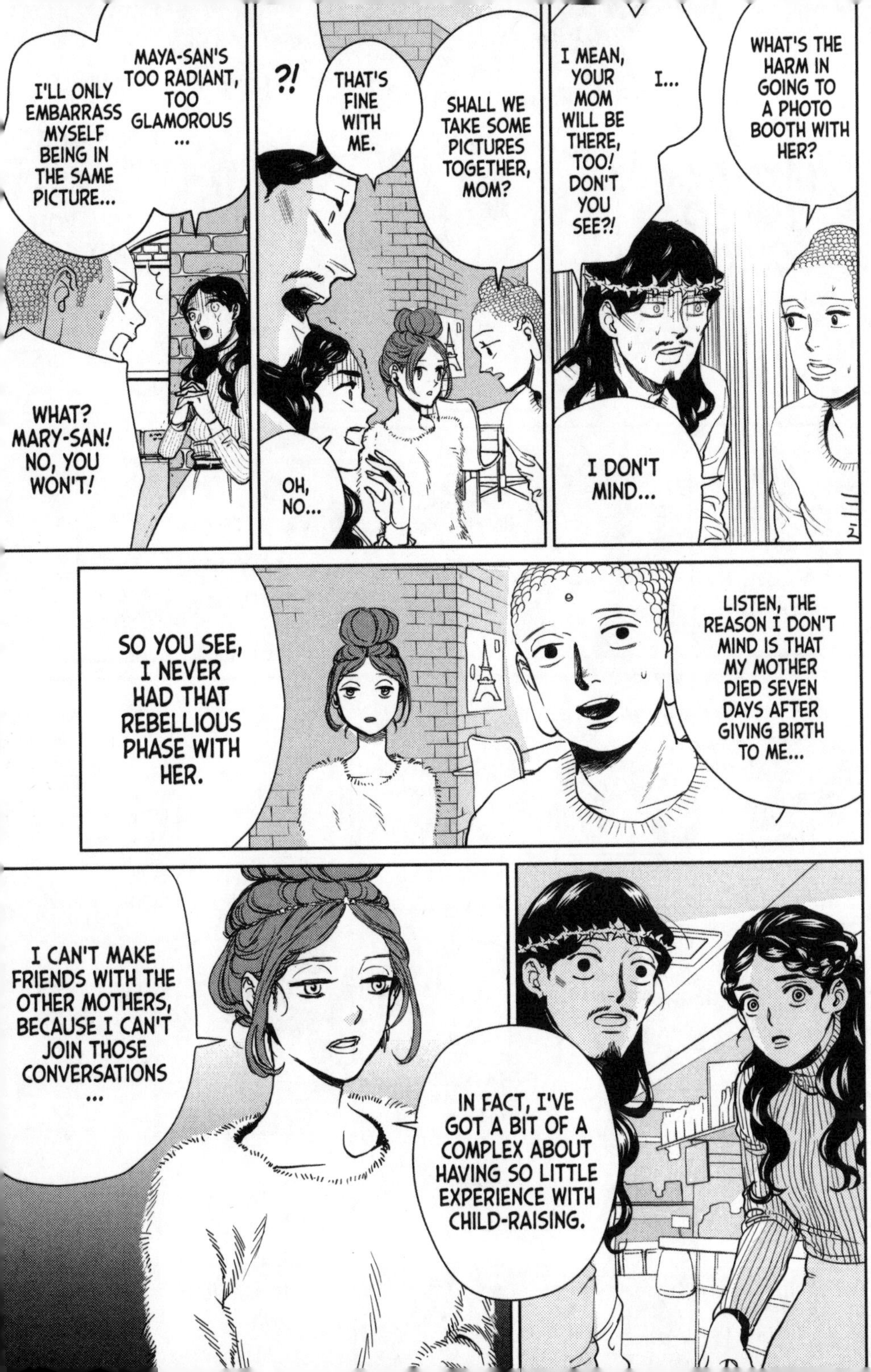
WHAT'S THE HARM IN GOING TO A PHOTO BOOTH WITH HER?
I...
I MEAN, YOUR MOM WILL BE THERE, TOO! DON'T YOU SEE?!
I DON'T MIND...
SHALL WE TAKE SOME PICTURES TOGETHER, MOM?
THAT'S FINE WITH ME.
?!
OH, NO...
MAYA-SAN'S TOO RADIANT, TOO GLAMOROUS ...
I'LL ONLY EMBARRASS MYSELF BEING IN THE SAME PICTURE...
WHAT? MARY-SAN! NO, YOU WON'T!
LISTEN, THE REASON I DON'T MIND IS THAT MY MOTHER DIED SEVEN DAYS AFTER GIVING BIRTH TO ME...
SO YOU SEE, I NEVER HAD THAT REBELLIOUS PHASE WITH HER.
I CAN'T MAKE FRIENDS WITH THE OTHER MOTHERS, BECAUSE I CAN'T JOIN THOSE CONVERSATIONS ...
IN FACT, I'VE GOT A BIT OF A COMPLEX ABOUT HAVING SO LITTLE EXPERIENCE WITH CHILD-RAISING.

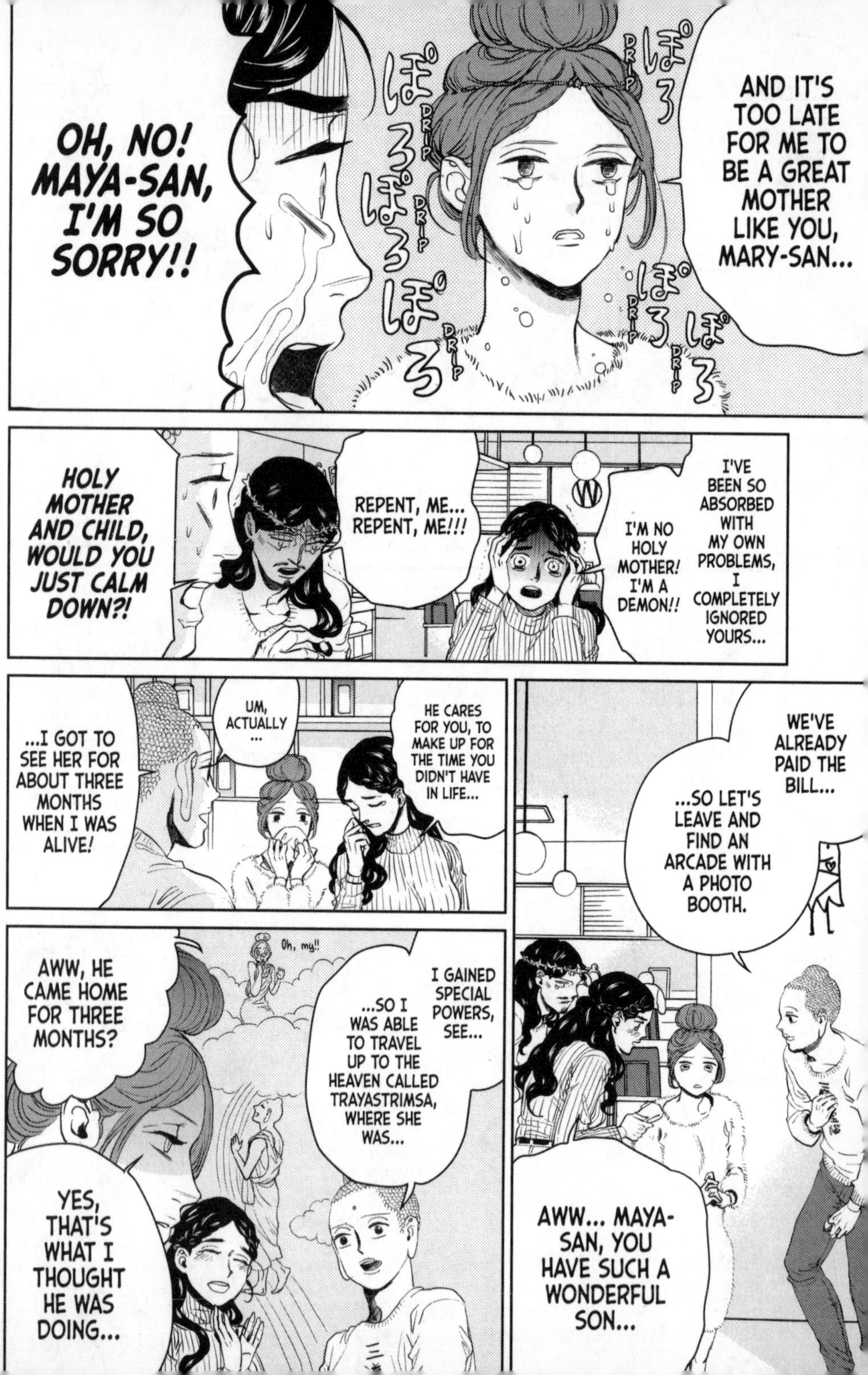
AND IT'S TOO LATE FOR ME TO BE A GREAT MOTHER LIKE YOU, MARY-SAN...
ぽろ DRIP
ぽろ DRIP
ぽろ DRIP
ぽろ DRIP
ぽろ DRIP
ぽろ DRIP
OH, NO! MAYA-SAN, I'M SO SORRY!!
I'VE BEEN SO ABSORBED WITH MY OWN PROBLEMS, I COMPLETELY IGNORED YOURS...
I'M NO HOLY MOTHER! I'M A DEMON!!
REPENT, ME... REPENT, ME!!!
HOLY MOTHER AND CHILD, WOULD YOU JUST CALM DOWN?!
WE'VE ALREADY PAID THE BILL...
...SO LET'S LEAVE AND FIND AN ARCADE WITH A PHOTO BOOTH.
HE CARES FOR YOU, TO MAKE UP FOR THE TIME YOU DIDN'T HAVE IN LIFE...
UM, ACTUALLY...
...I GOT TO SEE HER FOR ABOUT THREE MONTHS WHEN I WAS ALIVE!
AWW... MAYA-SAN, YOU HAVE SUCH A WONDERFUL SON...
I GAINED SPECIAL POWERS, SEE...
...SO I WAS ABLE TO TRAVEL UP TO THE HEAVEN CALLED TRAYASTRIMSA, WHERE SHE WAS...
Oh, my!!
AWW, HE CAME HOME FOR THREE MONTHS?
YES, THAT'S WHAT I THOUGHT HE WAS DOING...

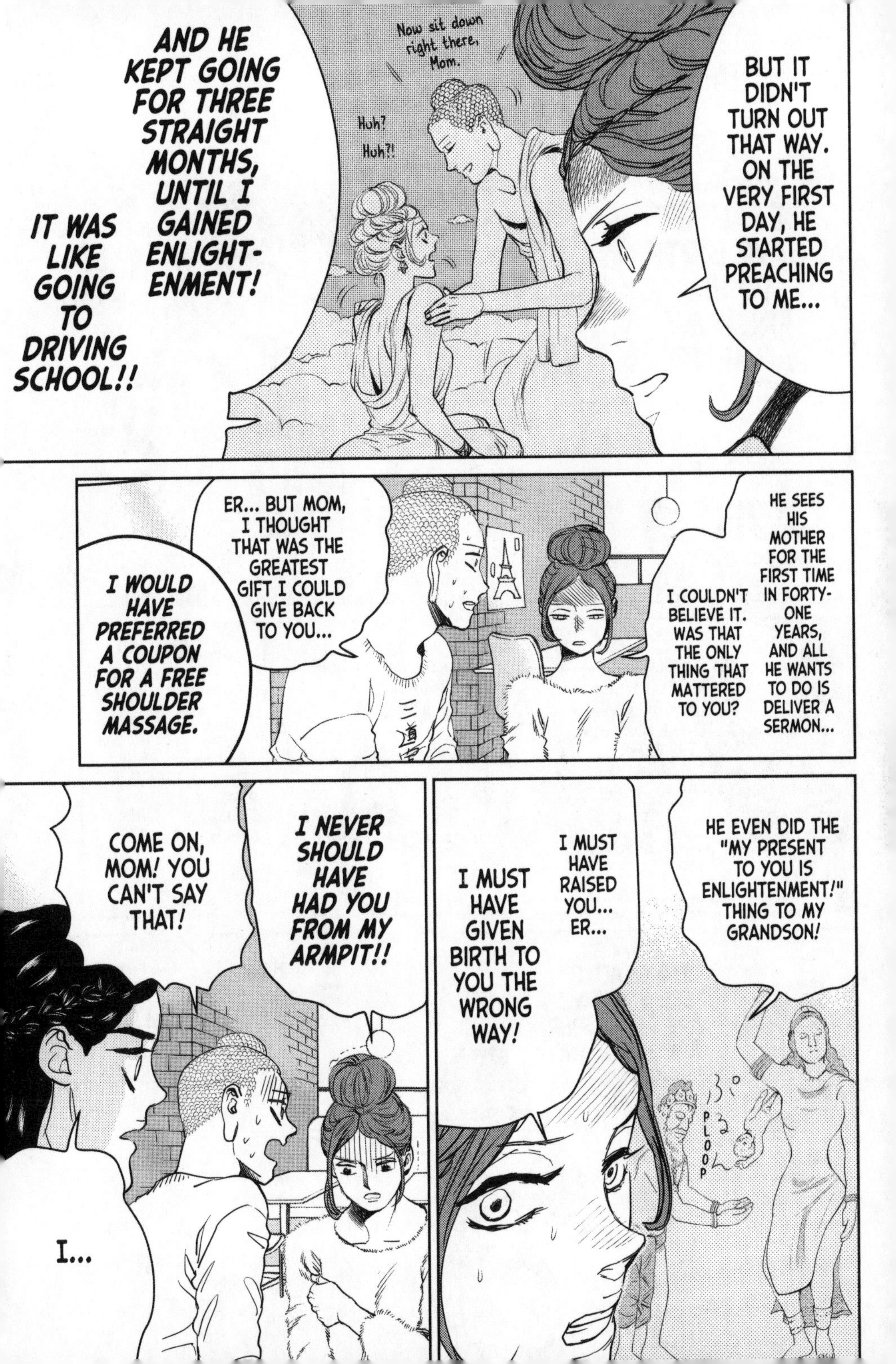

BUT IT DIDN'T TURN OUT THAT WAY. ON THE VERY FIRST DAY, HE STARTED PREACHING TO ME...
Now sit down right there, Mom.
Huh? Huh?!
AND HE KEPT GOING FOR THREE STRAIGHT MONTHS, UNTIL I GAINED ENLIGHTENMENT!
IT WAS LIKE GOING TO DRIVING SCHOOL!!
HE SEES HIS MOTHER FOR THE FIRST TIME IN FORTY-ONE YEARS, AND ALL HE WANTS TO DO IS DELIVER A SERMON...
I COULDN'T BELIEVE IT. WAS THAT THE ONLY THING THAT MATTERED TO YOU?
ER... BUT MOM, I THOUGHT THAT WAS THE GREATEST GIFT I COULD GIVE BACK TO YOU...
I WOULD HAVE PREFERRED A COUPON FOR A FREE SHOULDER MASSAGE.
HE EVEN DID THE "MY PRESENT TO YOU IS ENLIGHTENMENT!" THING TO MY GRANDSON!
I MUST HAVE RAISED YOU... ER...
I MUST HAVE GIVEN BIRTH TO YOU THE WRONG WAY!
PLOOP
I NEVER SHOULD HAVE HAD YOU FROM MY ARMPIT!!
COME ON, MOM! YOU CAN'T SAY THAT!
I...

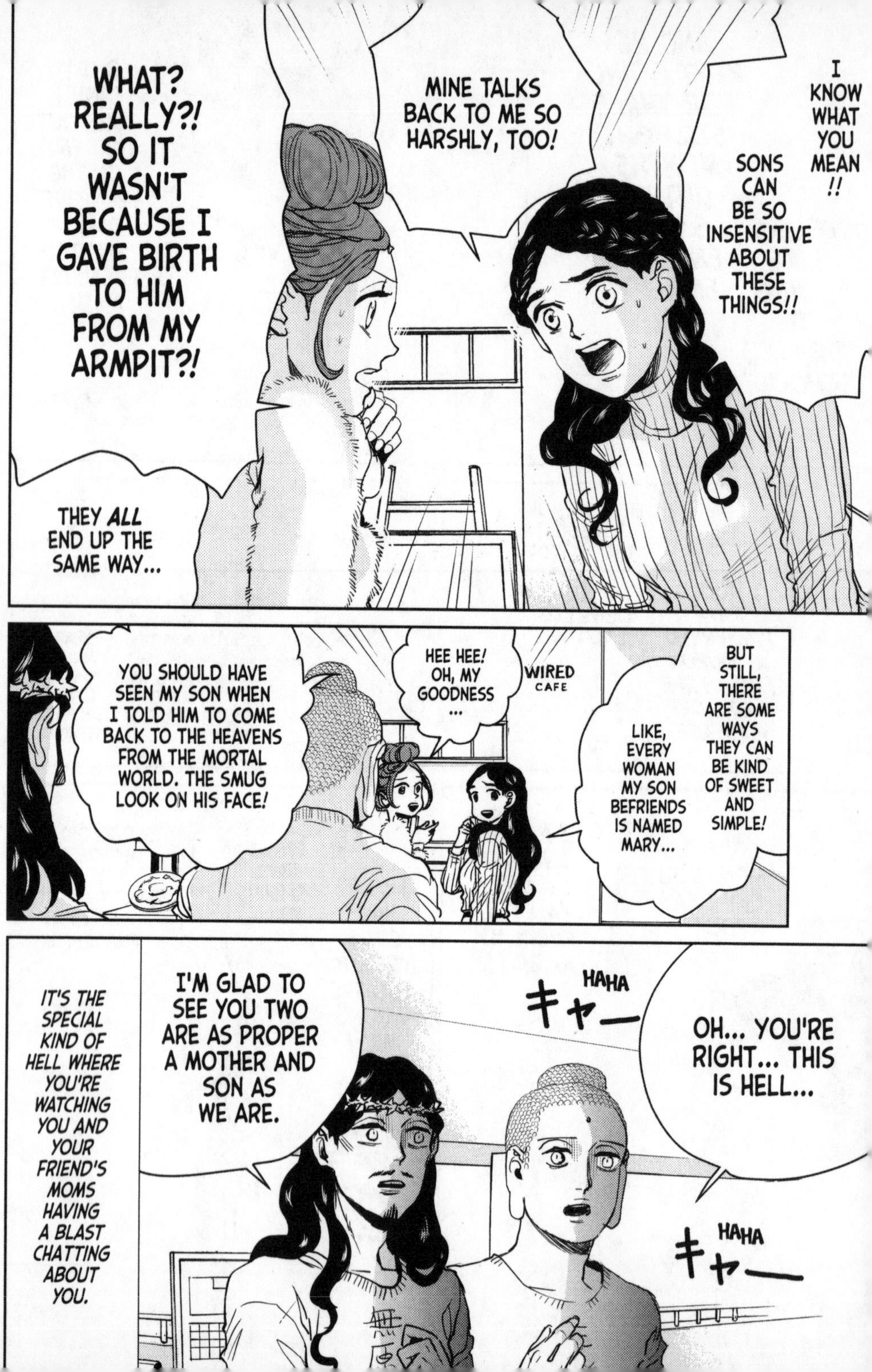
I KNOW WHAT YOU MEAN!!
SONS CAN BE SO INSENSITIVE ABOUT THESE THINGS!!
MINE TALKS BACK TO ME SO HARSHLY, TOO!
WHAT? REALLY?! SO IT WASN'T BECAUSE I GAVE BIRTH TO HIM FROM MY ARMPIT?!
THEY *ALL* END UP THE SAME WAY...
BUT STILL, THERE ARE SOME WAYS THEY CAN BE KIND OF SWEET AND SIMPLE!
LIKE, EVERY WOMAN MY SON BEFRIENDS IS NAMED MARY...
WIRED CAFE
HEE HEE! OH, MY GOODNESS ...
YOU SHOULD HAVE SEEN MY SON WHEN I TOLD HIM TO COME BACK TO THE HEAVENS FROM THE MORTAL WORLD. THE SMUG LOOK ON HIS FACE!
OH... YOU'RE RIGHT... THIS IS HELL...
キャー HAHA
キャー HAHA
I'M GLAD TO SEE YOU TWO ARE AS PROPER A MOTHER AND SON AS WE ARE.
IT'S THE SPECIAL KIND OF HELL WHERE YOU'RE WATCHING YOU AND YOUR FRIEND'S MOMS HAVING A BLAST CHATTING ABOUT YOU.

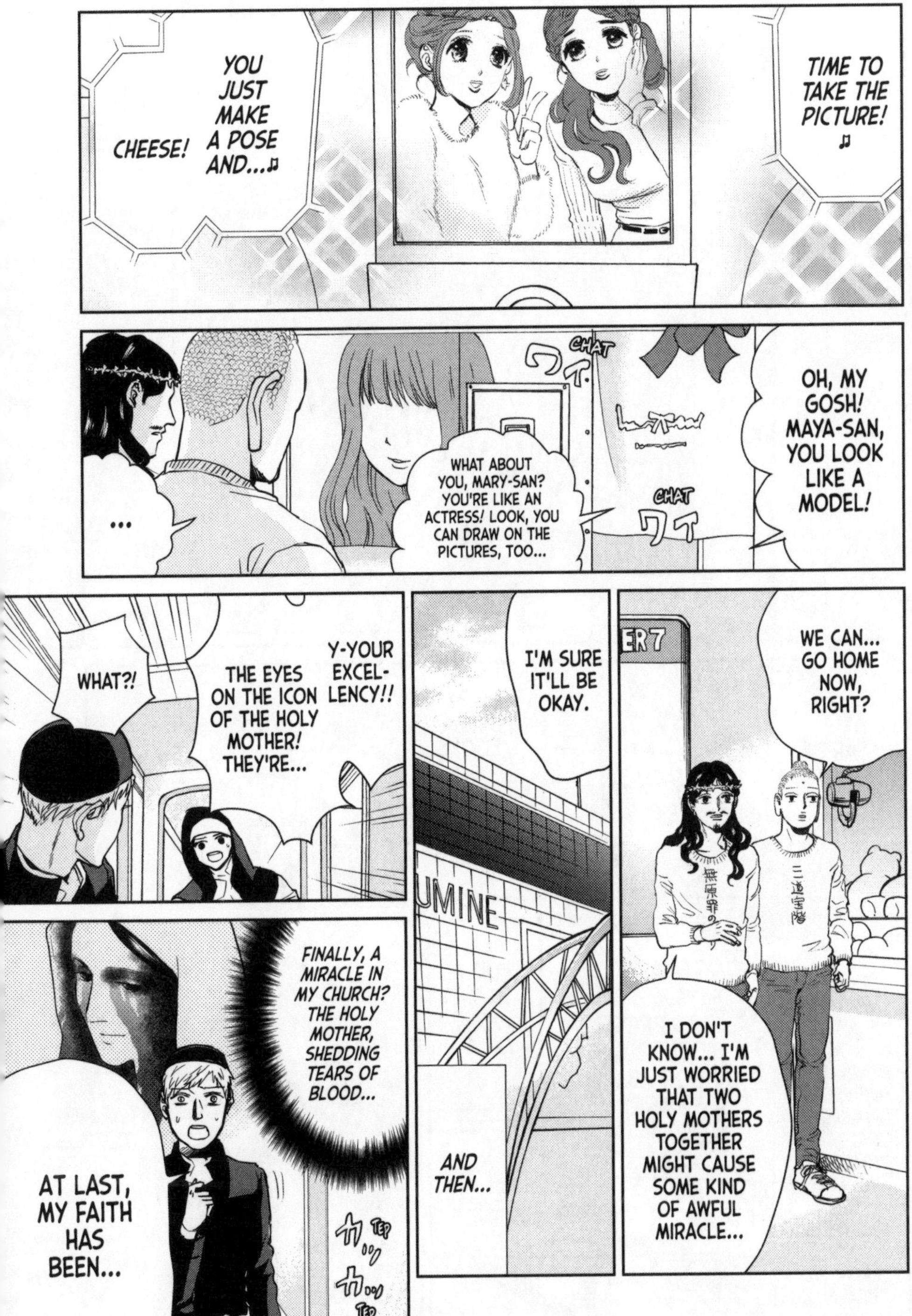
TIME TO TAKE THE PICTURE! ♫
YOU JUST MAKE A POSE AND...♫
CHEESE!
OH, MY GOSH! MAYA-SAN, YOU LOOK LIKE A MODEL!
ワイ CHAT
ワイ CHAT
WHAT ABOUT YOU, MARY-SAN? YOU'RE LIKE AN ACTRESS! LOOK, YOU CAN DRAW ON THE PICTURES, TOO...
...
WE CAN... GO HOME NOW, RIGHT?
I DON'T KNOW... I'M JUST WORRIED THAT TWO HOLY MOTHERS TOGETHER MIGHT CAUSE SOME KIND OF AWFUL MIRACLE...
I'M SURE IT'LL BE OKAY.
AND THEN...
Y-YOUR EXCEL-LENCY!!
THE EYES ON THE ICON OF THE HOLY MOTHER! THEY'RE...
WHAT?!
FINALLY, A MIRACLE IN MY CHURCH? THE HOLY MOTHER, SHEDDING TEARS OF BLOOD...
AT LAST, MY FAITH HAS BEEN...
カッ TEP
カッ TEP

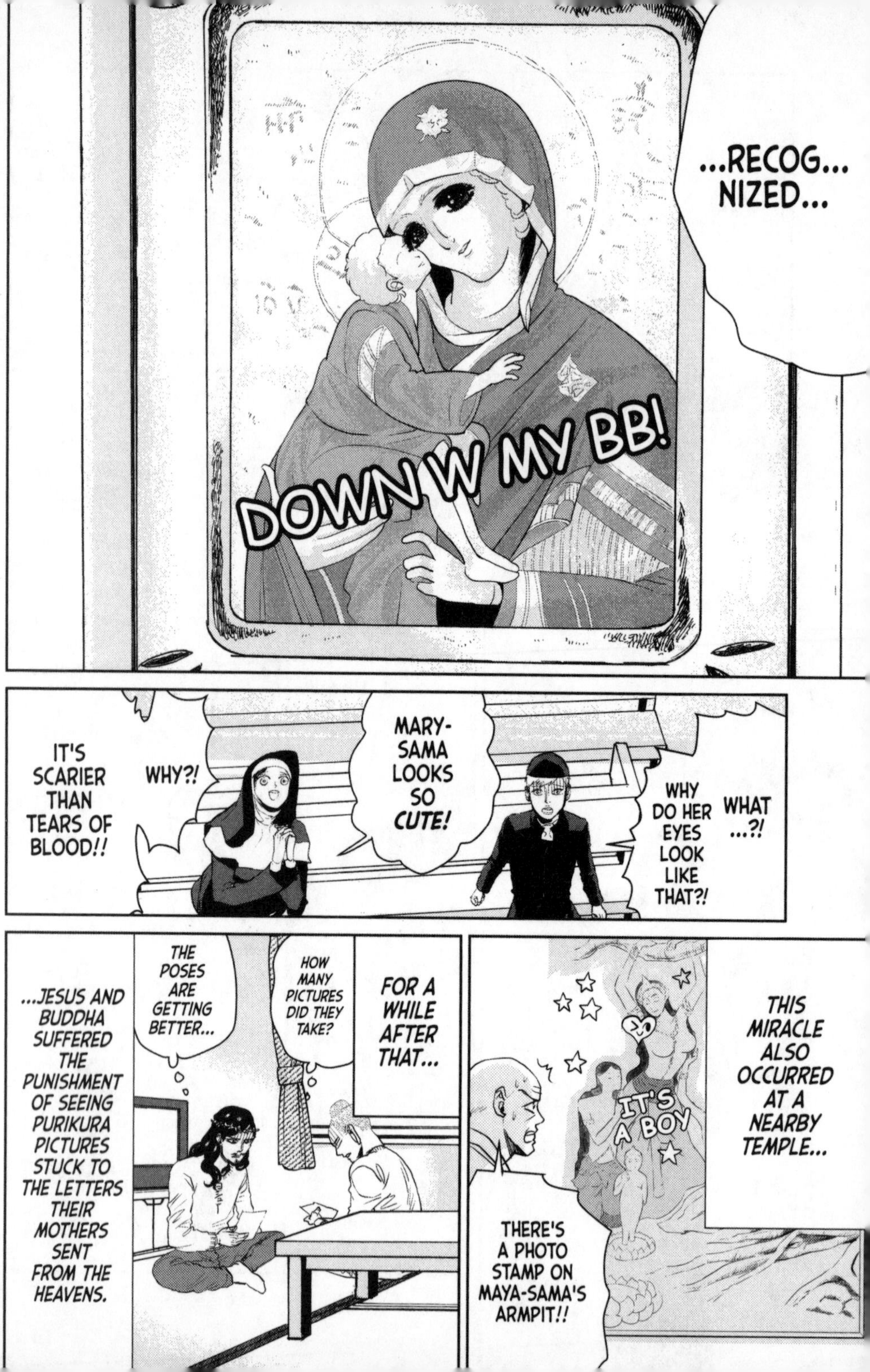
...RECOG... NIZED...
DOWN W MY BB!
WHAT ...?!
WHY DO HER EYES LOOK LIKE THAT?!
MARY-SAMA LOOKS SO CUTE!
WHY?!
IT'S SCARIER THAN TEARS OF BLOOD!!
THIS MIRACLE ALSO OCCURRED AT A NEARBY TEMPLE...
IT'S A BOY
THERE'S A PHOTO STAMP ON MAYA-SAMA'S ARMPIT!!
FOR A WHILE AFTER THAT...
HOW MANY PICTURES DID THEY TAKE?
THE POSES ARE GETTING BETTER...
...JESUS AND BUDDHA SUFFERED THE PUNISHMENT OF SEEING PURIKURA PICTURES STUCK TO THE LETTERS THEIR MOTHERS SENT FROM THE HEAVENS.

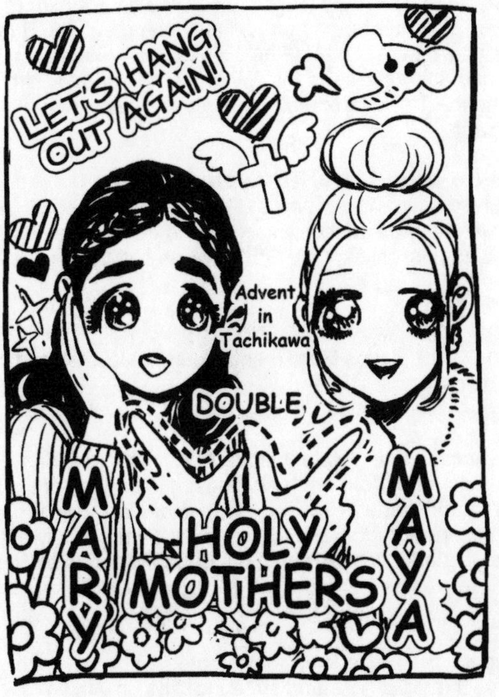
LET'S HANG OUT AGAIN!
Advent in Tachikawa
DOUBLE
MAYA
HOLY MOTHERS
MARY

CHAPTER 89 TRANSLATION NOTES

Mary over Cairo, page 1
Mass sightings of an apparition of the Virgin Mary were reported in Cairo between 1968 and 1971 over St. Mary's Coptic Church in Zeitoun, a district of the city. The sightings are colloquially referred to as "Our Lady of Zeitoun."

Immaculate Conception, page 5
The Catholic understanding of the Virgin Mary, which states that she herself was free of original sin from birth.

Assumption, page 5
The Assumption of Mary is the Catholic belief that Mary was physically taken up to Heaven at the end of her life, rather than suffering physical death.

Three ladders, page 5
Gautama Buddha's mother Maya is said to have died just seven days after his birth (from her armpit, as the story goes). Later in life, after he had gained enlightenment, the Buddha traveled beyond the mortal world to Trayastrimsa, one of the six heavens in Buddhist cosmology. There, he visited Maya and delivered sermons. When he returned to Earth, the Japanese call this event "Descending the Three Ladders," because the devas sent three ladders down from the heavens to Earth.

"Let she who has never been popular with men..." page 6
A parody of the famous phrase "Let he who is without sin cast the first stone," which Jesus said to the crowd that was gathered to stone an adulterous woman to death. The phrase refers to the sin that every human being possesses; only God is worthy of judging their sins.

Renoir & Doutor, page 6
Much like Starbucks, the Renoir and Doutor places Mary mentions are café chains ideal for spending time in a relaxed setting.

Exile, page 8
A long-running and very popular boy band known for its uniform black suits and many members. Several different "generations" of performers have phased in and out of the group over the years, and there have been some affiliated groups under the Exile umbrella (such as Generations) that operate separately. Mary's favorite singer Kiyoshi Hikawa is an *enka* singer whose style would stand in stark contrast with the modern R&B pop stylings of Exile.

Pandora's Box, page 9
The box in the myth opened by Pandora, the first human woman created by the gods, contains all of the evils in the world such as sickness and suffering. The only thing to remain trapped in the box is "hope."

W, page 17
The use of the letter W in Japanese is very often used as shorthand for the word "double" (for "double-u").

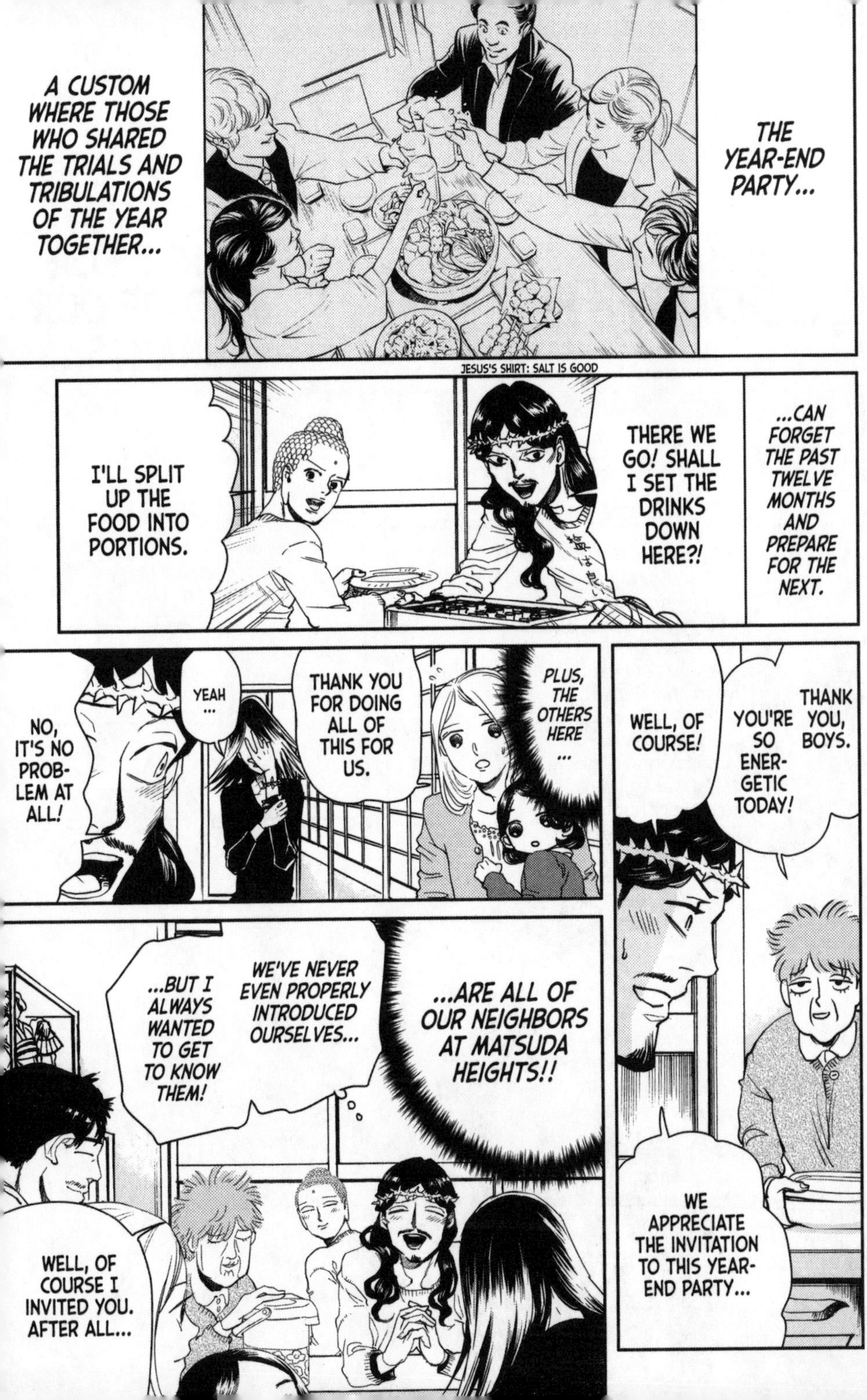
THE YEAR-END PARTY...
A CUSTOM WHERE THOSE WHO SHARED THE TRIALS AND TRIBULATIONS OF THE YEAR TOGETHER...
...CAN FORGET THE PAST TWELVE MONTHS AND PREPARE FOR THE NEXT.
JESUS'S SHIRT: SALT IS GOOD
THERE WE GO! SHALL I SET THE DRINKS DOWN HERE?!
I'LL SPLIT UP THE FOOD INTO PORTIONS.
THANK YOU, BOYS.
YOU'RE SO ENERGETIC TODAY!
WELL, OF COURSE!
WE APPRECIATE THE INVITATION TO THIS YEAR-END PARTY...
PLUS, THE OTHERS HERE...
THANK YOU FOR DOING ALL OF THIS FOR US.
YEAH...
NO, IT'S NO PROBLEM AT ALL!
...ARE ALL OF OUR NEIGHBORS AT MATSUDA HEIGHTS!!
WE'VE NEVER EVEN PROPERLY INTRODUCED OURSELVES...
...BUT I ALWAYS WANTED TO GET TO KNOW THEM!
WELL, OF COURSE I INVITED YOU. AFTER ALL...

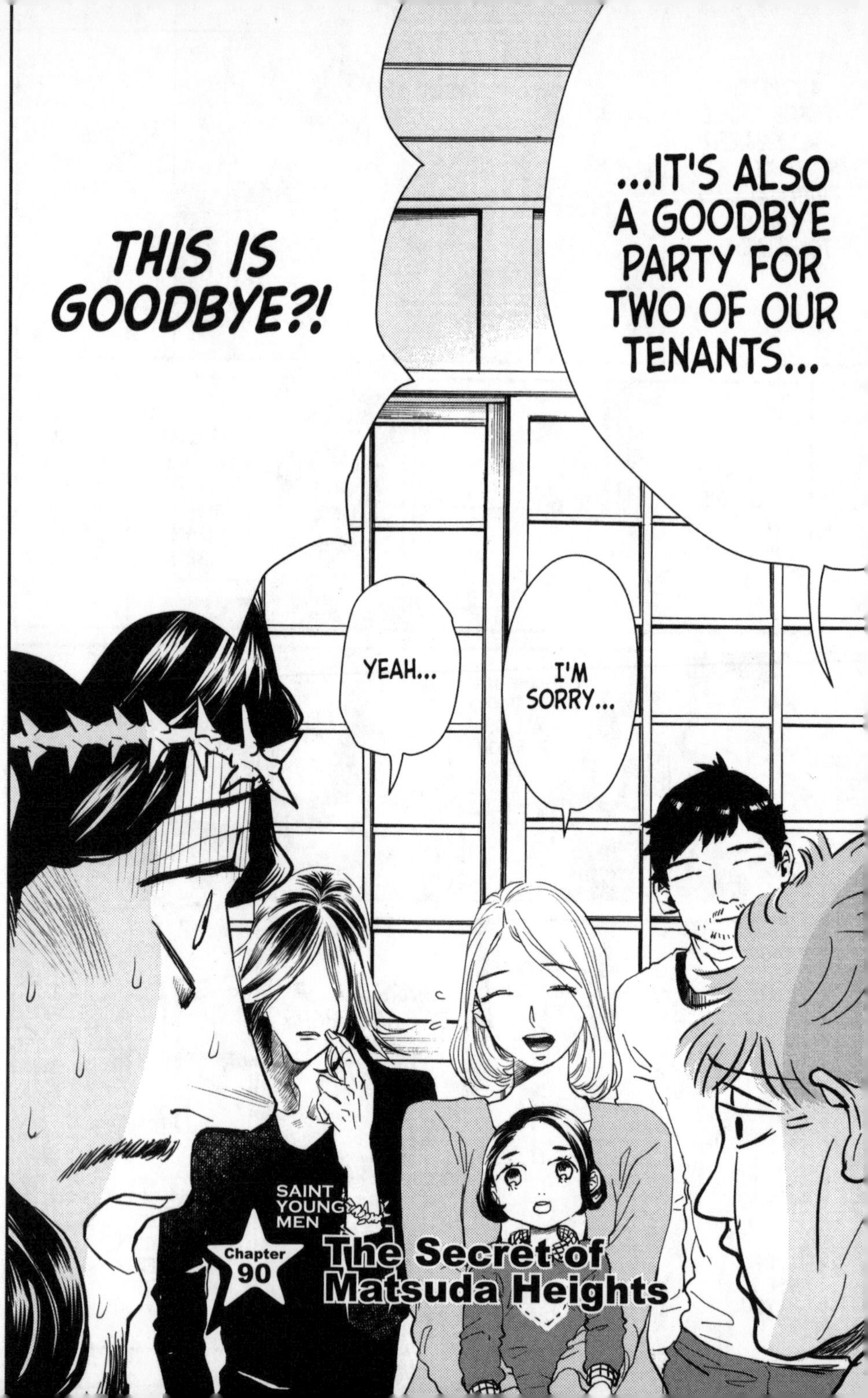
...IT'S ALSO A GOODBYE PARTY FOR TWO OF OUR TENANTS...
THIS IS GOODBYE?!
I'M SORRY...
YEAH...
SAINT YOUNG MEN
Chapter 90
The Secret of Matsuda Heights

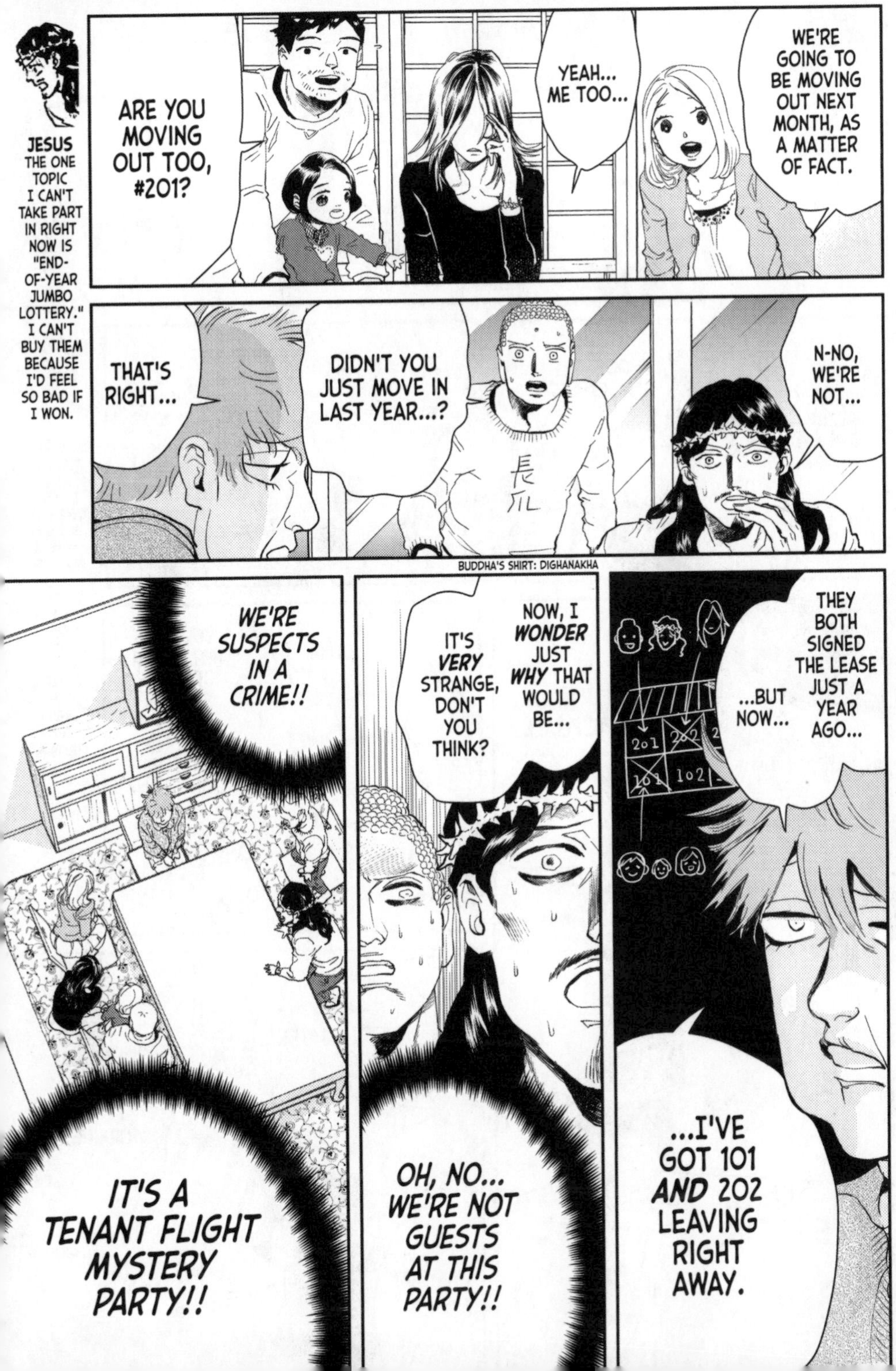
WE'RE GOING TO BE MOVING OUT NEXT MONTH, AS A MATTER OF FACT.
YEAH... ME TOO...
ARE YOU MOVING OUT TOO, #201?
JESUS
THE ONE TOPIC I CAN'T TAKE PART IN RIGHT NOW IS "END-OF-YEAR JUMBO LOTTERY." I CAN'T BUY THEM BECAUSE I'D FEEL SO BAD IF I WON.
N-NO, WE'RE NOT...
DIDN'T YOU JUST MOVE IN LAST YEAR...?
THAT'S RIGHT...
長爪
BUDDHA'S SHIRT: DIGHANAKHA
THEY BOTH SIGNED THE LEASE JUST A YEAR AGO...
...BUT NOW...
201
202
101
102
...I'VE GOT 101 AND 202 LEAVING RIGHT AWAY.
NOW, I WONDER JUST WHY THAT WOULD BE...
IT'S VERY STRANGE, DON'T YOU THINK?
OH, NO... WE'RE NOT GUESTS AT THIS PARTY!!
WE'RE SUSPECTS IN A CRIME!!
IT'S A TENANT FLIGHT MYSTERY PARTY!!

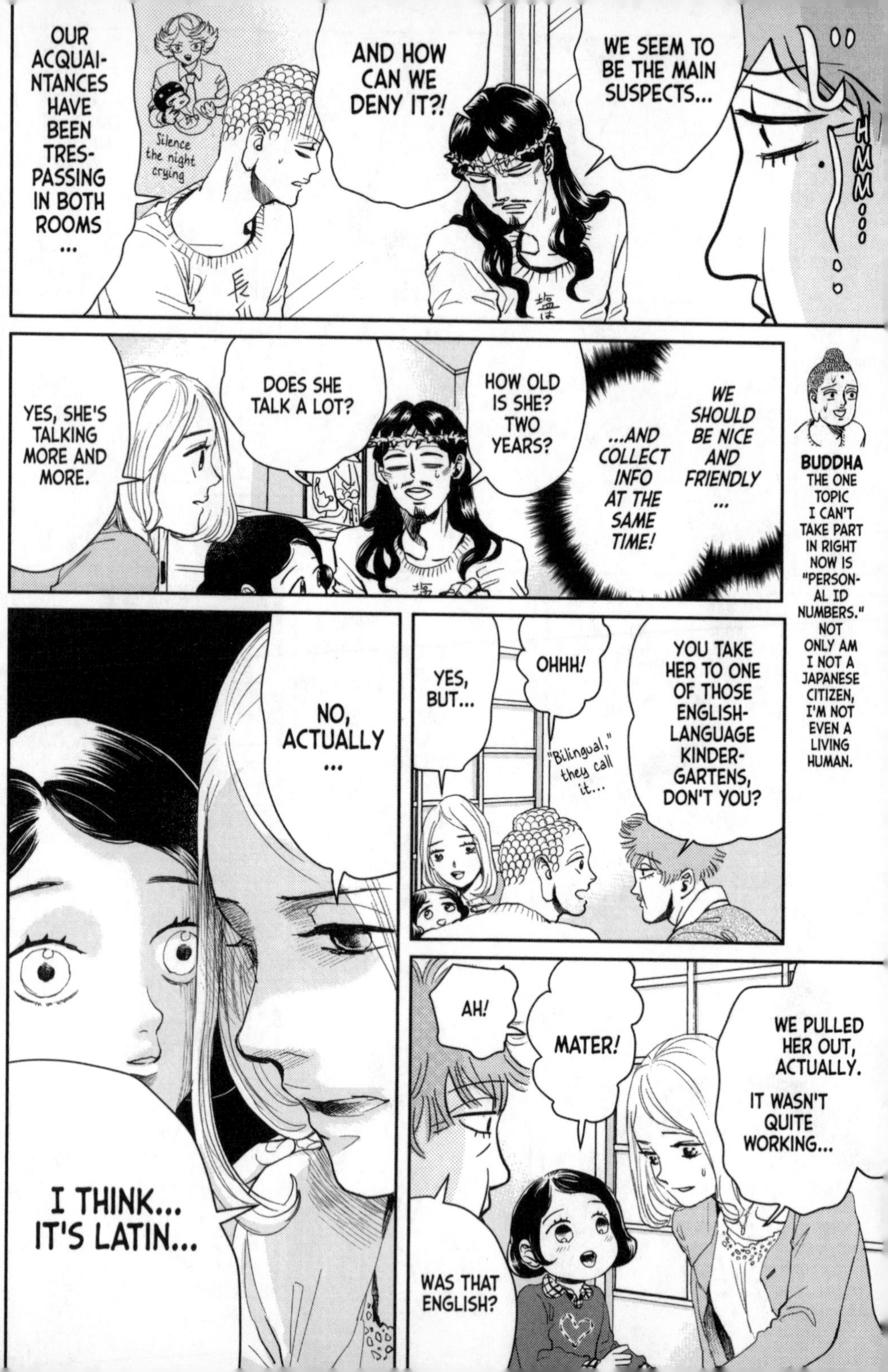
HMM...
WE SEEM TO BE THE MAIN SUSPECTS...
AND HOW CAN WE DENY IT?!
OUR ACQUAINTANCES HAVE BEEN TRESPASSING IN BOTH ROOMS...
Silence the night crying
WE SHOULD BE NICE AND FRIENDLY...
...AND COLLECT INFO AT THE SAME TIME!
HOW OLD IS SHE? TWO YEARS?
DOES SHE TALK A LOT?
YES, SHE'S TALKING MORE AND MORE.
BUDDHA THE ONE TOPIC I CAN'T TAKE PART IN RIGHT NOW IS "PERSONAL ID NUMBERS." NOT ONLY AM I NOT A JAPANESE CITIZEN, I'M NOT EVEN A LIVING HUMAN.
YOU TAKE HER TO ONE OF THOSE ENGLISH-LANGUAGE KINDERGARTENS, DON'T YOU?
"Bilingual," they call it...
OHHH!
YES, BUT...
WE PULLED HER OUT, ACTUALLY.
IT WASN'T QUITE WORKING...
MATER!
AH!
WAS THAT ENGLISH?
NO, ACTUALLY...
I THINK... IT'S LATIN...

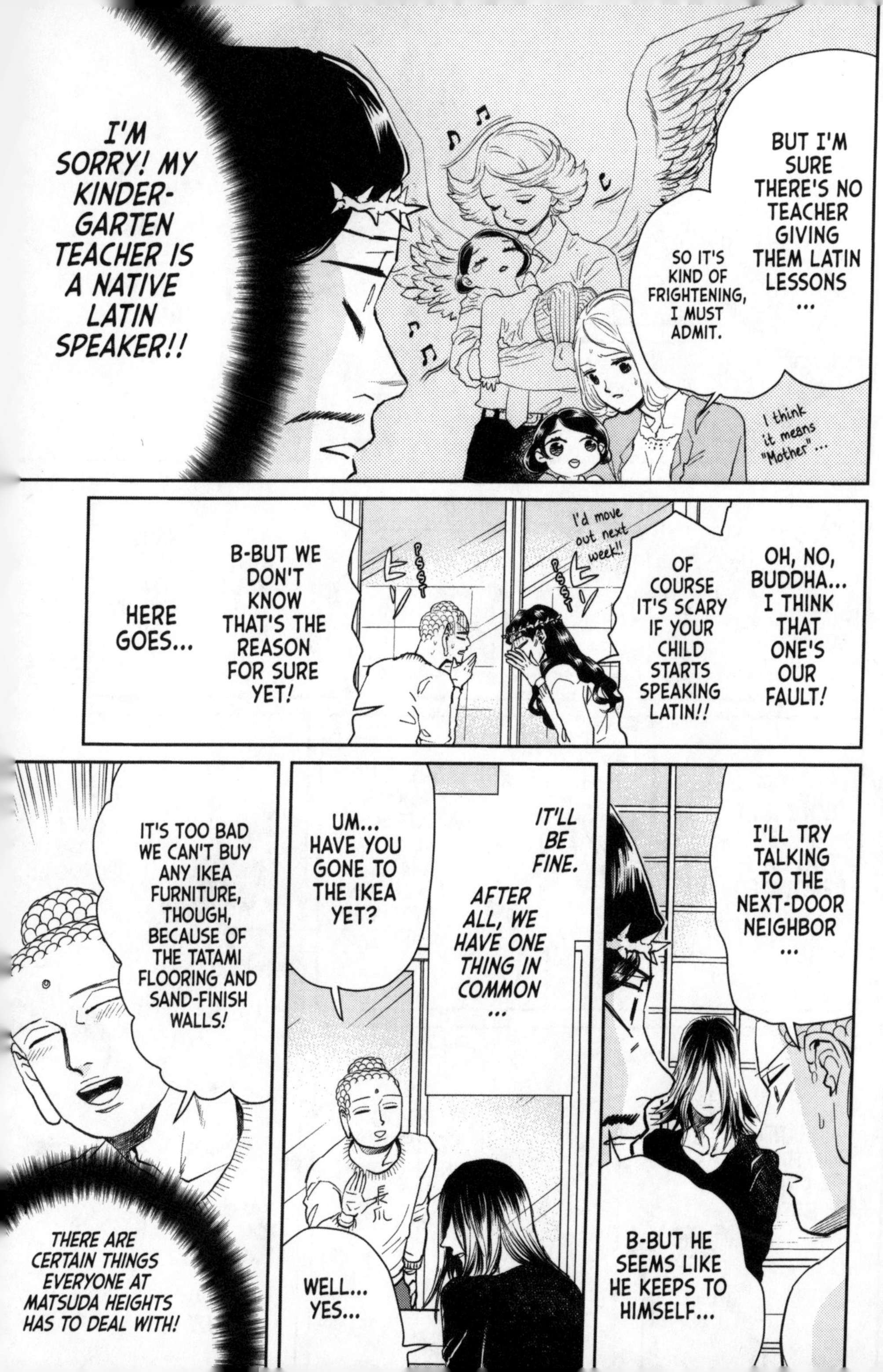
BUT I'M SURE THERE'S NO TEACHER GIVING THEM LATIN LESSONS ...
SO IT'S KIND OF FRIGHTENING, I MUST ADMIT.
I think it means "Mother"...
I'M SORRY! MY KINDER-GARTEN TEACHER IS A NATIVE LATIN SPEAKER!!
OH, NO, BUDDHA... I THINK THAT ONE'S OUR FAULT!
I'd move out next week!!
OF COURSE IT'S SCARY IF YOUR CHILD STARTS SPEAKING LATIN!!
PSST
PSST
B-BUT WE DON'T KNOW THAT'S THE REASON FOR SURE YET!
HERE GOES...
I'LL TRY TALKING TO THE NEXT-DOOR NEIGHBOR ...
B-BUT HE SEEMS LIKE HE KEEPS TO HIMSELF...
IT'LL BE FINE.
AFTER ALL, WE HAVE ONE THING IN COMMON ...
UM... HAVE YOU GONE TO THE IKEA YET?
WELL... YES...
IT'S TOO BAD WE CAN'T BUY ANY IKEA FURNITURE, THOUGH, BECAUSE OF THE TATAMI FLOORING AND SAND-FINISH WALLS!
THERE ARE CERTAIN THINGS EVERYONE AT MATSUDA HEIGHTS HAS TO DEAL WITH!

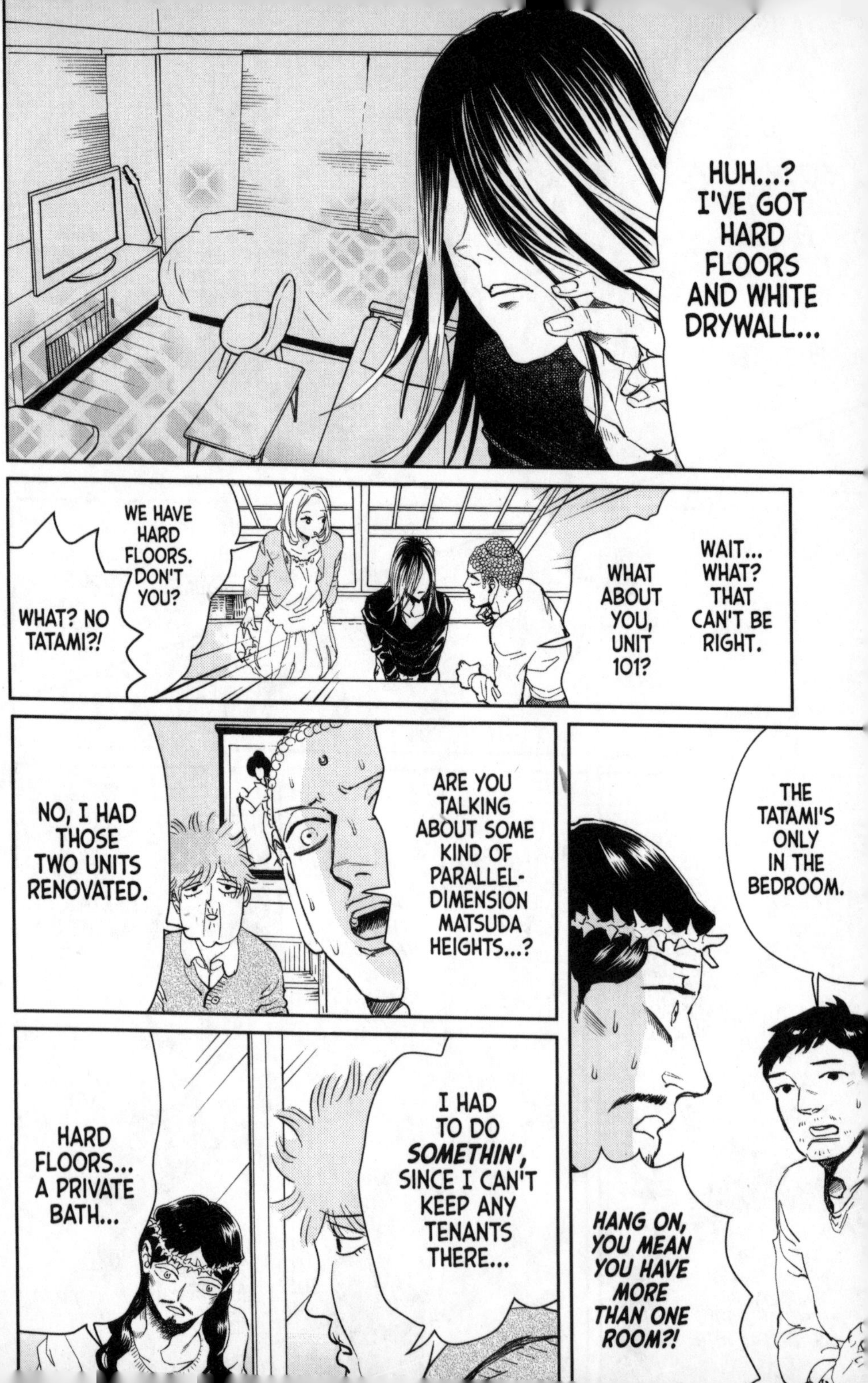
HUH...? I'VE GOT HARD FLOORS AND WHITE DRYWALL...
WAIT... WHAT? THAT CAN'T BE RIGHT.
WHAT ABOUT YOU, UNIT 101?
WE HAVE HARD FLOORS. DON'T YOU?
WHAT? NO TATAMI?!
THE TATAMI'S ONLY IN THE BEDROOM.
HANG ON, YOU MEAN YOU HAVE MORE THAN ONE ROOM?!
ARE YOU TALKING ABOUT SOME KIND OF PARALLEL-DIMENSION MATSUDA HEIGHTS...?
NO, I HAD THOSE TWO UNITS RENOVATED.
I HAD TO DO *SOMETHIN'*, SINCE I CAN'T KEEP ANY TENANTS THERE...
HARD FLOORS... A PRIVATE BATH...

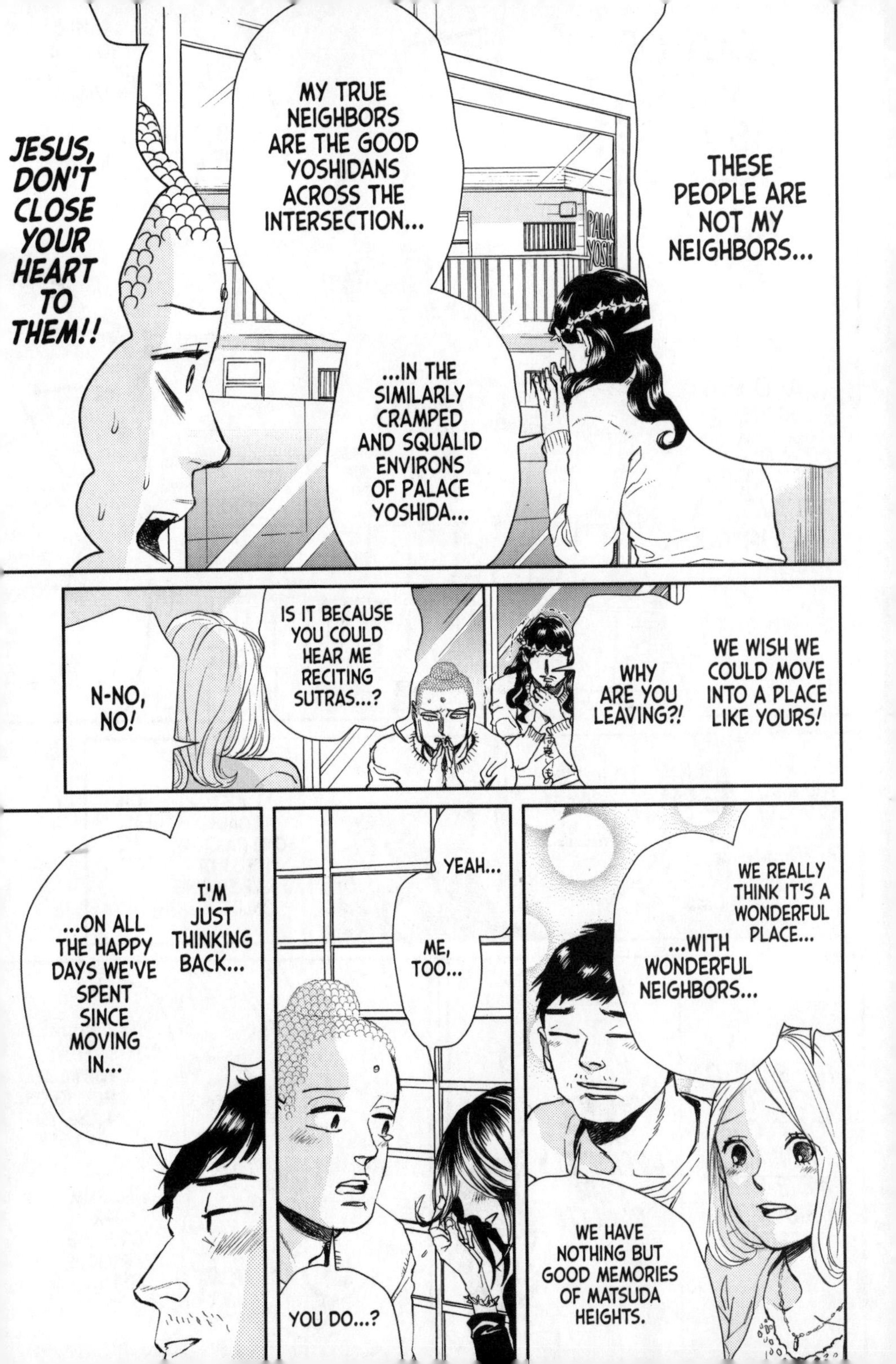
THESE PEOPLE ARE NOT MY NEIGHBORS...
MY TRUE NEIGHBORS ARE THE GOOD YOSHIDANS ACROSS THE INTERSECTION...
...IN THE SIMILARLY CRAMPED AND SQUALID ENVIRONS OF PALACE YOSHIDA...
JESUS, DON'T CLOSE YOUR HEART TO THEM!!
WE WISH WE COULD MOVE INTO A PLACE LIKE YOURS!
WHY ARE YOU LEAVING?!
IS IT BECAUSE YOU COULD HEAR ME RECITING SUTRAS...?
N-NO, NO!
WE REALLY THINK IT'S A WONDERFUL PLACE...
...WITH WONDERFUL NEIGHBORS...
WE HAVE NOTHING BUT GOOD MEMORIES OF MATSUDA HEIGHTS.
YEAH...
ME, TOO...
YOU DO...?
I'M JUST THINKING BACK...
...ON ALL THE HAPPY DAYS WE'VE SPENT SINCE MOVING IN...

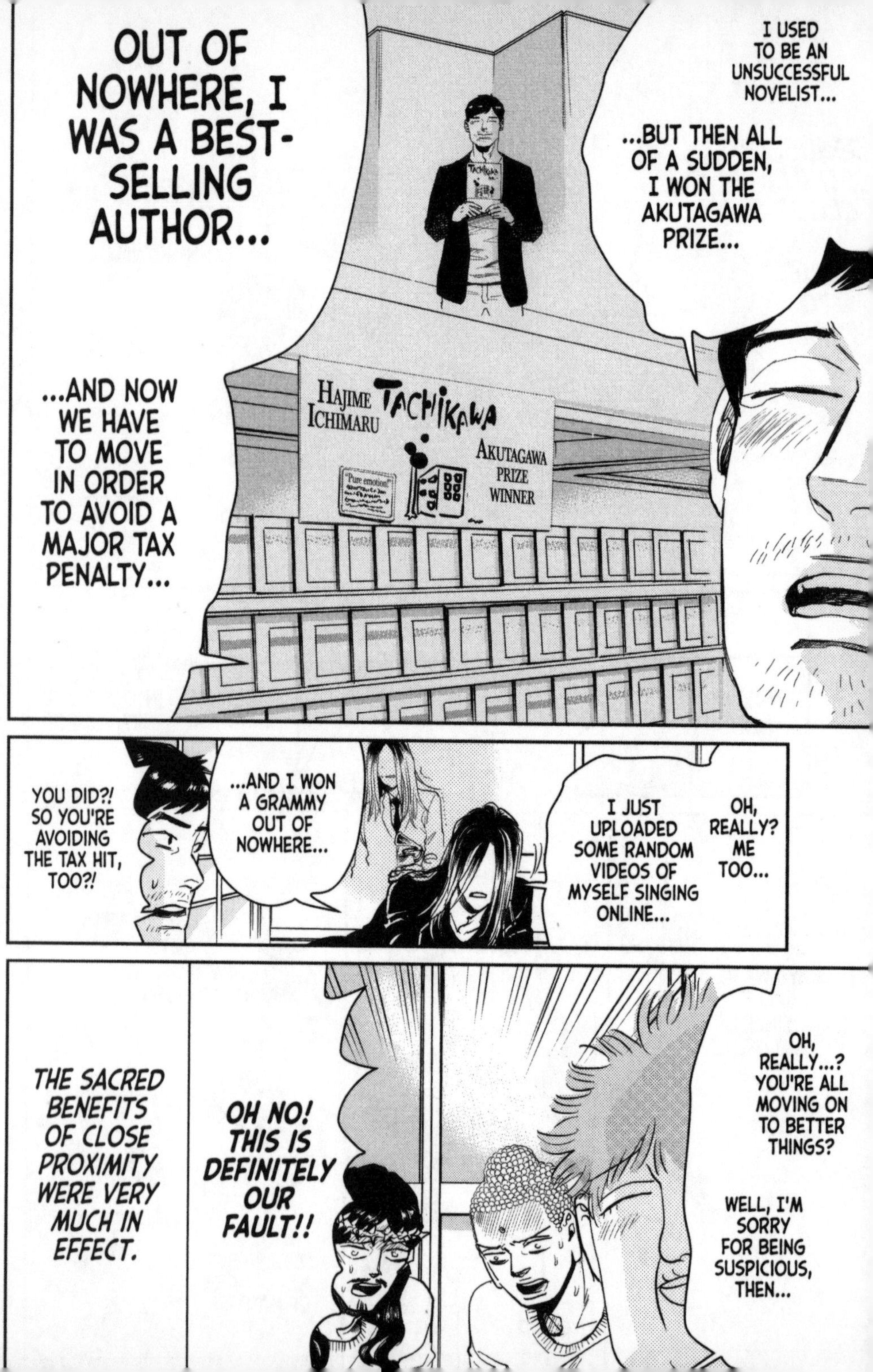
I USED TO BE AN UNSUCCESSFUL NOVELIST...
...BUT THEN ALL OF A SUDDEN, I WON THE AKUTAGAWA PRIZE...
OUT OF NOWHERE, I WAS A BEST-SELLING AUTHOR...
HAJIME ICHIMARU
TACHIKAWA
AKUTAGAWA PRIZE WINNER
"Pure emotion!"
...AND NOW WE HAVE TO MOVE IN ORDER TO AVOID A MAJOR TAX PENALTY...
OH, REALLY? ME TOO...
I JUST UPLOADED SOME RANDOM VIDEOS OF MYSELF SINGING ONLINE...
...AND I WON A GRAMMY OUT OF NOWHERE...
YOU DID?! SO YOU'RE AVOIDING THE TAX HIT, TOO?!
OH, REALLY...? YOU'RE ALL MOVING ON TO BETTER THINGS?
WELL, I'M SORRY FOR BEING SUSPICIOUS, THEN...
OH NO! THIS IS DEFINITELY OUR FAULT!!
THE SACRED BENEFITS OF CLOSE PROXIMITY WERE VERY MUCH IN EFFECT.

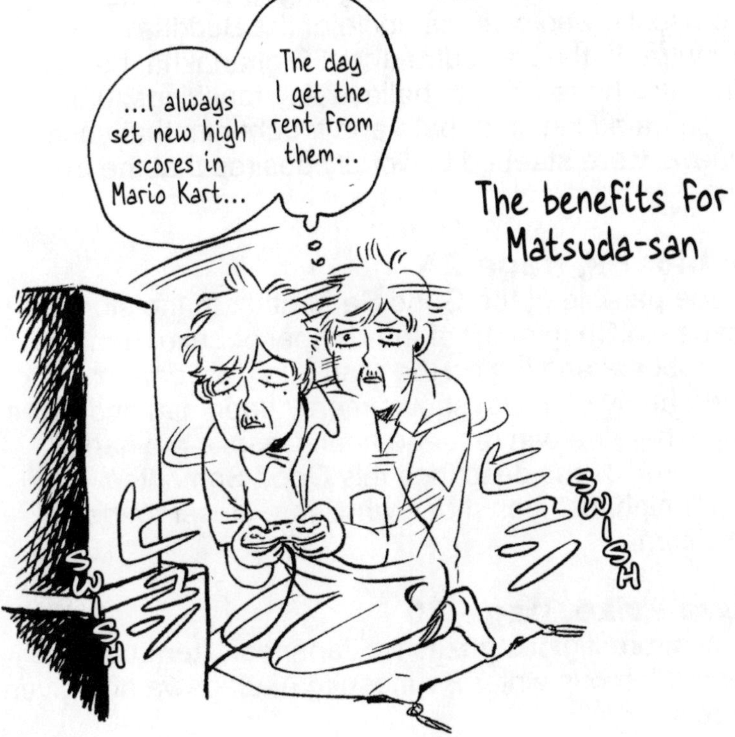
The benefits for Matsuda-san
The day I get the rent from them...
...I always set new high scores in Mario Kart...
SWISH
SWISH

CHAPTER 90 TRANSLATION NOTES

Salt is good, page 19

A passage from the Gospel of Mark, 9:50, in which Jesus says, "Salt is good, but if it loses its saltiness, how can you make it salty again? Have salt among yourselves, and be at peace with each other." It is interpreted as a statement on devotion to God, in which other worldly concerns can only dilute or bring impurity to the pureness of the kingdom of God.

Dighanakha, page 21

Dighanakha, whose name means "long fingernails," was a wandering ascetic who was the uncle of the Buddha's disciple Sariputra. In the Pali sutra about Dighanakha, he was a contrarian who refused to believe any teachings, until the Buddha defeated him in debate and taught him that such contrarian views were steeped in worldly desires that the truly wise eschew.

Good Yoshidans, page 25

A parody of the parable of the Good Samaritan. In the story Jesus describes in Chapter 10 of the Gospel of Luke, a man is beaten by robbers and left on the road. Only a Samaritan (normally the enemy of Jews) shows mercy upon him and takes him to an inn where he can rest and heal. Despite ordinarily being adversaries, Jesus describes this Good Samaritan as more of a "neighbor" than those who were closer to the unfortunate victim.

Akutagawa Prize, page 26

One of the most prestigious prizes for Japanese literature. It is named after the famous writer Ryûnosuke Akutagawa and given out twice a year.

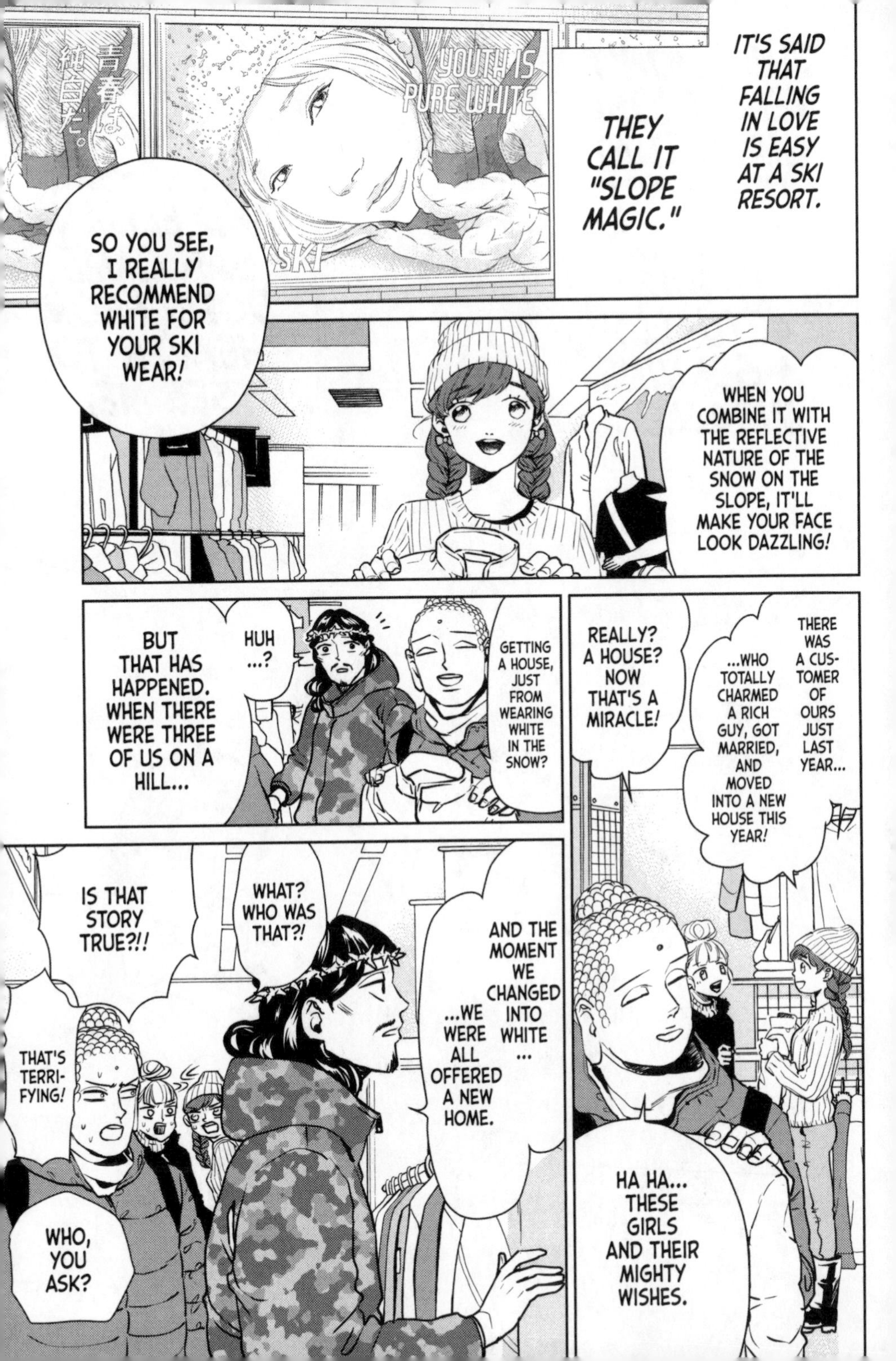
IT'S SAID THAT FALLING IN LOVE IS EASY AT A SKI RESORT.
THEY CALL IT "SLOPE MAGIC."
青春は純白だ。
YOUTH IS PURE WHITE
SKI
SO YOU SEE, I REALLY RECOMMEND WHITE FOR YOUR SKI WEAR!
WHEN YOU COMBINE IT WITH THE REFLECTIVE NATURE OF THE SNOW ON THE SLOPE, IT'LL MAKE YOUR FACE LOOK DAZZLING!
THERE WAS A CUS-TOMER OF OURS JUST LAST YEAR...
...WHO TOTALLY CHARMED A RICH GUY, GOT MARRIED, AND MOVED INTO A NEW HOUSE THIS YEAR!
REALLY? A HOUSE? NOW THAT'S A MIRACLE!
GETTING A HOUSE, JUST FROM WEARING WHITE IN THE SNOW?
HUH ...?
BUT THAT HAS HAPPENED. WHEN THERE WERE THREE OF US ON A HILL...
HA HA... THESE GIRLS AND THEIR MIGHTY WISHES.
AND THE MOMENT WE CHANGED INTO WHITE ...
...WE WERE ALL OFFERED A NEW HOME.
WHAT? WHO WAS THAT?!
IS THAT STORY TRUE?!!
THAT'S TERRI-FYING!
WHO, YOU ASK?

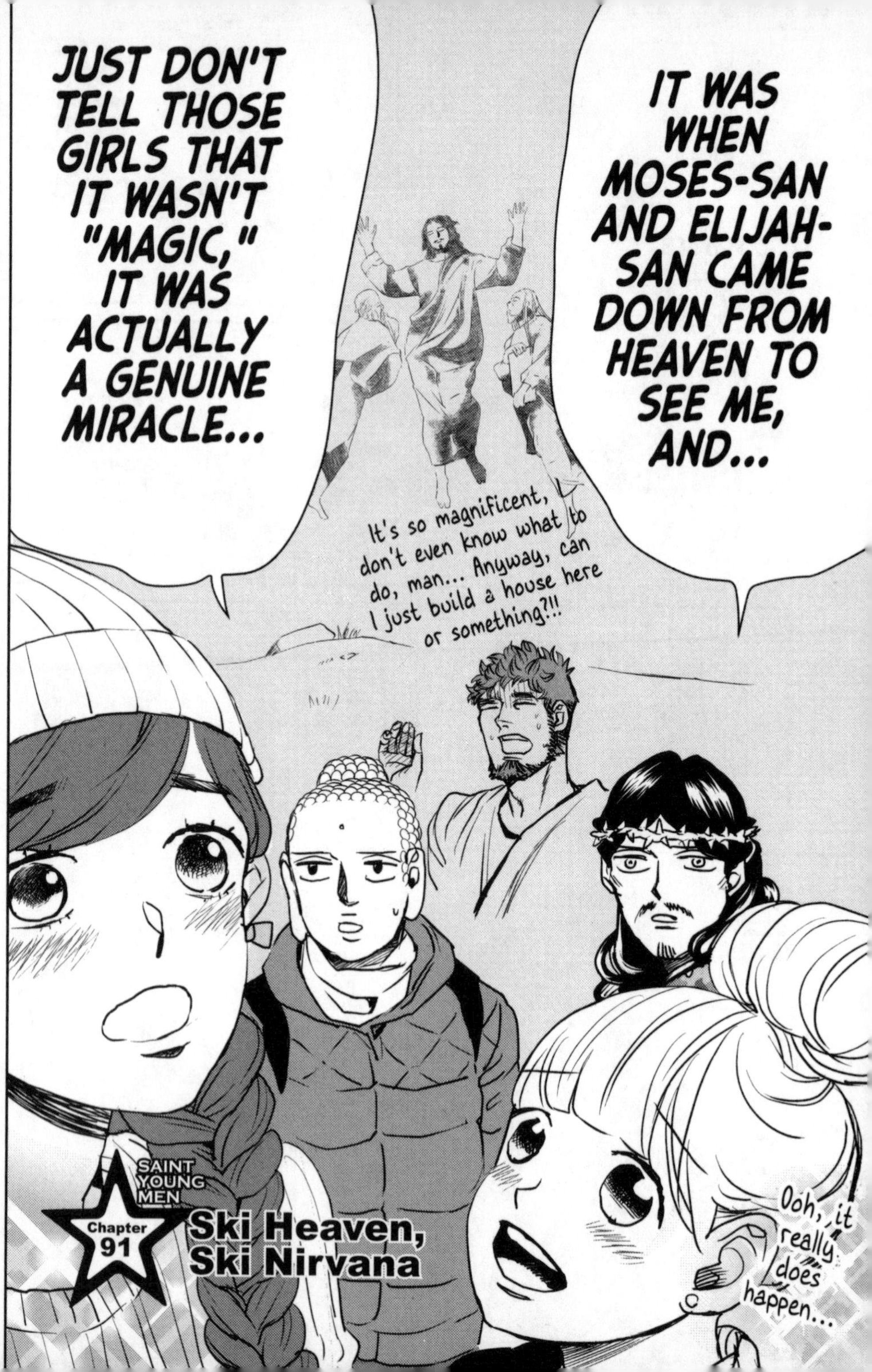
IT WAS WHEN MOSES-SAN AND ELIJAH-SAN CAME DOWN FROM HEAVEN TO SEE ME, AND...
JUST DON'T TELL THOSE GIRLS THAT IT WASN'T "MAGIC," IT WAS ACTUALLY A GENUINE MIRACLE...
It's so magnificent, to don't even know what do, man... Anyway, can I just build a house here or something?!!
SAINT YOUNG MEN
Chapter 91
Ski Heaven, Ski Nirvana
Ooh, it really does happen...

BUDDHA SO THOSE POLE THINGS YOU HOLD IN YOUR HANDS ARE CALLED "STOCKS" IN JAPAN? BUT THAT'S JUST FROM THE GERMAN WORD FOR "STAFF."

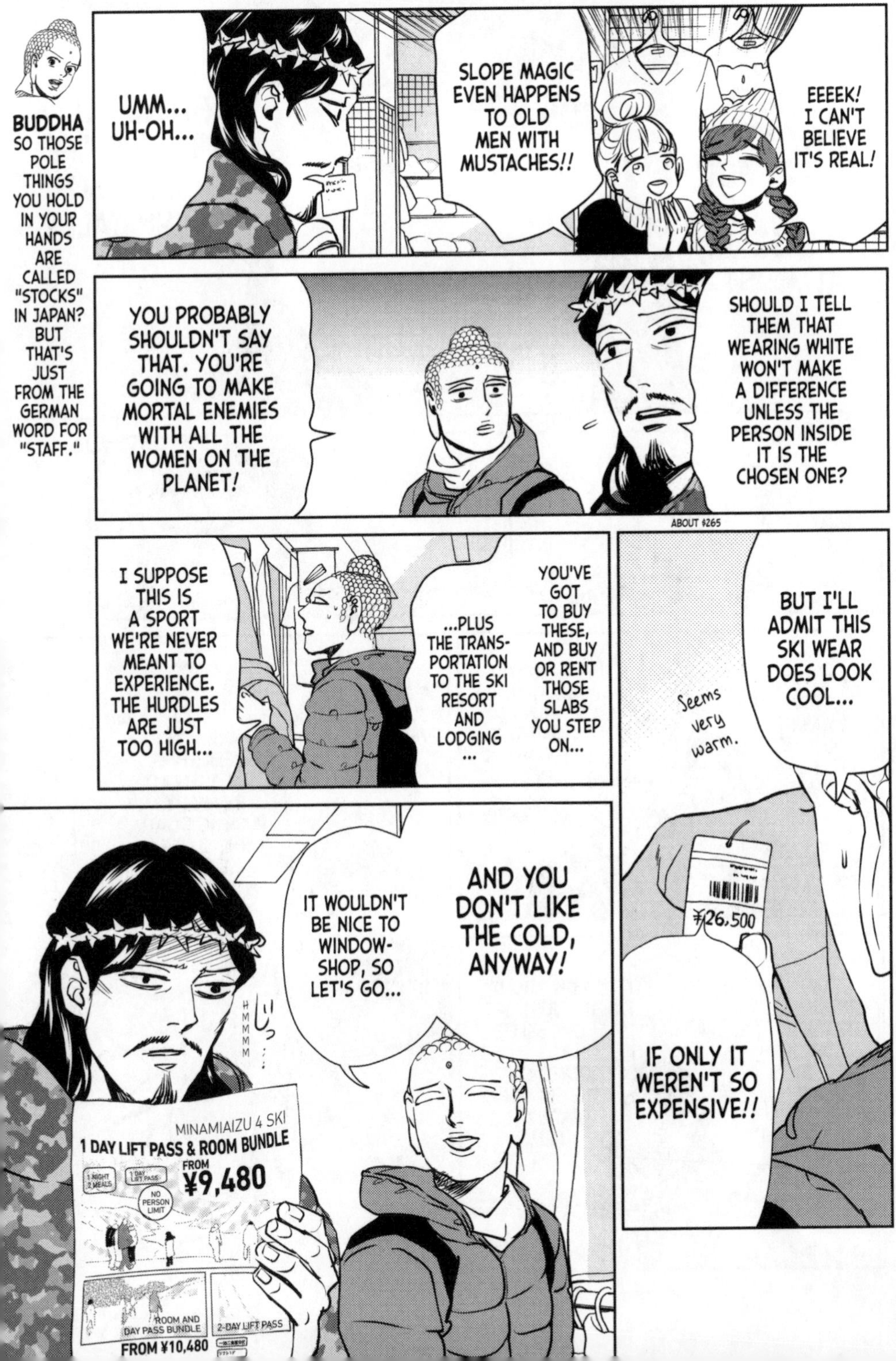
EEEEK! I CAN'T BELIEVE IT'S REAL!
SLOPE MAGIC EVEN HAPPENS TO OLD MEN WITH MUSTACHES!!
UMM... UH-OH...
SHOULD I TELL THEM THAT WEARING WHITE WON'T MAKE A DIFFERENCE UNLESS THE PERSON INSIDE IT IS THE CHOSEN ONE?
YOU PROBABLY SHOULDN'T SAY THAT. YOU'RE GOING TO MAKE MORTAL ENEMIES WITH ALL THE WOMEN ON THE PLANET!
ABOUT $265
BUT I'LL ADMIT THIS SKI WEAR DOES LOOK COOL...
Seems very warm.
¥26,500
IF ONLY IT WEREN'T SO EXPENSIVE!!
YOU'VE GOT TO BUY THESE, AND BUY OR RENT THOSE SLABS YOU STEP ON...
...PLUS THE TRANSPORTATION TO THE SKI RESORT AND LODGING...
I SUPPOSE THIS IS A SPORT WE'RE NEVER MEANT TO EXPERIENCE. THE HURDLES ARE JUST TOO HIGH...
AND YOU DON'T LIKE THE COLD, ANYWAY!
IT WOULDN'T BE NICE TO WINDOW-SHOP, SO LET'S GO...
HMMMM
MINAMIAIZU 4 SKI
1 DAY LIFT PASS & ROOM BUNDLE
FROM ¥9,480
1 NIGHT 2 MEALS
1 DAY LIFT PASS
NO PERSON LIMIT
ROOM AND DAY PASS BUNDLE
FROM ¥10,480
2-DAY LIFT PASS

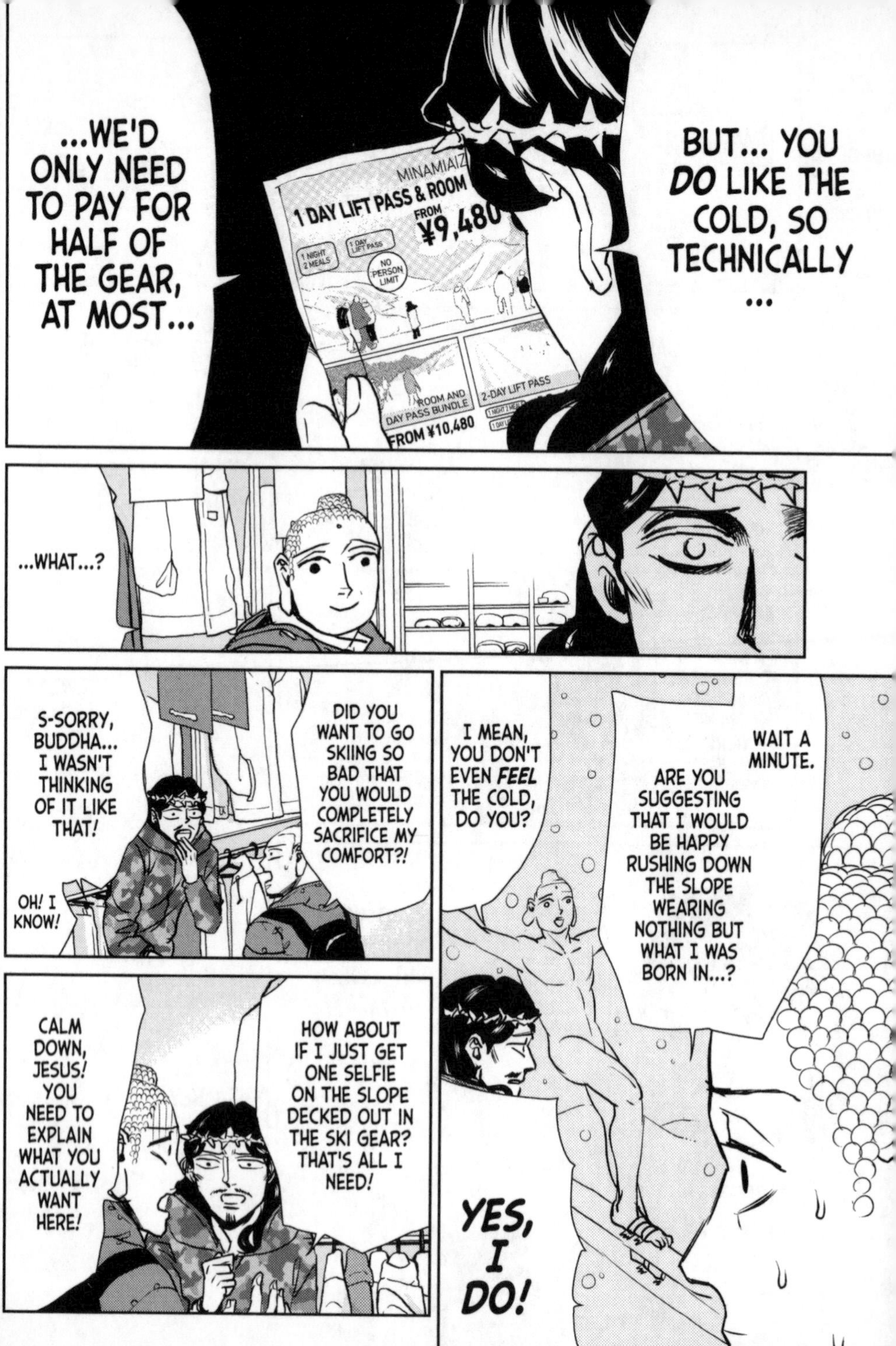
BUT... YOU *DO* LIKE THE COLD, SO TECHNICALLY ...
MINAMIAIZ
1 DAY LIFT PASS & ROOM
FROM ¥9,480
1 NIGHT 2 MEALS
1 DAY LIFT PASS
NO PERSON LIMIT
2-DAY LIFT PASS
ROOM AND DAY PASS BUNDLE
FROM ¥10,480
...WE'D ONLY NEED TO PAY FOR HALF OF THE GEAR, AT MOST...
...WHAT...?
WAIT A MINUTE.
ARE YOU SUGGESTING THAT I WOULD BE HAPPY RUSHING DOWN THE SLOPE WEARING NOTHING BUT WHAT I WAS BORN IN...?
I MEAN, YOU DON'T EVEN *FEEL* THE COLD, DO YOU?
YES, I DO!
DID YOU WANT TO GO SKIING SO BAD THAT YOU WOULD COMPLETELY SACRIFICE MY COMFORT?!
S-SORRY, BUDDHA... I WASN'T THINKING OF IT LIKE THAT!
OH! I KNOW!
HOW ABOUT IF I JUST GET ONE SELFIE ON THE SLOPE DECKED OUT IN THE SKI GEAR? THAT'S ALL I NEED!
CALM DOWN, JESUS! YOU NEED TO EXPLAIN WHAT YOU ACTUALLY WANT HERE!

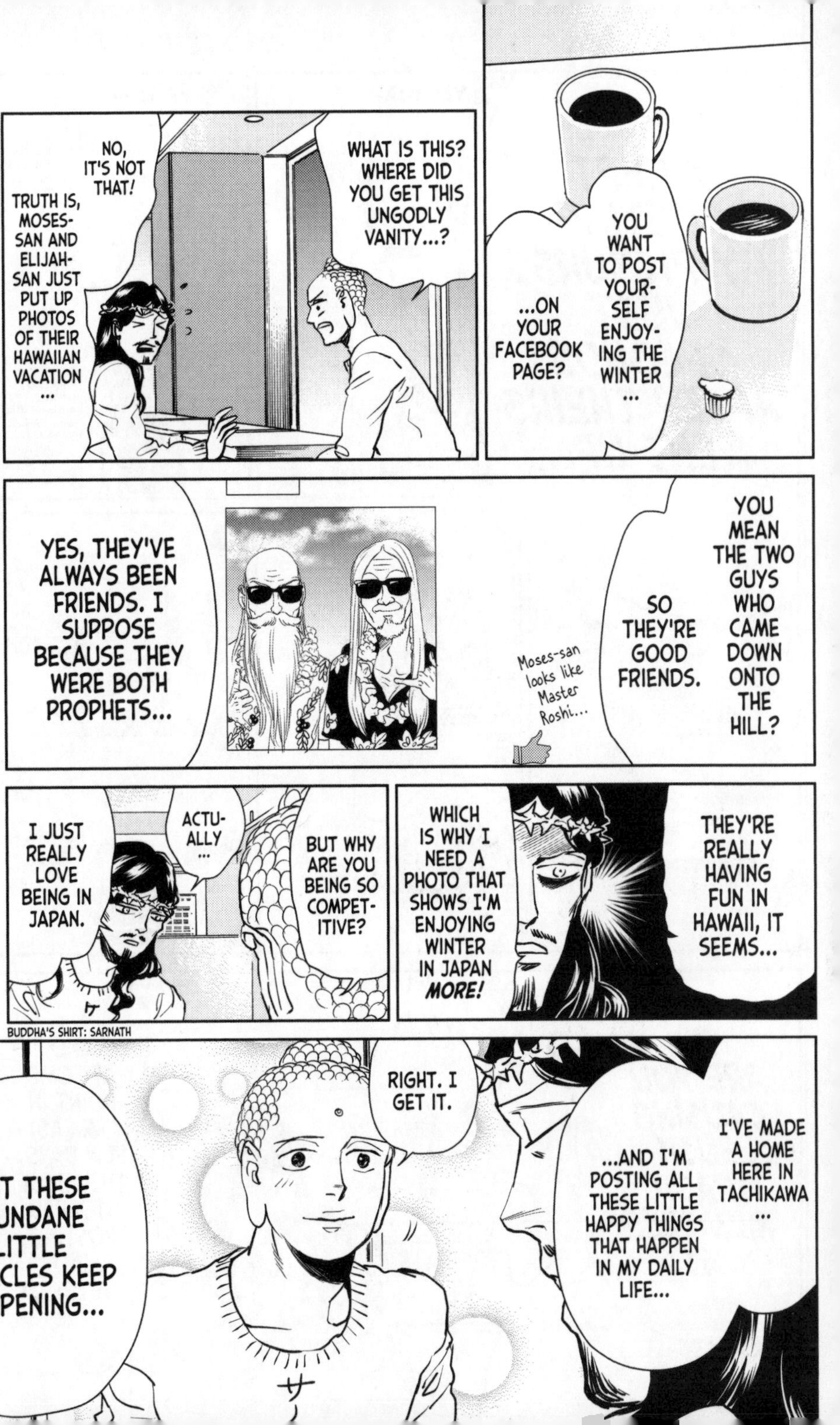
YOU WANT TO POST YOURSELF ENJOYING THE WINTER...
...ON YOUR FACEBOOK PAGE?
WHAT IS THIS? WHERE DID YOU GET THIS UNGODLY VANITY...?
NO, IT'S NOT THAT!
TRUTH IS, MOSES-SAN AND ELIJAH-SAN JUST PUT UP PHOTOS OF THEIR HAWAIIAN VACATION...
YOU MEAN THE TWO GUYS WHO CAME DOWN ONTO THE HILL?
SO THEY'RE GOOD FRIENDS.
Moses-san looks like Master Roshi...
YES, THEY'VE ALWAYS BEEN FRIENDS. I SUPPOSE BECAUSE THEY WERE BOTH PROPHETS...
THEY'RE REALLY HAVING FUN IN HAWAII, IT SEEMS...
WHICH IS WHY I NEED A PHOTO THAT SHOWS I'M ENJOYING WINTER IN JAPAN *MORE!*
BUT WHY ARE YOU BEING SO COMPETITIVE?
ACTUALLY...
I JUST REALLY LOVE BEING IN JAPAN.
BUDDHA'S SHIRT: SARNATH
I'VE MADE A HOME HERE IN TACHIKAWA...
...AND I'M POSTING ALL THESE LITTLE HAPPY THINGS THAT HAPPEN IN MY DAILY LIFE...
RIGHT. I GET IT.
BUT THESE MUNDANE LITTLE MIRACLES KEEP HAPPENING...

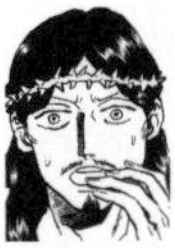

JESUS
SO THEY'RE CALLED "SKI POLES" RATHER THAN STICKS? AND IN FRANCE THEY'RE CALLED "BATONS," WHICH IS... WEIRD.

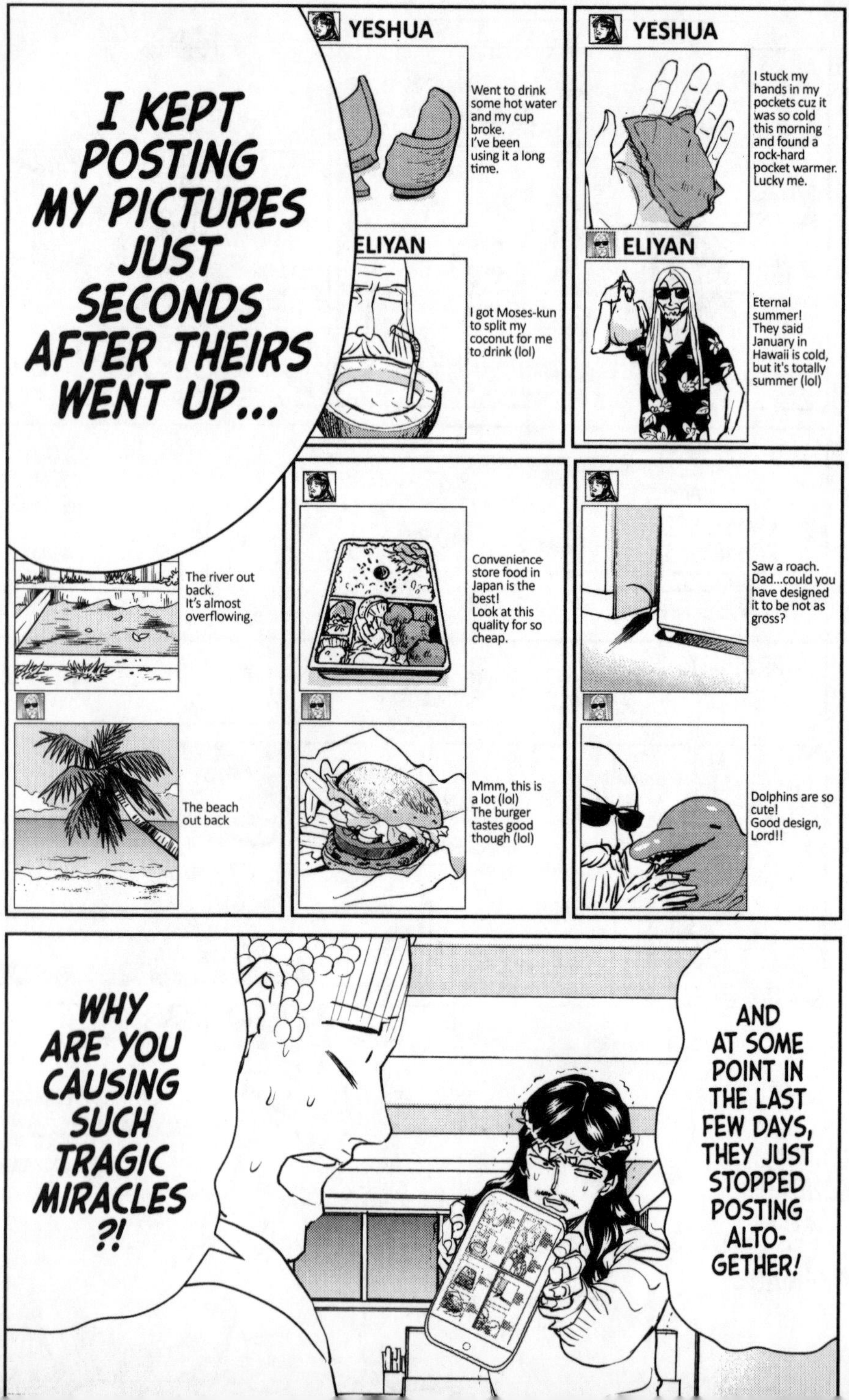
YESHUA
I stuck my hands in my pockets cuz it was so cold this morning and found a rock-hard pocket warmer. Lucky me.
ELIYAN
Eternal summer! They said January in Hawaii is cold, but it's totally summer (lol)
YESHUA
Went to drink some hot water and my cup broke. I've been using it a long time.
ELIYAN
I got Moses-kun to split my coconut for me to drink (lol)
Saw a roach. Dad...could you have designed it to be not as gross?
Dolphins are so cute! Good design, Lord!!
Convenience store food in Japan is the best! Look at this quality for so cheap.
Mmm, this is a lot (lol) The burger tastes good though (lol)
I KEPT POSTING MY PICTURES JUST SECONDS AFTER THEIRS WENT UP...
The river out back. It's almost overflowing.
The beach out back
AND AT SOME POINT IN THE LAST FEW DAYS, THEY JUST STOPPED POSTING ALTO-GETHER!
WHY ARE YOU CAUSING SUCH TRAGIC MIRACLES ?!

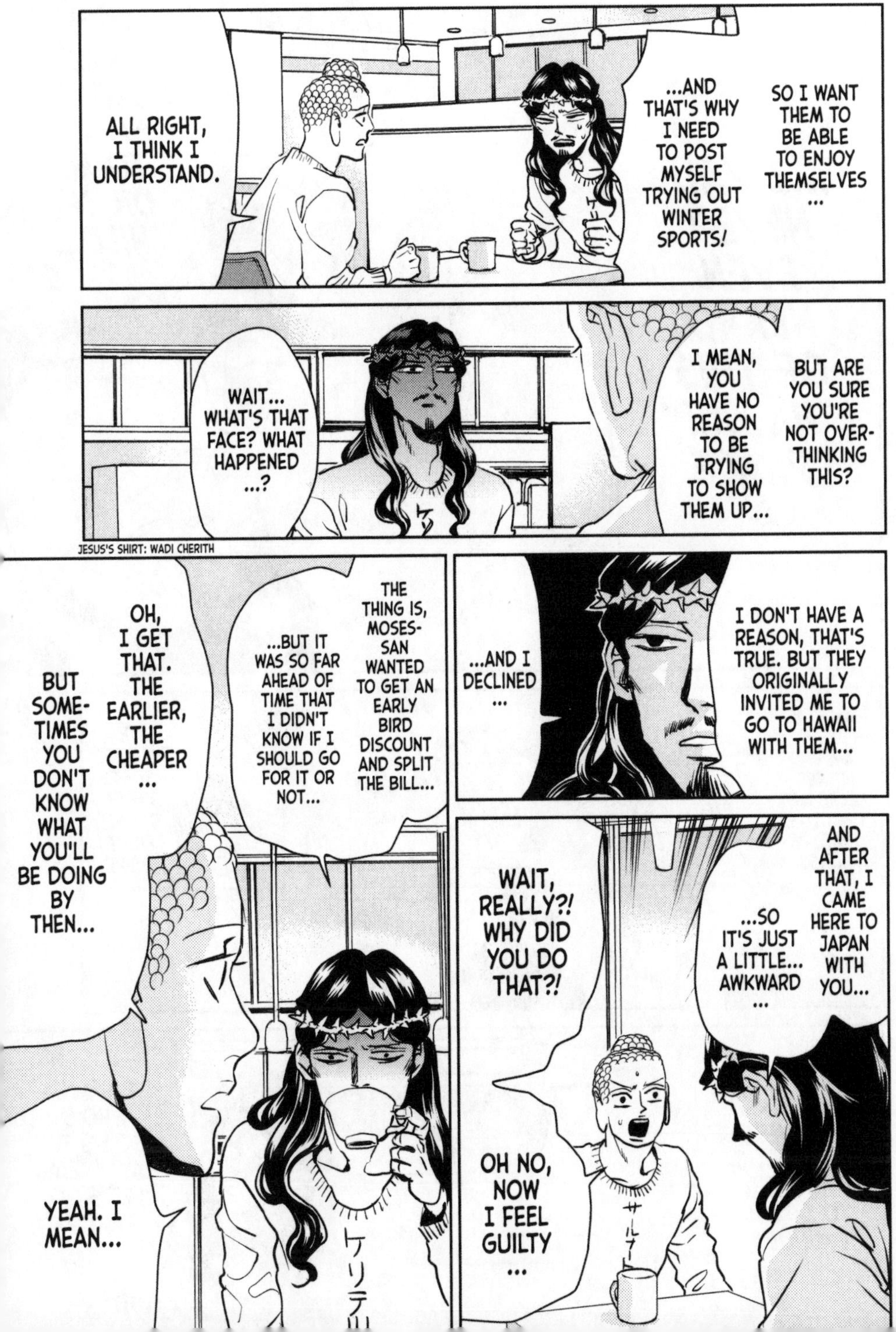
SO I WANT THEM TO BE ABLE TO ENJOY THEMSELVES...
...AND THAT'S WHY I NEED TO POST MYSELF TRYING OUT WINTER SPORTS!
ALL RIGHT, I THINK I UNDERSTAND.
BUT ARE YOU SURE YOU'RE NOT OVER-THINKING THIS?
I MEAN, YOU HAVE NO REASON TO BE TRYING TO SHOW THEM UP...
WAIT... WHAT'S THAT FACE? WHAT HAPPENED...?
JESUS'S SHIRT: WADI CHERITH
I DON'T HAVE A REASON, THAT'S TRUE. BUT THEY ORIGINALLY INVITED ME TO GO TO HAWAII WITH THEM...
...AND I DECLINED...
AND AFTER THAT, I CAME HERE TO JAPAN WITH YOU...
...SO IT'S JUST A LITTLE... AWKWARD...
WAIT, REALLY?! WHY DID YOU DO THAT?!
OH NO, NOW I FEEL GUILTY...
THE THING IS, MOSES-SAN WANTED TO GET AN EARLY BIRD DISCOUNT AND SPLIT THE BILL...
...BUT IT WAS SO FAR AHEAD OF TIME THAT I DIDN'T KNOW IF I SHOULD GO FOR IT OR NOT...
OH, I GET THAT. THE EARLIER, THE CHEAPER...
BUT SOMETIMES YOU DON'T KNOW WHAT YOU'LL BE DOING BY THEN...
YEAH. I MEAN...

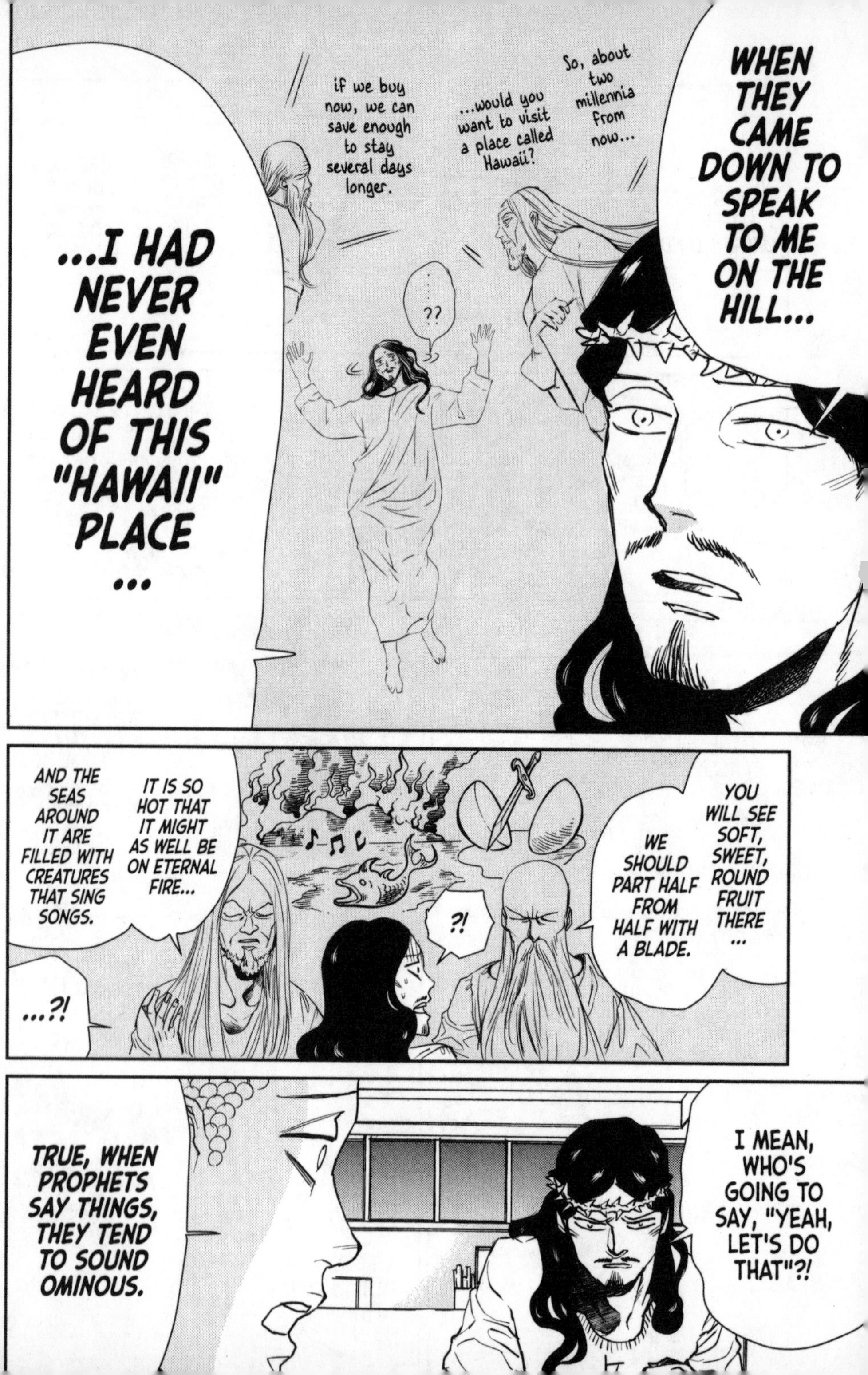
WHEN THEY CAME DOWN TO SPEAK TO ME ON THE HILL...
So, about two millennia from now...
...would you want to visit a place called Hawaii?
if we buy now, we can save enough to stay several days longer.
......??
...I HAD NEVER EVEN HEARD OF THIS "HAWAII" PLACE...
YOU WILL SEE SOFT, SWEET, ROUND FRUIT THERE...
WE SHOULD PART HALF FROM HALF WITH A BLADE.
?!
IT IS SO HOT THAT IT MIGHT AS WELL BE ON ETERNAL FIRE...
AND THE SEAS AROUND IT ARE FILLED WITH CREATURES THAT SING SONGS.
...?!
I MEAN, WHO'S GOING TO SAY, "YEAH, LET'S DO THAT"?!
TRUE, WHEN PROPHETS SAY THINGS, THEY TEND TO SOUND OMINOUS.

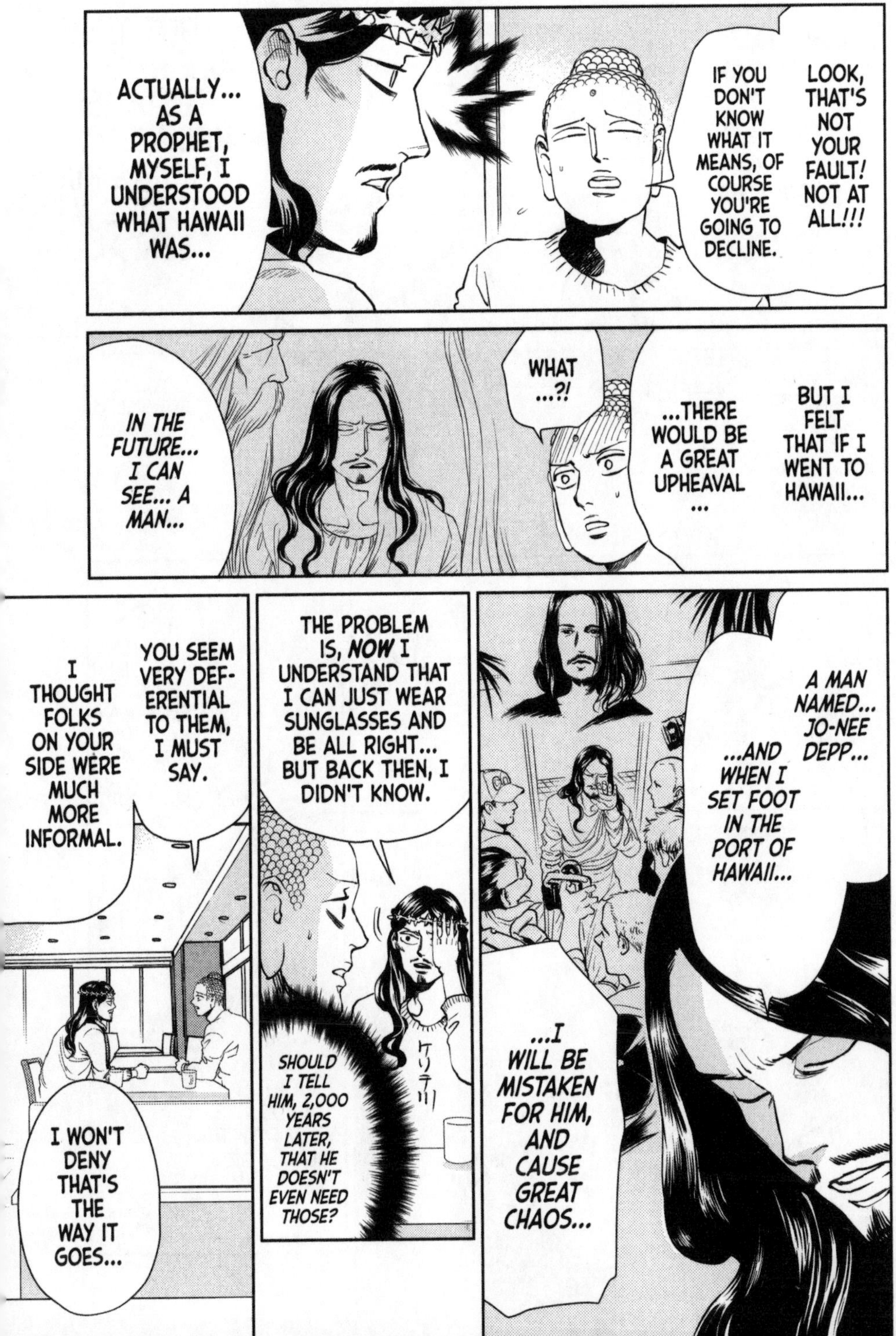
LOOK, THAT'S NOT YOUR FAULT! NOT AT ALL!!!
IF YOU DON'T KNOW WHAT IT MEANS, OF COURSE YOU'RE GOING TO DECLINE.
ACTUALLY... AS A PROPHET, MYSELF, I UNDERSTOOD WHAT HAWAII WAS...
BUT I FELT THAT IF I WENT TO HAWAII...
...THERE WOULD BE A GREAT UPHEAVAL...
WHAT ...?!
IN THE FUTURE... I CAN SEE... A MAN...
A MAN NAMED... JO-NEE DEPP...
...AND WHEN I SET FOOT IN THE PORT OF HAWAII...
...I WILL BE MISTAKEN FOR HIM, AND CAUSE GREAT CHAOS...
THE PROBLEM IS, NOW I UNDERSTAND THAT I CAN JUST WEAR SUNGLASSES AND BE ALL RIGHT... BUT BACK THEN, I DIDN'T KNOW.
SHOULD I TELL HIM, 2,000 YEARS LATER, THAT HE DOESN'T EVEN NEED THOSE?
YOU SEEM VERY DEFERENTIAL TO THEM, I MUST SAY.
I THOUGHT FOLKS ON YOUR SIDE WERE MUCH MORE INFORMAL.
I WON'T DENY THAT'S THE WAY IT GOES...

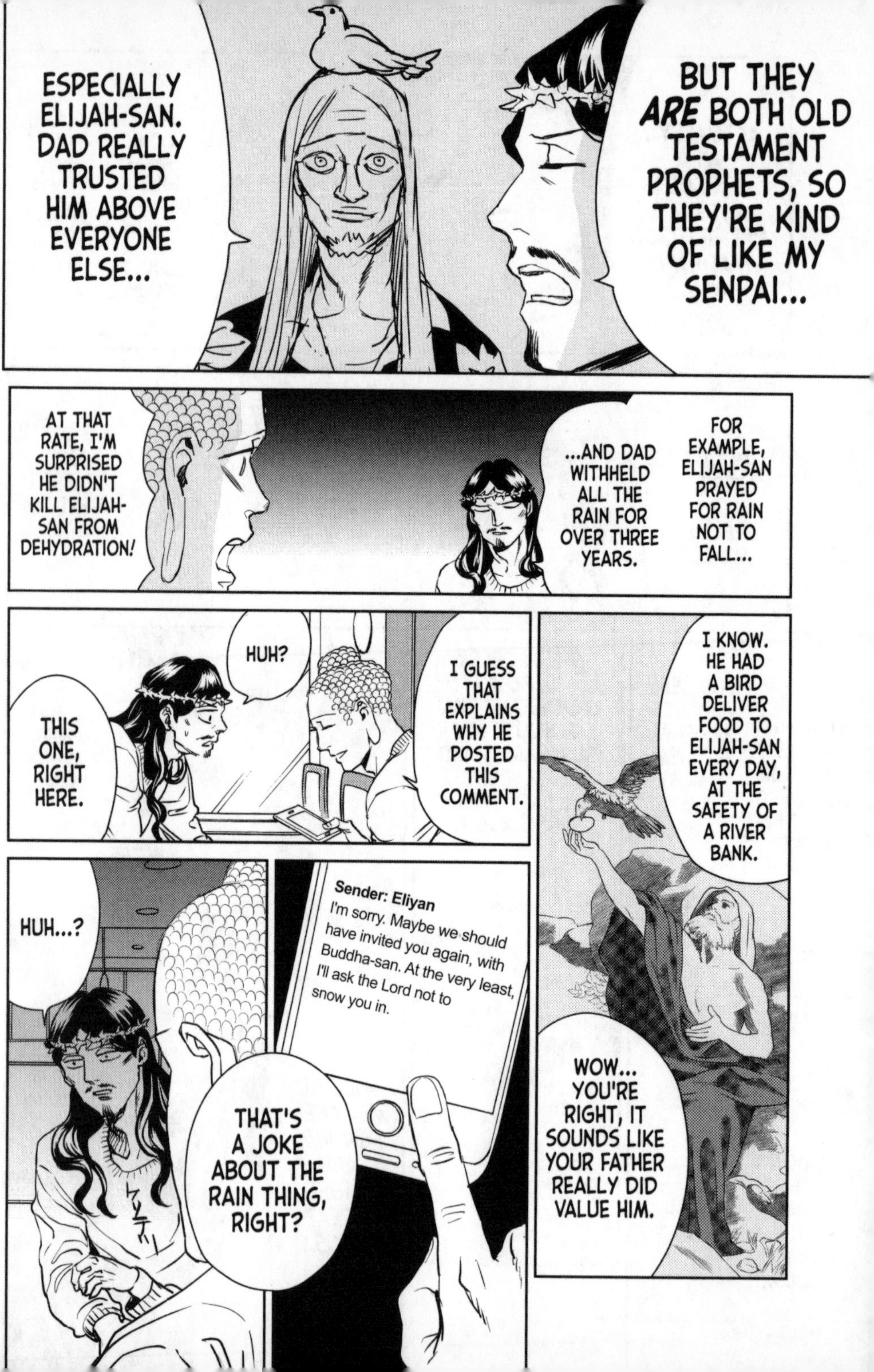
BUT THEY ARE BOTH OLD TESTAMENT PROPHETS, SO THEY'RE KIND OF LIKE MY SENPAI...
ESPECIALLY ELIJAH-SAN. DAD REALLY TRUSTED HIM ABOVE EVERYONE ELSE...
FOR EXAMPLE, ELIJAH-SAN PRAYED FOR RAIN NOT TO FALL...
...AND DAD WITHHELD ALL THE RAIN FOR OVER THREE YEARS.
AT THAT RATE, I'M SURPRISED HE DIDN'T KILL ELIJAH-SAN FROM DEHYDRATION!
I KNOW. HE HAD A BIRD DELIVER FOOD TO ELIJAH-SAN EVERY DAY, AT THE SAFETY OF A RIVER BANK.
WOW... YOU'RE RIGHT, IT SOUNDS LIKE YOUR FATHER REALLY DID VALUE HIM.
I GUESS THAT EXPLAINS WHY HE POSTED THIS COMMENT.
HUH?
THIS ONE, RIGHT HERE.
Sender: Eliyan
I'm sorry. Maybe we should have invited you again, with Buddha-san. At the very least, I'll ask the Lord not to snow you in.
THAT'S A JOKE ABOUT THE RAIN THING, RIGHT?
HUH...?

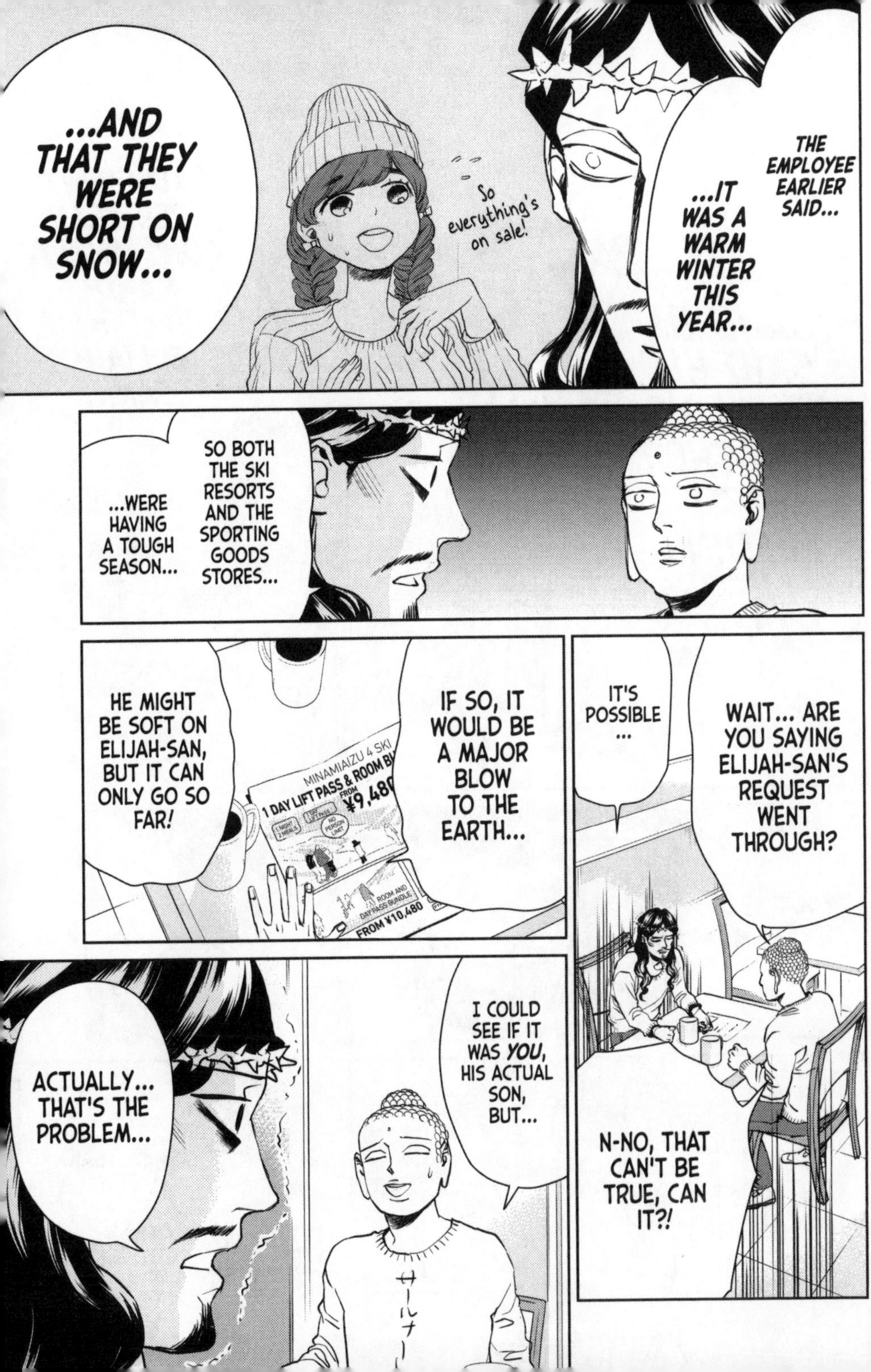
THE EMPLOYEE EARLIER SAID...
...IT WAS A WARM WINTER THIS YEAR...
So everything's on sale!
...AND THAT THEY WERE SHORT ON SNOW...
SO BOTH THE SKI RESORTS AND THE SPORTING GOODS STORES...
...WERE HAVING A TOUGH SEASON...
WAIT... ARE YOU SAYING ELIJAH-SAN'S REQUEST WENT THROUGH?
IT'S POSSIBLE ...
N-NO, THAT CAN'T BE TRUE, CAN IT?!
IF SO, IT WOULD BE A MAJOR BLOW TO THE EARTH...
HE MIGHT BE SOFT ON ELIJAH-SAN, BUT IT CAN ONLY GO SO FAR!
MINAMIAIZU 4 SKI
1 NIGHT 2 MEALS
NO PERSON LIMIT
ROOM AND DAY PASS BUNDLE
FROM ¥10,480
I COULD SEE IF IT WAS *YOU*, HIS ACTUAL SON, BUT...
ACTUALLY... THAT'S THE PROBLEM...

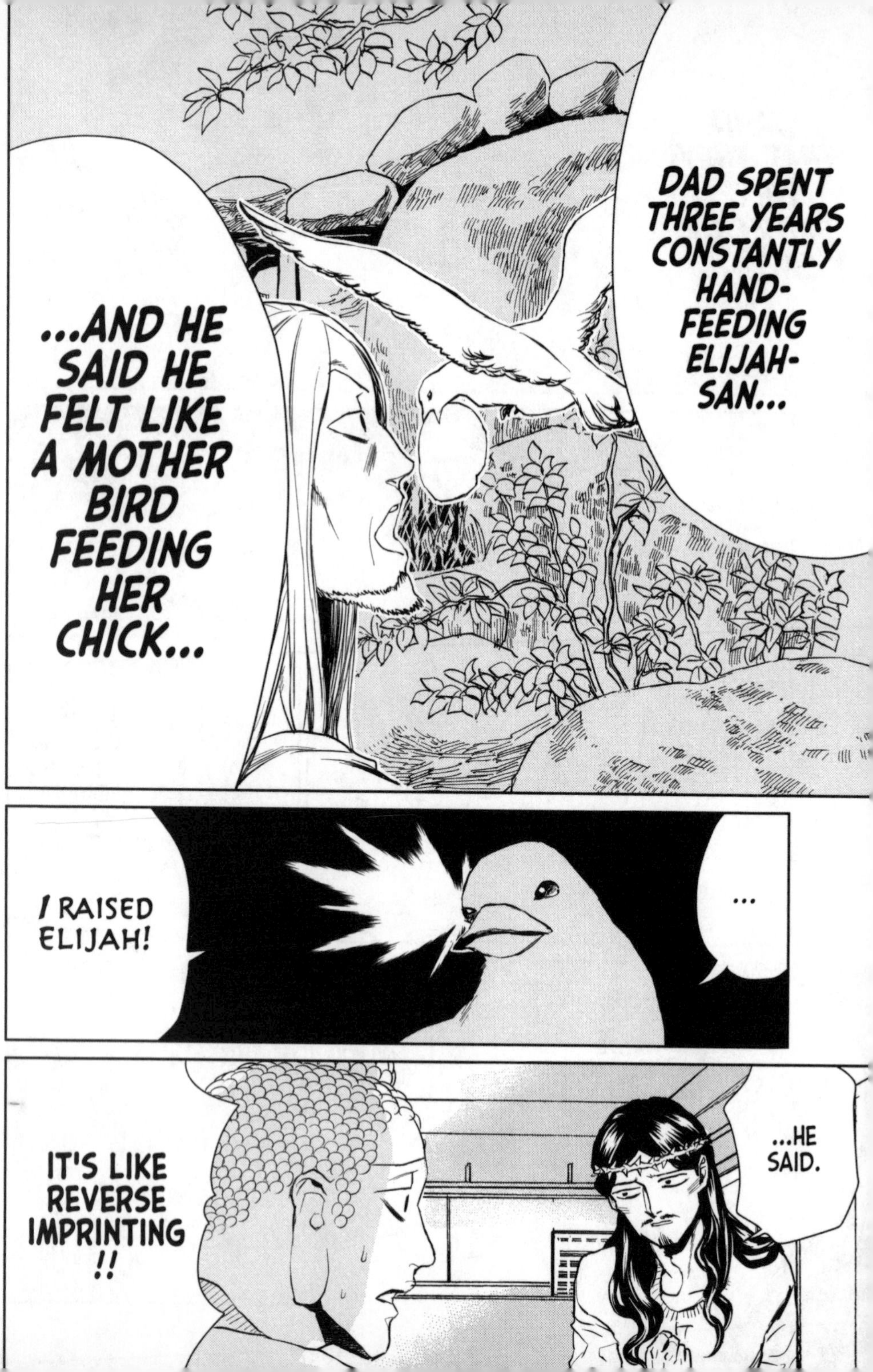
DAD SPENT THREE YEARS CONSTANTLY HAND-FEEDING ELIJAH-SAN...
...AND HE SAID HE FELT LIKE A MOTHER BIRD FEEDING HER CHICK...
...
I RAISED ELIJAH!
...HE SAID.
IT'S LIKE REVERSE IMPRINTING!!

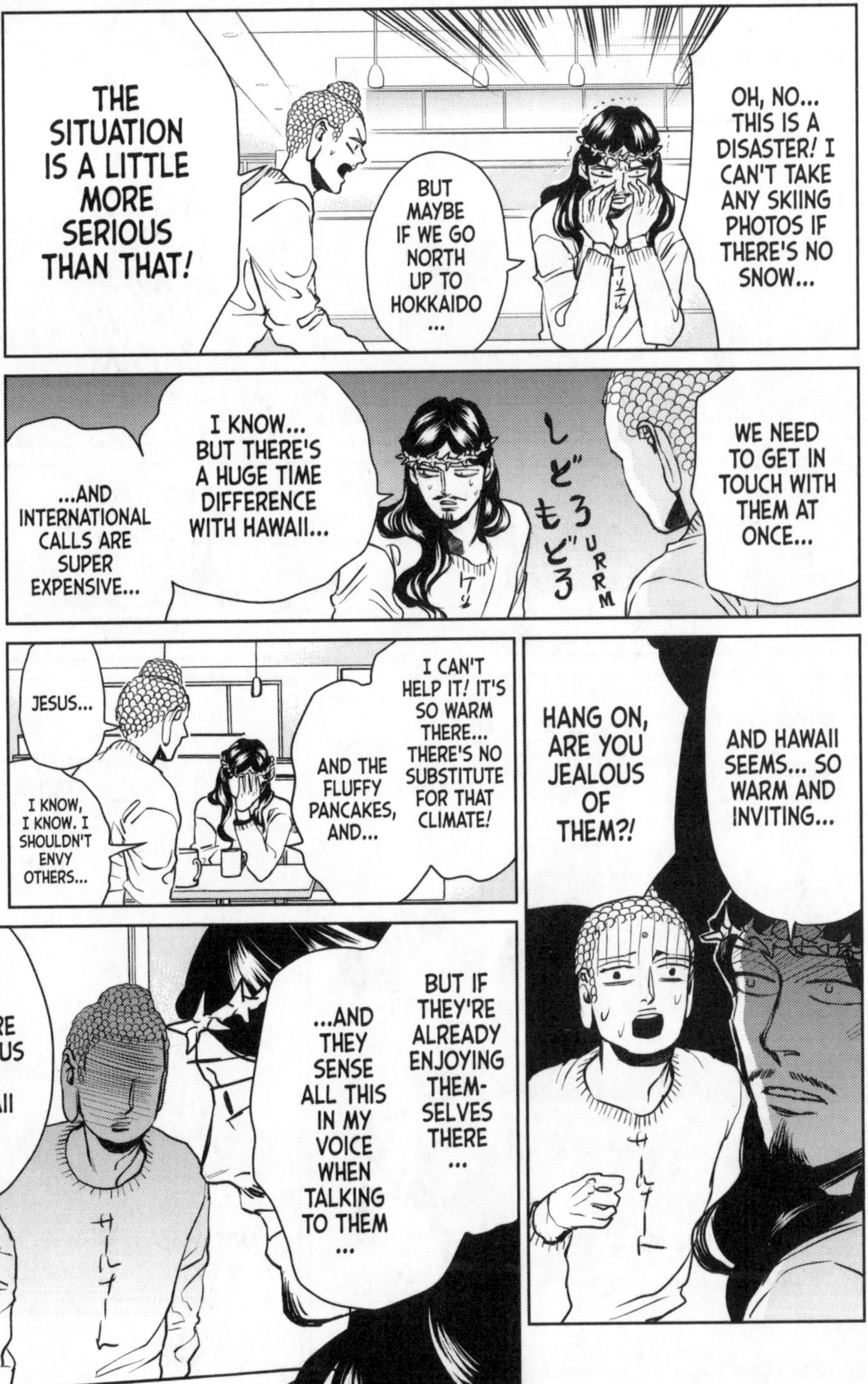
OH, NO... THIS IS A DISASTER! I CAN'T TAKE ANY SKIING PHOTOS IF THERE'S NO SNOW...
BUT MAYBE IF WE GO NORTH UP TO HOKKAIDO ...
THE SITUATION IS A LITTLE MORE SERIOUS THAN THAT!
WE NEED TO GET IN TOUCH WITH THEM AT ONCE...
しどろもどろ URRM
I KNOW... BUT THERE'S A HUGE TIME DIFFERENCE WITH HAWAII...
...AND INTERNATIONAL CALLS ARE SUPER EXPENSIVE...
AND HAWAII SEEMS... SO WARM AND INVITING...
HANG ON, ARE YOU JEALOUS OF THEM?!
I CAN'T HELP IT! IT'S SO WARM THERE... THERE'S NO SUBSTITUTE FOR THAT CLIMATE!
AND THE FLUFFY PANCAKES, AND...
JESUS...
I KNOW, I KNOW. I SHOULDN'T ENVY OTHERS...
BUT IF THEY'RE ALREADY ENJOYING THEM-SELVES THERE ...
...AND THEY SENSE ALL THIS IN MY VOICE WHEN TALKING TO THEM ...
SO YOU'RE JEALOUS OF HAWAII ...?

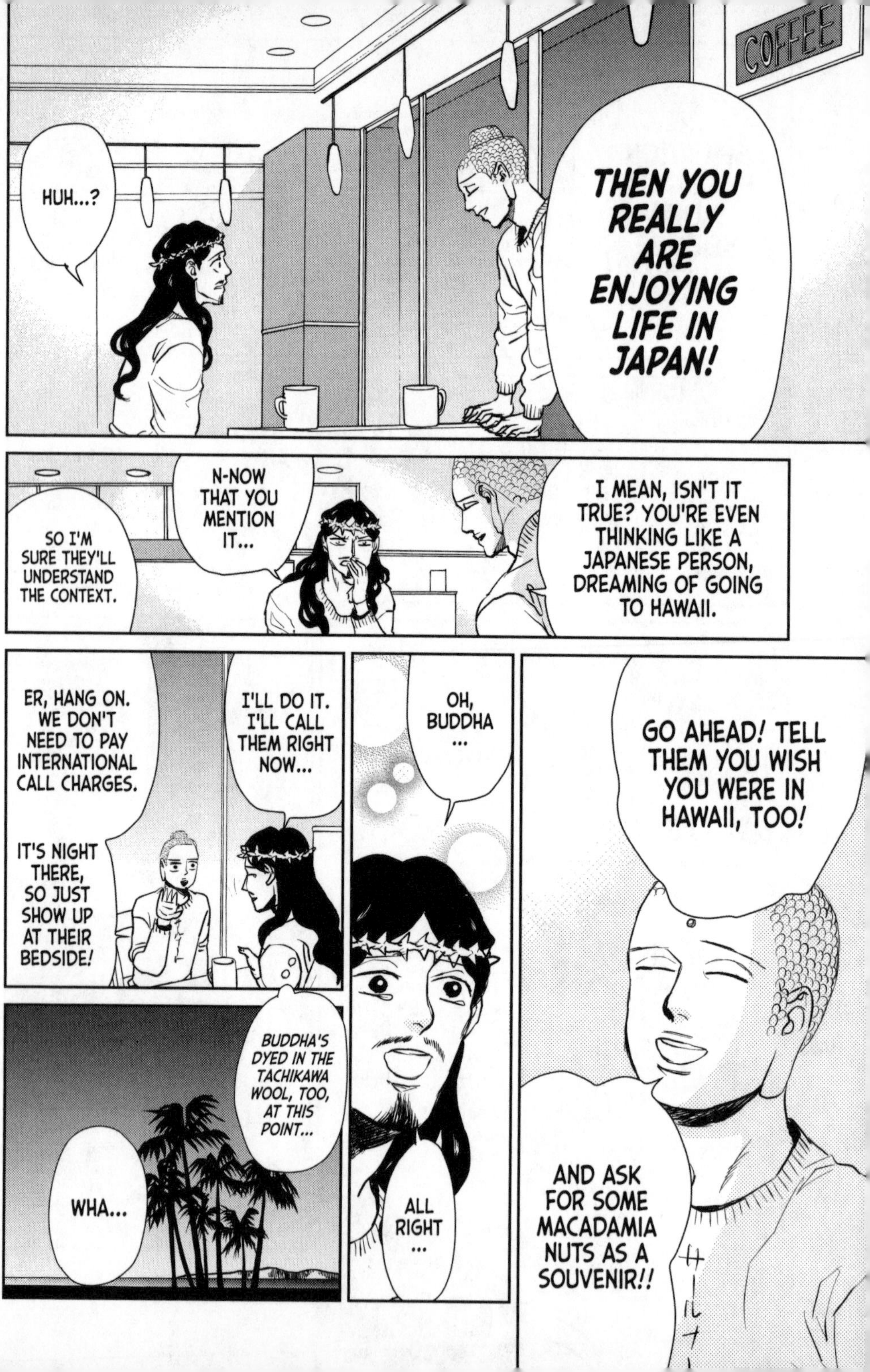
COFFEE
THEN YOU REALLY ARE ENJOYING LIFE IN JAPAN!
HUH...?
I MEAN, ISN'T IT TRUE? YOU'RE EVEN THINKING LIKE A JAPANESE PERSON, DREAMING OF GOING TO HAWAII.
N-NOW THAT YOU MENTION IT...
SO I'M SURE THEY'LL UNDERSTAND THE CONTEXT.
GO AHEAD! TELL THEM YOU WISH YOU WERE IN HAWAII, TOO!
AND ASK FOR SOME MACADAMIA NUTS AS A SOUVENIR!!
OH, BUDDHA...
ALL RIGHT...
I'LL DO IT. I'LL CALL THEM RIGHT NOW...
ER, HANG ON. WE DON'T NEED TO PAY INTERNATIONAL CALL CHARGES.
IT'S NIGHT THERE, SO JUST SHOW UP AT THEIR BEDSIDE!
BUDDHA'S DYED IN THE TACHIKAWA WOOL, TOO, AT THIS POINT...
WHA...

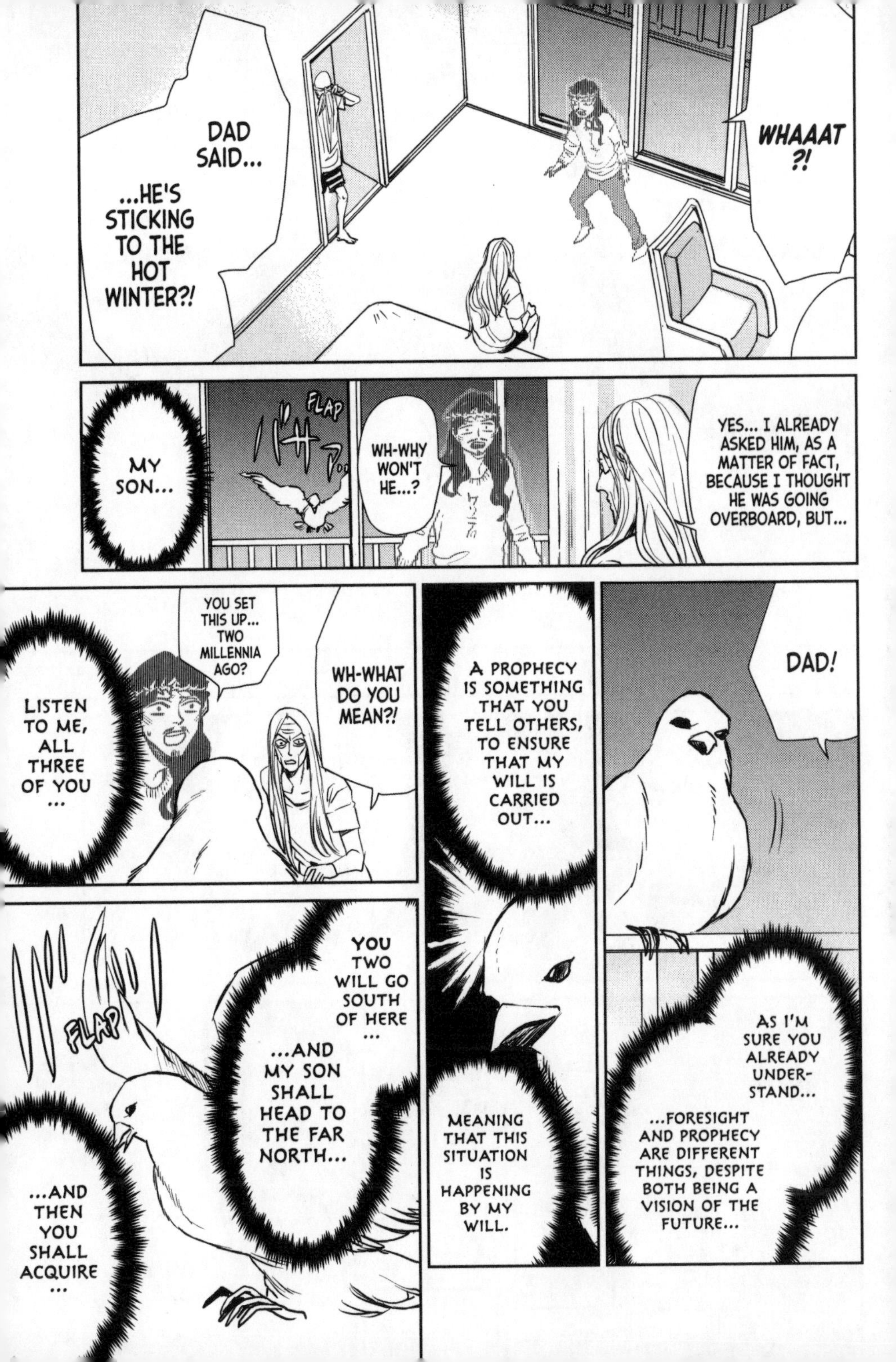
WHAAAT?!
DAD SAID... ...HE'S STICKING TO THE HOT WINTER?!
YES... I ALREADY ASKED HIM, AS A MATTER OF FACT, BECAUSE I THOUGHT HE WAS GOING OVERBOARD, BUT...
WH-WHY WON'T HE...?
FLAP
MY SON...
DAD!
AS I'M SURE YOU ALREADY UNDER-STAND...
...FORESIGHT AND PROPHECY ARE DIFFERENT THINGS, DESPITE BOTH BEING A VISION OF THE FUTURE...
A PROPHECY IS SOMETHING THAT YOU TELL OTHERS, TO ENSURE THAT MY WILL IS CARRIED OUT...
MEANING THAT THIS SITUATION IS HAPPENING BY MY WILL.
WH-WHAT DO YOU MEAN?!
YOU SET THIS UP... TWO MILLENNIA AGO?
LISTEN TO ME, ALL THREE OF YOU...
YOU TWO WILL GO SOUTH OF HERE...
...AND MY SON SHALL HEAD TO THE FAR NORTH...
FLAP
...AND THEN YOU SHALL ACQUIRE...

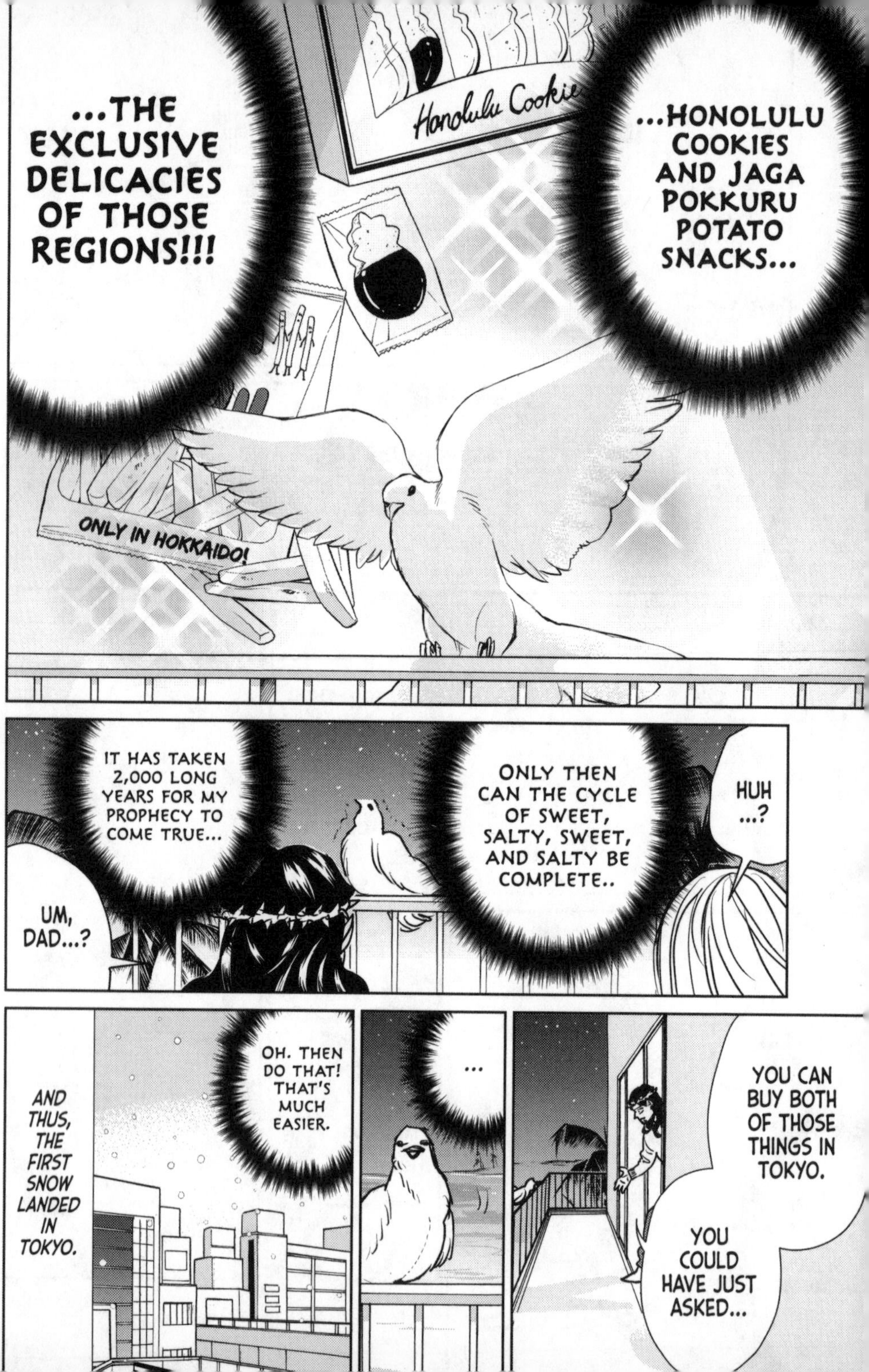

...HONOLULU COOKIES AND JAGA POKKURU POTATO SNACKS...
Honolulu Cookie
...THE EXCLUSIVE DELICACIES OF THOSE REGIONS!!!
ONLY IN HOKKAIDO!
HUH ...?
ONLY THEN CAN THE CYCLE OF SWEET, SALTY, SWEET, AND SALTY BE COMPLETE..
IT HAS TAKEN 2,000 LONG YEARS FOR MY PROPHECY TO COME TRUE...
UM, DAD...?
YOU CAN BUY BOTH OF THOSE THINGS IN TOKYO.
YOU COULD HAVE JUST ASKED...
...
OH. THEN DO THAT! THAT'S MUCH EASIER.
AND THUS, THE FIRST SNOW LANDED IN TOKYO.

Salty!! Salty!!
Sweet!! Sweet!! Sweet!!

SAINT☆YOUNG MEN

CHAPTER 91 TRANSLATION NOTES

The Transfiguration of Jesus, page 30
An event in which Jesus was accompanied by Peter, James, and John to pray on a mountain. While there, Jesus began to shine with a divine radiance, and the prophets Moses and Elijah appeared and spoke with him. As well, a voice from the sky called Jesus "Son." This event is held to be confirmation of Jesus's nature as the son of God. in the Gospels, Peter is confused by what he sees, and suggests that they set up tents for Moses and Elijah, as well.

Sarnath, page 33
Sarnath is the name of the place where Gautama Buddha is said to have given his first sermon to his followers. This was the establishment of his teaching of dharma.

Yeshua, page 34
The original Hebrew form of what would go on to be spelled Jesus, via the Greek and then Latin form. It is very similar to the root of the name Joshua, as well, of which the Hebrew form was Yehoshua.

Wadi Cherith, page 35
Cherith was a *wadi* (winter brook or stream) where the prophet Elijah hid himself during the three-year period of drought he foresaw.

Honolulu Cookies & Jaga Pokkuru, page 44
The Honolulu Cookie Company makes an assortment of shortbread cookies in the shape of pineapples featuring Hawaiian flavors like mango, lilikoi (passion fruit), coconut, and macadamia. *Jaga Pokkuru* (a combination of "potato" and the Ainu spirits named "koropokkuru") are a Hokkaido specialty snack. It looks like French fries, but rather than soft fried potato slivers, the pieces are crunchy and accentuate the natural potato flavor.

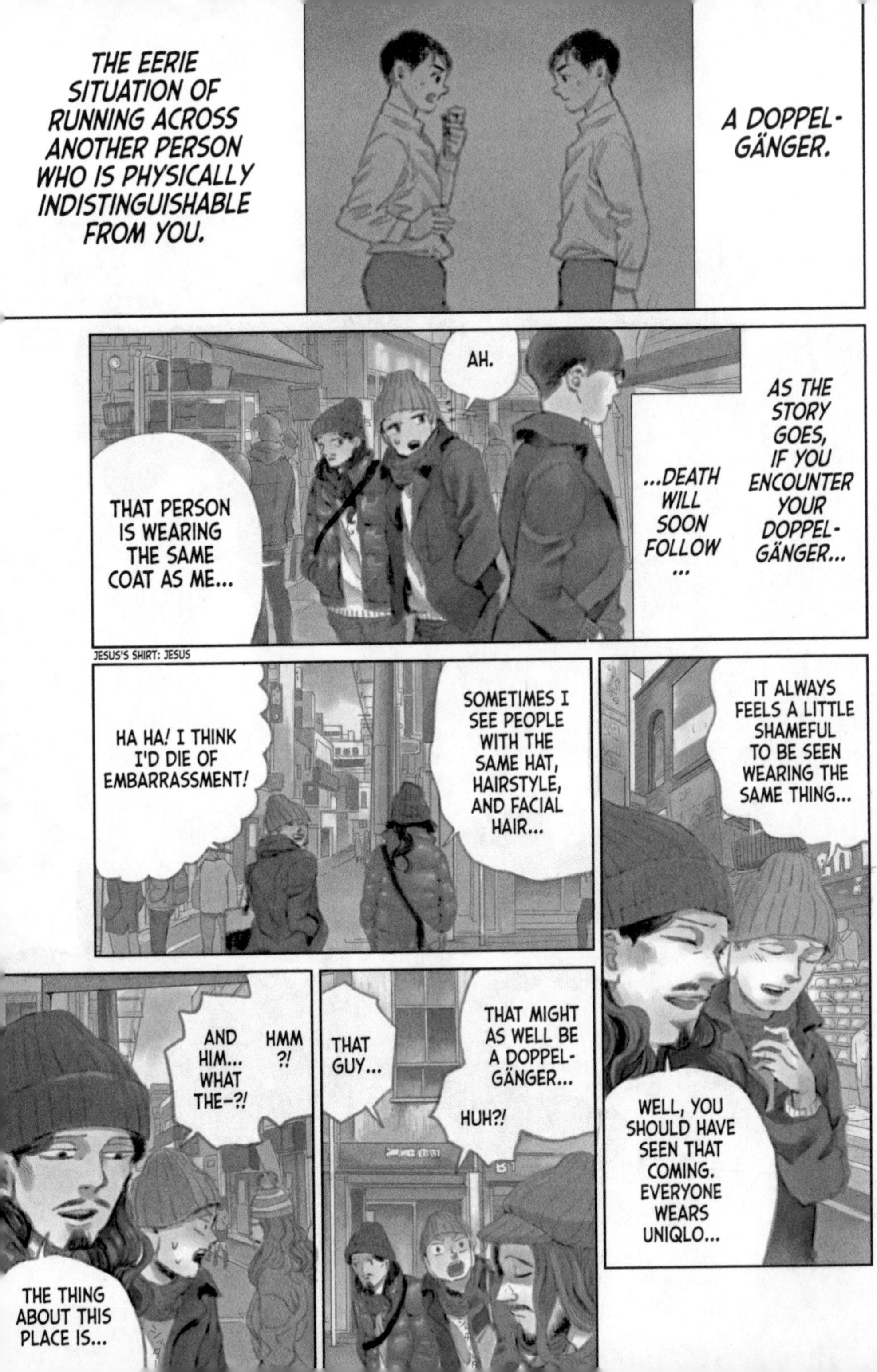
THE EERIE SITUATION OF RUNNING ACROSS ANOTHER PERSON WHO IS PHYSICALLY INDISTINGUISHABLE FROM YOU.
A DOPPEL-GÄNGER.
AS THE STORY GOES, IF YOU ENCOUNTER YOUR DOPPEL-GÄNGER...
...DEATH WILL SOON FOLLOW...
AH.
THAT PERSON IS WEARING THE SAME COAT AS ME...
JESUS'S SHIRT: JESUS
IT ALWAYS FEELS A LITTLE SHAMEFUL TO BE SEEN WEARING THE SAME THING...
WELL, YOU SHOULD HAVE SEEN THAT COMING. EVERYONE WEARS UNIQLO...
SOMETIMES I SEE PEOPLE WITH THE SAME HAT, HAIRSTYLE, AND FACIAL HAIR...
HA HA! I THINK I'D DIE OF EMBARRASSMENT!
THAT MIGHT AS WELL BE A DOPPEL-GÄNGER...
THAT GUY...
HUH?!
HMM ?!
AND HIM... WHAT THE–?!
THE THING ABOUT THIS PLACE IS...

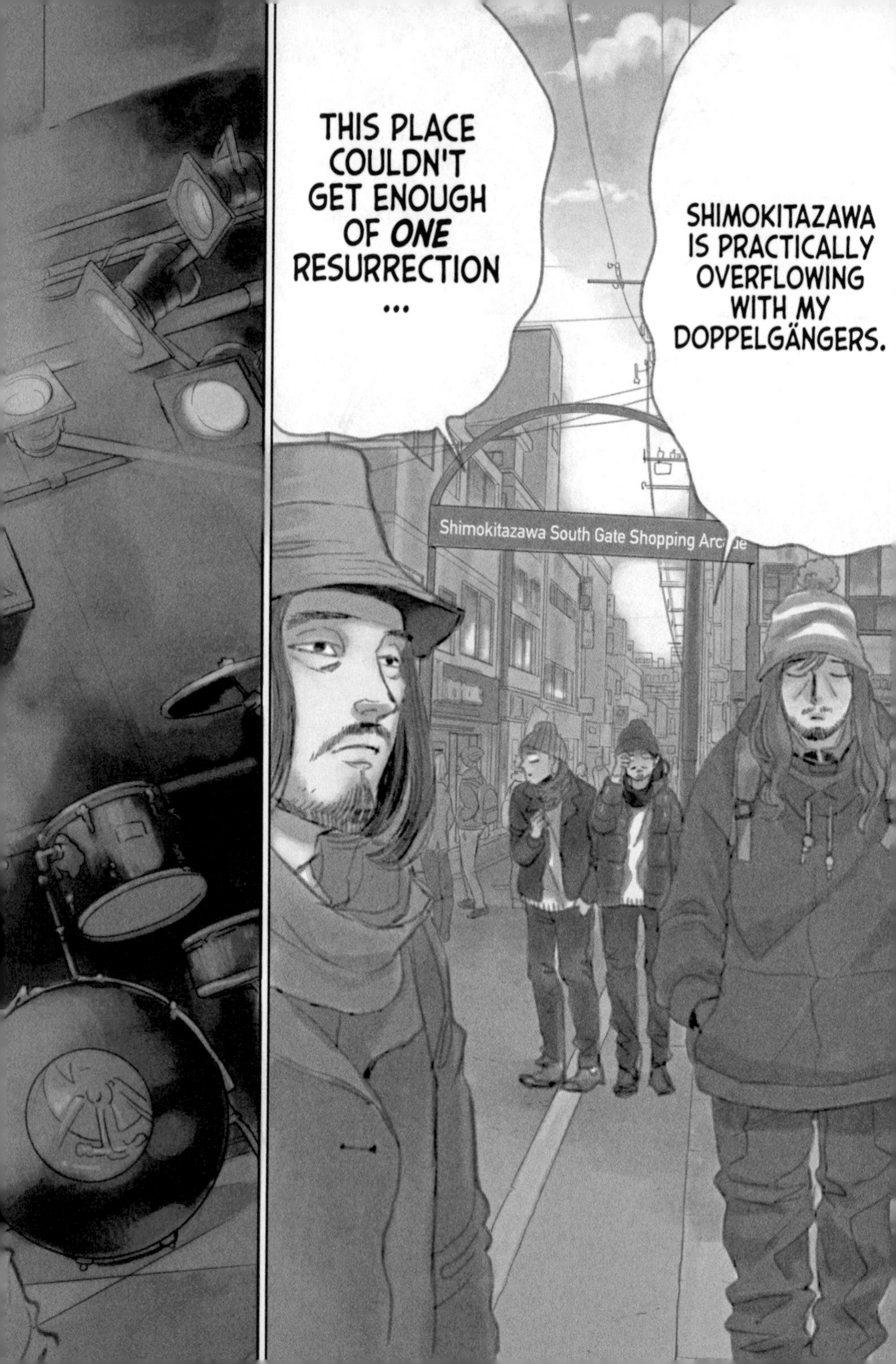
SHIMOKITAZAWA IS PRACTICALLY OVERFLOWING WITH MY DOPPELGÄNGERS.
THIS PLACE COULDN'T GET ENOUGH OF *ONE* RESURRECTION ...
Shimokitazawa South Gate Shopping Arc

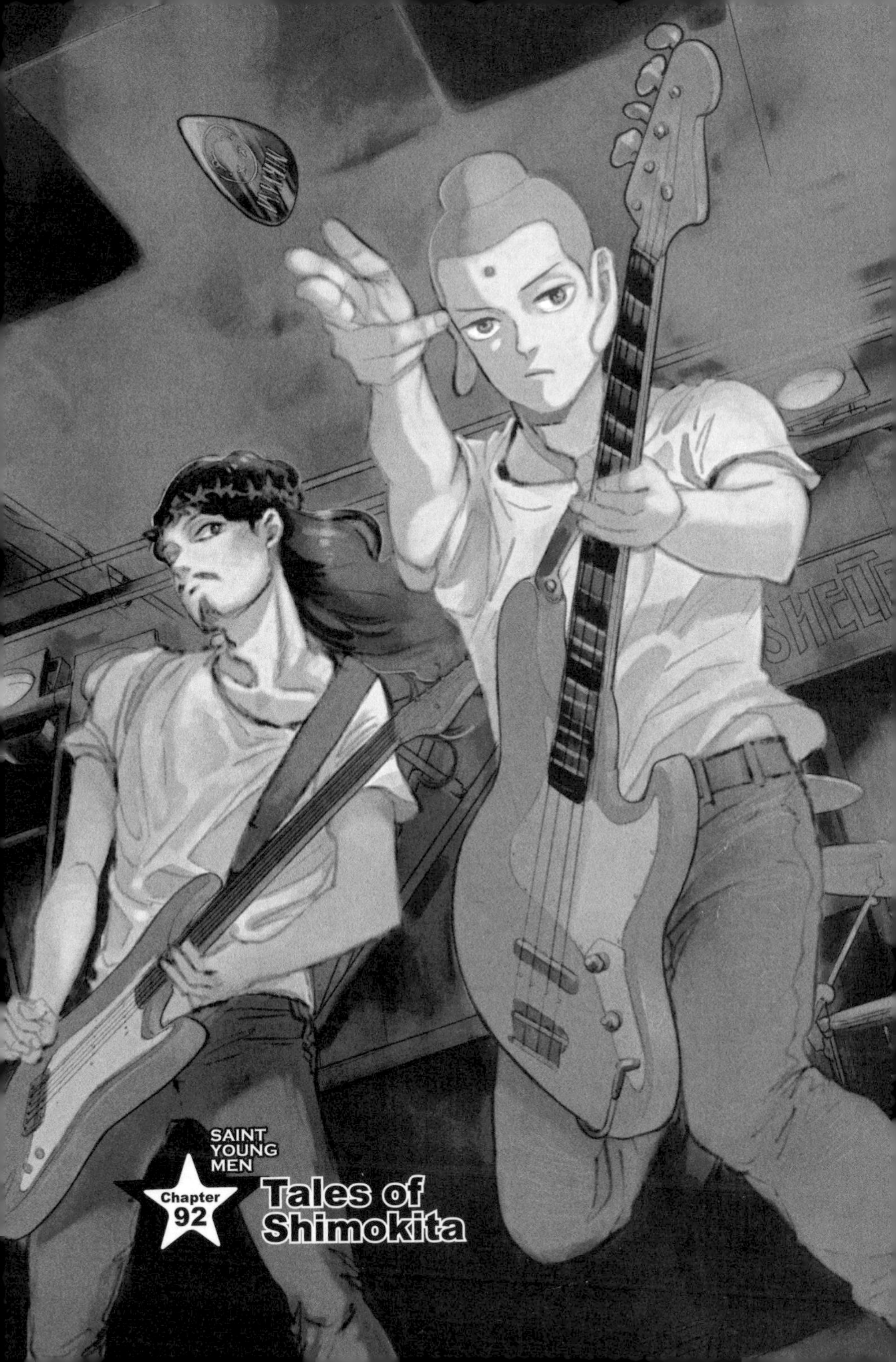
SAINT YOUNG MEN
Chapter 92
Tales of Shimokita
SHELT

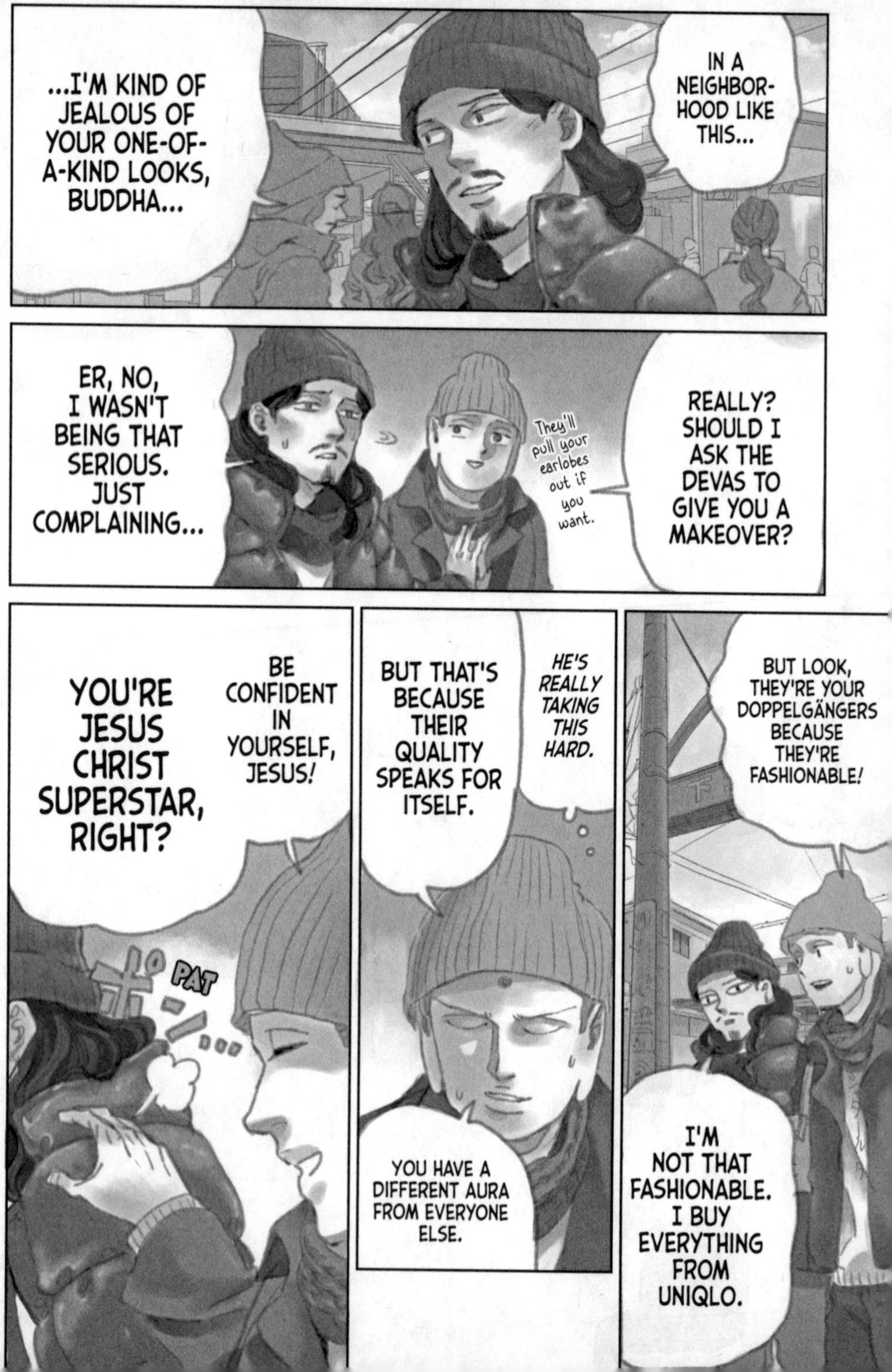
IN A NEIGHBOR-HOOD LIKE THIS...
...I'M KIND OF JEALOUS OF YOUR ONE-OF-A-KIND LOOKS, BUDDHA...
REALLY? SHOULD I ASK THE DEVAS TO GIVE YOU A MAKEOVER?
They'll pull your earlobes out if you want.
ER, NO, I WASN'T BEING THAT SERIOUS. JUST COMPLAINING...
BUT LOOK, THEY'RE YOUR DOPPELGÄNGERS BECAUSE THEY'RE FASHIONABLE!
I'M NOT THAT FASHIONABLE. I BUY EVERYTHING FROM UNIQLO.
HE'S REALLY TAKING THIS HARD.
BUT THAT'S BECAUSE THEIR QUALITY SPEAKS FOR ITSELF.
YOU HAVE A DIFFERENT AURA FROM EVERYONE ELSE.
BE CONFIDENT IN YOURSELF, JESUS!
YOU'RE JESUS CHRIST SUPERSTAR, RIGHT?
PAT
...

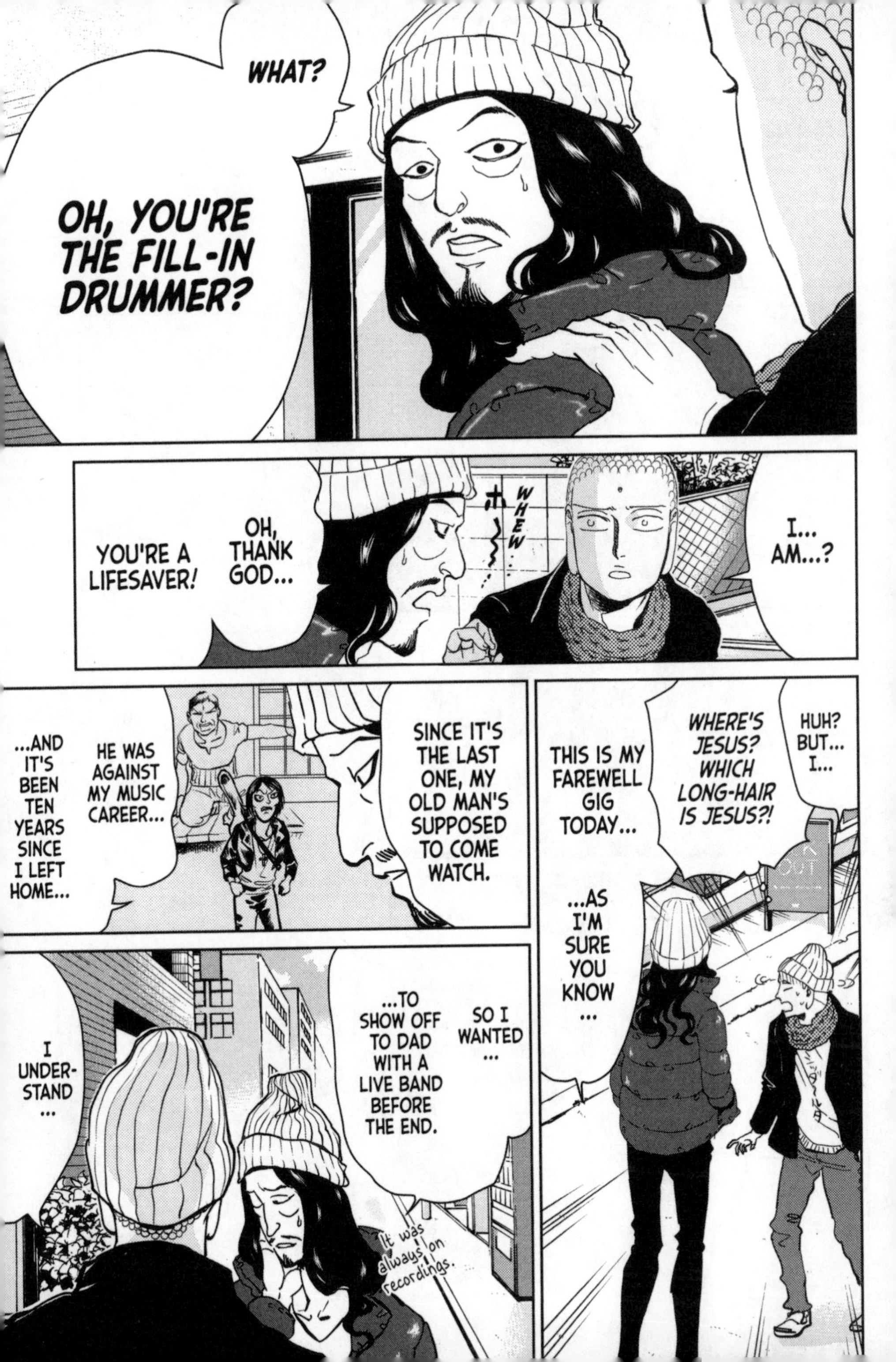
WHAT?
OH, YOU'RE THE FILL-IN DRUMMER?
I... AM...?
WHEW
OH, THANK GOD...
YOU'RE A LIFESAVER!
HUH? BUT... I...
WHERE'S JESUS? WHICH LONG-HAIR IS JESUS?!
THIS IS MY FAREWELL GIG TODAY...
...AS I'M SURE YOU KNOW ...
SINCE IT'S THE LAST ONE, MY OLD MAN'S SUPPOSED TO COME WATCH.
HE WAS AGAINST MY MUSIC CAREER...
...AND IT'S BEEN TEN YEARS SINCE I LEFT HOME...
SO I WANTED ...
...TO SHOW OFF TO DAD WITH A LIVE BAND BEFORE THE END.
It was always on recordings.
I UNDER-STAND ...

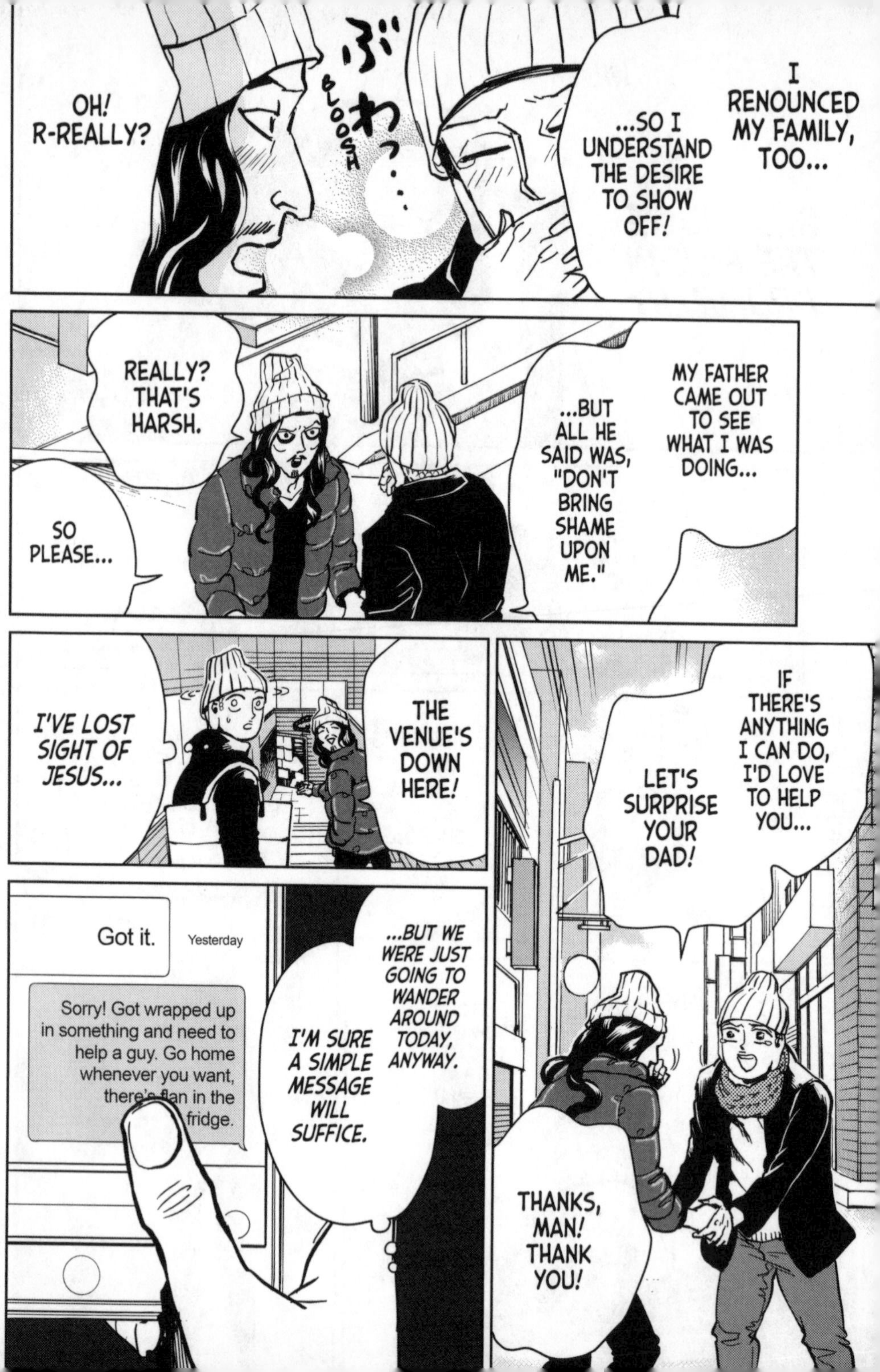
I RENOUNCED MY FAMILY, TOO...
...SO I UNDERSTAND THE DESIRE TO SHOW OFF!
ぶわっ...
BLOOSH
OH! R-REALLY?
MY FATHER CAME OUT TO SEE WHAT I WAS DOING...
...BUT ALL HE SAID WAS, "DON'T BRING SHAME UPON ME."
REALLY? THAT'S HARSH.
SO PLEASE...
IF THERE'S ANYTHING I CAN DO, I'D LOVE TO HELP YOU...
LET'S SURPRISE YOUR DAD!
THANKS, MAN! THANK YOU!
THE VENUE'S DOWN HERE!
I'VE LOST SIGHT OF JESUS...
...BUT WE WERE JUST GOING TO WANDER AROUND TODAY, ANYWAY.
I'M SURE A SIMPLE MESSAGE WILL SUFFICE.
Got it.
Yesterday
Sorry! Got wrapped up in something and need to help a guy. Go home whenever you want, there's flan in the fridge.

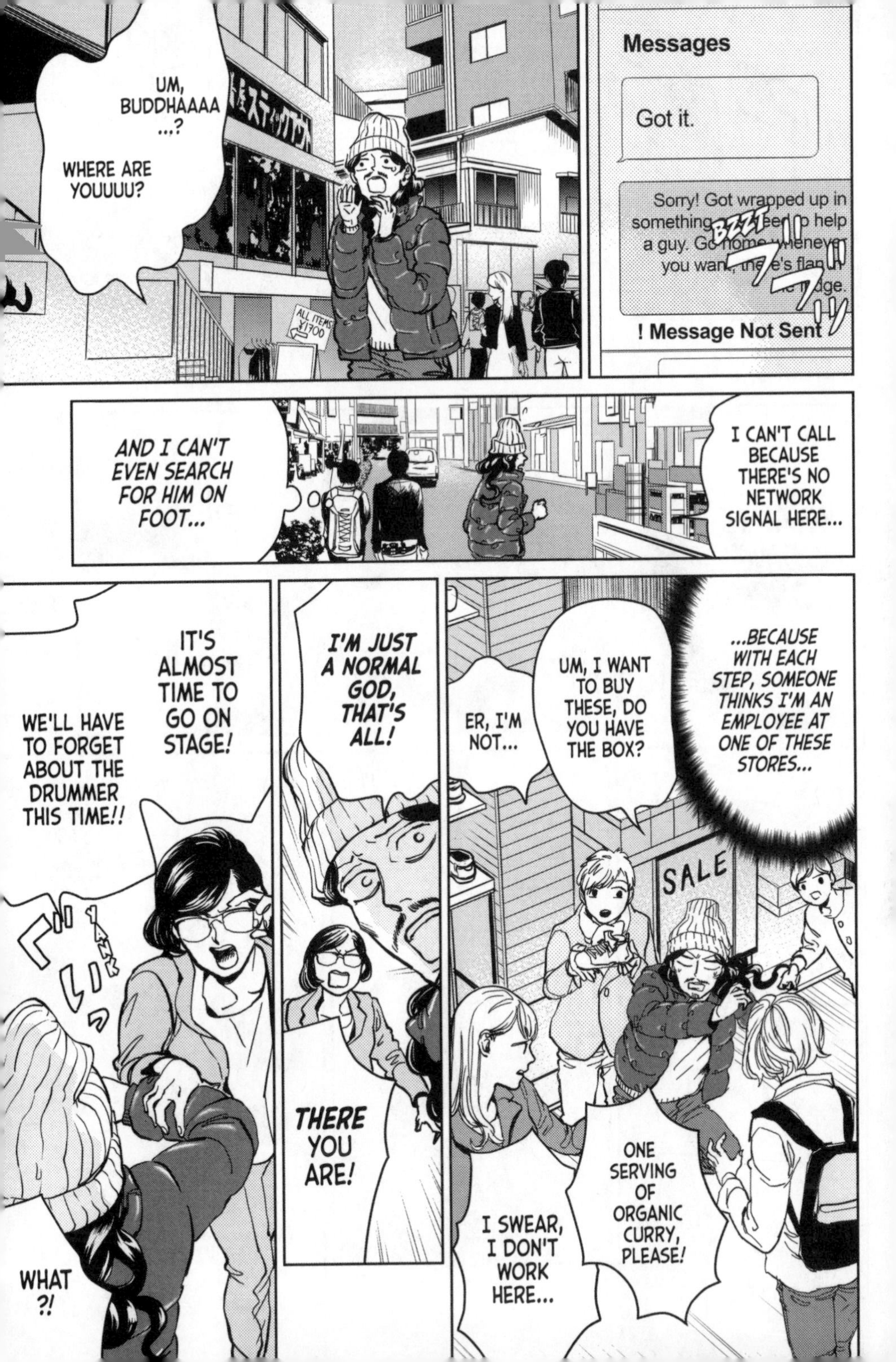
Messages
Got it.
Sorry! Got wrapped up in
BZZT
! Message Not Sent
UM, BUDDHAAAA ...?
WHERE ARE YOUUUU?
ALL ITEMS ¥1700
I CAN'T CALL BECAUSE THERE'S NO NETWORK SIGNAL HERE...
AND I CAN'T EVEN SEARCH FOR HIM ON FOOT...
...BECAUSE WITH EACH STEP, SOMEONE THINKS I'M AN EMPLOYEE AT ONE OF THESE STORES...
UM, I WANT TO BUY THESE, DO YOU HAVE THE BOX?
ER, I'M NOT...
SALE
ONE SERVING OF ORGANIC CURRY, PLEASE!
I SWEAR, I DON'T WORK HERE...
I'M JUST A NORMAL GOD, THAT'S ALL!
THERE YOU ARE!
IT'S ALMOST TIME TO GO ON STAGE!
WE'LL HAVE TO FORGET ABOUT THE DRUMMER THIS TIME!!
YANK
WHAT?!

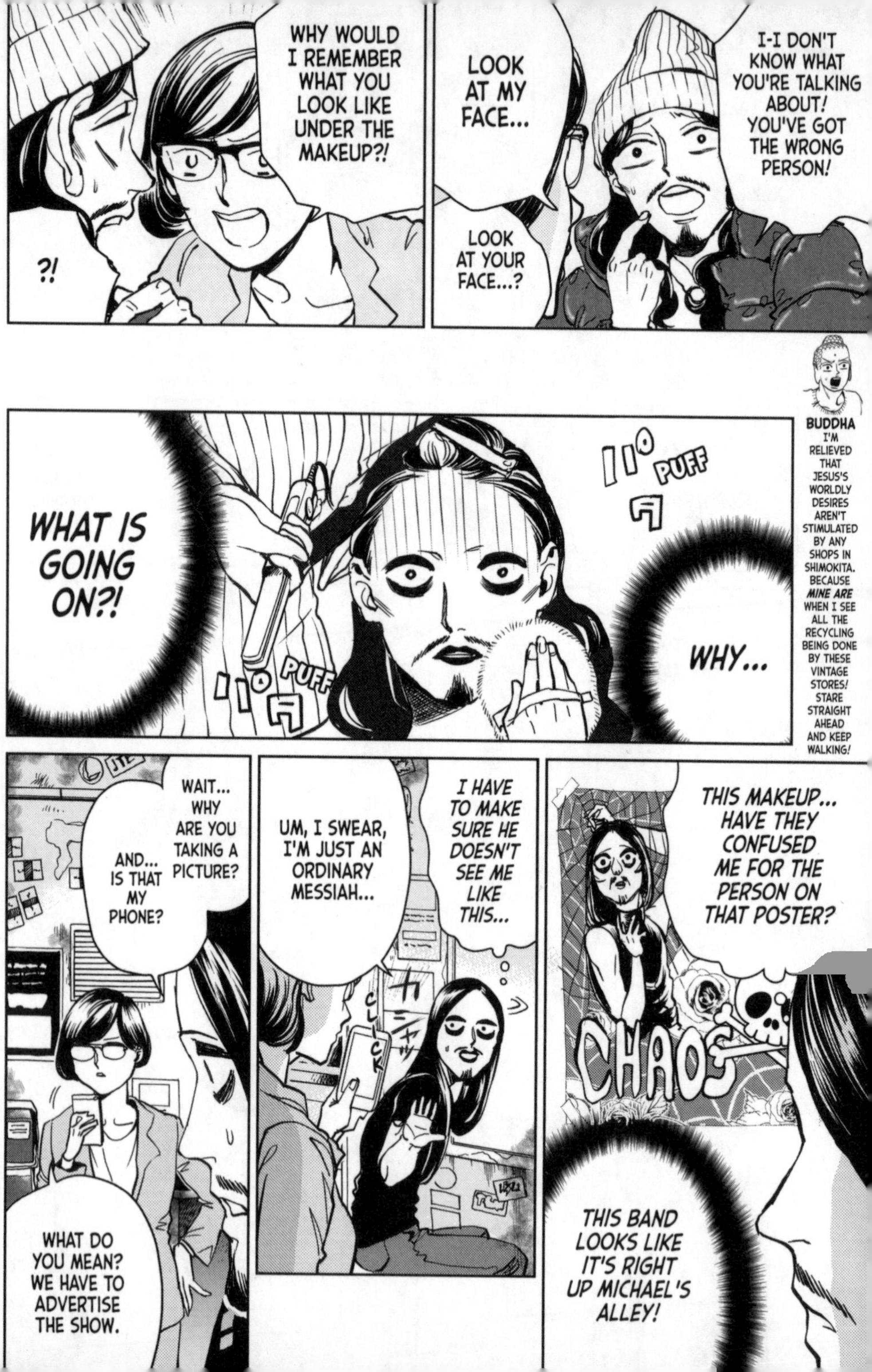
I-I DON'T KNOW WHAT YOU'RE TALKING ABOUT! YOU'VE GOT THE WRONG PERSON!
LOOK AT MY FACE...
LOOK AT YOUR FACE...?
WHY WOULD I REMEMBER WHAT YOU LOOK LIKE UNDER THE MAKEUP?!
?!
PUFF
WHY...
PUFF
WHAT IS GOING ON?!
THIS MAKEUP... HAVE THEY CONFUSED ME FOR THE PERSON ON THAT POSTER?
CHAOS
THIS BAND LOOKS LIKE IT'S RIGHT UP MICHAEL'S ALLEY!
I HAVE TO MAKE SURE HE DOESN'T SEE ME LIKE THIS...
UM, I SWEAR, I'M JUST AN ORDINARY MESSIAH...
CLICK
WAIT... WHY ARE YOU TAKING A PICTURE?
AND... IS THAT MY PHONE?
WHAT DO YOU MEAN? WE HAVE TO ADVERTISE THE SHOW.
BUDDHA
I'M RELIEVED THAT JESUS'S WORLDLY DESIRES AREN'T STIMULATED BY ANY SHOPS IN SHIMOKITA. BECAUSE *MINE ARE* WHEN I SEE ALL THE RECYCLING BEING DONE BY THESE VINTAGE STORES! STARE STRAIGHT AHEAD AND KEEP WALKING!

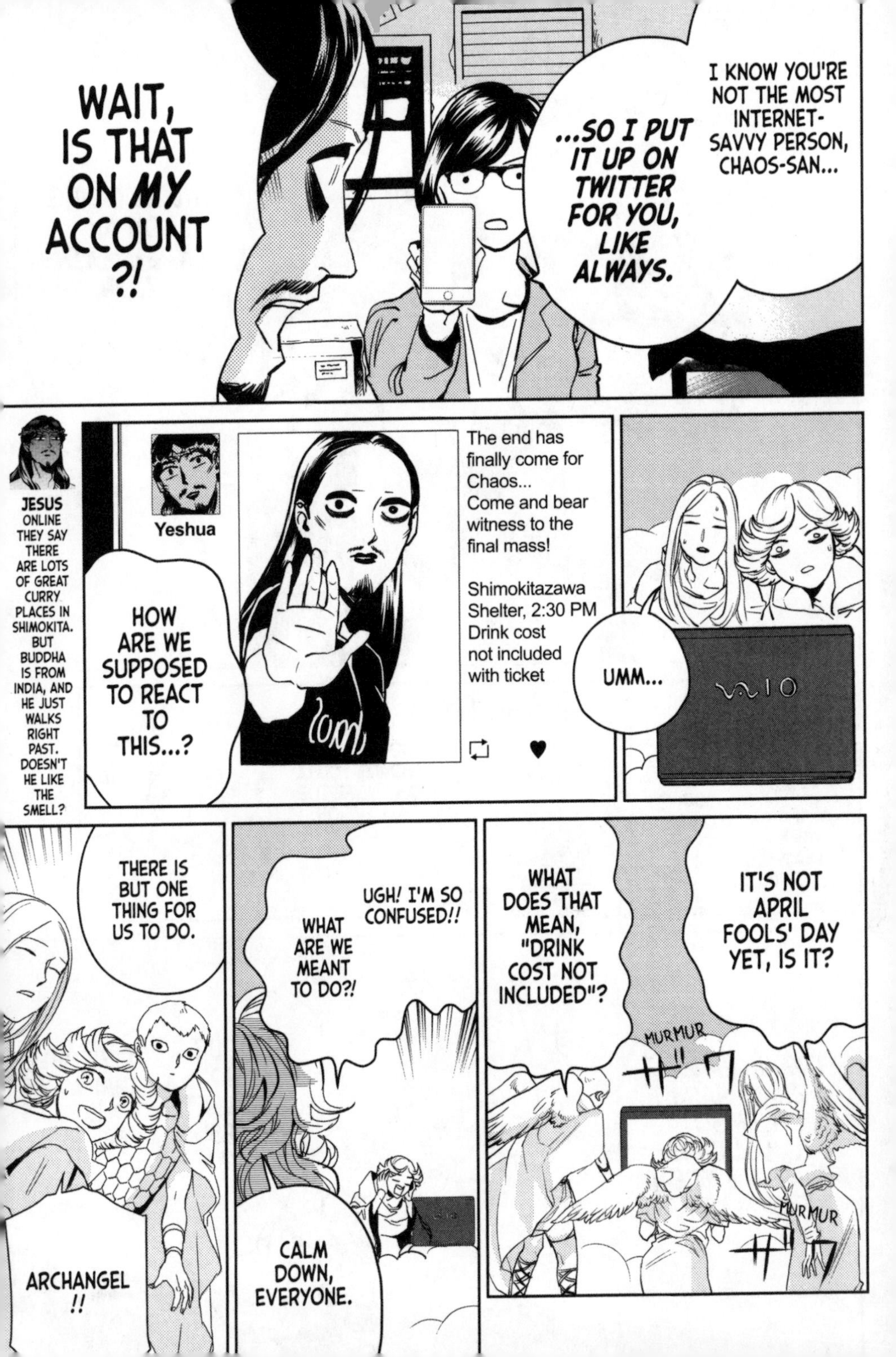
I KNOW YOU'RE NOT THE MOST INTERNET-SAVVY PERSON, CHAOS-SAN...
...SO I PUT IT UP ON TWITTER FOR YOU, LIKE ALWAYS.
WAIT, IS THAT ON *MY* ACCOUNT?!
UMM...
Yeshua
The end has finally come for Chaos... Come and bear witness to the final mass!
Shimokitazawa Shelter, 2:30 PM Drink cost not included with ticket
HOW ARE WE SUPPOSED TO REACT TO THIS...?
JESUS ONLINE THEY SAY THERE ARE LOTS OF GREAT CURRY PLACES IN SHIMOKITA. BUT BUDDHA IS FROM INDIA, AND HE JUST WALKS RIGHT PAST. DOESN'T HE LIKE THE SMELL?
IT'S NOT APRIL FOOLS' DAY YET, IS IT?
WHAT DOES THAT MEAN, "DRINK COST NOT INCLUDED"?
MURMUR
MURMUR
UGH! I'M SO CONFUSED!!
WHAT ARE WE MEANT TO DO?!
CALM DOWN, EVERYONE.
THERE IS BUT ONE THING FOR US TO DO.
ARCHANGEL!!

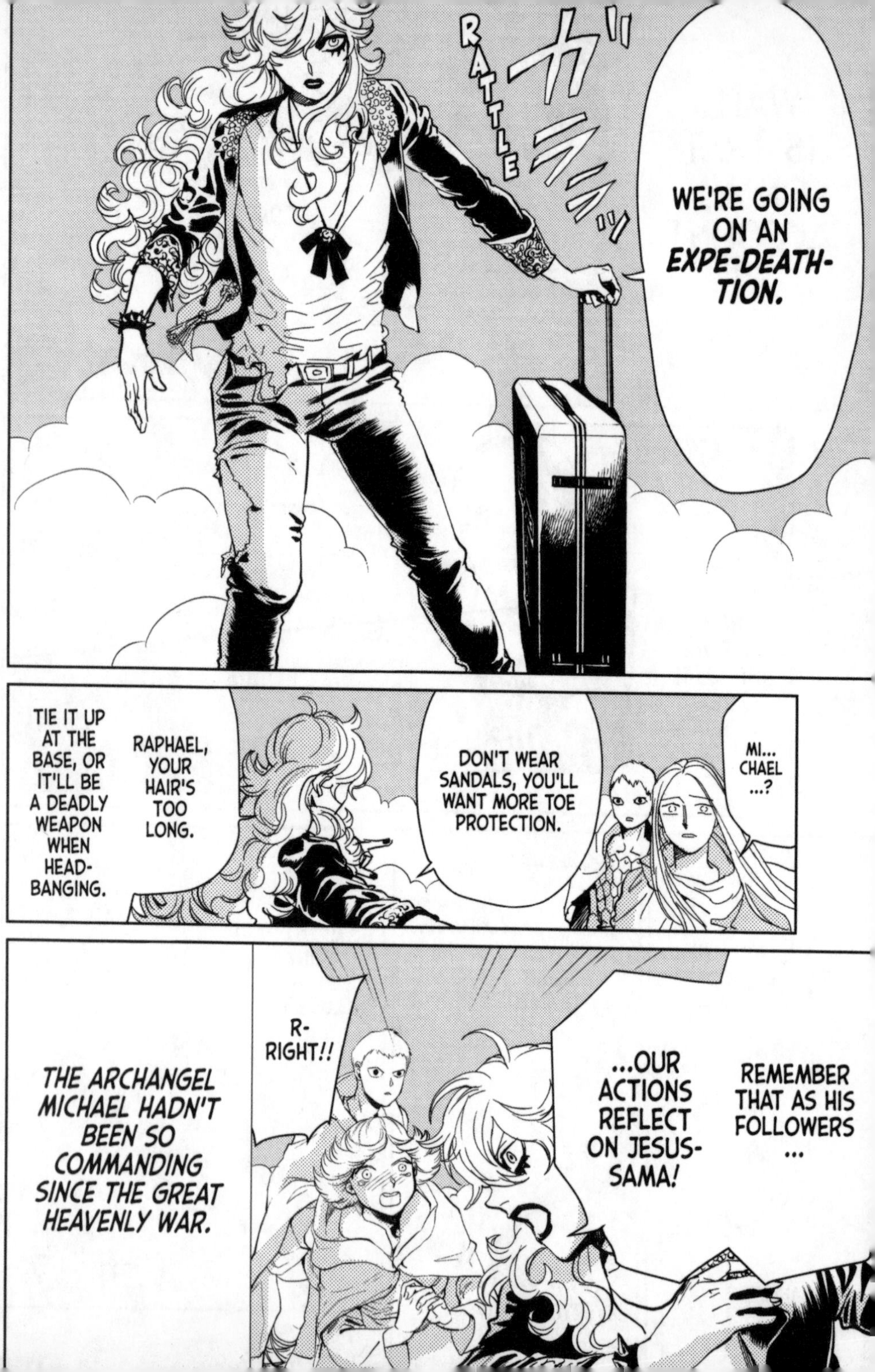
WE'RE GOING ON AN *EXPE-DEATH-TION.*
RATTLE
MI... CHAEL ...?
DON'T WEAR SANDALS, YOU'LL WANT MORE TOE PROTECTION.
RAPHAEL, YOUR HAIR'S TOO LONG.
TIE IT UP AT THE BASE, OR IT'LL BE A DEADLY WEAPON WHEN HEAD-BANGING.
REMEMBER THAT AS HIS FOLLOWERS ...
...OUR ACTIONS REFLECT ON JESUS-SAMA!
R- RIGHT!!
THE ARCHANGEL MICHAEL HADN'T BEEN SO COMMANDING SINCE THE GREAT HEAVENLY WAR.

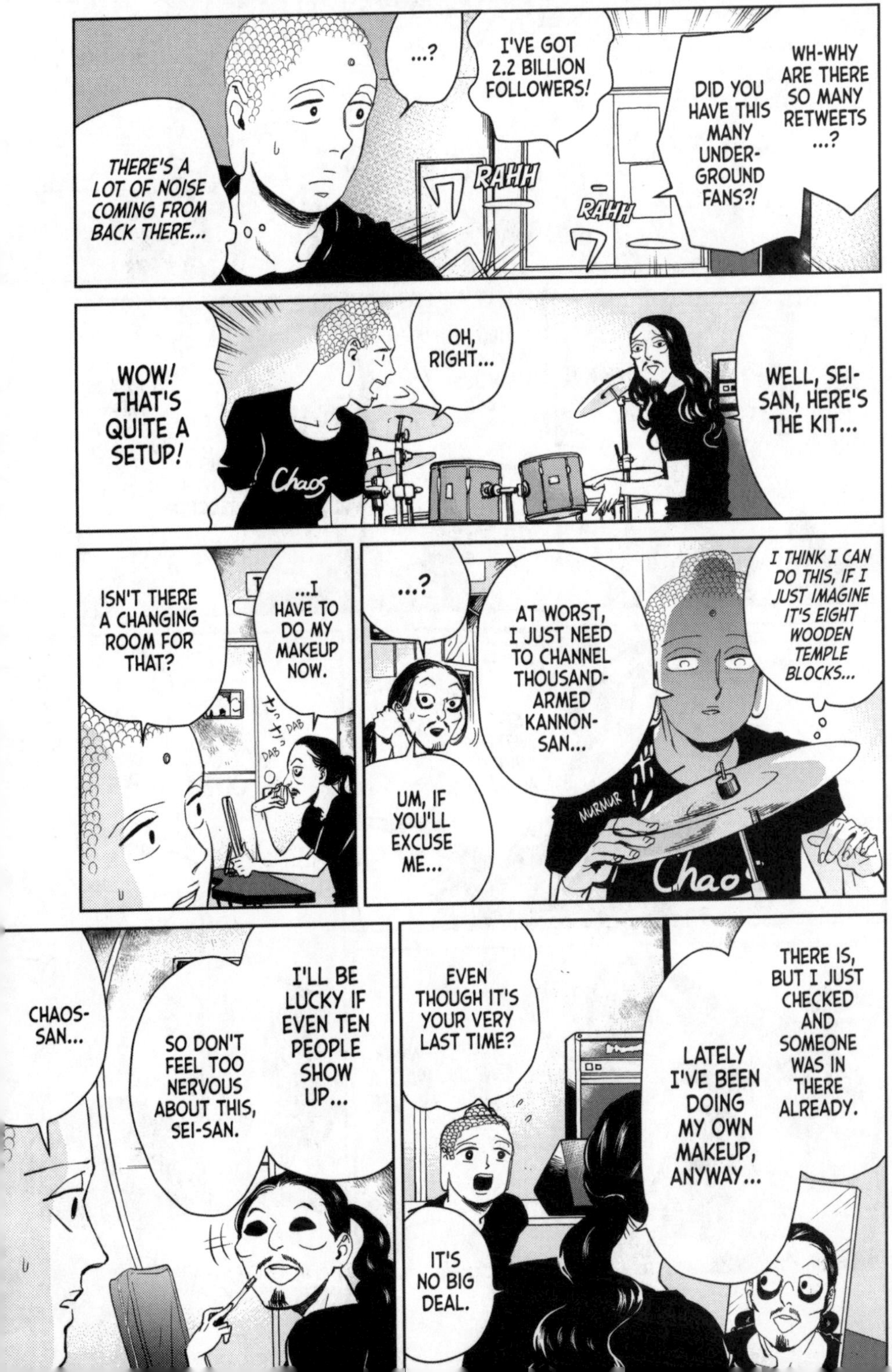
WH-WHY ARE THERE SO MANY RETWEETS ...?
DID YOU HAVE THIS MANY UNDER-GROUND FANS?!
I'VE GOT 2.2 BILLION FOLLOWERS!
RAHH
RAHH
...?
THERE'S A LOT OF NOISE COMING FROM BACK THERE...
WELL, SEI-SAN, HERE'S THE KIT...
OH, RIGHT...
WOW! THAT'S QUITE A SETUP!
I THINK I CAN DO THIS, IF I JUST IMAGINE IT'S EIGHT WOODEN TEMPLE BLOCKS...
AT WORST, I JUST NEED TO CHANNEL THOUSAND-ARMED KANNON-SAN...
MURMUR
...?
UM, IF YOU'LL EXCUSE ME...
...I HAVE TO DO MY MAKEUP NOW.
DAB
DAB
ISN'T THERE A CHANGING ROOM FOR THAT?
THERE IS, BUT I JUST CHECKED AND SOMEONE WAS IN THERE ALREADY.
LATELY I'VE BEEN DOING MY OWN MAKEUP, ANYWAY...
EVEN THOUGH IT'S YOUR VERY LAST TIME?
IT'S NO BIG DEAL.
I'LL BE LUCKY IF EVEN TEN PEOPLE SHOW UP...
SO DON'T FEEL TOO NERVOUS ABOUT THIS, SEI-SAN.
CHAOS-SAN...

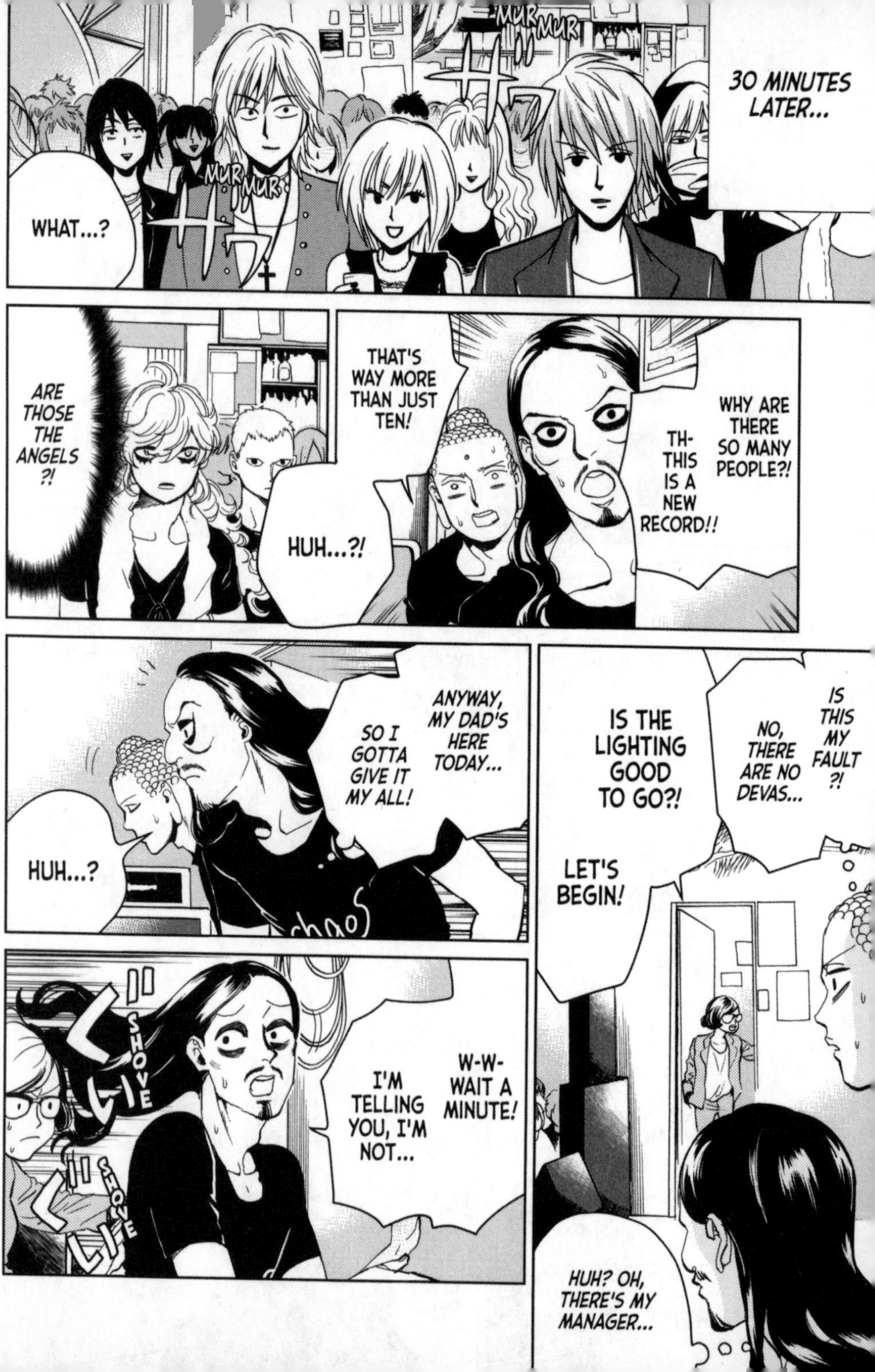
30 MINUTES LATER...
MUR MUR
MUR MUR
WHAT...?
WHY ARE THERE SO MANY PEOPLE?!
TH- THIS IS A NEW RECORD!!
THAT'S WAY MORE THAN JUST TEN!
HUH...?!
ARE THOSE THE ANGELS?!
IS THIS MY FAULT?!
NO, THERE ARE NO DEVAS...
IS THE LIGHTING GOOD TO GO?!
LET'S BEGIN!
HUH? OH, THERE'S MY MANAGER...
ANYWAY, MY DAD'S HERE TODAY...
SO I GOTTA GIVE IT MY ALL!
HUH...?
W-W-WAIT A MINUTE!
I'M TELLING YOU, I'M NOT...
SHOVE
SHOVE

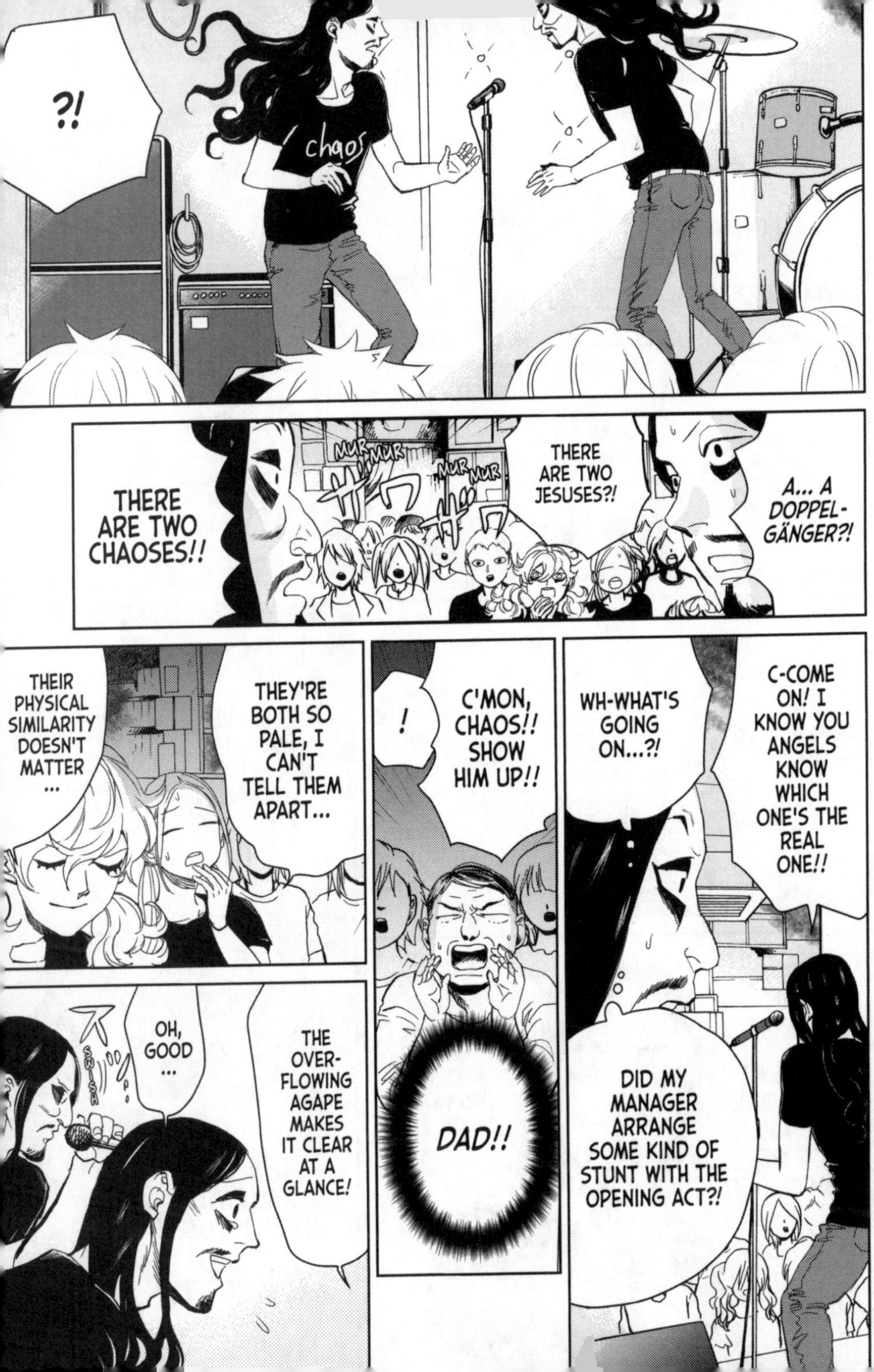
?!
A... A DOPPEL-GÄNGER?!
THERE ARE TWO JESUSES?!
MUR MUR
MUR MUR
THERE ARE TWO CHAOSES!!
C-COME ON! I KNOW YOU ANGELS KNOW WHICH ONE'S THE REAL ONE!!
WH-WHAT'S GOING ON...?!
DID MY MANAGER ARRANGE SOME KIND OF STUNT WITH THE OPENING ACT?!
C'MON, CHAOS!! SHOW HIM UP!!
!
DAD!!
THEY'RE BOTH SO PALE, I CAN'T TELL THEM APART...
THEIR PHYSICAL SIMILARITY DOESN'T MATTER ...
THE OVER-FLOWING AGAPE MAKES IT CLEAR AT A GLANCE!
OH, GOOD ...
SWISH

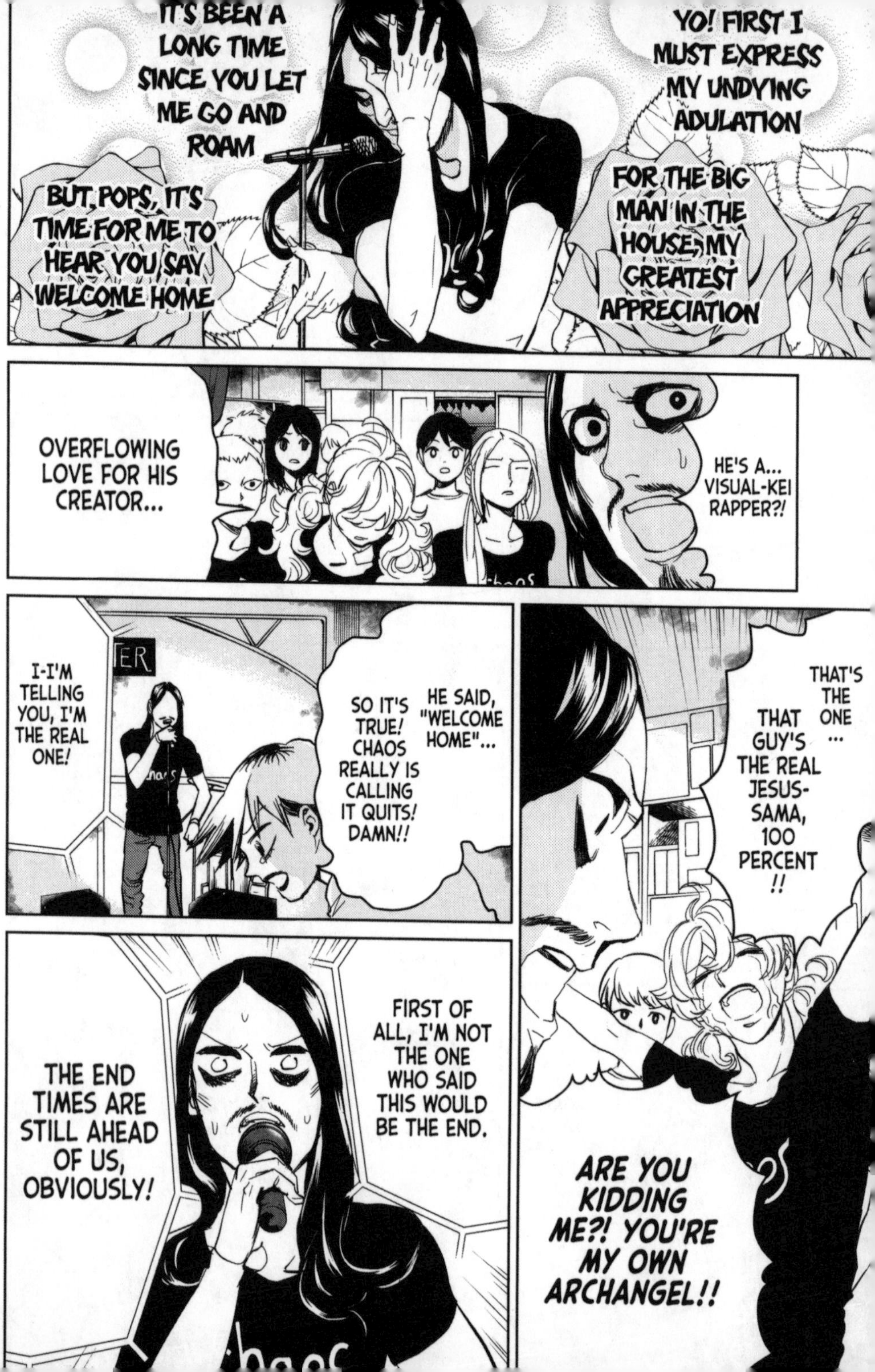
YO! FIRST I MUST EXPRESS MY UNDYING ADULATION
FOR THE BIG MAN IN THE HOUSE, MY GREATEST APPRECIATION
IT'S BEEN A LONG TIME SINCE YOU LET ME GO AND ROAM
BUT, POPS, IT'S TIME FOR ME TO HEAR YOU SAY WELCOME HOME
HE'S A... VISUAL-KEI RAPPER?!
OVERFLOWING LOVE FOR HIS CREATOR...
THAT'S THE ONE ...
THAT GUY'S THE REAL JESUS-SAMA, 100 PERCENT !!
ARE YOU KIDDING ME?! YOU'RE MY OWN ARCHANGEL!!
HE SAID, "WELCOME HOME"...
SO IT'S TRUE! CHAOS REALLY IS CALLING IT QUITS! DAMN!!
I-I'M TELLING YOU, I'M THE REAL ONE!
FIRST OF ALL, I'M NOT THE ONE WHO SAID THIS WOULD BE THE END.
THE END TIMES ARE STILL AHEAD OF US, OBVIOUSLY!

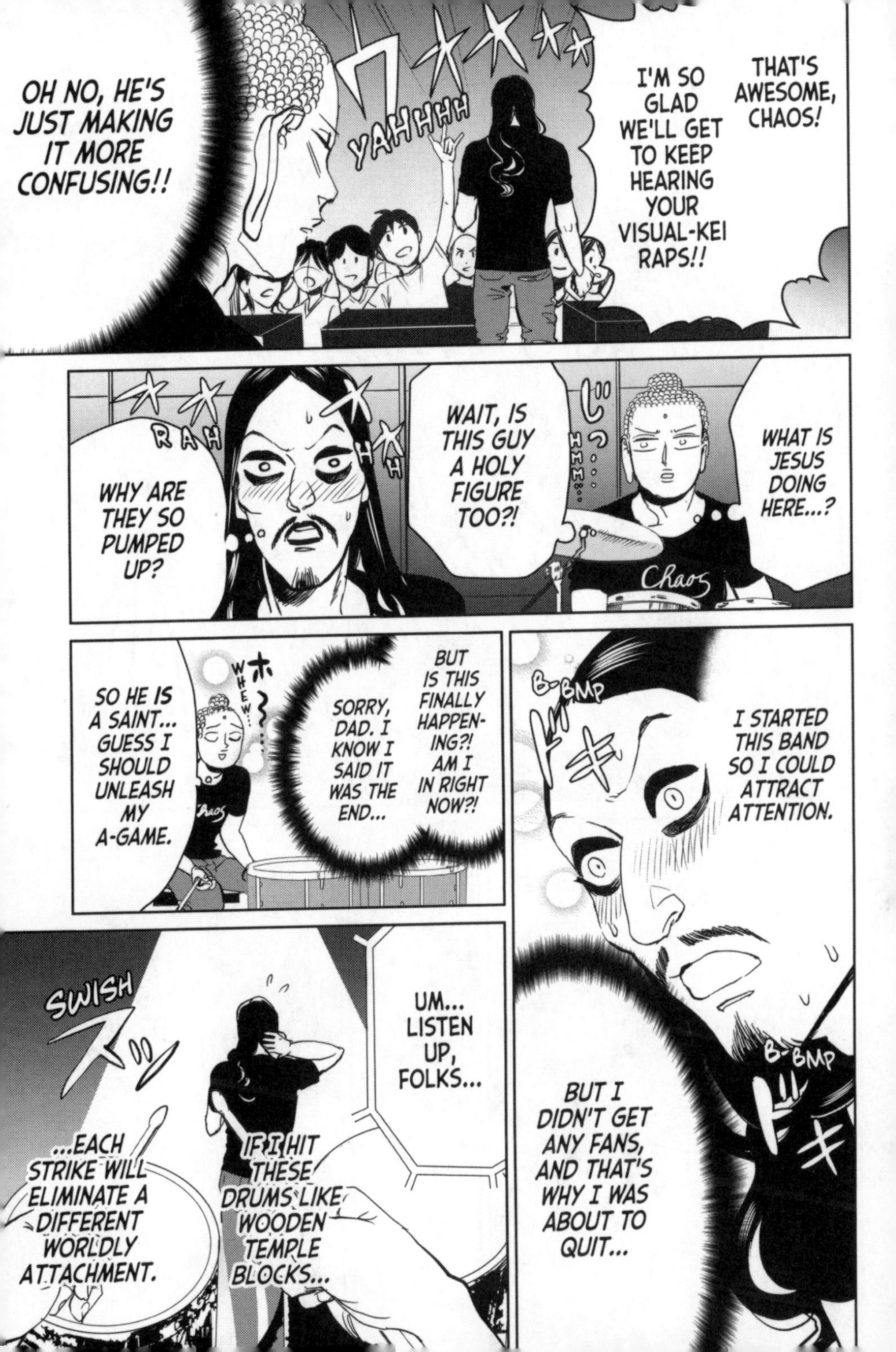
THAT'S AWESOME, CHAOS!
I'M SO GLAD WE'LL GET TO KEEP HEARING YOUR VISUAL-KEI RAPS!!
YAHHHH
OH NO, HE'S JUST MAKING IT MORE CONFUSING!!
WHAT IS JESUS DOING HERE...?
HMMM...
Chaos
WAIT, IS THIS GUY A HOLY FIGURE TOO?!
RAHHH
WHY ARE THEY SO PUMPED UP?
B-BMP
I STARTED THIS BAND SO I COULD ATTRACT ATTENTION.
B-BMP
BUT I DIDN'T GET ANY FANS, AND THAT'S WHY I WAS ABOUT TO QUIT...
BUT IS THIS FINALLY HAPPENING?! AM I IN RIGHT NOW?!
SORRY, DAD. I KNOW I SAID IT WAS THE END...
WHEW...
SO HE IS A SAINT... GUESS I SHOULD UNLEASH MY A-GAME.
UM... LISTEN UP, FOLKS...
IF I HIT THESE DRUMS LIKE WOODEN TEMPLE BLOCKS...
...EACH STRIKE WILL ELIMINATE A DIFFERENT WORLDLY ATTACHMENT.
SWISH

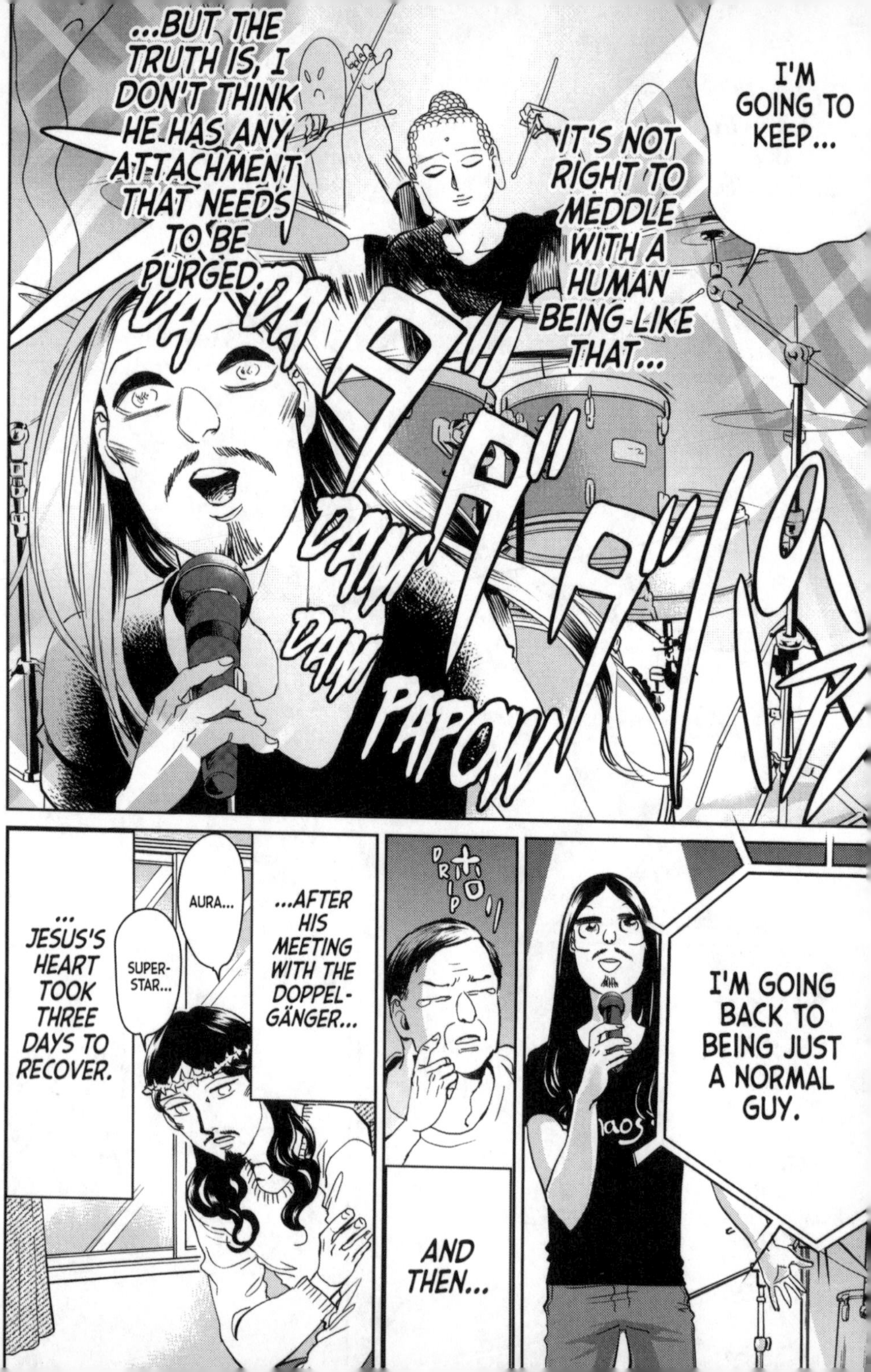
I'M GOING TO KEEP...
IT'S NOT RIGHT TO MEDDLE WITH A HUMAN BEING LIKE THAT...
...BUT THE TRUTH IS, I DON'T THINK HE HAS ANY ATTACHMENT THAT NEEDS TO BE PURGED.
DA DA
DAM DAM
PAPOW
I'M GOING BACK TO BEING JUST A NORMAL GUY.
DRIP
...AFTER HIS MEETING WITH THE DOPPEL-GÄNGER...
AND THEN...
AURA...
SUPER-STAR...
...JESUS'S HEART TOOK THREE DAYS TO RECOVER.

THANKS TO SHIMOKITAZAWA'S SHELTER FOR THE REFERENCE PHOTOS.

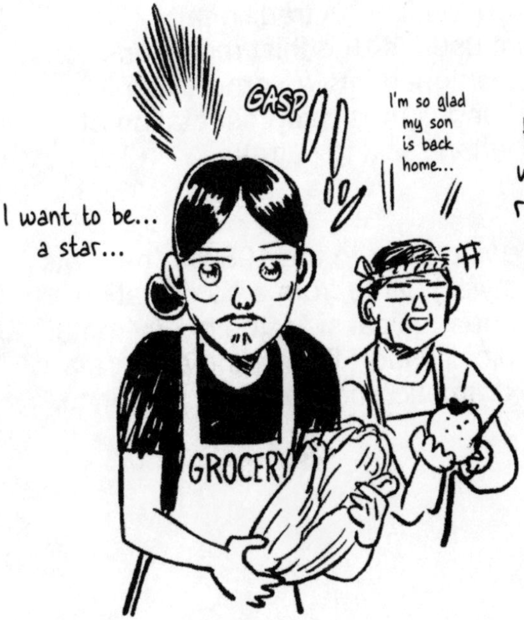

I'm so glad my son is back home...
GASP
I want to be... a star...
GROCERY

*Worldly attachments banished by the wooden block will return in about a month, so don't worry, fans of Chaos.

SAINT ☆ YOUNG MEN

CHAPTER 92 TRANSLATION NOTES

Uniqlo, page 47

A popular Japanese clothing retailer that has recently expanded further into international markets. Known for having simple styles that everyone can wear that are cheap and reliable.

Shimokitazawa, page 48

A neighborhood in Tokyo known for its many vintage clothes shops, music venues, and other subculture-based independent businesses. In short, a hipster area. Known as "Shimokita" for short.

Wooden temple blocks, page 57

Also known as *mokugyo* or "wooden fish." A traditional, hollowed percussion instrument used in Buddhist recitations and ceremonies and typically fashioned into an ornate fish shape. The fish "never sleeps" and is thus a representation of wakefulness and mindfulness when reciting sutras.

Visual-kei, page 60

A genre of music and fashion going back to the 1980s. The roots of *visual-kei* (meaning "visual style") came from a combination of glam rock and goth, and on the musical side, the heavy metal and punk of the 80's. Artists typically sport flashy and elaborate makeup and costumes, and a dramatic, moody stage presence.

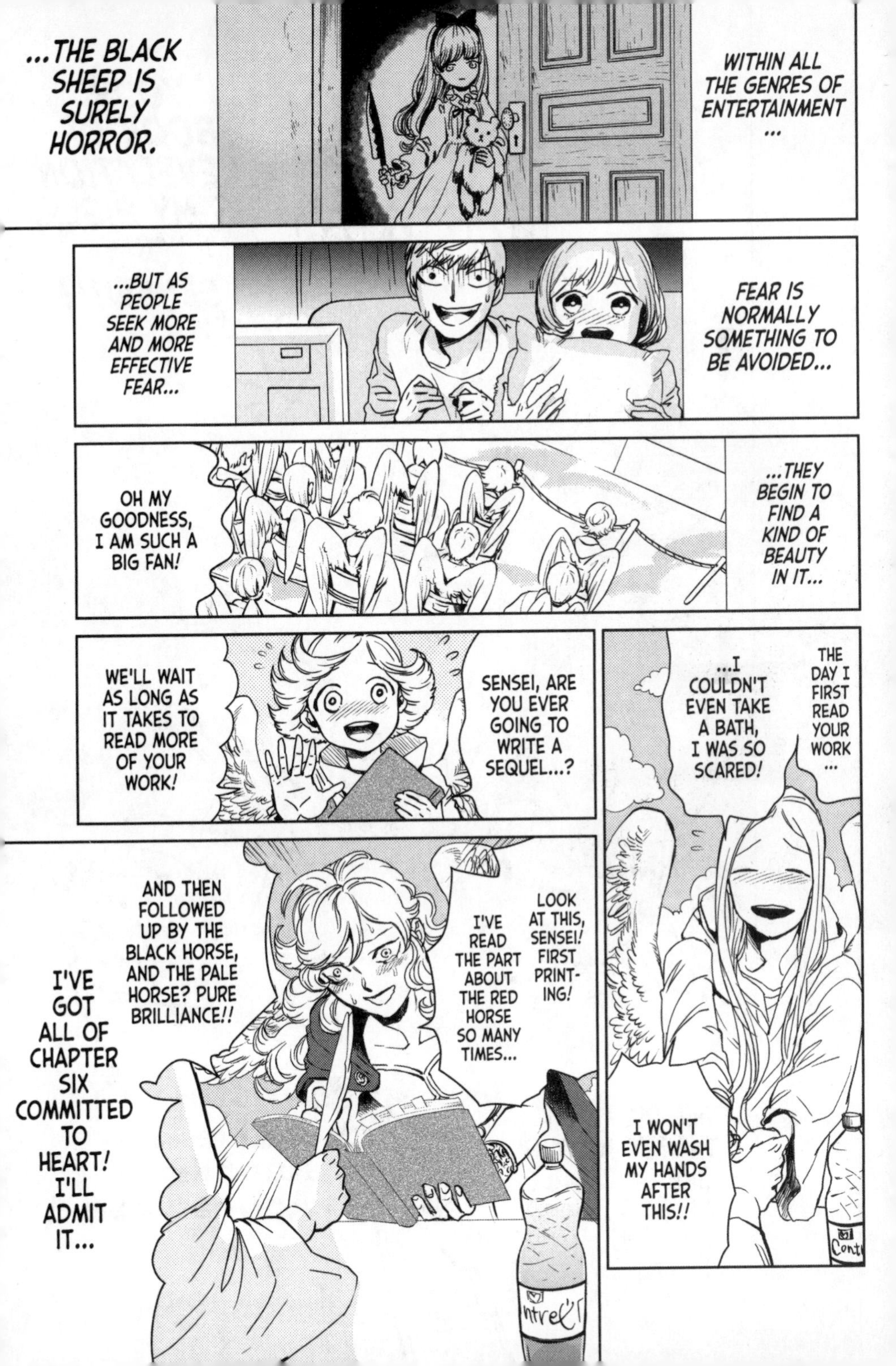
WITHIN ALL THE GENRES OF ENTERTAINMENT ...
...THE BLACK SHEEP IS SURELY HORROR.
FEAR IS NORMALLY SOMETHING TO BE AVOIDED...
...BUT AS PEOPLE SEEK MORE AND MORE EFFECTIVE FEAR...
...THEY BEGIN TO FIND A KIND OF BEAUTY IN IT...
OH MY GOODNESS, I AM SUCH A BIG FAN!
THE DAY I FIRST READ YOUR WORK ...
...I COULDN'T EVEN TAKE A BATH, I WAS SO SCARED!
I WON'T EVEN WASH MY HANDS AFTER THIS!!
SENSEI, ARE YOU EVER GOING TO WRITE A SEQUEL...?
WE'LL WAIT AS LONG AS IT TAKES TO READ MORE OF YOUR WORK!
LOOK AT THIS, SENSEI! FIRST PRINTING!
I'VE READ THE PART ABOUT THE RED HORSE SO MANY TIMES...
AND THEN FOLLOWED UP BY THE BLACK HORSE, AND THE PALE HORSE? PURE BRILLIANCE!!
I'VE GOT ALL OF CHAPTER SIX COMMITTED TO HEART! I'LL ADMIT IT...

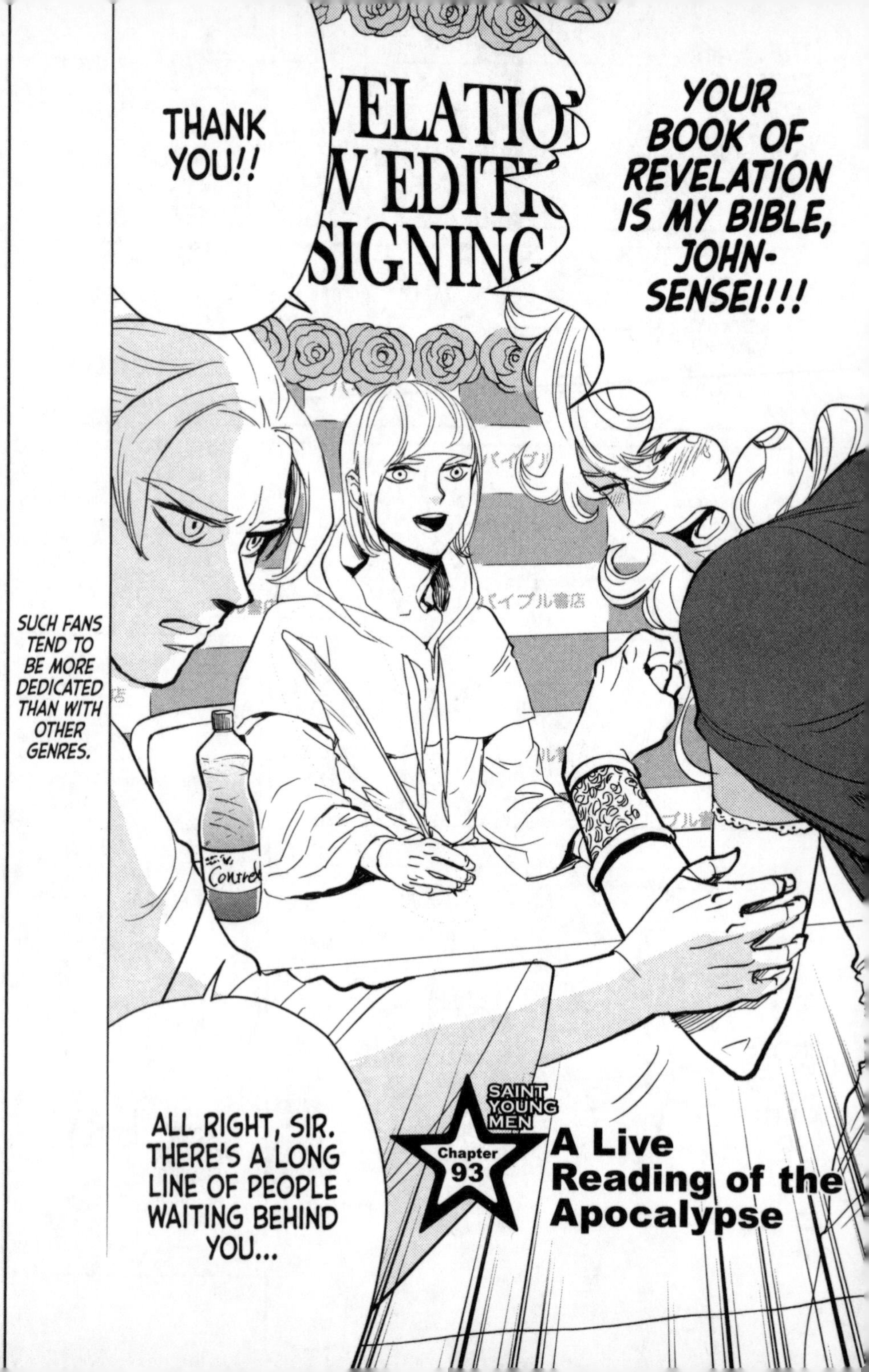
YOUR BOOK OF REVELATION IS MY BIBLE, JOHN-SENSEI!!!
THANK YOU!!
SAINT YOUNG MEN
Chapter 93
A Live Reading of the Apocalypse
SUCH FANS TEND TO BE MORE DEDICATED THAN WITH OTHER GENRES.
ALL RIGHT, SIR. THERE'S A LONG LINE OF PEOPLE WAITING BEHIND YOU...

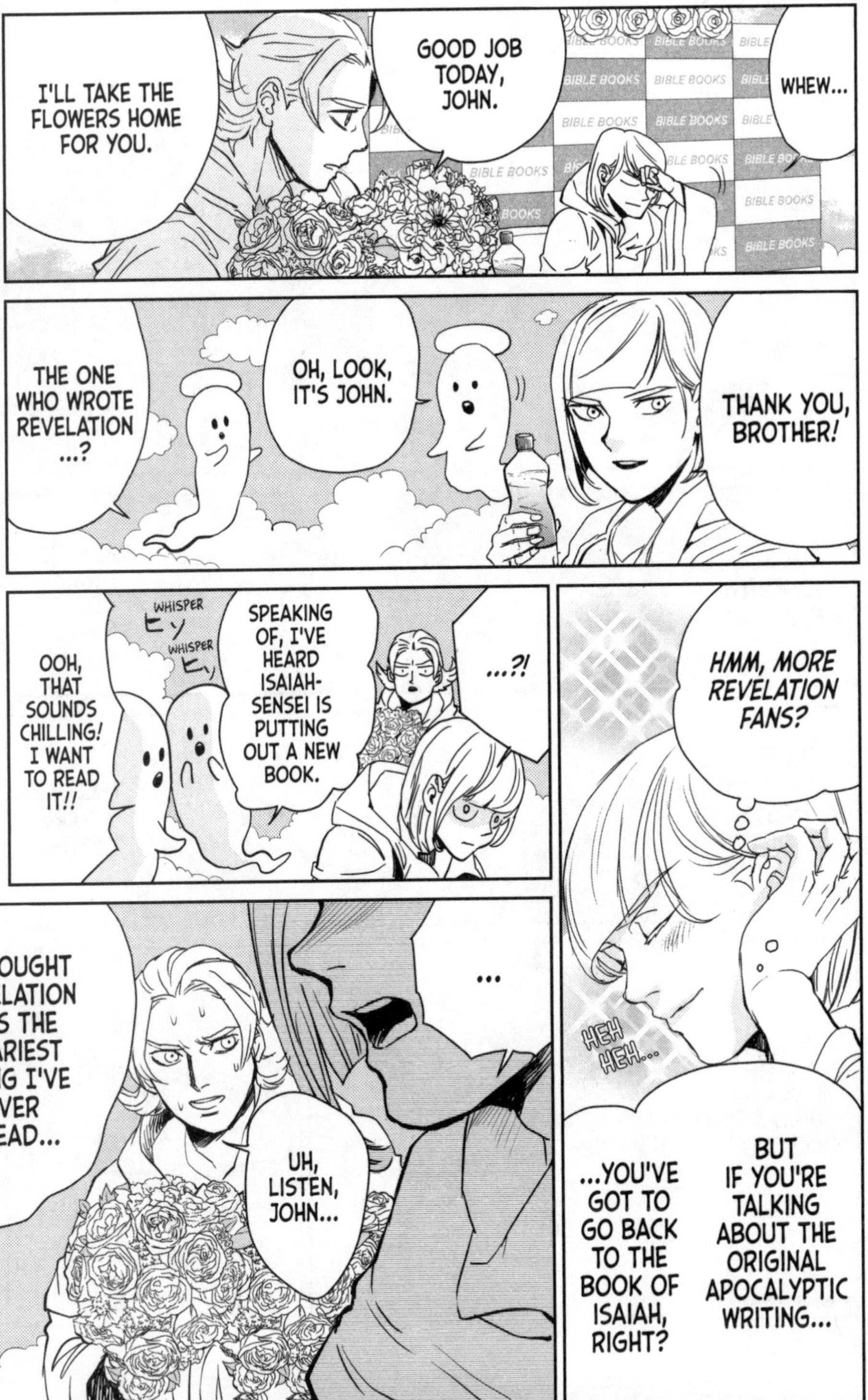
WHEW...
GOOD JOB TODAY, JOHN.
I'LL TAKE THE FLOWERS HOME FOR YOU.
BIBLE BOOKS
THANK YOU, BROTHER!
OH, LOOK, IT'S JOHN.
THE ONE WHO WROTE REVELATION ...?
HMM, MORE REVELATION FANS?
HEH HEH...
BUT IF YOU'RE TALKING ABOUT THE ORIGINAL APOCALYPTIC WRITING...
...YOU'VE GOT TO GO BACK TO THE BOOK OF ISAIAH, RIGHT?
...?!
SPEAKING OF, I'VE HEARD ISAIAH-SENSEI IS PUTTING OUT A NEW BOOK.
WHISPER ヒソ
WHISPER ヒ
OOH, THAT SOUNDS CHILLING! I WANT TO READ IT!!
...
I THOUGHT REVELATION WAS THE SCARIEST THING I'VE EVER READ...
UH, LISTEN, JOHN...

JESUS THE BOOK I DON'T WANT ANYONE TO SEE IS MY "ENGLISH CONVERSATION FOR BEGINNERS." WHEN I WAS ALIVE, I'D NEVER EVEN HEARD THE ENGLISH LANGUAGE!

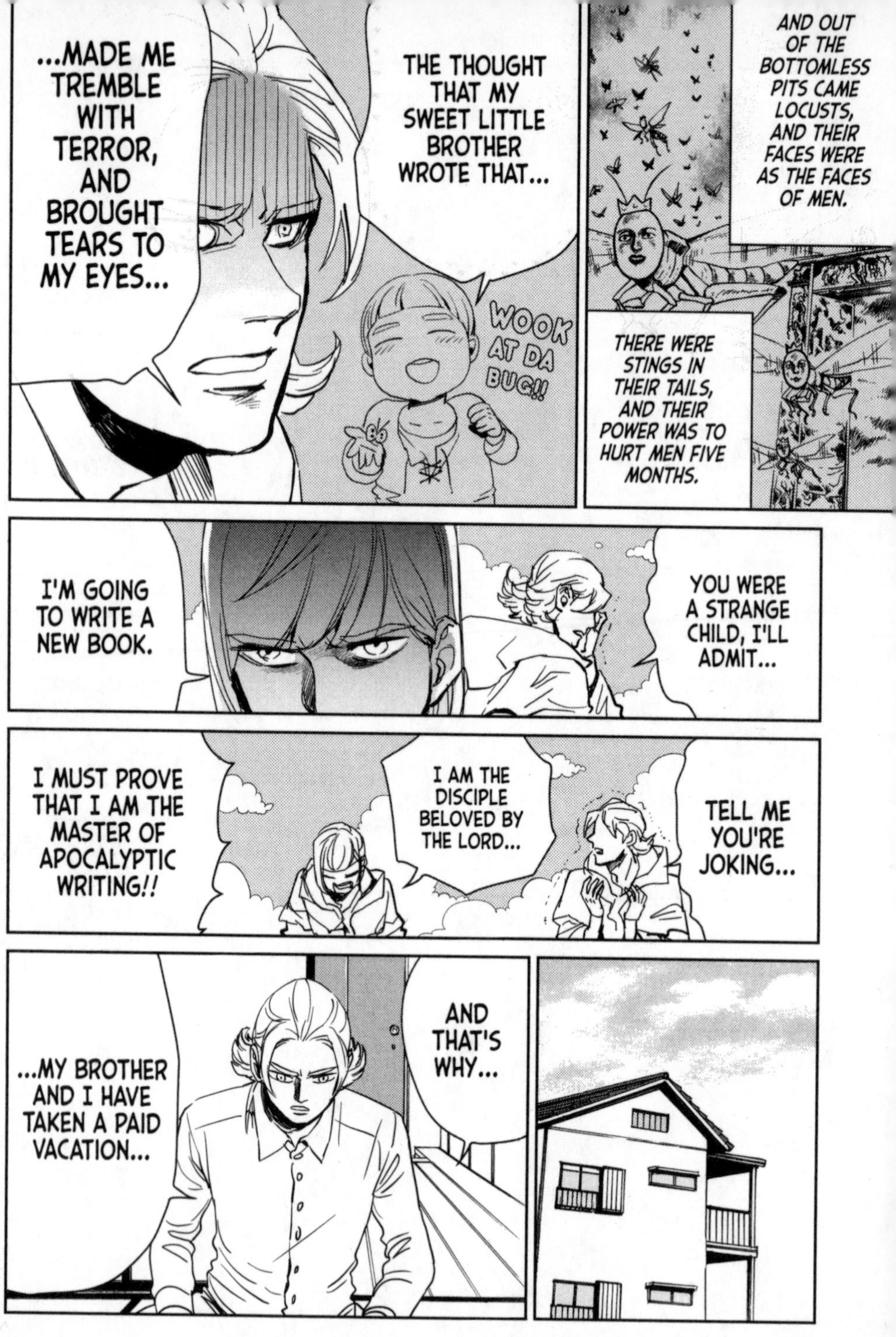
AND OUT OF THE BOTTOMLESS PITS CAME LOCUSTS, AND THEIR FACES WERE AS THE FACES OF MEN.
THERE WERE STINGS IN THEIR TAILS, AND THEIR POWER WAS TO HURT MEN FIVE MONTHS.
THE THOUGHT THAT MY SWEET LITTLE BROTHER WROTE THAT...
WOOK AT DA BUG!!
...MADE ME TREMBLE WITH TERROR, AND BROUGHT TEARS TO MY EYES...
YOU WERE A STRANGE CHILD, I'LL ADMIT...
I'M GOING TO WRITE A NEW BOOK.
TELL ME YOU'RE JOKING...
I AM THE DISCIPLE BELOVED BY THE LORD...
I MUST PROVE THAT I AM THE MASTER OF APOCALYPTIC WRITING!!
AND THAT'S WHY...
...MY BROTHER AND I HAVE TAKEN A PAID VACATION...

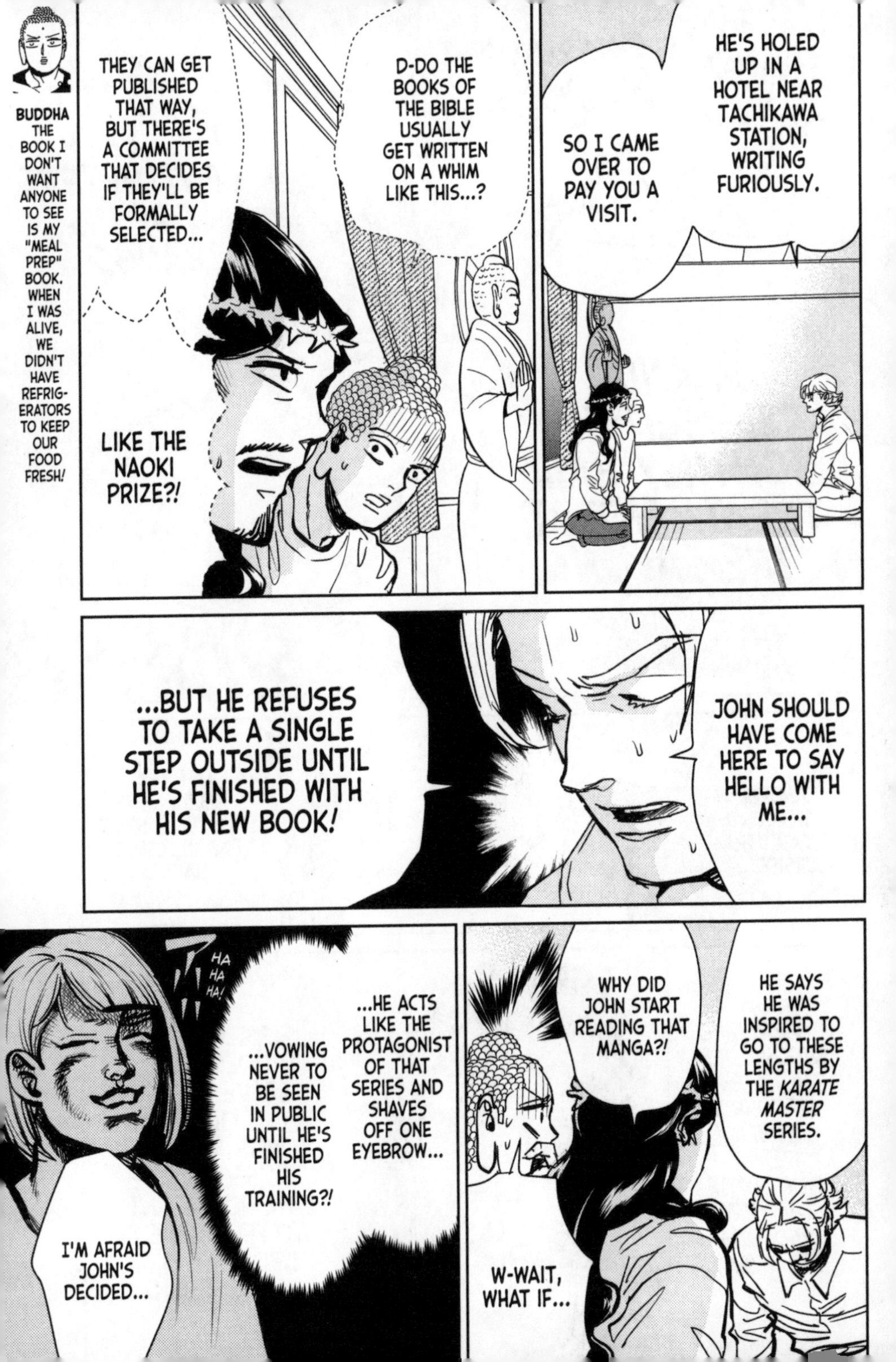
BUDDHA
THE BOOK I DON'T WANT ANYONE TO SEE IS MY "MEAL PREP" BOOK. WHEN I WAS ALIVE, WE DIDN'T HAVE REFRIGERATORS TO KEEP OUR FOOD FRESH!
HE'S HOLED UP IN A HOTEL NEAR TACHIKAWA STATION, WRITING FURIOUSLY.
SO I CAME OVER TO PAY YOU A VISIT.
D-DO THE BOOKS OF THE BIBLE USUALLY GET WRITTEN ON A WHIM LIKE THIS...?
THEY CAN GET PUBLISHED THAT WAY, BUT THERE'S A COMMITTEE THAT DECIDES IF THEY'LL BE FORMALLY SELECTED...
LIKE THE NAOKI PRIZE?!
JOHN SHOULD HAVE COME HERE TO SAY HELLO WITH ME...
...BUT HE REFUSES TO TAKE A SINGLE STEP OUTSIDE UNTIL HE'S FINISHED WITH HIS NEW BOOK!
HE SAYS HE WAS INSPIRED TO GO TO THESE LENGTHS BY THE *KARATE MASTER* SERIES.
WHY DID JOHN START READING THAT MANGA?!
W-WAIT, WHAT IF...
...HE ACTS LIKE THE PROTAGONIST OF THAT SERIES AND SHAVES OFF ONE EYEBROW...
...VOWING NEVER TO BE SEEN IN PUBLIC UNTIL HE'S FINISHED HIS TRAINING?!
HA HA HA!
I'M AFRAID JOHN'S DECIDED...

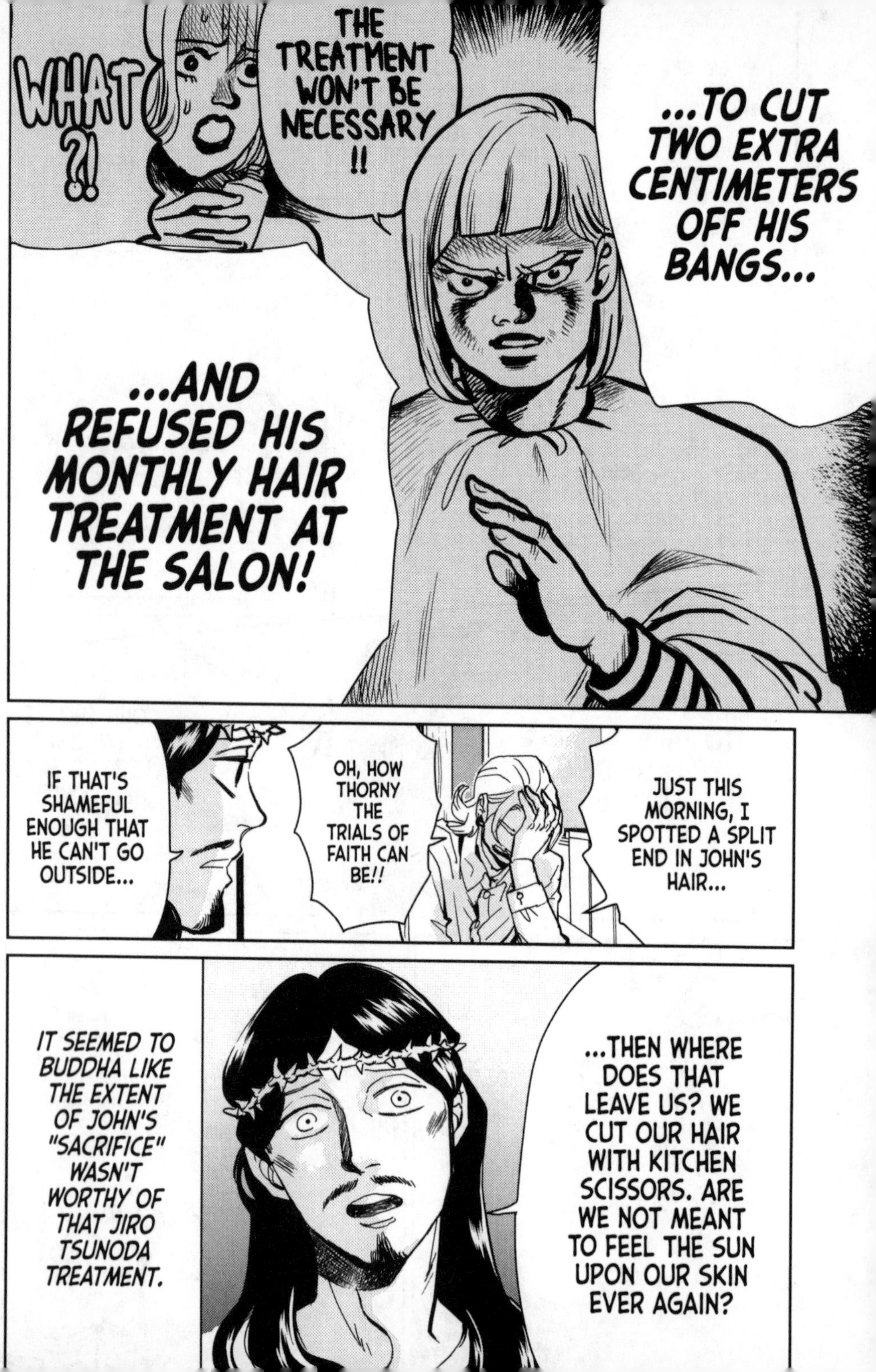
...TO CUT TWO EXTRA CENTIMETERS OFF HIS BANGS...
THE TREATMENT WON'T BE NECESSARY !!
WHAT ?!
...AND REFUSED HIS MONTHLY HAIR TREATMENT AT THE SALON!
JUST THIS MORNING, I SPOTTED A SPLIT END IN JOHN'S HAIR...
OH, HOW THORNY THE TRIALS OF FAITH CAN BE!!
IF THAT'S SHAMEFUL ENOUGH THAT HE CAN'T GO OUTSIDE...
...THEN WHERE DOES THAT LEAVE US? WE CUT OUR HAIR WITH KITCHEN SCISSORS. ARE WE NOT MEANT TO FEEL THE SUN UPON OUR SKIN EVER AGAIN?
IT SEEMED TO BUDDHA LIKE THE EXTENT OF JOHN'S "SACRIFICE" WASN'T WORTHY OF THAT JIRO TSUNODA TREATMENT.

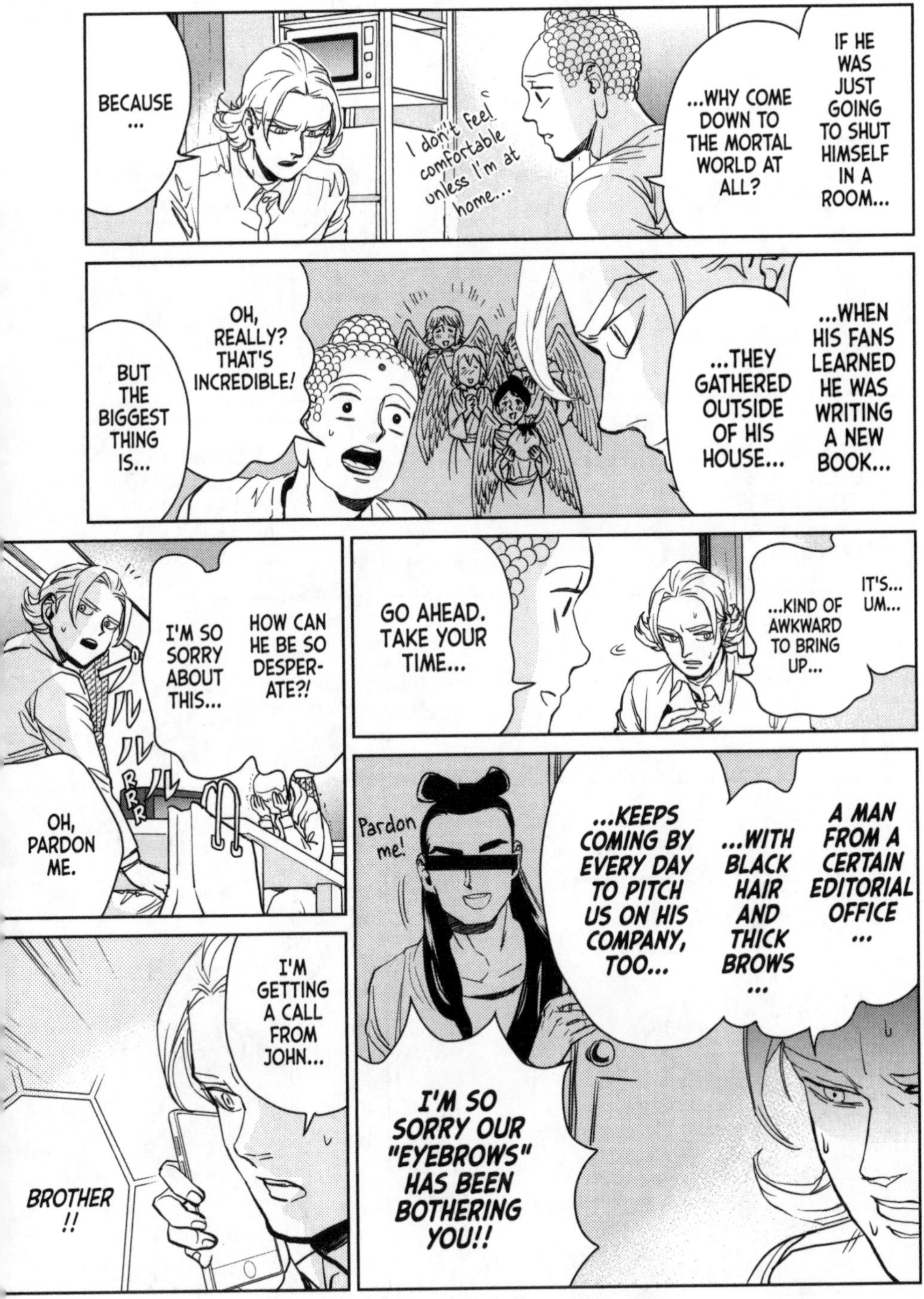
IF HE WAS JUST GOING TO SHUT HIMSELF IN A ROOM...
...WHY COME DOWN TO THE MORTAL WORLD AT ALL?
I don't feel comfortable unless I'm at home...
BECAUSE ...
...WHEN HIS FANS LEARNED HE WAS WRITING A NEW BOOK...
...THEY GATHERED OUTSIDE OF HIS HOUSE...
OH, REALLY? THAT'S INCREDIBLE!
BUT THE BIGGEST THING IS...
IT'S... UM...
...KIND OF AWKWARD TO BRING UP...
GO AHEAD. TAKE YOUR TIME...
A MAN FROM A CERTAIN EDITORIAL OFFICE ...
...WITH BLACK HAIR AND THICK BROWS ...
...KEEPS COMING BY EVERY DAY TO PITCH US ON HIS COMPANY, TOO...
Pardon me!
I'M SO SORRY OUR "EYEBROWS" HAS BEEN BOTHERING YOU!!
HOW CAN HE BE SO DESPERATE?!
I'M SO SORRY ABOUT THIS...
ルルル
RRR
OH, PARDON ME.
I'M GETTING A CALL FROM JOHN...
BROTHER !!

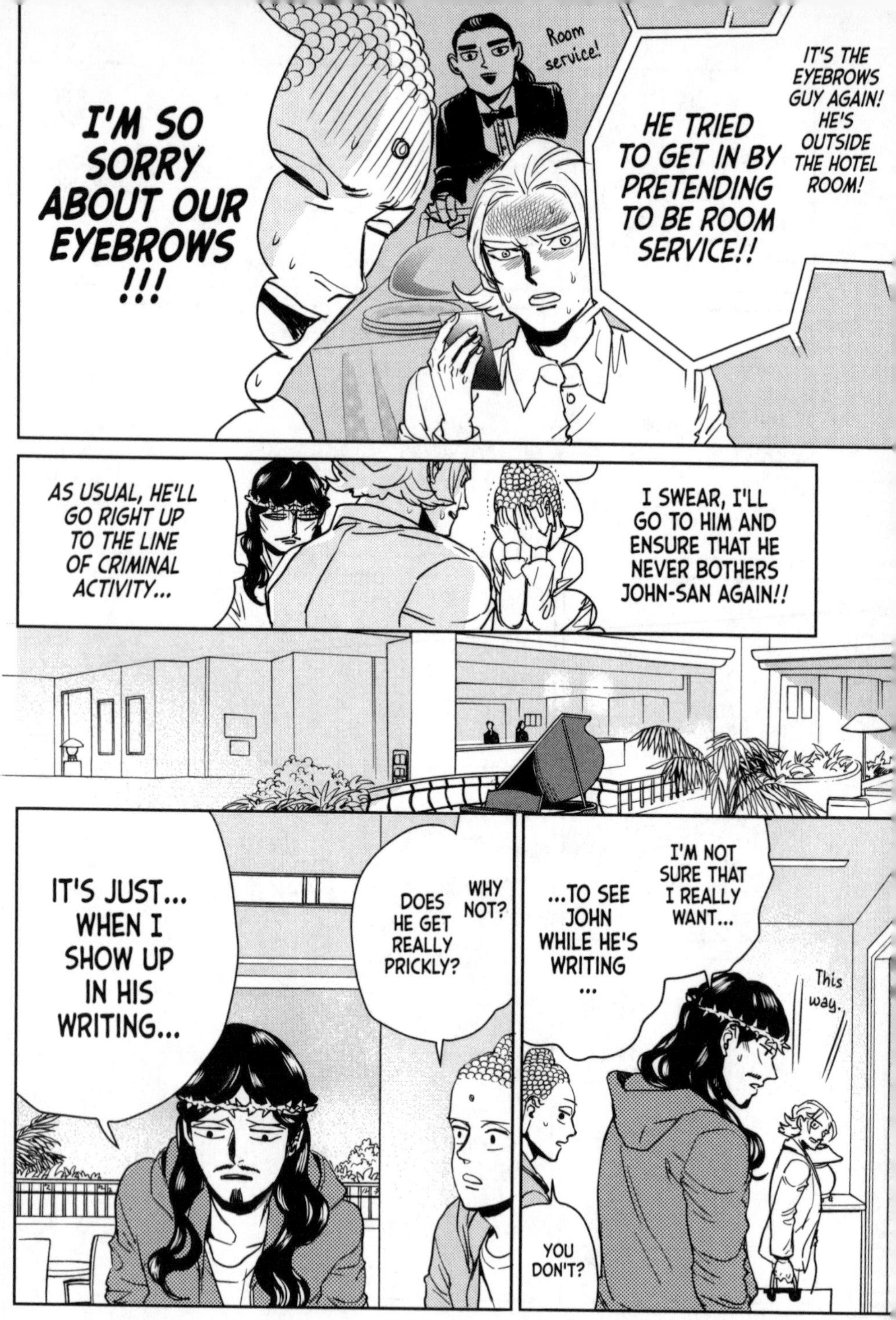
IT'S THE EYEBROWS GUY AGAIN! HE'S OUTSIDE THE HOTEL ROOM!
HE TRIED TO GET IN BY PRETENDING TO BE ROOM SERVICE!!
Room service!
I'M SO SORRY ABOUT OUR EYEBROWS!!!
I SWEAR, I'LL GO TO HIM AND ENSURE THAT HE NEVER BOTHERS JOHN-SAN AGAIN!!
AS USUAL, HE'LL GO RIGHT UP TO THE LINE OF CRIMINAL ACTIVITY...
I'M NOT SURE THAT I REALLY WANT...
...TO SEE JOHN WHILE HE'S WRITING ...
This way.
YOU DON'T?
WHY NOT?
DOES HE GET REALLY PRICKLY?
IT'S JUST... WHEN I SHOW UP IN HIS WRITING...

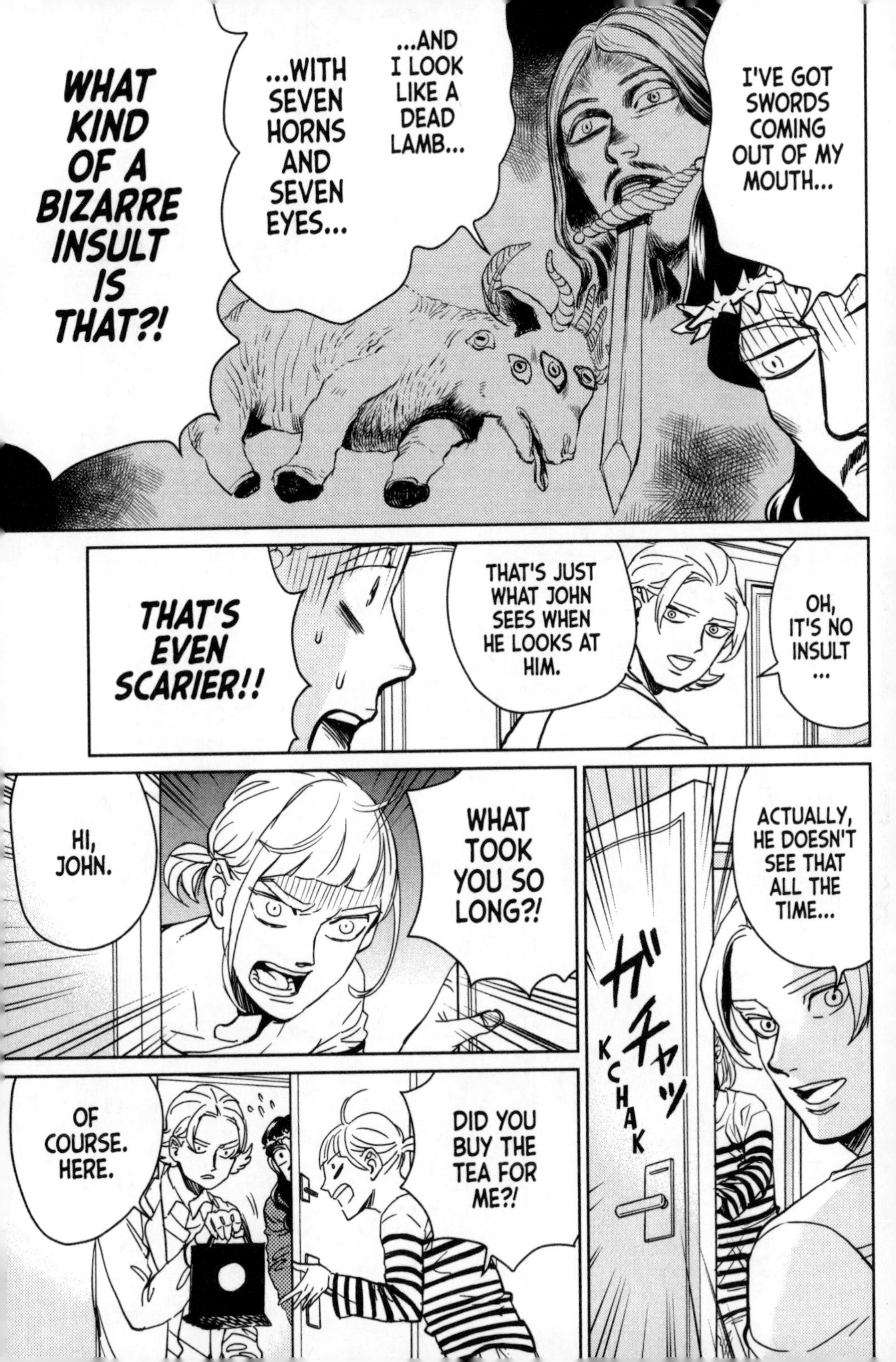
I'VE GOT SWORDS COMING OUT OF MY MOUTH...
...AND I LOOK LIKE A DEAD LAMB...
...WITH SEVEN HORNS AND SEVEN EYES...
WHAT KIND OF A BIZARRE INSULT IS THAT?!
OH, IT'S NO INSULT ...
THAT'S JUST WHAT JOHN SEES WHEN HE LOOKS AT HIM.
THAT'S EVEN SCARIER!!
ACTUALLY, HE DOESN'T SEE THAT ALL THE TIME...
ガチャッ
KCHAK
WHAT TOOK YOU SO LONG?!
HI, JOHN.
DID YOU BUY THE TEA FOR ME?!
OF COURSE. HERE.

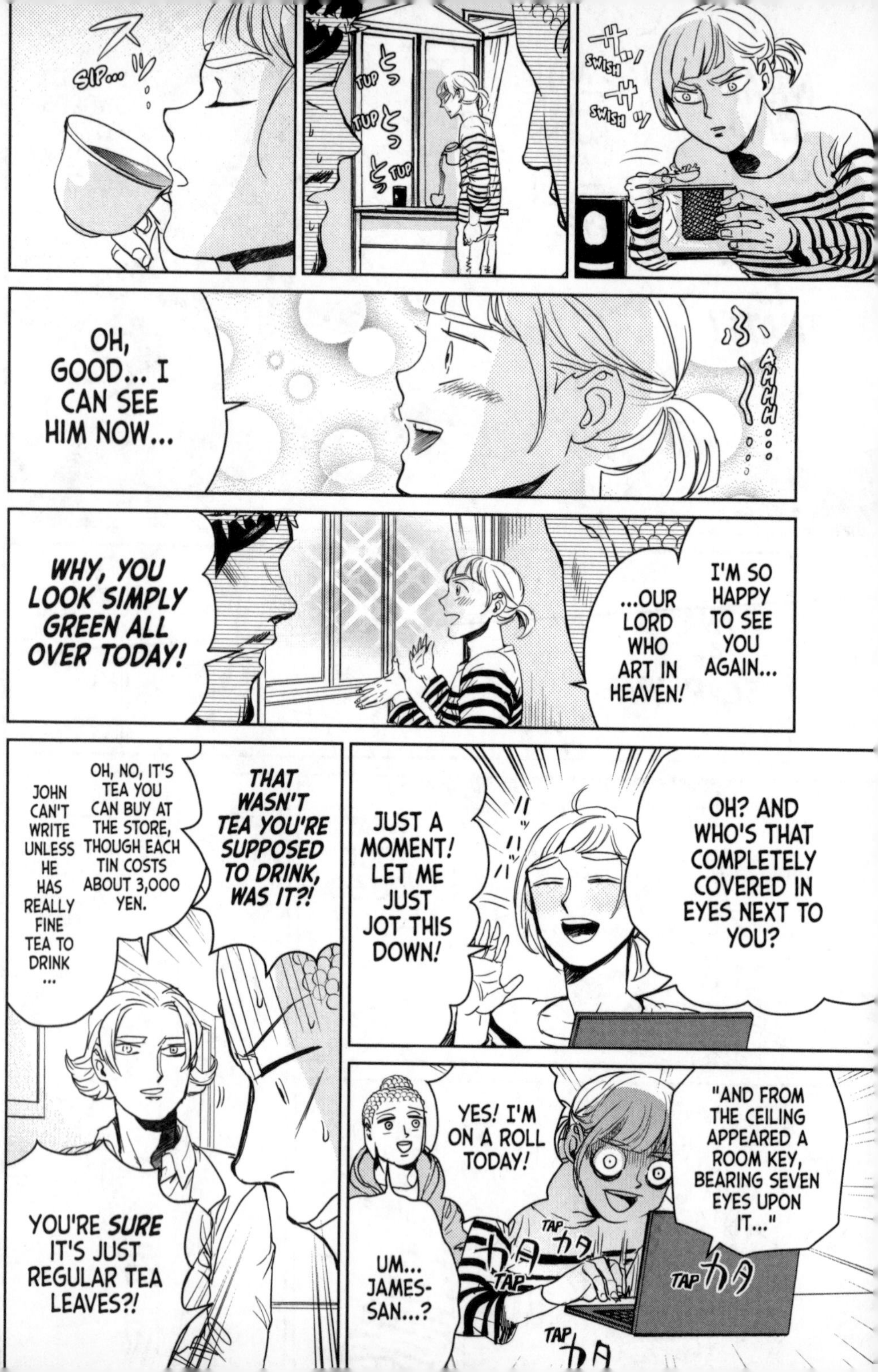

SWISH
SWISH
TUP
TUP
TUP
SIP...
AHHH...
OH, GOOD... I CAN SEE HIM NOW...
I'M SO HAPPY TO SEE YOU AGAIN...
...OUR LORD WHO ART IN HEAVEN!
WHY, YOU LOOK SIMPLY GREEN ALL OVER TODAY!
OH? AND WHO'S THAT COMPLETELY COVERED IN EYES NEXT TO YOU?
JUST A MOMENT! LET ME JUST JOT THIS DOWN!
"AND FROM THE CEILING APPEARED A ROOM KEY, BEARING SEVEN EYES UPON IT..."
YES! I'M ON A ROLL TODAY!
TAP
TAP
TAP
TAP
UM... JAMES-SAN...?
THAT WASN'T TEA YOU'RE SUPPOSED TO DRINK, WAS IT?!
OH, NO, IT'S TEA YOU CAN BUY AT THE STORE, THOUGH EACH TIN COSTS ABOUT 3,000 YEN.
JOHN CAN'T WRITE UNLESS HE HAS REALLY FINE TEA TO DRINK...
YOU'RE SURE IT'S JUST REGULAR TEA LEAVES?!

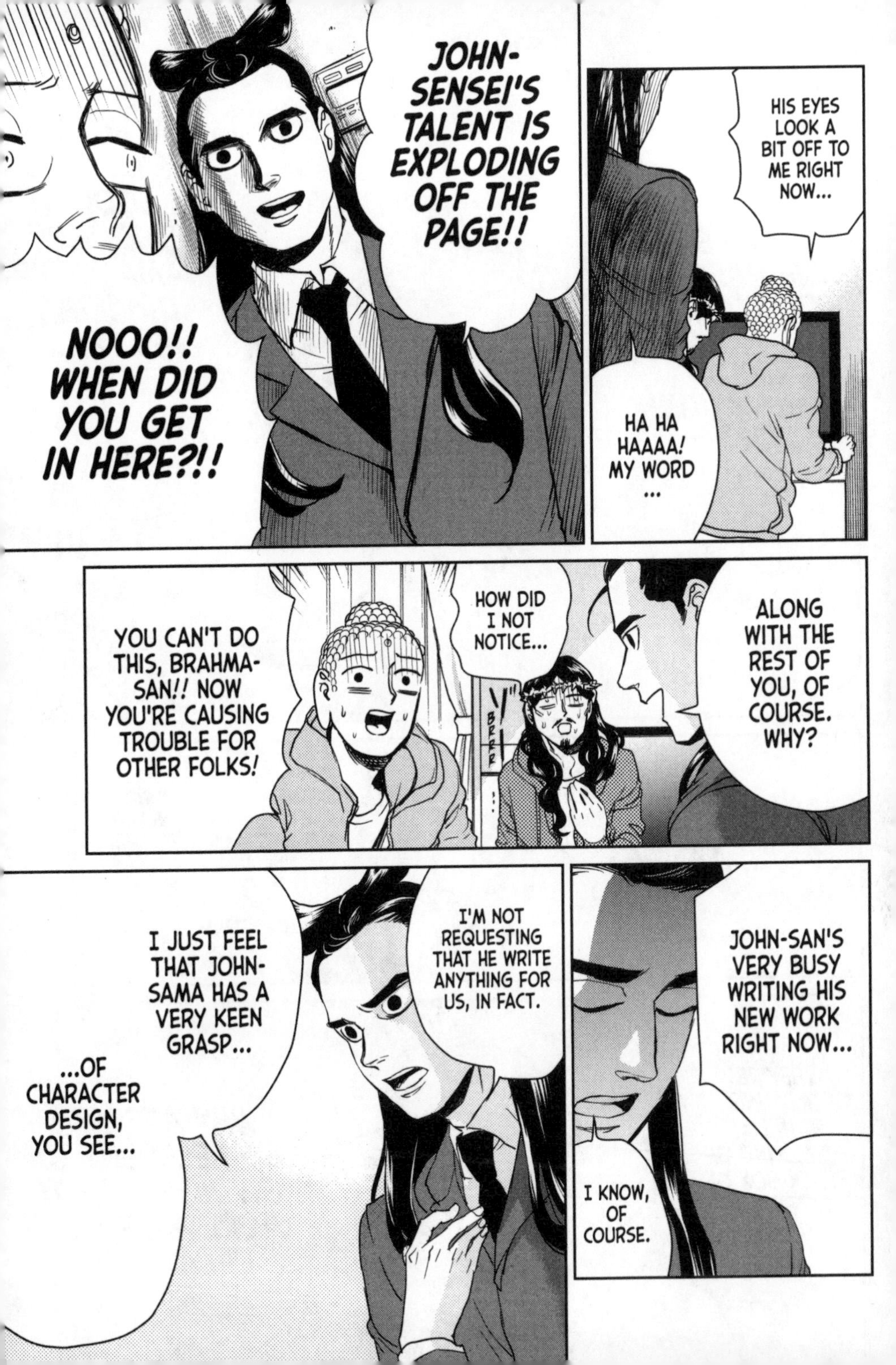

HIS EYES LOOK A BIT OFF TO ME RIGHT NOW...
HA HA HAAAA! MY WORD ...
JOHN-SENSEI'S TALENT IS EXPLODING OFF THE PAGE!!
NOOO!! WHEN DID YOU GET IN HERE?!!
ALONG WITH THE REST OF YOU, OF COURSE. WHY?
HOW DID I NOT NOTICE...
YOU CAN'T DO THIS, BRAHMA-SAN!! NOW YOU'RE CAUSING TROUBLE FOR OTHER FOLKS!
JOHN-SAN'S VERY BUSY WRITING HIS NEW WORK RIGHT NOW...
I KNOW, OF COURSE.
I'M NOT REQUESTING THAT HE WRITE ANYTHING FOR US, IN FACT.
I JUST FEEL THAT JOHN-SAMA HAS A VERY KEEN GRASP...
...OF CHARACTER DESIGN, YOU SEE...

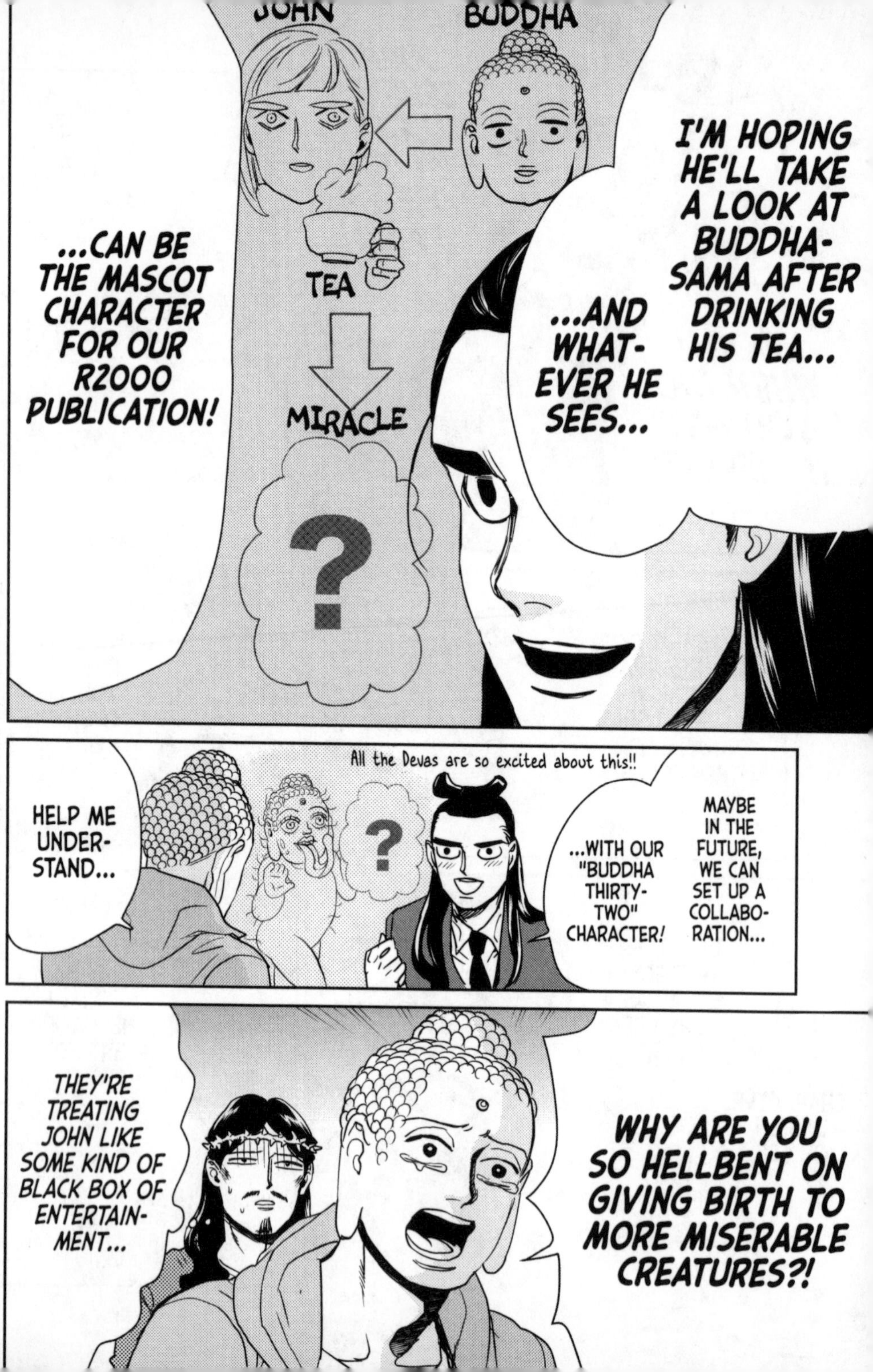
I'M HOPING HE'LL TAKE A LOOK AT BUDDHA-SAMA AFTER DRINKING HIS TEA...
...AND WHAT-EVER HE SEES...
BUDDHA
JOHN
TEA
MIRACLE
?
...CAN BE THE MASCOT CHARACTER FOR OUR R2000 PUBLICATION!
MAYBE IN THE FUTURE, WE CAN SET UP A COLLABO-RATION...
...WITH OUR "BUDDHA THIRTY-TWO" CHARACTER!
All the Devas are so excited about this!!
?
HELP ME UNDER-STAND...
WHY ARE YOU SO HELLBENT ON GIVING BIRTH TO MORE MISERABLE CREATURES?!
THEY'RE TREATING JOHN LIKE SOME KIND OF BLACK BOX OF ENTERTAIN-MENT...

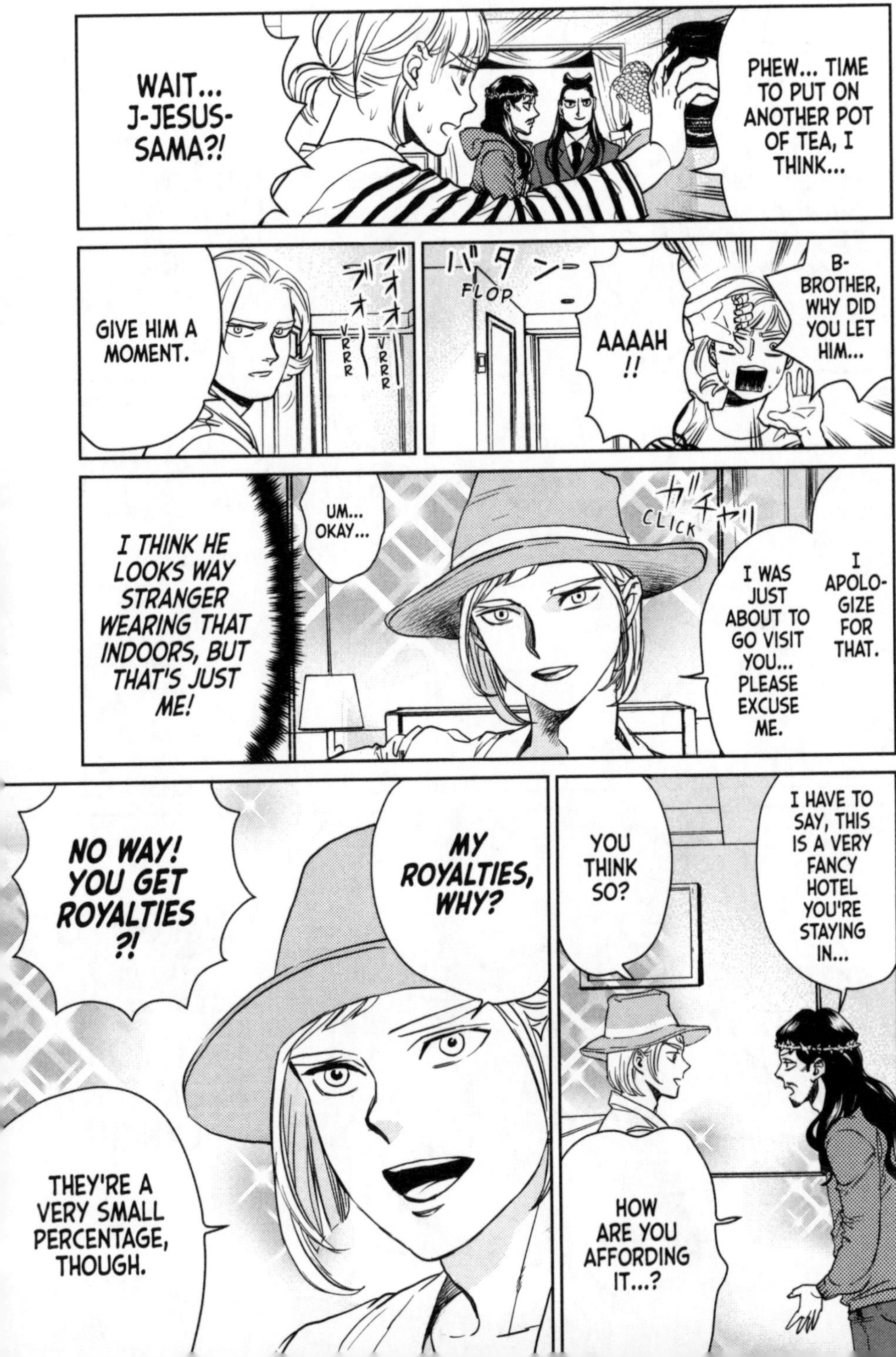
PHEW... TIME TO PUT ON ANOTHER POT OF TEA, I THINK...
WAIT... J-JESUS-SAMA?!
B-BROTHER, WHY DID YOU LET HIM...
AAAAH!!
バタン
FLOP
VRRR VRRR
GIVE HIM A MOMENT.
ガチャリ
CLICK
I APOLOGIZE FOR THAT.
I WAS JUST ABOUT TO GO VISIT YOU... PLEASE EXCUSE ME.
UM... OKAY...
I THINK HE LOOKS WAY STRANGER WEARING THAT INDOORS, BUT THAT'S JUST ME!
I HAVE TO SAY, THIS IS A VERY FANCY HOTEL YOU'RE STAYING IN...
YOU THINK SO?
HOW ARE YOU AFFORDING IT...?
MY ROYALTIES, WHY?
NO WAY! YOU GET ROYALTIES?!
THEY'RE A VERY SMALL PERCENTAGE, THOUGH.

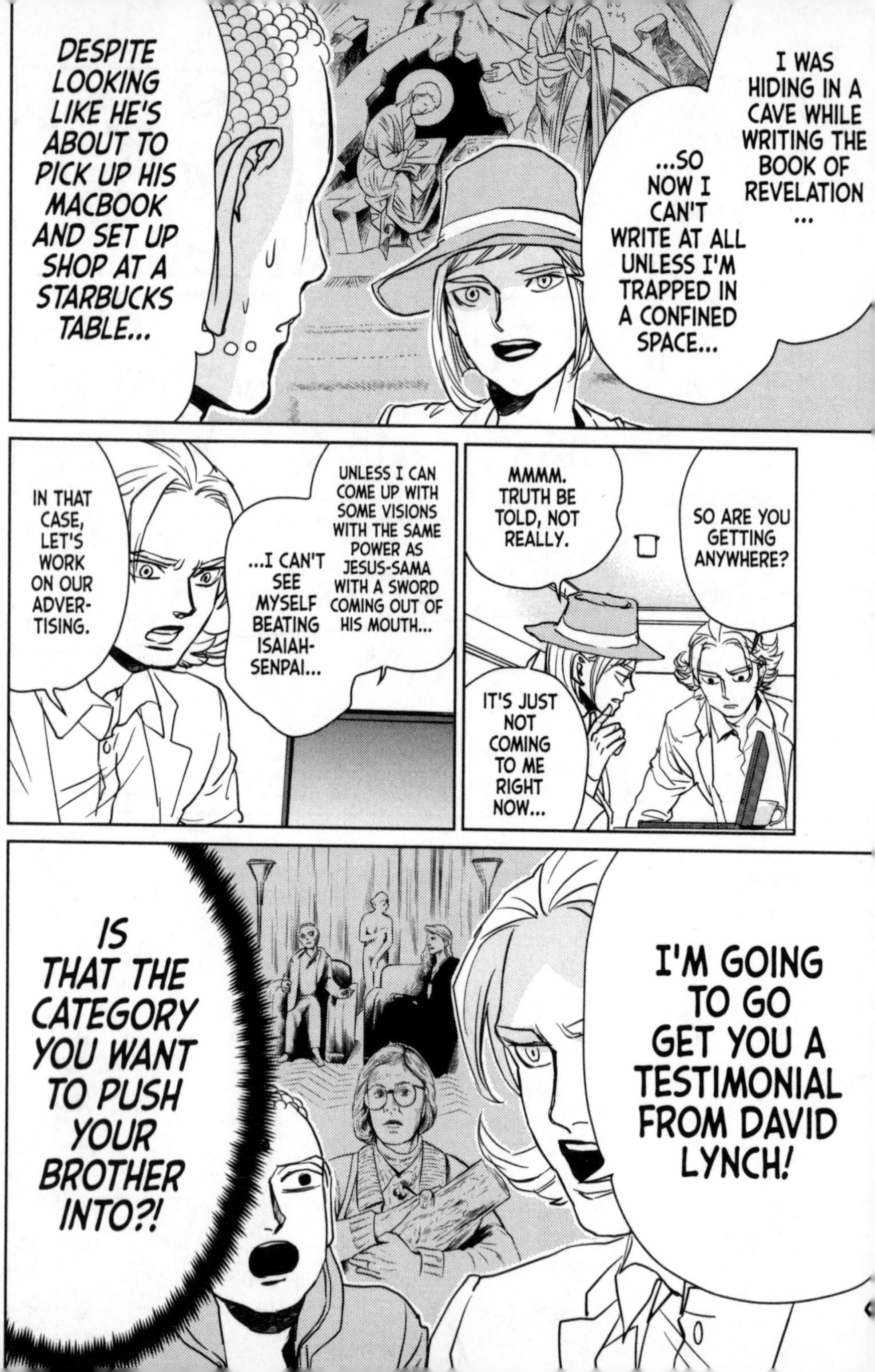
I WAS HIDING IN A CAVE WHILE WRITING THE BOOK OF REVELATION ...
...SO NOW I CAN'T WRITE AT ALL UNLESS I'M TRAPPED IN A CONFINED SPACE...
DESPITE LOOKING LIKE HE'S ABOUT TO PICK UP HIS MACBOOK AND SET UP SHOP AT A STARBUCKS TABLE...
SO ARE YOU GETTING ANYWHERE?
MMMM. TRUTH BE TOLD, NOT REALLY.
IT'S JUST NOT COMING TO ME RIGHT NOW...
UNLESS I CAN COME UP WITH SOME VISIONS WITH THE SAME POWER AS JESUS-SAMA WITH A SWORD COMING OUT OF HIS MOUTH...
...I CAN'T SEE MYSELF BEATING ISAIAH-SENPAI...
IN THAT CASE, LET'S WORK ON OUR ADVERTISING.
I'M GOING TO GO GET YOU A TESTIMONIAL FROM DAVID LYNCH!
IS THAT THE CATEGORY YOU WANT TO PUSH YOUR BROTHER INTO?!

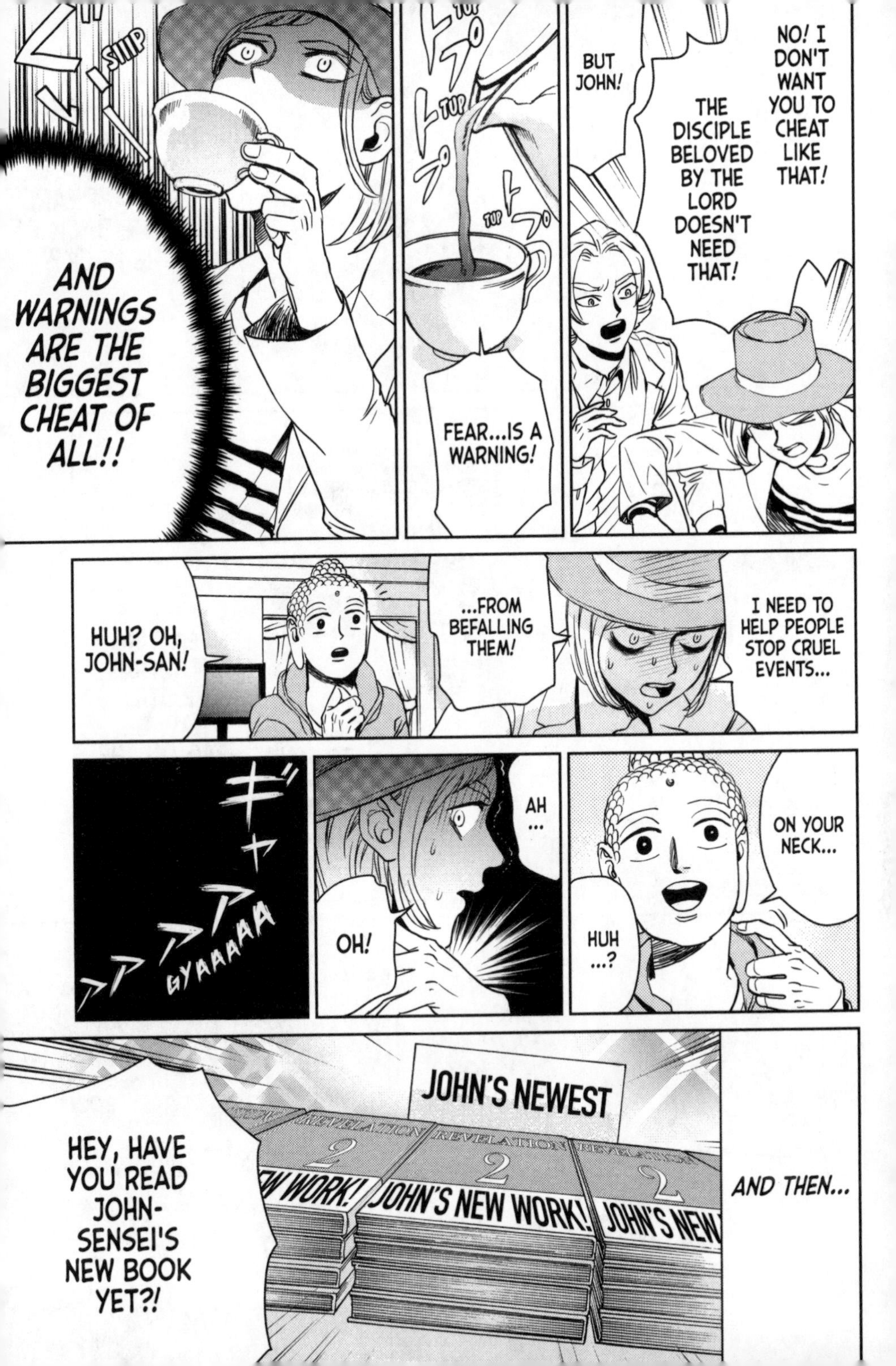
NO! I DON'T WANT YOU TO CHEAT LIKE THAT!
THE DISCIPLE BELOVED BY THE LORD DOESN'T NEED THAT!
BUT JOHN!
TUP TUP TUP
FEAR...IS A WARNING!
SIIIP
AND WARNINGS ARE THE BIGGEST CHEAT OF ALL!!
I NEED TO HELP PEOPLE STOP CRUEL EVENTS...
...FROM BEFALLING THEM!
HUH? OH, JOHN-SAN!
ON YOUR NECK...
HUH ...?
AH ...
OH!
GYAAAAA
AND THEN...
JOHN'S NEWEST
REVELATION 2
JOHN'S NEW WORK!
HEY, HAVE YOU READ JOHN-SENSEI'S NEW BOOK YET?!

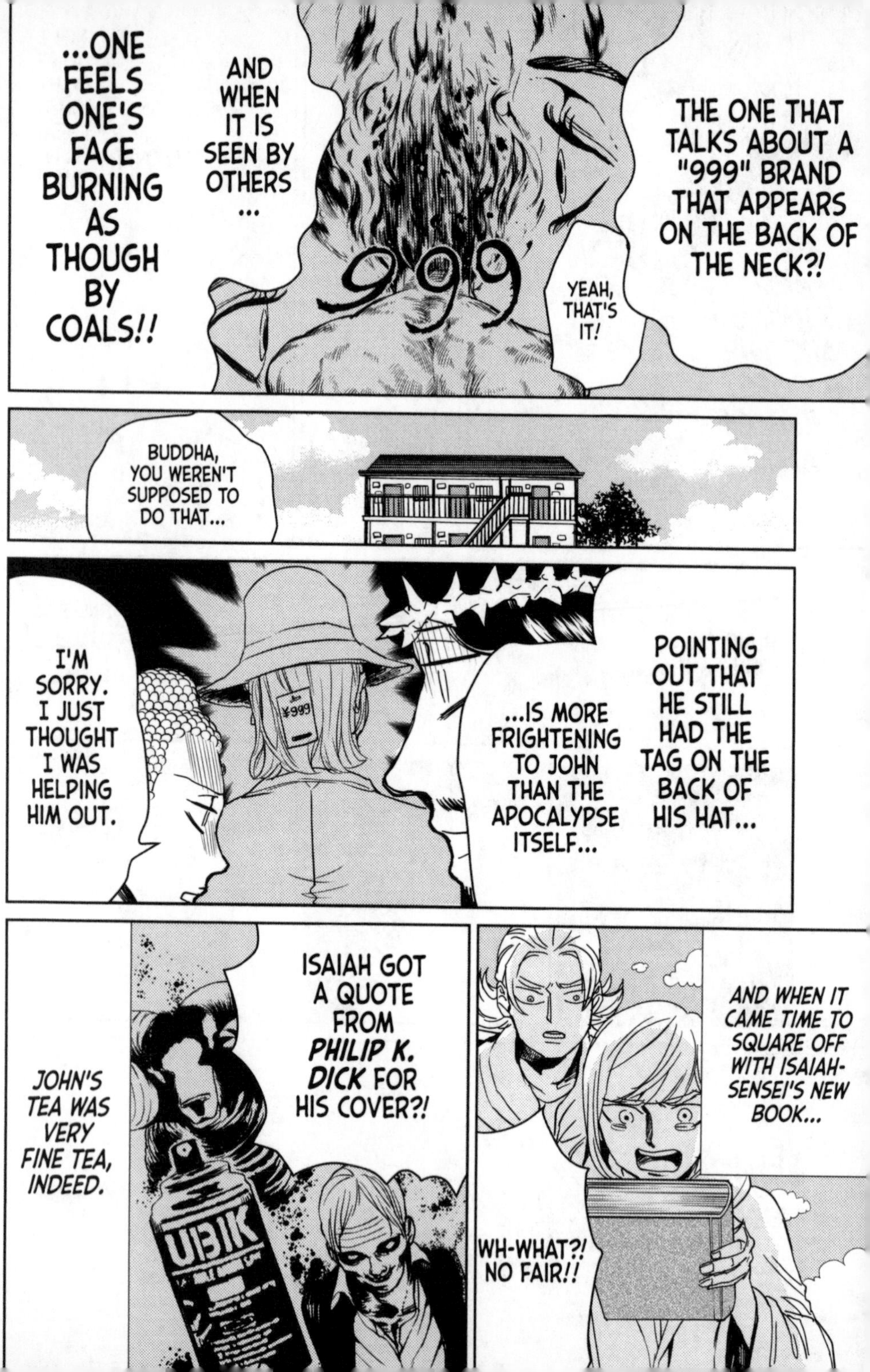
THE ONE THAT TALKS ABOUT A "999" BRAND THAT APPEARS ON THE BACK OF THE NECK?!
YEAH, THAT'S IT!
AND WHEN IT IS SEEN BY OTHERS ...
...ONE FEELS ONE'S FACE BURNING AS THOUGH BY COALS!!
999
BUDDHA, YOU WEREN'T SUPPOSED TO DO THAT...
POINTING OUT THAT HE STILL HAD THE TAG ON THE BACK OF HIS HAT...
...IS MORE FRIGHTENING TO JOHN THAN THE APOCALYPSE ITSELF...
¥999
I'M SORRY. I JUST THOUGHT I WAS HELPING HIM OUT.
AND WHEN IT CAME TIME TO SQUARE OFF WITH ISAIAH-SENSEI'S NEW BOOK...
WH-WHAT?! NO FAIR!!
ISAIAH GOT A QUOTE FROM *PHILIP K. DICK* FOR HIS COVER?!
JOHN'S TEA WAS VERY FINE TEA, INDEED.
UBIK

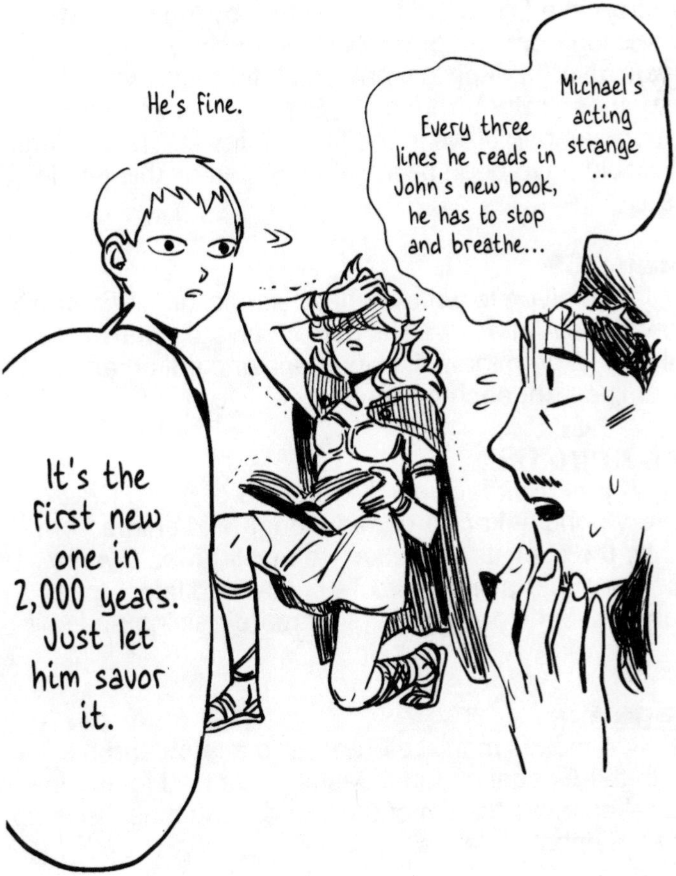
Michael's acting strange ...
Every three lines he reads in John's new book, he has to stop and breathe...
He's fine.
It's the first new one in 2,000 years. Just let him savor it.

CHAPTER 93 TRANSLATION NOTES

Chapter Six, page 65

Chapter Six of the Book of Revelation contains the descriptions of the infamous "Four Horsemen of the Apocalypse." The first horseman is on a white horse, symbolizing Conquest. Next comes the rider on the red horse, symbolizing War. The rider on the black horse symbolizes Famine, and the rider on the pale horse symbolizes Death.

Isaiah, page 67

The Book of Isaiah from the Old Testament, written by the prophet Isaiah, contains a section from Chapters 24-27 sometimes referred to as the "little apocalypse." It depicts what Isaiah foresees when the people of Israel and Judah return from exile, in fanciful imagery that made it a popular book among Jews in the time of Jesus. Theologians surmise that John would have been heavily influenced by this text in writing Revelation.

Naoki Prize, page 69

A literary award in Japan given to writers of popular fiction, in contrast to the literary fiction of the Akutagawa Prize. Both awards were created by Kan Kikuchi, a prominent literary magazine editor, and were intended to complement each other.

Karate Master, page 69

Originally known as *Karate Baka Ichidai* ("A Lifetime of Being Crazy About Karate"). A very popular karate-based manga and anime from the 1970s inspired by the exploits of the karate master Mas Oyama, written by Ikki Kajiwara and drawn by Jiro Tsunoda (and later, Joya Kagemaru). It is famous for its depictions of extreme training and self-sacrifice.

Dead lamb, page 73

The Book of Revelation makes many references to a lamb and the actions it will take. In the Gospel of John, Jesus is referred to as the "Lamb of God who takes away the sin of the world," and thus the lamb is understood to be a symbol of Jesus.

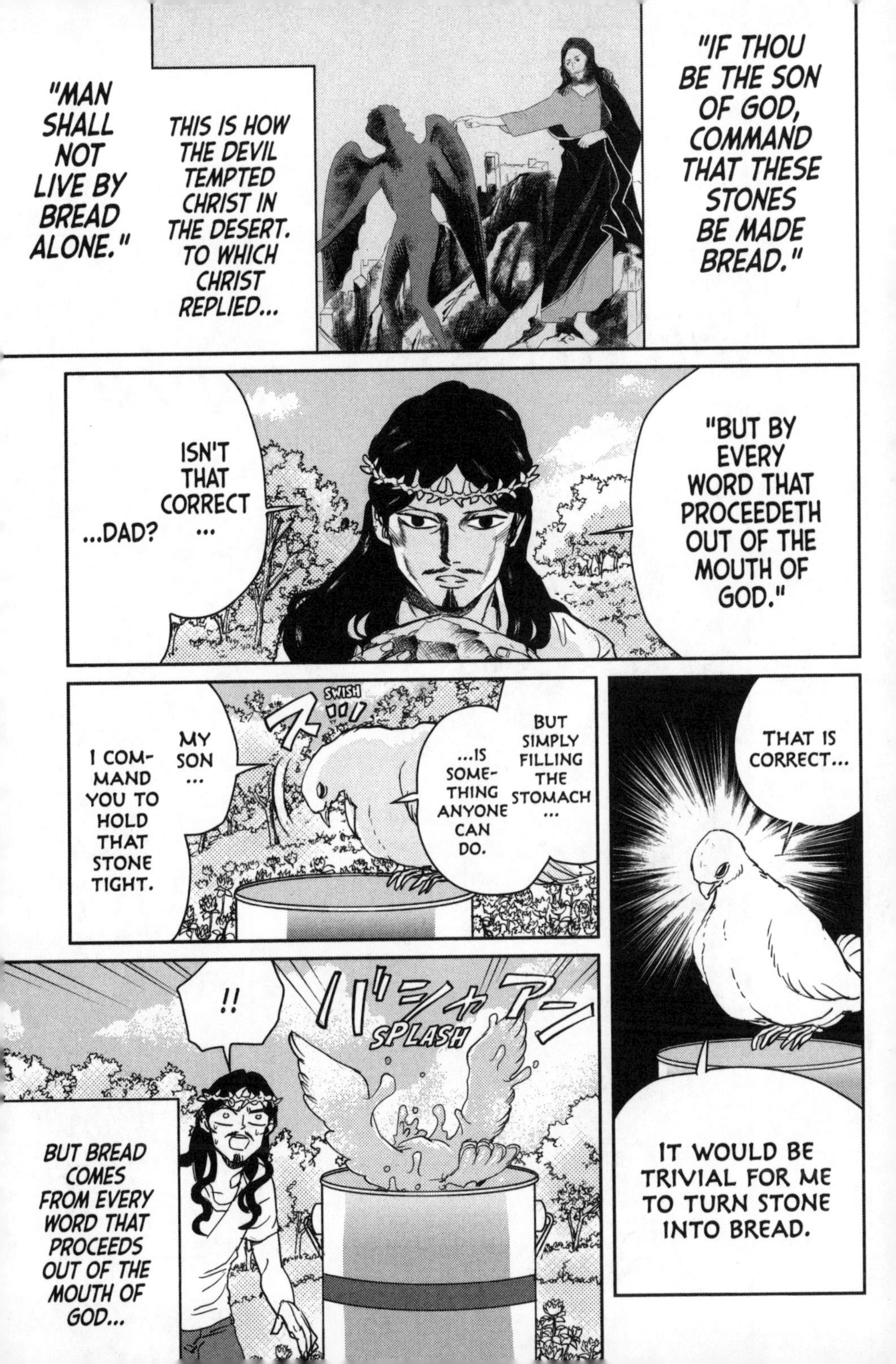
"IF THOU BE THE SON OF GOD, COMMAND THAT THESE STONES BE MADE BREAD."
THIS IS HOW THE DEVIL TEMPTED CHRIST IN THE DESERT. TO WHICH CHRIST REPLIED...
"MAN SHALL NOT LIVE BY BREAD ALONE."
"BUT BY EVERY WORD THAT PROCEEDETH OUT OF THE MOUTH OF GOD."
ISN'T THAT CORRECT ...
...DAD?
THAT IS CORRECT...
IT WOULD BE TRIVIAL FOR ME TO TURN STONE INTO BREAD.
BUT SIMPLY FILLING THE STOMACH ...
...IS SOME-THING ANYONE CAN DO.
SWISH
MY SON ...
I COM-MAND YOU TO HOLD THAT STONE TIGHT.
SPLASH
!!
BUT BREAD COMES FROM EVERY WORD THAT PROCEEDS OUT OF THE MOUTH OF GOD...

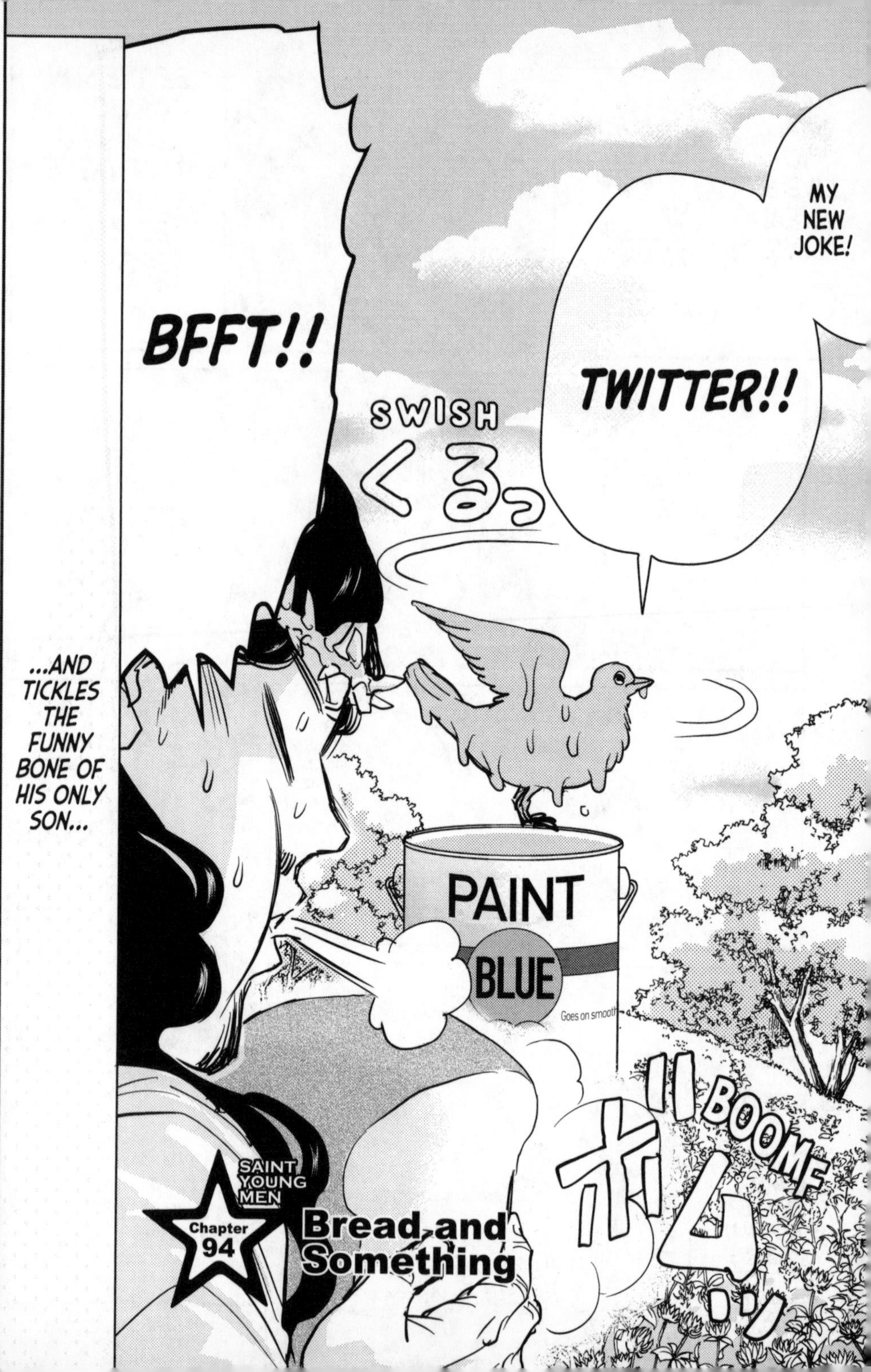
MY NEW JOKE!
TWITTER!!
SWISH
くるっ
BFFT!!
...AND TICKLES THE FUNNY BONE OF HIS ONLY SON...
PAINT
BLUE
Goes on smooth
BOOMF
ボムッ
SAINT YOUNG MEN
Chapter 94
Bread and Something

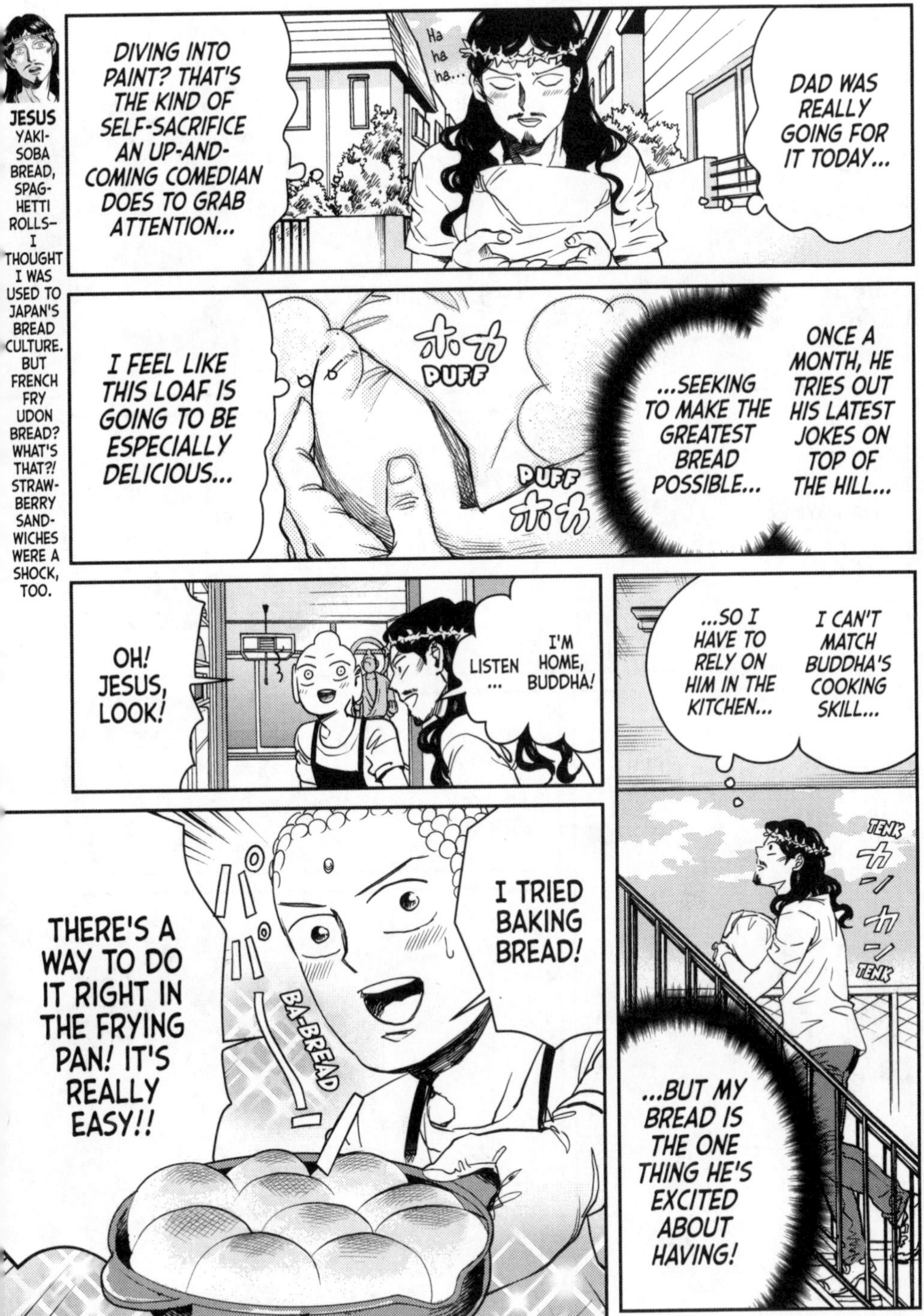
JESUS
YAKISOBA BREAD, SPAGHETTI ROLLS—I THOUGHT I WAS USED TO JAPAN'S BREAD CULTURE. BUT FRENCH FRY UDON BREAD? WHAT'S THAT?! STRAWBERRY SANDWICHES WERE A SHOCK, TOO.
DAD WAS REALLY GOING FOR IT TODAY...
Ha ha ha...
DIVING INTO PAINT? THAT'S THE KIND OF SELF-SACRIFICE AN UP-AND-COMING COMEDIAN DOES TO GRAB ATTENTION...
ONCE A MONTH, HE TRIES OUT HIS LATEST JOKES ON TOP OF THE HILL...
...SEEKING TO MAKE THE GREATEST BREAD POSSIBLE...
PUFF
PUFF
I FEEL LIKE THIS LOAF IS GOING TO BE ESPECIALLY DELICIOUS...
I CAN'T MATCH BUDDHA'S COOKING SKILL...
...SO I HAVE TO RELY ON HIM IN THE KITCHEN...
TENK
TENK
...BUT MY BREAD IS THE ONE THING HE'S EXCITED ABOUT HAVING!
I'M HOME, BUDDHA!
LISTEN ...
OH! JESUS, LOOK!
I TRIED BAKING BREAD!
BA-BREAD
THERE'S A WAY TO DO IT RIGHT IN THE FRYING PAN! IT'S REALLY EASY!!

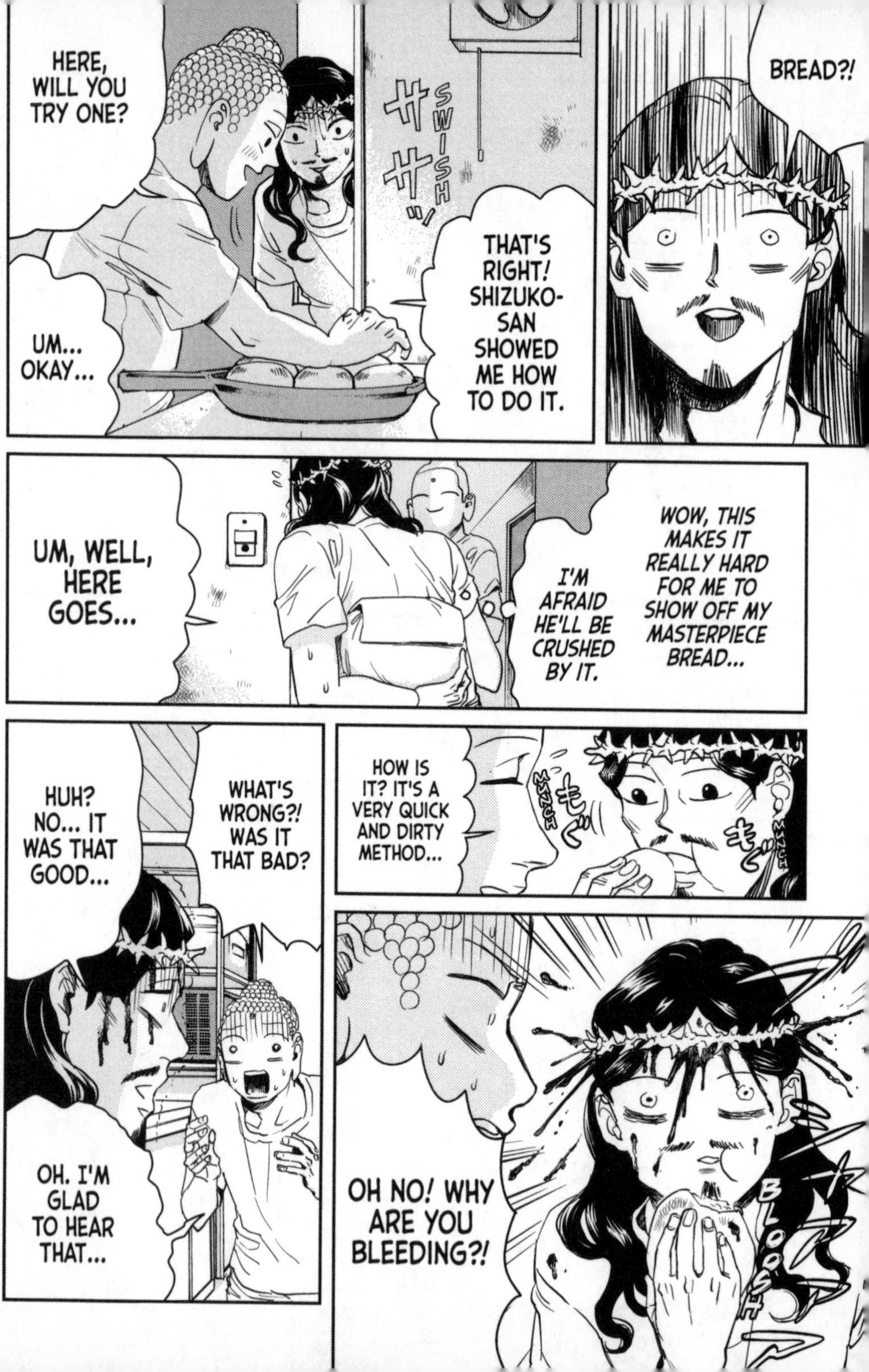
BREAD?!
SWISH
THAT'S RIGHT! SHIZUKO-SAN SHOWED ME HOW TO DO IT.
HERE, WILL YOU TRY ONE?
UM... OKAY...
WOW, THIS MAKES IT REALLY HARD FOR ME TO SHOW OFF MY MASTERPIECE BREAD...
I'M AFRAID HE'LL BE CRUSHED BY IT.
UM, WELL, HERE GOES...
MUNCH
HOW IS IT? IT'S A VERY QUICK AND DIRTY METHOD...
MUNCH
BLOOSH
OH NO! WHY ARE YOU BLEEDING?!
WHAT'S WRONG?! WAS IT THAT BAD?
HUH? NO... IT WAS THAT GOOD...
OH. I'M GLAD TO HEAR THAT...

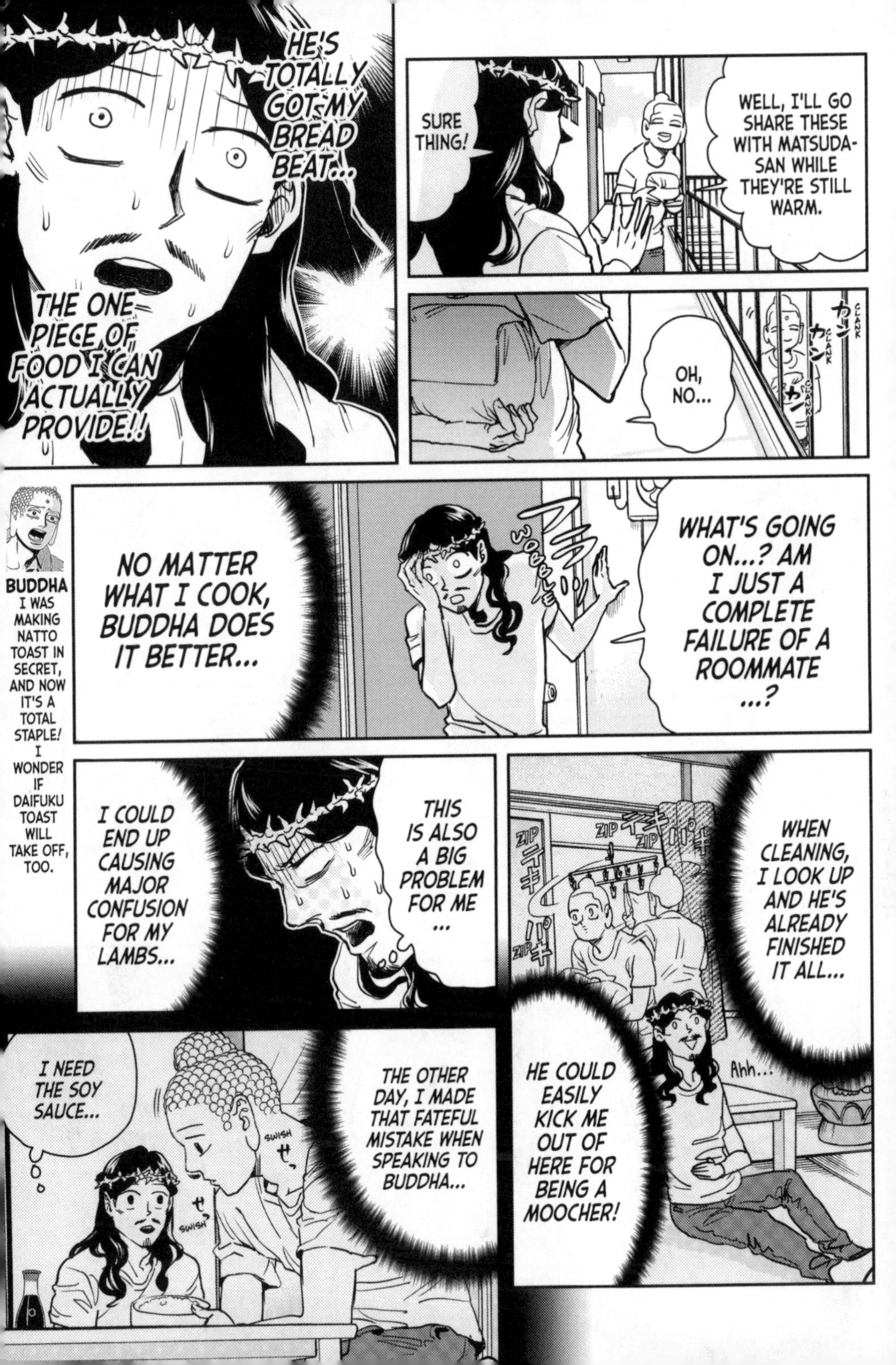
WELL, I'LL GO SHARE THESE WITH MATSUDA-SAN WHILE THEY'RE STILL WARM.
SURE THING!
CLANK CLANK CLANK
OH, NO...
HE'S TOTALLY GOT MY BREAD BEAT...
THE ONE PIECE OF FOOD I CAN ACTUALLY PROVIDE!!
WHAT'S GOING ON...? AM I JUST A COMPLETE FAILURE OF A ROOMMATE ...?
WOBBLE
NO MATTER WHAT I COOK, BUDDHA DOES IT BETTER...
WHEN CLEANING, I LOOK UP AND HE'S ALREADY FINISHED IT ALL...
ZIP ZIP ZIP ZIP
THIS IS ALSO A BIG PROBLEM FOR ME ...
I COULD END UP CAUSING MAJOR CONFUSION FOR MY LAMBS...
HE COULD EASILY KICK ME OUT OF HERE FOR BEING A MOOCHER!
Ahh...
THE OTHER DAY, I MADE THAT FATEFUL MISTAKE WHEN SPEAKING TO BUDDHA...
SWISH SWISH
I NEED THE SOY SAUCE...
BUDDHA
I WAS MAKING NATTO TOAST IN SECRET, AND NOW IT'S A TOTAL STAPLE! I WONDER IF DAIFUKU TOAST WILL TAKE OFF, TOO.

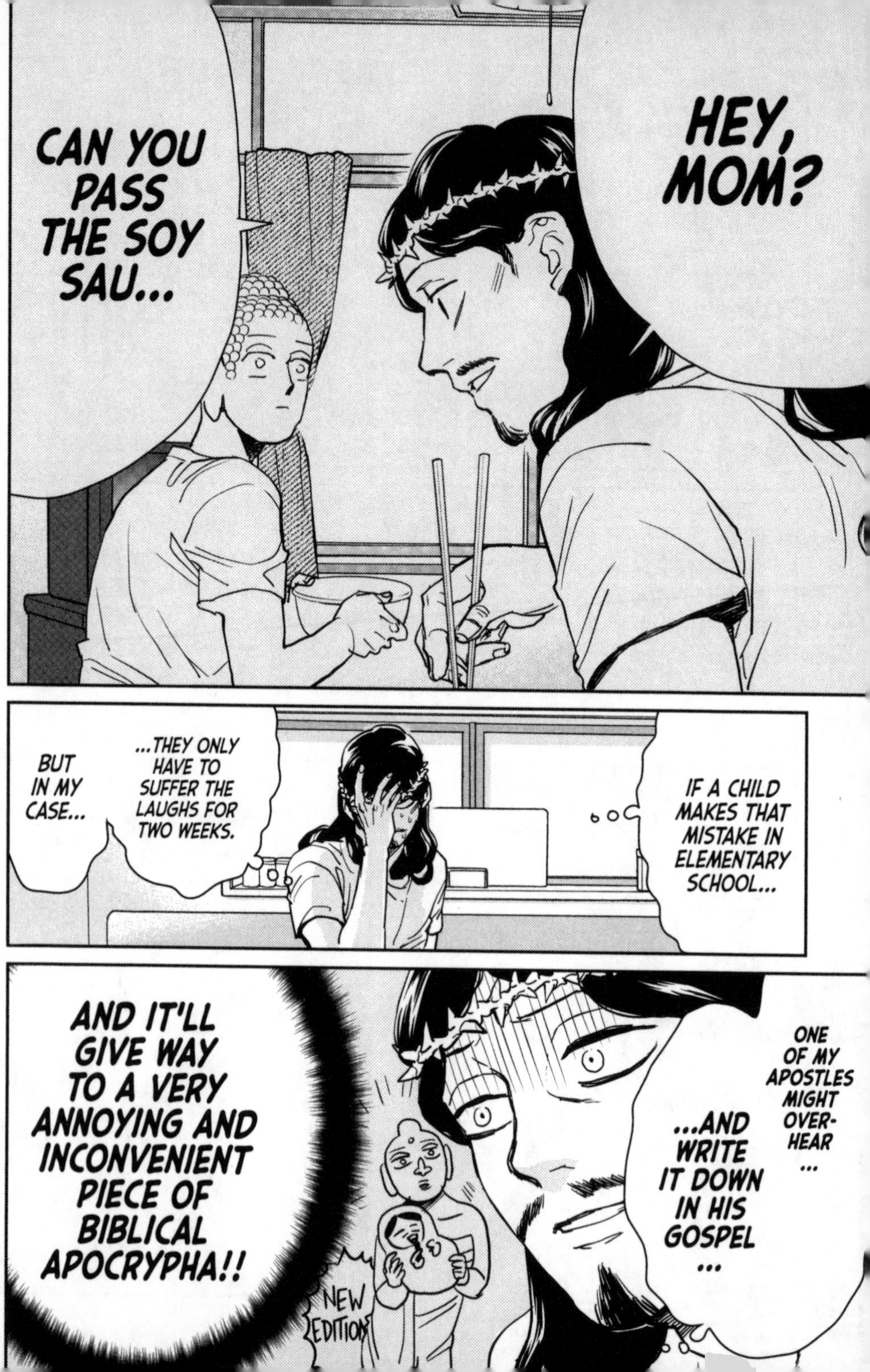
HEY, MOM?
CAN YOU PASS THE SOY SAU...
IF A CHILD MAKES THAT MISTAKE IN ELEMENTARY SCHOOL...
...THEY ONLY HAVE TO SUFFER THE LAUGHS FOR TWO WEEKS.
BUT IN MY CASE...
ONE OF MY APOSTLES MIGHT OVER-HEAR...
...AND WRITE IT DOWN IN HIS GOSPEL...
AND IT'LL GIVE WAY TO A VERY ANNOYING AND INCONVENIENT PIECE OF BIBLICAL APOCRYPHA!!
NEW EDITION

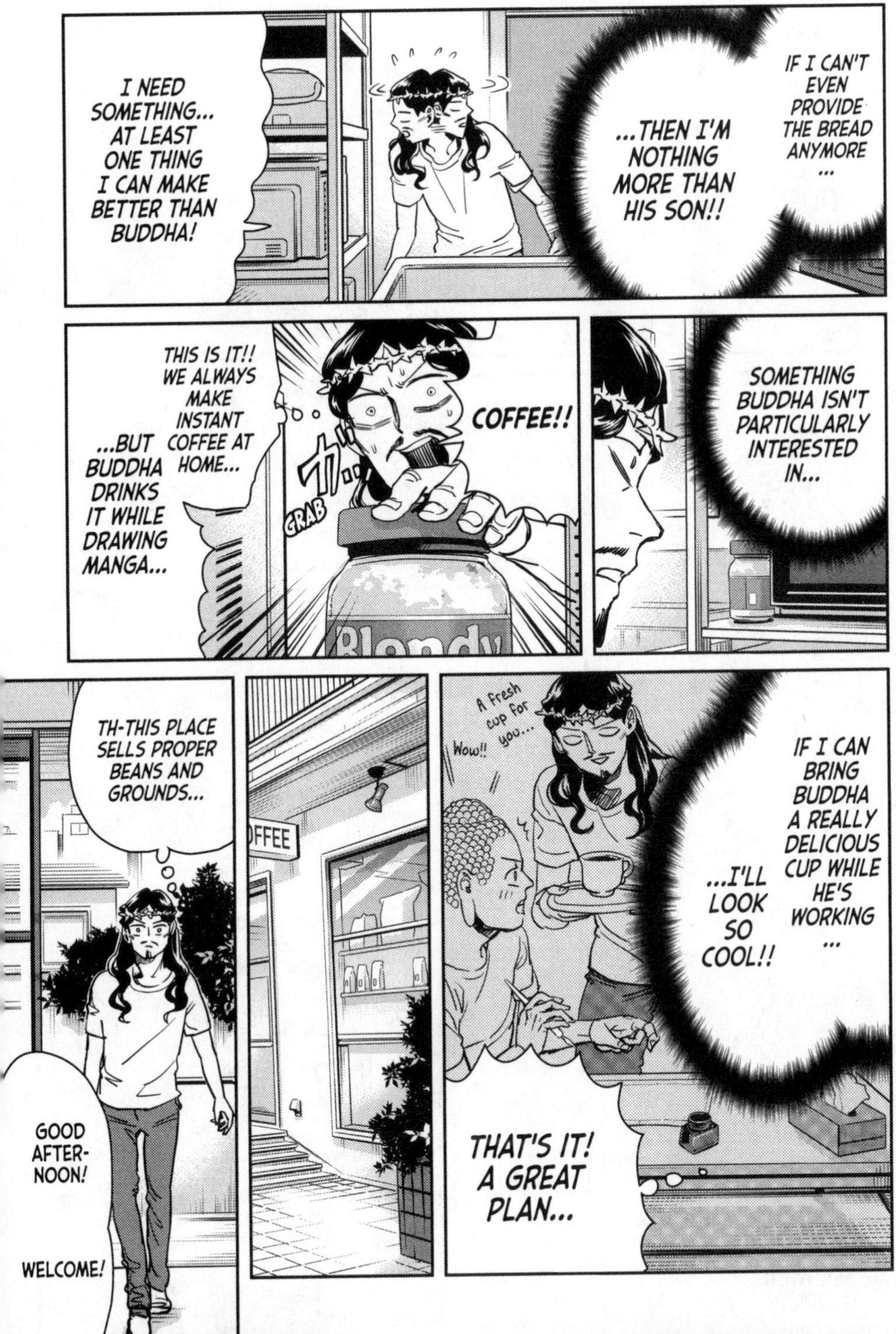
IF I CAN'T EVEN PROVIDE THE BREAD ANYMORE ...
...THEN I'M NOTHING MORE THAN HIS SON!!
I NEED SOMETHING... AT LEAST ONE THING I CAN MAKE BETTER THAN BUDDHA!
SOMETHING BUDDHA ISN'T PARTICULARLY INTERESTED IN...
COFFEE!!
GRAB
Blondy
THIS IS IT!! WE ALWAYS MAKE INSTANT COFFEE AT HOME...
...BUT BUDDHA DRINKS IT WHILE DRAWING MANGA...
IF I CAN BRING BUDDHA A REALLY DELICIOUS CUP WHILE HE'S WORKING ...
...I'LL LOOK SO COOL!!
A Fresh cup for you...
Wow!!
THAT'S IT! A GREAT PLAN...
OFFEE
TH-THIS PLACE SELLS PROPER BEANS AND GROUNDS...
GOOD AFTER-NOON!
WELCOME!

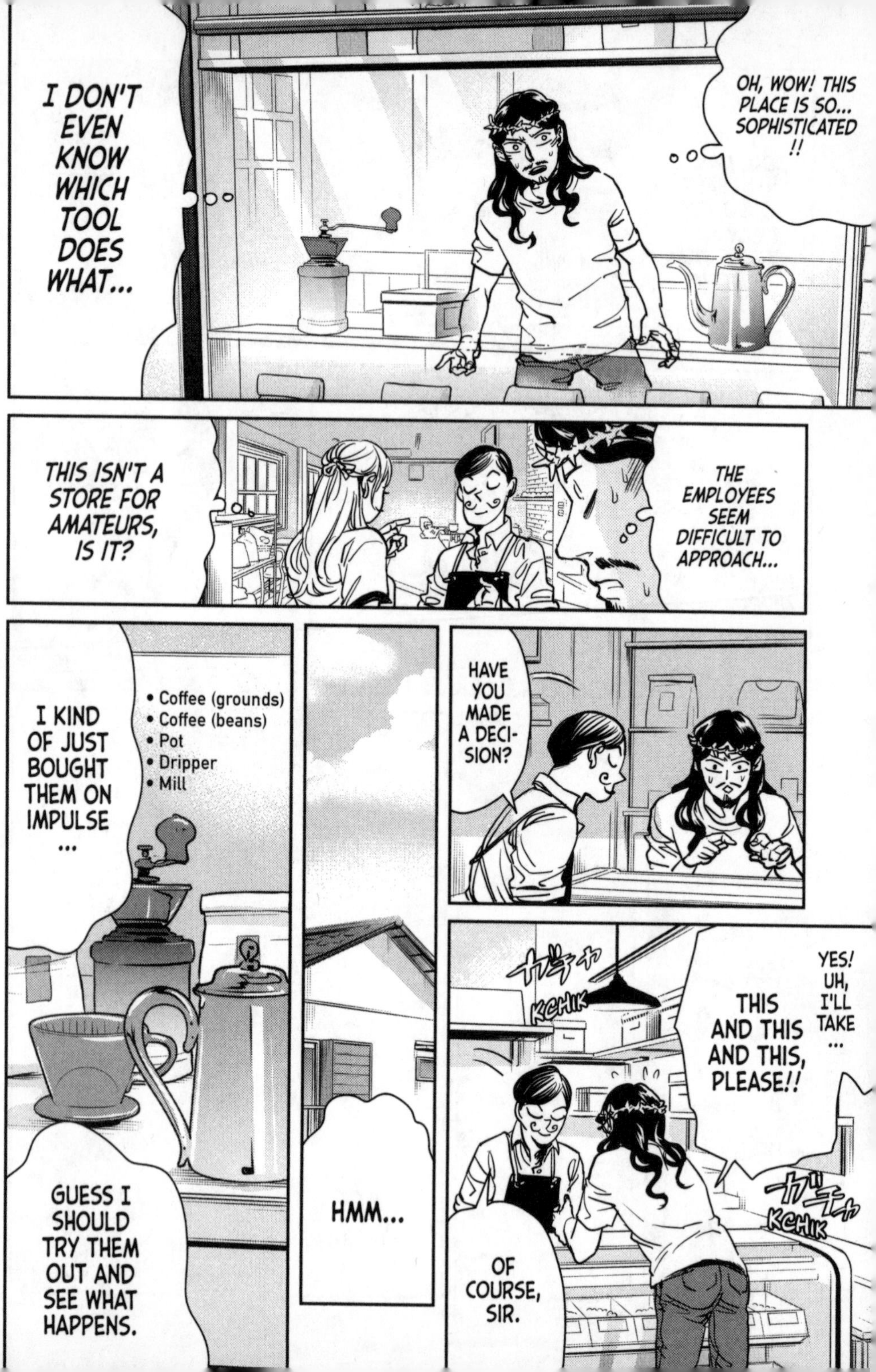
OH, WOW! THIS PLACE IS SO... SOPHISTICATED!!
I DON'T EVEN KNOW WHICH TOOL DOES WHAT...
THE EMPLOYEES SEEM DIFFICULT TO APPROACH...
THIS ISN'T A STORE FOR AMATEURS, IS IT?
HAVE YOU MADE A DECISION?
YES! UH, I'LL TAKE...
THIS AND THIS AND THIS, PLEASE!!
KCHIK
KCHIK
OF COURSE, SIR.
HMM...
I KIND OF JUST BOUGHT THEM ON IMPULSE...
• Coffee (grounds)
• Coffee (beans)
• Pot
• Dripper
• Mill
GUESS I SHOULD TRY THEM OUT AND SEE WHAT HAPPENS.

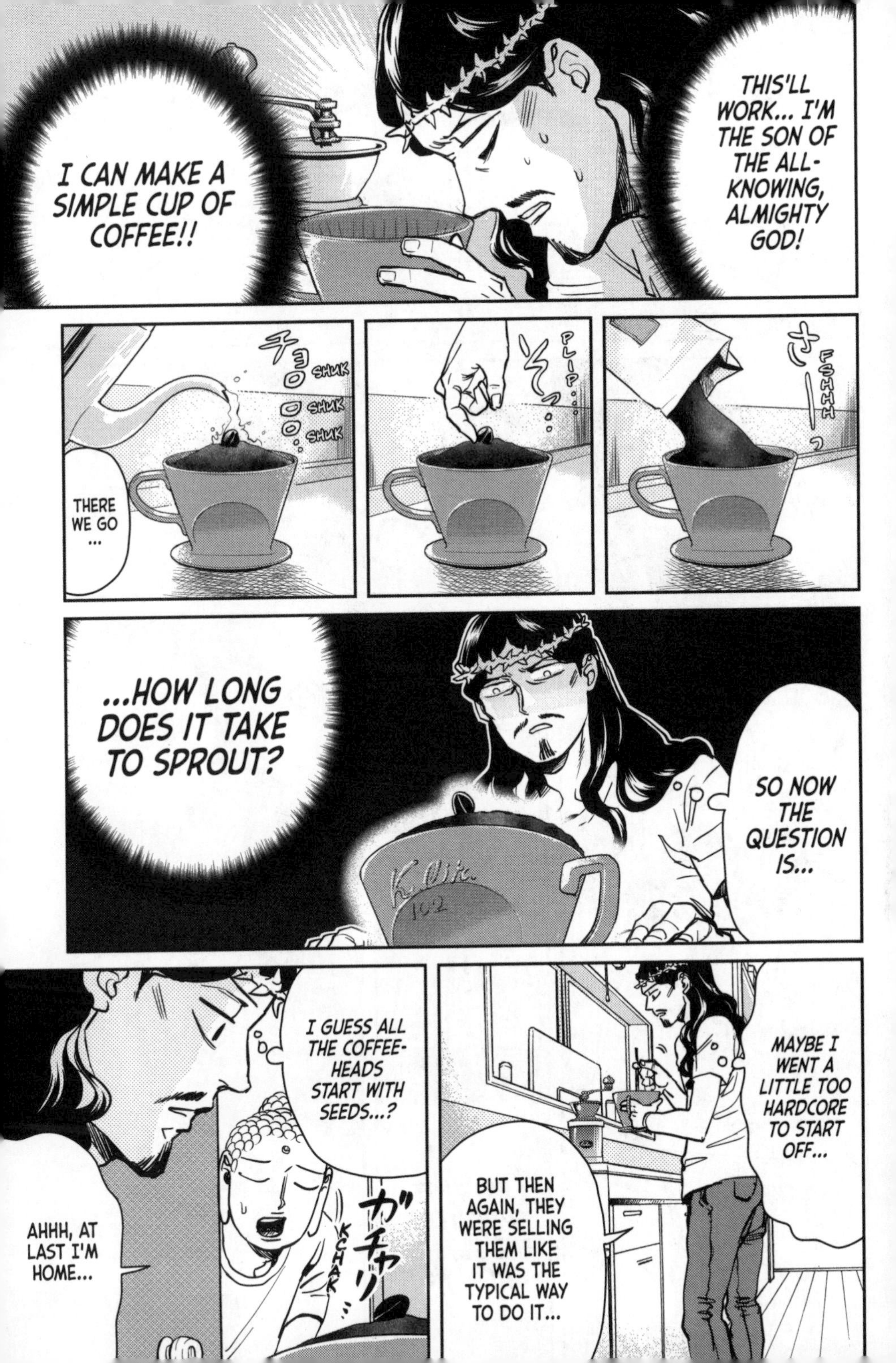
THIS'LL WORK... I'M THE SON OF THE ALL-KNOWING, ALMIGHTY GOD!
I CAN MAKE A SIMPLE CUP OF COFFEE!!
さーっ
FSHHH
そっ
PLIP...
チョロロロ
SHUK SHUK SHUK
THERE WE GO...
SO NOW THE QUESTION IS...
...HOW LONG DOES IT TAKE TO SPROUT?
MAYBE I WENT A LITTLE TOO HARDCORE TO START OFF...
BUT THEN AGAIN, THEY WERE SELLING THEM LIKE IT WAS THE TYPICAL WAY TO DO IT...
I GUESS ALL THE COFFEE-HEADS START WITH SEEDS...?
ガチャリ
KCHAK
AHHH, AT LAST I'M HOME...

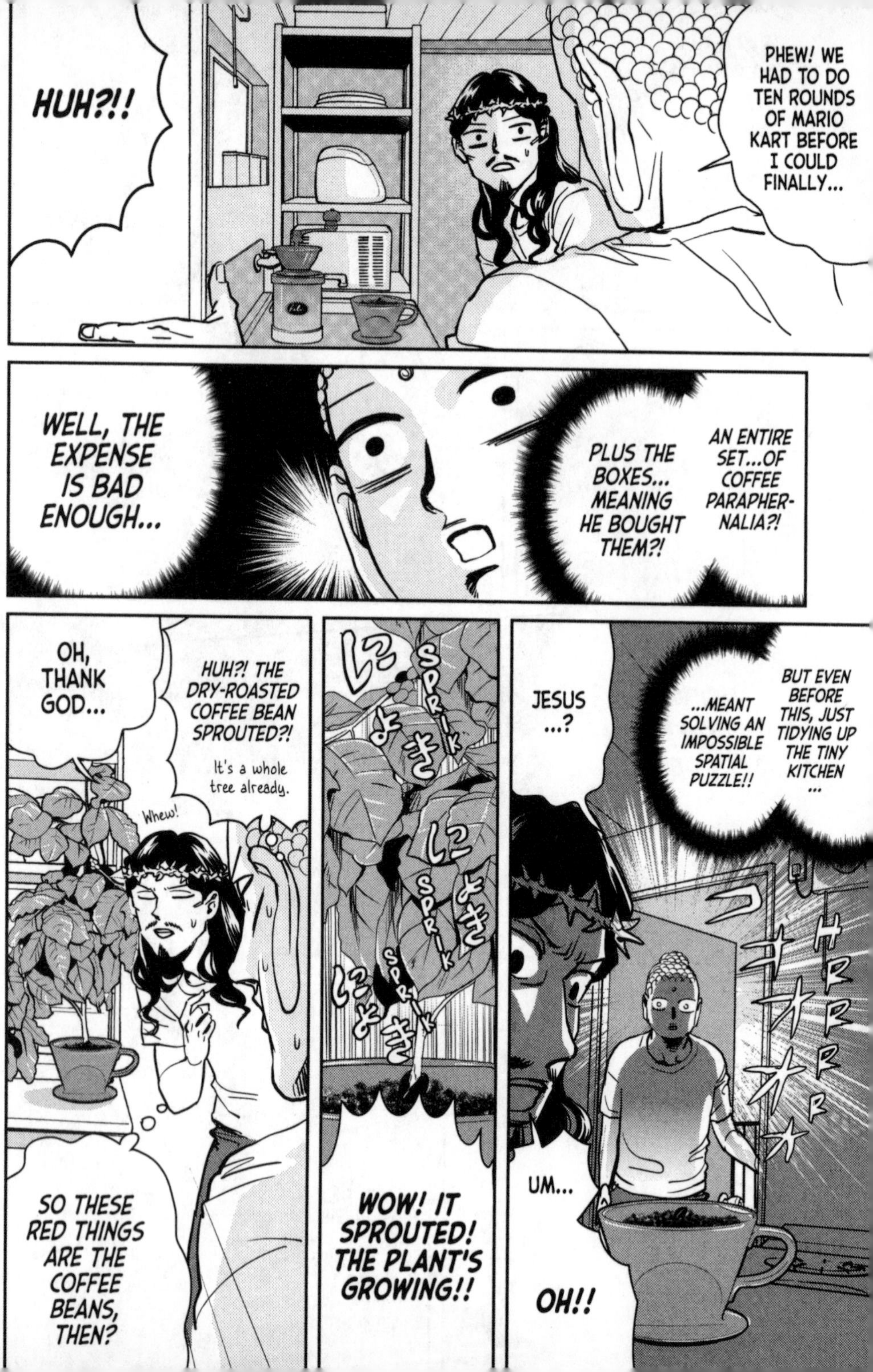
PHEW! WE HAD TO DO TEN ROUNDS OF MARIO KART BEFORE I COULD FINALLY...
HUH?!!
AN ENTIRE SET...OF COFFEE PARAPHER-NALIA?!
PLUS THE BOXES... MEANING HE BOUGHT THEM?!
WELL, THE EXPENSE IS BAD ENOUGH...
BUT EVEN BEFORE THIS, JUST TIDYING UP THE TINY KITCHEN ...
...MEANT SOLVING AN IMPOSSIBLE SPATIAL PUZZLE!!
JESUS ...?
HRRRRRR
UM...
OH!!
SPRIK
SPRIK
SPRIK
WOW! IT SPROUTED! THE PLANT'S GROWING!!
HUH?! THE DRY-ROASTED COFFEE BEAN SPROUTED?!
It's a whole tree already.
OH, THANK GOD...
Whew!
SO THESE RED THINGS ARE THE COFFEE BEANS, THEN?

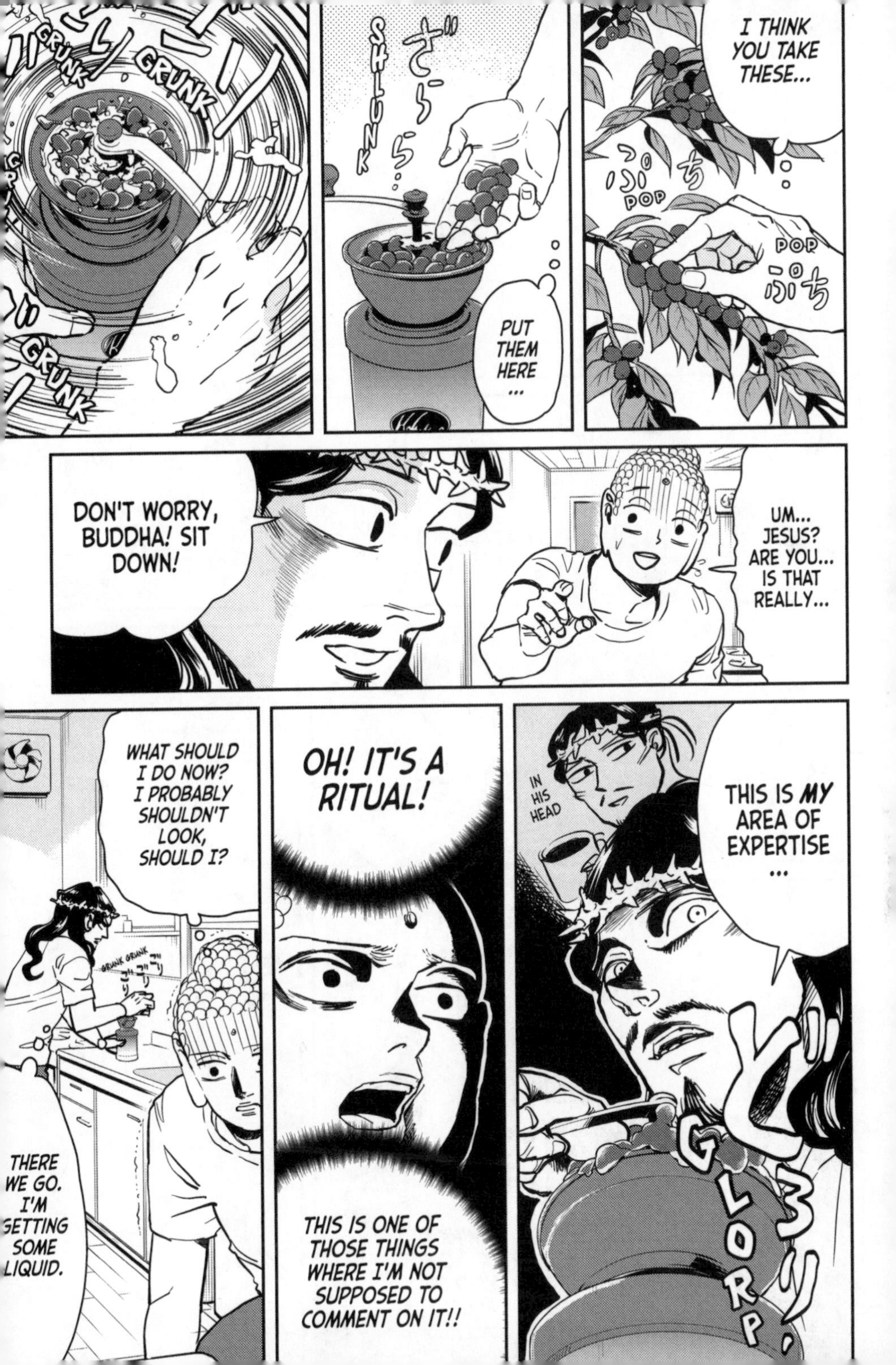

I THINK YOU TAKE THESE...
POP ぷち
POP ぷち
SHLUNK ざらら
PUT THEM HERE...
GRUNK
GRUNK
GRUNK
UM... JESUS? ARE YOU... IS THAT REALLY...
DON'T WORRY, BUDDHA! SIT DOWN!
IN HIS HEAD
THIS IS MY AREA OF EXPERTISE...
GLORP
OH! IT'S A RITUAL!
THIS IS ONE OF THOSE THINGS WHERE I'M NOT SUPPOSED TO COMMENT ON IT!!
WHAT SHOULD I DO NOW? I PROBABLY SHOULDN'T LOOK, SHOULD I?
GRUNK GRUNK
THERE WE GO. I'M GETTING SOME LIQUID.

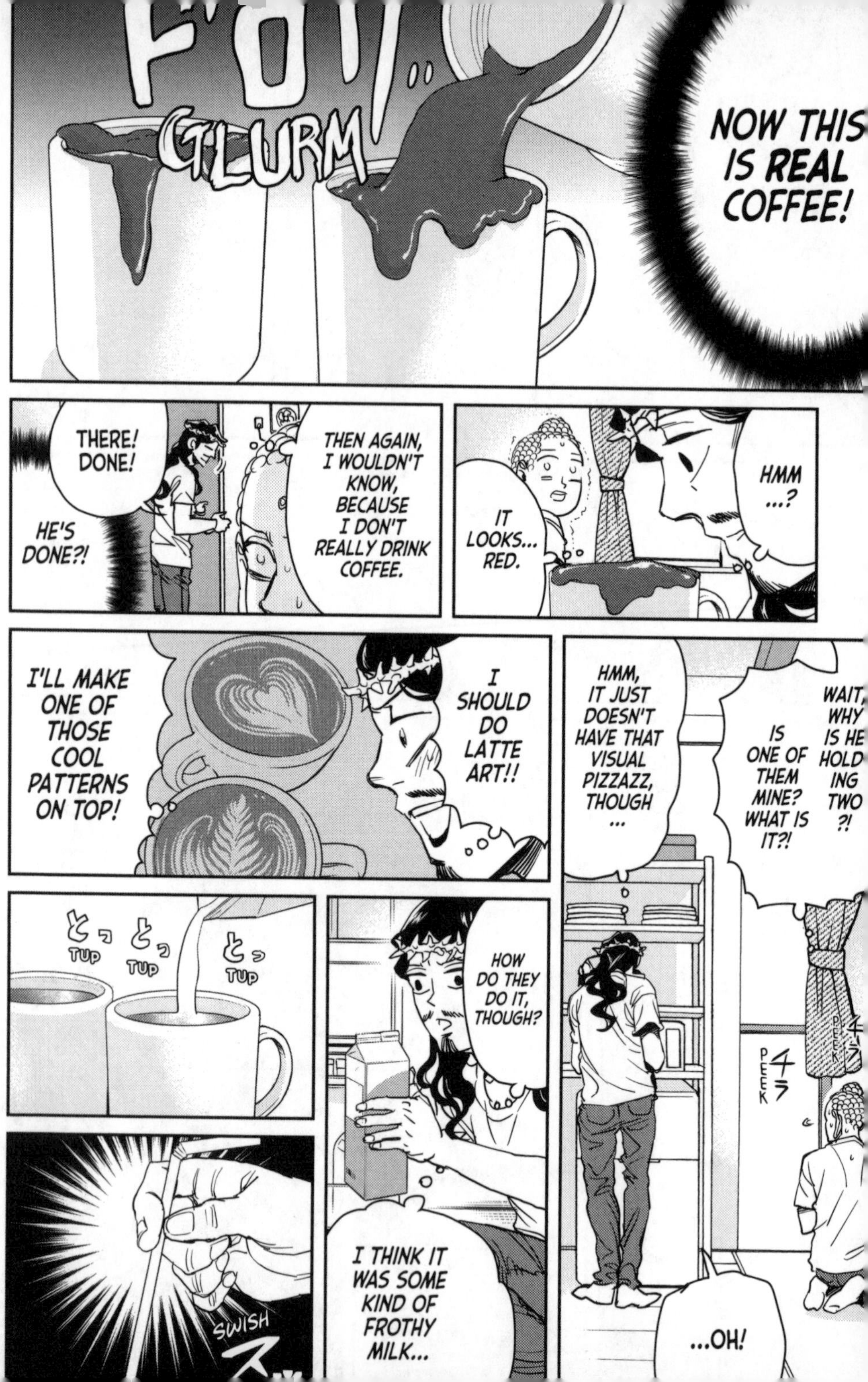
NOW THIS IS REAL COFFEE!
GLURM
HMM ...?
IT LOOKS... RED.
THEN AGAIN, I WOULDN'T KNOW, BECAUSE I DON'T REALLY DRINK COFFEE.
THERE! DONE!
HE'S DONE?!
WAIT, WHY IS HE HOLDING TWO ?!
IS ONE OF THEM MINE? WHAT IS IT?!
HMM, IT JUST DOESN'T HAVE THAT VISUAL PIZZAZZ, THOUGH ...
PEEK
PEEK
...OH!
I SHOULD DO LATTE ART!!
I'LL MAKE ONE OF THOSE COOL PATTERNS ON TOP!
HOW DO THEY DO IT, THOUGH?
I THINK IT WAS SOME KIND OF FROTHY MILK...
とっ TUP
とっ TUP
とっ TUP
SWISH

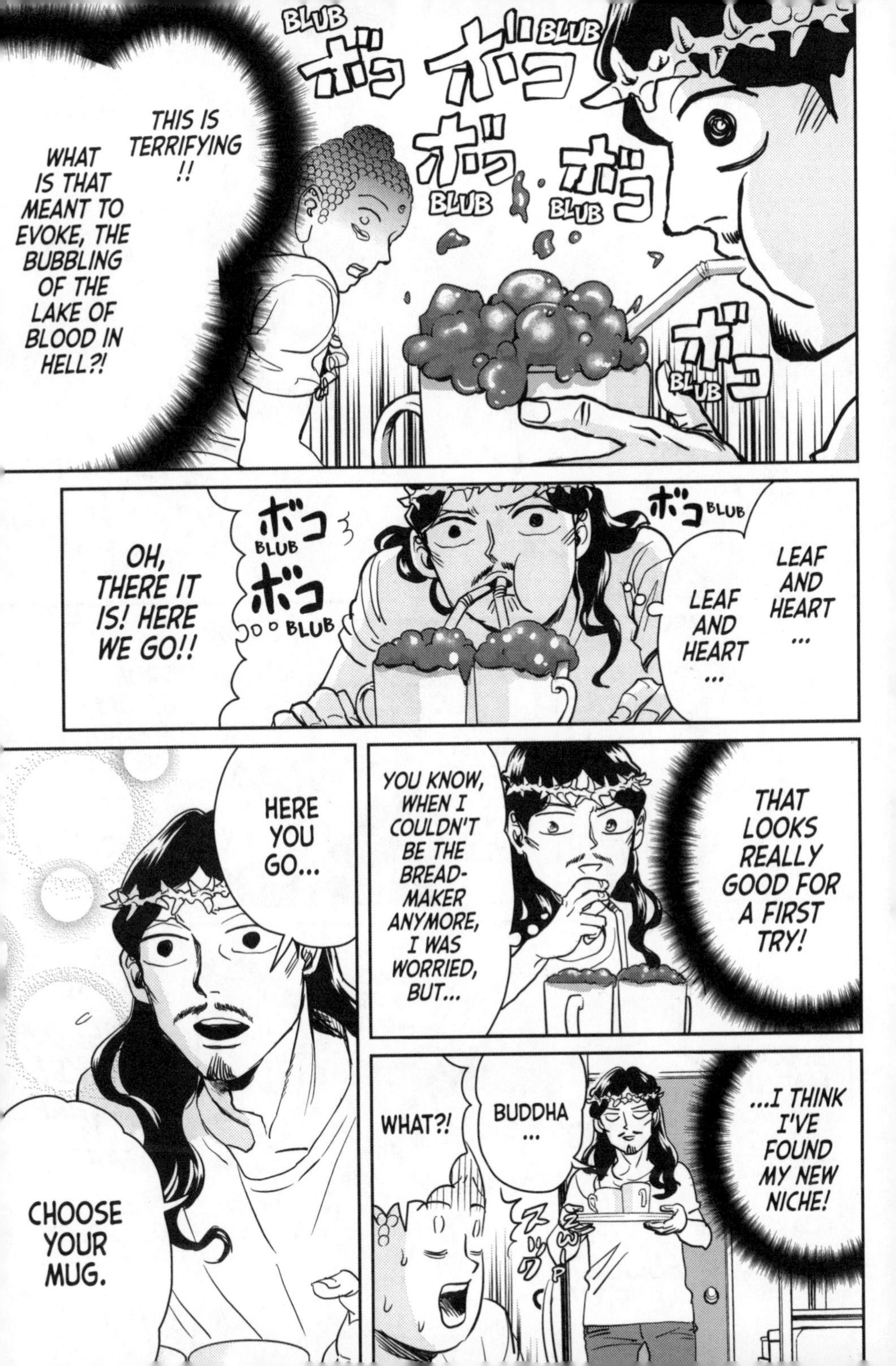
ボコ BLUB
ボッ BLUB
ボッ BLUB
ボッ BLUB
ボコ BLUB
THIS IS TERRIFYING!!
WHAT IS THAT MEANT TO EVOKE, THE BUBBLING OF THE LAKE OF BLOOD IN HELL?!
LEAF AND HEART...
LEAF AND HEART...
ボコ BLUB
ボコ BLUB
ボコ BLUB
OH, THERE IT IS! HERE WE GO!!
THAT LOOKS REALLY GOOD FOR A FIRST TRY!
YOU KNOW, WHEN I COULDN'T BE THE BREAD-MAKER ANYMORE, I WAS WORRIED, BUT...
...I THINK I'VE FOUND MY NEW NICHE!
BUDDHA...
WHAT?!
HERE YOU GO...
CHOOSE YOUR MUG.

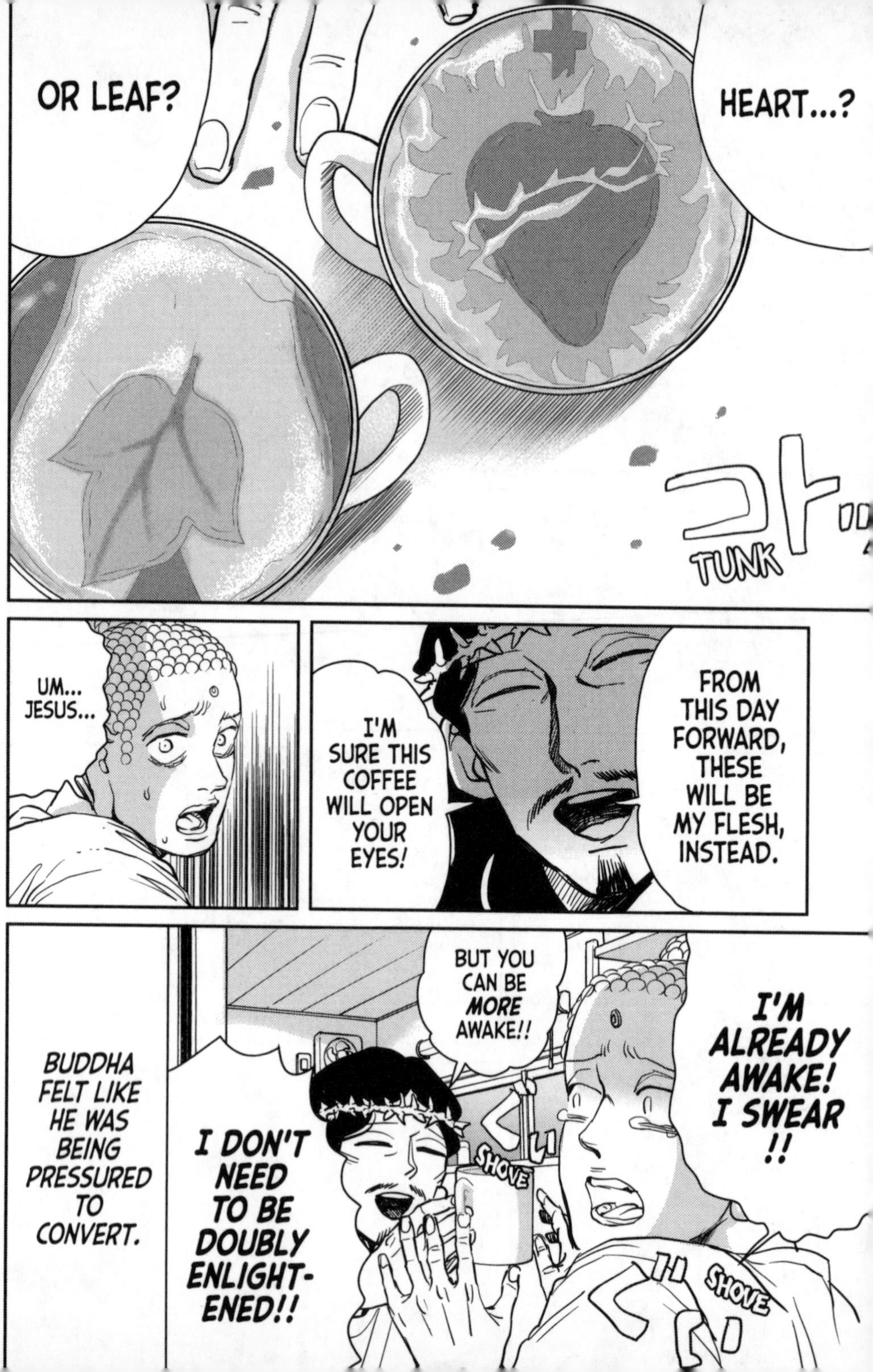
HEART...?
OR LEAF?
コトッ
TUNK
FROM THIS DAY FORWARD, THESE WILL BE MY FLESH, INSTEAD.
I'M SURE THIS COFFEE WILL OPEN YOUR EYES!
UM... JESUS...
I'M ALREADY AWAKE! I SWEAR!!
BUT YOU CAN BE *MORE* AWAKE!!
SHOVE
SHOVE
I DON'T NEED TO BE DOUBLY ENLIGHTENED!!
BUDDHA FELT LIKE HE WAS BEING PRESSURED TO CONVERT.

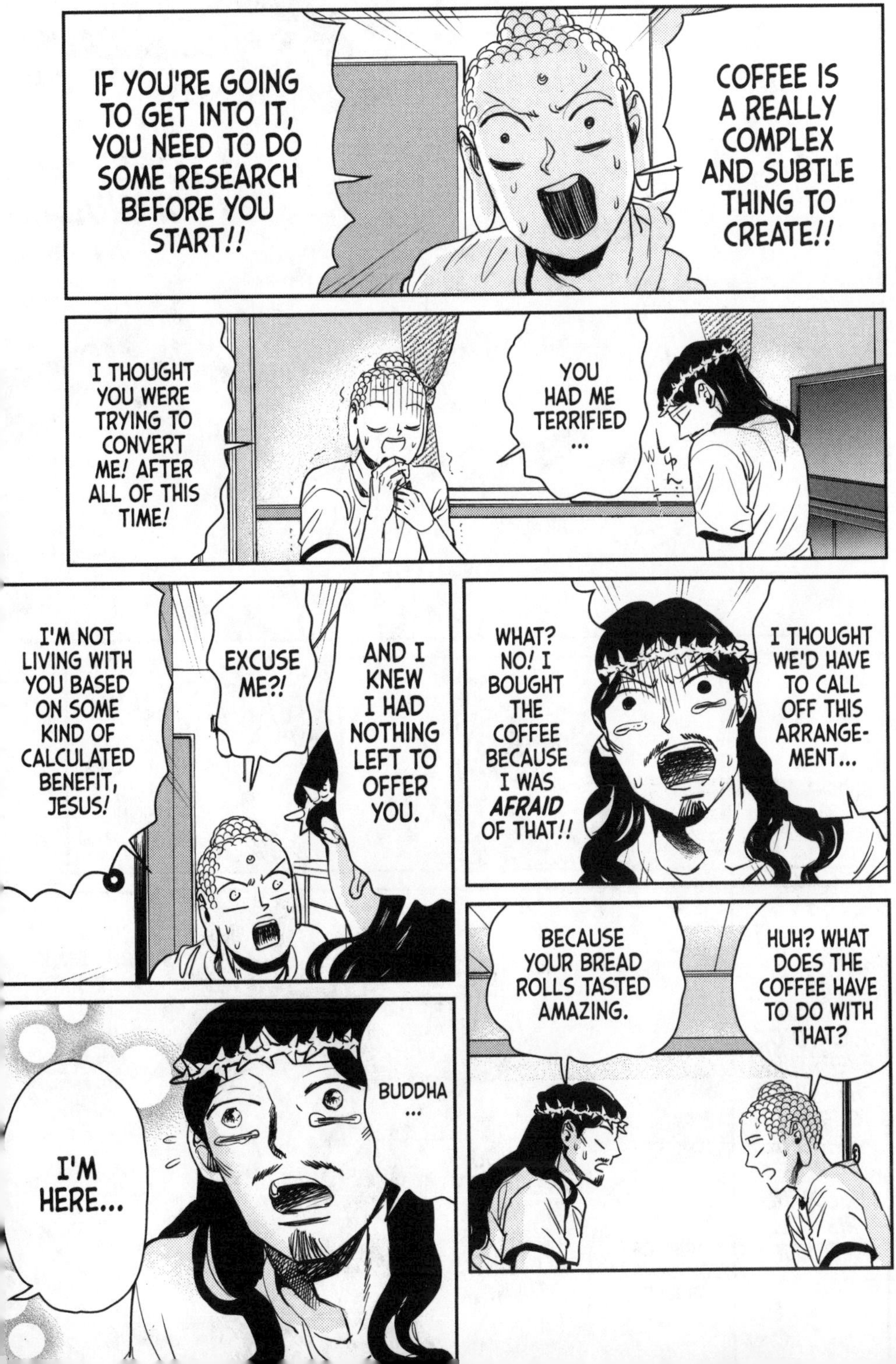
COFFEE IS A REALLY COMPLEX AND SUBTLE THING TO CREATE!!
IF YOU'RE GOING TO GET INTO IT, YOU NEED TO DO SOME RESEARCH BEFORE YOU START!!
YOU HAD ME TERRIFIED ...
しゅん
WILT
I THOUGHT YOU WERE TRYING TO CONVERT ME! AFTER ALL OF THIS TIME!
I THOUGHT WE'D HAVE TO CALL OFF THIS ARRANGE-MENT...
WHAT? NO! I BOUGHT THE COFFEE BECAUSE I WAS *AFRAID* OF THAT!!
AND I KNEW I HAD NOTHING LEFT TO OFFER YOU.
EXCUSE ME?!
I'M NOT LIVING WITH YOU BASED ON SOME KIND OF CALCULATED BENEFIT, JESUS!
HUH? WHAT DOES THE COFFEE HAVE TO DO WITH THAT?
BECAUSE YOUR BREAD ROLLS TASTED AMAZING.
BUDDHA ...
I'M HERE...

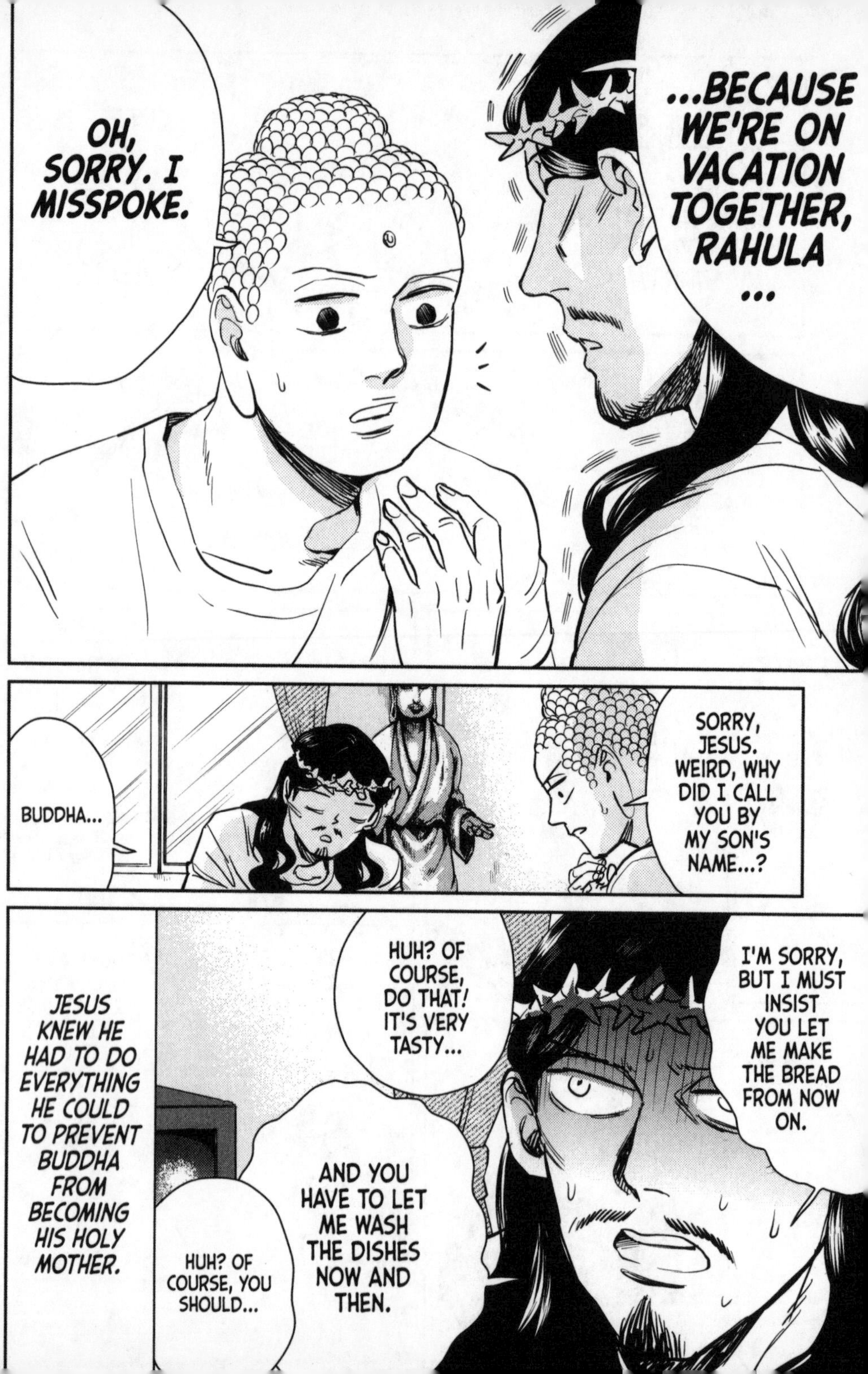
...BECAUSE WE'RE ON VACATION TOGETHER, RAHULA ...
OH, SORRY. I MISSPOKE.
SORRY, JESUS. WEIRD, WHY DID I CALL YOU BY MY SON'S NAME...?
BUDDHA...
I'M SORRY, BUT I MUST INSIST YOU LET ME MAKE THE BREAD FROM NOW ON.
HUH? OF COURSE, DO THAT! IT'S VERY TASTY...
AND YOU HAVE TO LET ME WASH THE DISHES NOW AND THEN.
HUH? OF COURSE, YOU SHOULD...
JESUS KNEW HE HAD TO DO EVERYTHING HE COULD TO PREVENT BUDDHA FROM BECOMING HIS HOLY MOTHER.

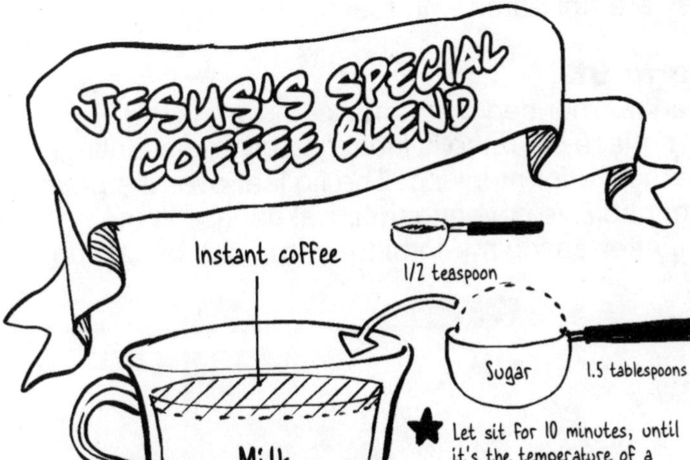
JESUS'S SPECIAL COFFEE BLEND
Instant coffee
1/2 teaspoon
Sugar
1.5 tablespoons
Milk
Let sit for 10 minutes, until it's the temperature of a lukewarm pool in summer!
Jesus's pinpoint advice
if you have a tin of Milo powder, that tastes even better!!

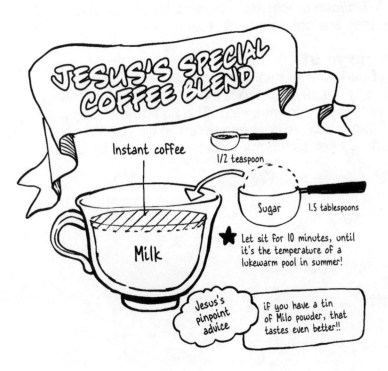

SAINT ☆ YOUNG MEN

CHAPTER 94 TRANSLATION NOTES

Natto, page 87
One of the most famous "acquired tastes" of Japan, *natto* is a mixture of fermented whole soybeans in a very sticky and stringy paste. It has an extremely pungent smell. *Natto* is quite popular as a kind of health food, and is often eaten for breakfast with rice or, as is popular lately, toast.

Daifuku, page 87
A kind of *mochi* (glutinous rice cake) filled with sweet red bean paste (*anko*). *Daifuku mochi* are a classic Japanese sweet, but unlike *natto*, they are not eaten with toast.

Latte art, page 96
The burning heart surrounded by thorns is known as the "Sacred Heart," a piece of Catholic iconography representing Christ's boundless love for mankind. The fig leaf over the groin represents Adam and Eve covering their nakedness in the Garden of Eden, after eating the forbidden fruit and becoming aware.

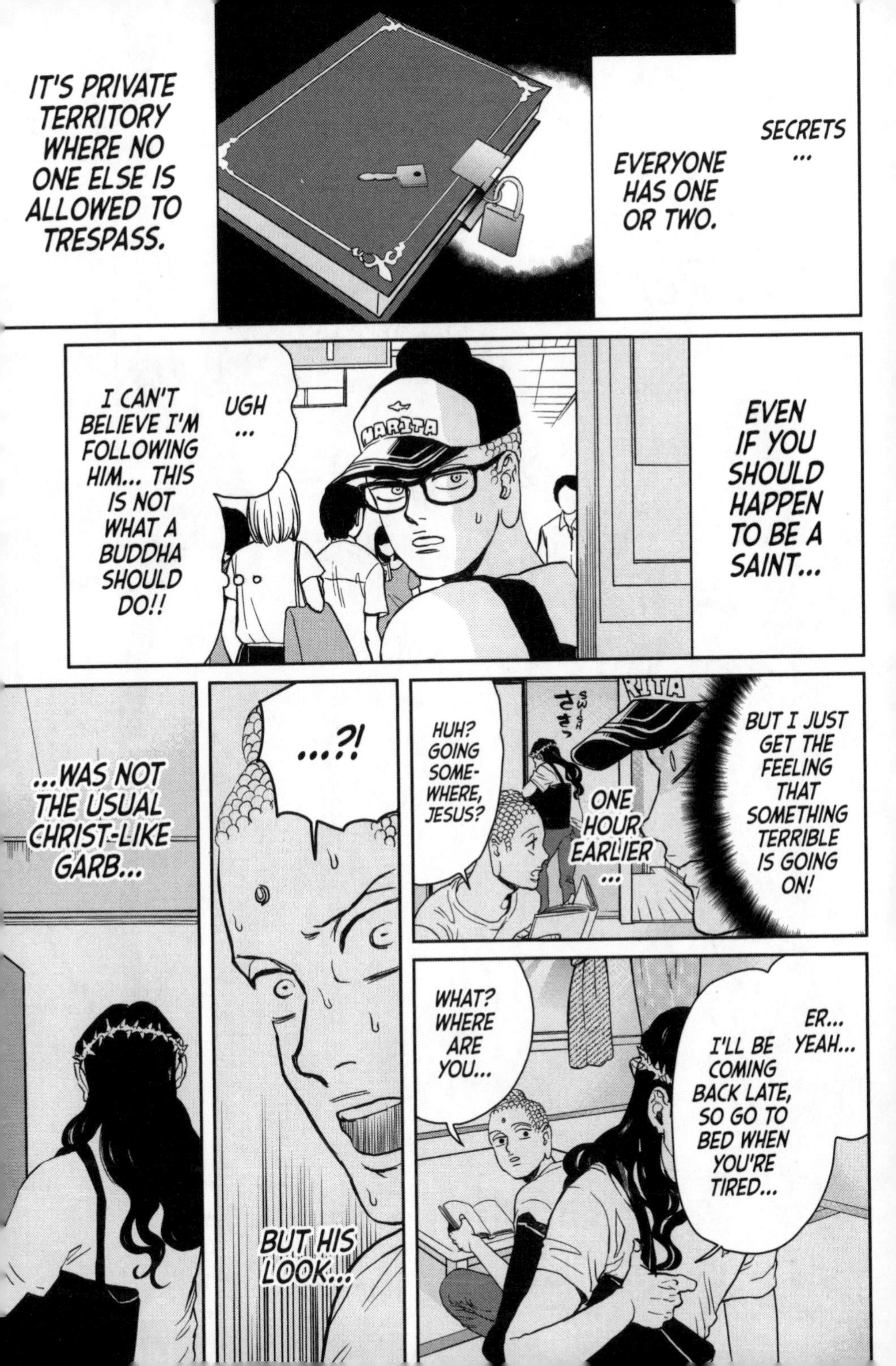
SECRETS ...
EVERYONE HAS ONE OR TWO.
IT'S PRIVATE TERRITORY WHERE NO ONE ELSE IS ALLOWED TO TRESPASS.
EVEN IF YOU SHOULD HAPPEN TO BE A SAINT...
UGH ...
NARITA
I CAN'T BELIEVE I'M FOLLOWING HIM... THIS IS NOT WHAT A BUDDHA SHOULD DO!!
BUT I JUST GET THE FEELING THAT SOMETHING TERRIBLE IS GOING ON!
さきっ SWISH
ONE HOUR EARLIER ...
HUH? GOING SOME-WHERE, JESUS?
ER... YEAH...
I'LL BE COMING BACK LATE, SO GO TO BED WHEN YOU'RE TIRED...
WHAT? WHERE ARE YOU...
...?!
BUT HIS LOOK...
...WAS NOT THE USUAL CHRIST-LIKE GARB...

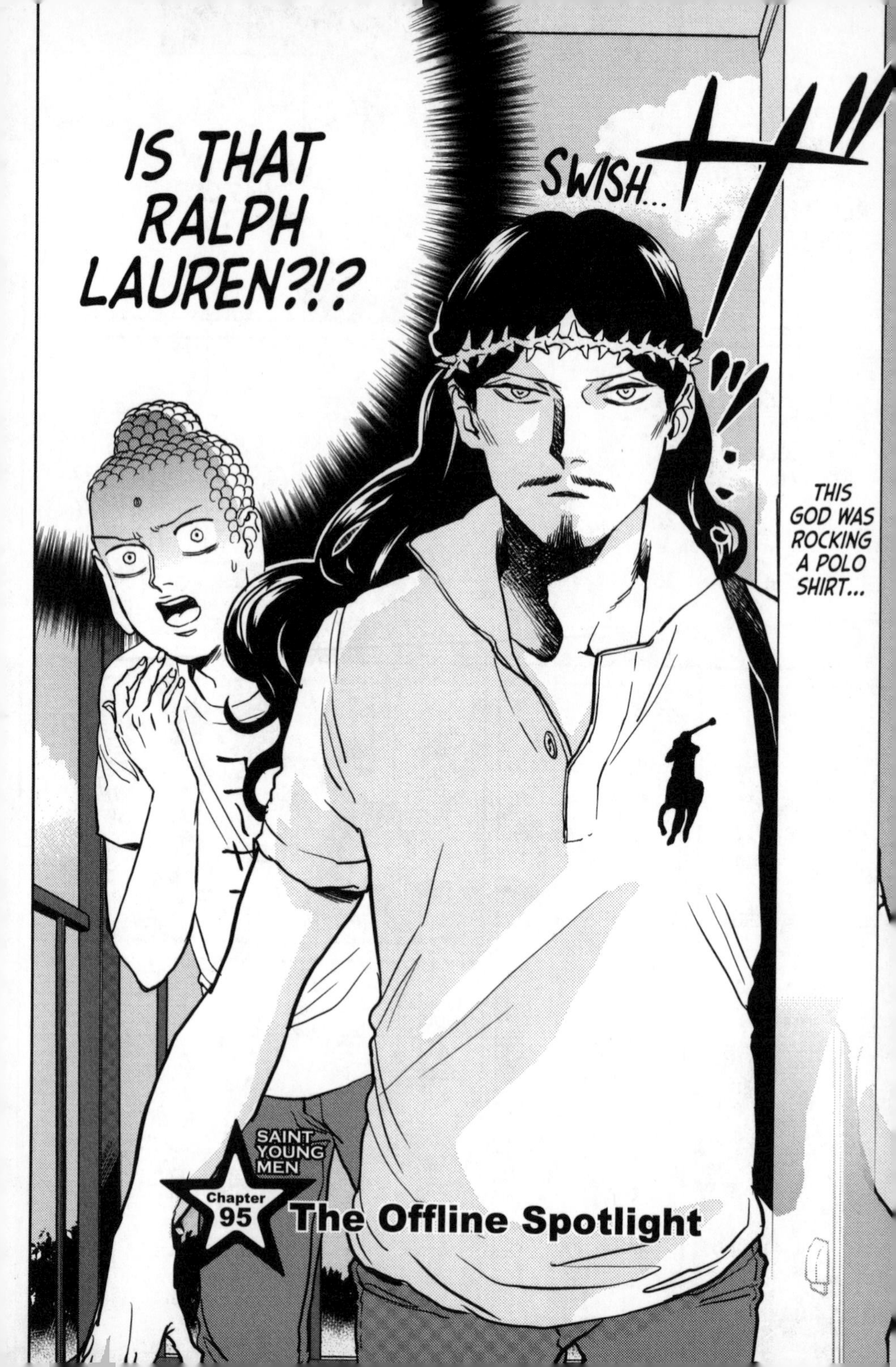
SWISH...
IS THAT RALPH LAUREN?!?
THIS GOD WAS ROCKING A POLO SHIRT...
SAINT YOUNG MEN
Chapter 95
The Offline Spotlight

JESUS USES A CHEAP PLASTIC UMBRELLA. NO BIG SWEAT IF YOU LOSE IT, AND EASY TO LEND TO OTHERS. SHARE THE AGAPE!

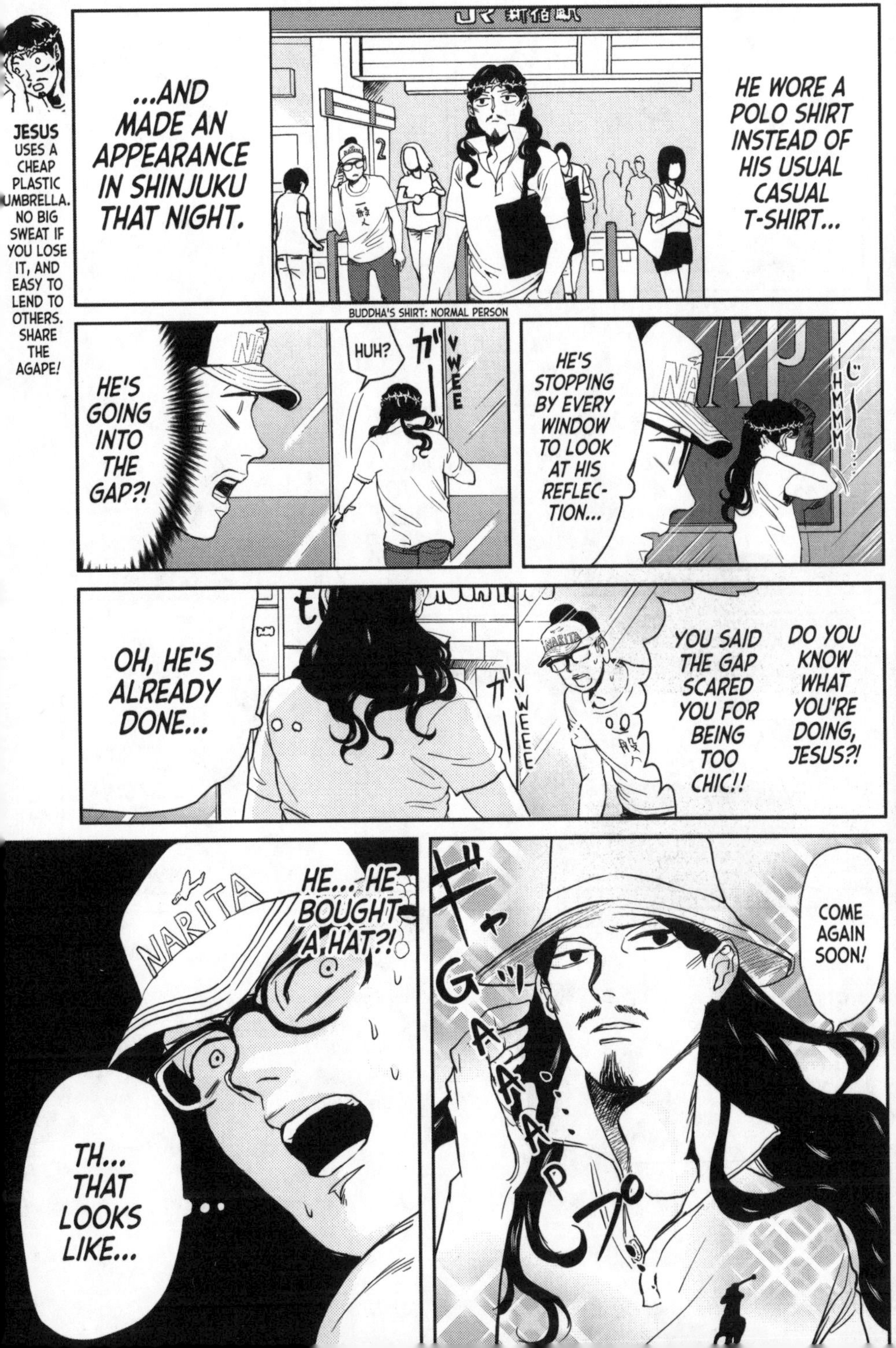
HE WORE A POLO SHIRT INSTEAD OF HIS USUAL CASUAL T-SHIRT...
...AND MADE AN APPEARANCE IN SHINJUKU THAT NIGHT.
BUDDHA'S SHIRT: NORMAL PERSON
HMMM
HE'S STOPPING BY EVERY WINDOW TO LOOK AT HIS REFLECTION...
VWEE
HUH?
HE'S GOING INTO THE GAP?!
DO YOU KNOW WHAT YOU'RE DOING, JESUS?!
YOU SAID THE GAP SCARED YOU FOR BEING TOO CHIC!!
VWEEE
OH, HE'S ALREADY DONE...
COME AGAIN SOON!
GAAAAP
HE... HE BOUGHT A HAT?!
TH... THAT LOOKS LIKE...

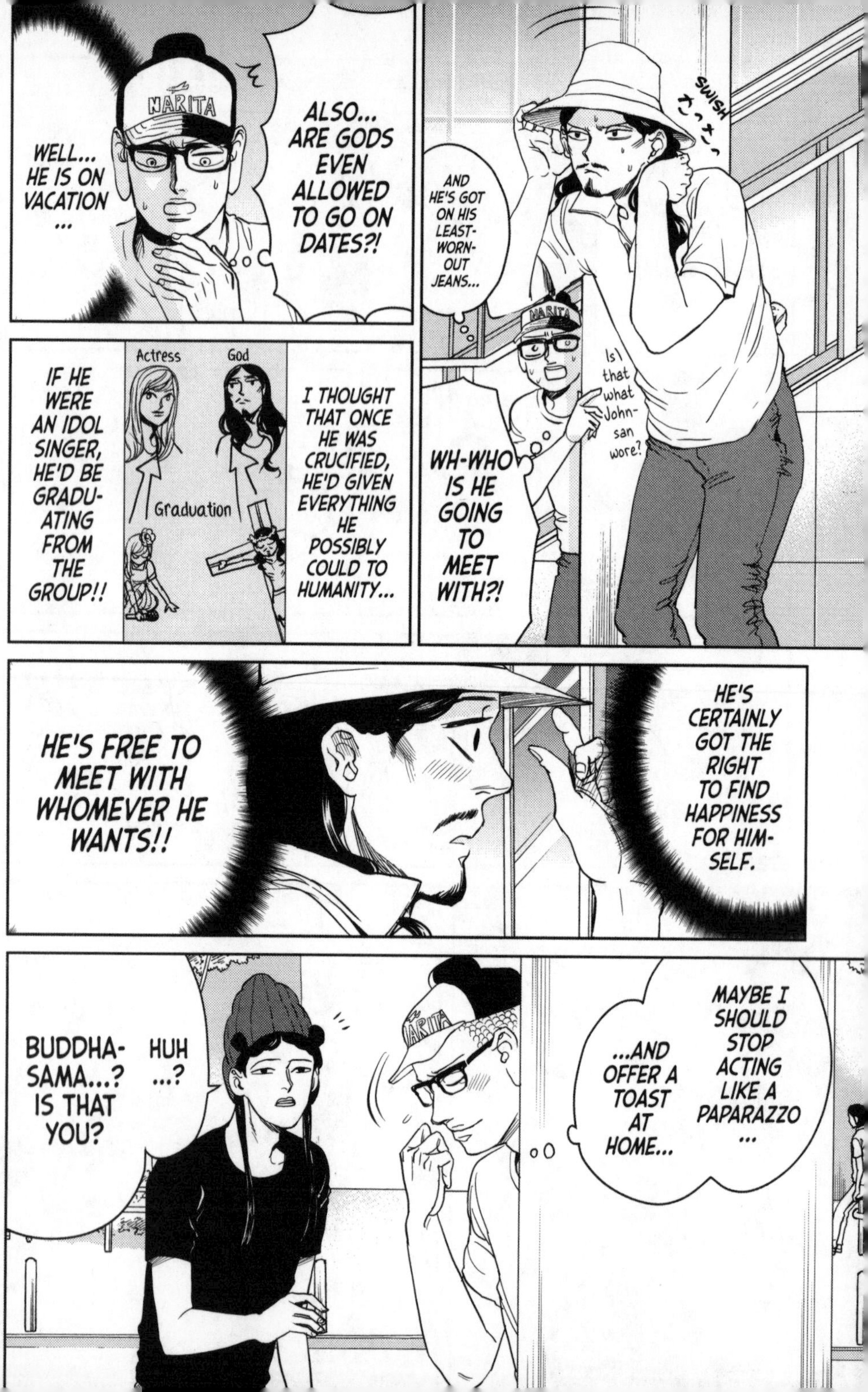
SWISH
さっさっ
AND HE'S GOT ON HIS LEAST-WORN-OUT JEANS...
Is that what John-san wore?
WH-WHO IS HE GOING TO MEET WITH?!
ALSO... ARE GODS EVEN ALLOWED TO GO ON DATES?!
WELL... HE IS ON VACATION...
I THOUGHT THAT ONCE HE WAS CRUCIFIED, HE'D GIVEN EVERYTHING HE POSSIBLY COULD TO HUMANITY...
God
Actress
Graduation
IF HE WERE AN IDOL SINGER, HE'D BE GRADUATING FROM THE GROUP!!
HE'S CERTAINLY GOT THE RIGHT TO FIND HAPPINESS FOR HIMSELF.
HE'S FREE TO MEET WITH WHOMEVER HE WANTS!!
MAYBE I SHOULD STOP ACTING LIKE A PAPARAZZO...
...AND OFFER A TOAST AT HOME...
HUH...?
BUDDHA-SAMA...? IS THAT YOU?

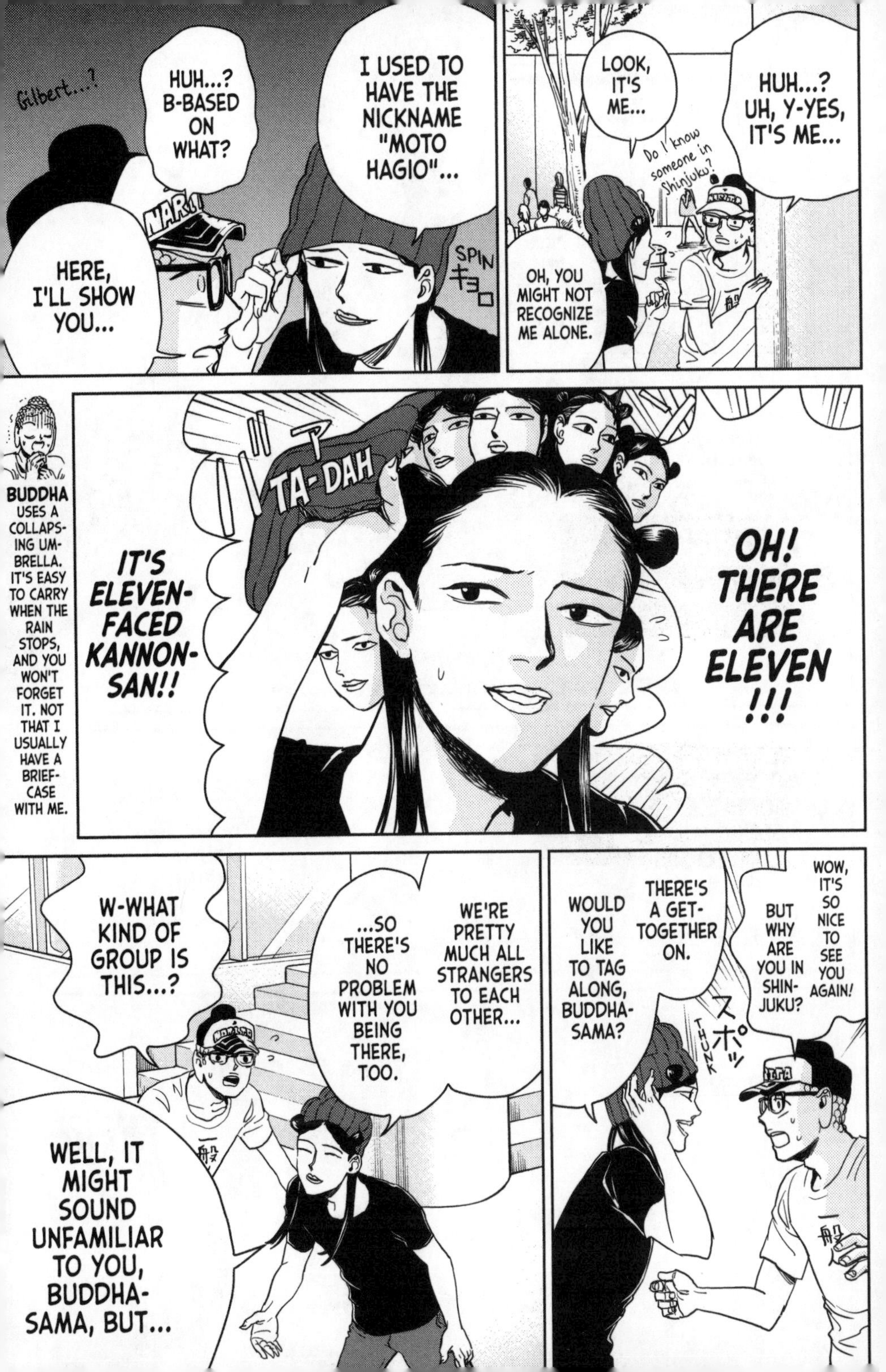
LOOK, IT'S ME...
HUH...? UH, Y-YES, IT'S ME...
Do I know someone in Shinjuku?
OH, YOU MIGHT NOT RECOGNIZE ME ALONE.
I USED TO HAVE THE NICKNAME "MOTO HAGIO"...
HUH...? B-BASED ON WHAT?
Gilbert...?
SPIN
キョロ
HERE, I'LL SHOW YOU...
TA-DAH
OH! THERE ARE ELEVEN!!!
IT'S ELEVEN-FACED KANNON-SAN!!
BUDDHA USES A COLLAPSING UMBRELLA. IT'S EASY TO CARRY WHEN THE RAIN STOPS, AND YOU WON'T FORGET IT. NOT THAT I USUALLY HAVE A BRIEFCASE WITH ME.
WOW, IT'S SO NICE TO SEE YOU AGAIN!
BUT WHY ARE YOU IN SHINJUKU?
THUNK
スポッ
THERE'S A GET-TOGETHER ON.
WOULD YOU LIKE TO TAG ALONG, BUDDHA-SAMA?
W-WHAT KIND OF GROUP IS THIS...?
WELL, IT MIGHT SOUND UNFAMILIAR TO YOU, BUDDHA-SAMA, BUT...
WE'RE PRETTY MUCH ALL STRANGERS TO EACH OTHER...
...SO THERE'S NO PROBLEM WITH YOU BEING THERE, TOO.

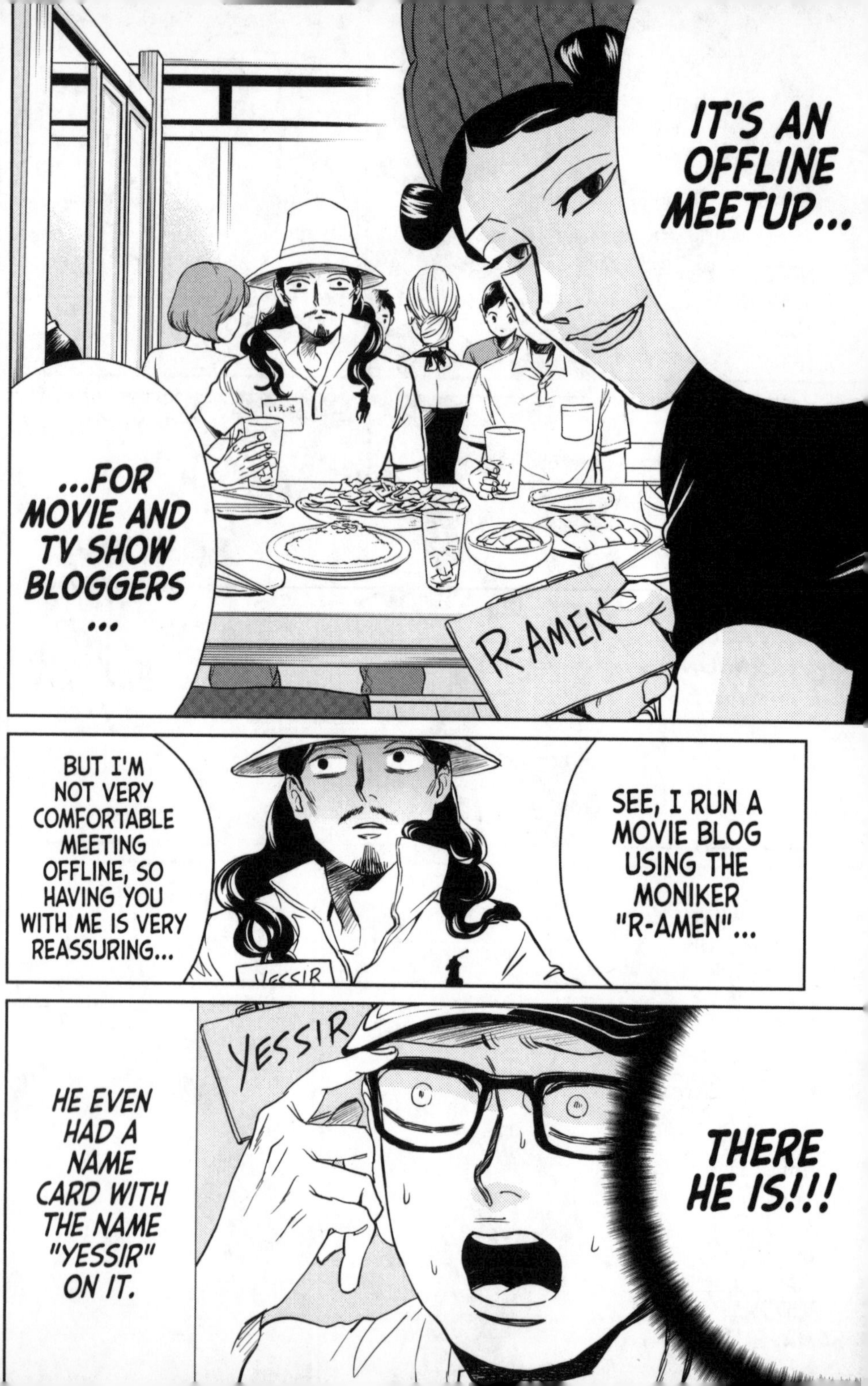
IT'S AN OFFLINE MEETUP...
...FOR MOVIE AND TV SHOW BLOGGERS ...
R-AMEN
SEE, I RUN A MOVIE BLOG USING THE MONIKER "R-AMEN"...
BUT I'M NOT VERY COMFORTABLE MEETING OFFLINE, SO HAVING YOU WITH ME IS VERY REASSURING...
THERE HE IS!!!
YESSIR
HE EVEN HAD A NAME CARD WITH THE NAME "YESSIR" ON IT.

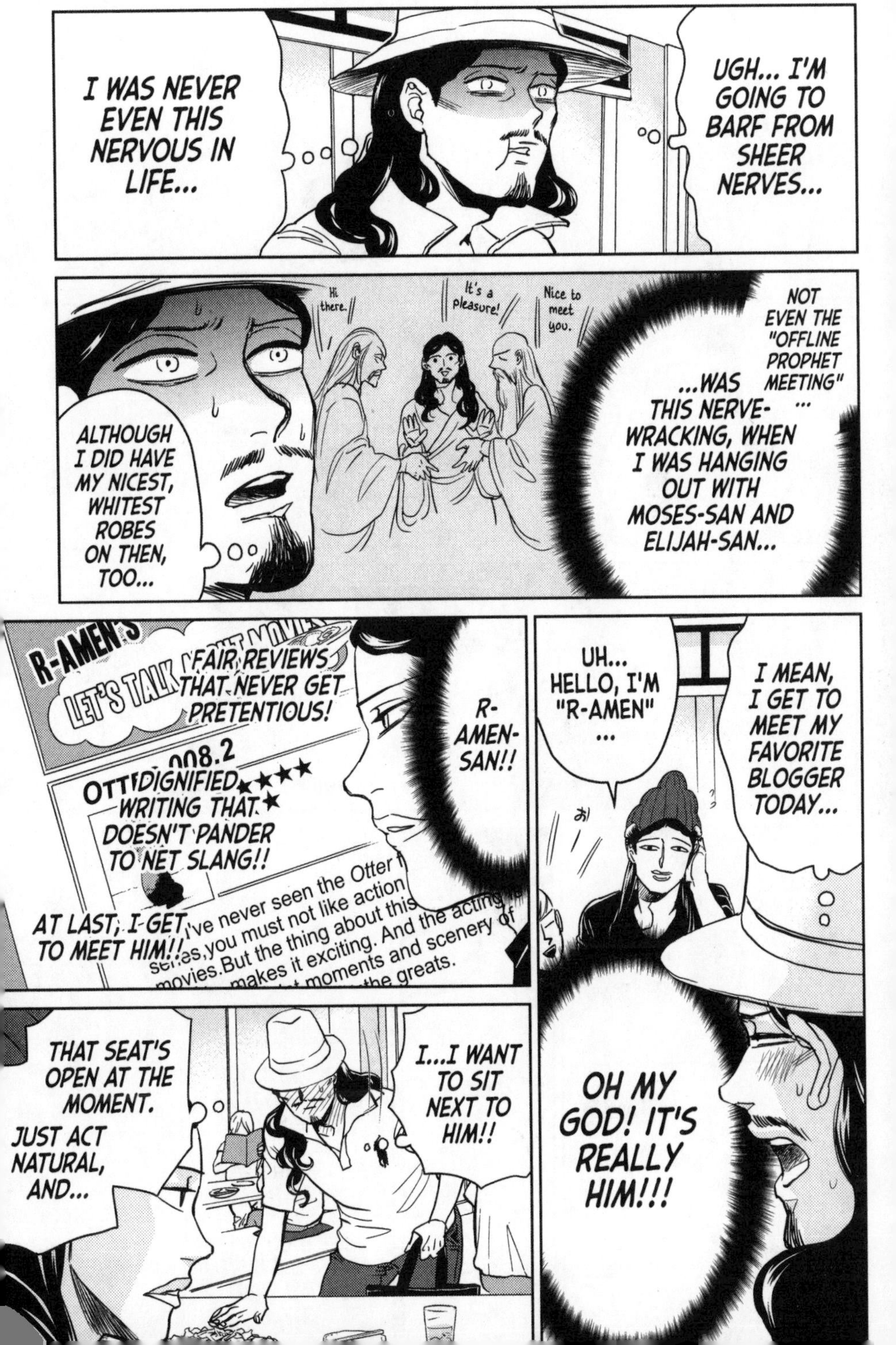
UGH... I'M GOING TO BARF FROM SHEER NERVES...
I WAS NEVER EVEN THIS NERVOUS IN LIFE...
NOT EVEN THE "OFFLINE PROPHET MEETING" ...
...WAS THIS NERVE-WRACKING, WHEN I WAS HANGING OUT WITH MOSES-SAN AND ELIJAH-SAN...
Nice to meet you.
It's a pleasure!
Hi there.
ALTHOUGH I DID HAVE MY NICEST, WHITEST ROBES ON THEN, TOO...
I MEAN, I GET TO MEET MY FAVORITE BLOGGER TODAY...
UH... HELLO, I'M "R-AMEN" ...
OH MY GOD! IT'S REALLY HIM!!!
R-AMEN-SAN!!
R-AMEN'S
LET'S TALK
FAIR REVIEWS THAT NEVER GET PRETENTIOUS!
DIGNIFIED WRITING THAT DOESN'T PANDER TO NET SLANG!!
AT LAST, I GET TO MEET HIM!!
I...I WANT TO SIT NEXT TO HIM!!
THAT SEAT'S OPEN AT THE MOMENT.
JUST ACT NATURAL, AND...

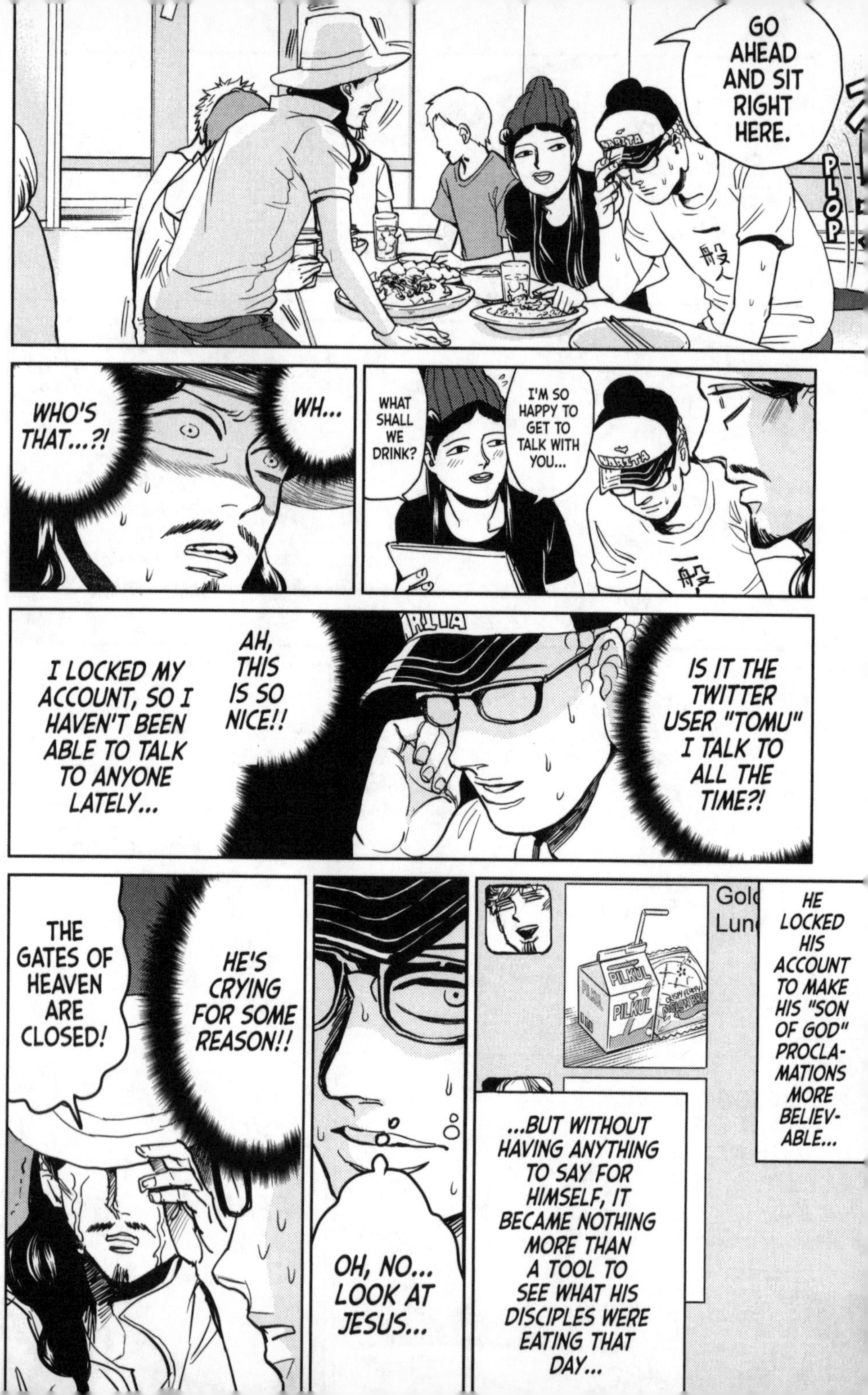
GO AHEAD AND SIT RIGHT HERE.
PLOP
I'M SO HAPPY TO GET TO TALK WITH YOU...
WHAT SHALL WE DRINK?
WH...
WHO'S THAT...?!
IS IT THE TWITTER USER "TOMU" I TALK TO ALL THE TIME?!
AH, THIS IS SO NICE!!
I LOCKED MY ACCOUNT, SO I HAVEN'T BEEN ABLE TO TALK TO ANYONE LATELY...
HE LOCKED HIS ACCOUNT TO MAKE HIS "SON OF GOD" PROCLA-MATIONS MORE BELIEV-ABLE...
PILKUL
...BUT WITHOUT HAVING ANYTHING TO SAY FOR HIMSELF, IT BECAME NOTHING MORE THAN A TOOL TO SEE WHAT HIS DISCIPLES WERE EATING THAT DAY...
HE'S CRYING FOR SOME REASON!!
OH, NO... LOOK AT JESUS...
THE GATES OF HEAVEN ARE CLOSED!

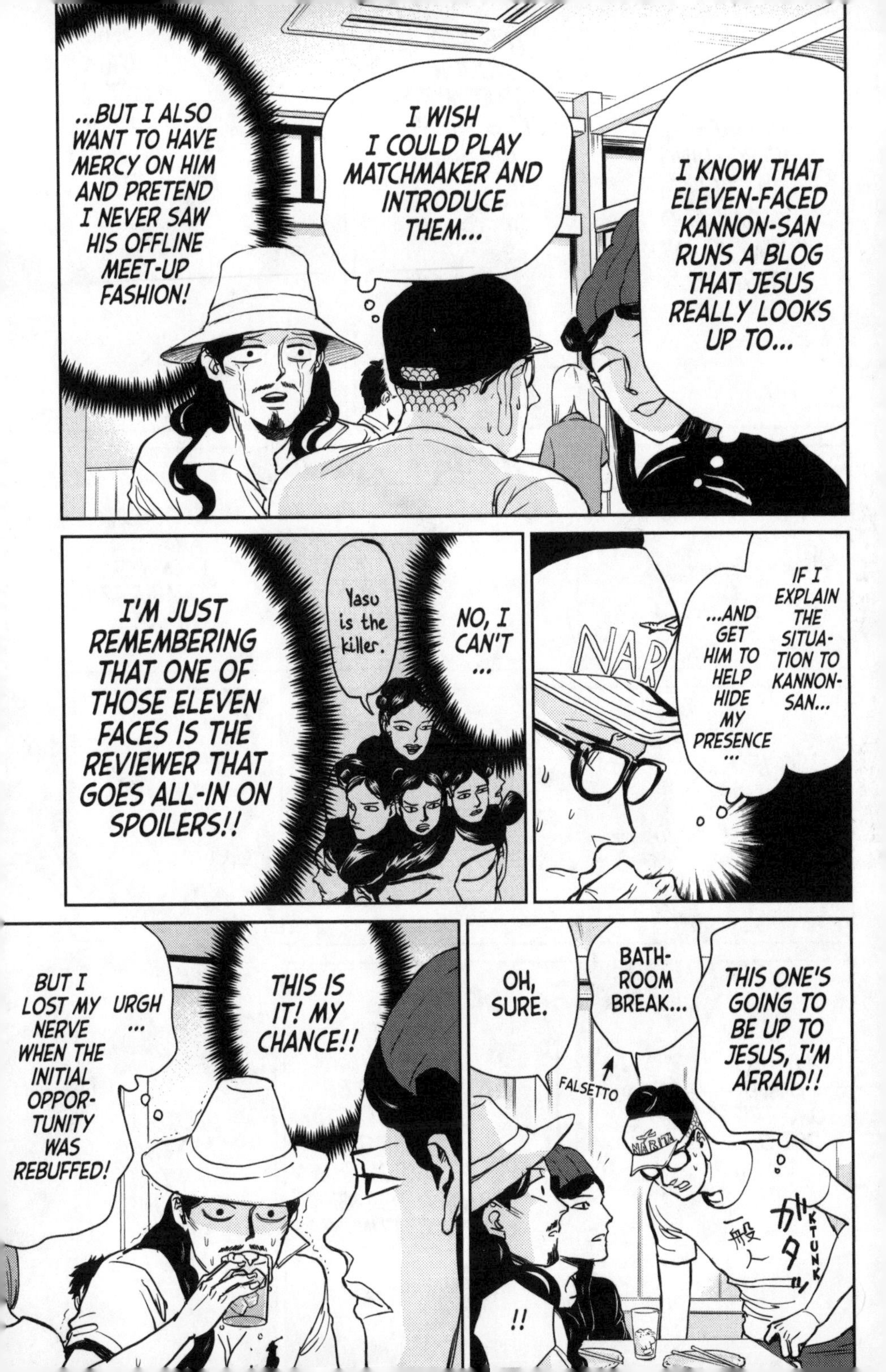
I KNOW THAT ELEVEN-FACED KANNON-SAN RUNS A BLOG THAT JESUS REALLY LOOKS UP TO...
I WISH I COULD PLAY MATCHMAKER AND INTRODUCE THEM...
...BUT I ALSO WANT TO HAVE MERCY ON HIM AND PRETEND I NEVER SAW HIS OFFLINE MEET-UP FASHION!
IF I EXPLAIN THE SITUATION TO KANNON-SAN...
...AND GET HIM TO HELP HIDE MY PRESENCE...
NAR
NO, I CAN'T...
Yasu is the killer.
I'M JUST REMEMBERING THAT ONE OF THOSE ELEVEN FACES IS THE REVIEWER THAT GOES ALL-IN ON SPOILERS!!
THIS ONE'S GOING TO BE UP TO JESUS, I'M AFRAID!!
BATH-ROOM BREAK...
FALSETTO
OH, SURE.
NARITA
一般
ガタッ KTUNK
!!
THIS IS IT! MY CHANCE!!
URGH...
BUT I LOST MY NERVE WHEN THE INITIAL OPPORTUNITY WAS REBUFFED!

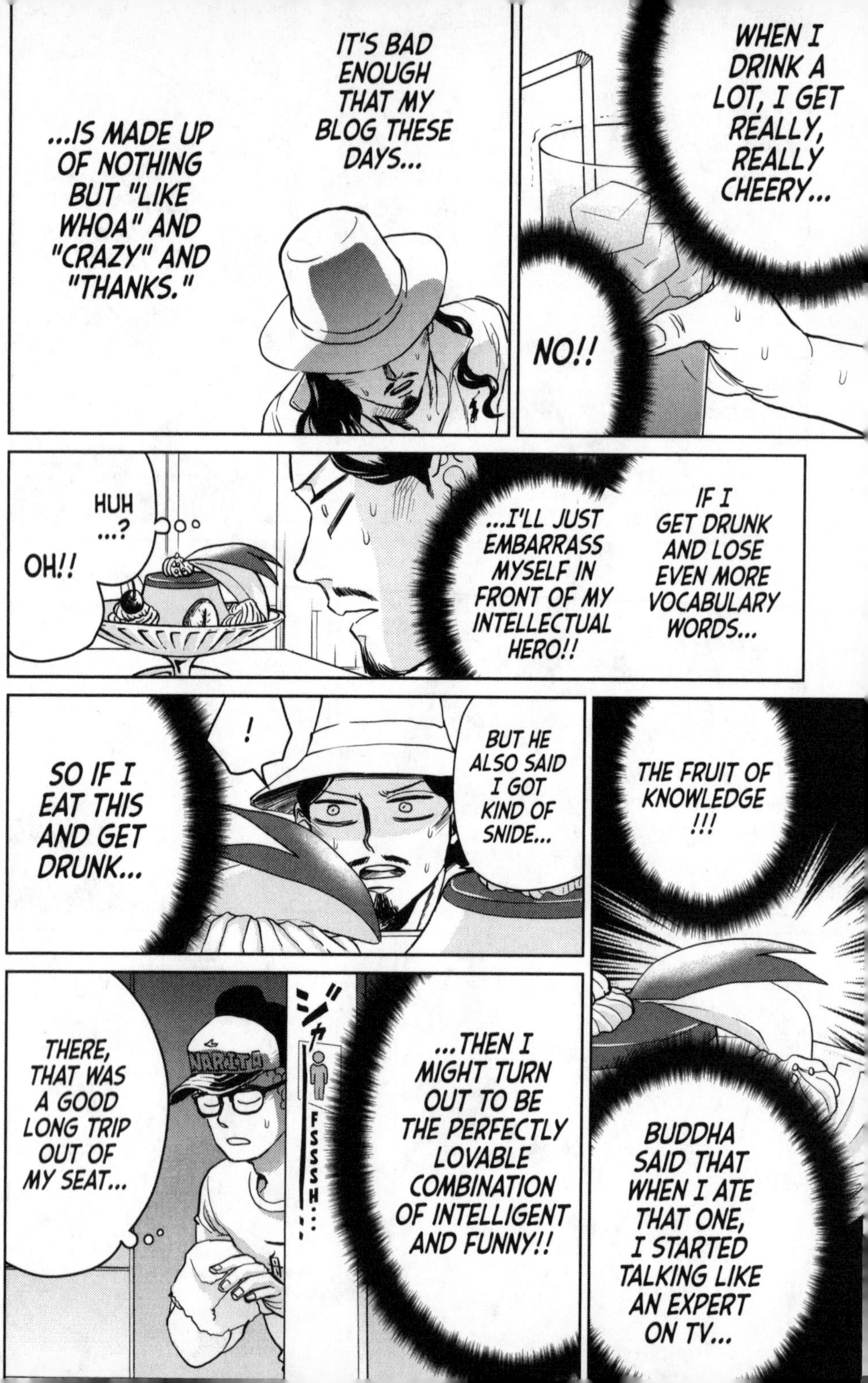
WHEN I DRINK A LOT, I GET REALLY, REALLY CHEERY...
NO!!
IT'S BAD ENOUGH THAT MY BLOG THESE DAYS...
...IS MADE UP OF NOTHING BUT "LIKE WHOA" AND "CRAZY" AND "THANKS."
IF I GET DRUNK AND LOSE EVEN MORE VOCABULARY WORDS...
...I'LL JUST EMBARRASS MYSELF IN FRONT OF MY INTELLECTUAL HERO!!
HUH ...?
OH!!
THE FRUIT OF KNOWLEDGE !!!
BUDDHA SAID THAT WHEN I ATE THAT ONE, I STARTED TALKING LIKE AN EXPERT ON TV...
!
BUT HE ALSO SAID I GOT KIND OF SNIDE...
SO IF I EAT THIS AND GET DRUNK...
...THEN I MIGHT TURN OUT TO BE THE PERFECTLY LOVABLE COMBINATION OF INTELLIGENT AND FUNNY!!
FSSSSH...
THERE, THAT WAS A GOOD LONG TRIP OUT OF MY SEAT...

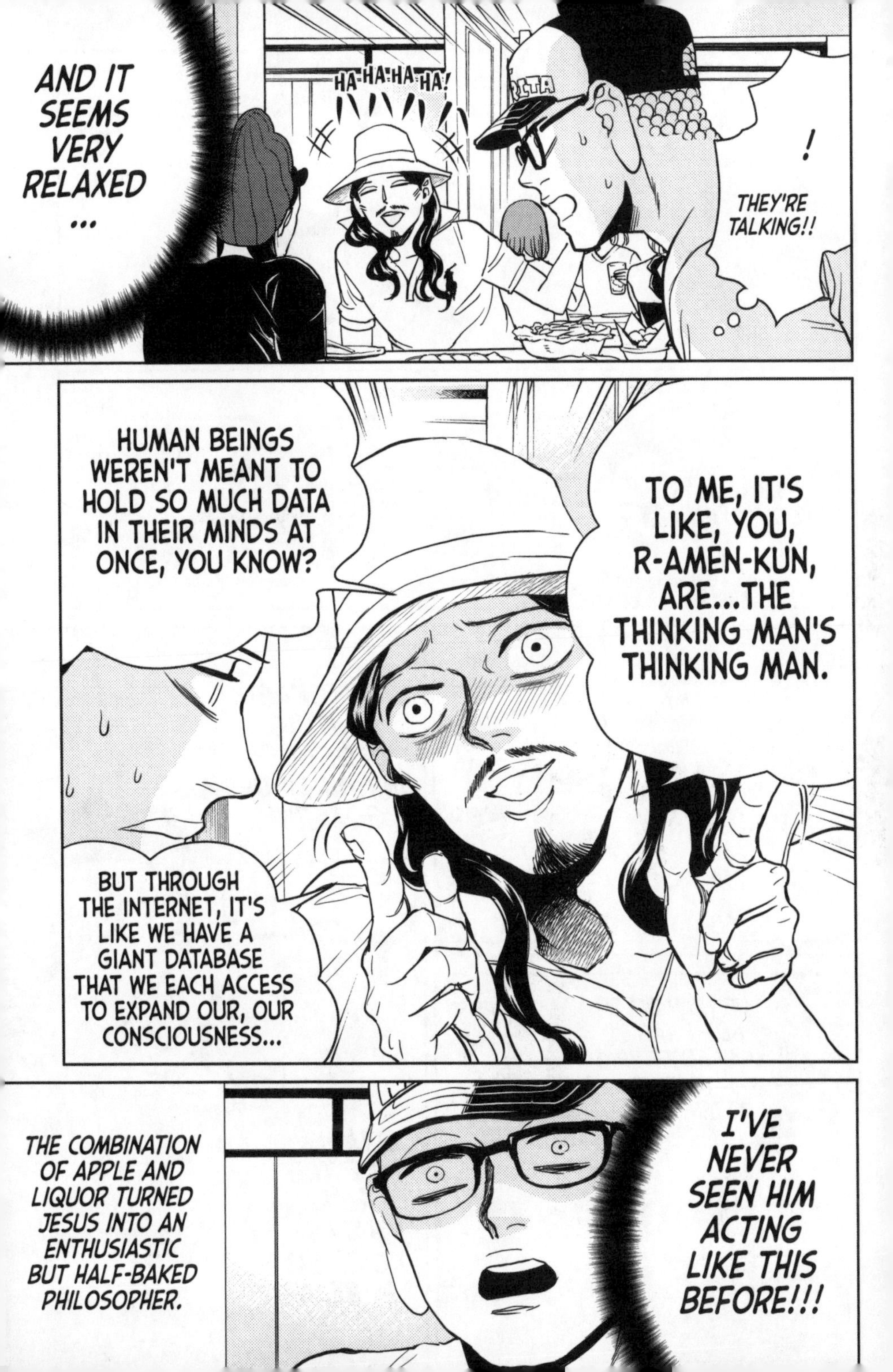
!
THEY'RE TALKING!!
HA-HA-HA-HA!
AND IT SEEMS VERY RELAXED ...
TO ME, IT'S LIKE, YOU, R-AMEN-KUN, ARE...THE THINKING MAN'S THINKING MAN.
HUMAN BEINGS WEREN'T MEANT TO HOLD SO MUCH DATA IN THEIR MINDS AT ONCE, YOU KNOW?
BUT THROUGH THE INTERNET, IT'S LIKE WE HAVE A GIANT DATABASE THAT WE EACH ACCESS TO EXPAND OUR, OUR CONSCIOUSNESS...
I'VE NEVER SEEN HIM ACTING LIKE THIS BEFORE!!!
THE COMBINATION OF APPLE AND LIQUOR TURNED JESUS INTO AN ENTHUSIASTIC BUT HALF-BAKED PHILOSOPHER.

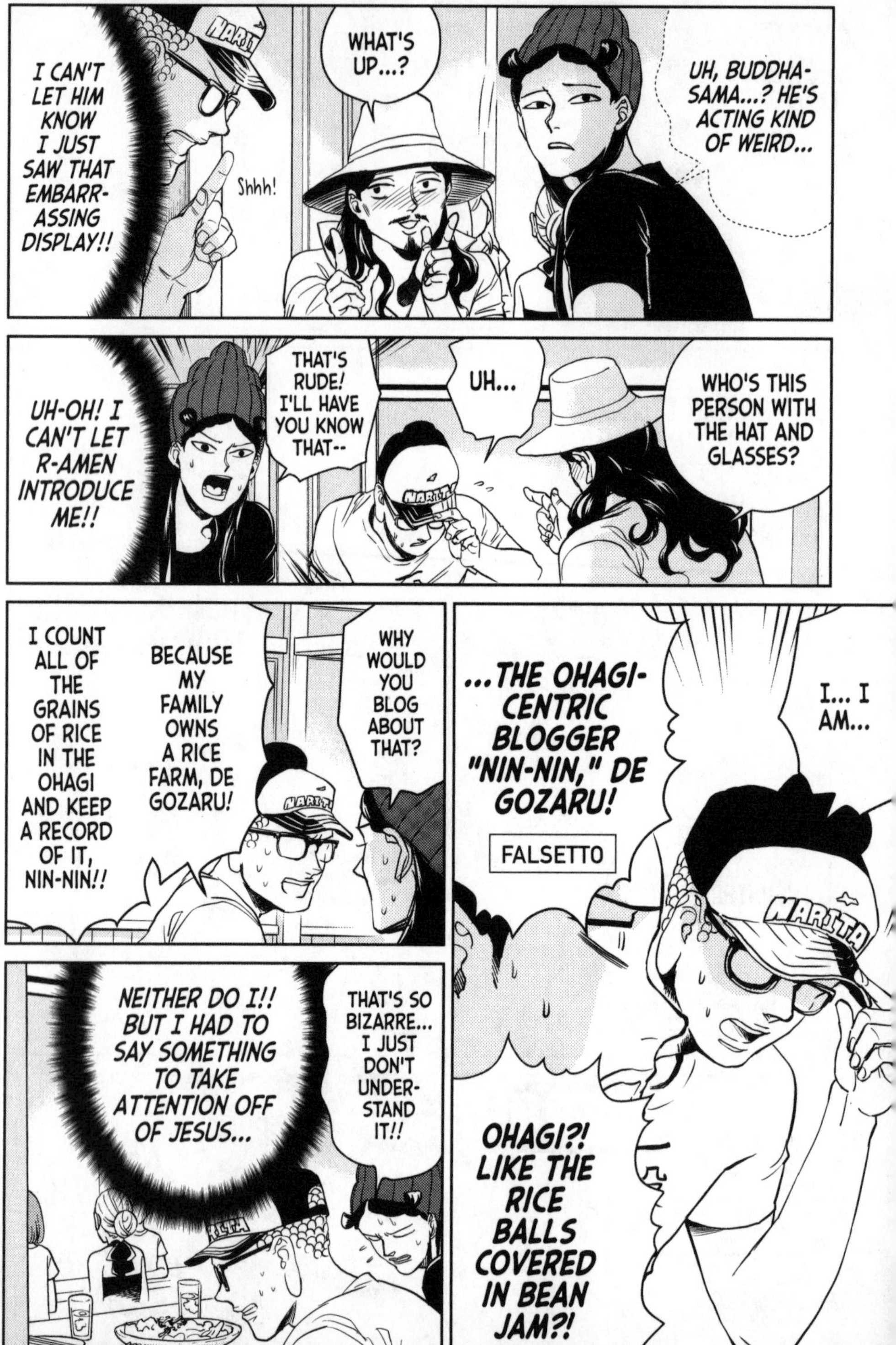
UH, BUDDHA-SAMA...? HE'S ACTING KIND OF WEIRD...
WHAT'S UP...?
Shhh!
I CAN'T LET HIM KNOW I JUST SAW THAT EMBARR-ASSING DISPLAY!!
WHO'S THIS PERSON WITH THE HAT AND GLASSES?
UH...
THAT'S RUDE! I'LL HAVE YOU KNOW THAT--
UH-OH! I CAN'T LET R-AMEN INTRODUCE ME!!
I... I AM...
...THE OHAGI-CENTRIC BLOGGER "NIN-NIN," DE GOZARU!
FALSETTO
OHAGI?! LIKE THE RICE BALLS COVERED IN BEAN JAM?!
WHY WOULD YOU BLOG ABOUT THAT?
BECAUSE MY FAMILY OWNS A RICE FARM, DE GOZARU!
I COUNT ALL OF THE GRAINS OF RICE IN THE OHAGI AND KEEP A RECORD OF IT, NIN-NIN!!
THAT'S SO BIZARRE... I JUST DON'T UNDER-STAND IT!!
NEITHER DO I!! BUT I HAD TO SAY SOMETHING TO TAKE ATTENTION OFF OF JESUS...

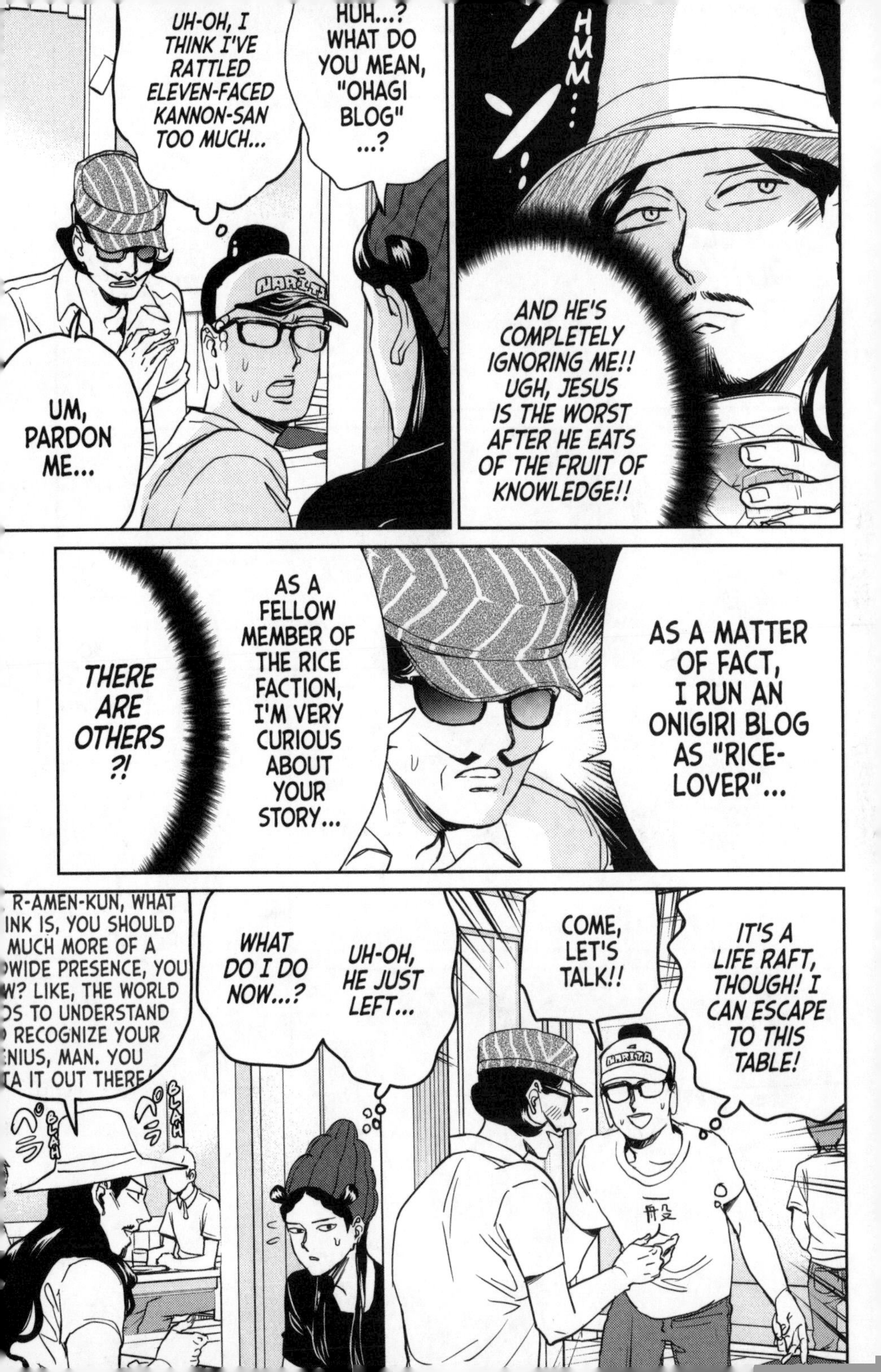
HMM...
AND HE'S COMPLETELY IGNORING ME!! UGH, JESUS IS THE WORST AFTER HE EATS OF THE FRUIT OF KNOWLEDGE!!
HUH...? WHAT DO YOU MEAN, "OHAGI BLOG" ...?
UH-OH, I THINK I'VE RATTLED ELEVEN-FACED KANNON-SAN TOO MUCH...
UM, PARDON ME...
AS A MATTER OF FACT, I RUN AN ONIGIRI BLOG AS "RICE-LOVER"...
AS A FELLOW MEMBER OF THE RICE FACTION, I'M VERY CURIOUS ABOUT YOUR STORY...
THERE ARE OTHERS?!
IT'S A LIFE RAFT, THOUGH! I CAN ESCAPE TO THIS TABLE!
COME, LET'S TALK!!
UH-OH, HE JUST LEFT...
WHAT DO I DO NOW...?
R-AMEN-KUN, WHAT INK IS, YOU SHOULD MUCH MORE OF A DWIDE PRESENCE, YOU W? LIKE, THE WORLD DS TO UNDERSTAND RECOGNIZE YOUR ENIUS, MAN. YOU TA IT OUT THERE!
BLAH BLAH

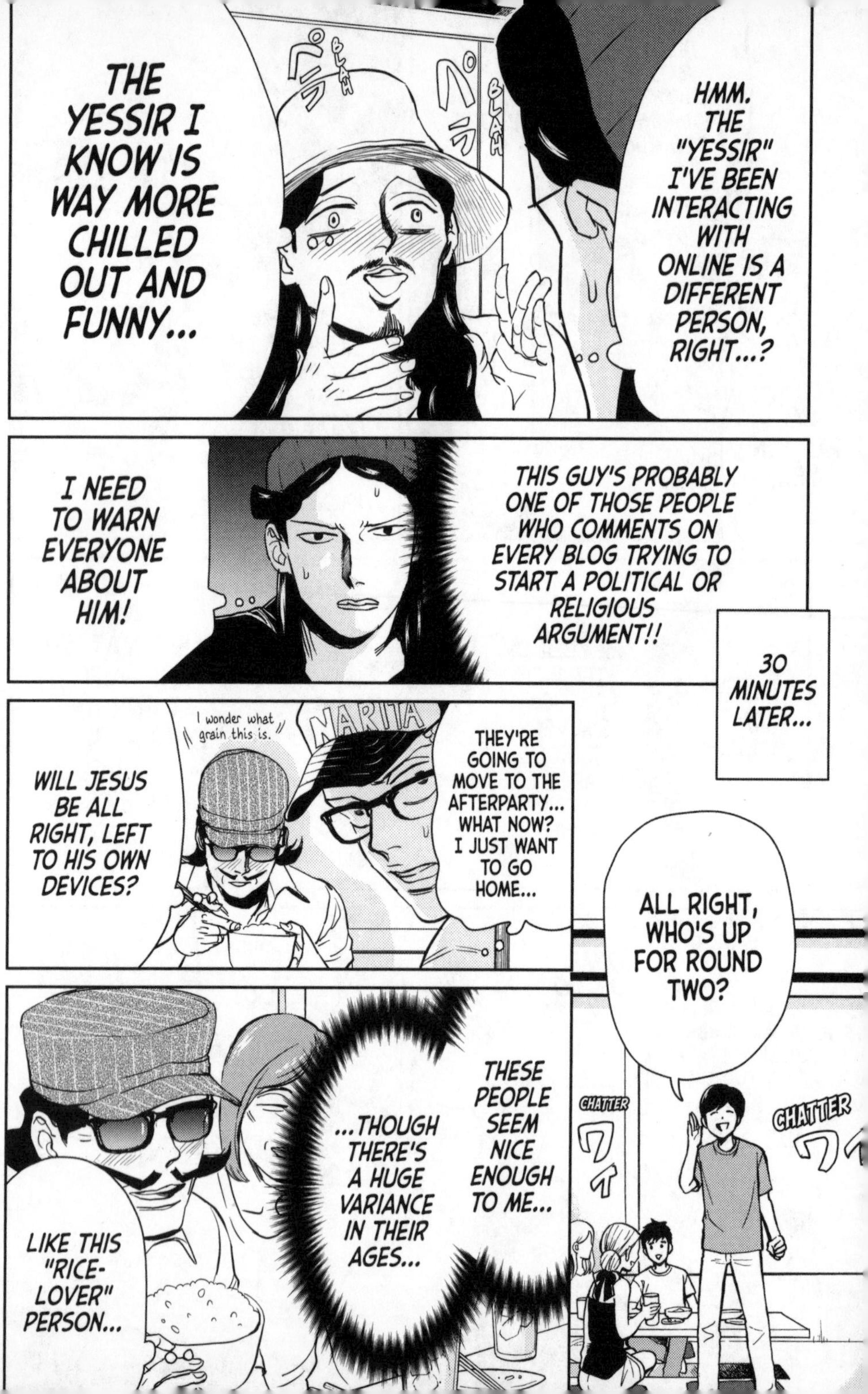

HMM. THE "YESSIR" I'VE BEEN INTERACTING WITH ONLINE IS A DIFFERENT PERSON, RIGHT...?
ペラ BLAH
ペラ BLAH
THE YESSIR I KNOW IS WAY MORE CHILLED OUT AND FUNNY...
THIS GUY'S PROBABLY ONE OF THOSE PEOPLE WHO COMMENTS ON EVERY BLOG TRYING TO START A POLITICAL OR RELIGIOUS ARGUMENT!!
I NEED TO WARN EVERYONE ABOUT HIM!
30 MINUTES LATER...
THEY'RE GOING TO MOVE TO THE AFTERPARTY... WHAT NOW? I JUST WANT TO GO HOME...
NARITA
I wonder what grain this is.
WILL JESUS BE ALL RIGHT, LEFT TO HIS OWN DEVICES?
ALL RIGHT, WHO'S UP FOR ROUND TWO?
ワイ CHATTER
ワイ CHATTER
THESE PEOPLE SEEM NICE ENOUGH TO ME...
...THOUGH THERE'S A HUGE VARIANCE IN THEIR AGES...
LIKE THIS "RICE-LOVER" PERSON...

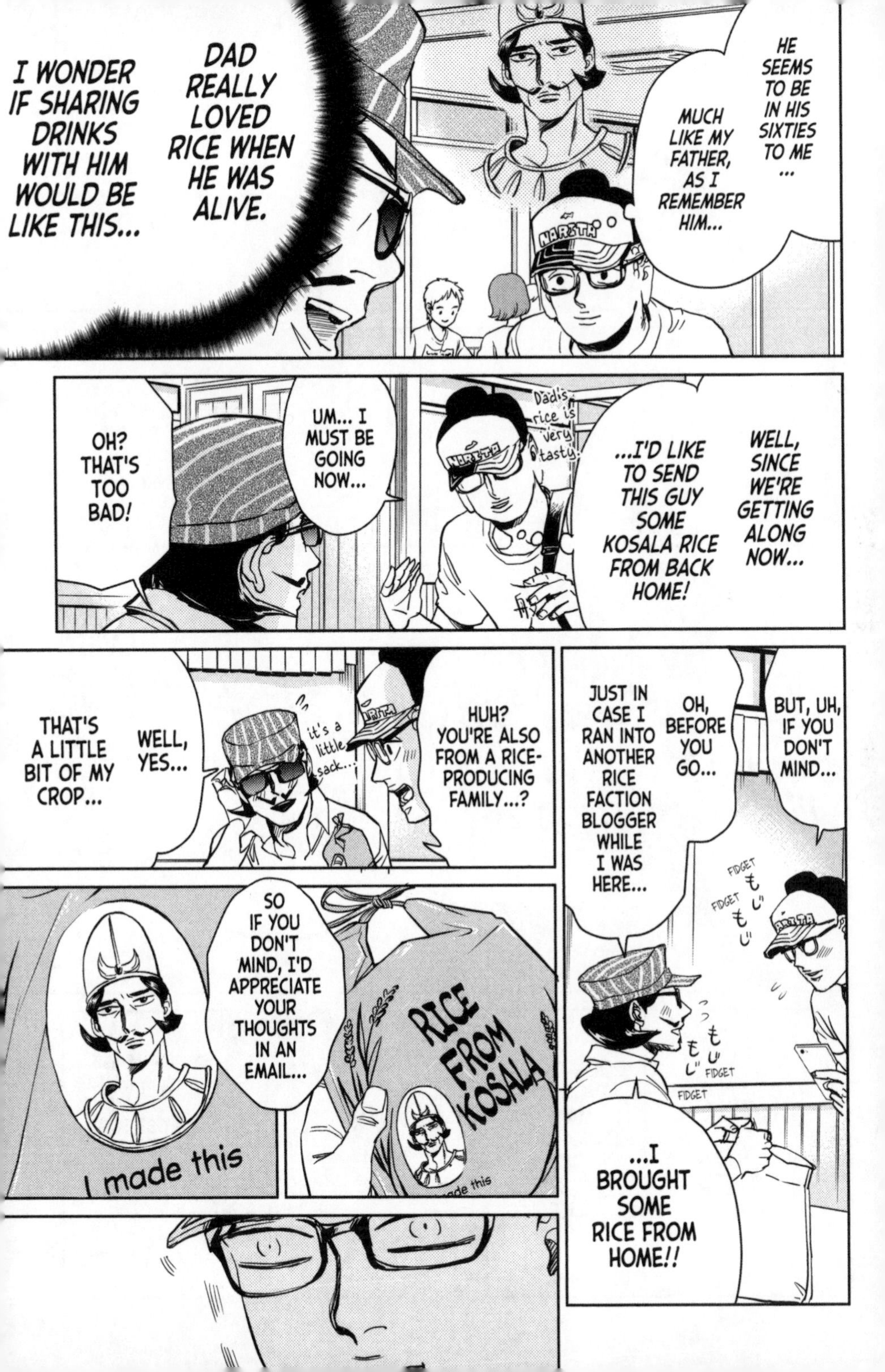
HE SEEMS TO BE IN HIS SIXTIES TO ME ...
MUCH LIKE MY FATHER, AS I REMEMBER HIM...
DAD REALLY LOVED RICE WHEN HE WAS ALIVE.
I WONDER IF SHARING DRINKS WITH HIM WOULD BE LIKE THIS...
WELL, SINCE WE'RE GETTING ALONG NOW...
...I'D LIKE TO SEND THIS GUY SOME KOSALA RICE FROM BACK HOME!
Dad's rice is very tasty
UM... I MUST BE GOING NOW...
OH? THAT'S TOO BAD!
BUT, UH, IF YOU DON'T MIND...
OH, BEFORE YOU GO...
JUST IN CASE I RAN INTO ANOTHER RICE FACTION BLOGGER WHILE I WAS HERE...
FIDGET もじ FIDGET もじ
もじ もじ FIDGET FIDGET
...I BROUGHT SOME RICE FROM HOME!!
HUH? YOU'RE ALSO FROM A RICE-PRODUCING FAMILY...?
it's a little sack...
WELL, YES...
THAT'S A LITTLE BIT OF MY CROP...
SO IF YOU DON'T MIND, I'D APPRECIATE YOUR THOUGHTS IN AN EMAIL...
RICE FROM KOSALA
I made this

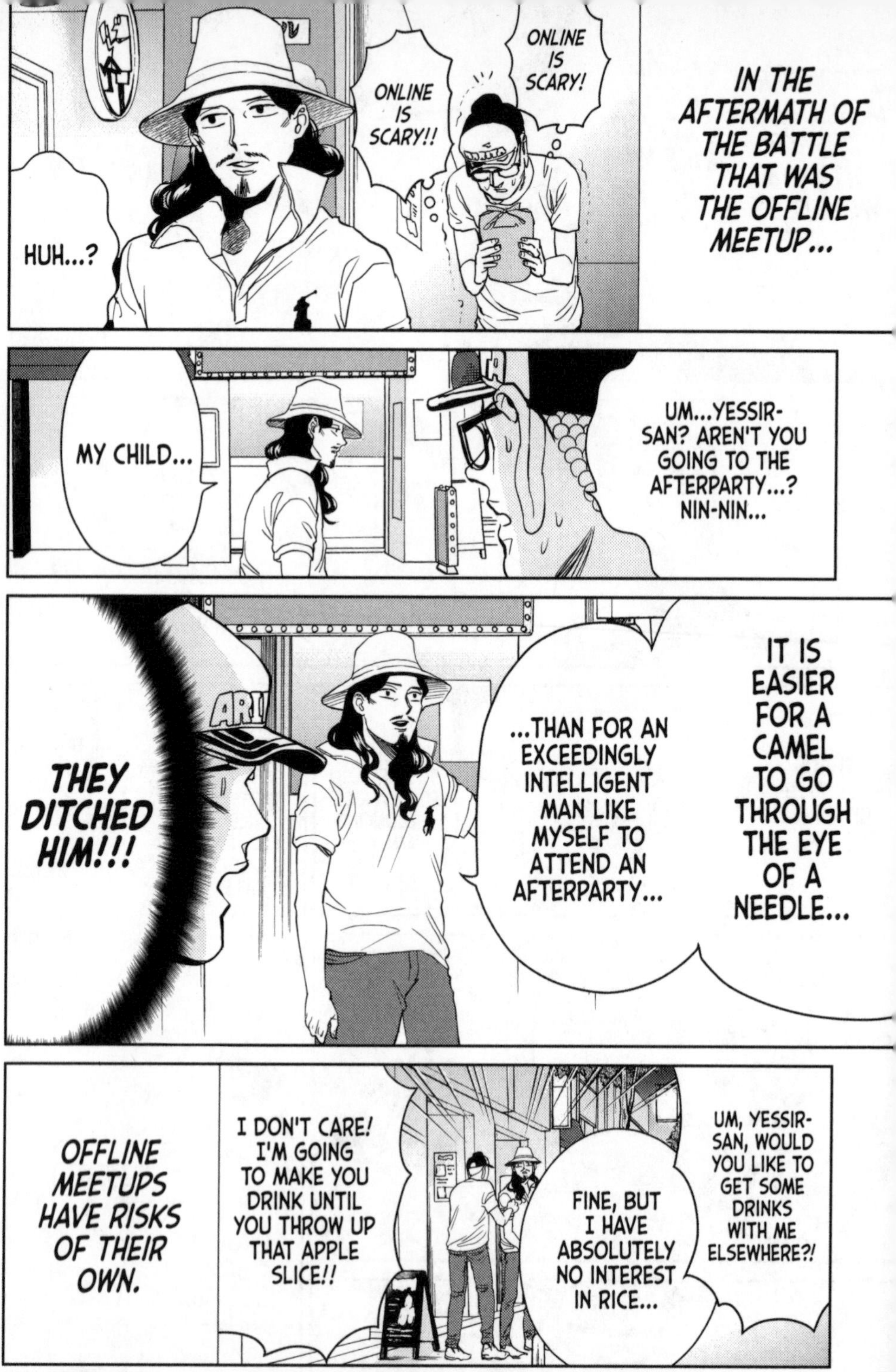
IN THE AFTERMATH OF THE BATTLE THAT WAS THE OFFLINE MEETUP...
ONLINE IS SCARY!
ONLINE IS SCARY!!
HUH...?
UM...YESSIR-SAN? AREN'T YOU GOING TO THE AFTERPARTY...? NIN-NIN...
MY CHILD...
IT IS EASIER FOR A CAMEL TO GO THROUGH THE EYE OF A NEEDLE...
...THAN FOR AN EXCEEDINGLY INTELLIGENT MAN LIKE MYSELF TO ATTEND AN AFTERPARTY...
THEY DITCHED HIM!!!
UM, YESSIR-SAN, WOULD YOU LIKE TO GET SOME DRINKS WITH ME ELSEWHERE?!
FINE, BUT I HAVE ABSOLUTELY NO INTEREST IN RICE...
I DON'T CARE! I'M GOING TO MAKE YOU DRINK UNTIL YOU THROW UP THAT APPLE SLICE!!
OFFLINE MEETUPS HAVE RISKS OF THEIR OWN.

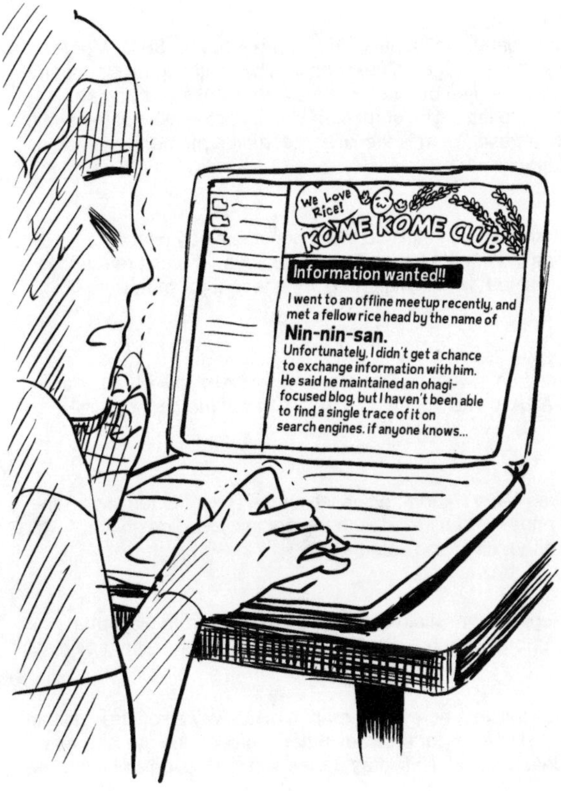
We Love Rice!
KOME KOME CLUB
Information wanted!!
I went to an offline meetup recently, and met a fellow rice head by the name of
Nin-nin-san.
Unfortunately, I didn't get a chance to exchange information with him. He said he maintained an ohagi-focused blog, but I haven't been able to find a single trace of it on search engines. if anyone knows...

CHAPTER 95 TRANSLATION NOTES

Graduation, page 104
When a member of an idol pop group becomes so popular that she essentially outgrows them into launching a solo career, the Japanese term for "graduation" is typically applied.

Moto Hagio, page 105
An influential and visionary manga artist credited with helping launch the *shōjo* manga form. She has drawn highly regarded series in several genres, including romance, science fiction, gothic horror, and boys' love. *They Were Eleven* (The tense of the Japanese title is closer to "There Are Eleven") is one of her most famous works, about a spaceship crew of ten cadets who suddenly realize there are eleven members present, and no one can remember who the imposter is.
The name of "Gilbert" pronounced in the French style, however, is typically associated with the protagonist of Keiko Takemiya's seminal BL manga *The Poem of Wind and Trees*. Takemiya was a contemporary of Hagio's and shared many influences with her.

Yasu is the killer, page 109
A reference and cultural meme arising from the influential 1983 game *Portopia Serial Murder Case,* written by Yuji Horii, the creator of the *Dragon Quest* series. The sleuthing mystery game was well known (especially once it was released on the Nintendo Famicom) for having an unusually rich story for video games at the time. The surprising identity of the killer at the end of the game was so memorable that the phrase "Yasu is the killer" became a meme, joining other famous "single-phrase spoilers" in Japan.

Apple + liquor, page 111
In the original Japanese, Jesus's transformation in this scene is punctuated by a lot of unnecessary English words, which has the effect of sounding pretentious. The text references him sounding like the comedian Lou Oshiba, whose signature Japanese-English mixture is so distinct that it's called "Lou-ese."

Ohagi, page 112
A type of traditional Japanese treat made of sweet rice surrounded by *azuki* (sweet red bean) paste. *Ohagi* is made with unfiltered *azuki* paste, meaning that the skin of the beans is still present for added texture.

Nin-nin, page 112
A reference to the classic manga/anime *Ninja Hattori-kun*, in which the titular Hattori says "nin-nin!" as a catchphrase, and typically ends his sentences with the archaic form "de gozaru," which often pops up in other period pieces about ninja and samurai.

Kosala, page 115
The ancient Indian kingdom that subjugated the Shakya clan which gave birth to Gautama Buddha. In addition, the name of the Buddha's father, Suddhodana, means "one who grows rice."

Camel, page 116
A famous quote from the story of Jesus telling a rich young man to give away all of his wealth in order to reach Heaven. The quote is, "It is easier for a camel to pass through the eye of a needle than for a rich man to enter the kingdom of God." This story appears in the Gospels of Matthew, Mark, and Luke.

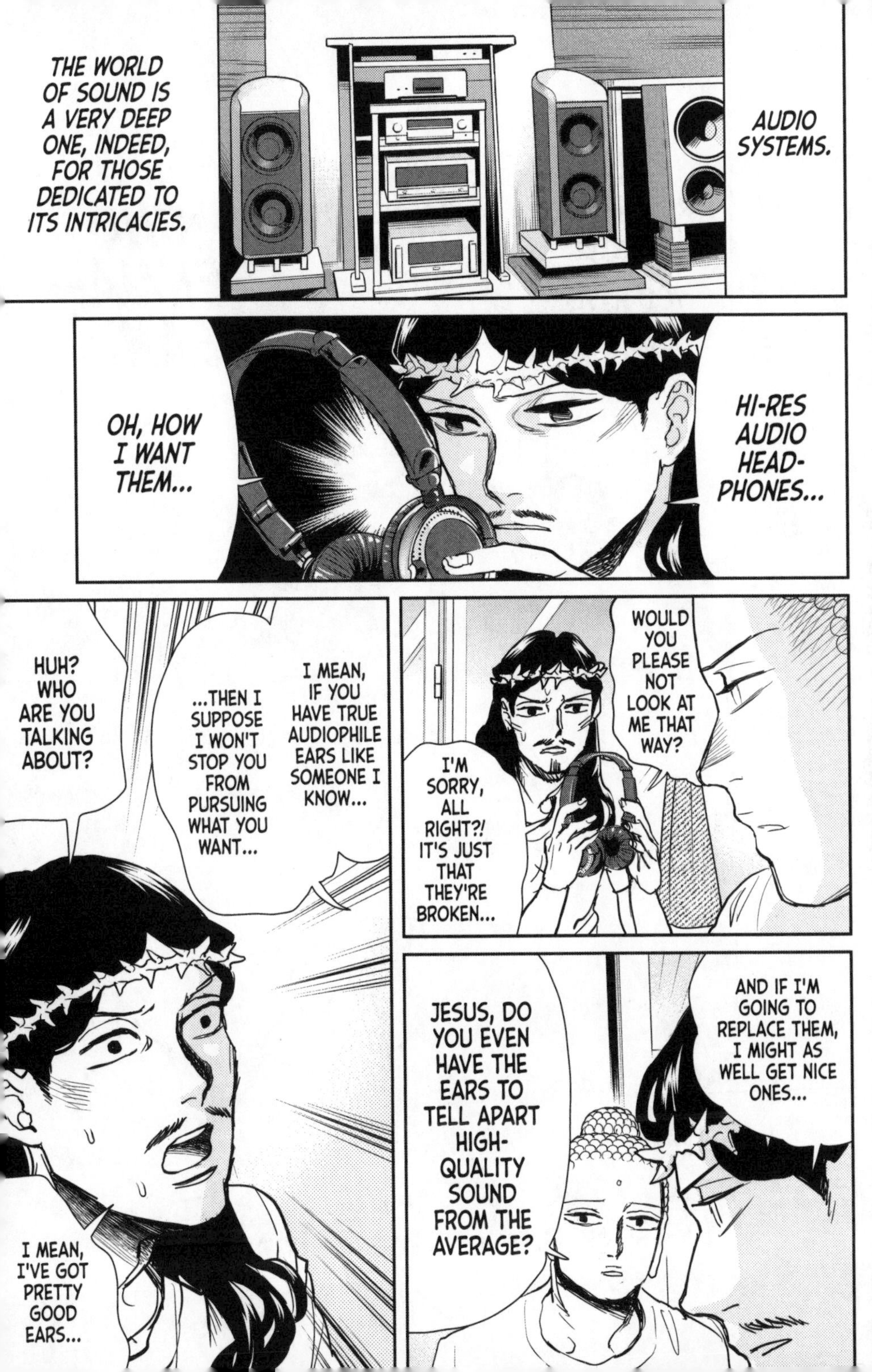

AUDIO SYSTEMS.
THE WORLD OF SOUND IS A VERY DEEP ONE, INDEED, FOR THOSE DEDICATED TO ITS INTRICACIES.
HI-RES AUDIO HEAD-PHONES...
OH, HOW I WANT THEM...
WOULD YOU PLEASE NOT LOOK AT ME THAT WAY?
I'M SORRY, ALL RIGHT?! IT'S JUST THAT THEY'RE BROKEN...
AND IF I'M GOING TO REPLACE THEM, I MIGHT AS WELL GET NICE ONES...
JESUS, DO YOU EVEN HAVE THE EARS TO TELL APART HIGH-QUALITY SOUND FROM THE AVERAGE?
I MEAN, IF YOU HAVE TRUE AUDIOPHILE EARS LIKE SOMEONE I KNOW...
...THEN I SUPPOSE I WON'T STOP YOU FROM PURSUING WHAT YOU WANT...
HUH? WHO ARE YOU TALKING ABOUT?
I MEAN, I'VE GOT PRETTY GOOD EARS...

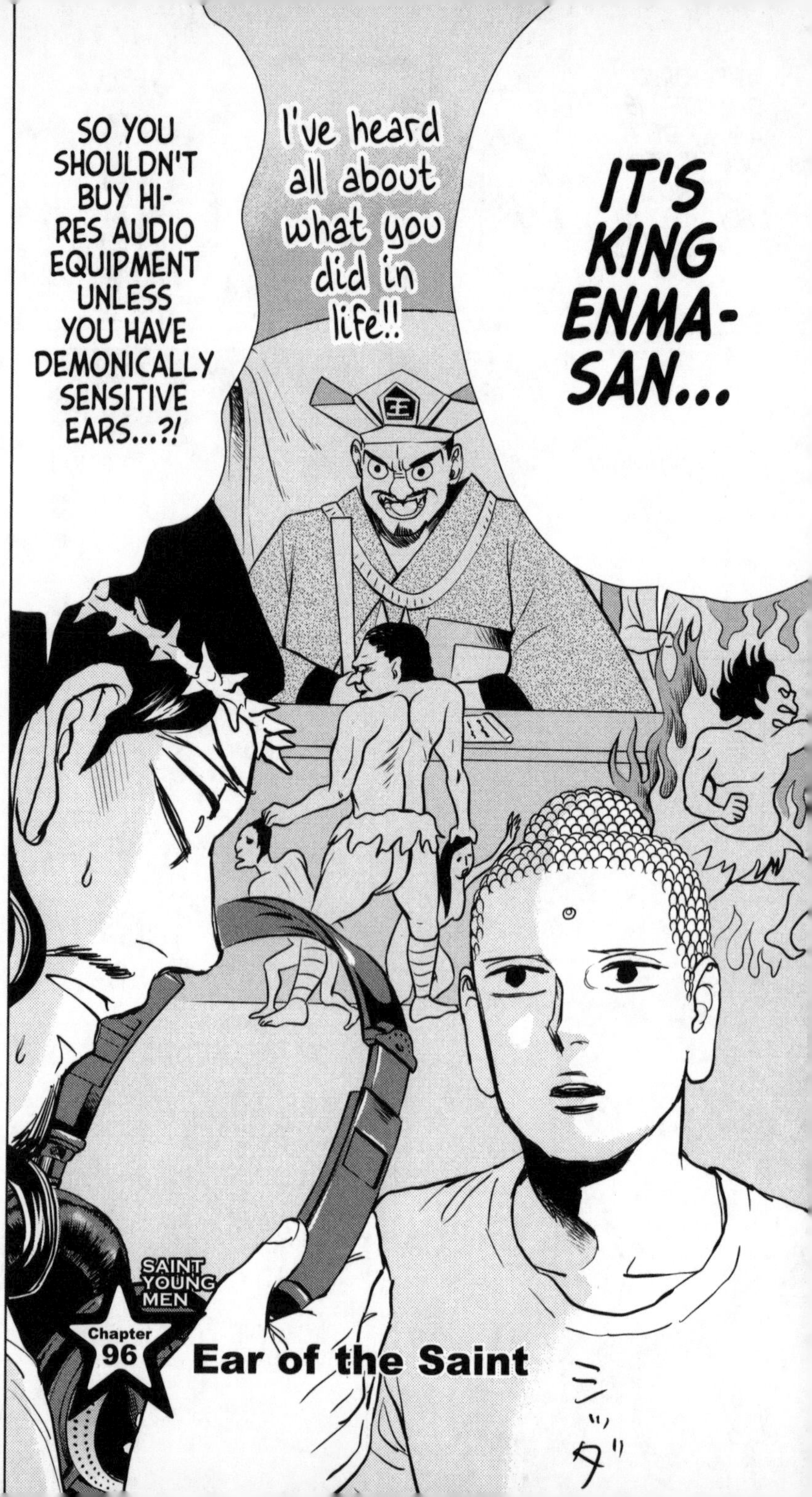
IT'S KING ENMA-SAN...
I've heard all about what you did in life!!
SO YOU SHOULDN'T BUY HI-RES AUDIO EQUIPMENT UNLESS YOU HAVE DEMONICALLY SENSITIVE EARS...?!
SAINT YOUNG MEN
Chapter 96
Ear of the Saint
シッダ

IN JAPAN, SHARP HEARING IS CALLED "EARS OF HELL," BECAUSE OF HOW ENMA HEARS EVERYTHING ON THE SURFACE.

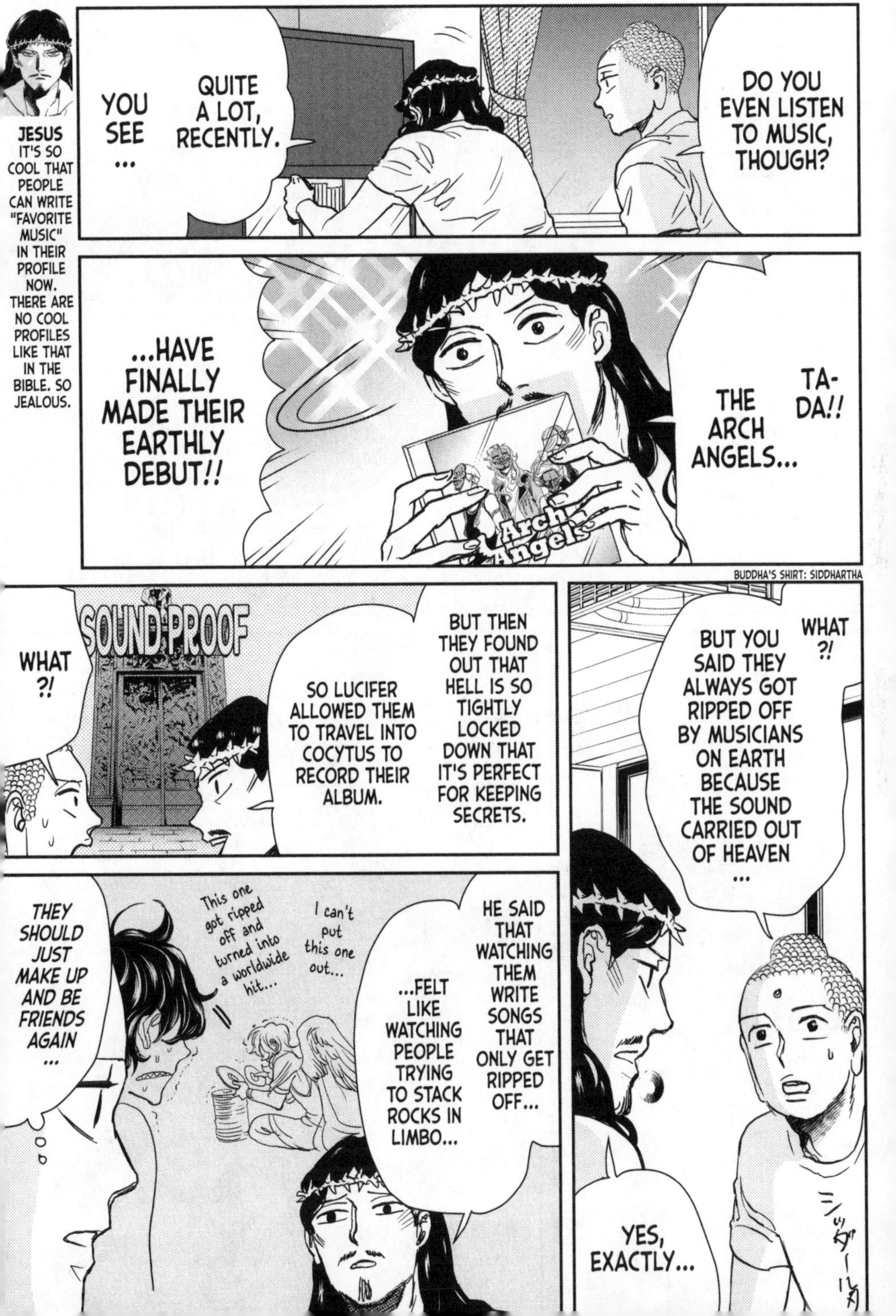
DO YOU EVEN LISTEN TO MUSIC, THOUGH?
QUITE A LOT, RECENTLY.
YOU SEE ...
TA-DA!!
THE ARCH ANGELS...
...HAVE FINALLY MADE THEIR EARTHLY DEBUT!!
Arch Angels
BUDDHA'S SHIRT: SIDDHARTHA
WHAT?!
BUT YOU SAID THEY ALWAYS GOT RIPPED OFF BY MUSICIANS ON EARTH BECAUSE THE SOUND CARRIED OUT OF HEAVEN ...
YES, EXACTLY...
BUT THEN THEY FOUND OUT THAT HELL IS SO TIGHTLY LOCKED DOWN THAT IT'S PERFECT FOR KEEPING SECRETS.
SO LUCIFER ALLOWED THEM TO TRAVEL INTO COCYTUS TO RECORD THEIR ALBUM.
SOUND-PROOF
WHAT?!
HE SAID THAT WATCHING THEM WRITE SONGS THAT ONLY GET RIPPED OFF...
...FELT LIKE WATCHING PEOPLE TRYING TO STACK ROCKS IN LIMBO...
I can't put this one out...
This one got ripped off and turned into a worldwide hit...
THEY SHOULD JUST MAKE UP AND BE FRIENDS AGAIN ...
JESUS
IT'S SO COOL THAT PEOPLE CAN WRITE "FAVORITE MUSIC" IN THEIR PROFILE NOW. THERE ARE NO COOL PROFILES LIKE THAT IN THE BIBLE. SO JEALOUS.

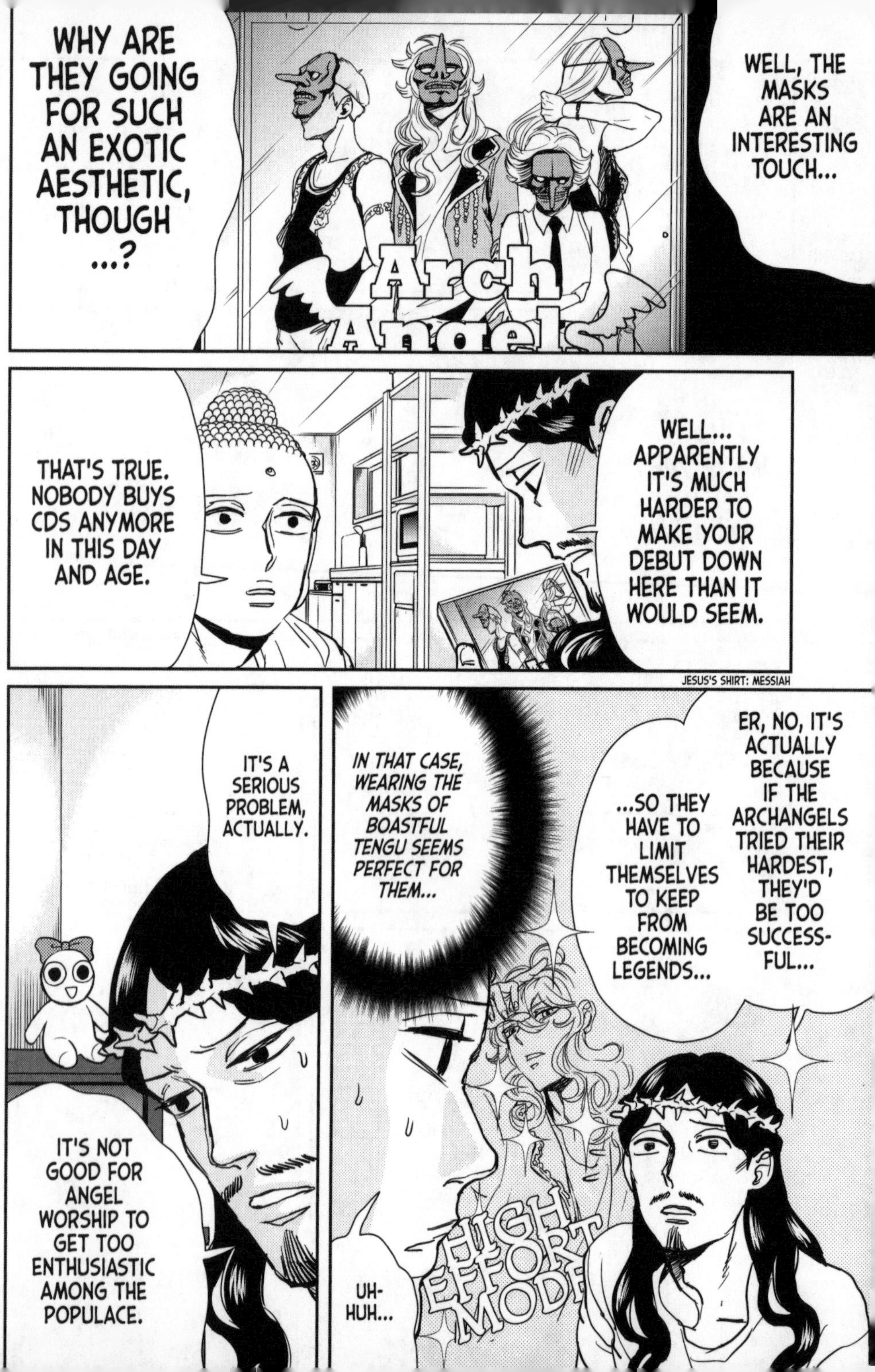
WELL, THE MASKS ARE AN INTERESTING TOUCH...
Arch Angels
WHY ARE THEY GOING FOR SUCH AN EXOTIC AESTHETIC, THOUGH ...?
WELL... APPARENTLY IT'S MUCH HARDER TO MAKE YOUR DEBUT DOWN HERE THAN IT WOULD SEEM.
THAT'S TRUE. NOBODY BUYS CDS ANYMORE IN THIS DAY AND AGE.
JESUS'S SHIRT: MESSIAH
ER, NO, IT'S ACTUALLY BECAUSE IF THE ARCHANGELS TRIED THEIR HARDEST, THEY'D BE TOO SUCCESS-FUL...
...SO THEY HAVE TO LIMIT THEMSELVES TO KEEP FROM BECOMING LEGENDS...
HIGH EFFORT MODE
IN THAT CASE, WEARING THE MASKS OF BOASTFUL TENGU SEEMS PERFECT FOR THEM...
UH-HUH...
IT'S A SERIOUS PROBLEM, ACTUALLY.
IT'S NOT GOOD FOR ANGEL WORSHIP TO GET TOO ENTHUSIASTIC AMONG THE POPULACE.

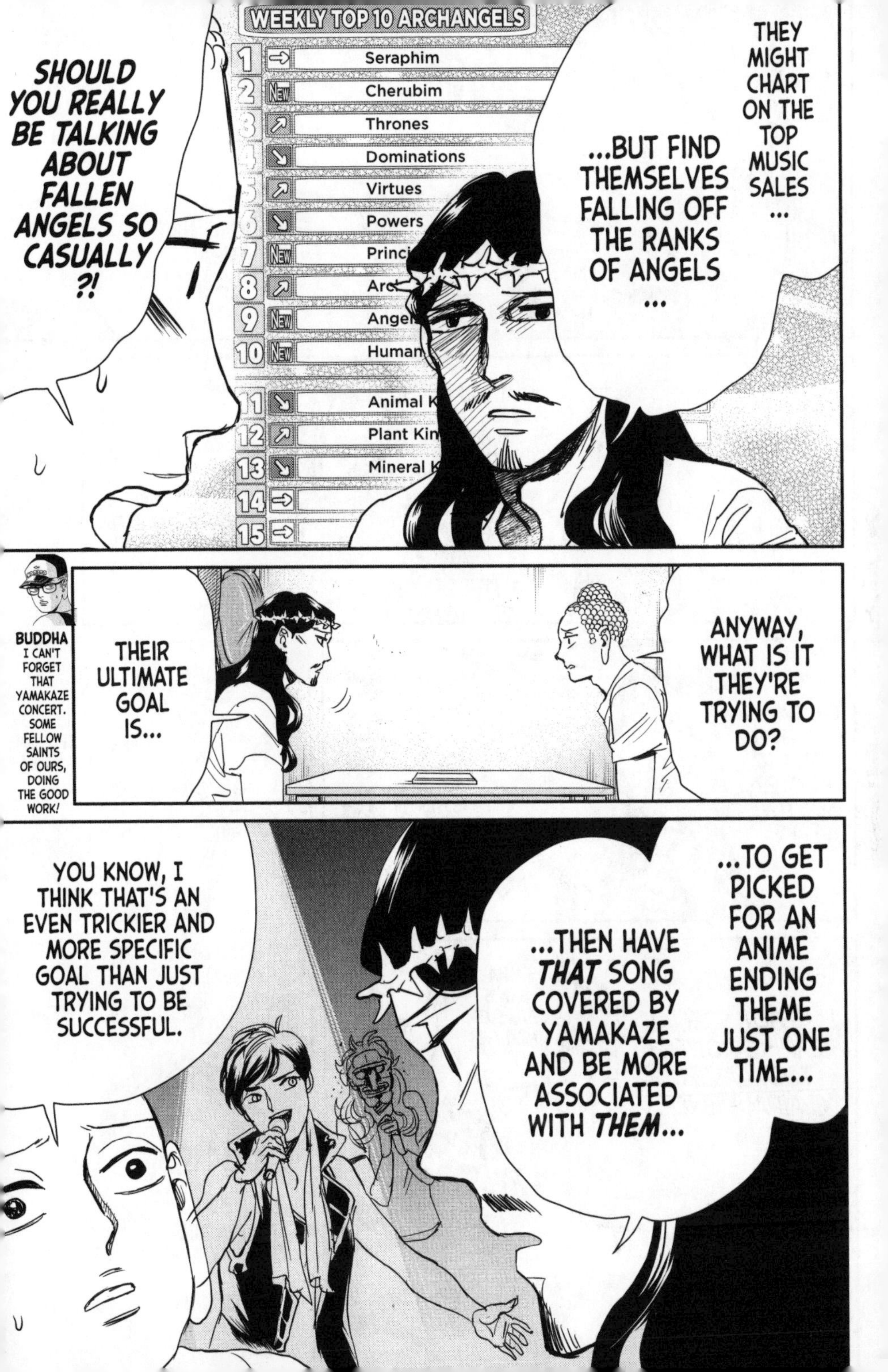
THEY MIGHT CHART ON THE TOP MUSIC SALES ...
...BUT FIND THEMSELVES FALLING OFF THE RANKS OF ANGELS ...
WEEKLY TOP 10 ARCHANGELS
1 Seraphim
2 NEW Cherubim
3 Thrones
4 Dominations
5 Virtues
6 Powers
7 NEW Princi
8 Arc
9 NEW Angel
10 NEW Human
11 Animal K
12 Plant Kin
13 Mineral K
14
15
SHOULD YOU REALLY BE TALKING ABOUT FALLEN ANGELS SO CASUALLY ?!
ANYWAY, WHAT IS IT THEY'RE TRYING TO DO?
THEIR ULTIMATE GOAL IS...
BUDDHA I CAN'T FORGET THAT YAMAKAZE CONCERT. SOME FELLOW SAINTS OF OURS, DOING THE GOOD WORK!
...TO GET PICKED FOR AN ANIME ENDING THEME JUST ONE TIME...
...THEN HAVE *THAT* SONG COVERED BY YAMAKAZE AND BE MORE ASSOCIATED WITH *THEM*...
YOU KNOW, I THINK THAT'S AN EVEN TRICKIER AND MORE SPECIFIC GOAL THAN JUST TRYING TO BE SUCCESSFUL.

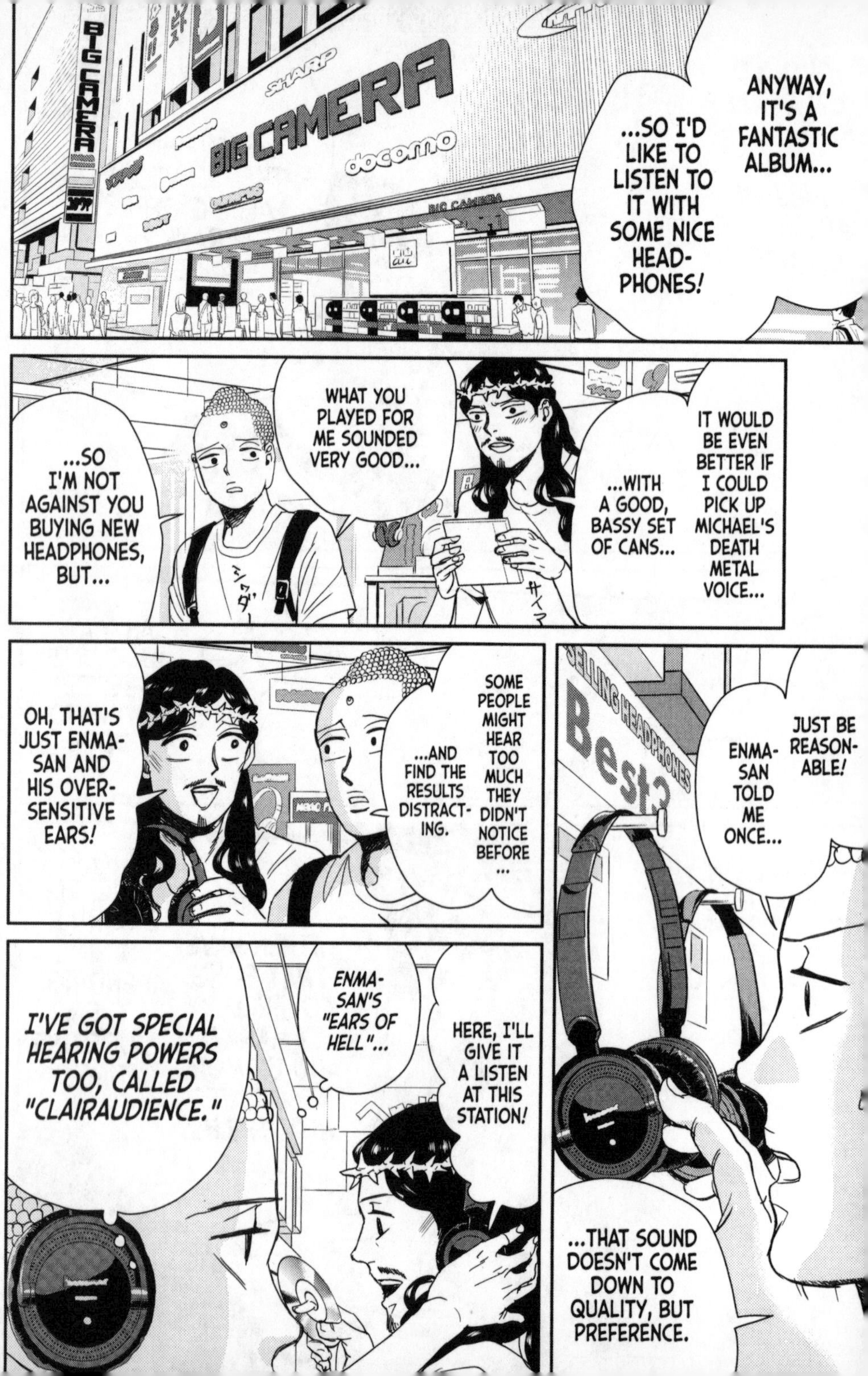
BIG CAMERA
SHARP
docomo
ANYWAY, IT'S A FANTASTIC ALBUM...
...SO I'D LIKE TO LISTEN TO IT WITH SOME NICE HEADPHONES!
IT WOULD BE EVEN BETTER IF I COULD PICK UP MICHAEL'S DEATH METAL VOICE...
...WITH A GOOD, BASSY SET OF CANS...
WHAT YOU PLAYED FOR ME SOUNDED VERY GOOD...
...SO I'M NOT AGAINST YOU BUYING NEW HEADPHONES, BUT...
SELLING HEADPHONES
Best3
JUST BE REASONABLE!
ENMA-SAN TOLD ME ONCE...
...THAT SOUND DOESN'T COME DOWN TO QUALITY, BUT PREFERENCE.
SOME PEOPLE MIGHT HEAR TOO MUCH THEY DIDN'T NOTICE BEFORE...
...AND FIND THE RESULTS DISTRACTING.
OH, THAT'S JUST ENMA-SAN AND HIS OVER-SENSITIVE EARS!
HERE, I'LL GIVE IT A LISTEN AT THIS STATION!
ENMA-SAN'S "EARS OF HELL"...
I'VE GOT SPECIAL HEARING POWERS TOO, CALLED "CLAIRAUDIENCE."

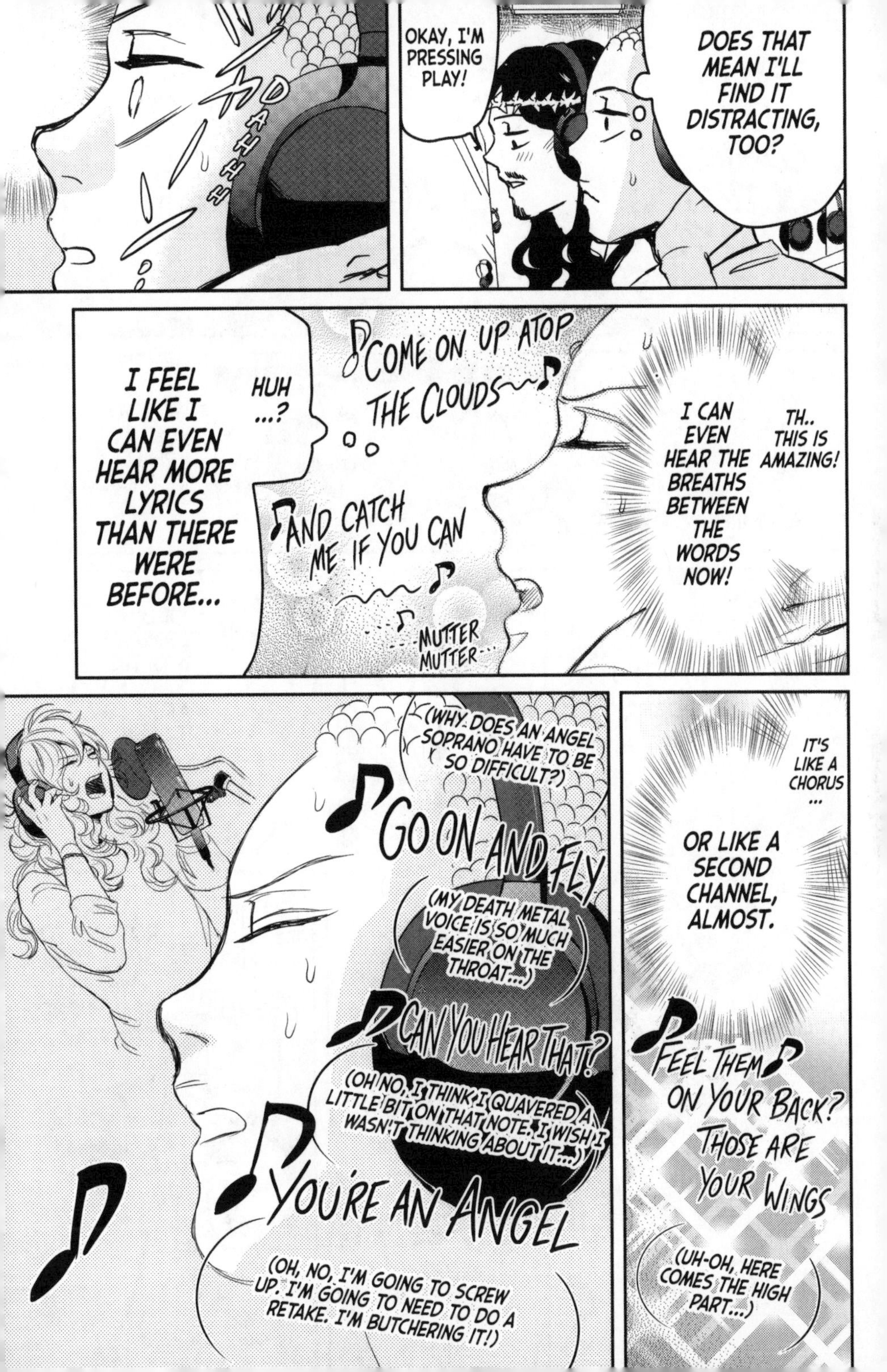
DOES THAT MEAN I'LL FIND IT DISTRACTING, TOO?
OKAY, I'M PRESSING PLAY!
DAHHHH
TH.. THIS IS AMAZING!
I CAN EVEN HEAR THE BREATHS BETWEEN THE WORDS NOW!
COME ON UP ATOP THE CLOUDS
AND CATCH ME IF YOU CAN
MUTTER MUTTER
HUH ...?
I FEEL LIKE I CAN EVEN HEAR MORE LYRICS THAN THERE WERE BEFORE...
IT'S LIKE A CHORUS ...
OR LIKE A SECOND CHANNEL, ALMOST.
FEEL THEM ON YOUR BACK? THOSE ARE YOUR WINGS
(UH-OH, HERE COMES THE HIGH PART...)
(WHY DOES AN ANGEL SOPRANO HAVE TO BE SO DIFFICULT?)
GO ON AND FLY
(MY DEATH METAL VOICE IS SO MUCH EASIER ON THE THROAT...)
CAN YOU HEAR THAT?
(OH NO, I THINK I QUAVERED A LITTLE BIT ON THAT NOTE. I WISH I WASN'T THINKING ABOUT IT...)
YOU'RE AN ANGEL
(OH, NO, I'M GOING TO SCREW UP. I'M GOING TO NEED TO DO A RETAKE. I'M BUTCHERING IT!)

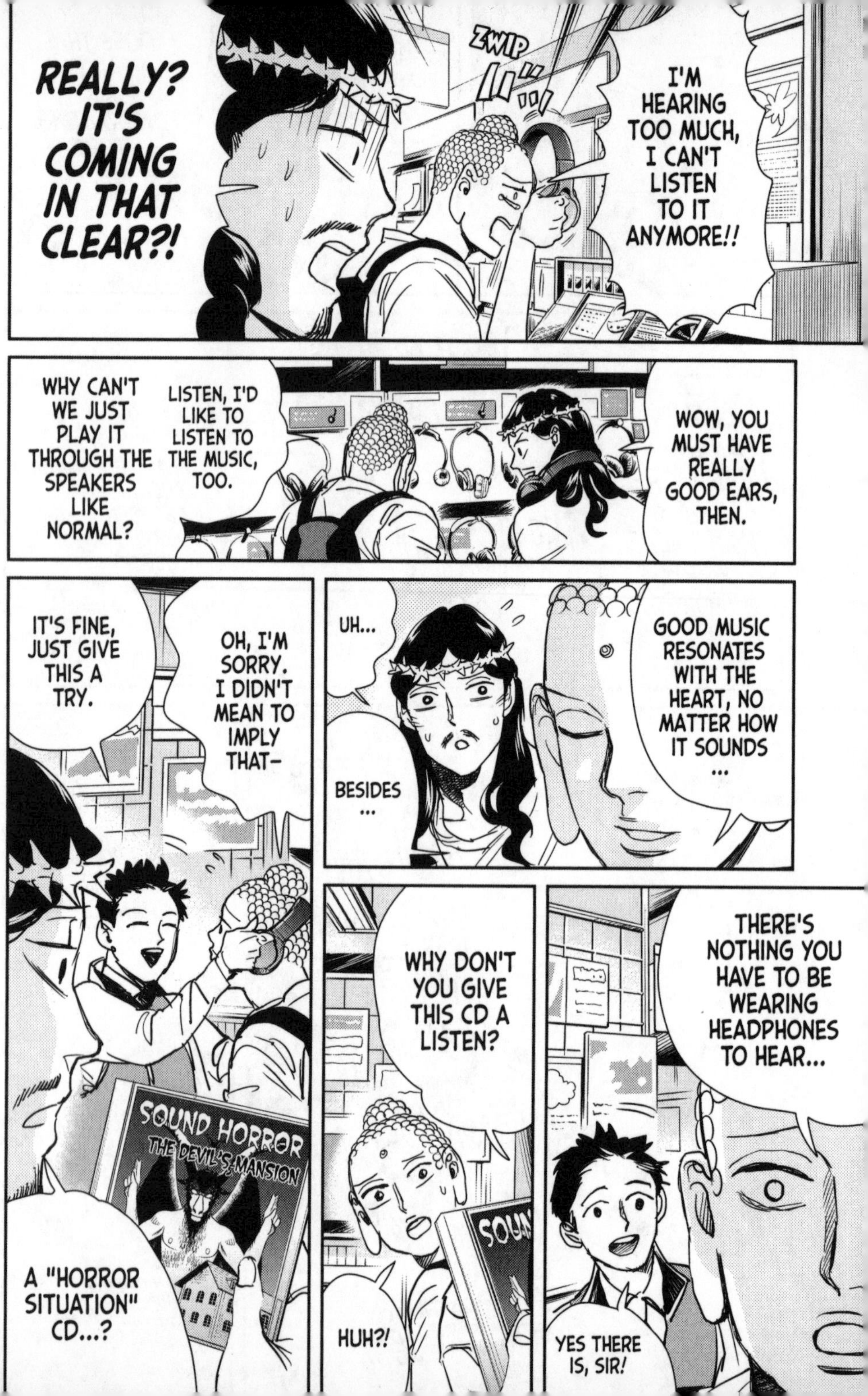
ZWIP
I'M HEARING TOO MUCH, I CAN'T LISTEN TO IT ANYMORE!!
REALLY? IT'S COMING IN THAT CLEAR?!
WOW, YOU MUST HAVE REALLY GOOD EARS, THEN.
LISTEN, I'D LIKE TO LISTEN TO THE MUSIC, TOO.
WHY CAN'T WE JUST PLAY IT THROUGH THE SPEAKERS LIKE NORMAL?
GOOD MUSIC RESONATES WITH THE HEART, NO MATTER HOW IT SOUNDS ...
UH...
BESIDES ...
THERE'S NOTHING YOU HAVE TO BE WEARING HEADPHONES TO HEAR...
YES THERE IS, SIR!
WHY DON'T YOU GIVE THIS CD A LISTEN?
HUH?!
OH, I'M SORRY. I DIDN'T MEAN TO IMPLY THAT—
IT'S FINE, JUST GIVE THIS A TRY.
SOUND HORROR
THE DEVIL'S MANSION
A "HORROR SITUATION" CD...?

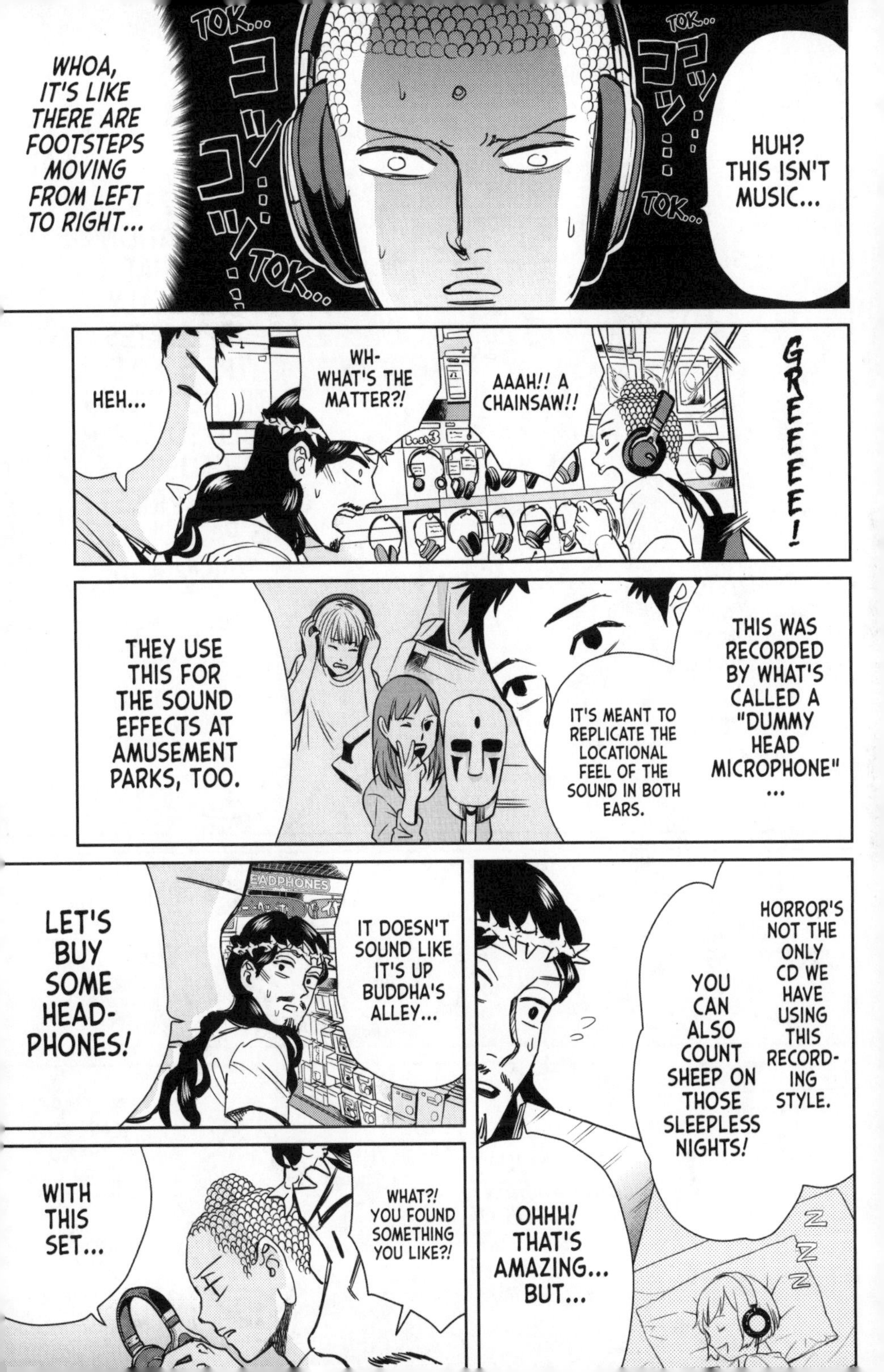
HUH? THIS ISN'T MUSIC...
TOK...
コッ
TOK...
コッ
TOK...
コッ
TOK...
WHOA, IT'S LIKE THERE ARE FOOTSTEPS MOVING FROM LEFT TO RIGHT...
GREEEEE!
AAAH!! A CHAINSAW!!
WH- WHAT'S THE MATTER?!
HEH...
THIS WAS RECORDED BY WHAT'S CALLED A "DUMMY HEAD MICROPHONE"...
IT'S MEANT TO REPLICATE THE LOCATIONAL FEEL OF THE SOUND IN BOTH EARS.
THEY USE THIS FOR THE SOUND EFFECTS AT AMUSEMENT PARKS, TOO.
HORROR'S NOT THE ONLY CD WE HAVE USING THIS RECORDING STYLE.
YOU CAN ALSO COUNT SHEEP ON THOSE SLEEPLESS NIGHTS!
Z Z Z
OHHH! THAT'S AMAZING... BUT...
IT DOESN'T SOUND LIKE IT'S UP BUDDHA'S ALLEY...
LET'S BUY SOME HEAD-PHONES!
WHAT?! YOU FOUND SOMETHING YOU LIKE?!
WITH THIS SET...

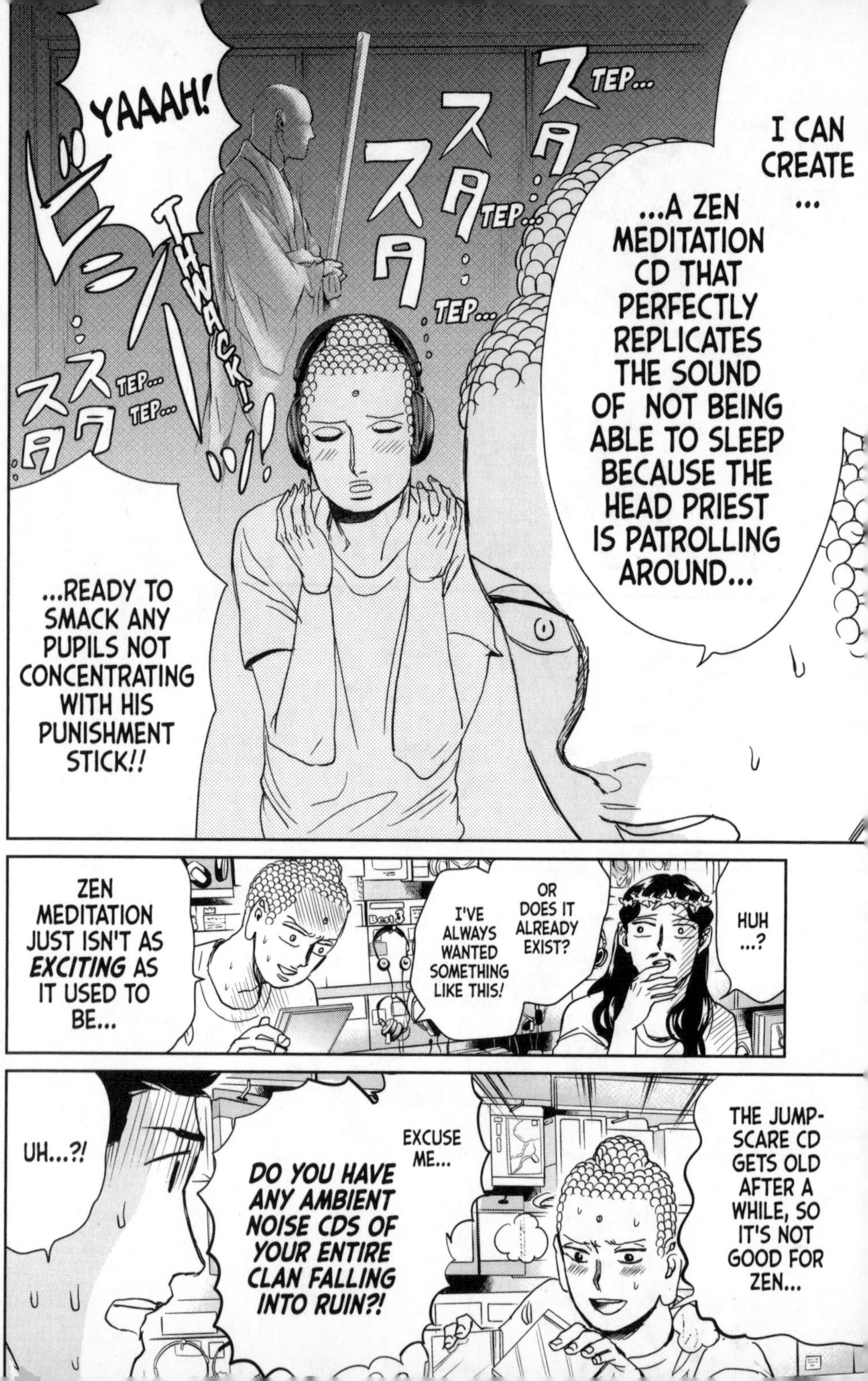
I CAN CREATE...
...A ZEN MEDITATION CD THAT PERFECTLY REPLICATES THE SOUND OF NOT BEING ABLE TO SLEEP BECAUSE THE HEAD PRIEST IS PATROLLING AROUND...
TEP...
TEP...
TEP...
YAAAH!
THWACK!
TEP... TEP...
...READY TO SMACK ANY PUPILS NOT CONCENTRATING WITH HIS PUNISHMENT STICK!!
HUH ...?
OR DOES IT ALREADY EXIST?
I'VE ALWAYS WANTED SOMETHING LIKE THIS!
ZEN MEDITATION JUST ISN'T AS *EXCITING* AS IT USED TO BE...
THE JUMP-SCARE CD GETS OLD AFTER A WHILE, SO IT'S NOT GOOD FOR ZEN...
EXCUSE ME...
DO YOU HAVE ANY AMBIENT NOISE CDS OF YOUR ENTIRE CLAN FALLING INTO RUIN?!
UH...?!

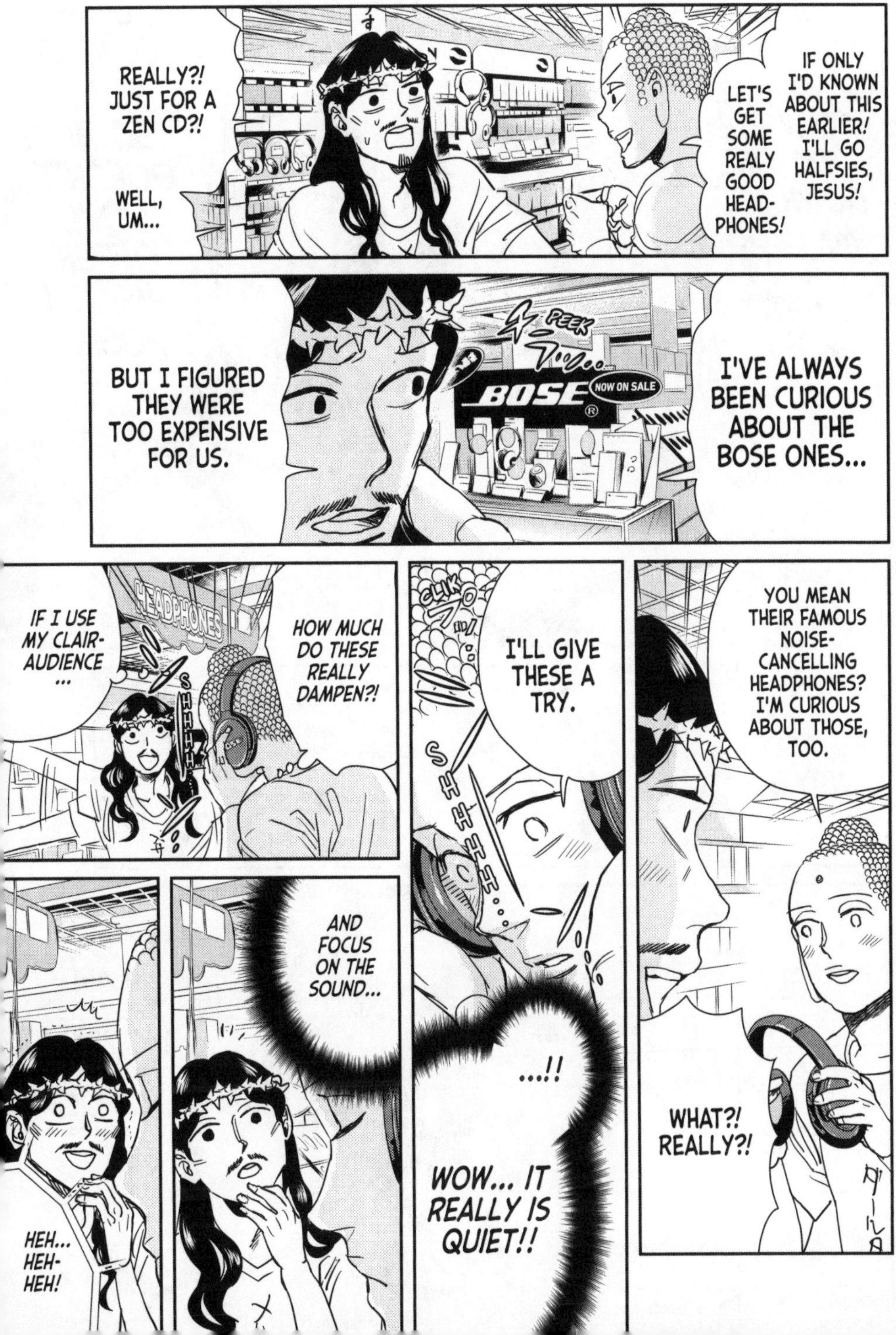
IF ONLY I'D KNOWN ABOUT THIS EARLIER! I'LL GO HALFSIES, JESUS!
LET'S GET SOME REALY GOOD HEAD-PHONES!
REALLY?! JUST FOR A ZEN CD?!
WELL, UM...
I'VE ALWAYS BEEN CURIOUS ABOUT THE BOSE ONES...
PEEK
BOSE
NOW ON SALE
BUT I FIGURED THEY WERE TOO EXPENSIVE FOR US.
YOU MEAN THEIR FAMOUS NOISE-CANCELLING HEADPHONES? I'M CURIOUS ABOUT THOSE, TOO.
WHAT?! REALLY?!
CLIK
I'LL GIVE THESE A TRY.
...!!
WOW... IT REALLY IS QUIET!!
HOW MUCH DO THESE REALLY DAMPEN?!
HEADPHONES
IF I USE MY CLAIR-AUDIENCE...
SHHHH
AND FOCUS ON THE SOUND...
HEH... HEH-HEH!

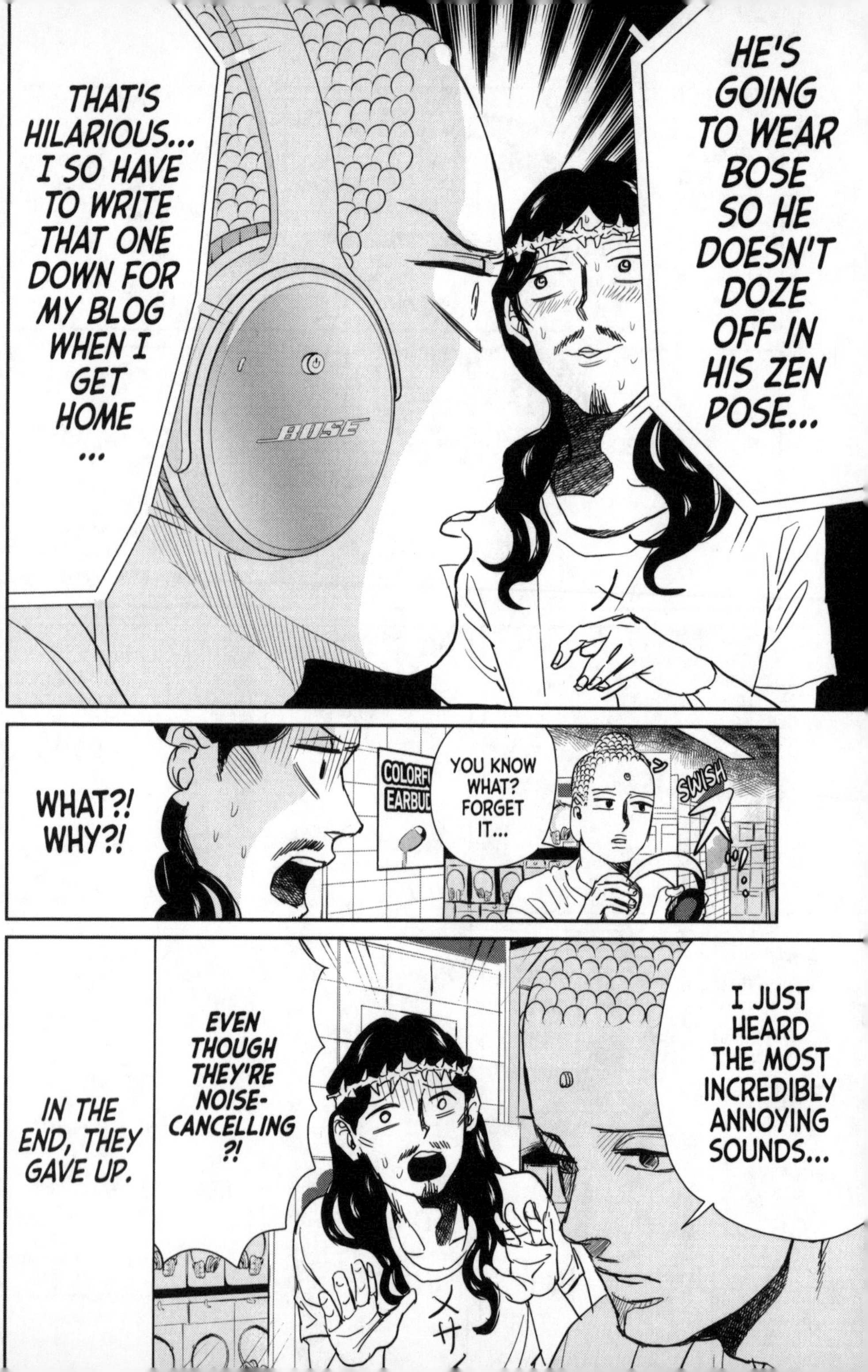
HE'S GOING TO WEAR BOSE SO HE DOESN'T DOZE OFF IN HIS ZEN POSE...
THAT'S HILARIOUS... I SO HAVE TO WRITE THAT ONE DOWN FOR MY BLOG WHEN I GET HOME ...
BOSE
SWISH
YOU KNOW WHAT? FORGET IT...
WHAT?! WHY?!
I JUST HEARD THE MOST INCREDIBLY ANNOYING SOUNDS...
EVEN THOUGH THEY'RE NOISE-CANCELLING ?!
IN THE END, THEY GAVE UP.

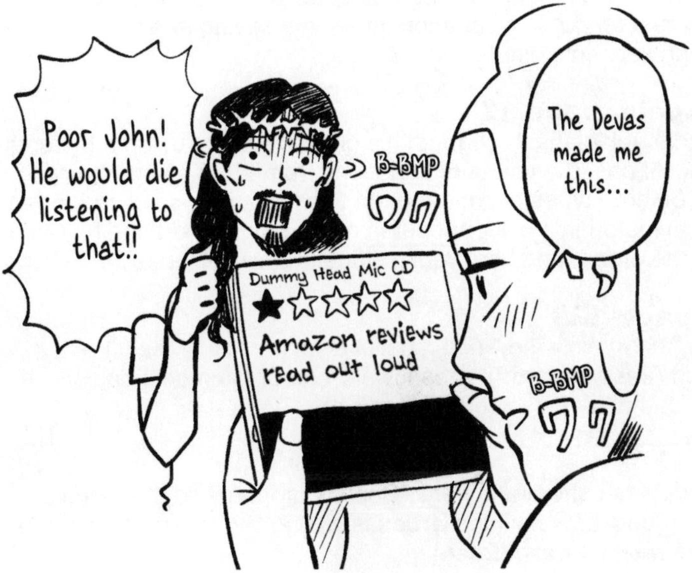
The Devas made me this...
B-BMP
B-BMP
Dummy Head Mic CD
Amazon reviews read out loud
Poor John! He would die listening to that!!

CHAPTER 96 TRANSLATION NOTES

Enma, page 120

The Buddhist king of Hell who rules over the dead and accursed. As mentioned in the text, the Japanese term for sharp hearing, *jigoku-mimi*, means "Hell ears" or "ears of Hell," because of the way that Enma hears about the wicked deeds of the dead in passing judgment upon them.

Stacking rocks in Limbo, page 121

In Japanese Buddhism, there is a children's limbo called *Sai no Kawara*, which is a riverbed of souls. The souls of children trapped there must build towers of stones to climb out of their purgatory, only for terrible *oni* (ogres) to come along and kick them over.

Tengu, page 122

A type of being in Japanese folklore. *Tengu* can be represented in human or crow-like form, but most typically are humanoid with very long noses. Depending on the depiction, *tengu* can be anywhere from frightening to humorous, but one of their most defining characteristics is arrogance. The phrase "to become a *tengu*" is a common Japanese saying meaning that someone is acting very conceited.

Ranks of angels, page 123

Various Christian theologians throughout history have constructed a hierarchy of classes of angels based on certain quotations from the Bible, grouping three "spheres" of three types each. Although this hierarchy is not supported directly by biblical material, it does appear in much religious art; the hierarchy also appears in the order seen here within Dante's *Divine Comedy*.

Yamakaze, page 123

A term meaning "mountain wind," and most likely a parody of the ultra-popular boy band Arashi ("storm"). Arashi were one of the most popular groups throughout the 2010s. (See Chapter 53.)

Bose, page 130

in the original Japanese, the brand name Bose is pronounced the same as the word *bôzu*, or "priest." So originally, Jesus was joking to himself that the *bôzu* (priest) was wearing *bôzu* (Bose).

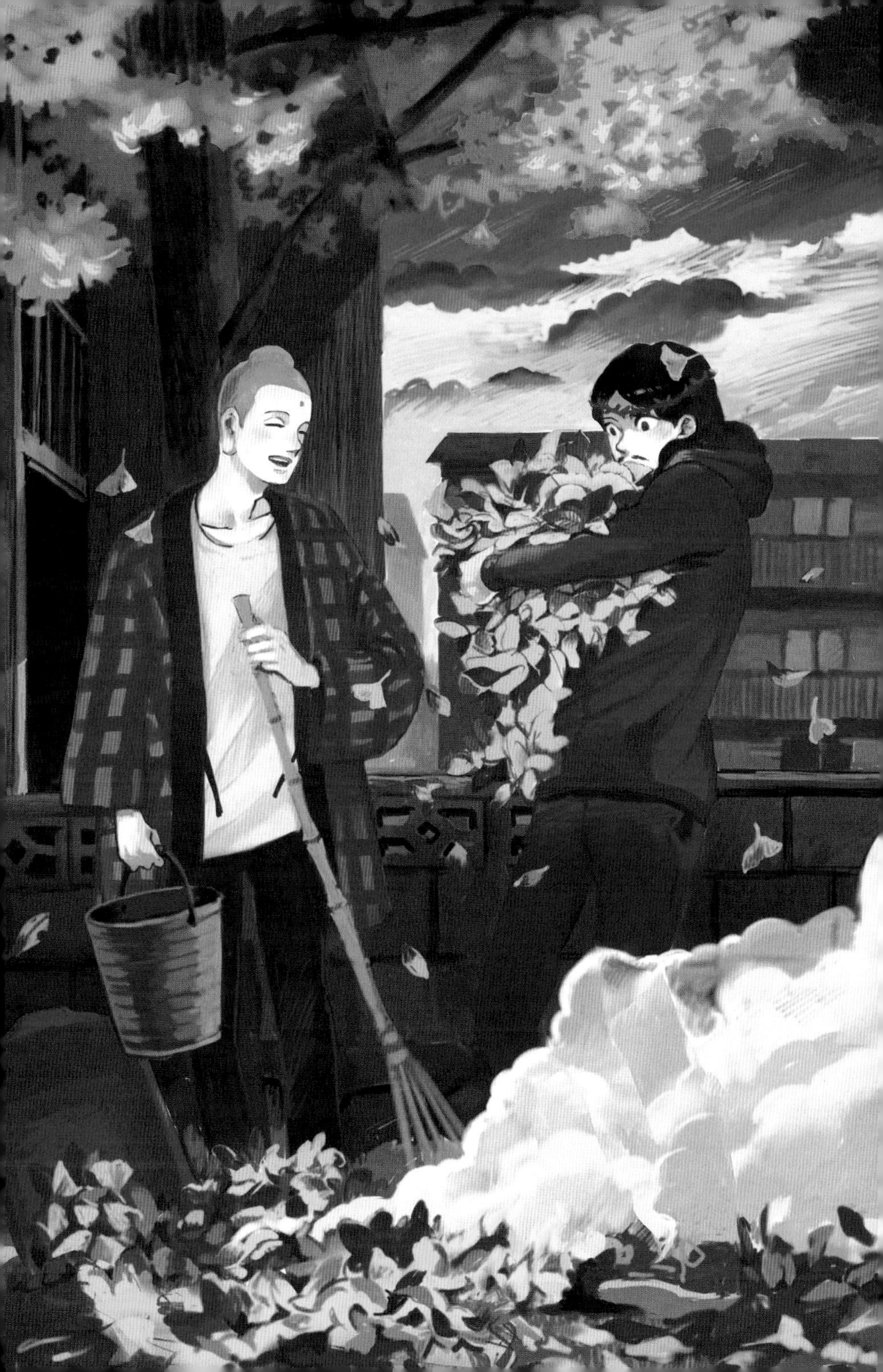

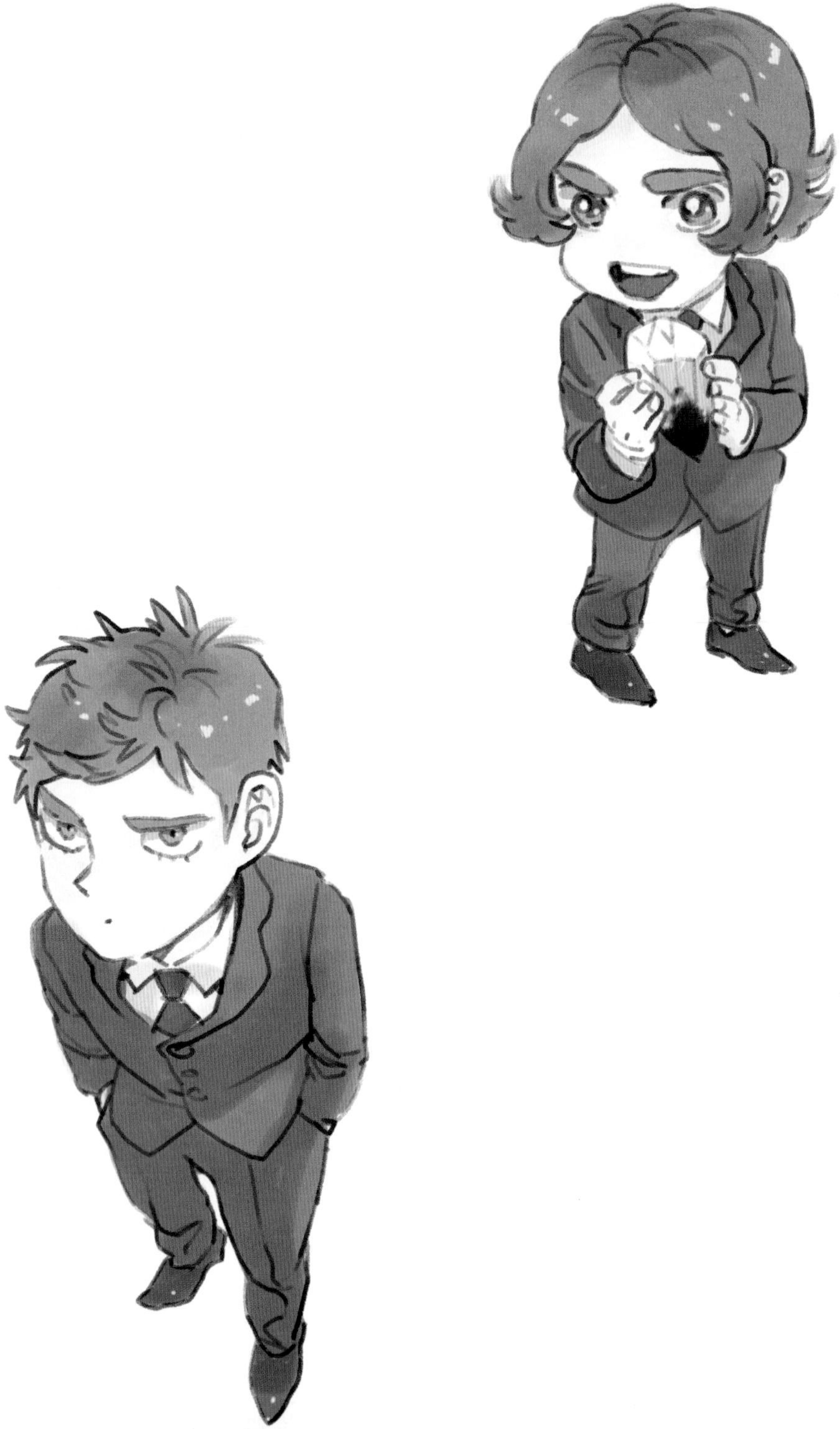

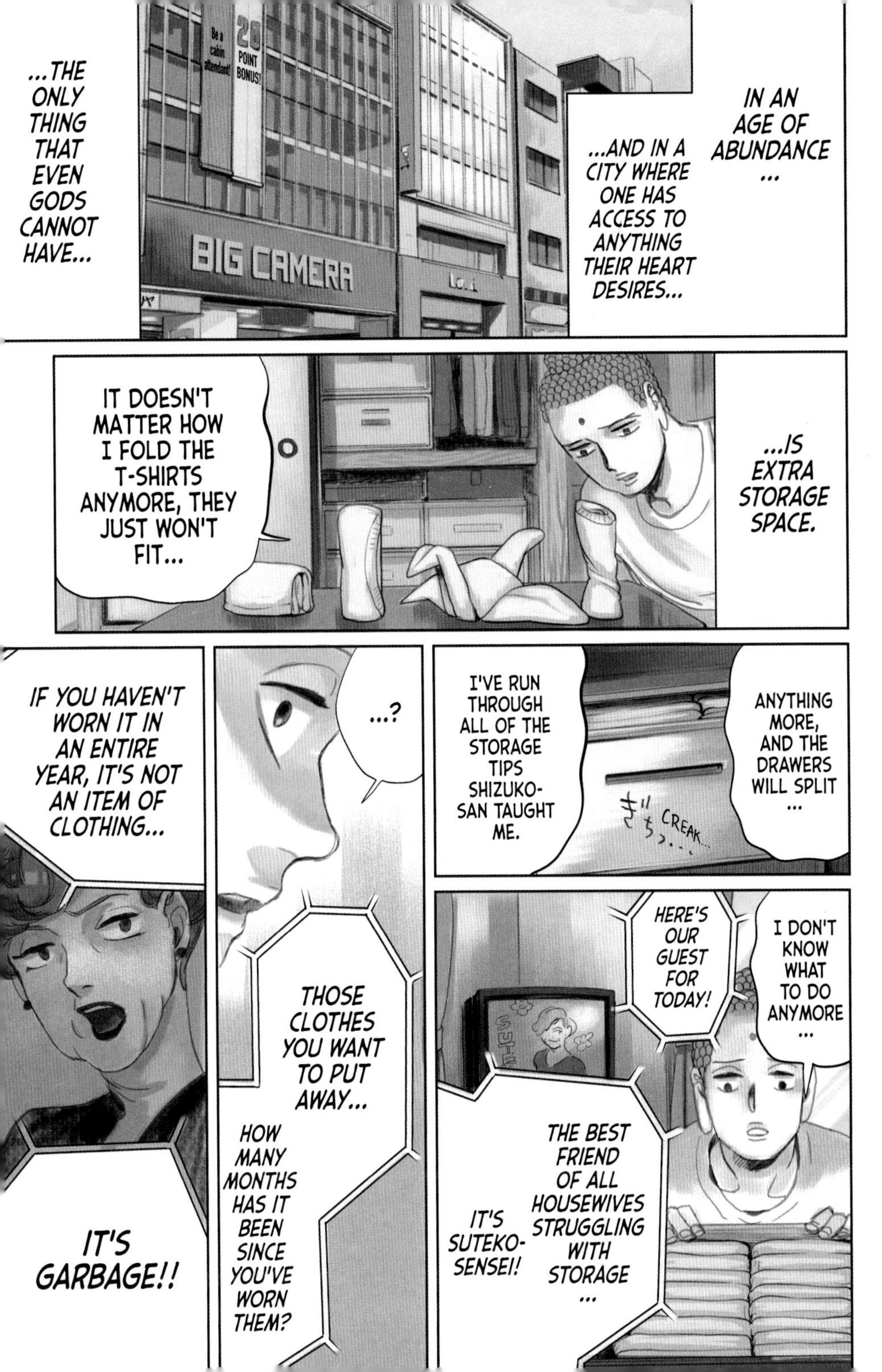
IN AN AGE OF ABUNDANCE...
...AND IN A CITY WHERE ONE HAS ACCESS TO ANYTHING THEIR HEART DESIRES...
Be a cabin attendant!
20 POINT BONUS!
BIG CAMERA
...THE ONLY THING THAT EVEN GODS CANNOT HAVE...
...IS EXTRA STORAGE SPACE.
IT DOESN'T MATTER HOW I FOLD THE T-SHIRTS ANYMORE, THEY JUST WON'T FIT...
ANYTHING MORE, AND THE DRAWERS WILL SPLIT...
I'VE RUN THROUGH ALL OF THE STORAGE TIPS SHIZUKO-SAN TAUGHT ME.
ぎちっ... CREAK...
I DON'T KNOW WHAT TO DO ANYMORE...
HERE'S OUR GUEST FOR TODAY!
THE BEST FRIEND OF ALL HOUSEWIVES STRUGGLING WITH STORAGE...
IT'S SUTEKO-SENSEI!
...?
THOSE CLOTHES YOU WANT TO PUT AWAY...
HOW MANY MONTHS HAS IT BEEN SINCE YOU'VE WORN THEM?
IF YOU HAVEN'T WORN IT IN AN ENTIRE YEAR, IT'S NOT AN ITEM OF CLOTHING...
IT'S GARBAGE!!

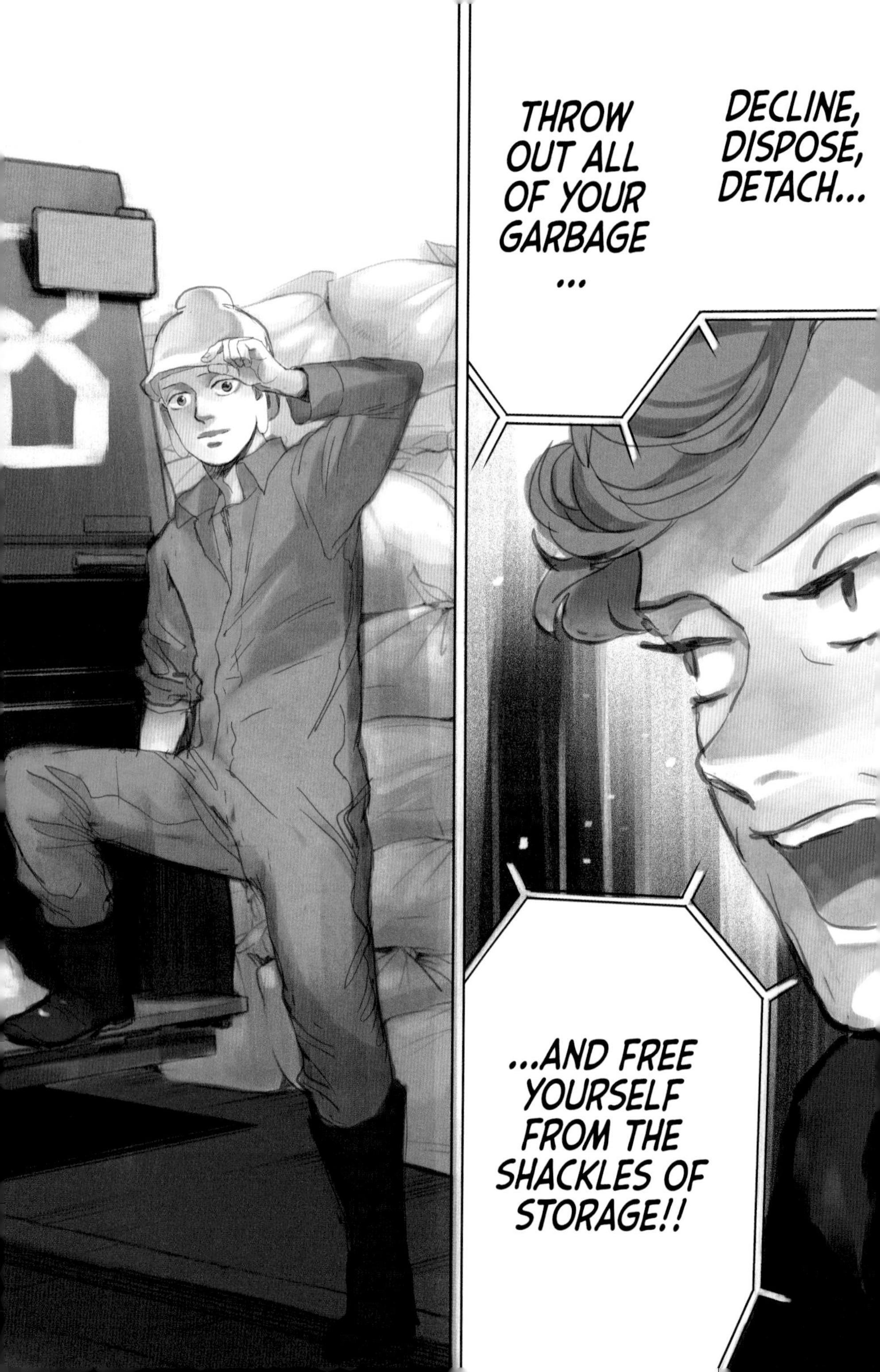
DECLINE, DISPOSE, DETACH...
THROW OUT ALL OF YOUR GARBAGE ...
...AND FREE YOURSELF FROM THE SHACKLES OF STORAGE!!

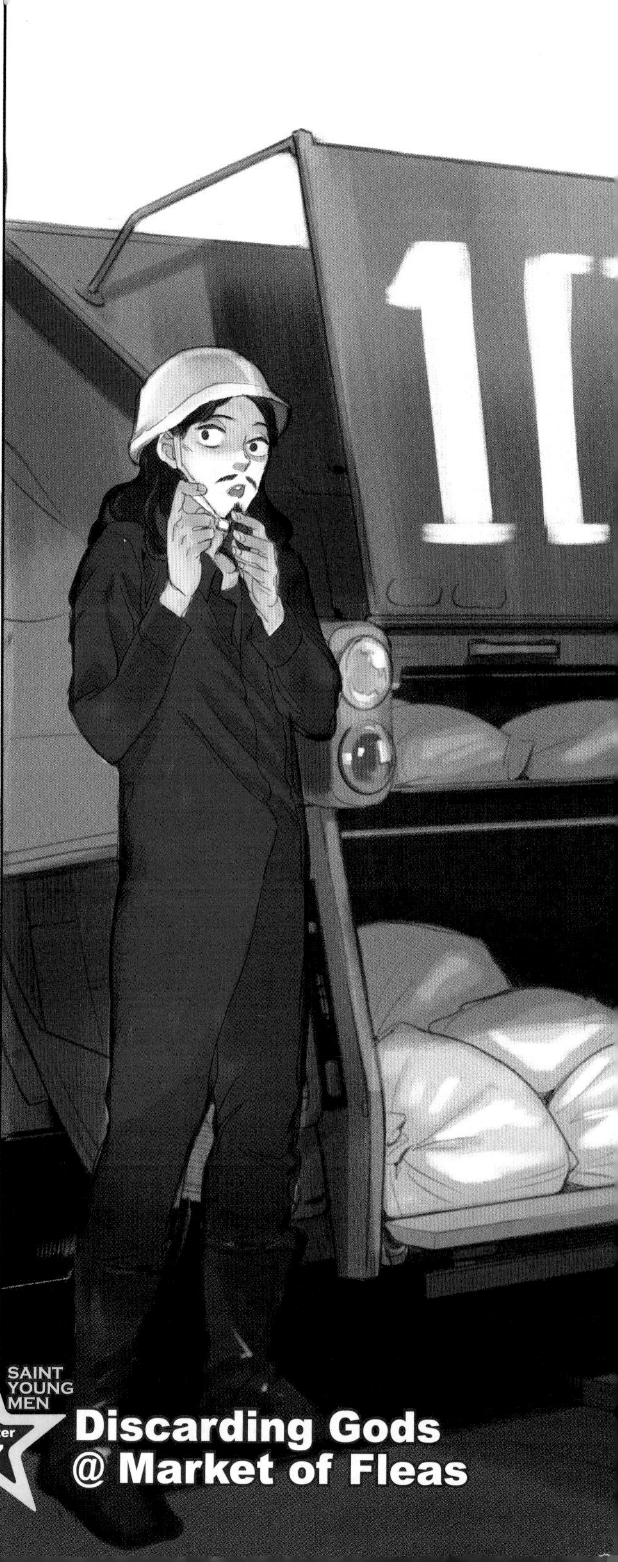
SAINT YOUNG MEN
Chapter 97
Discarding Gods @ Market of Fleas
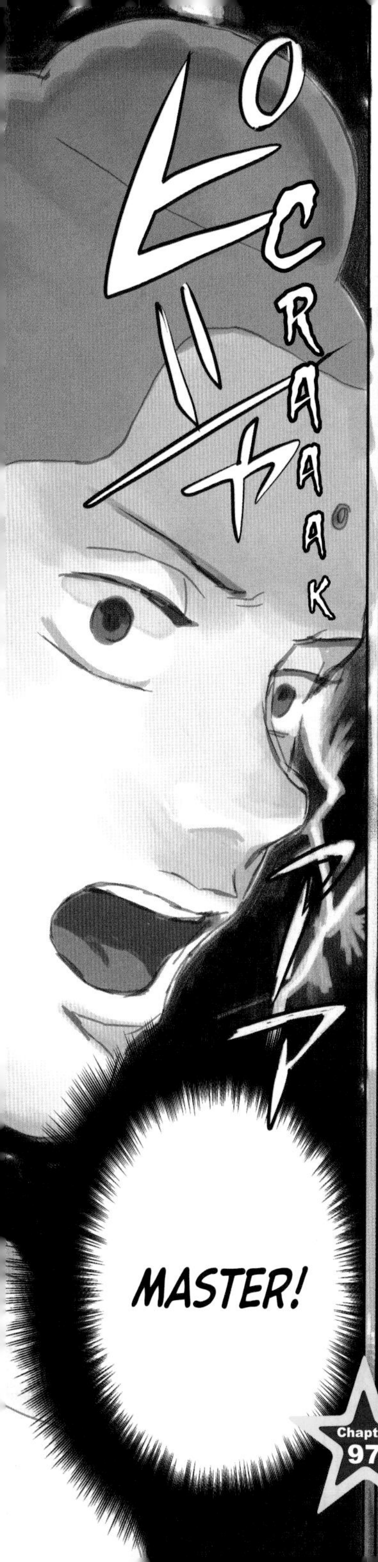
CRAAAK
MASTER!

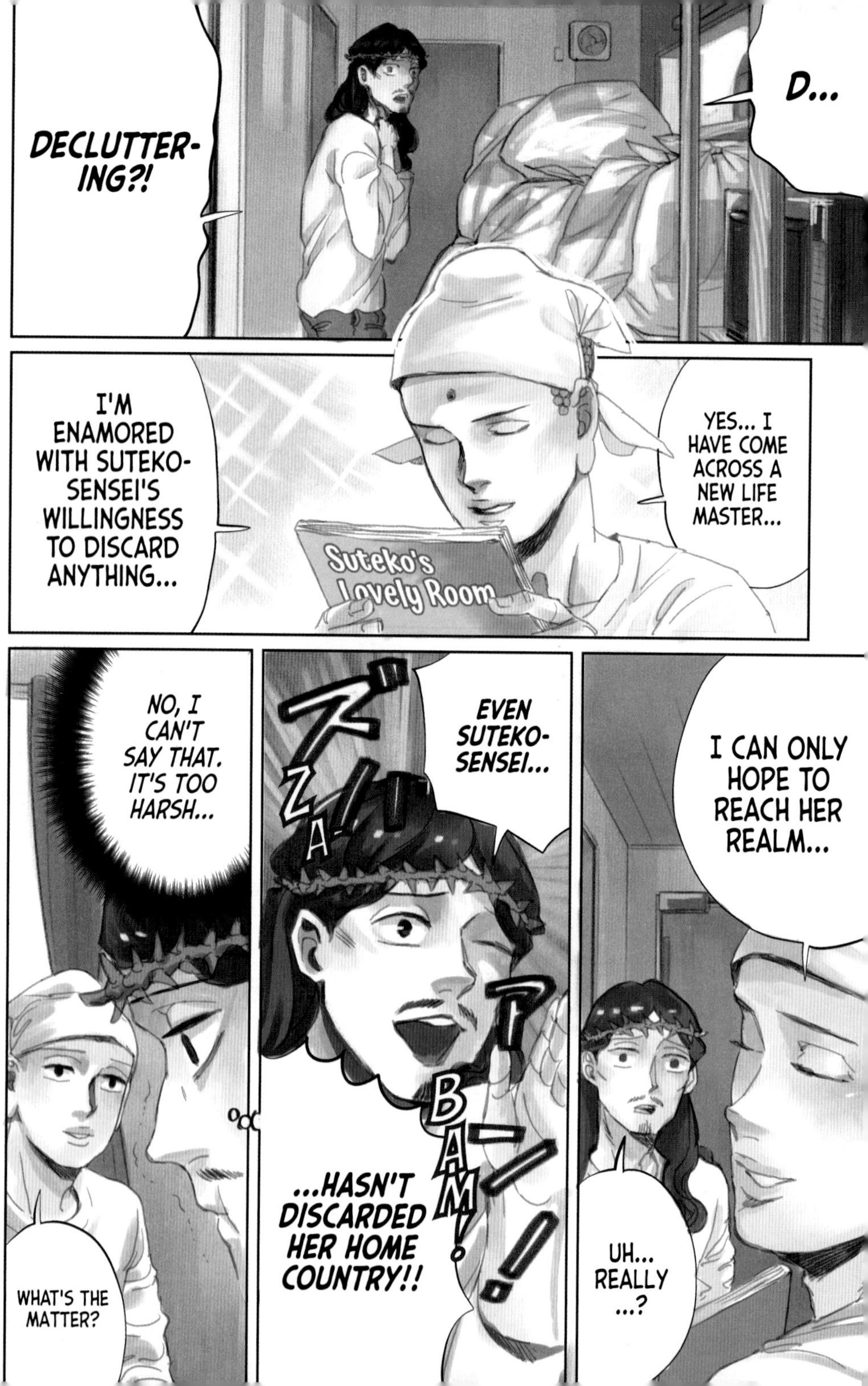
D...
DECLUTTER-ING?!
YES... I HAVE COME ACROSS A NEW LIFE MASTER...
I'M ENAMORED WITH SUTEKO-SENSEI'S WILLINGNESS TO DISCARD ANYTHING...
Suteko's Lovely Room
I CAN ONLY HOPE TO REACH HER REALM...
UH... REALLY ...?
EVEN SUTEKO-SENSEI...
ZA!
BAM!
...HASN'T DISCARDED HER HOME COUNTRY!!
NO, I CAN'T SAY THAT. IT'S TOO HARSH...
WHAT'S THE MATTER?

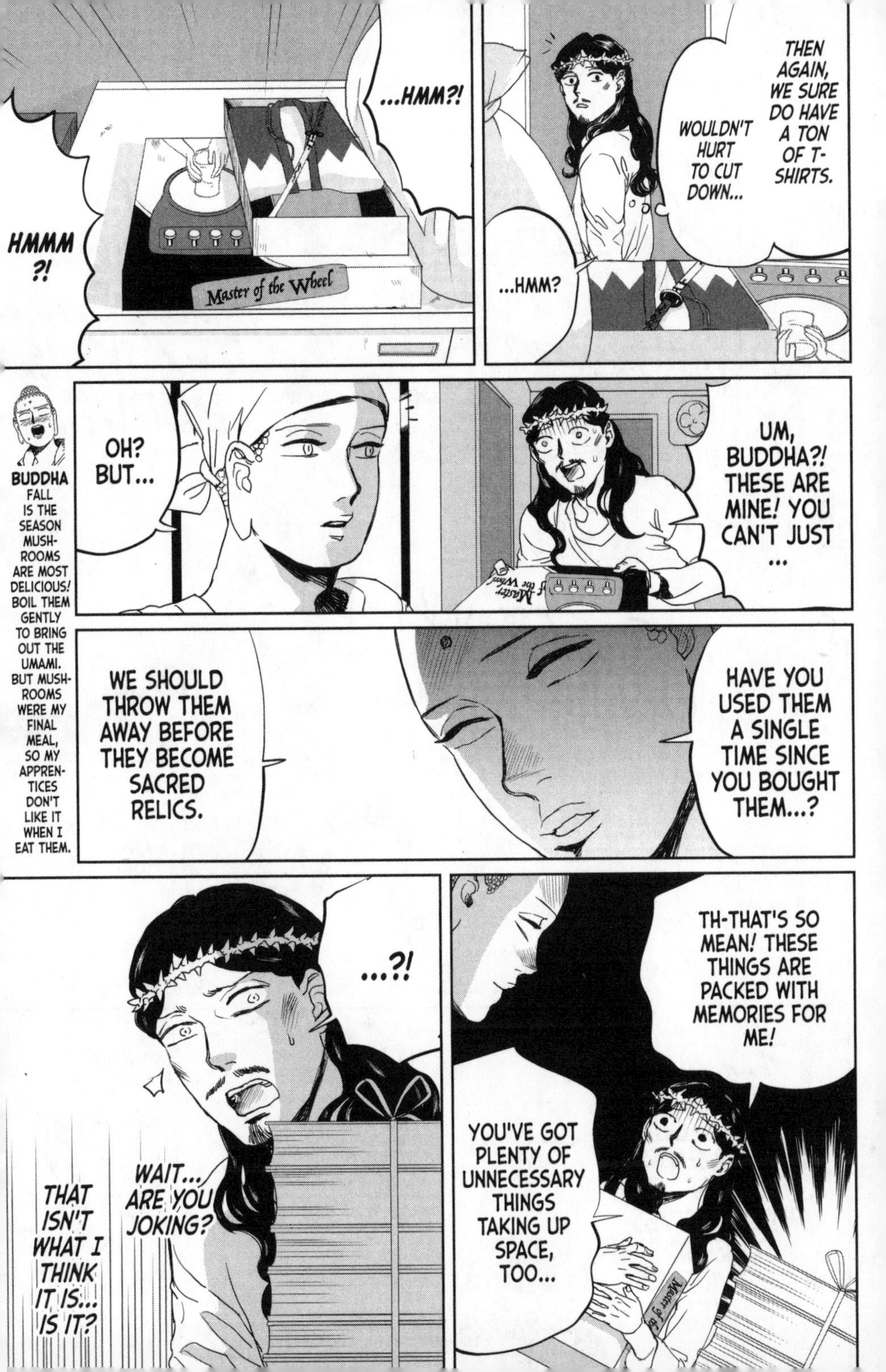
THEN AGAIN, WE SURE DO HAVE A TON OF T-SHIRTS.
WOULDN'T HURT TO CUT DOWN...
...HMM?
...HMM?!
HMMM ?!
Master of the Wheel
UM, BUDDHA?! THESE ARE MINE! YOU CAN'T JUST ...
OH? BUT...
HAVE YOU USED THEM A SINGLE TIME SINCE YOU BOUGHT THEM...?
WE SHOULD THROW THEM AWAY BEFORE THEY BECOME SACRED RELICS.
BUDDHA
FALL IS THE SEASON MUSHROOMS ARE MOST DELICIOUS! BOIL THEM GENTLY TO BRING OUT THE UMAMI. BUT MUSHROOMS WERE MY FINAL MEAL, SO MY APPRENTICES DON'T LIKE IT WHEN I EAT THEM.
TH-THAT'S SO MEAN! THESE THINGS ARE PACKED WITH MEMORIES FOR ME!
YOU'VE GOT PLENTY OF UNNECESSARY THINGS TAKING UP SPACE, TOO...
...?!
WAIT... ARE YOU JOKING?
THAT ISN'T WHAT I THINK IT IS... IS IT?

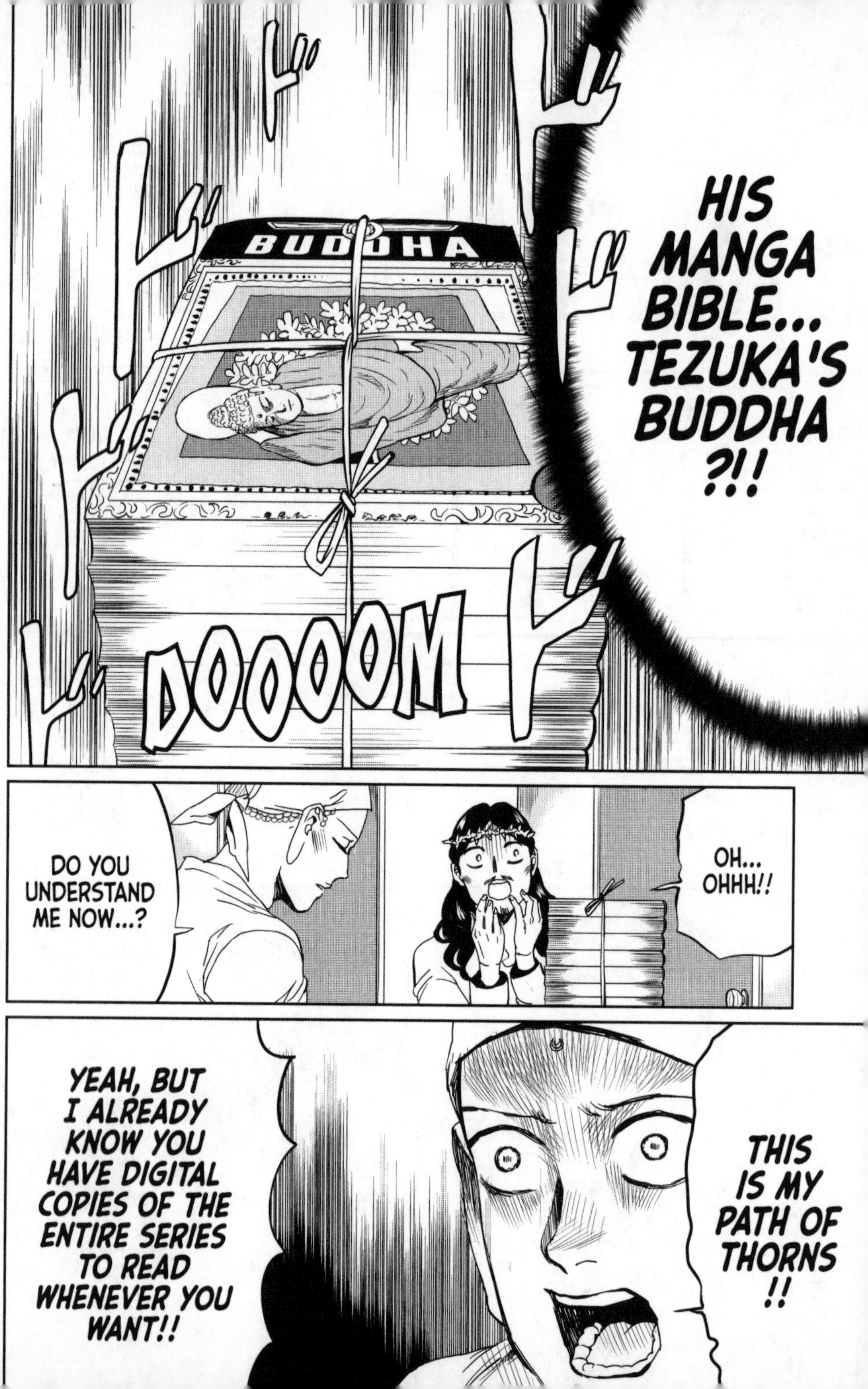
HIS MANGA BIBLE... TEZUKA'S BUDDHA ?!!
BUDDHA
DOOOM
OH... OHHH!!
DO YOU UNDERSTAND ME NOW...?
THIS IS MY PATH OF THORNS !!
YEAH, BUT I ALREADY KNOW YOU HAVE DIGITAL COPIES OF THE ENTIRE SERIES TO READ WHENEVER YOU WANT!!

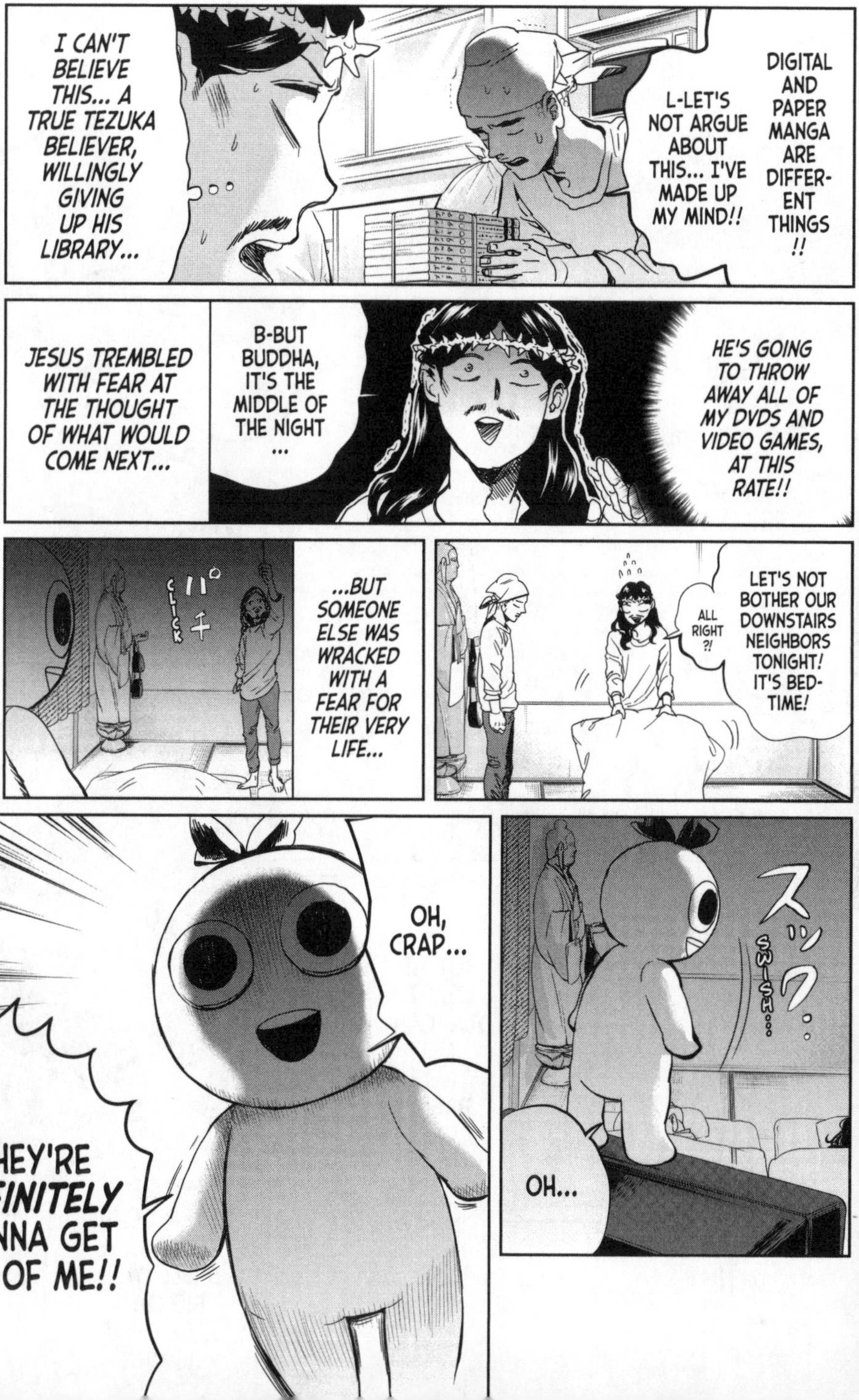
DIGITAL AND PAPER MANGA ARE DIFFERENT THINGS!!
L-LET'S NOT ARGUE ABOUT THIS... I'VE MADE UP MY MIND!!
I CAN'T BELIEVE THIS... A TRUE TEZUKA BELIEVER, WILLINGLY GIVING UP HIS LIBRARY...
HE'S GOING TO THROW AWAY ALL OF MY DVDS AND VIDEO GAMES, AT THIS RATE!!
B-BUT BUDDHA, IT'S THE MIDDLE OF THE NIGHT...
JESUS TREMBLED WITH FEAR AT THE THOUGHT OF WHAT WOULD COME NEXT...
LET'S NOT BOTHER OUR DOWNSTAIRS NEIGHBORS TONIGHT! IT'S BED-TIME!
ALL RIGHT?!
...BUT SOMEONE ELSE WAS WRACKED WITH A FEAR FOR THEIR VERY LIFE...
CLICK
SWISH...
OH...
OH, CRAP...
THEY'RE DEFINITELY GONNA GET RID OF ME!!

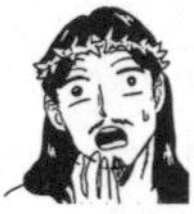

JESUS
FALL IS THE SEASON FOR PIKE!! TRADITIONALLY, THEY USE FANS TO BLOW AWAY THE SMOKINESS OF THE GRILLING. I WANT A TINY PORTABLE GRILL TO COOK IT, BUT WHENEVER I ASK, BUDDHA PRETENDS HE CAN'T HEAR ME.

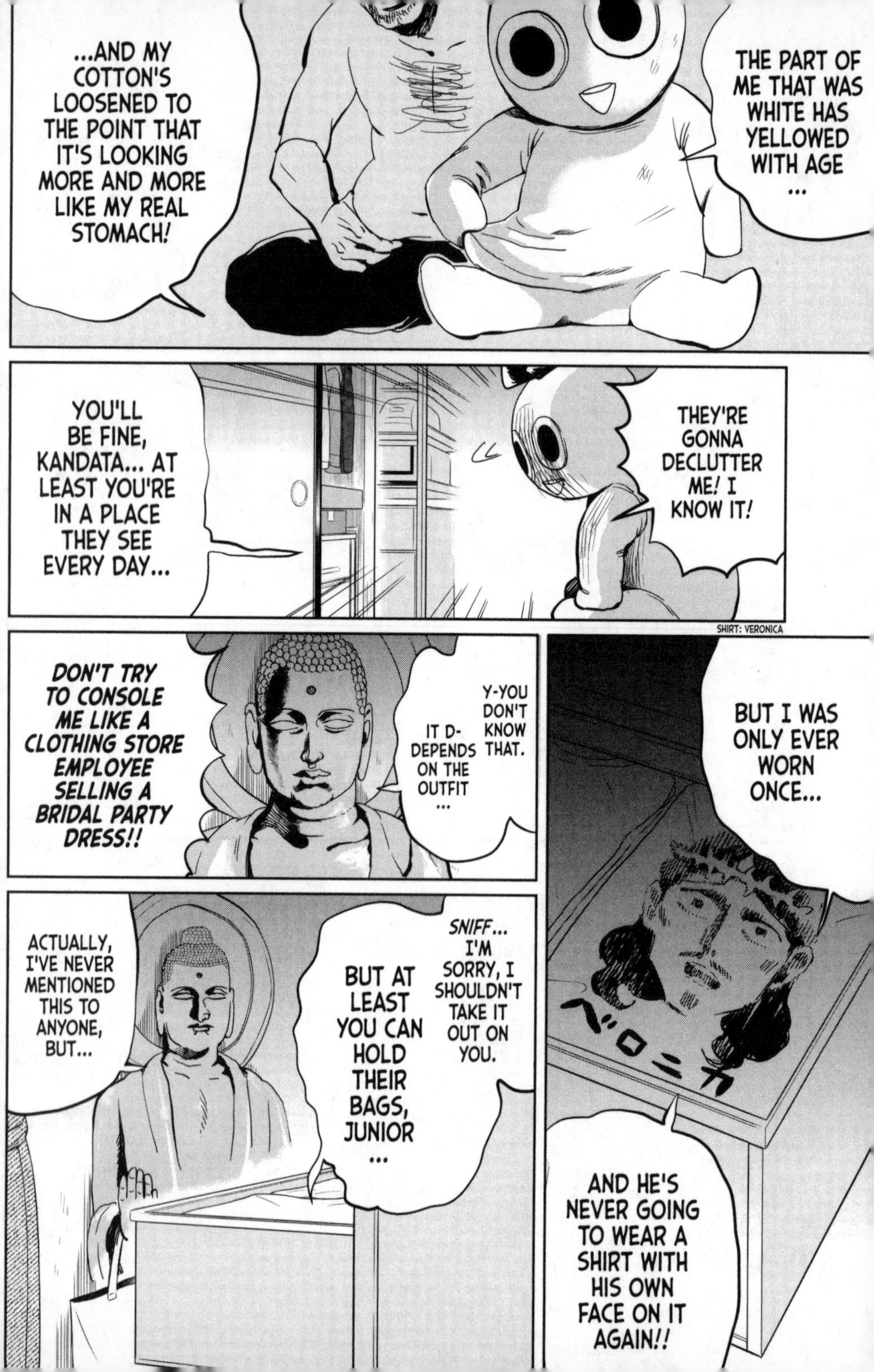

THE PART OF ME THAT WAS WHITE HAS YELLOWED WITH AGE...
...AND MY COTTON'S LOOSENED TO THE POINT THAT IT'S LOOKING MORE AND MORE LIKE MY REAL STOMACH!
THEY'RE GONNA DECLUTTER ME! I KNOW IT!
YOU'LL BE FINE, KANDATA... AT LEAST YOU'RE IN A PLACE THEY SEE EVERY DAY...
SHIRT: VERONICA
BUT I WAS ONLY EVER WORN ONCE...
ベロニカ
AND HE'S NEVER GOING TO WEAR A SHIRT WITH HIS OWN FACE ON IT AGAIN!!
Y-YOU DON'T KNOW THAT.
IT D-DEPENDS ON THE OUTFIT...
DON'T TRY TO CONSOLE ME LIKE A CLOTHING STORE EMPLOYEE SELLING A BRIDAL PARTY DRESS!!
SNIFF... I'M SORRY, I SHOULDN'T TAKE IT OUT ON YOU.
BUT AT LEAST YOU CAN HOLD THEIR BAGS, JUNIOR...
ACTUALLY, I'VE NEVER MENTIONED THIS TO ANYONE, BUT...

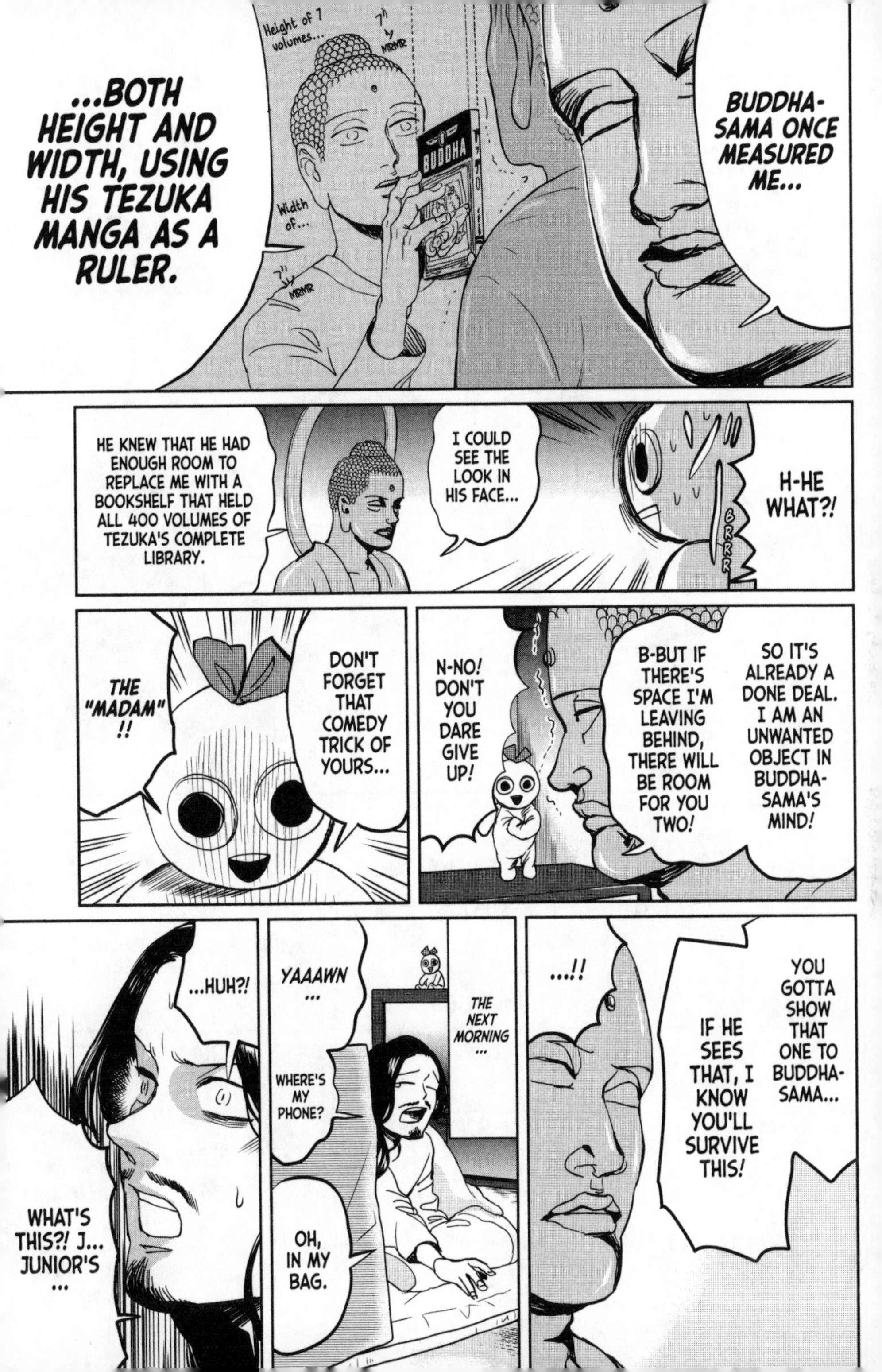
BUDDHA-SAMA ONCE MEASURED ME...
Height of 7 volumes...
MRMR
Width of...
MRMR
...BOTH HEIGHT AND WIDTH, USING HIS TEZUKA MANGA AS A RULER.
H-HE WHAT?!
BRRR
I COULD SEE THE LOOK IN HIS FACE...
HE KNEW THAT HE HAD ENOUGH ROOM TO REPLACE ME WITH A BOOKSHELF THAT HELD ALL 400 VOLUMES OF TEZUKA'S COMPLETE LIBRARY.
SO IT'S ALREADY A DONE DEAL. I AM AN UNWANTED OBJECT IN BUDDHA-SAMA'S MIND!
B-BUT IF THERE'S SPACE I'M LEAVING BEHIND, THERE WILL BE ROOM FOR YOU TWO!
N-NO! DON'T YOU DARE GIVE UP!
DON'T FORGET THAT COMEDY TRICK OF YOURS...
THE "MADAM"!!
YOU GOTTA SHOW THAT ONE TO BUDDHA-SAMA...
IF HE SEES THAT, I KNOW YOU'LL SURVIVE THIS!
...!!
THE NEXT MORNING...
YAAAWN...
WHERE'S MY PHONE?
OH, IN MY BAG.
...HUH?!
WHAT'S THIS?! J... JUNIOR'S...

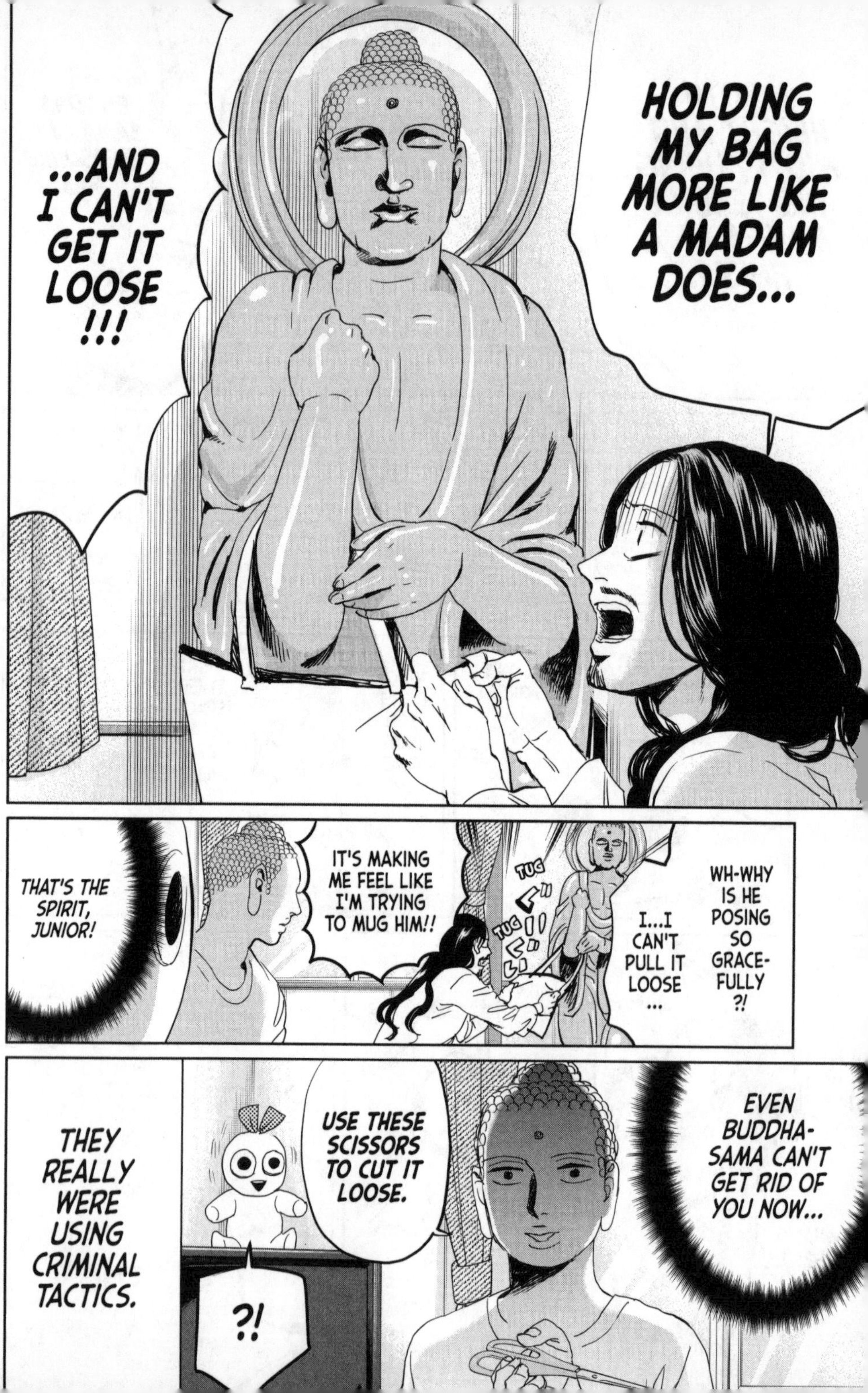
HOLDING MY BAG MORE LIKE A MADAM DOES...
...AND I CAN'T GET IT LOOSE !!!
WH-WHY IS HE POSING SO GRACE-FULLY ?!
I...I CAN'T PULL IT LOOSE ...
TUG
TUG
IT'S MAKING ME FEEL LIKE I'M TRYING TO MUG HIM!!
THAT'S THE SPIRIT, JUNIOR!
EVEN BUDDHA-SAMA CAN'T GET RID OF YOU NOW...
USE THESE SCISSORS TO CUT IT LOOSE.
?!
THEY REALLY WERE USING CRIMINAL TACTICS.

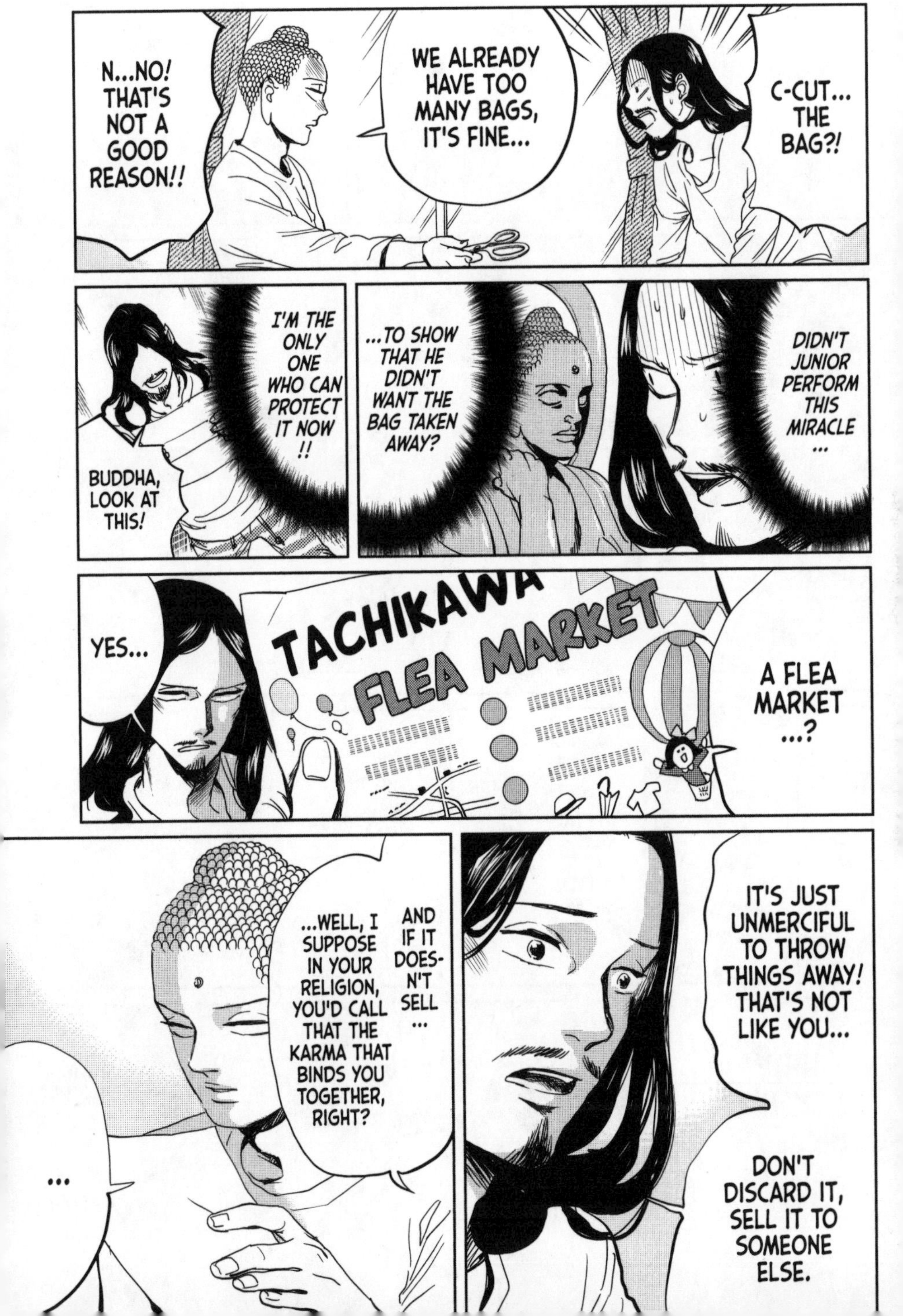
C-CUT... THE BAG?!
WE ALREADY HAVE TOO MANY BAGS, IT'S FINE...
N...NO! THAT'S NOT A GOOD REASON!!
DIDN'T JUNIOR PERFORM THIS MIRACLE ...
...TO SHOW THAT HE DIDN'T WANT THE BAG TAKEN AWAY?
I'M THE ONLY ONE WHO CAN PROTECT IT NOW !!
BUDDHA, LOOK AT THIS!
A FLEA MARKET ...?
TACHIKAWA FLEA MARKET
YES...
IT'S JUST UNMERCIFUL TO THROW THINGS AWAY! THAT'S NOT LIKE YOU...
DON'T DISCARD IT, SELL IT TO SOMEONE ELSE.
AND IF IT DOESN'T SELL ...
...WELL, I SUPPOSE IN YOUR RELIGION, YOU'D CALL THAT THE KARMA THAT BINDS YOU TOGETHER, RIGHT?
...

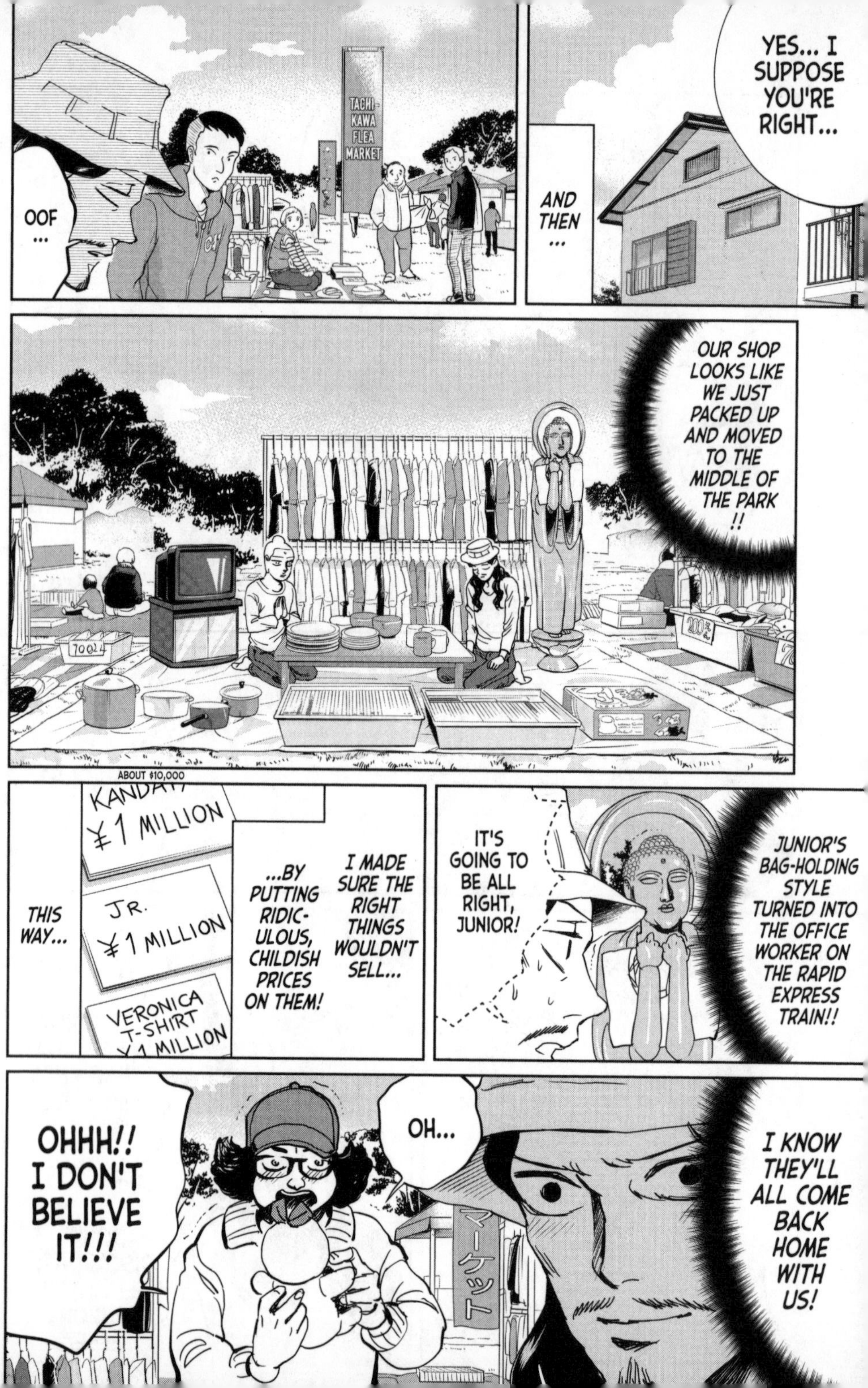
YES... I SUPPOSE YOU'RE RIGHT...
AND THEN ...
TACHI-KAWA FLEA MARKET
OOF ...
OUR SHOP LOOKS LIKE WE JUST PACKED UP AND MOVED TO THE MIDDLE OF THE PARK !!
JUNIOR'S BAG-HOLDING STYLE TURNED INTO THE OFFICE WORKER ON THE RAPID EXPRESS TRAIN!!
IT'S GOING TO BE ALL RIGHT, JUNIOR!
I MADE SURE THE RIGHT THINGS WOULDN'T SELL...
...BY PUTTING RIDICULOUS, CHILDISH PRICES ON THEM!
¥1 MILLION
JR. ¥1 MILLION
VERONICA T-SHIRT ¥1 MILLION
THIS WAY...
ABOUT $10,000
I KNOW THEY'LL ALL COME BACK HOME WITH US!
OH...
マーケット
OHHH!! I DON'T BELIEVE IT!!!

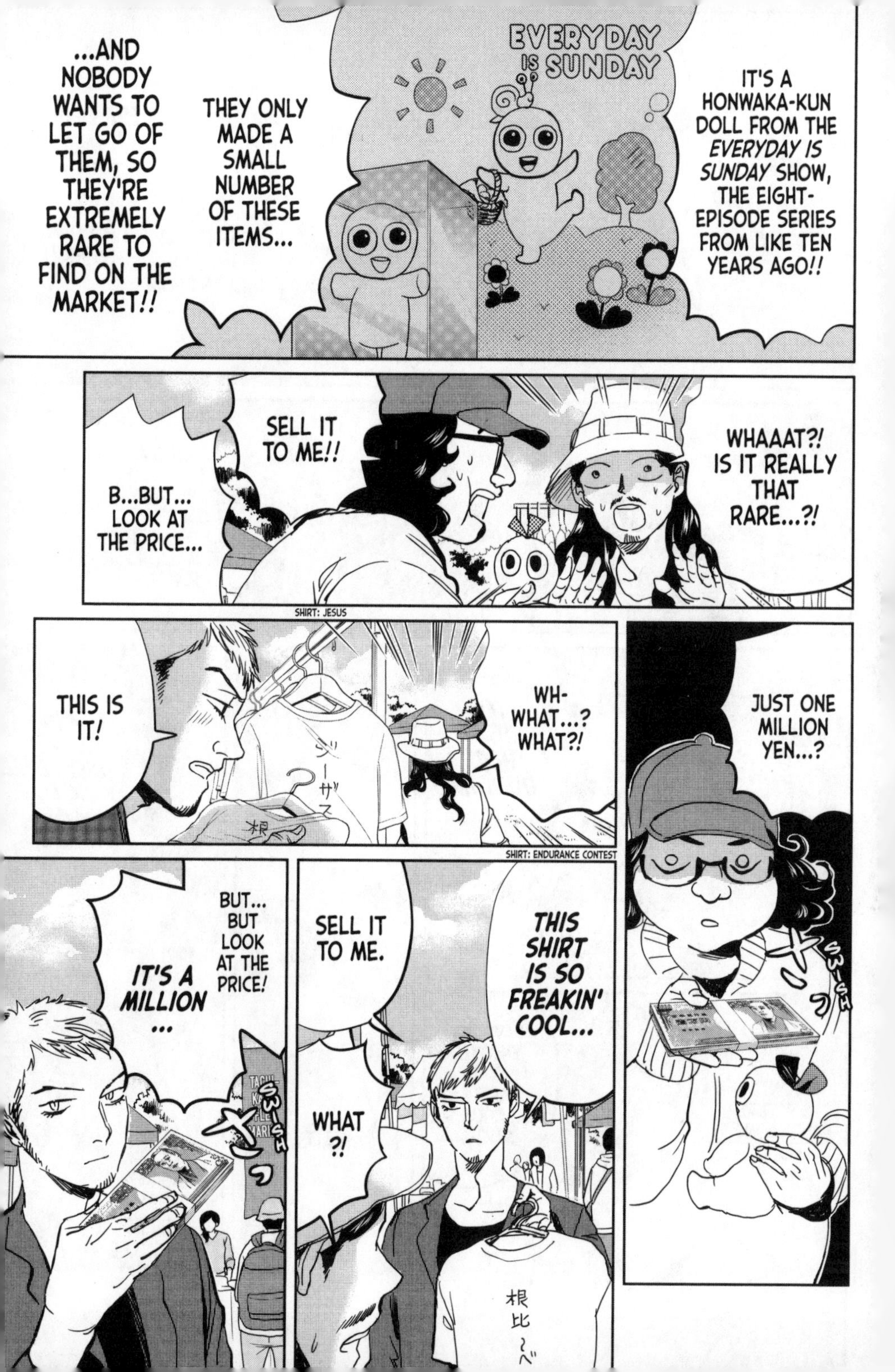
IT'S A HONWAKA-KUN DOLL FROM THE *EVERYDAY IS SUNDAY* SHOW, THE EIGHT-EPISODE SERIES FROM LIKE TEN YEARS AGO!!
EVERYDAY IS SUNDAY
THEY ONLY MADE A SMALL NUMBER OF THESE ITEMS...
...AND NOBODY WANTS TO LET GO OF THEM, SO THEY'RE EXTREMELY RARE TO FIND ON THE MARKET!!
WHAAAT?! IS IT REALLY THAT RARE...?!
SELL IT TO ME!!
B...BUT... LOOK AT THE PRICE...
SHIRT: JESUS
JUST ONE MILLION YEN...?
SWISH
WH-WHAT...? WHAT?!
ジーザス
THIS IS IT!
SHIRT: ENDURANCE CONTEST
THIS SHIRT IS SO FREAKIN' COOL...
SELL IT TO ME.
WHAT?!
根比べ
BUT... BUT LOOK AT THE PRICE!
IT'S A MILLION...
SWISH

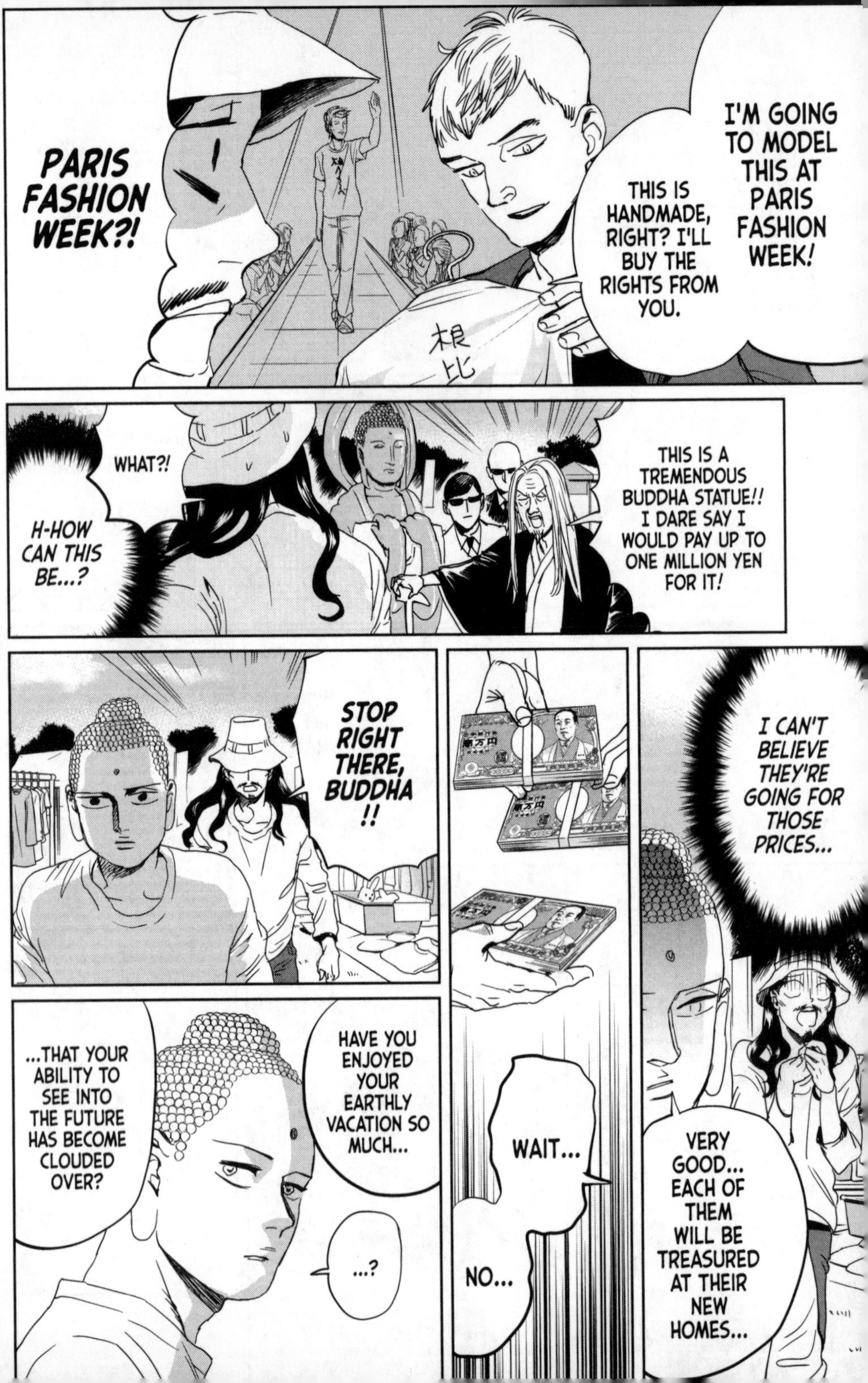
I'M GOING TO MODEL THIS AT PARIS FASHION WEEK!
THIS IS HANDMADE, RIGHT? I'LL BUY THE RIGHTS FROM YOU.
PARIS FASHION WEEK?!
根比
THIS IS A TREMENDOUS BUDDHA STATUE!! I DARE SAY I WOULD PAY UP TO ONE MILLION YEN FOR IT!
WHAT?!
H-HOW CAN THIS BE...?
I CAN'T BELIEVE THEY'RE GOING FOR THOSE PRICES...
VERY GOOD... EACH OF THEM WILL BE TREASURED AT THEIR NEW HOMES...
WAIT...
NO...
STOP RIGHT THERE, BUDDHA!!
HAVE YOU ENJOYED YOUR EARTHLY VACATION SO MUCH...
...THAT YOUR ABILITY TO SEE INTO THE FUTURE HAS BECOME CLOUDED OVER?
...?

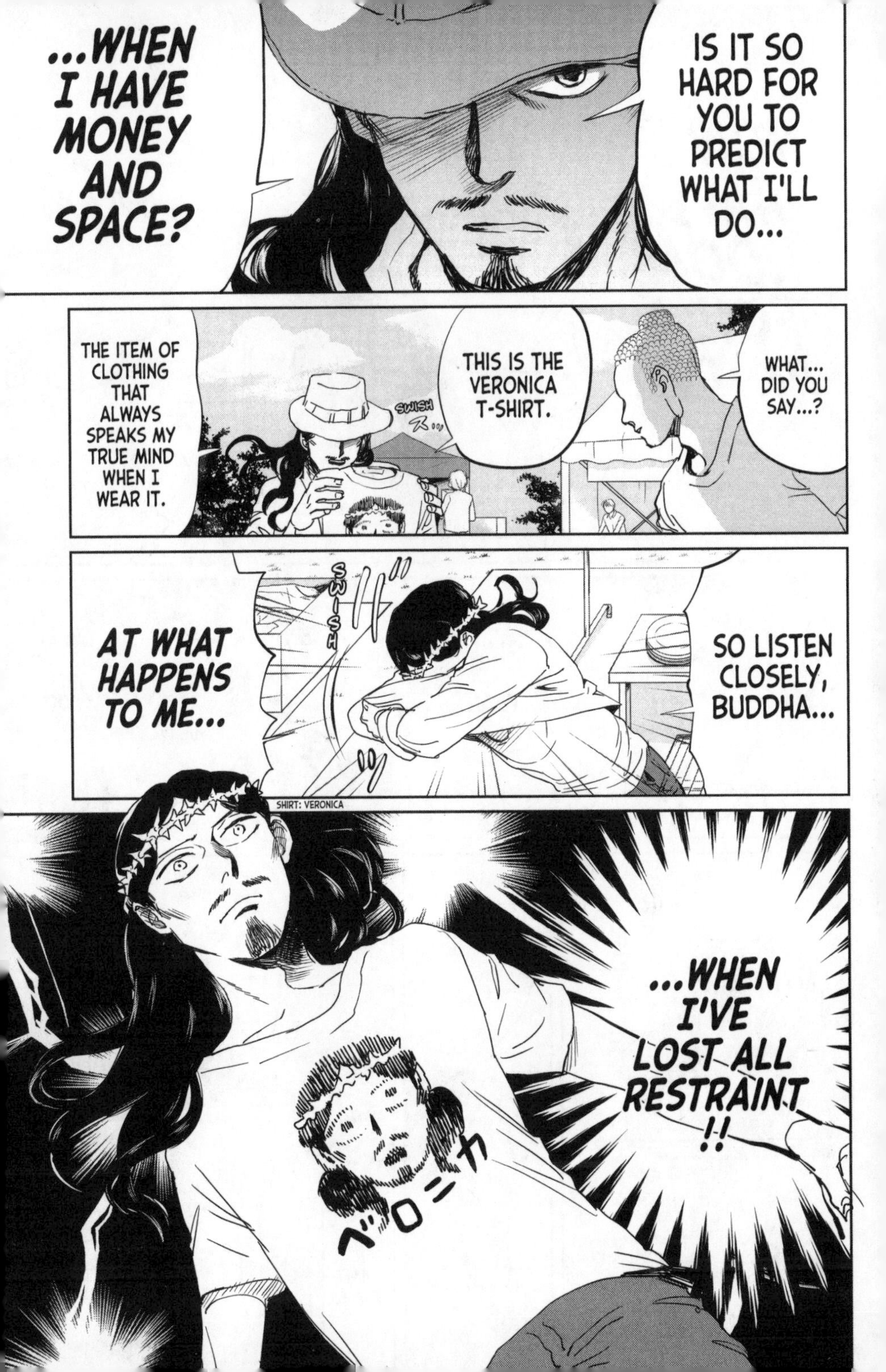
IS IT SO HARD FOR YOU TO PREDICT WHAT I'LL DO...
...WHEN I HAVE MONEY AND SPACE?
WHAT... DID YOU SAY...?
THIS IS THE VERONICA T-SHIRT.
SWISH
THE ITEM OF CLOTHING THAT ALWAYS SPEAKS MY TRUE MIND WHEN I WEAR IT.
SO LISTEN CLOSELY, BUDDHA...
SWISH
AT WHAT HAPPENS TO ME...
SHIRT: VERONICA
...WHEN I'VE LOST ALL RESTRAINT!!
ベロニカ

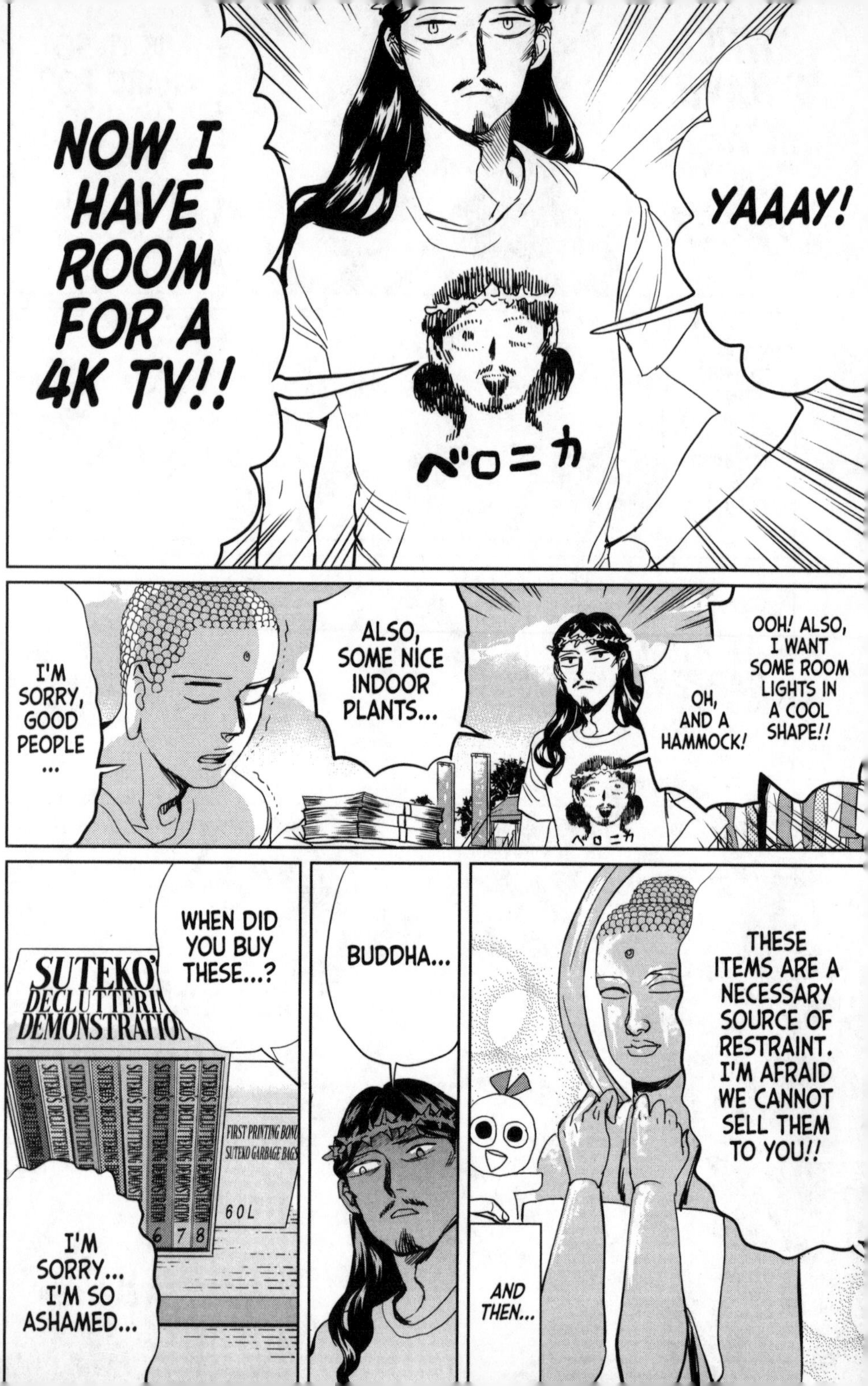
NOW I HAVE ROOM FOR A 4K TV!!
YAAAY!
ベロニカ
OOH! ALSO, I WANT SOME ROOM LIGHTS IN A COOL SHAPE!!
OH, AND A HAMMOCK!
ALSO, SOME NICE INDOOR PLANTS...
I'M SORRY, GOOD PEOPLE...
ベロニカ
THESE ITEMS ARE A NECESSARY SOURCE OF RESTRAINT. I'M AFRAID WE CANNOT SELL THEM TO YOU!!
AND THEN...
BUDDHA...
WHEN DID YOU BUY THESE...?
SUTEKO'
DECLUTTERI
DEMONSTRATIO
FIRST PRINTING BONU
SUTEKO GARBAGE BAGS
60L
6 7 8
I'M SORRY... I'M SO ASHAMED...

"Everyday is Sunday"
The Legendary Finale

Tomorrow...
at long
last...

...it will be
Monday...

SAINT☆YOUNG MEN

CHAPTER 97 TRANSLATION NOTES

Suteko-sensei, page 1
The name Suteko means "discarding child." It is technically a real name, although very rare, and in this case is clearly meant to refer to decluttering gurus like Marie Kondo.

108, page 3
The number 108 on the garbage truck is a reference to *bonnô*, or "worldly desires," which are attachments that tie an individual to earthly experience and prevent them from achieving nirvana.

Endurance Contest, page 13
This word in Japanese is pronounced *konkurabe*, but is written with the "a" extended, which intentionally makes it sound like "conclave," referring to the papal conclave, the meeting of Catholic cardinals to select the next pope.

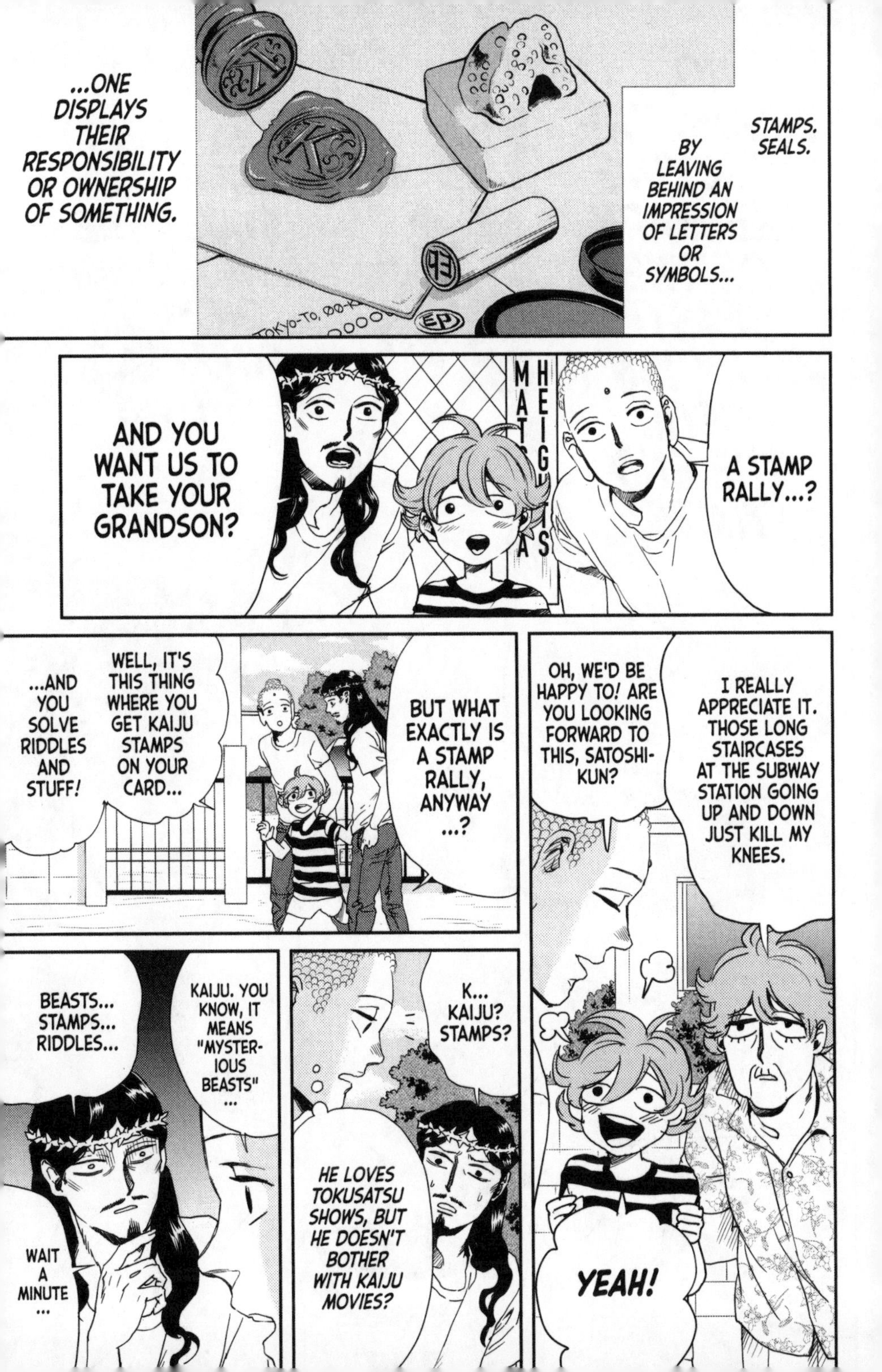
STAMPS. SEALS.
BY LEAVING BEHIND AN IMPRESSION OF LETTERS OR SYMBOLS...
...ONE DISPLAYS THEIR RESPONSIBILITY OR OWNERSHIP OF SOMETHING.
A STAMP RALLY...?
HEIGHTS
AND YOU WANT US TO TAKE YOUR GRANDSON?
I REALLY APPRECIATE IT. THOSE LONG STAIRCASES AT THE SUBWAY STATION GOING UP AND DOWN JUST KILL MY KNEES.
OH, WE'D BE HAPPY TO! ARE YOU LOOKING FORWARD TO THIS, SATOSHI-KUN?
YEAH!
BUT WHAT EXACTLY IS A STAMP RALLY, ANYWAY ...?
WELL, IT'S THIS THING WHERE YOU GET KAIJU STAMPS ON YOUR CARD...
...AND YOU SOLVE RIDDLES AND STUFF!
K... KAIJU? STAMPS?
HE LOVES TOKUSATSU SHOWS, BUT HE DOESN'T BOTHER WITH KAIJU MOVIES?
KAIJU. YOU KNOW, IT MEANS "MYSTER-IOUS BEASTS" ...
BEASTS... STAMPS... RIDDLES...
WAIT A MINUTE ...

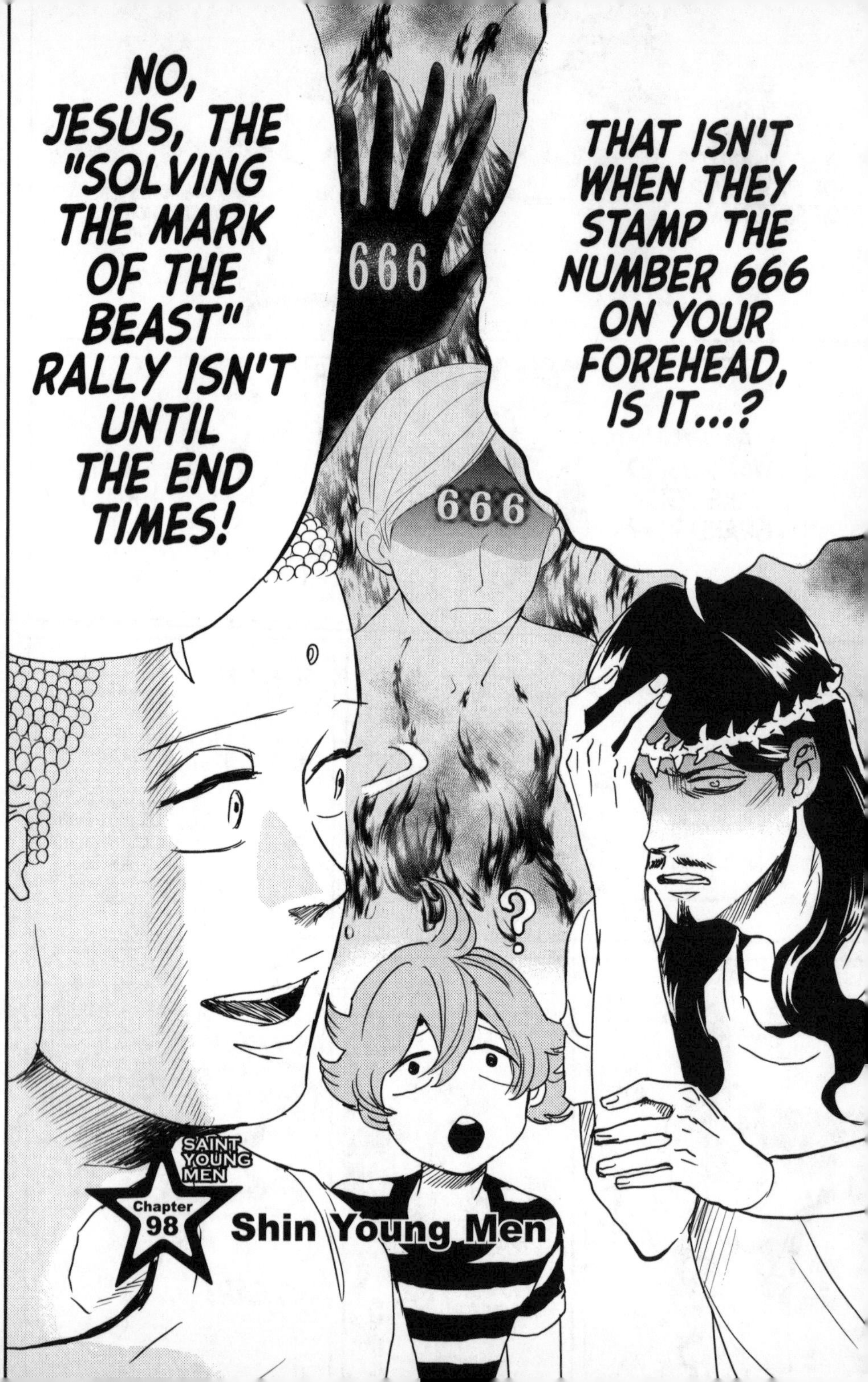
THAT ISN'T WHEN THEY STAMP THE NUMBER 666 ON YOUR FOREHEAD, IS IT...?
NO, JESUS, THE "SOLVING THE MARK OF THE BEAST" RALLY ISN'T UNTIL THE END TIMES!
666
666
?
SAINT YOUNG MEN
Chapter 98
Shin Young Men

BUDDHA
I HEAR THERE'S A TREND OF COLLECTING RED SHUIN STAMPS FROM TEMPLES. I'D GO, BUT MY VISIT THERE WOULD ONLY CAUSE A STIR... IT'S HARDER TO WEAR DISGUISES IN THE SUMMER.

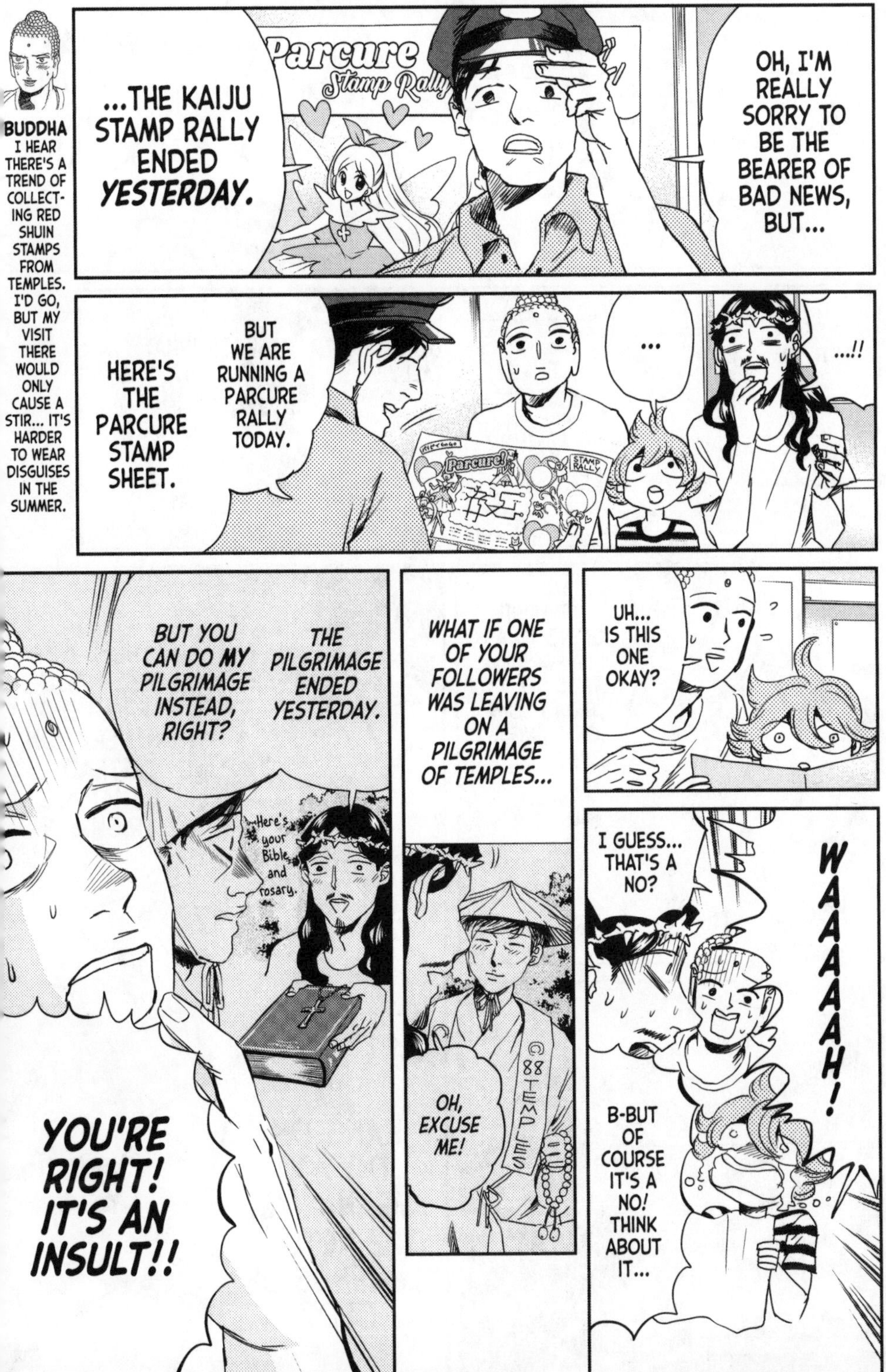

Parcure
Stamp Rally
OH, I'M REALLY SORRY TO BE THE BEARER OF BAD NEWS, BUT...
...THE KAIJU STAMP RALLY ENDED YESTERDAY.
...!!
...
BUT WE ARE RUNNING A PARCURE RALLY TODAY.
HERE'S THE PARCURE STAMP SHEET.
Parcure!
STAMP RALLY
UH... IS THIS ONE OKAY?
WAAAAAH!
I GUESS... THAT'S A NO?
B-BUT OF COURSE IT'S A NO! THINK ABOUT IT...
WHAT IF ONE OF YOUR FOLLOWERS WAS LEAVING ON A PILGRIMAGE OF TEMPLES...
88 TEMPLES
OH, EXCUSE ME!
THE PILGRIMAGE ENDED YESTERDAY.
BUT YOU CAN DO MY PILGRIMAGE INSTEAD, RIGHT?
Here's your Bible and rosary.
YOU'RE RIGHT! IT'S AN INSULT!!

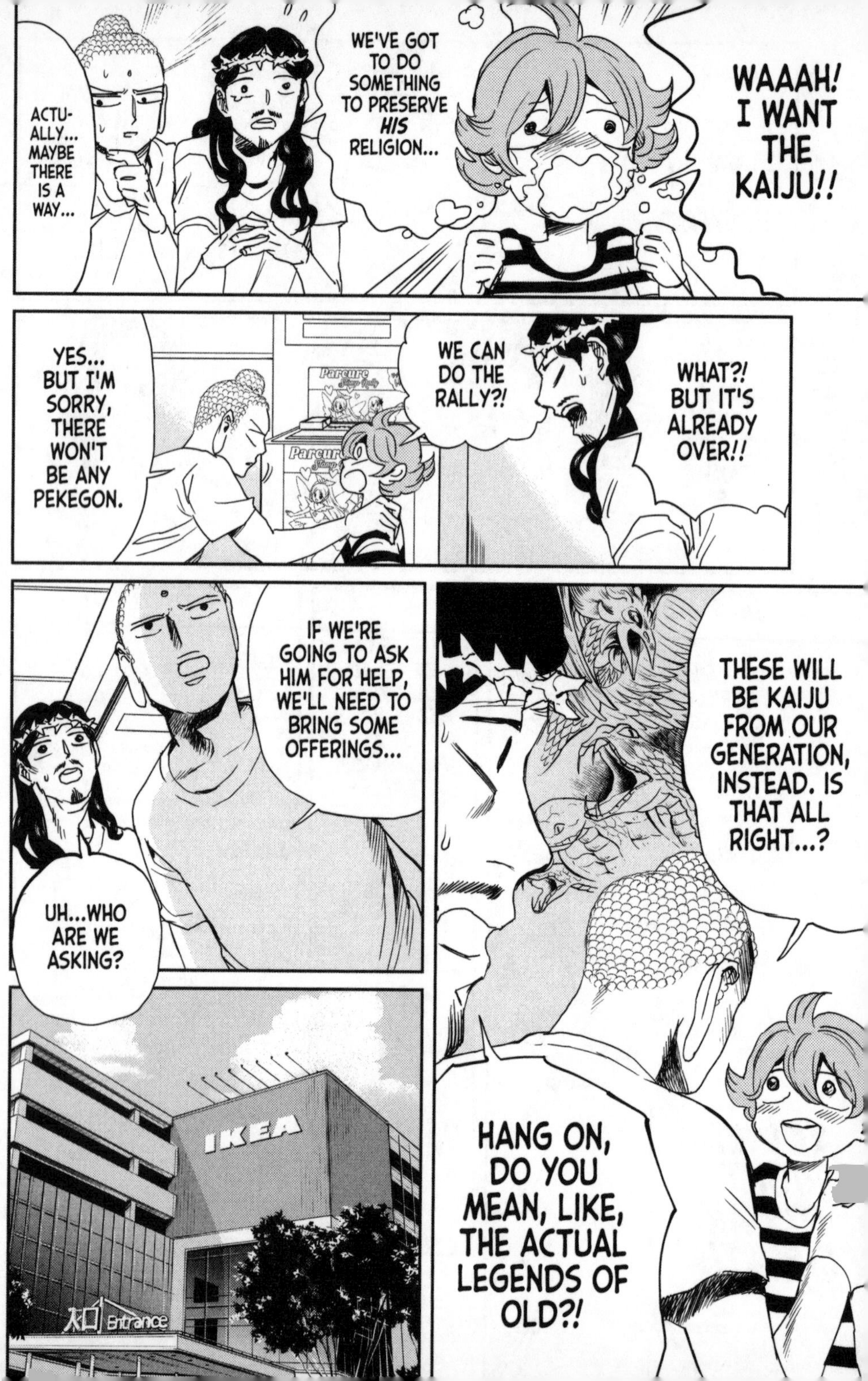
WAAAH! I WANT THE KAIJU!!
WE'VE GOT TO DO SOMETHING TO PRESERVE *HIS* RELIGION...
ACTU-ALLY... MAYBE THERE IS A WAY...
WHAT?! BUT IT'S ALREADY OVER!!
WE CAN DO THE RALLY?!
YES... BUT I'M SORRY, THERE WON'T BE ANY PEKEGON.
THESE WILL BE KAIJU FROM OUR GENERATION, INSTEAD. IS THAT ALL RIGHT...?
HANG ON, DO YOU MEAN, LIKE, THE ACTUAL LEGENDS OF OLD?!
IF WE'RE GOING TO ASK HIM FOR HELP, WE'LL NEED TO BRING SOME OFFERINGS...
UH...WHO ARE WE ASKING?
IKEA
入口 Entrance

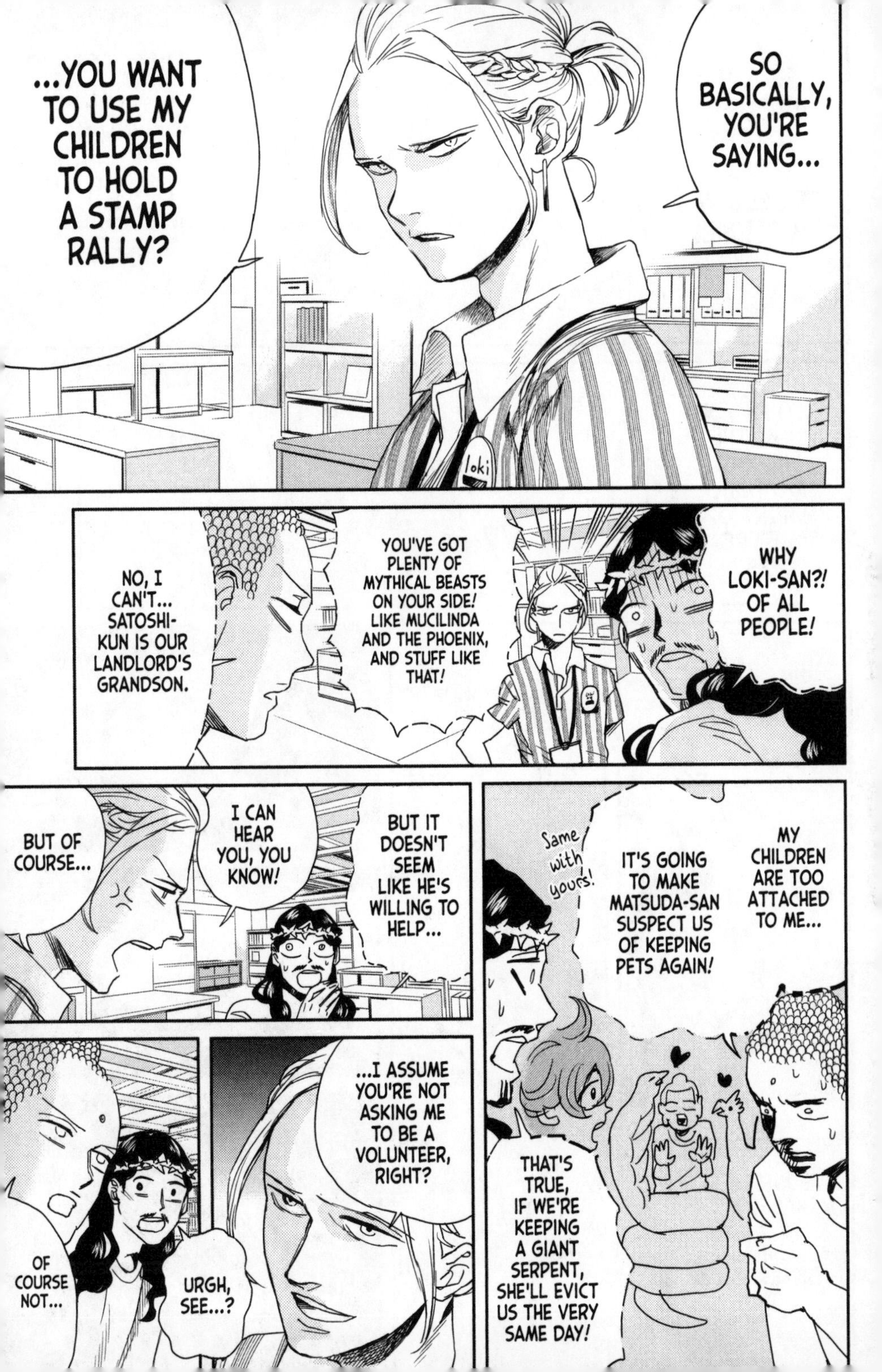
SO BASICALLY, YOU'RE SAYING...
...YOU WANT TO USE MY CHILDREN TO HOLD A STAMP RALLY?
loki
WHY LOKI-SAN?! OF ALL PEOPLE!
YOU'VE GOT PLENTY OF MYTHICAL BEASTS ON YOUR SIDE! LIKE MUCILINDA AND THE PHOENIX, AND STUFF LIKE THAT!
NO, I CAN'T... SATOSHI-KUN IS OUR LANDLORD'S GRANDSON.
MY CHILDREN ARE TOO ATTACHED TO ME...
IT'S GOING TO MAKE MATSUDA-SAN SUSPECT US OF KEEPING PETS AGAIN!
Same with yours!
THAT'S TRUE, IF WE'RE KEEPING A GIANT SERPENT, SHE'LL EVICT US THE VERY SAME DAY!
BUT IT DOESN'T SEEM LIKE HE'S WILLING TO HELP...
I CAN HEAR YOU, YOU KNOW!
BUT OF COURSE...
...I ASSUME YOU'RE NOT ASKING ME TO BE A VOLUNTEER, RIGHT?
URGH, SEE...?
OF COURSE NOT...

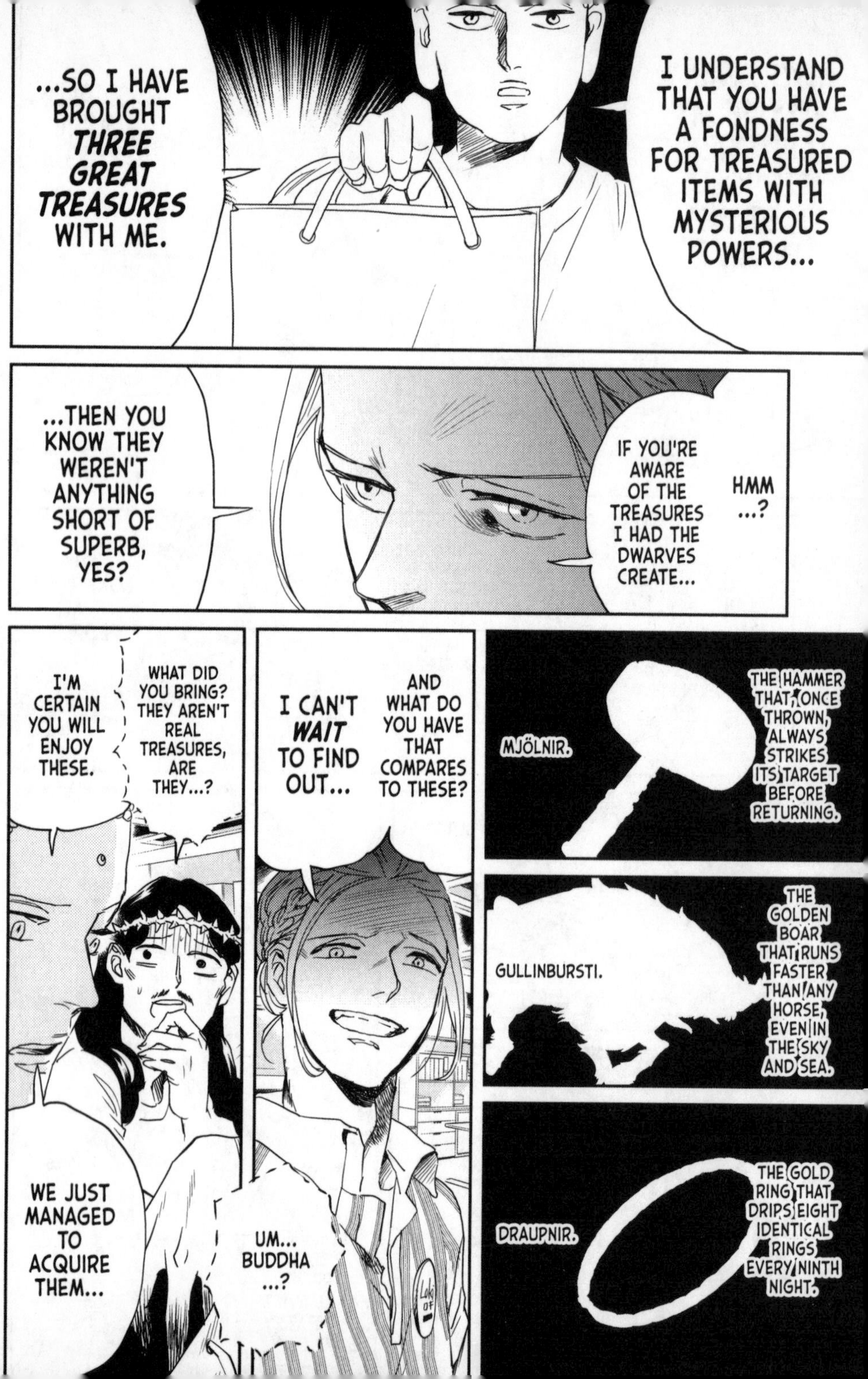
I UNDERSTAND THAT YOU HAVE A FONDNESS FOR TREASURED ITEMS WITH MYSTERIOUS POWERS...
...SO I HAVE BROUGHT *THREE GREAT TREASURES* WITH ME.
HMM ...?
IF YOU'RE AWARE OF THE TREASURES I HAD THE DWARVES CREATE...
...THEN YOU KNOW THEY WEREN'T ANYTHING SHORT OF SUPERB, YES?
THE HAMMER THAT, ONCE THROWN, ALWAYS STRIKES ITS TARGET BEFORE RETURNING.
MJÖLNIR.
THE GOLDEN BOAR THAT RUNS FASTER THAN ANY HORSE, EVEN IN THE SKY AND SEA.
GULLINBURSTI.
THE GOLD RING THAT DRIPS EIGHT IDENTICAL RINGS EVERY NINTH NIGHT.
DRAUPNIR.
AND WHAT DO YOU HAVE THAT COMPARES TO THESE?
I CAN'T *WAIT* TO FIND OUT...
UM... BUDDHA ...?
WHAT DID YOU BRING? THEY AREN'T REAL TREASURES, ARE THEY...?
I'M CERTAIN YOU WILL ENJOY THESE.
WE JUST MANAGED TO ACQUIRE THEM...

THE GLOOPY AND FLOWING, YET NEVER STICKING TO THE HANDS...
...THINGY!!
THE EXTENDABLE AND RETRACTABLE UPON A SINGLE SWING...
...WHATSIT!!
THE LONG, WHISTLING, HOLLOW...
...WHIPPY GUY!!
WHAT... ARE THOSE ...?
HEY... YOU GOT THOSE FROM THAT TOY STORE WE STOPPED AT...
SEE, LOKI-SAN SEEMS TO HAVE A WEAKNESS FOR STRANGE, INEXPLICABLE THINGS...
YES, I'LL ADMIT THEY *ARE* STRANGE!
BUT I DON'T THINK IT'S THE KIND OF STRANGE HE'S LOOKING FOR...
IT'S NOT JUST A CHOICE OF OPTIONS, RIGHT? I GET ALL THREE?
REALLY?! IT'S **EXACTLY** *THE KIND OF STRANGE HE'S LOOKING FOR?!!*

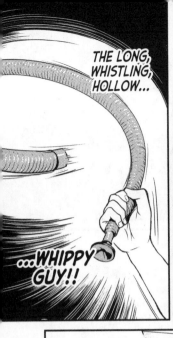

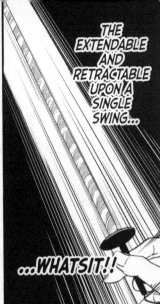

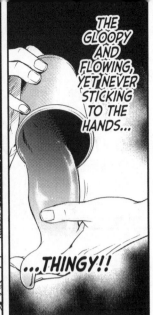

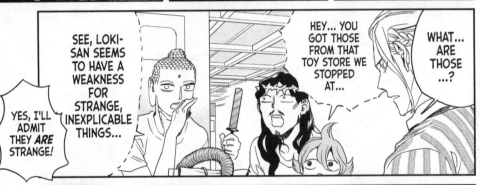

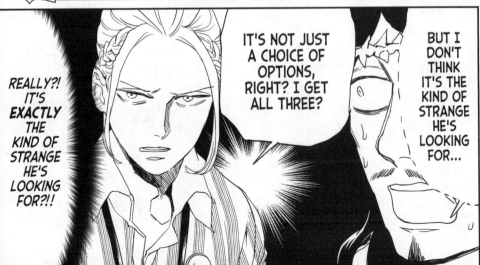

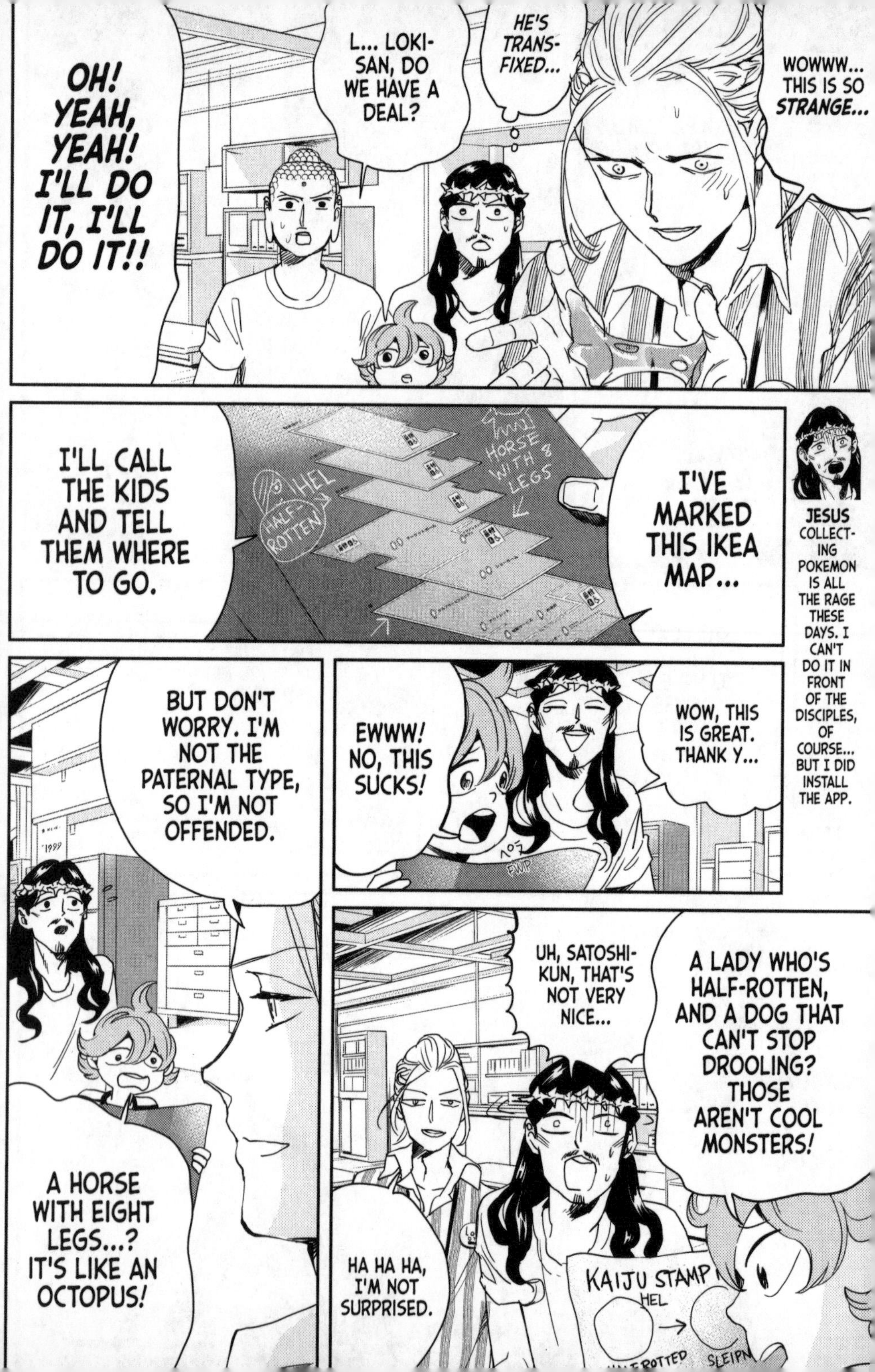
WOWWW... THIS IS SO STRANGE...
HE'S TRANS-FIXED...
L... LOKI-SAN, DO WE HAVE A DEAL?
OH! YEAH, YEAH! I'LL DO IT, I'LL DO IT!!
I'VE MARKED THIS IKEA MAP...
HORSE WITH 8 LEGS
HEL
HALF-ROTTEN
I'LL CALL THE KIDS AND TELL THEM WHERE TO GO.
JESUS
COLLECTING POKEMON IS ALL THE RAGE THESE DAYS. I CAN'T DO IT IN FRONT OF THE DISCIPLES, OF COURSE... BUT I DID INSTALL THE APP.
WOW, THIS IS GREAT. THANK Y...
EWWW! NO, THIS SUCKS!
FWP
A LADY WHO'S HALF-ROTTEN, AND A DOG THAT CAN'T STOP DROOLING? THOSE AREN'T COOL MONSTERS!
UH, SATOSHI-KUN, THAT'S NOT VERY NICE...
HA HA HA, I'M NOT SURPRISED.
KAIJU STAMP
HEL
BUT DON'T WORRY. I'M NOT THE PATERNAL TYPE, SO I'M NOT OFFENDED.
A HORSE WITH EIGHT LEGS...? IT'S LIKE AN OCTOPUS!

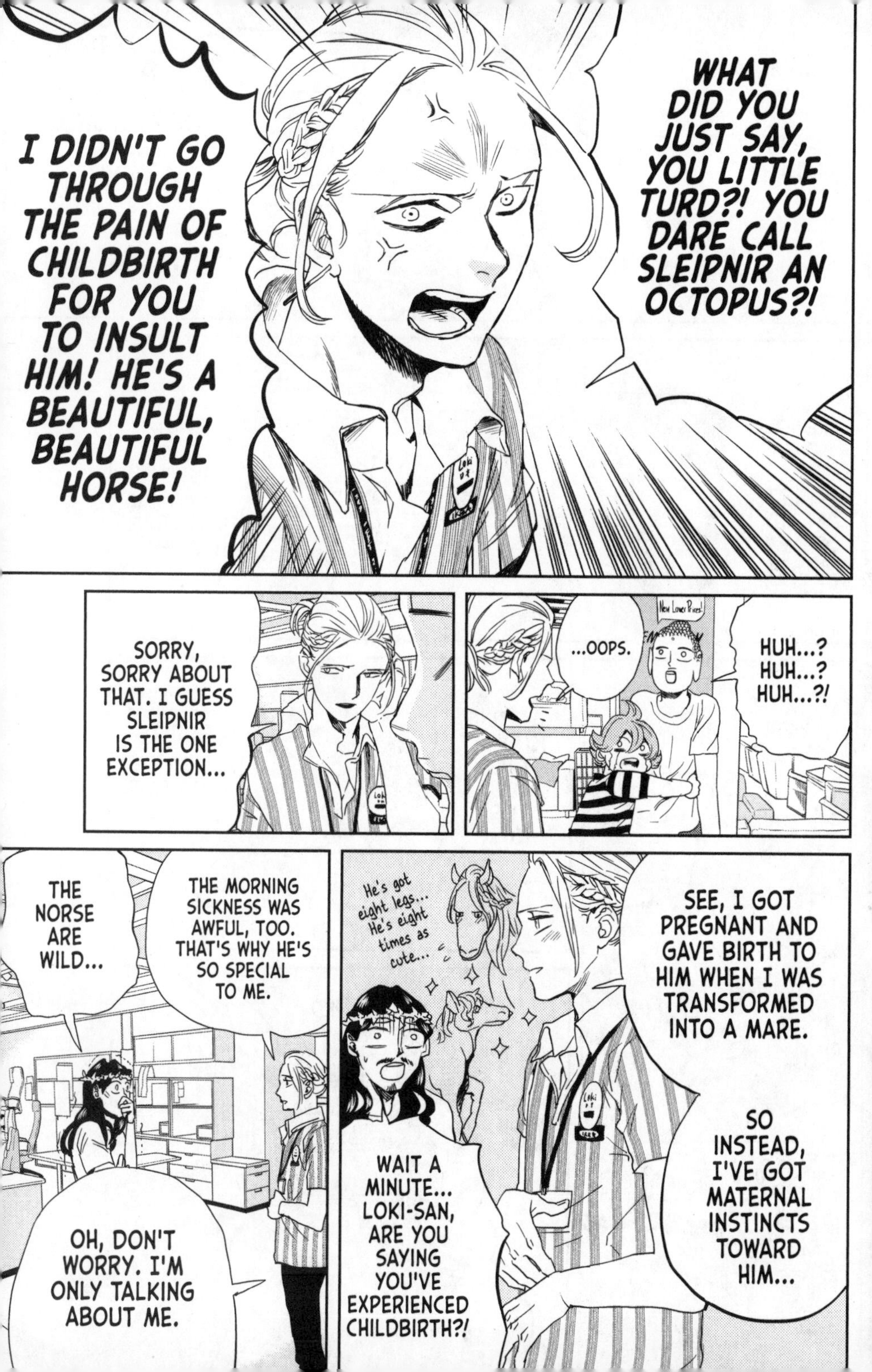
WHAT DID YOU JUST SAY, YOU LITTLE TURD?! YOU DARE CALL SLEIPNIR AN OCTOPUS?!
I DIDN'T GO THROUGH THE PAIN OF CHILDBIRTH FOR YOU TO INSULT HIM! HE'S A BEAUTIFUL, BEAUTIFUL HORSE!
HUH...? HUH...? HUH...?!
New Lower Prices!
...OOPS.
SORRY, SORRY ABOUT THAT. I GUESS SLEIPNIR IS THE ONE EXCEPTION...
SEE, I GOT PREGNANT AND GAVE BIRTH TO HIM WHEN I WAS TRANSFORMED INTO A MARE.
He's got eight legs... He's eight times as cute...
SO INSTEAD, I'VE GOT MATERNAL INSTINCTS TOWARD HIM...
WAIT A MINUTE... LOKI-SAN, ARE YOU SAYING YOU'VE EXPERIENCED CHILDBIRTH?!
THE MORNING SICKNESS WAS AWFUL, TOO. THAT'S WHY HE'S SO SPECIAL TO ME.
THE NORSE ARE WILD...
OH, DON'T WORRY. I'M ONLY TALKING ABOUT ME.

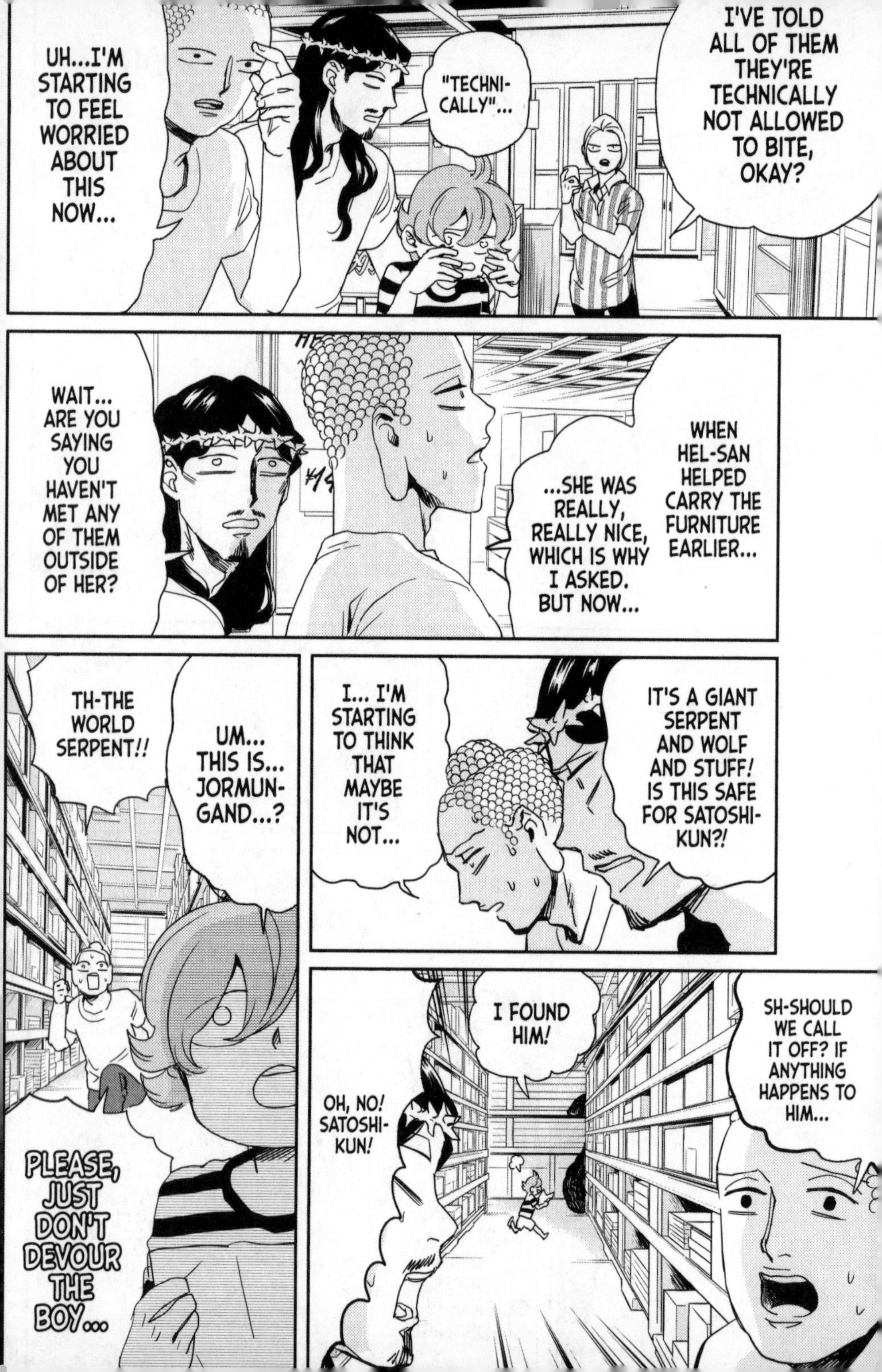
I'VE TOLD ALL OF THEM THEY'RE TECHNICALLY NOT ALLOWED TO BITE, OKAY?
"TECHNICALLY"...
UH...I'M STARTING TO FEEL WORRIED ABOUT THIS NOW...
WHEN HEL-SAN HELPED CARRY THE FURNITURE EARLIER...
...SHE WAS REALLY, REALLY NICE, WHICH IS WHY I ASKED. BUT NOW...
WAIT... ARE YOU SAYING YOU HAVEN'T MET ANY OF THEM OUTSIDE OF HER?
IT'S A GIANT SERPENT AND WOLF AND STUFF! IS THIS SAFE FOR SATOSHI-KUN?!
I... I'M STARTING TO THINK THAT MAYBE IT'S NOT...
SH-SHOULD WE CALL IT OFF? IF ANYTHING HAPPENS TO HIM...
I FOUND HIM!
OH, NO! SATOSHI-KUN!
UM... THIS IS... JORMUNGAND...?
TH-THE WORLD SERPENT!!
PLEASE, JUST DON'T DEVOUR THE BOY...

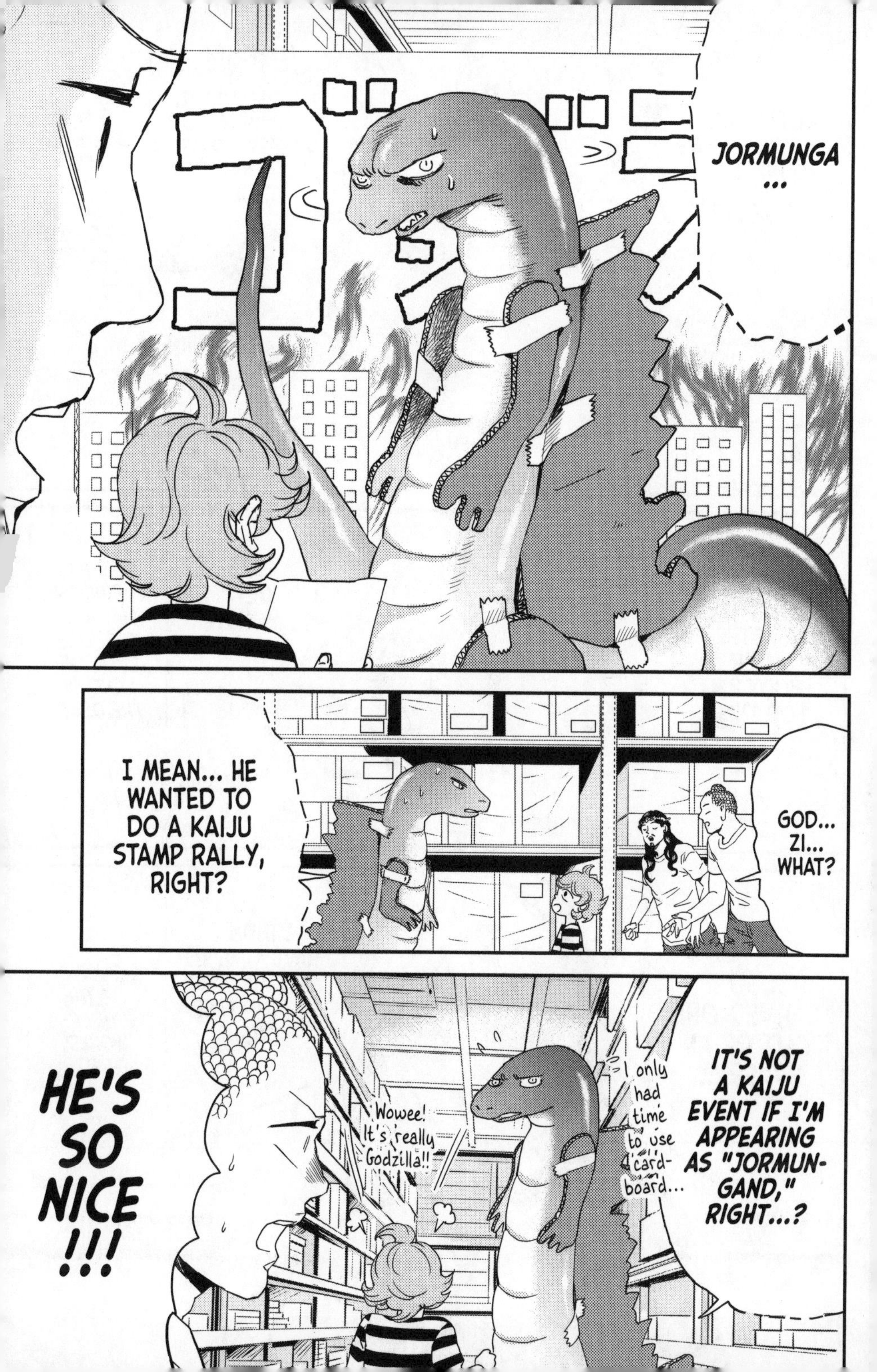
JORMUNGA...
GOD... ZI... WHAT?
I MEAN... HE WANTED TO DO A KAIJU STAMP RALLY, RIGHT?
IT'S NOT A KAIJU EVENT IF I'M APPEARING AS "JORMUNGAND," RIGHT...?
I only had time to use cardboard...
Wowee! It's really Godzilla!!
HE'S SO NICE!!!

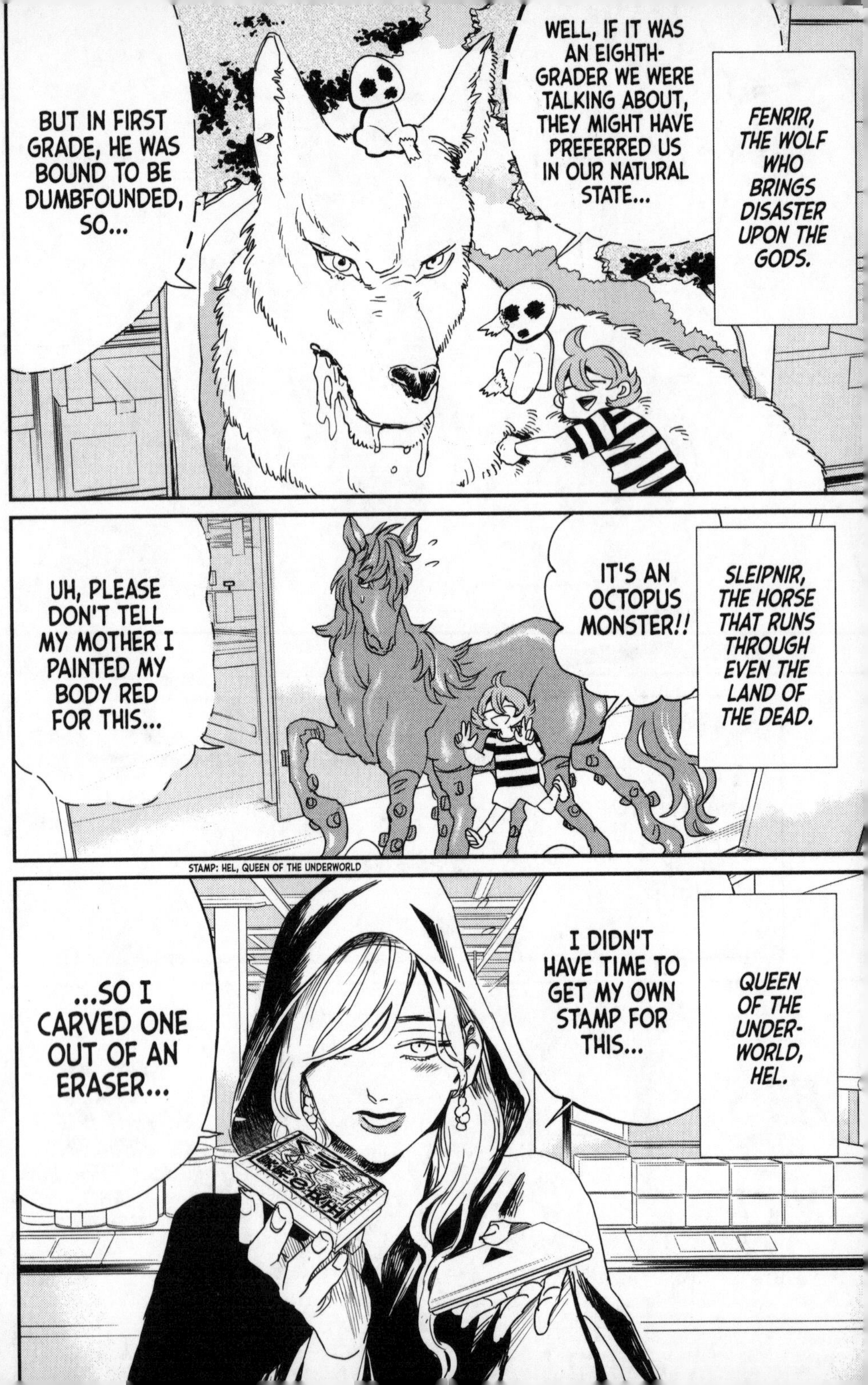
FENRIR, THE WOLF WHO BRINGS DISASTER UPON THE GODS.
WELL, IF IT WAS AN EIGHTH-GRADER WE WERE TALKING ABOUT, THEY MIGHT HAVE PREFERRED US IN OUR NATURAL STATE...
BUT IN FIRST GRADE, HE WAS BOUND TO BE DUMBFOUNDED, SO...
SLEIPNIR, THE HORSE THAT RUNS THROUGH EVEN THE LAND OF THE DEAD.
IT'S AN OCTOPUS MONSTER!!
UH, PLEASE DON'T TELL MY MOTHER I PAINTED MY BODY RED FOR THIS...
STAMP: HEL, QUEEN OF THE UNDERWORLD
QUEEN OF THE UNDER-WORLD, HEL.
I DIDN'T HAVE TIME TO GET MY OWN STAMP FOR THIS...
...SO I CARVED ONE OUT OF AN ERASER...

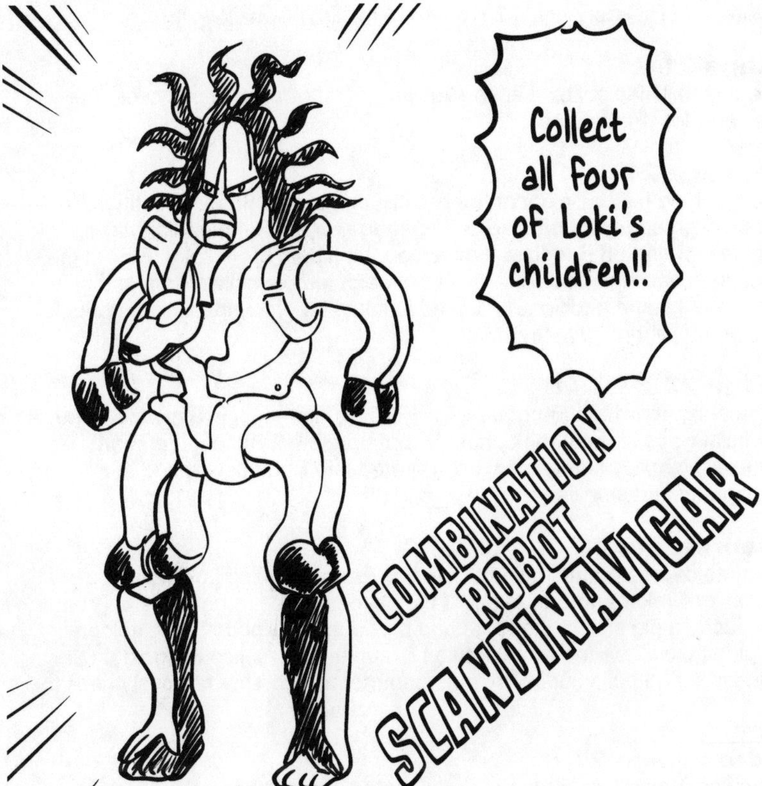
Collect all four of Loki's children!!
COMBINATION ROBOT SCANDINAVIGAR

SAINT☆YOUNG MEN

CHAPTER 98 TRANSLATION NOTES

Kaiju, page 19
A term ("mysterious beasts," or usually just translated to "giant monsters") that refers to the genre of giant monster movies exemplified by the *Godzilla* series. Although modern developments in *kaiju* movies use contemporary technology like CG, classic kaiju movies fall under the *tokusatsu* (special effects live-action) umbrella due to physical effects like actors in monster suits fighting on miniaturized city sets. Jesus's tastes in *tokusatsu*, apparently, exclusively focus on *sentai* series based on teams of color-coordinated heroes.

Shin Young Men, page 20
This title is a parody of Hideaki Anno's 2016 *kaiju* film, *Shin Godzilla*.

ParCure, page 21
A parody of the popular magical girl series *PreCure* (*Pretty Cure*). In this case, the abbreviation is short for "Party Cure."

Pilgrimage, page 21
Pilgrimages have a long history in Japan for both Buddhist and Shinto practitioners. The most famous pilgrimage is the Shikoku Pilgrimage, or 88-Temple Pilgrimage, because it involves touring 88 Buddhist temples on the island of Shikoku. Part of the pilgrimage involves receiving special stamps from each temple called a *shuin* that is fashioned by the monks and additionally signed in ink, either in a special stampbook, or on the robes of the pilgrims directly.

Phoenix, page 23
The Chinese phoenix, known as *Fenghuang* or *Hô-ô* in Japanese, is a mythical bird, similar in superficial ways to the Greek phoenix, but unrelated. Although primarily a symbol of Chinese myth, it is sometimes incorporated into Buddhist art and symbology as a sign of prosperity and stability.

Loki's treasures, page 24
The three treasures come from a story in the *Prose Edda*, in which Loki makes a bet with the dwarves Brokkr and Eitri to see if they can produce three items of great quality. Brokkr places a pig skin in the forge and produces Gullinbursti, the golden boar. Then he puts gold in the forge and makes Draupnir, the replicating gold ring. Lastly, he inserts iron and pulls out Mjölnir, the hammer, which Thor famously uses for himself.

Loki's children, page 27
According to the sagas used as source material, Loki has three children: Fenrir the giant wolf; Jormungand the World Serpent; and Hel, the ruler of the land of Hel (or Helheim), a realm where some gods go after death, especially after old age or sickness. Hel is described as being partially blue of skin. After his death, Baldr spends his time trapped under Hel's watch. The eight-legged horse Sleipnir, however, he birthed to the stallion Svadilfari while transformed into a mare.

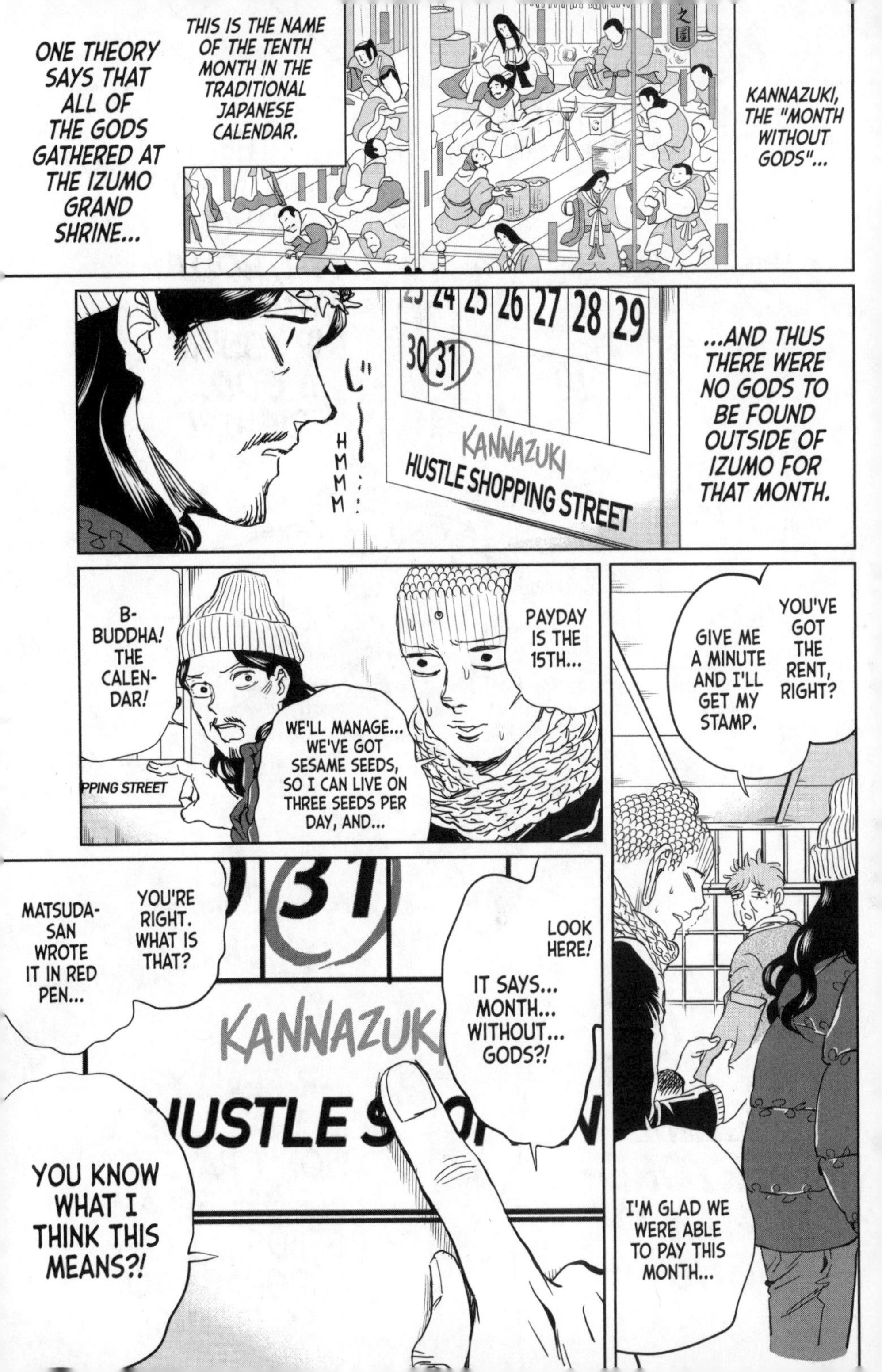
KANNAZUKI, THE "MONTH WITHOUT GODS"...
THIS IS THE NAME OF THE TENTH MONTH IN THE TRADITIONAL JAPANESE CALENDAR.
ONE THEORY SAYS THAT ALL OF THE GODS GATHERED AT THE IZUMO GRAND SHRINE...
...AND THUS THERE WERE NO GODS TO BE FOUND OUTSIDE OF IZUMO FOR THAT MONTH.
24 25 26 27 28 29
30 31
KANNAZUKI
HUSTLE SHOPPING STREET
HMMM
YOU'VE GOT THE RENT, RIGHT?
GIVE ME A MINUTE AND I'LL GET MY STAMP.
I'M GLAD WE WERE ABLE TO PAY THIS MONTH...
PAYDAY IS THE 15TH...
WE'LL MANAGE... WE'VE GOT SESAME SEEDS, SO I CAN LIVE ON THREE SEEDS PER DAY, AND...
B-BUDDHA! THE CALENDAR!
PPING STREET
31
KANNAZUKI
HUSTLE S
LOOK HERE!
IT SAYS... MONTH... WITHOUT... GODS?!
YOU'RE RIGHT. WHAT IS THAT?
MATSUDA-SAN WROTE IT IN RED PEN...
YOU KNOW WHAT I THINK THIS MEANS?!

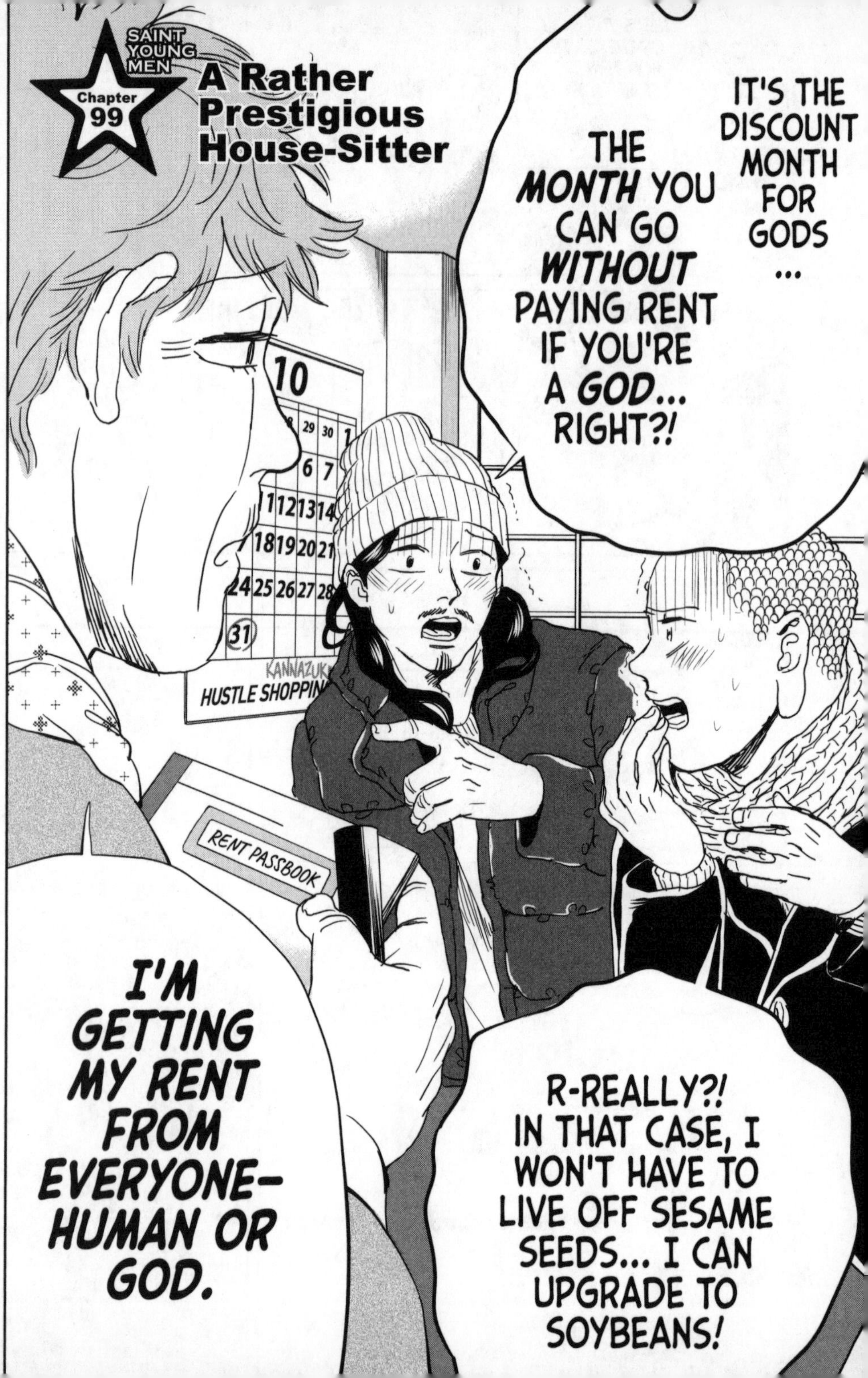
SAINT YOUNG MEN
Chapter 99
A Rather Prestigious House-Sitter
IT'S THE DISCOUNT MONTH FOR GODS ...
THE *MONTH* YOU CAN GO *WITHOUT* PAYING RENT IF YOU'RE A *GOD*... RIGHT?!
KANNAZUKI
RENT PASSBOOK
R-REALLY?! IN THAT CASE, I WON'T HAVE TO LIVE OFF SESAME SEEDS... I CAN UPGRADE TO SOYBEANS!
I'M GETTING MY RENT FROM EVERYONE- HUMAN OR GOD.

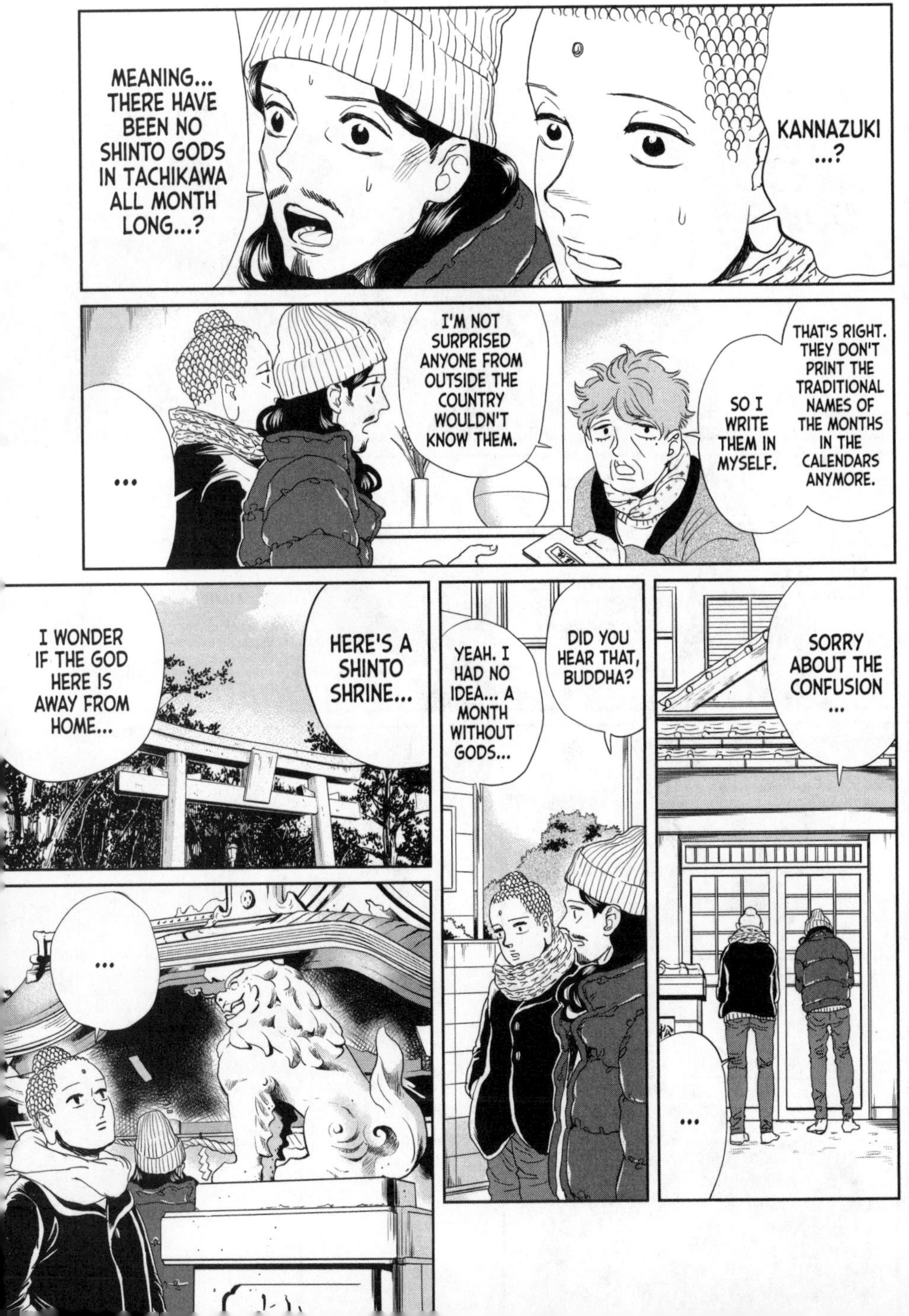
KANNAZUKI ...?
MEANING... THERE HAVE BEEN NO SHINTO GODS IN TACHIKAWA ALL MONTH LONG...?
THAT'S RIGHT. THEY DON'T PRINT THE TRADITIONAL NAMES OF THE MONTHS IN THE CALENDARS ANYMORE.
SO I WRITE THEM IN MYSELF.
I'M NOT SURPRISED ANYONE FROM OUTSIDE THE COUNTRY WOULDN'T KNOW THEM.
...
SORRY ABOUT THE CONFUSION ...
...
DID YOU HEAR THAT, BUDDHA?
YEAH. I HAD NO IDEA... A MONTH WITHOUT GODS...
HERE'S A SHINTO SHRINE...
I WONDER IF THE GOD HERE IS AWAY FROM HOME...
...

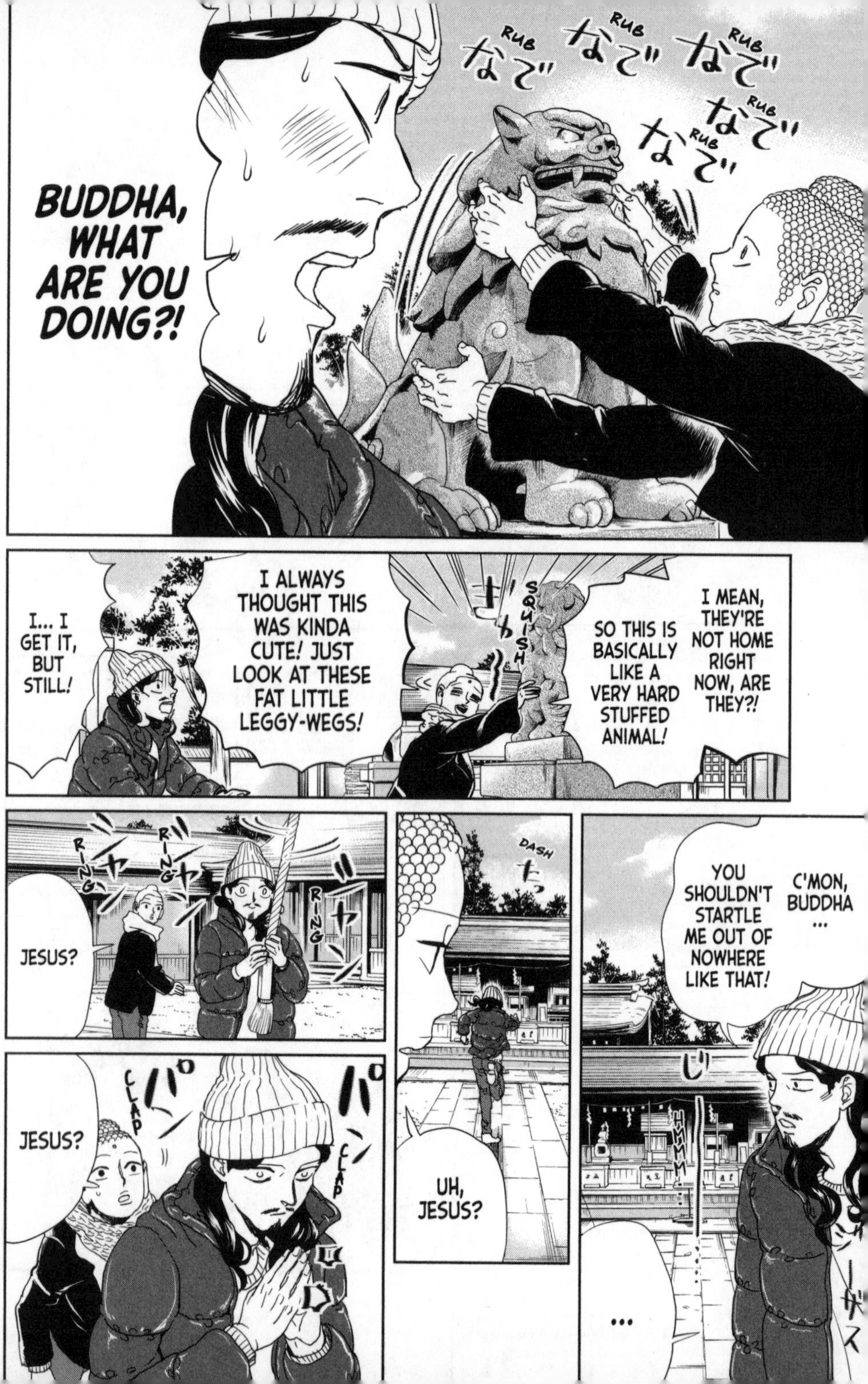
RUB なで
RUB なで
RUB なで
RUB なで
RUB なで
BUDDHA, WHAT ARE YOU DOING?!
I MEAN, THEY'RE NOT HOME RIGHT NOW, ARE THEY?!
SO THIS IS BASICALLY LIKE A VERY HARD STUFFED ANIMAL!
SQUISH
I ALWAYS THOUGHT THIS WAS KINDA CUTE! JUST LOOK AT THESE FAT LITTLE LEGGY-WEGS!
I... I GET IT, BUT STILL!
C'MON, BUDDHA ...
YOU SHOULDN'T STARTLE ME OUT OF NOWHERE LIKE THAT!
HMMMM...
...
DASH
UH, JESUS?
RING
RING
RING
JESUS?
CLAP
CLAP
JESUS?

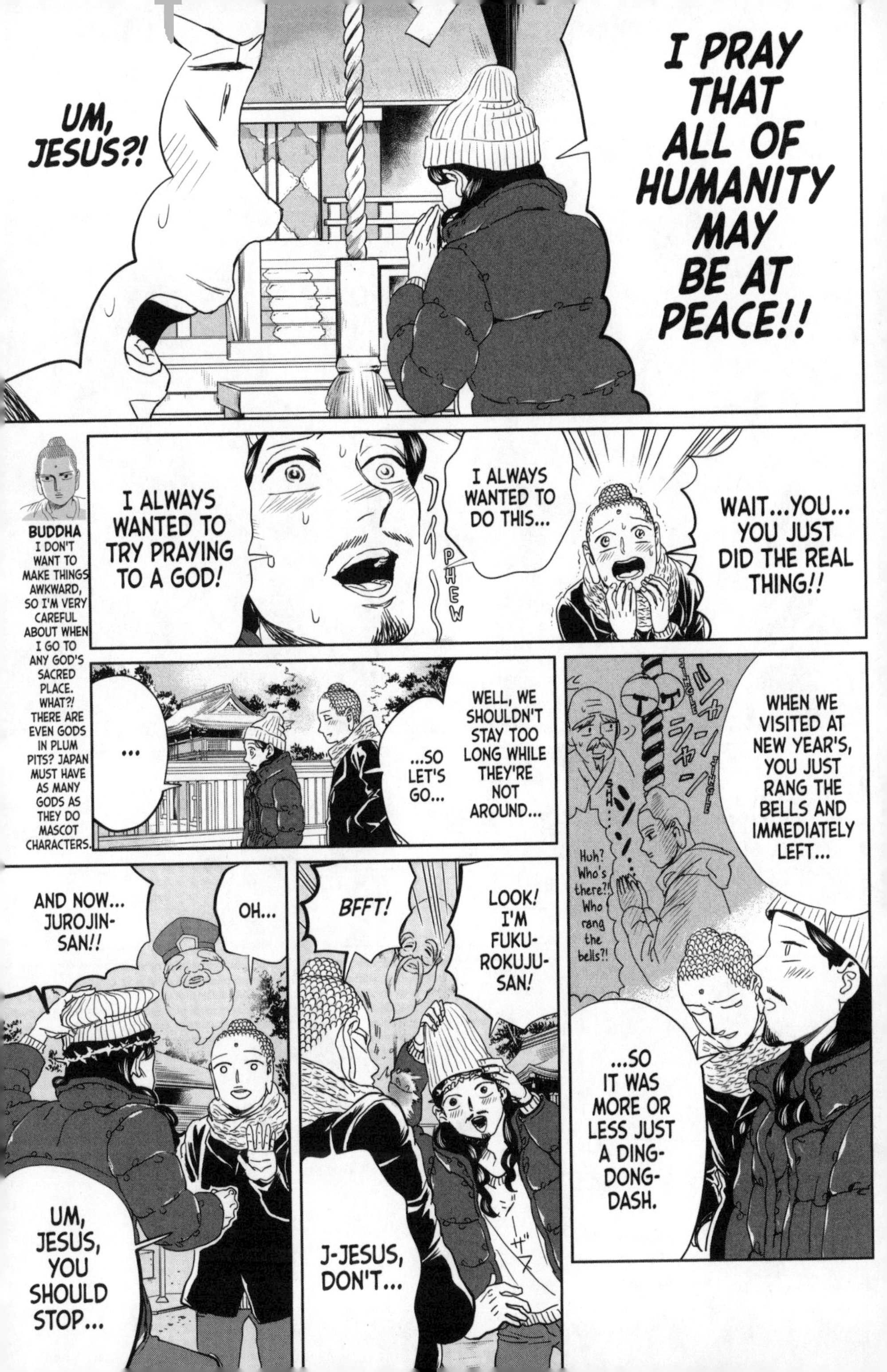
I PRAY THAT ALL OF HUMANITY MAY BE AT PEACE!!
UM, JESUS?!
WAIT...YOU... YOU JUST DID THE REAL THING!!
I ALWAYS WANTED TO DO THIS...
PHEW
I ALWAYS WANTED TO TRY PRAYING TO A GOD!
WHEN WE VISITED AT NEW YEAR'S, YOU JUST RANG THE BELLS AND IMMEDIATELY LEFT...
Huh? Who's there?! Who rang the bells?!
...SO IT WAS MORE OR LESS JUST A DING-DONG-DASH.
WELL, WE SHOULDN'T STAY TOO LONG WHILE THEY'RE NOT AROUND...
...SO LET'S GO...
...
LOOK! I'M FUKU-ROKUJU-SAN!
BFFT!
J-JESUS, DON'T...
OH...
AND NOW... JUROJIN-SAN!!
UM, JESUS, YOU SHOULD STOP...
BUDDHA
I DON'T WANT TO MAKE THINGS AWKWARD, SO I'M VERY CAREFUL ABOUT WHEN I GO TO ANY GOD'S SACRED PLACE. WHAT?! THERE ARE EVEN GODS IN PLUM PITS? JAPAN MUST HAVE AS MANY GODS AS THEY DO MASCOT CHARACTERS.

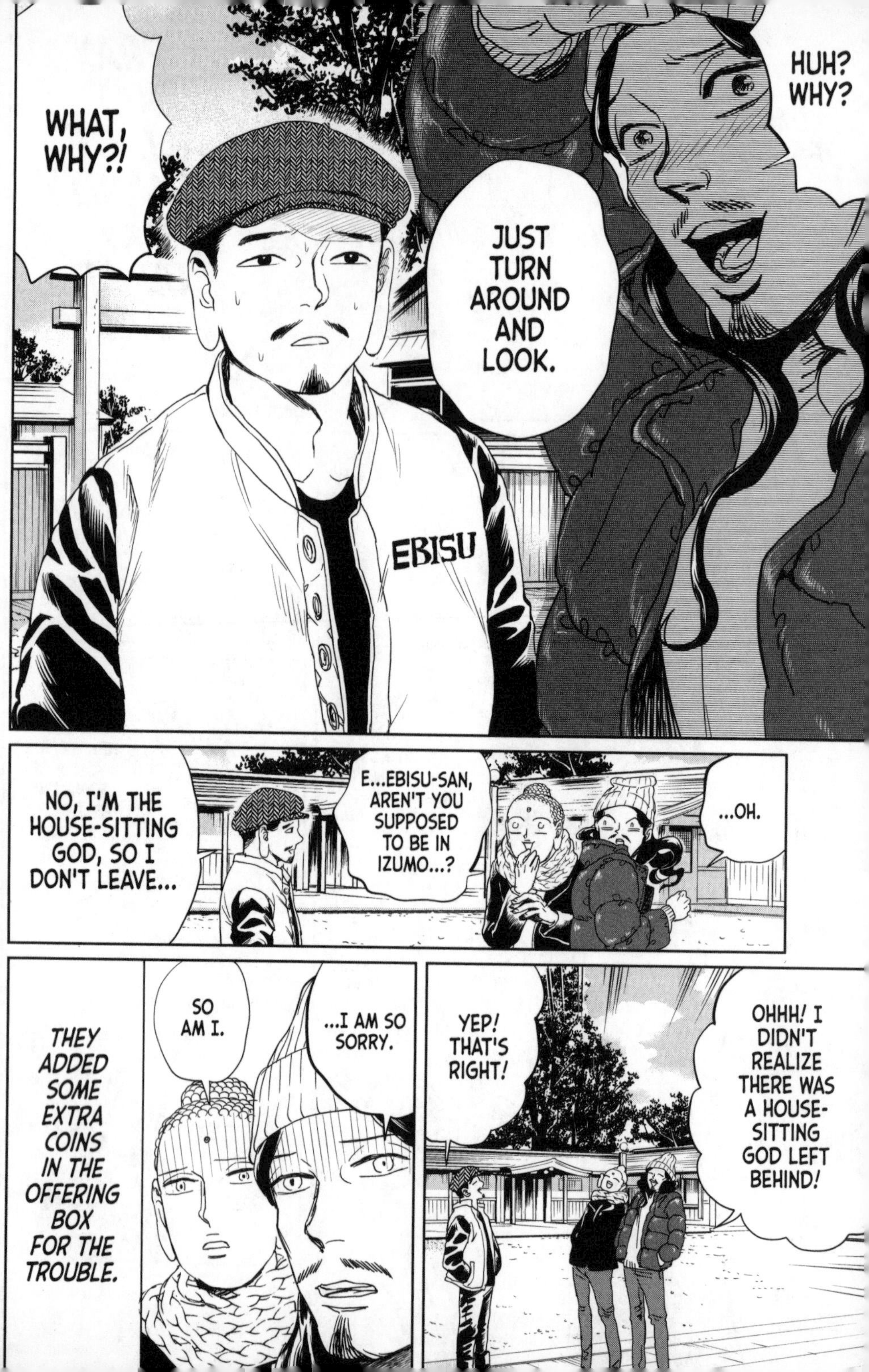
HUH? WHY?
JUST TURN AROUND AND LOOK.
WHAT, WHY?!
EBISU
...OH.
E...EBISU-SAN, AREN'T YOU SUPPOSED TO BE IN IZUMO...?
NO, I'M THE HOUSE-SITTING GOD, SO I DON'T LEAVE...
OHHH! I DIDN'T REALIZE THERE WAS A HOUSE-SITTING GOD LEFT BEHIND!
YEP! THAT'S RIGHT!
...I AM SO SORRY.
SO AM I.
THEY ADDED SOME EXTRA COINS IN THE OFFERING BOX FOR THE TROUBLE.

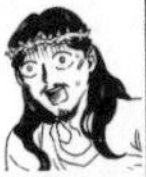

JESUS AFTER POSTING ON AN ANONYMOUS MESSAGE BOARD, HE ALWAYS GETS NERVOUS WHEN HE SEES SOMEONE SAY, "A GOD WALKS AMONG US." THE CONCEPT OF GOD HAS REALLY BEEN COMMODITIZED ONLINE! (SAW THAT PRETENTIOUS PHRASE ON Y*HOO ANSWERS ONCE.)

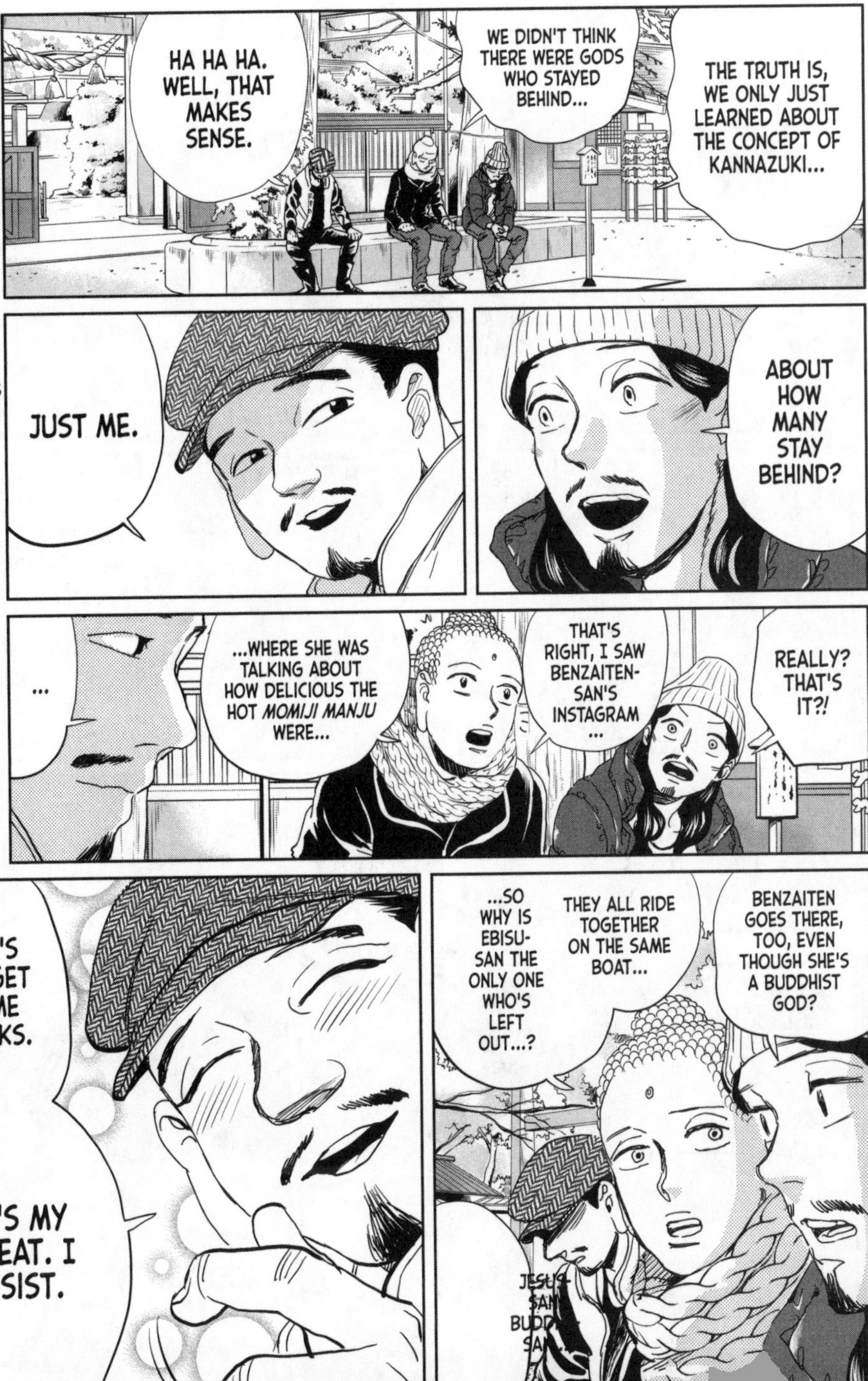
THE TRUTH IS, WE ONLY JUST LEARNED ABOUT THE CONCEPT OF KANNAZUKI...
WE DIDN'T THINK THERE WERE GODS WHO STAYED BEHIND...
HA HA HA. WELL, THAT MAKES SENSE.
ABOUT HOW MANY STAY BEHIND?
JUST ME.
REALLY? THAT'S IT?!
THAT'S RIGHT, I SAW BENZAITEN-SAN'S INSTAGRAM ...
...WHERE SHE WAS TALKING ABOUT HOW DELICIOUS THE HOT *MOMIJI MANJU* WERE...
...
BENZAITEN GOES THERE, TOO, EVEN THOUGH SHE'S A BUDDHIST GOD?
THEY ALL RIDE TOGETHER ON THE SAME BOAT...
...SO WHY IS EBISU-SAN THE ONLY ONE WHO'S LEFT OUT...?
LET'S GO GET SOME DRINKS.
IT'S MY TREAT. I INSIST.

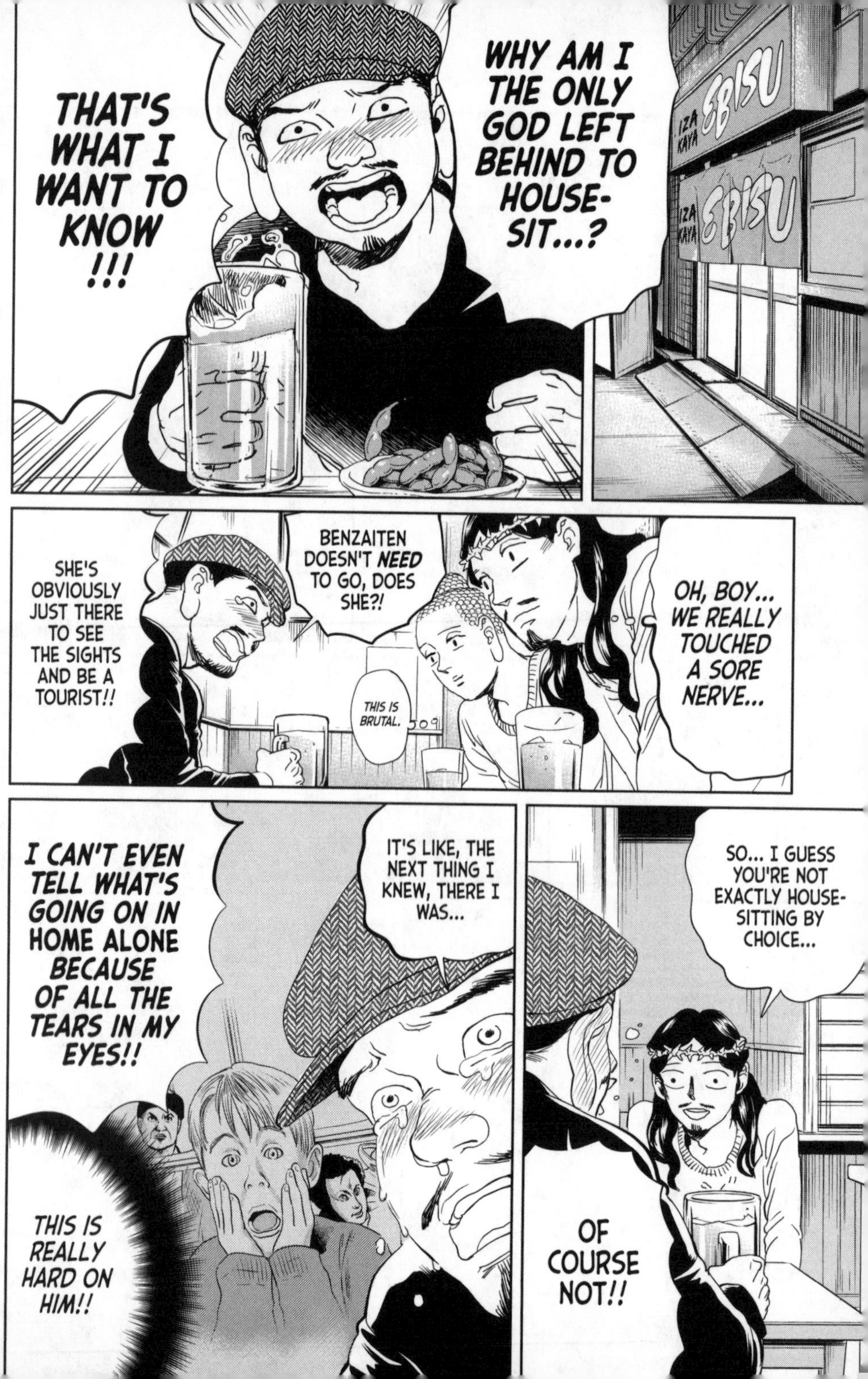

IZA KAYA EBISU
IZA KAYA EBISU
WHY AM I THE ONLY GOD LEFT BEHIND TO HOUSE-SIT...?
THAT'S WHAT I WANT TO KNOW!!!
OH, BOY... WE REALLY TOUCHED A SORE NERVE...
BENZAITEN DOESN'T *NEED* TO GO, DOES SHE?!
SHE'S OBVIOUSLY JUST THERE TO SEE THE SIGHTS AND BE A TOURIST!!
THIS IS BRUTAL.
SO... I GUESS YOU'RE NOT EXACTLY HOUSE-SITTING BY CHOICE...
OF COURSE NOT!!
IT'S LIKE, THE NEXT THING I KNEW, THERE I WAS...
I CAN'T EVEN TELL WHAT'S GOING ON IN HOME ALONE BECAUSE OF ALL THE TEARS IN MY EYES!!
THIS IS REALLY HARD ON HIM!!

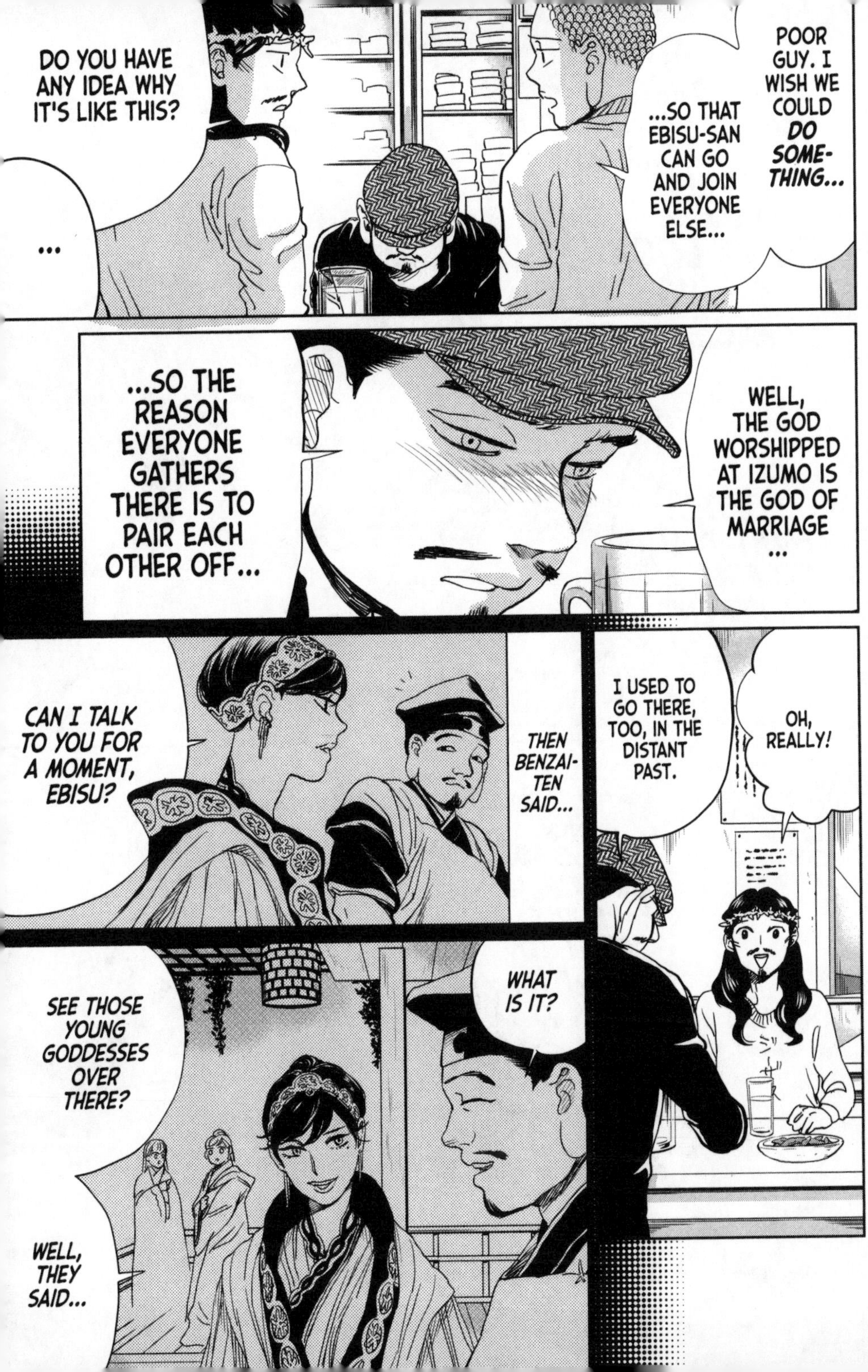
POOR GUY. I WISH WE COULD *DO SOME-THING...*
...SO THAT EBISU-SAN CAN GO AND JOIN EVERYONE ELSE...
DO YOU HAVE ANY IDEA WHY IT'S LIKE THIS?
...
WELL, THE GOD WORSHIPPED AT IZUMO IS THE GOD OF MARRIAGE ...
...SO THE REASON EVERYONE GATHERS THERE IS TO PAIR EACH OTHER OFF...
OH, REALLY!
I USED TO GO THERE, TOO, IN THE DISTANT PAST.
THEN BENZAI-TEN SAID...
CAN I TALK TO YOU FOR A MOMENT, EBISU?
WHAT IS IT?
SEE THOSE YOUNG GODDESSES OVER THERE?
WELL, THEY SAID...

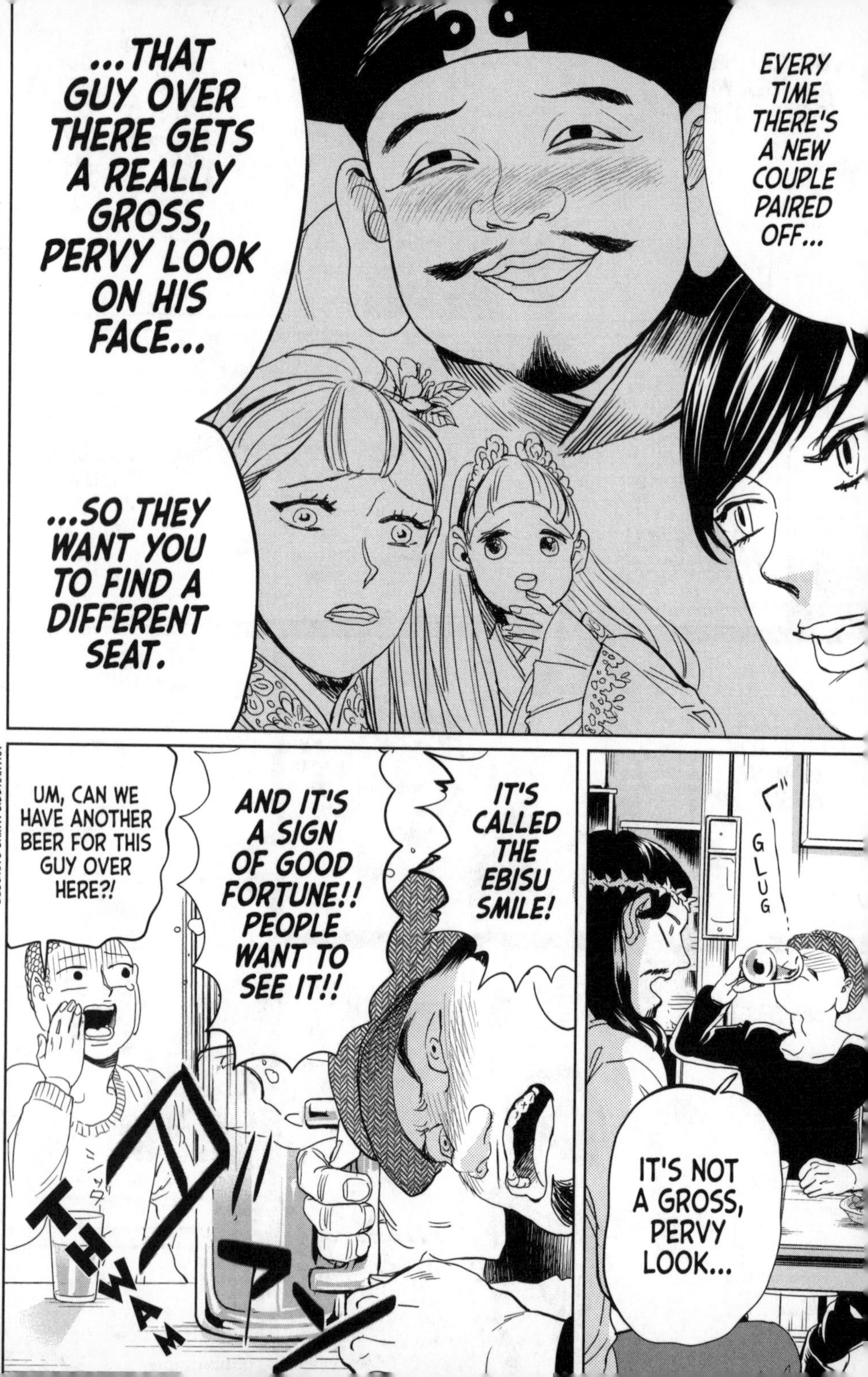
EVERY TIME THERE'S A NEW COUPLE PAIRED OFF...
...THAT GUY OVER THERE GETS A REALLY GROSS, PERVY LOOK ON HIS FACE...
...SO THEY WANT YOU TO FIND A DIFFERENT SEAT.
GLUG
IT'S NOT A GROSS, PERVY LOOK...
IT'S CALLED THE EBISU SMILE!
AND IT'S A SIGN OF GOOD FORTUNE!! PEOPLE WANT TO SEE IT!!
UM, CAN WE HAVE ANOTHER BEER FOR THIS GUY OVER HERE?!
THWAM

BUDDHA'S SHIRT: SIDDHARTHA

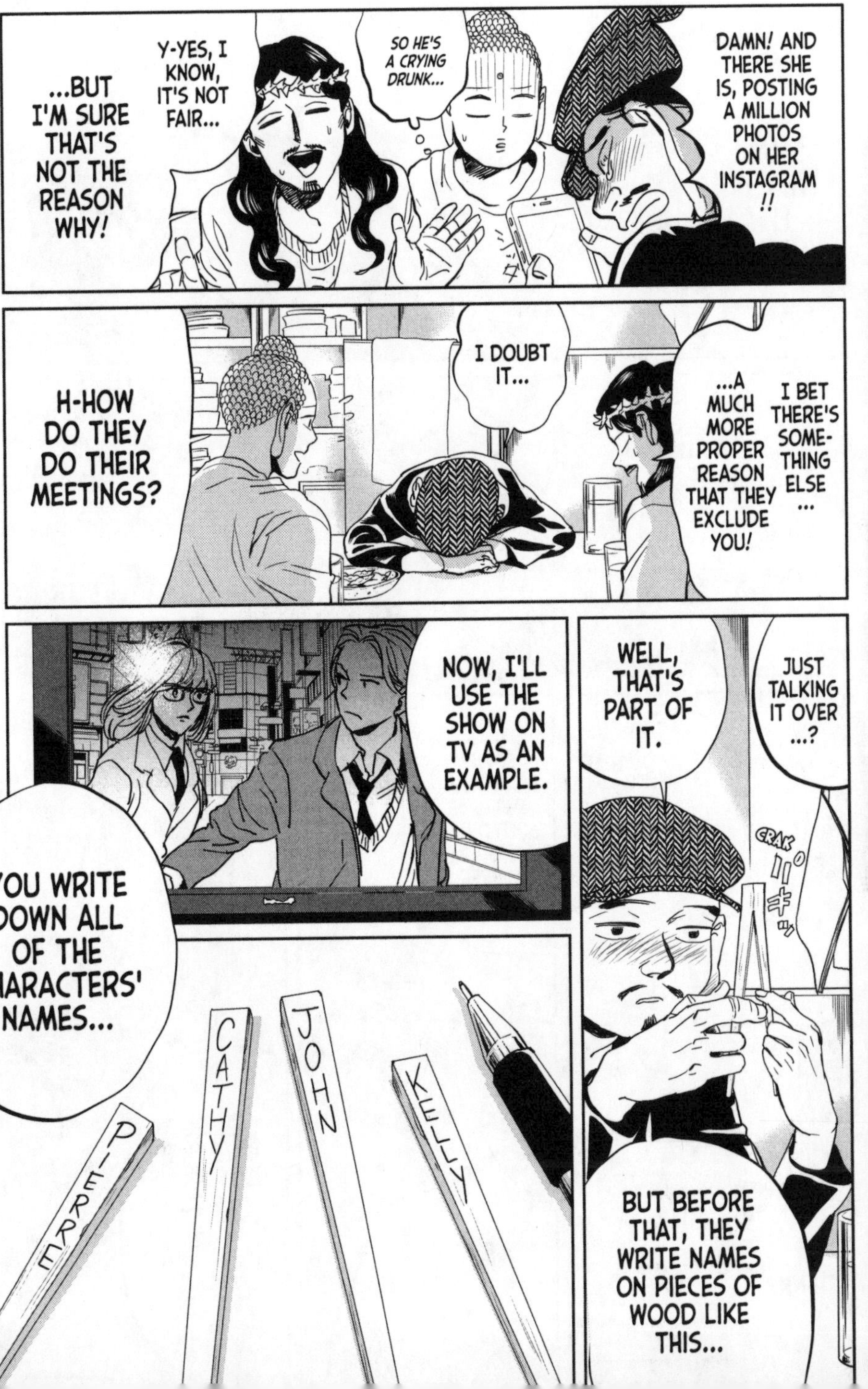
DAMN! AND THERE SHE IS, POSTING A MILLION PHOTOS ON HER INSTAGRAM!!
SO HE'S A CRYING DRUNK...
Y-YES, I KNOW, IT'S NOT FAIR...
...BUT I'M SURE THAT'S NOT THE REASON WHY!
I BET THERE'S SOME-THING ELSE...
...A MUCH MORE PROPER REASON THAT THEY EXCLUDE YOU!
I DOUBT IT...
H-HOW DO THEY DO THEIR MEETINGS?
JUST TALKING IT OVER...?
WELL, THAT'S PART OF IT.
CRAK
BUT BEFORE THAT, THEY WRITE NAMES ON PIECES OF WOOD LIKE THIS...
NOW, I'LL USE THE SHOW ON TV AS AN EXAMPLE.
YOU WRITE DOWN ALL OF THE CHARACTERS' NAMES...
KELLY
JOHN
CATHY
PIERRE

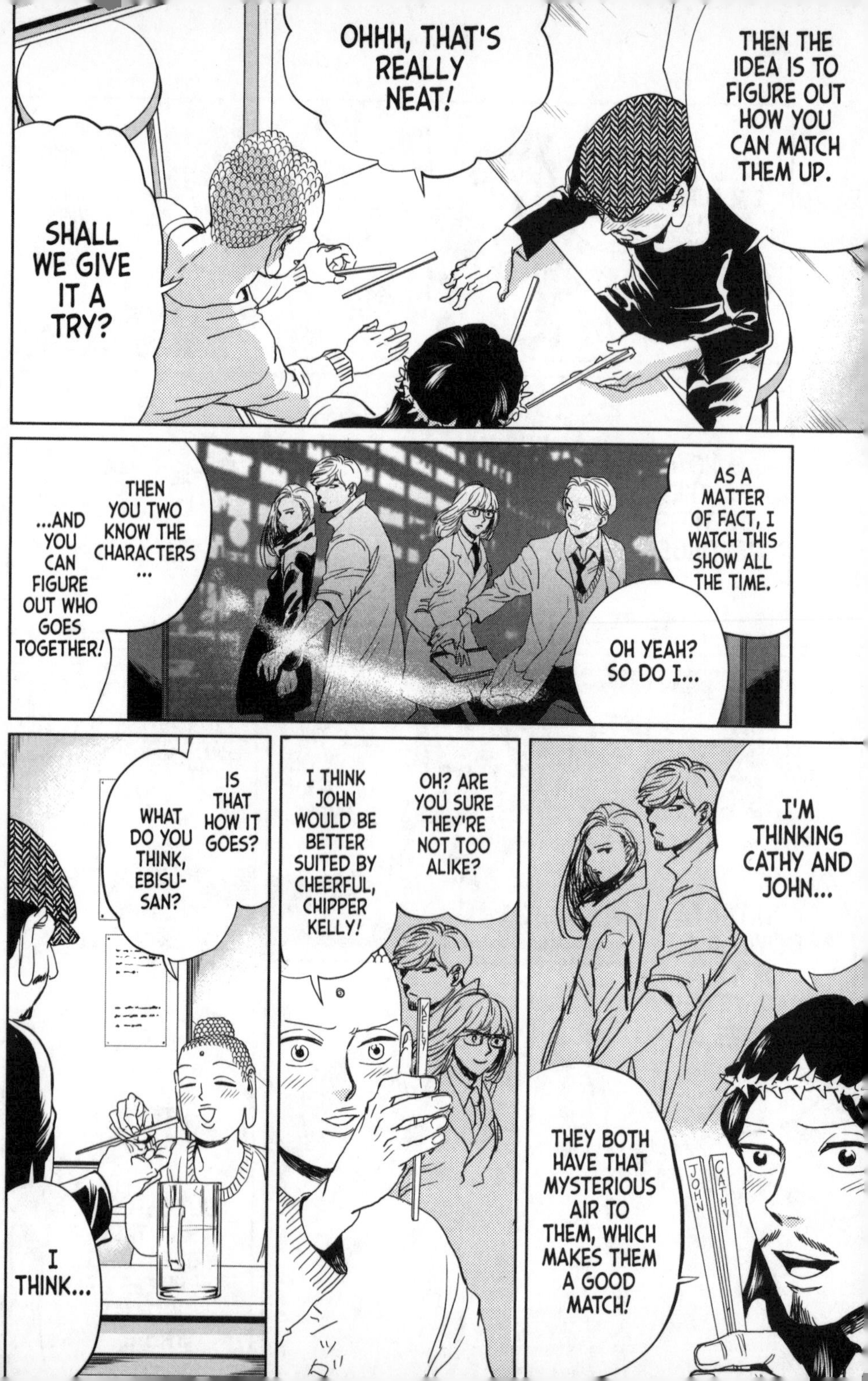
THEN THE IDEA IS TO FIGURE OUT HOW YOU CAN MATCH THEM UP.
OHHH, THAT'S REALLY NEAT!
SHALL WE GIVE IT A TRY?
AS A MATTER OF FACT, I WATCH THIS SHOW ALL THE TIME.
OH YEAH? SO DO I...
THEN YOU TWO KNOW THE CHARACTERS...
...AND YOU CAN FIGURE OUT WHO GOES TOGETHER!
I'M THINKING CATHY AND JOHN...
THEY BOTH HAVE THAT MYSTERIOUS AIR TO THEM, WHICH MAKES THEM A GOOD MATCH!
CATHY
JOHN
OH? ARE YOU SURE THEY'RE NOT TOO ALIKE?
I THINK JOHN WOULD BE BETTER SUITED BY CHEERFUL, CHIPPER KELLY!
KELLY
IS THAT HOW IT GOES?
WHAT DO YOU THINK, EBISU-SAN?
I THINK...

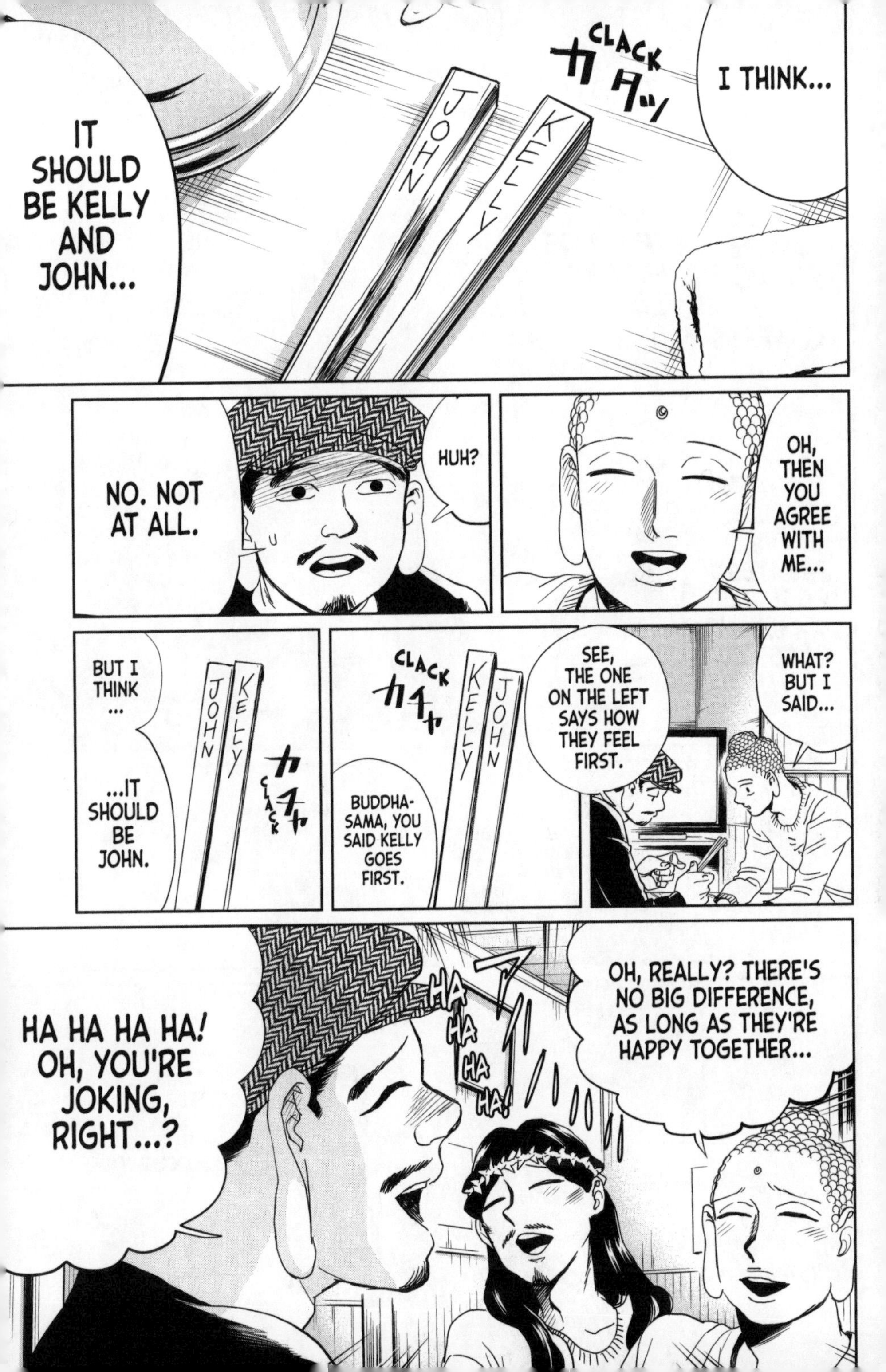
I THINK...
CLACK
カタッ
JOHN
KELLY
IT SHOULD BE KELLY AND JOHN...
OH, THEN YOU AGREE WITH ME...
HUH?
NO. NOT AT ALL.
WHAT? BUT I SAID...
SEE, THE ONE ON THE LEFT SAYS HOW THEY FEEL FIRST.
CLACK
カチャ
KELLY
JOHN
BUDDHA-SAMA, YOU SAID KELLY GOES FIRST.
BUT I THINK ...
JOHN
KELLY
CLACK
カチャ
...IT SHOULD BE JOHN.
OH, REALLY? THERE'S NO BIG DIFFERENCE, AS LONG AS THEY'RE HAPPY TOGETHER...
HA HA HA HA!
HA HA HA HA! OH, YOU'RE JOKING, RIGHT...?

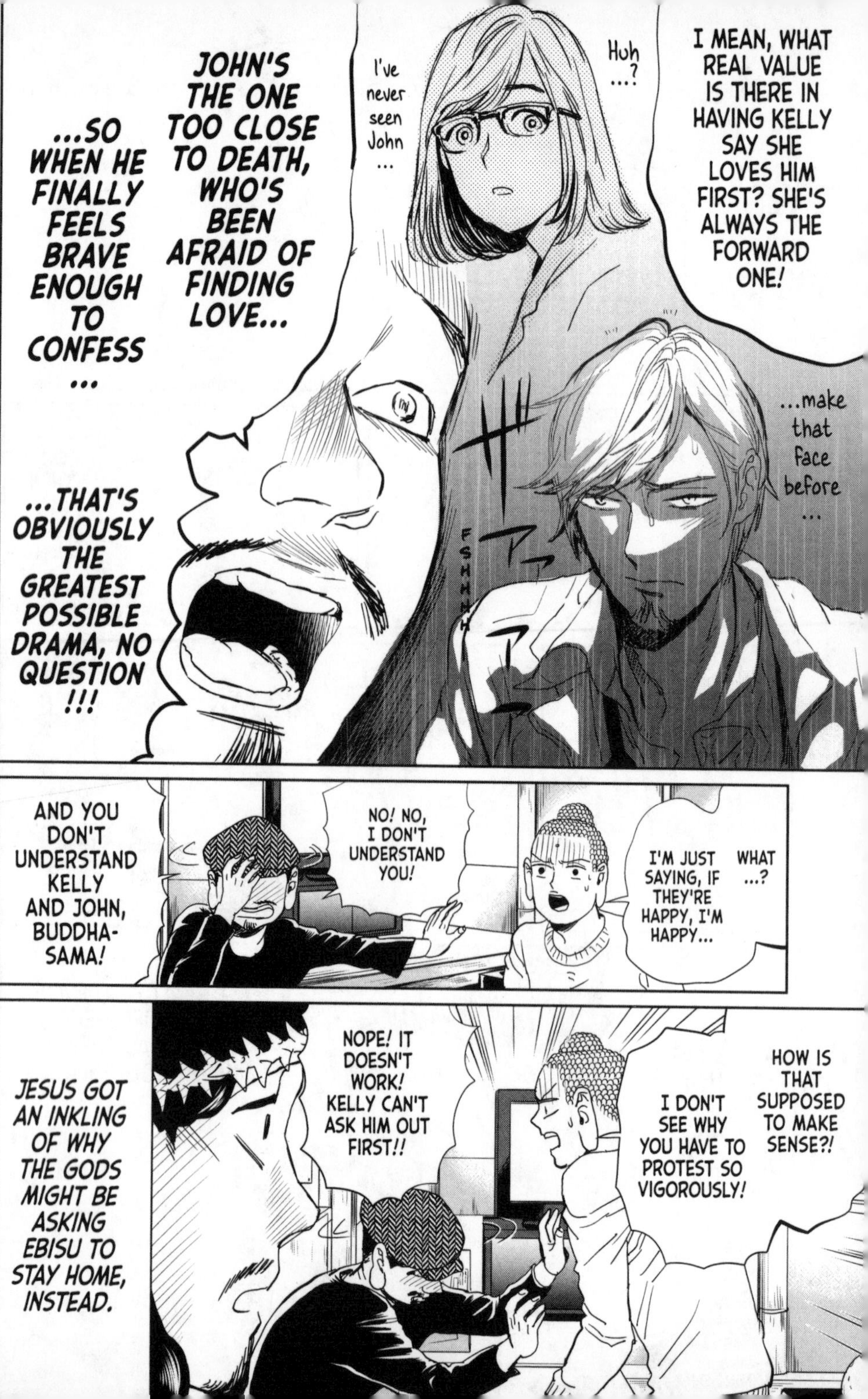
I MEAN, WHAT REAL VALUE IS THERE IN HAVING KELLY SAY SHE LOVES HIM FIRST? SHE'S ALWAYS THE FORWARD ONE!
Huh...?
I've never seen John...
...make that face before...
JOHN'S THE ONE TOO CLOSE TO DEATH, WHO'S BEEN AFRAID OF FINDING LOVE...
...SO WHEN HE FINALLY FEELS BRAVE ENOUGH TO CONFESS...
...THAT'S OBVIOUSLY THE GREATEST POSSIBLE DRAMA, NO QUESTION!!!
FSHHHH
WHAT...?
I'M JUST SAYING, IF THEY'RE HAPPY, I'M HAPPY...
NO! NO, I DON'T UNDERSTAND YOU!
AND YOU DON'T UNDERSTAND KELLY AND JOHN, BUDDHA-SAMA!
HOW IS THAT SUPPOSED TO MAKE SENSE?!
I DON'T SEE WHY YOU HAVE TO PROTEST SO VIGOROUSLY!
NOPE! IT DOESN'T WORK! KELLY CAN'T ASK HIM OUT FIRST!!
JESUS GOT AN INKLING OF WHY THE GODS MIGHT BE ASKING EBISU TO STAY HOME, INSTEAD.

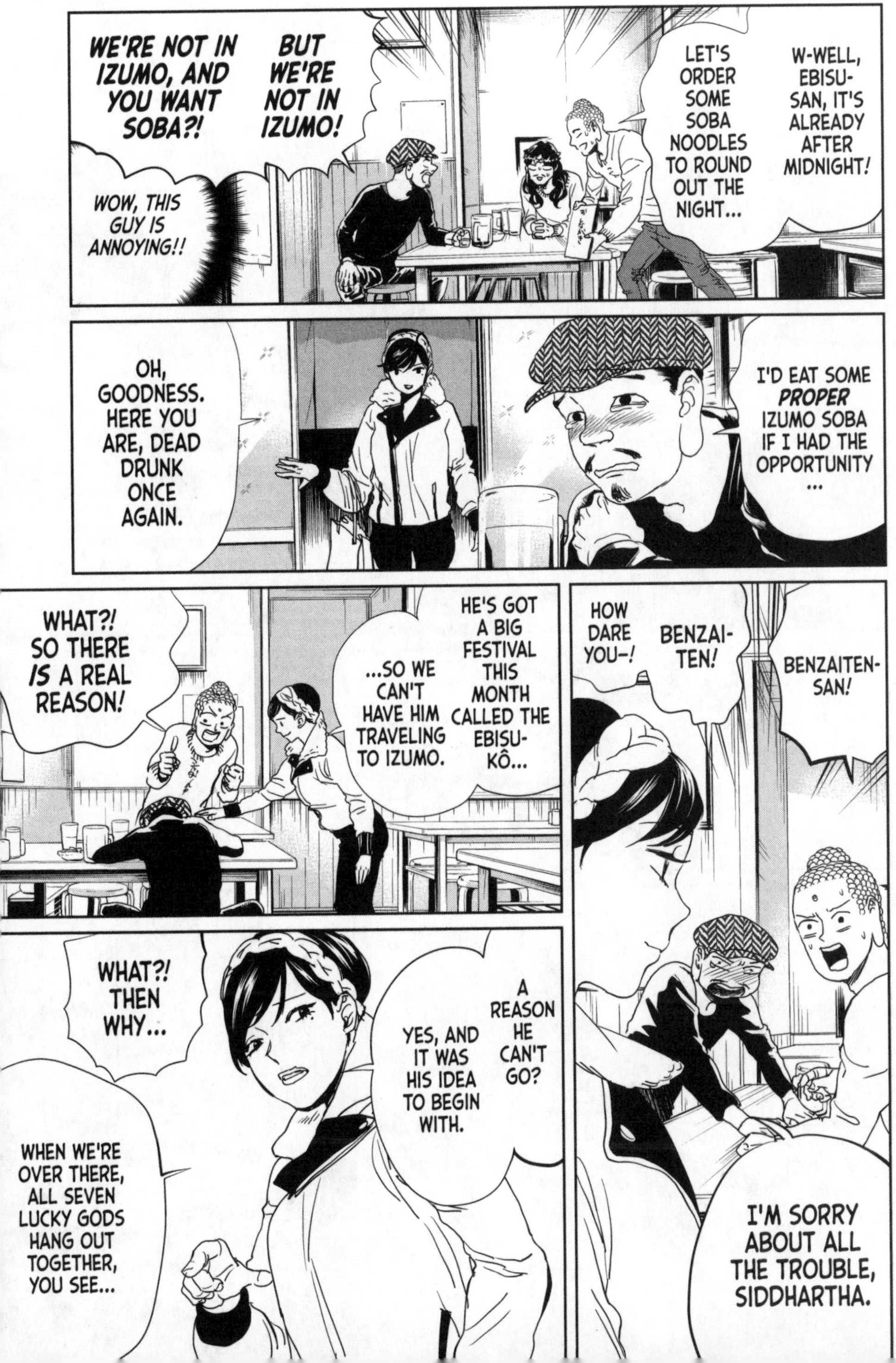
W-WELL, EBISU-SAN, IT'S ALREADY AFTER MIDNIGHT!
LET'S ORDER SOME SOBA NOODLES TO ROUND OUT THE NIGHT...
BUT WE'RE NOT IN IZUMO!
WE'RE NOT IN IZUMO, AND YOU WANT SOBA?!
WOW, THIS GUY IS ANNOYING!!
I'D EAT SOME *PROPER* IZUMO SOBA IF I HAD THE OPPORTUNITY ...
OH, GOODNESS. HERE YOU ARE, DEAD DRUNK ONCE AGAIN.
BENZAITEN-SAN!
BENZAITEN!
HOW DARE YOU–!
I'M SORRY ABOUT ALL THE TROUBLE, SIDDHARTHA.
HE'S GOT A BIG FESTIVAL THIS MONTH CALLED THE EBISU-KÔ...
...SO WE CAN'T HAVE HIM TRAVELING TO IZUMO.
WHAT?! SO THERE *IS* A REAL REASON!
A REASON HE CAN'T GO?
YES, AND IT WAS HIS IDEA TO BEGIN WITH.
WHAT?! THEN WHY...
WHEN WE'RE OVER THERE, ALL SEVEN LUCKY GODS HANG OUT TOGETHER, YOU SEE...

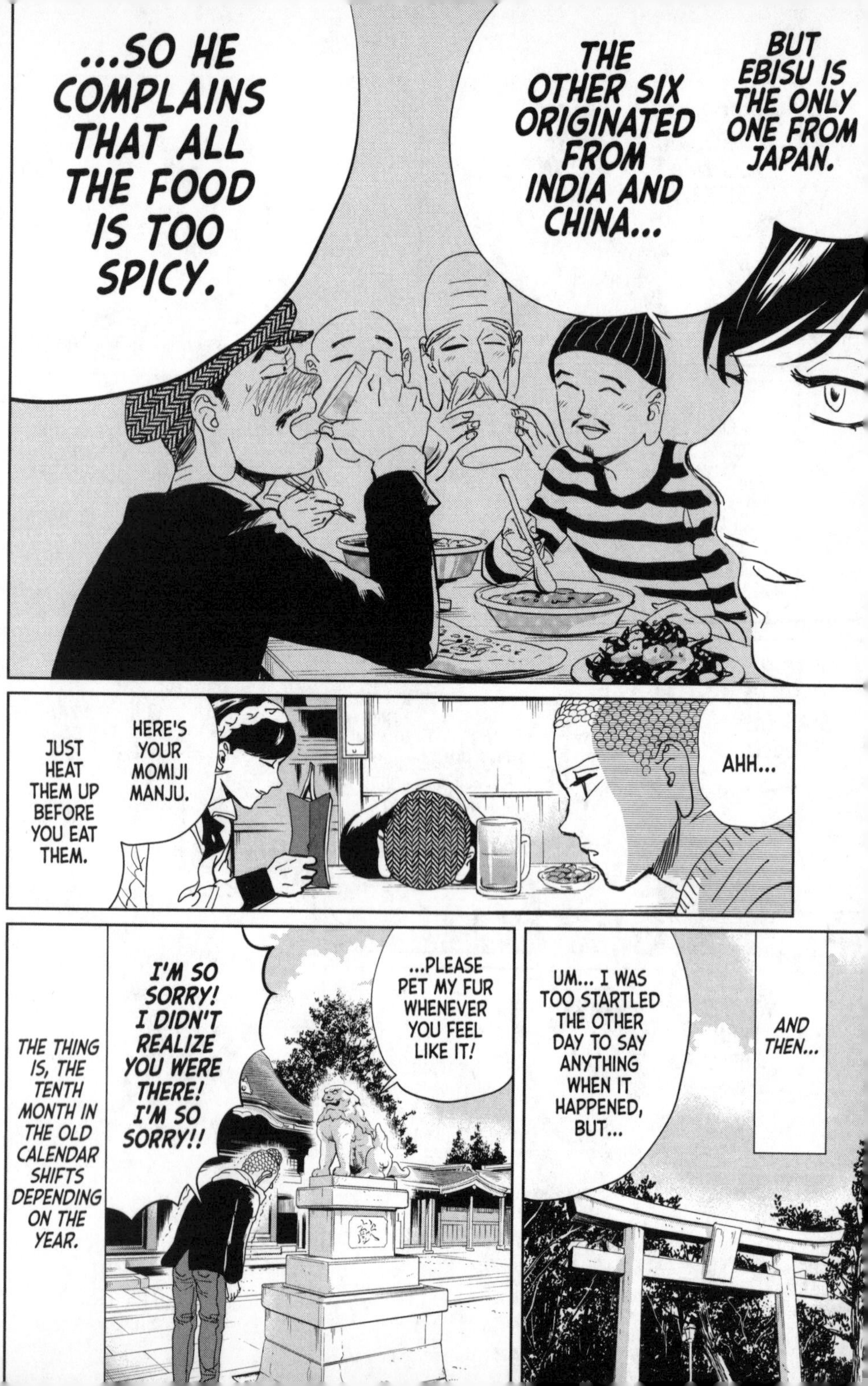
BUT EBISU IS THE ONLY ONE FROM JAPAN.
THE OTHER SIX ORIGINATED FROM INDIA AND CHINA...
...SO HE COMPLAINS THAT ALL THE FOOD IS TOO SPICY.
AHH...
HERE'S YOUR MOMIJI MANJU.
JUST HEAT THEM UP BEFORE YOU EAT THEM.
AND THEN...
UM... I WAS TOO STARTLED THE OTHER DAY TO SAY ANYTHING WHEN IT HAPPENED, BUT...
...PLEASE PET MY FUR WHENEVER YOU FEEL LIKE IT!
I'M SO SORRY! I DIDN'T REALIZE YOU WERE THERE! I'M SO SORRY!!
THE THING IS, THE TENTH MONTH IN THE OLD CALENDAR SHIFTS DEPENDING ON THE YEAR.

After the tummy rubs have been allowed
Ahhh...
It is an ill omen!!

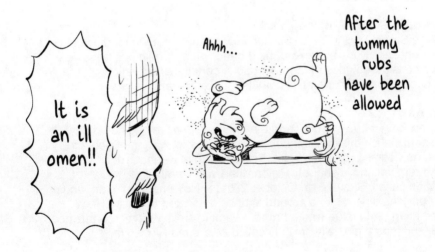

CHAPTER 99 TRANSLATION NOTES

Izumo, page 37

A city on the far western end of the island of Honshu known for its soba (buckwheat) noodles, and the Izumo-Taisha, or Izumo Grand Shrine, the oldest Shinto shrine. According to Shinto mythology, "Izumo" is the name of the realm of the gods, and is thus the place where all of the gods go during Kannazuki, the "month without gods" that corresponds to October.

Komainu, page 40

The stone statues, often called "lion dogs," that stand guard outside of Shinto shrines. They always come in pairs, and typically one has an opened mouth, while the other's is closed.

Shinto shrines, page 41

The common custom when visiting Shinto shrines, after donating for an offering, is to pull on the rope bearing one or more large bells to ring them, then bow, clap your hands, and bow again and pray. This calls upon the god revered at the shrine to bring good fortune. The gods are said to reside at these shrines, which is why the concept of a month in which all the gods are absent is so remarkable.

Fukurokuju & Jurojin, page 41

Two of the Seven Lucky Gods (*Shichifukujin*) of Japan. Fukurokuju is almost always identified by his elongated, bald head, while Jurojin has headwear. Both are considered gods of longevity, so in certain configurations of the Seven Lucky Gods, Fukurokuju is omitted for redundancy.

Ebisu, page 42

One of the Seven Lucky Gods, and the only one to have originated entirely from Japan. He is considered the fisherman's god for his gift of bountiful catches, as well as a god of wealth. In the month of Kannazuki, he is the only god who remains in his shrine(s) rather than visit Izumo, and thus there is a celebration called Ebisu-kô on October 20th (or November 20th, depending on the year) in some regions around shrines dedicated to Ebisu. He is depicted in art and statue with a broad, beaming smile that represents good fortune, and thus a big, jolly smile is called *ebisu-gao* ("Ebisu face").

Momiji manju, page 43

A type of *manju* cake typically made and sold on the island of Itsukushima, where the Itsukushima Shrine is another famous Shinto site. The manju, filled with sweet red bean paste, is shaped like a Japanese maple (*momiji*) leaf.

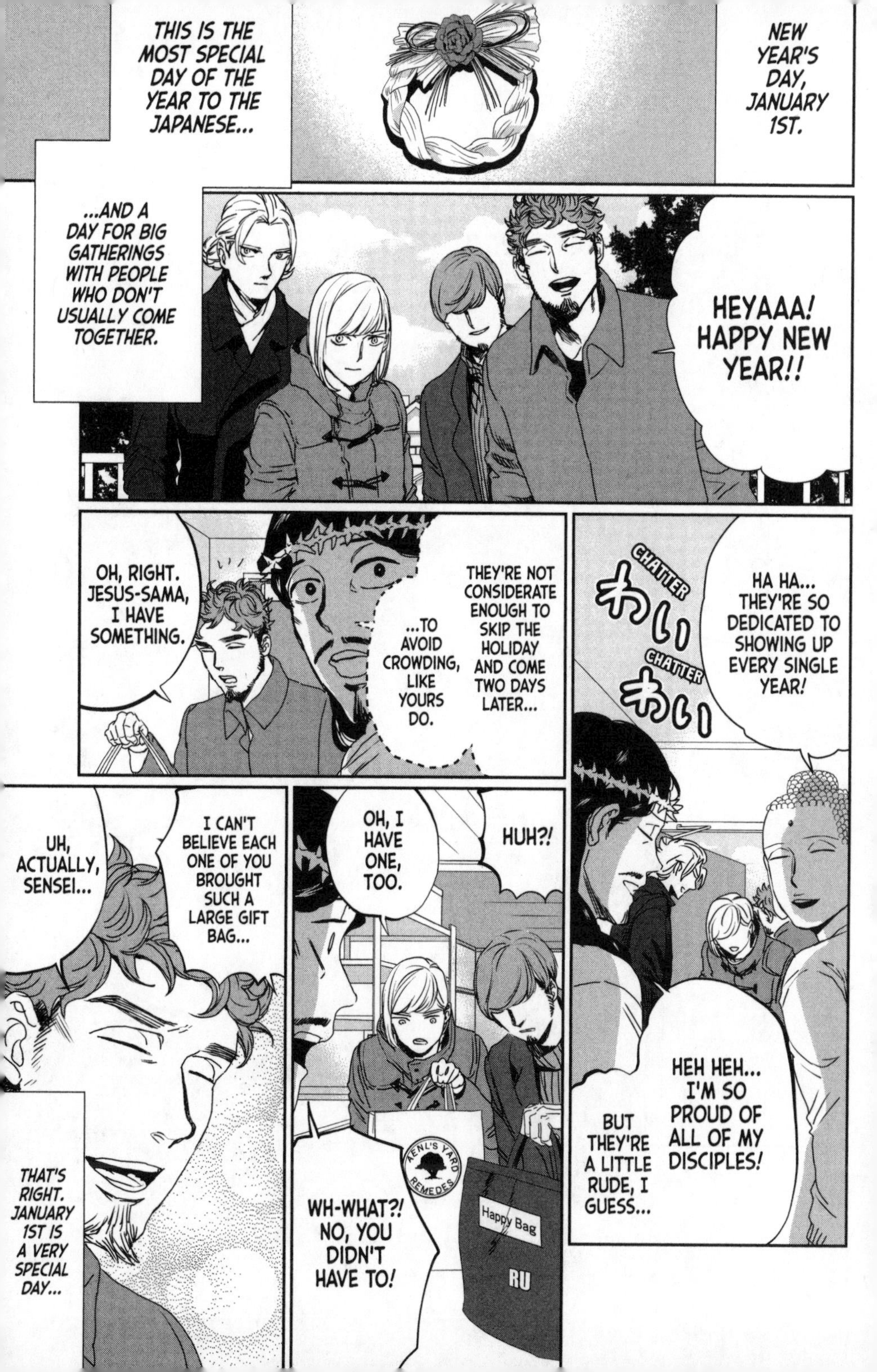
NEW YEAR'S DAY, JANUARY 1ST.
THIS IS THE MOST SPECIAL DAY OF THE YEAR TO THE JAPANESE...
...AND A DAY FOR BIG GATHERINGS WITH PEOPLE WHO DON'T USUALLY COME TOGETHER.
HEYAAA! HAPPY NEW YEAR!!
HA HA... THEY'RE SO DEDICATED TO SHOWING UP EVERY SINGLE YEAR!
CHATTER
わい
CHATTER
わい
HEH HEH... I'M SO PROUD OF ALL OF MY DISCIPLES!
BUT THEY'RE A LITTLE RUDE, I GUESS...
THEY'RE NOT CONSIDERATE ENOUGH TO SKIP THE HOLIDAY AND COME TWO DAYS LATER...
...TO AVOID CROWDING, LIKE YOURS DO.
OH, RIGHT. JESUS-SAMA, I HAVE SOMETHING.
HUH?!
OH, I HAVE ONE, TOO.
AENL'S YARD REMEDES
Happy Bag
RU
WH-WHAT?! NO, YOU DIDN'T HAVE TO!
I CAN'T BELIEVE EACH ONE OF YOU BROUGHT SUCH A LARGE GIFT BAG...
UH, ACTUALLY, SENSEI...
THAT'S RIGHT. JANUARY 1ST IS A VERY SPECIAL DAY...

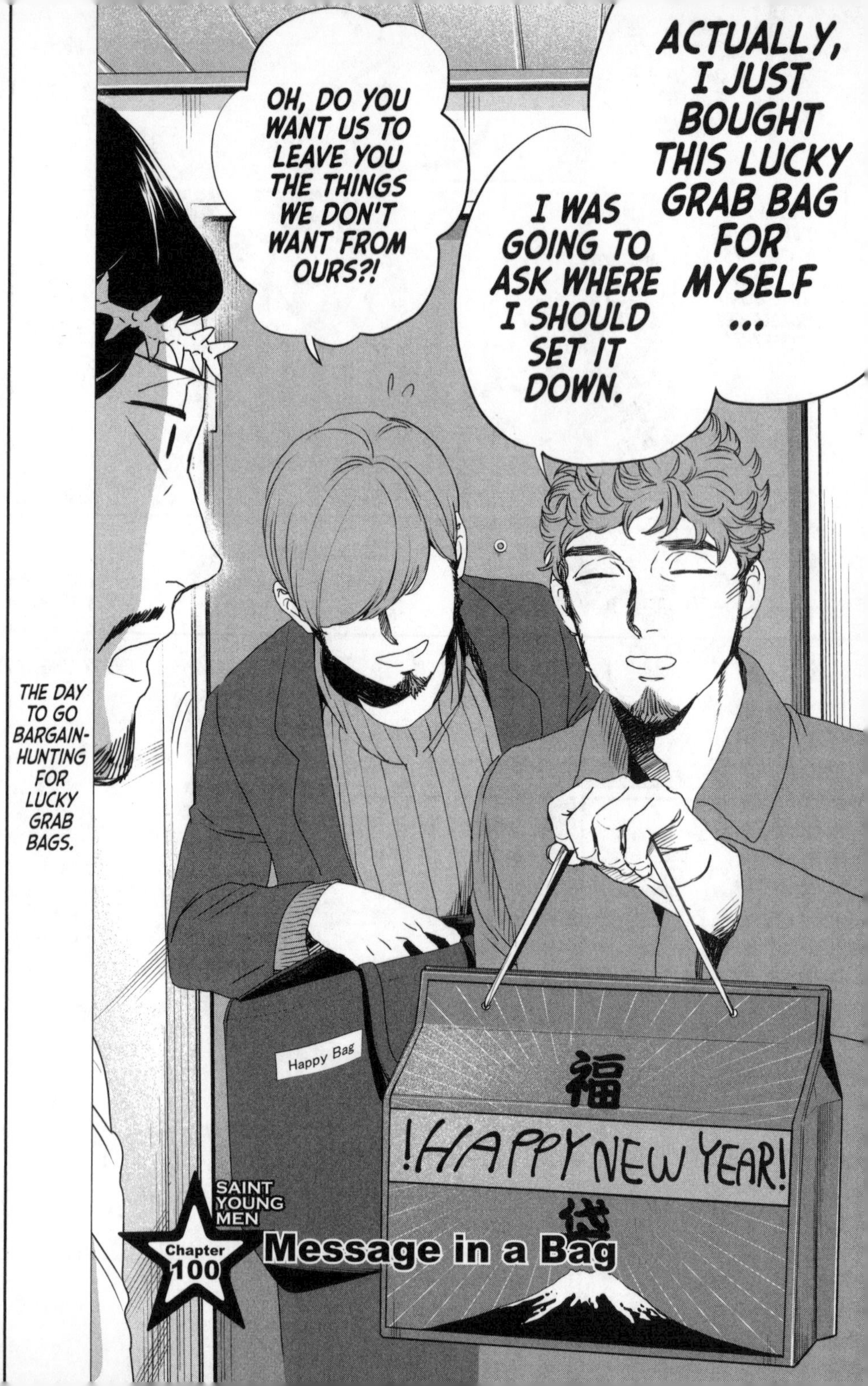
ACTUALLY, I JUST BOUGHT THIS LUCKY GRAB BAG FOR MYSELF ...
I WAS GOING TO ASK WHERE I SHOULD SET IT DOWN.
OH, DO YOU WANT US TO LEAVE YOU THE THINGS WE DON'T WANT FROM OURS?!
THE DAY TO GO BARGAIN-HUNTING FOR LUCKY GRAB BAGS.
Happy Bag
福
!HAPPY NEW YEAR!
SAINT YOUNG MEN
Chapter 100
Message in a Bag

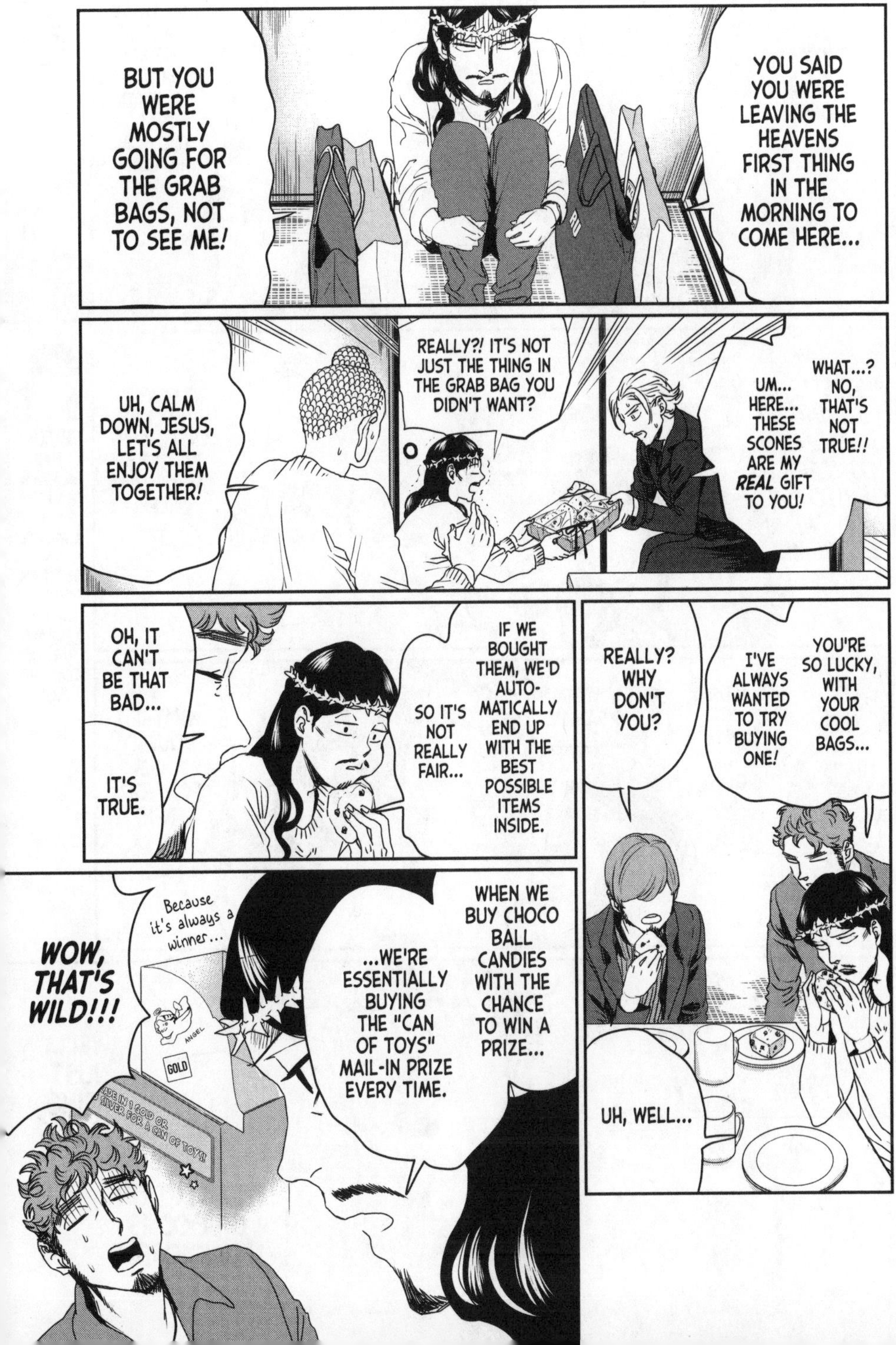
YOU SAID YOU WERE LEAVING THE HEAVENS FIRST THING IN THE MORNING TO COME HERE...
BUT YOU WERE MOSTLY GOING FOR THE GRAB BAGS, NOT TO SEE ME!
WHAT...? NO, THAT'S NOT TRUE!!
UM... HERE... THESE SCONES ARE MY *REAL* GIFT TO YOU!
REALLY?! IT'S NOT JUST THE THING IN THE GRAB BAG YOU DIDN'T WANT?
UH, CALM DOWN, JESUS, LET'S ALL ENJOY THEM TOGETHER!
YOU'RE SO LUCKY, WITH YOUR COOL BAGS...
I'VE ALWAYS WANTED TO TRY BUYING ONE!
REALLY? WHY DON'T YOU?
UH, WELL...
IF WE BOUGHT THEM, WE'D AUTO-MATICALLY END UP WITH THE BEST POSSIBLE ITEMS INSIDE.
SO IT'S NOT REALLY FAIR...
OH, IT CAN'T BE THAT BAD...
IT'S TRUE.
WHEN WE BUY CHOCO BALL CANDIES WITH THE CHANCE TO WIN A PRIZE...
...WE'RE ESSENTIALLY BUYING THE "CAN OF TOYS" MAIL-IN PRIZE EVERY TIME.
Because it's always a winner...
ANGEL
GOLD
WOW, THAT'S WILD!!!

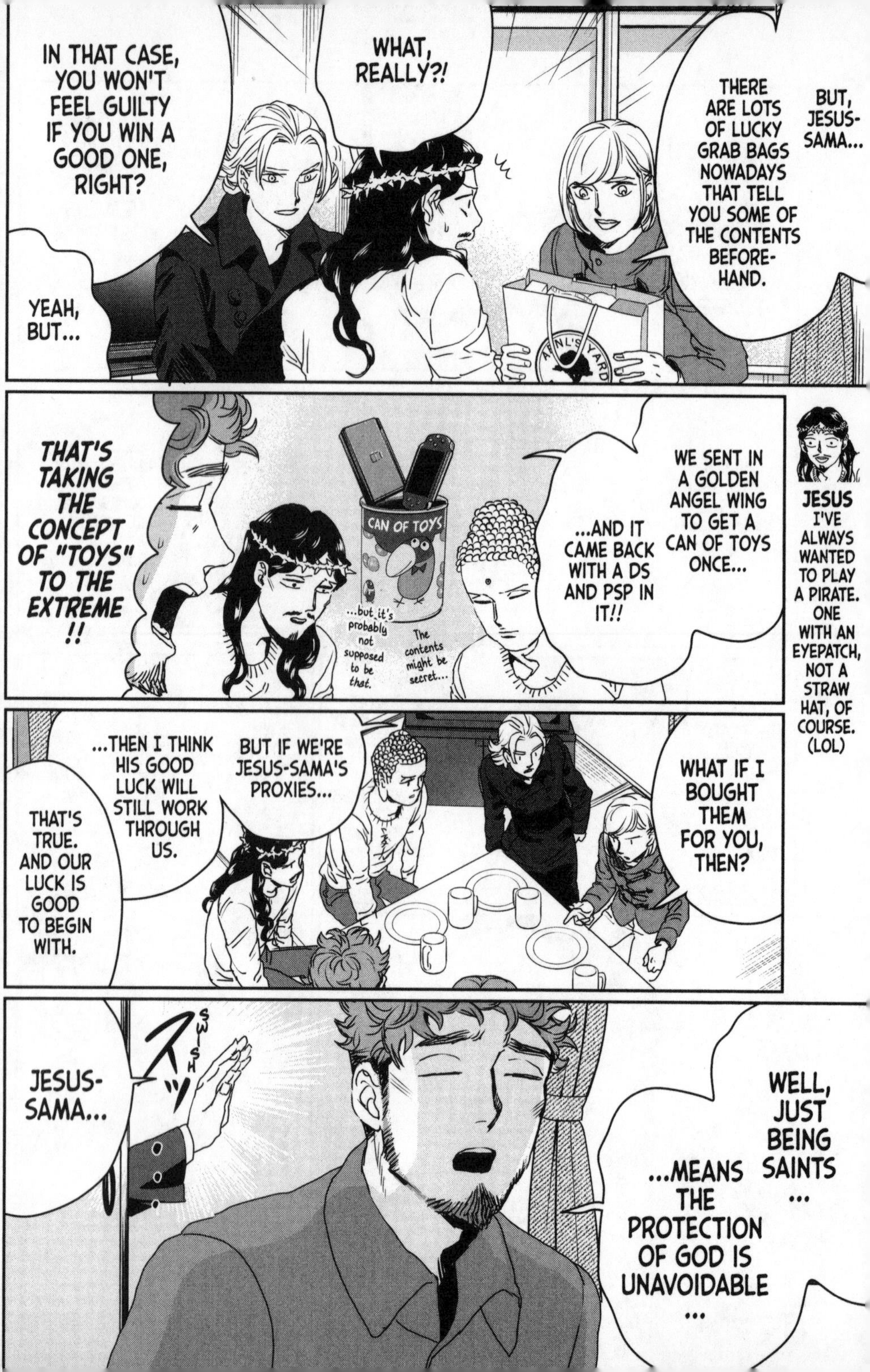
BUT, JESUS-SAMA...
THERE ARE LOTS OF LUCKY GRAB BAGS NOWADAYS THAT TELL YOU SOME OF THE CONTENTS BEFOREHAND.
WHAT, REALLY?!
IN THAT CASE, YOU WON'T FEEL GUILTY IF YOU WIN A GOOD ONE, RIGHT?
YEAH, BUT...
WE SENT IN A GOLDEN ANGEL WING TO GET A CAN OF TOYS ONCE...
...AND IT CAME BACK WITH A DS AND PSP IN IT!!
CAN OF TOYS
The contents might be secret...
...but it's probably not supposed to be that.
THAT'S TAKING THE CONCEPT OF "TOYS" TO THE EXTREME!!
WHAT IF I BOUGHT THEM FOR YOU, THEN?
BUT IF WE'RE JESUS-SAMA'S PROXIES...
...THEN I THINK HIS GOOD LUCK WILL STILL WORK THROUGH US.
THAT'S TRUE. AND OUR LUCK IS GOOD TO BEGIN WITH.
WELL, JUST BEING SAINTS...
...MEANS THE PROTECTION OF GOD IS UNAVOIDABLE...
SWISH
JESUS-SAMA...
JESUS
I'VE ALWAYS WANTED TO PLAY A PIRATE. ONE WITH AN EYEPATCH, NOT A STRAW HAT, OF COURSE. (LOL)

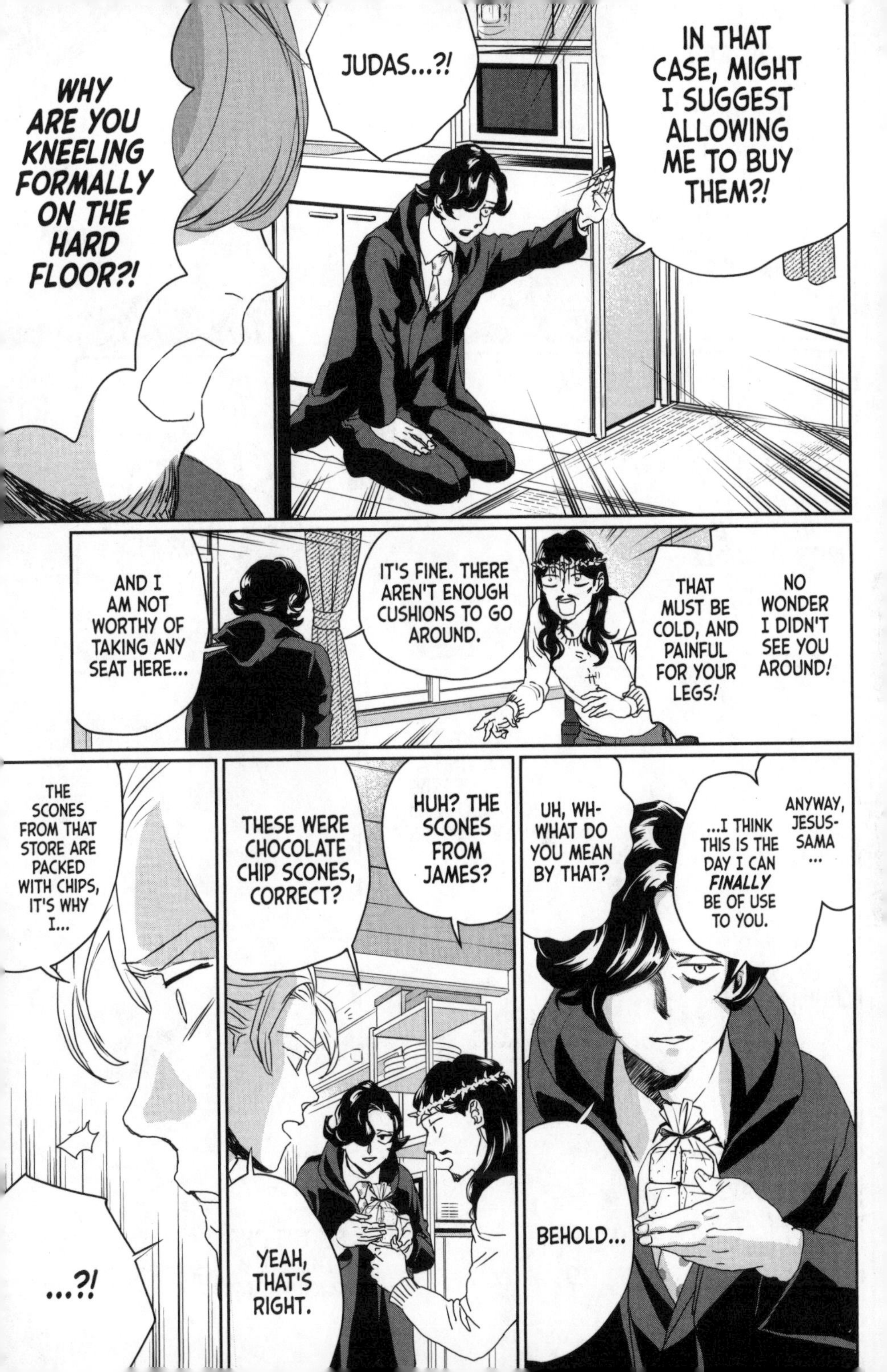
IN THAT CASE, MIGHT I SUGGEST ALLOWING ME TO BUY THEM?!
JUDAS...?!
WHY ARE YOU KNEELING FORMALLY ON THE HARD FLOOR?!
NO WONDER I DIDN'T SEE YOU AROUND!
THAT MUST BE COLD, AND PAINFUL FOR YOUR LEGS!
IT'S FINE. THERE AREN'T ENOUGH CUSHIONS TO GO AROUND.
AND I AM NOT WORTHY OF TAKING ANY SEAT HERE...
ANYWAY, JESUS-SAMA ...
...I THINK THIS IS THE DAY I CAN FINALLY BE OF USE TO YOU.
UH, WH-WHAT DO YOU MEAN BY THAT?
BEHOLD...
HUH? THE SCONES FROM JAMES?
THESE WERE CHOCOLATE CHIP SCONES, CORRECT?
YEAH, THAT'S RIGHT.
THE SCONES FROM THAT STORE ARE PACKED WITH CHIPS, IT'S WHY I...
...?!

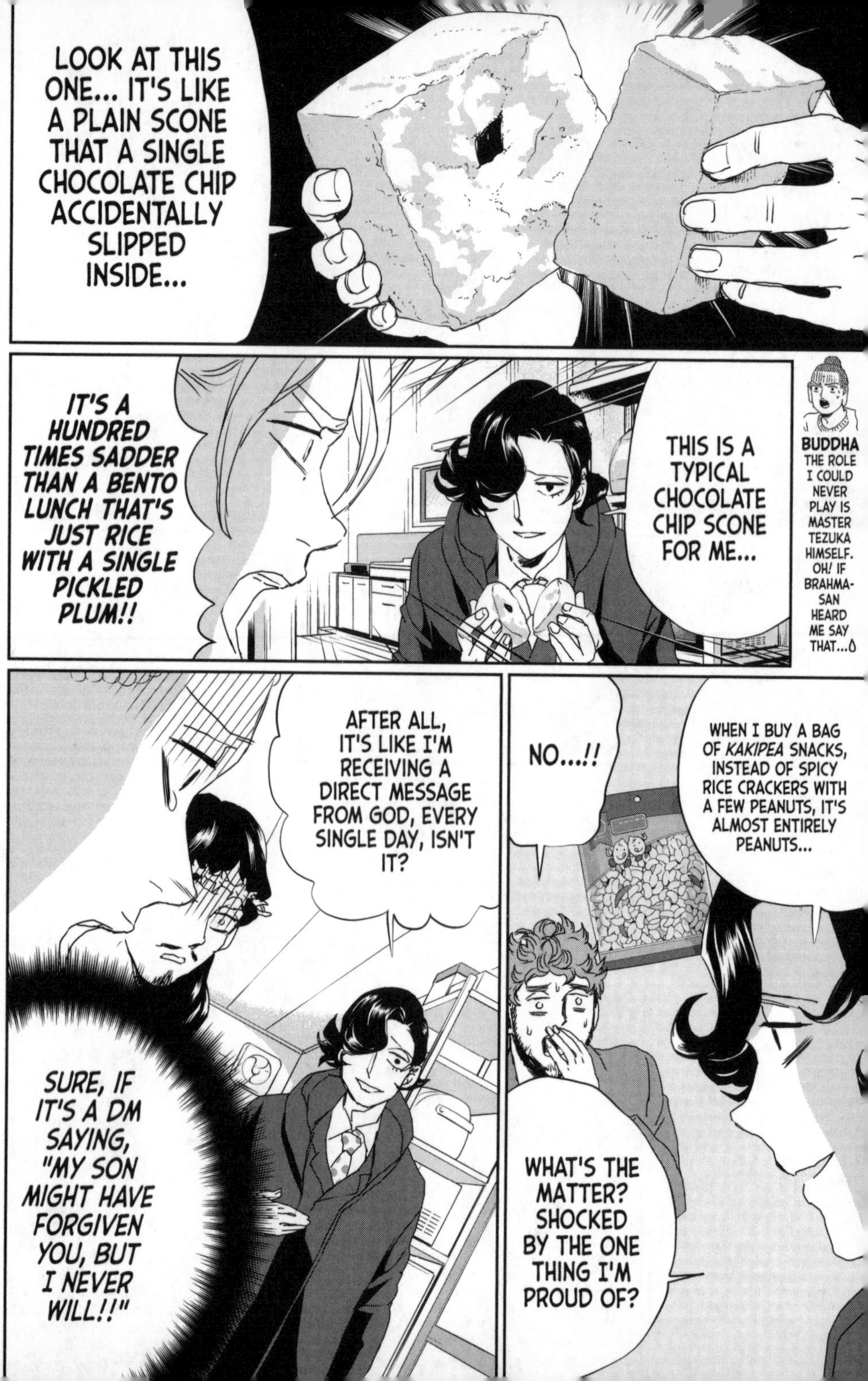
LOOK AT THIS ONE... IT'S LIKE A PLAIN SCONE THAT A SINGLE CHOCOLATE CHIP ACCIDENTALLY SLIPPED INSIDE...
BUDDHA
THE ROLE I COULD NEVER PLAY IS MASTER TEZUKA HIMSELF. OH! IF BRAHMA-SAN HEARD ME SAY THAT...
THIS IS A TYPICAL CHOCOLATE CHIP SCONE FOR ME...
IT'S A HUNDRED TIMES SADDER THAN A BENTO LUNCH THAT'S JUST RICE WITH A SINGLE PICKLED PLUM!!
WHEN I BUY A BAG OF *KAKIPEA* SNACKS, INSTEAD OF SPICY RICE CRACKERS WITH A FEW PEANUTS, IT'S ALMOST ENTIRELY PEANUTS...
NO...!!
WHAT'S THE MATTER? SHOCKED BY THE ONE THING I'M PROUD OF?
AFTER ALL, IT'S LIKE I'M RECEIVING A DIRECT MESSAGE FROM GOD, EVERY SINGLE DAY, ISN'T IT?
SURE, IF IT'S A DM SAYING, "MY SON MIGHT HAVE FORGIVEN YOU, BUT I NEVER WILL!!"

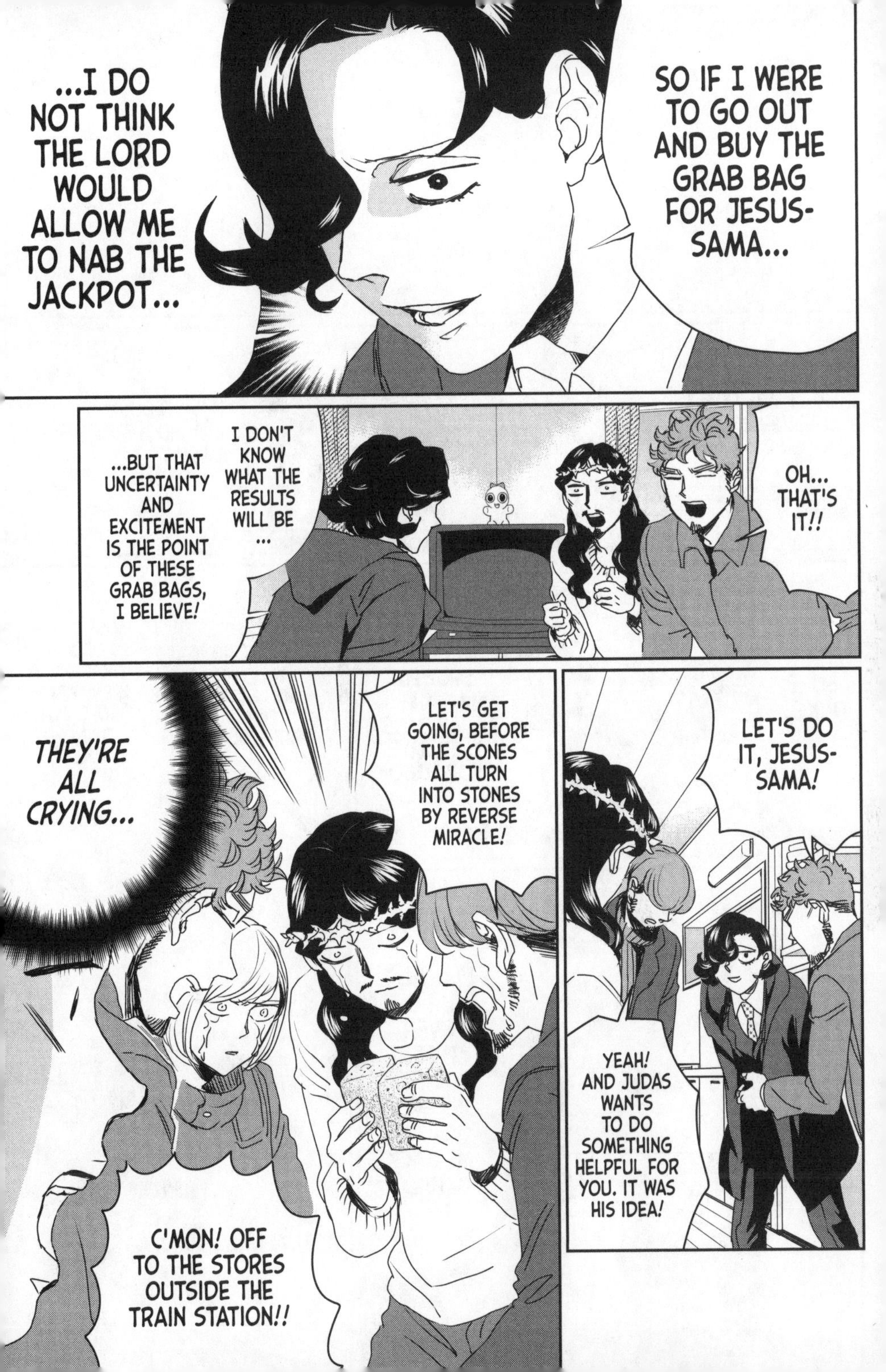
SO IF I WERE TO GO OUT AND BUY THE GRAB BAG FOR JESUS-SAMA...
...I DO NOT THINK THE LORD WOULD ALLOW ME TO NAB THE JACKPOT...
OH... THAT'S IT!!
I DON'T KNOW WHAT THE RESULTS WILL BE ...
...BUT THAT UNCERTAINTY AND EXCITEMENT IS THE POINT OF THESE GRAB BAGS, I BELIEVE!
LET'S DO IT, JESUS-SAMA!
YEAH! AND JUDAS WANTS TO DO SOMETHING HELPFUL FOR YOU. IT WAS HIS IDEA!
LET'S GET GOING, BEFORE THE SCONES ALL TURN INTO STONES BY REVERSE MIRACLE!
THEY'RE ALL CRYING...
C'MON! OFF TO THE STORES OUTSIDE THE TRAIN STATION!!

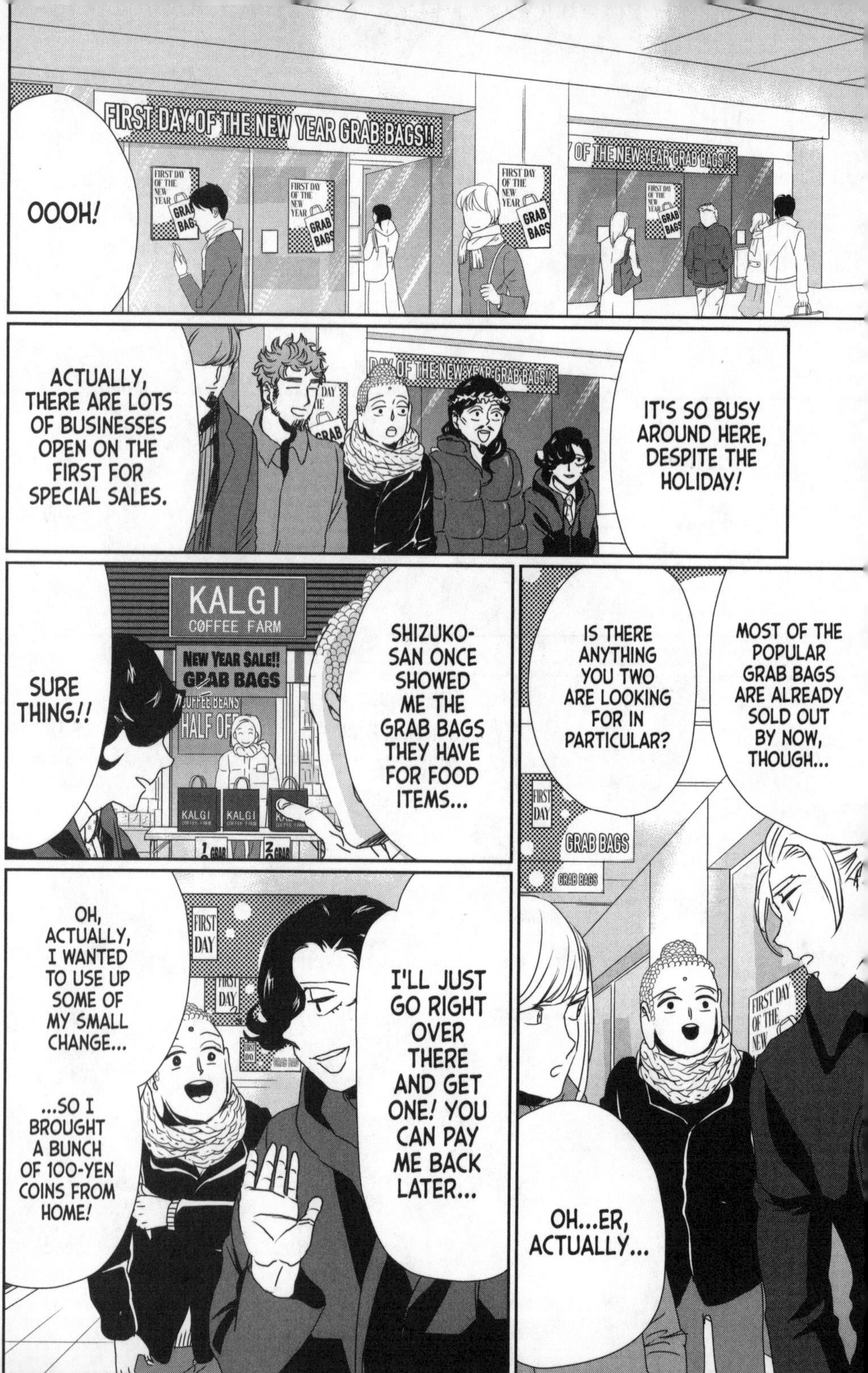
FIRST DAY OF THE NEW YEAR GRAB BAGS!!
OOOH!
IT'S SO BUSY AROUND HERE, DESPITE THE HOLIDAY!
ACTUALLY, THERE ARE LOTS OF BUSINESSES OPEN ON THE FIRST FOR SPECIAL SALES.
MOST OF THE POPULAR GRAB BAGS ARE ALREADY SOLD OUT BY NOW, THOUGH...
IS THERE ANYTHING YOU TWO ARE LOOKING FOR IN PARTICULAR?
KALGI COFFEE FARM
NEW YEAR SALE!! GRAB BAGS
SHIZUKO-SAN ONCE SHOWED ME THE GRAB BAGS THEY HAVE FOR FOOD ITEMS...
SURE THING!!
OH...ER, ACTUALLY...
I'LL JUST GO RIGHT OVER THERE AND GET ONE! YOU CAN PAY ME BACK LATER...
OH, ACTUALLY, I WANTED TO USE UP SOME OF MY SMALL CHANGE...
...SO I BROUGHT A BUNCH OF 100-YEN COINS FROM HOME!

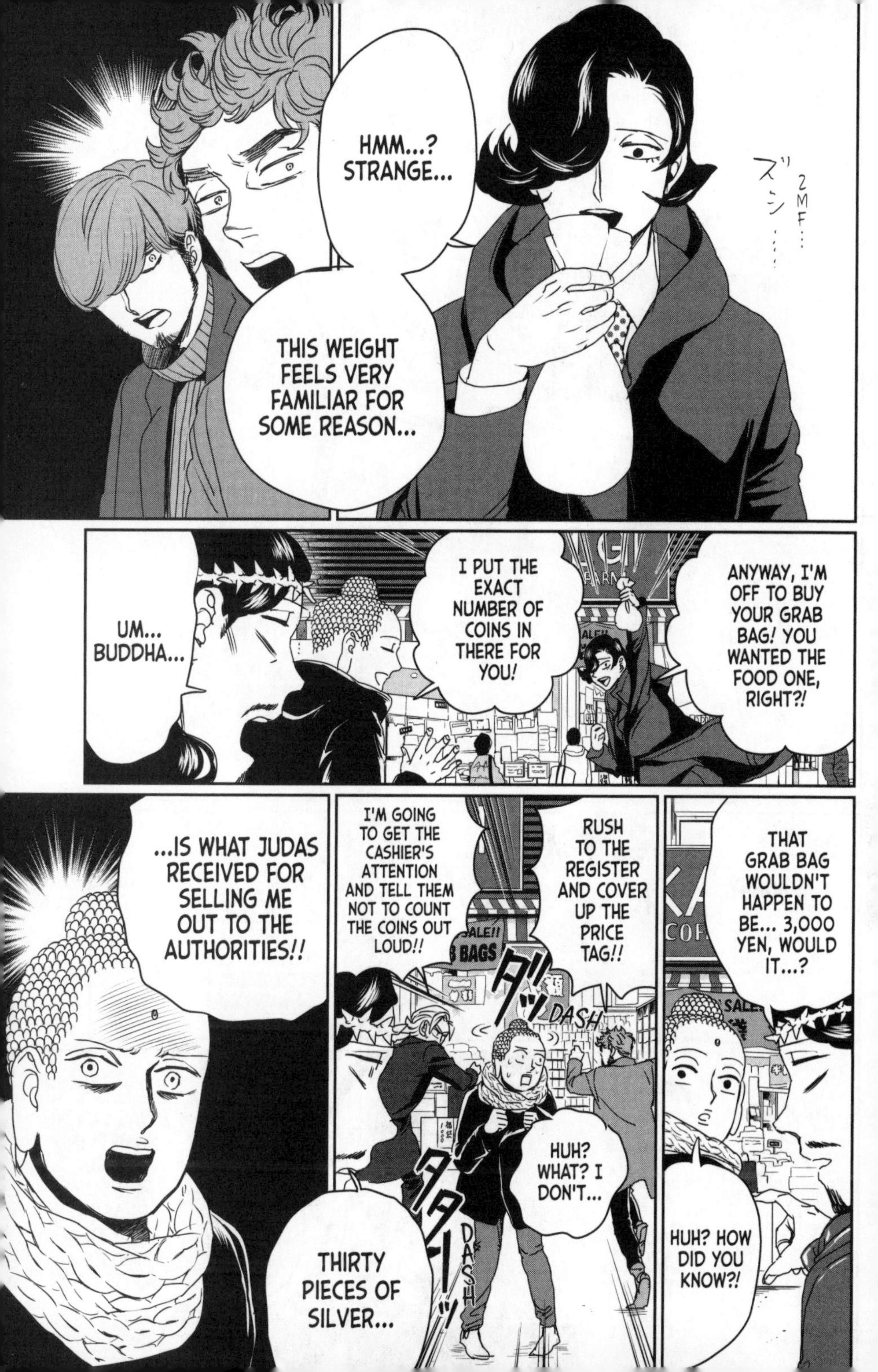
ズシン……
ZMF...
HMM...? STRANGE...
THIS WEIGHT FEELS VERY FAMILIAR FOR SOME REASON...
ANYWAY, I'M OFF TO BUY YOUR GRAB BAG! YOU WANTED THE FOOD ONE, RIGHT?!
I PUT THE EXACT NUMBER OF COINS IN THERE FOR YOU!
UM... BUDDHA...
THAT GRAB BAG WOULDN'T HAPPEN TO BE... 3,000 YEN, WOULD IT...?
HUH? HOW DID YOU KNOW?!
RUSH TO THE REGISTER AND COVER UP THE PRICE TAG!!
I'M GOING TO GET THE CASHIER'S ATTENTION AND TELL THEM NOT TO COUNT THE COINS OUT LOUD!!
SALE!!
BAGS
ダッ DASH
HUH? WHAT? I DON'T...
タタ— DASH
THIRTY PIECES OF SILVER...
...IS WHAT JUDAS RECEIVED FOR SELLING ME OUT TO THE AUTHORITIES!!

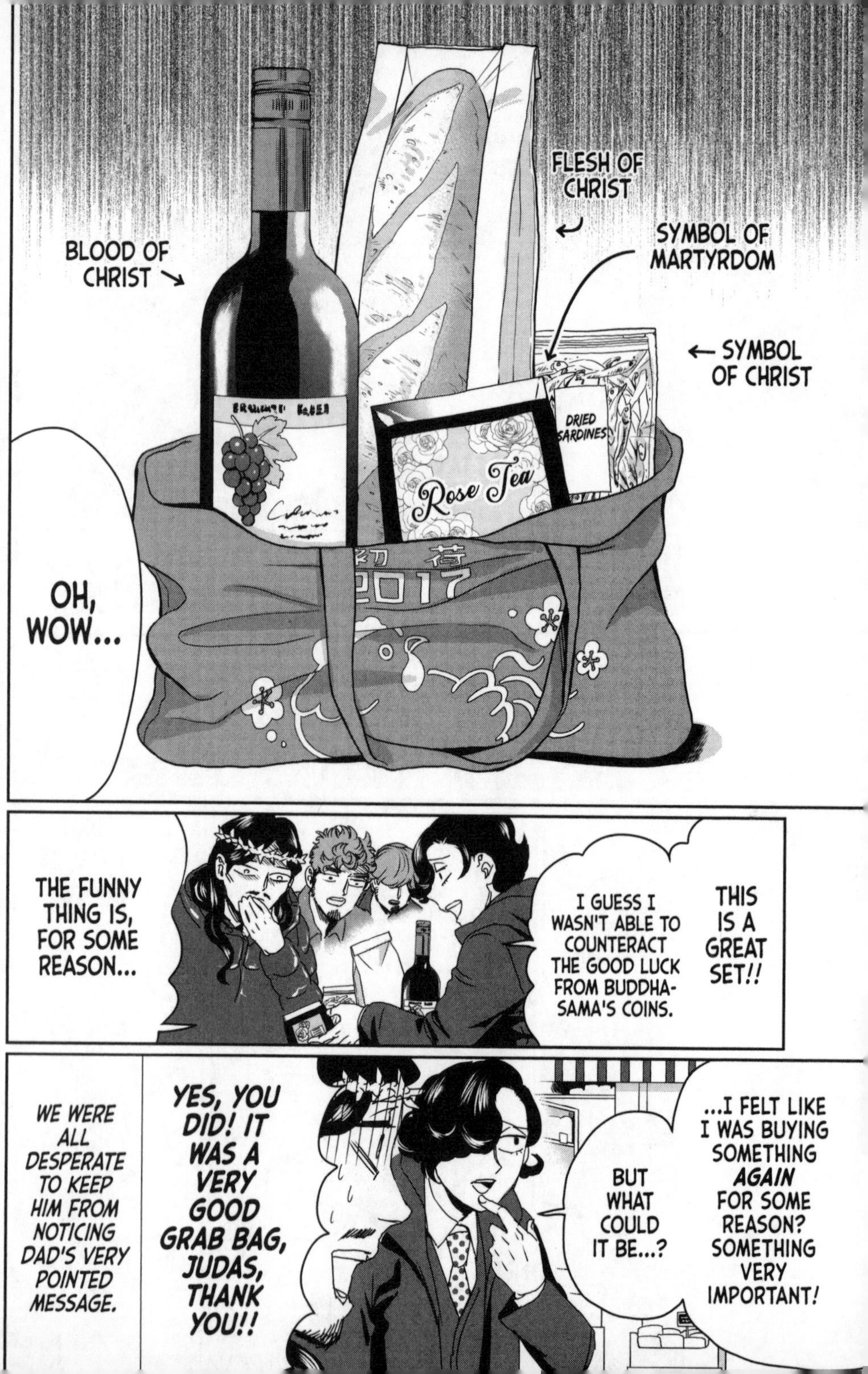

← SYMBOL OF CHRIST
SYMBOL OF MARTYRDOM
FLESH OF CHRIST
BLOOD OF CHRIST →
DRIED SARDINES
Rose Tea
2017
OH, WOW...
THIS IS A GREAT SET!!
I GUESS I WASN'T ABLE TO COUNTERACT THE GOOD LUCK FROM BUDDHA-SAMA'S COINS.
THE FUNNY THING IS, FOR SOME REASON...
...I FELT LIKE I WAS BUYING SOMETHING AGAIN FOR SOME REASON? SOMETHING VERY IMPORTANT!
BUT WHAT COULD IT BE...?
YES, YOU DID! IT WAS A VERY GOOD GRAB BAG, JUDAS, THANK YOU!!
WE WERE ALL DESPERATE TO KEEP HIM FROM NOTICING DAD'S VERY POINTED MESSAGE.

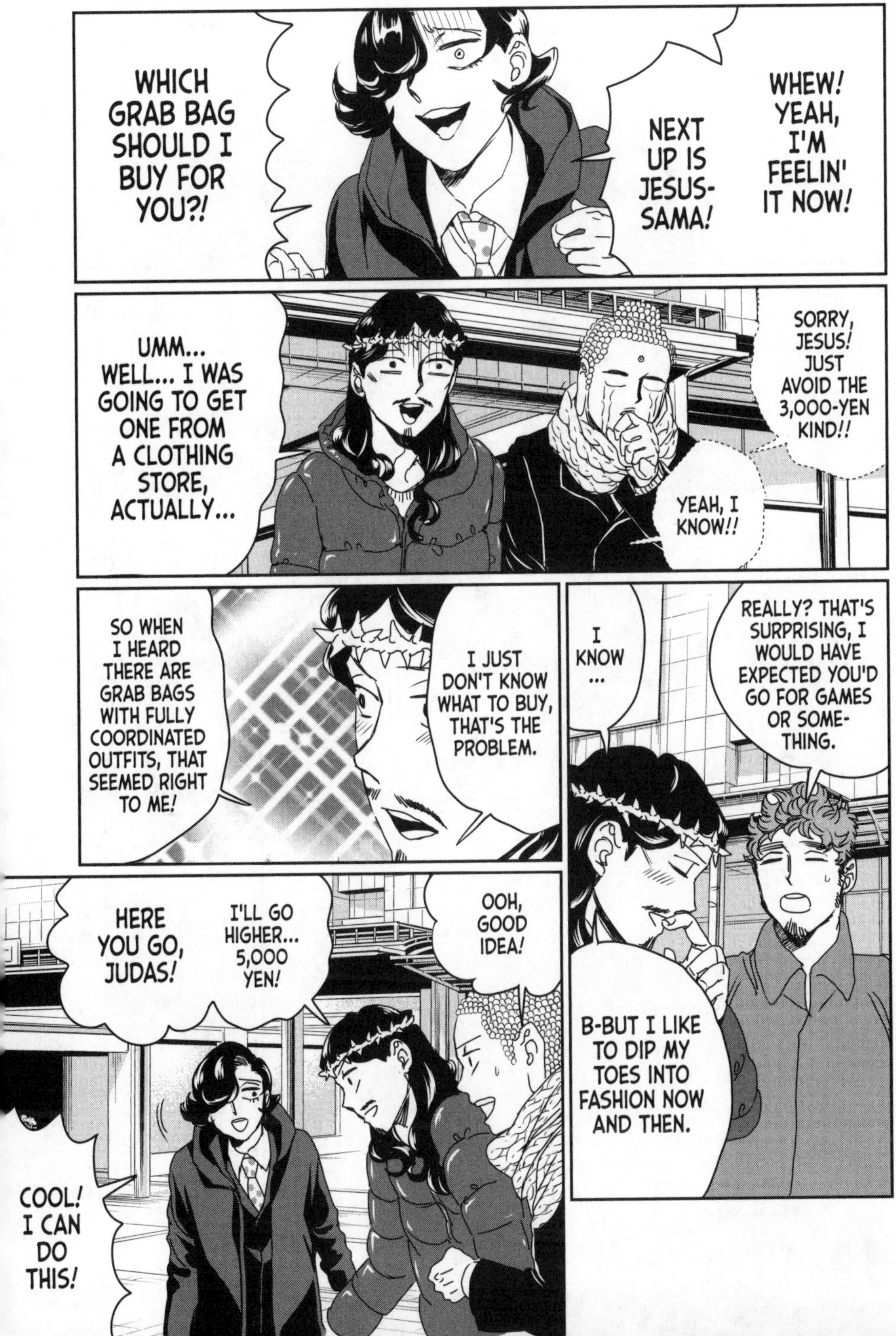
WHEW! YEAH, I'M FEELIN' IT NOW!
NEXT UP IS JESUS-SAMA!
WHICH GRAB BAG SHOULD I BUY FOR YOU?!
SORRY, JESUS! JUST AVOID THE 3,000-YEN KIND!!
YEAH, I KNOW!!
UMM... WELL... I WAS GOING TO GET ONE FROM A CLOTHING STORE, ACTUALLY...
REALLY? THAT'S SURPRISING, I WOULD HAVE EXPECTED YOU'D GO FOR GAMES OR SOME-THING.
I KNOW ...
B-BUT I LIKE TO DIP MY TOES INTO FASHION NOW AND THEN.
I JUST DON'T KNOW WHAT TO BUY, THAT'S THE PROBLEM.
SO WHEN I HEARD THERE ARE GRAB BAGS WITH FULLY COORDINATED OUTFITS, THAT SEEMED RIGHT TO ME!
OOH, GOOD IDEA!
I'LL GO HIGHER... 5,000 YEN!
HERE YOU GO, JUDAS!
COOL! I CAN DO THIS!

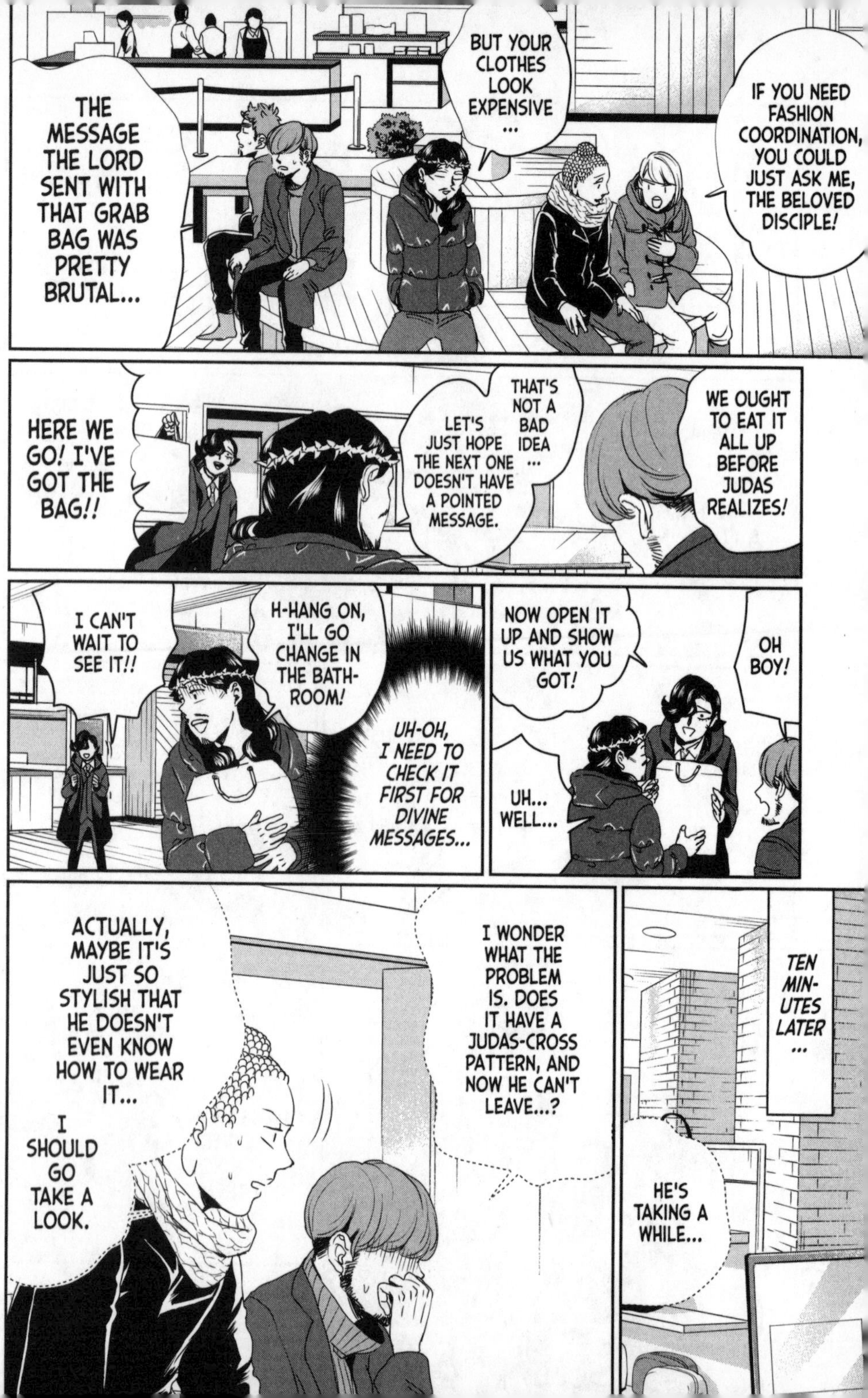
IF YOU NEED FASHION COORDINATION, YOU COULD JUST ASK ME, THE BELOVED DISCIPLE!
BUT YOUR CLOTHES LOOK EXPENSIVE...
THE MESSAGE THE LORD SENT WITH THAT GRAB BAG WAS PRETTY BRUTAL...
WE OUGHT TO EAT IT ALL UP BEFORE JUDAS REALIZES!
THAT'S NOT A BAD IDEA...
LET'S JUST HOPE THE NEXT ONE DOESN'T HAVE A POINTED MESSAGE.
HERE WE GO! I'VE GOT THE BAG!!
OH BOY!
NOW OPEN IT UP AND SHOW US WHAT YOU GOT!
UH... WELL...
H-HANG ON, I'LL GO CHANGE IN THE BATH-ROOM!
I CAN'T WAIT TO SEE IT!!
UH-OH, I NEED TO CHECK IT FIRST FOR DIVINE MESSAGES...
TEN MIN-UTES LATER...
HE'S TAKING A WHILE...
I WONDER WHAT THE PROBLEM IS. DOES IT HAVE A JUDAS-CROSS PATTERN, AND NOW HE CAN'T LEAVE...?
ACTUALLY, MAYBE IT'S JUST SO STYLISH THAT HE DOESN'T EVEN KNOW HOW TO WEAR IT...
I SHOULD GO TAKE A LOOK.

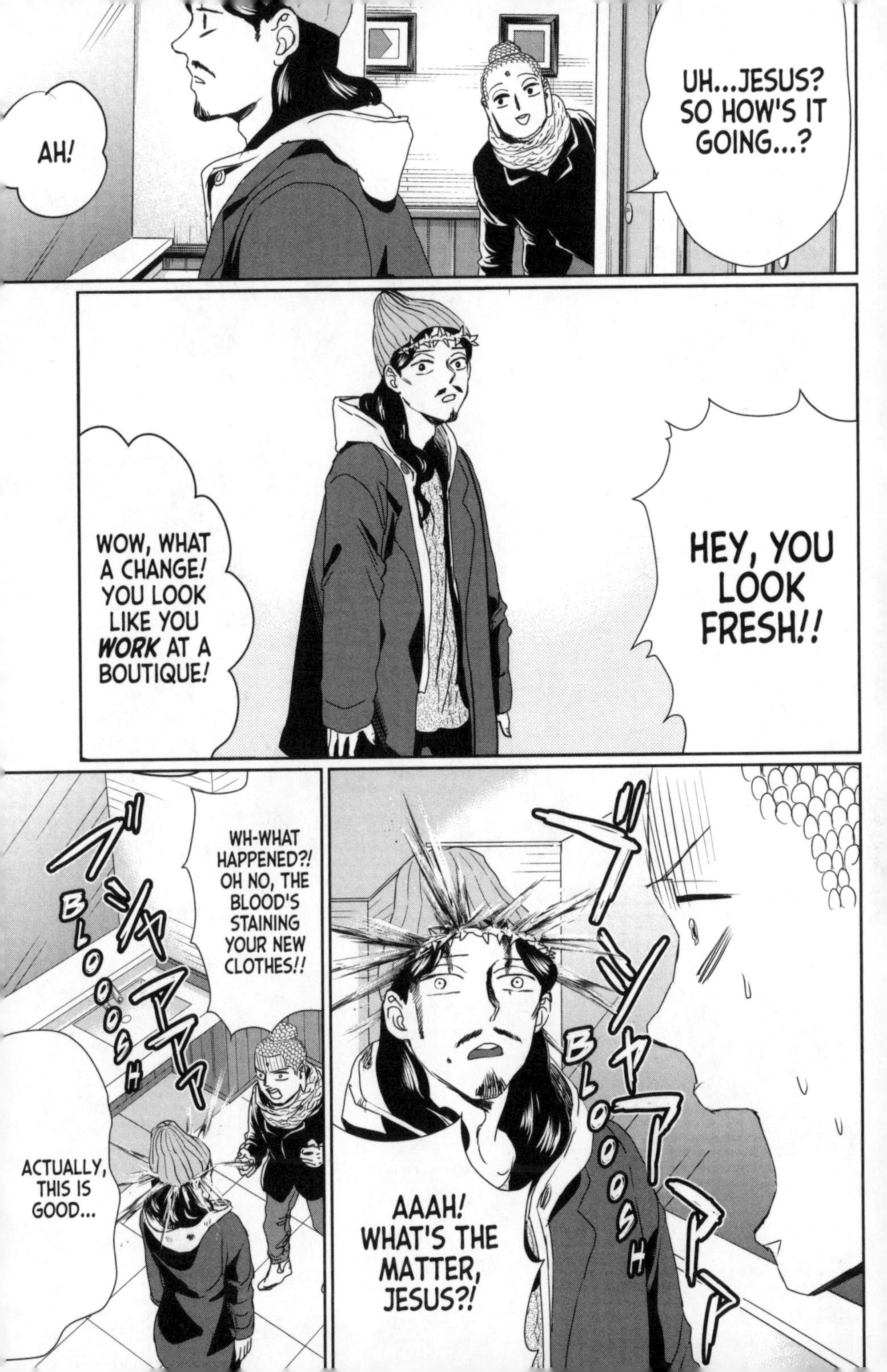
UH...JESUS? SO HOW'S IT GOING...?
AH!
HEY, YOU LOOK FRESH!!
WOW, WHAT A CHANGE! YOU LOOK LIKE YOU *WORK* AT A BOUTIQUE!
BLOOOOSH
AAAH! WHAT'S THE MATTER, JESUS?!
WH-WHAT HAPPENED?! OH NO, THE BLOOD'S STAINING YOUR NEW CLOTHES!!
BLOOOOSH
ACTUALLY, THIS IS GOOD...

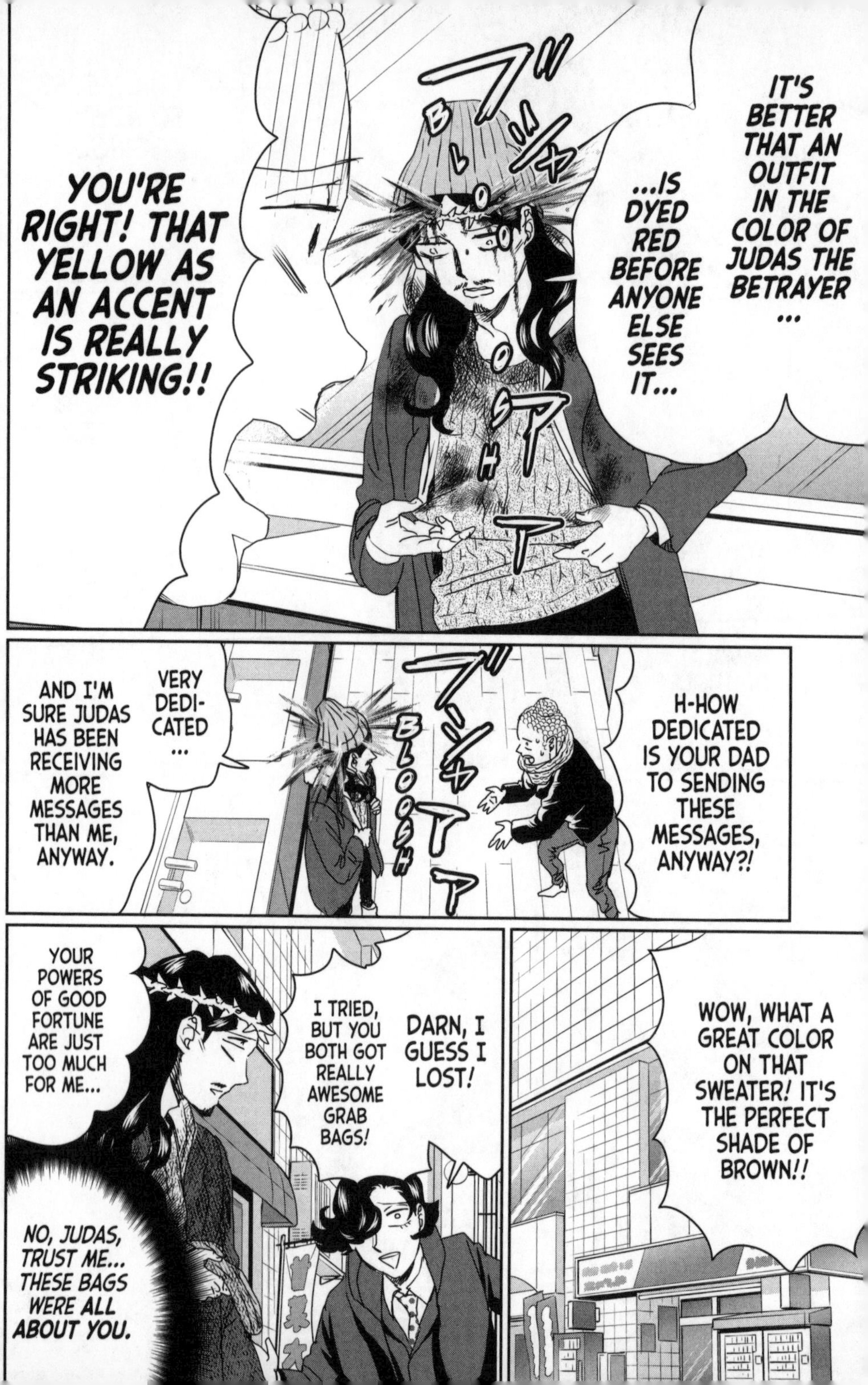
IT'S BETTER THAT AN OUTFIT IN THE COLOR OF JUDAS THE BETRAYER ...
...IS DYED RED BEFORE ANYONE ELSE SEES IT...
BLOOOSH
YOU'RE RIGHT! THAT YELLOW AS AN ACCENT IS REALLY STRIKING!!
H-HOW DEDICATED IS YOUR DAD TO SENDING THESE MESSAGES, ANYWAY?!
BLOOSH
VERY DEDI-CATED ...
AND I'M SURE JUDAS HAS BEEN RECEIVING MORE MESSAGES THAN ME, ANYWAY.
WOW, WHAT A GREAT COLOR ON THAT SWEATER! IT'S THE PERFECT SHADE OF BROWN!!
DARN, I GUESS I LOST!
I TRIED, BUT YOU BOTH GOT REALLY AWESOME GRAB BAGS!
YOUR POWERS OF GOOD FORTUNE ARE JUST TOO MUCH FOR ME...
NO, JUDAS, TRUST ME... THESE BAGS WERE ALL ABOUT YOU.

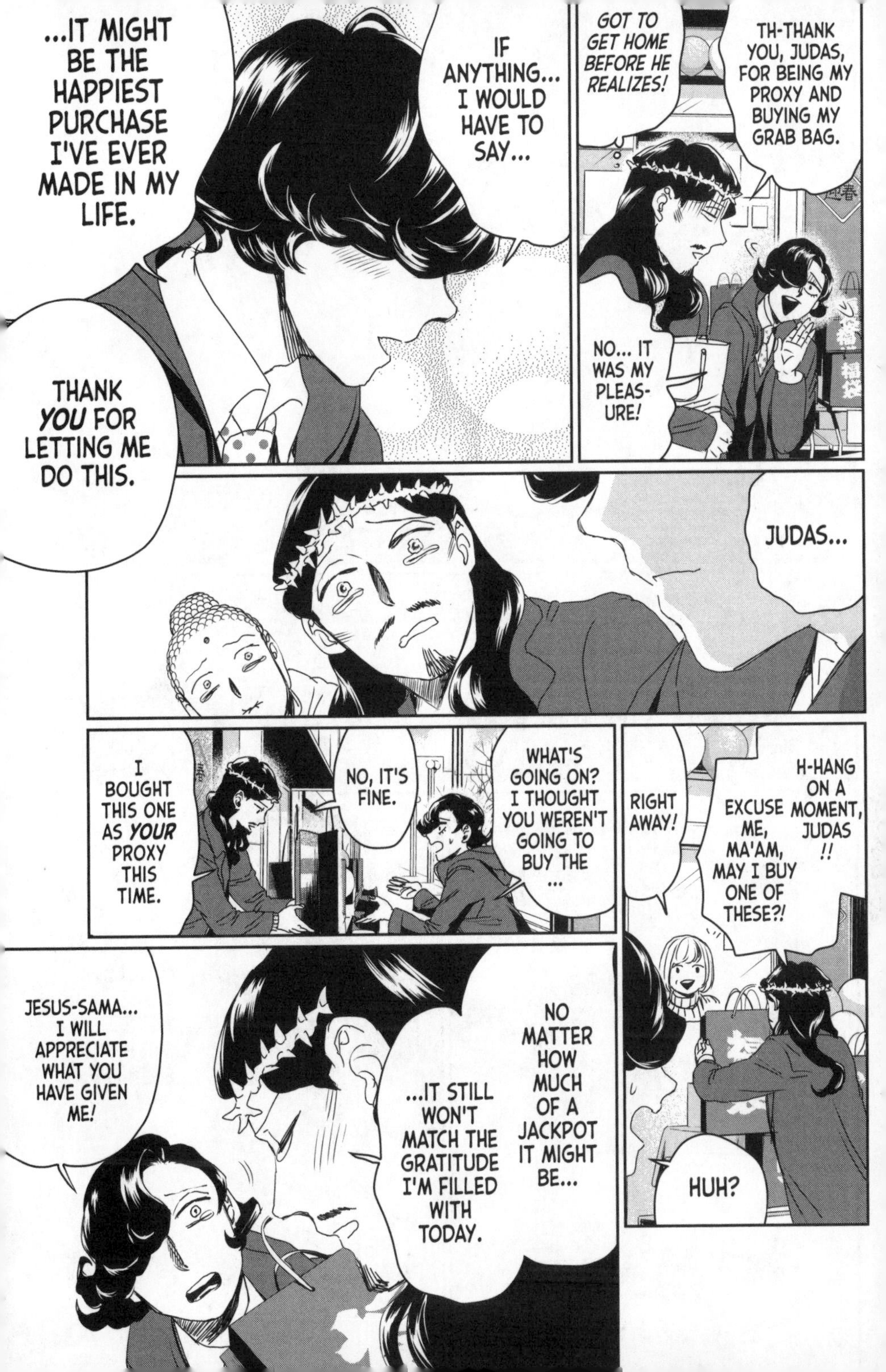
TH-THANK YOU, JUDAS, FOR BEING MY PROXY AND BUYING MY GRAB BAG.
GOT TO GET HOME BEFORE HE REALIZES!
NO... IT WAS MY PLEAS-URE!
IF ANYTHING... I WOULD HAVE TO SAY...
...IT MIGHT BE THE HAPPIEST PURCHASE I'VE EVER MADE IN MY LIFE.
THANK *YOU* FOR LETTING ME DO THIS.
JUDAS...
H-HANG ON A MOMENT, JUDAS !!
EXCUSE ME, MA'AM, MAY I BUY ONE OF THESE?!
RIGHT AWAY!
HUH?
WHAT'S GOING ON? I THOUGHT YOU WEREN'T GOING TO BUY THE ...
NO, IT'S FINE.
I BOUGHT THIS ONE AS *YOUR* PROXY THIS TIME.
NO MATTER HOW MUCH OF A JACKPOT IT MIGHT BE...
...IT STILL WON'T MATCH THE GRATITUDE I'M FILLED WITH TODAY.
JESUS-SAMA... I WILL APPRECIATE WHAT YOU HAVE GIVEN ME!

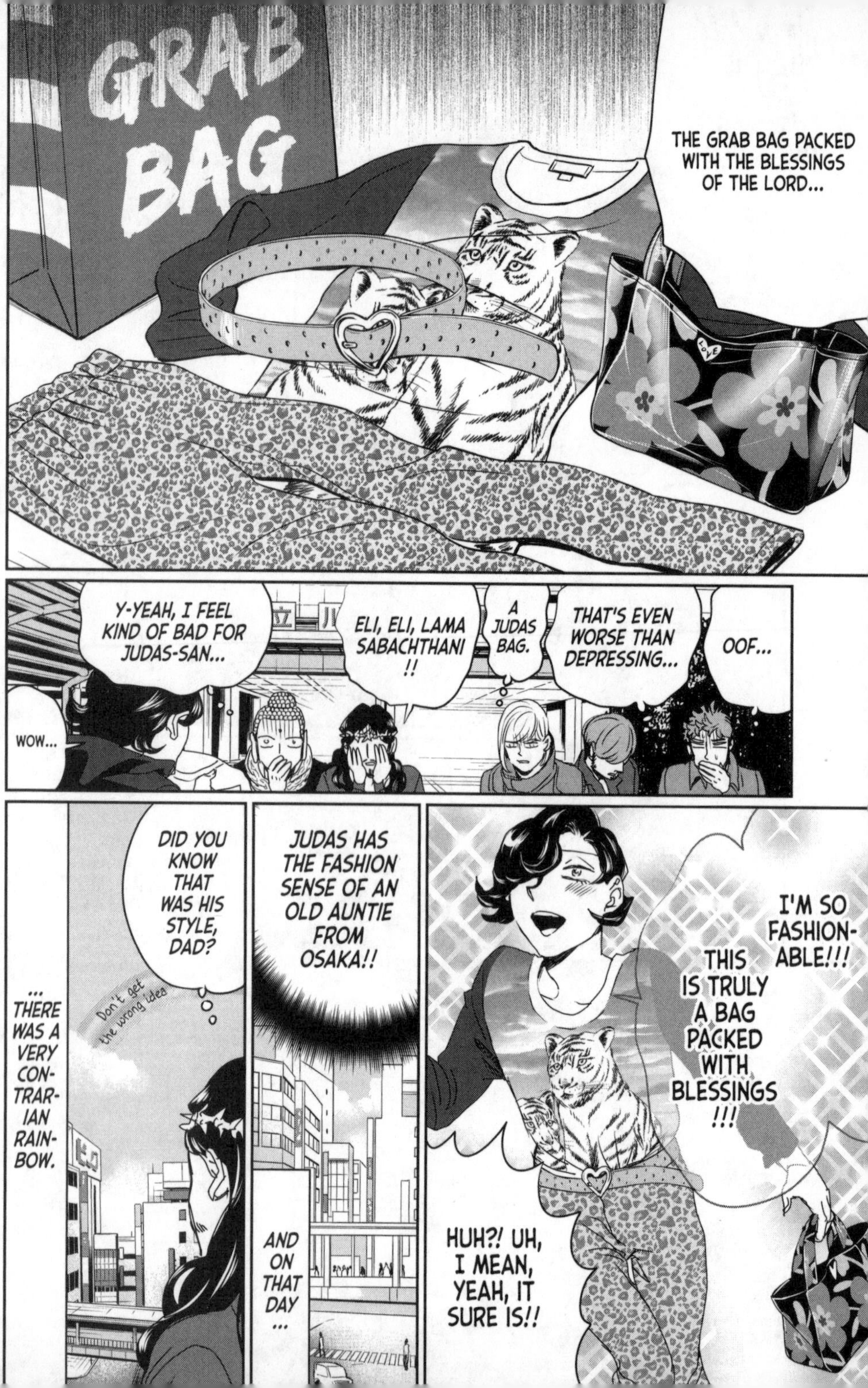
GRAB BAG
THE GRAB BAG PACKED WITH THE BLESSINGS OF THE LORD...
OOF...
THAT'S EVEN WORSE THAN DEPRESSING...
A JUDAS BAG.
ELI, ELI, LAMA SABACHTHANI!!
Y-YEAH, I FEEL KIND OF BAD FOR JUDAS-SAN...
WOW...
I'M SO FASHION-ABLE!!!
THIS IS TRULY A BAG PACKED WITH BLESSINGS!!!
HUH?! UH, I MEAN, YEAH, IT SURE IS!!
JUDAS HAS THE FASHION SENSE OF AN OLD AUNTIE FROM OSAKA!!
AND ON THAT DAY...
DID YOU KNOW THAT WAS HIS STYLE, DAD?
Don't get the wrong idea
...THERE WAS A VERY CONTRAR-IAN RAIN-BOW.

Judas Ratios

I'm used to it.

Curry

Obanyaki

Shaved Ice

Pocky

SAINT☆YOUNG MEN

CHAPTER 100 TRANSLATION NOTES

Lucky grab bags, page 56
A New Year's practice in Japan called *fukubukuro* ("lucky bag") in which stores make grab bags of products (usually blind, but sometimes they will advertise the exact products) for a modest price, but containing items worth more than the tag, and in some cases, significantly more valuable. This custom is designed to get shoppers into the store to buy other items, as well.

Choco Ball, page 57
A brand of candy snacks, featuring a flavored candy shell around some kind of filling, such as peanuts, caramel, or rice crisp. They are famous for their mail-in promotion; each box is opened up with a tab on the top, and on the inside can be either a silver or (rarer) gold "angel" tag. One gold angel or five silver angels can be traded in for an exclusive "Can of Toys." In recent years, the manufacturer, Morinaga, has created a different can on a yearly basis.

Hinomaru bento, page 60
A type of boxed lunch named after the Japanese flag (*hi-no-maru*, or "circle of sun") because on the bed of white rice is nothing more than a single *umeboshi* pickled plum. While *umeboshi* are treasured for their salt content, the humble simplicity of a *hinomaru* bento is so apparent on first glance that it's the poster child of "miserable" lunches.

Kakipea, page 60
A classic salty snack mix, consisting of a mix of peanuts and spicy rice crackers that are colored orange. The rice crackers are shaped to look like persimmon seeds, called *kaki no tane*, hence the name "kaki-pea." The proper ratio has more rice crackers than peanuts, because the crackers have the flavor and the peanuts are meant to provide a softer, nutty reprieve.

Osaka, page 70
Within Japan, different regions and cities have stereotypes about their residents and culture. As the second-largest metropolitan area in Japan after Tokyo, Osaka is often described as having a chip on its shoulder in relation to the capital. The people are louder and livelier and less inclined to be reserved, according to the generalization. Iin particular, middle-aged women from Osaka are stereotypically loud in every sense, and completely unconcerned with good taste.

Obanyaki, page 71
A sweet baked item, more commonly known as *imagawayaki*, which resembles an American biscuit in size, but with the outer consistency of a pancake. Like many traditional Japanese sweets, it is filled with *anko* sweet bean paste. it is cooked in special rounded molds to give it that particular cylindrical look.

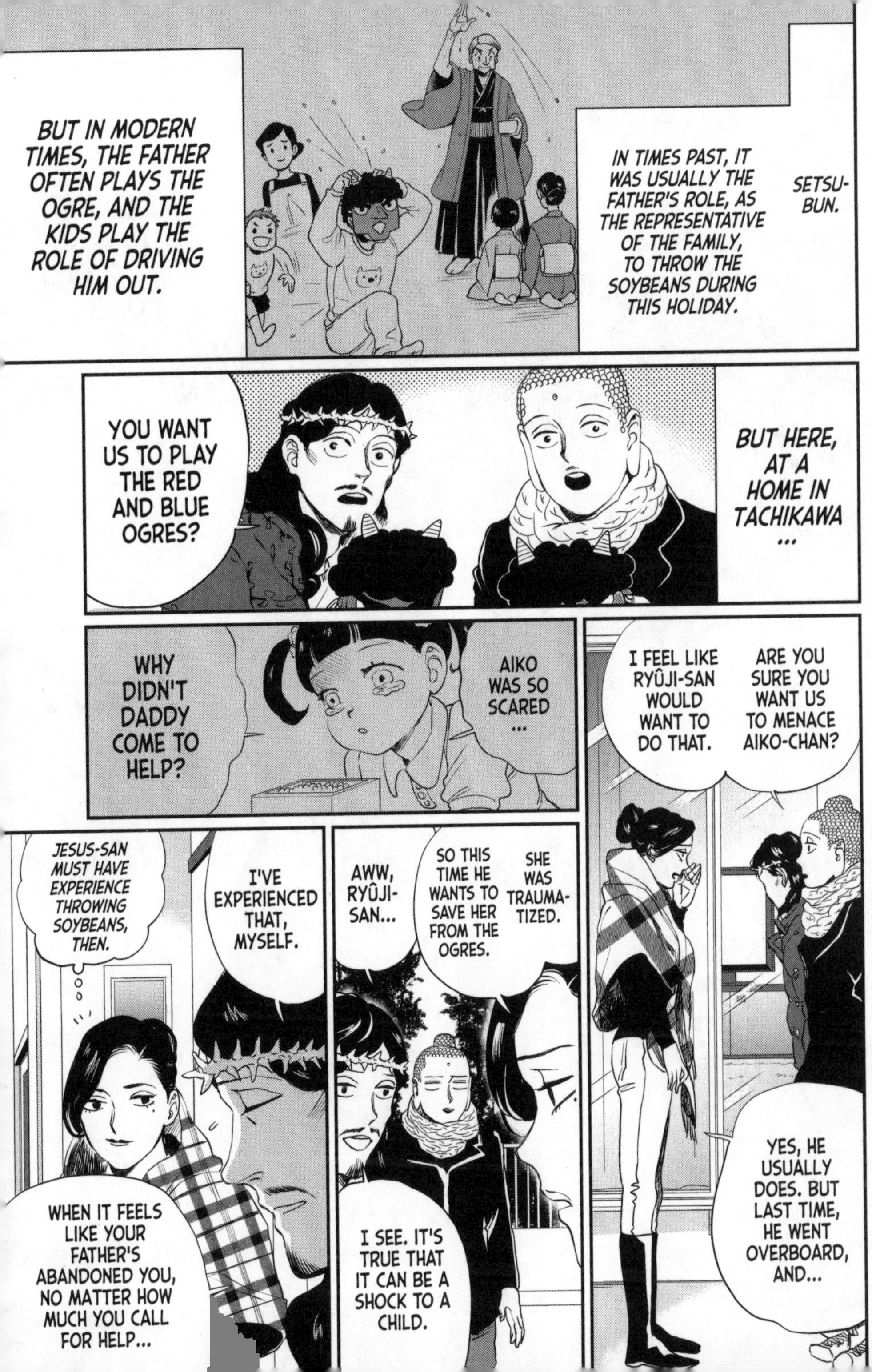
SETSU-BUN.
IN TIMES PAST, IT WAS USUALLY THE FATHER'S ROLE, AS THE REPRESENTATIVE OF THE FAMILY, TO THROW THE SOYBEANS DURING THIS HOLIDAY.
BUT IN MODERN TIMES, THE FATHER OFTEN PLAYS THE OGRE, AND THE KIDS PLAY THE ROLE OF DRIVING HIM OUT.
BUT HERE, AT A HOME IN TACHIKAWA ...
YOU WANT US TO PLAY THE RED AND BLUE OGRES?
ARE YOU SURE YOU WANT US TO MENACE AIKO-CHAN?
I FEEL LIKE RYŪJI-SAN WOULD WANT TO DO THAT.
YES, HE USUALLY DOES. BUT LAST TIME, HE WENT OVERBOARD, AND...
AIKO WAS SO SCARED ...
WHY DIDN'T DADDY COME TO HELP?
SHE WAS TRAUMATIZED.
SO THIS TIME HE WANTS TO SAVE HER FROM THE OGRES.
AWW, RYŪJI-SAN...
I SEE. IT'S TRUE THAT IT CAN BE A SHOCK TO A CHILD.
I'VE EXPERIENCED THAT, MYSELF.
JESUS-SAN MUST HAVE EXPERIENCE THROWING SOYBEANS, THEN.
WHEN IT FEELS LIKE YOUR FATHER'S ABANDONED YOU, NO MATTER HOW MUCH YOU CALL FOR HELP...

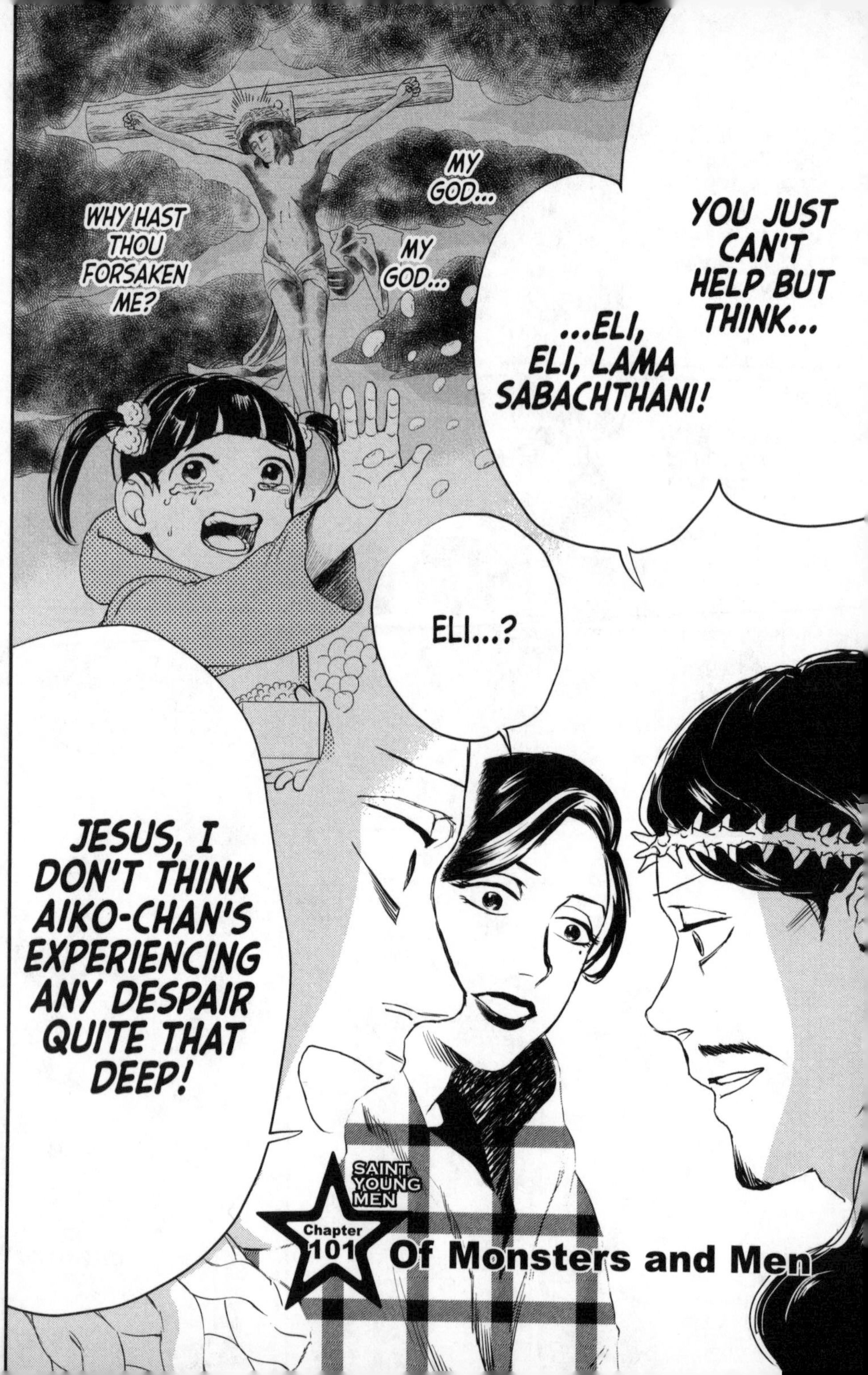
YOU JUST CAN'T HELP BUT THINK...
...ELI, ELI, LAMA SABACHTHANI!
MY GOD...
MY GOD...
WHY HAST THOU FORSAKEN ME?
ELI...?
JESUS, I DON'T THINK AIKO-CHAN'S EXPERIENCING ANY DESPAIR QUITE THAT DEEP!
SAINT YOUNG MEN
Chapter 101
Of Monsters and Men

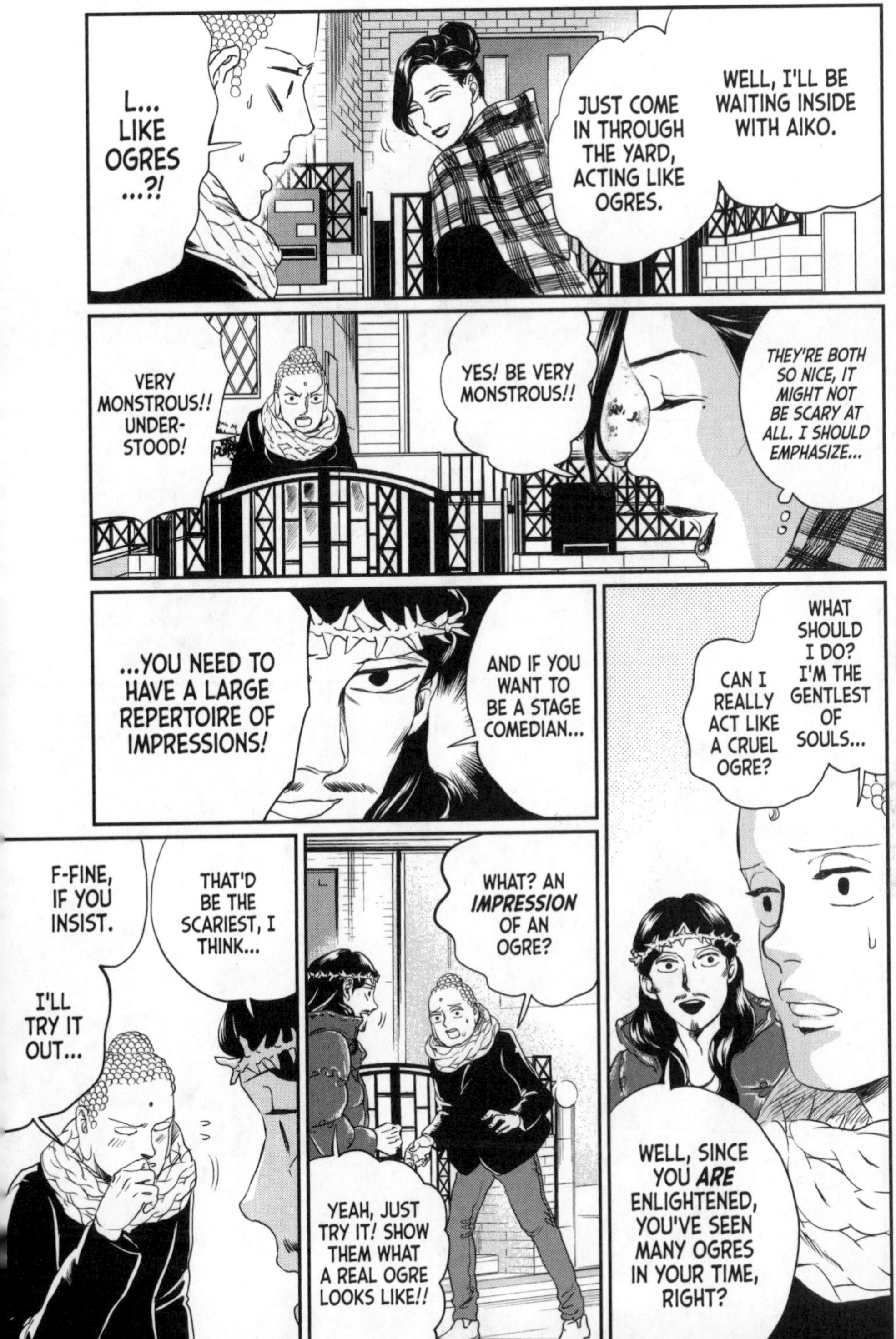
WELL, I'LL BE WAITING INSIDE WITH AIKO.
JUST COME IN THROUGH THE YARD, ACTING LIKE OGRES.
L... LIKE OGRES ...?!
THEY'RE BOTH SO NICE, IT MIGHT NOT BE SCARY AT ALL. I SHOULD EMPHASIZE...
YES! BE VERY MONSTROUS!!
VERY MONSTROUS!! UNDER-STOOD!
WHAT SHOULD I DO? I'M THE GENTLEST OF SOULS...
CAN I REALLY ACT LIKE A CRUEL OGRE?
WELL, SINCE YOU ARE ENLIGHTENED, YOU'VE SEEN MANY OGRES IN YOUR TIME, RIGHT?
AND IF YOU WANT TO BE A STAGE COMEDIAN...
...YOU NEED TO HAVE A LARGE REPERTOIRE OF IMPRESSIONS!
WHAT? AN IMPRESSION OF AN OGRE?
YEAH, JUST TRY IT! SHOW THEM WHAT A REAL OGRE LOOKS LIKE!!
THAT'D BE THE SCARIEST, I THINK...
F-FINE, IF YOU INSIST.
I'LL TRY IT OUT...

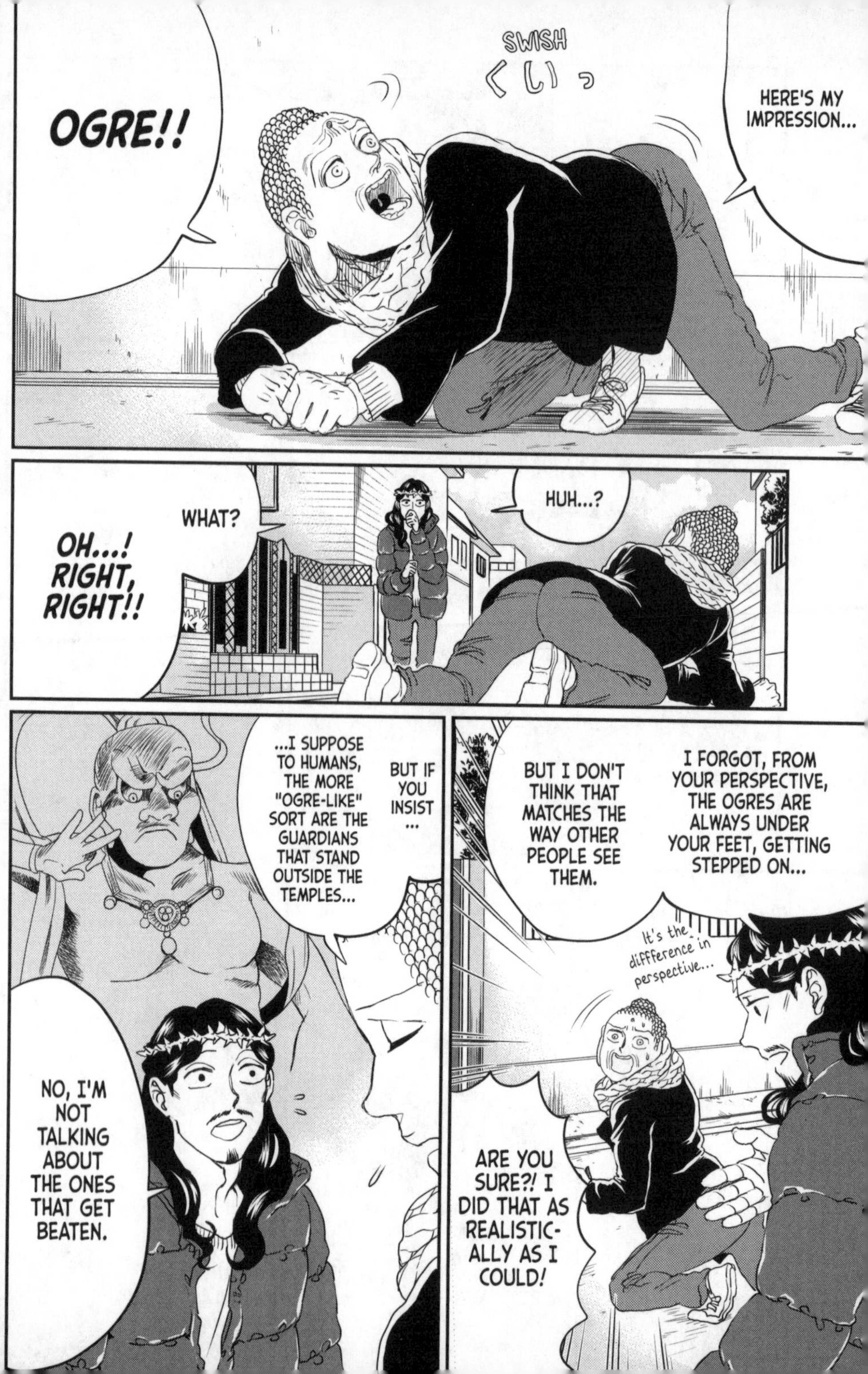
HERE'S MY IMPRESSION...
SWISH
くしっ
OGRE!!
HUH...?
WHAT?
OH...! RIGHT, RIGHT!!
I FORGOT, FROM YOUR PERSPECTIVE, THE OGRES ARE ALWAYS UNDER YOUR FEET, GETTING STEPPED ON...
BUT I DON'T THINK THAT MATCHES THE WAY OTHER PEOPLE SEE THEM.
It's the difference in perspective...
ARE YOU SURE?! I DID THAT AS REALISTIC-ALLY AS I COULD!
BUT IF YOU INSIST ...
...I SUPPOSE TO HUMANS, THE MORE "OGRE-LIKE" SORT ARE THE GUARDIANS THAT STAND OUTSIDE THE TEMPLES...
NO, I'M NOT TALKING ABOUT THE ONES THAT GET BEATEN.

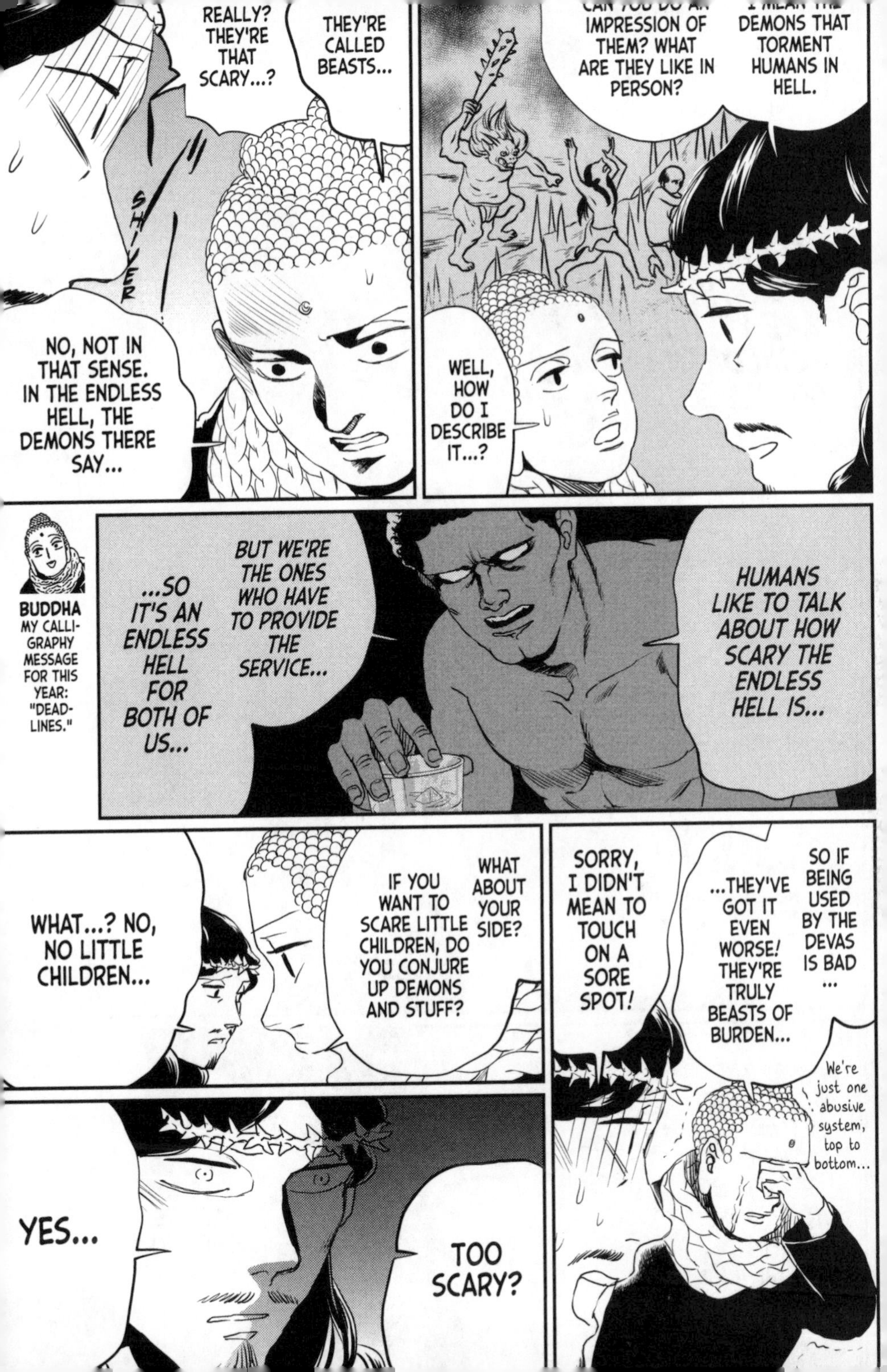
I MEAN THE DEMONS THAT TORMENT HUMANS IN HELL.
CAN YOU DO AN IMPRESSION OF THEM? WHAT ARE THEY LIKE IN PERSON?
WELL, HOW DO I DESCRIBE IT...?
THEY'RE CALLED BEASTS...
REALLY? THEY'RE THAT SCARY...?
SHIVER
NO, NOT IN THAT SENSE. IN THE ENDLESS HELL, THE DEMONS THERE SAY...
HUMANS LIKE TO TALK ABOUT HOW SCARY THE ENDLESS HELL IS...
BUT WE'RE THE ONES WHO HAVE TO PROVIDE THE SERVICE...
...SO IT'S AN ENDLESS HELL FOR BOTH OF US...
BUDDHA
MY CALLIGRAPHY MESSAGE FOR THIS YEAR: "DEADLINES."
SO IF BEING USED BY THE DEVAS IS BAD ...
...THEY'VE GOT IT EVEN WORSE! THEY'RE TRULY BEASTS OF BURDEN...
SORRY, I DIDN'T MEAN TO TOUCH ON A SORE SPOT!
We're just one abusive system, top to bottom...
WHAT ABOUT YOUR SIDE?
IF YOU WANT TO SCARE LITTLE CHILDREN, DO YOU CONJURE UP DEMONS AND STUFF?
WHAT...? NO, NO LITTLE CHILDREN...
TOO SCARY?
YES...

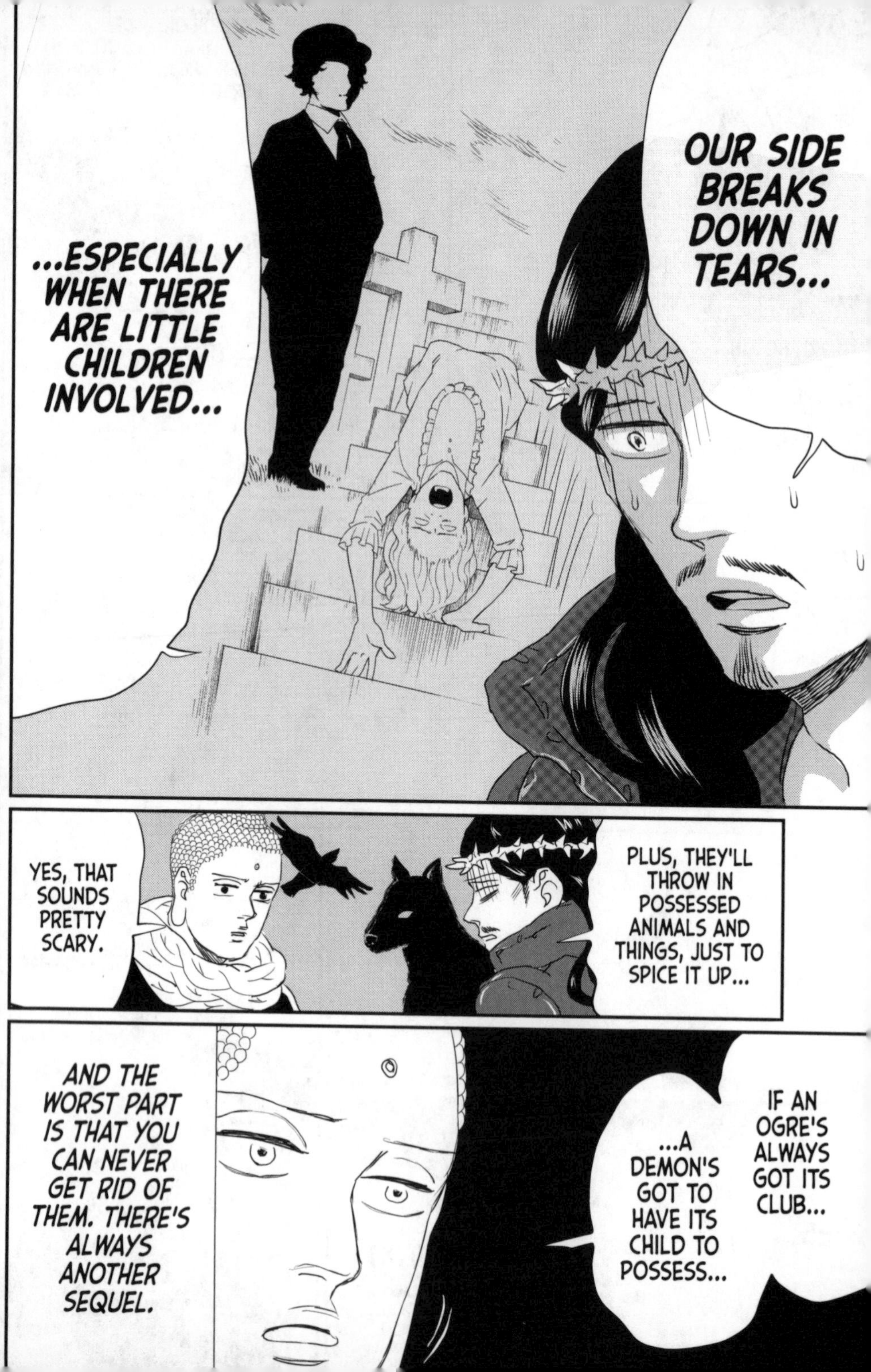
OUR SIDE BREAKS DOWN IN TEARS...
...ESPECIALLY WHEN THERE ARE LITTLE CHILDREN INVOLVED...
PLUS, THEY'LL THROW IN POSSESSED ANIMALS AND THINGS, JUST TO SPICE IT UP...
YES, THAT SOUNDS PRETTY SCARY.
IF AN OGRE'S ALWAYS GOT ITS CLUB...
...A DEMON'S GOT TO HAVE ITS CHILD TO POSSESS...
AND THE WORST PART IS THAT YOU CAN NEVER GET RID OF THEM. THERE'S ALWAYS ANOTHER SEQUEL.

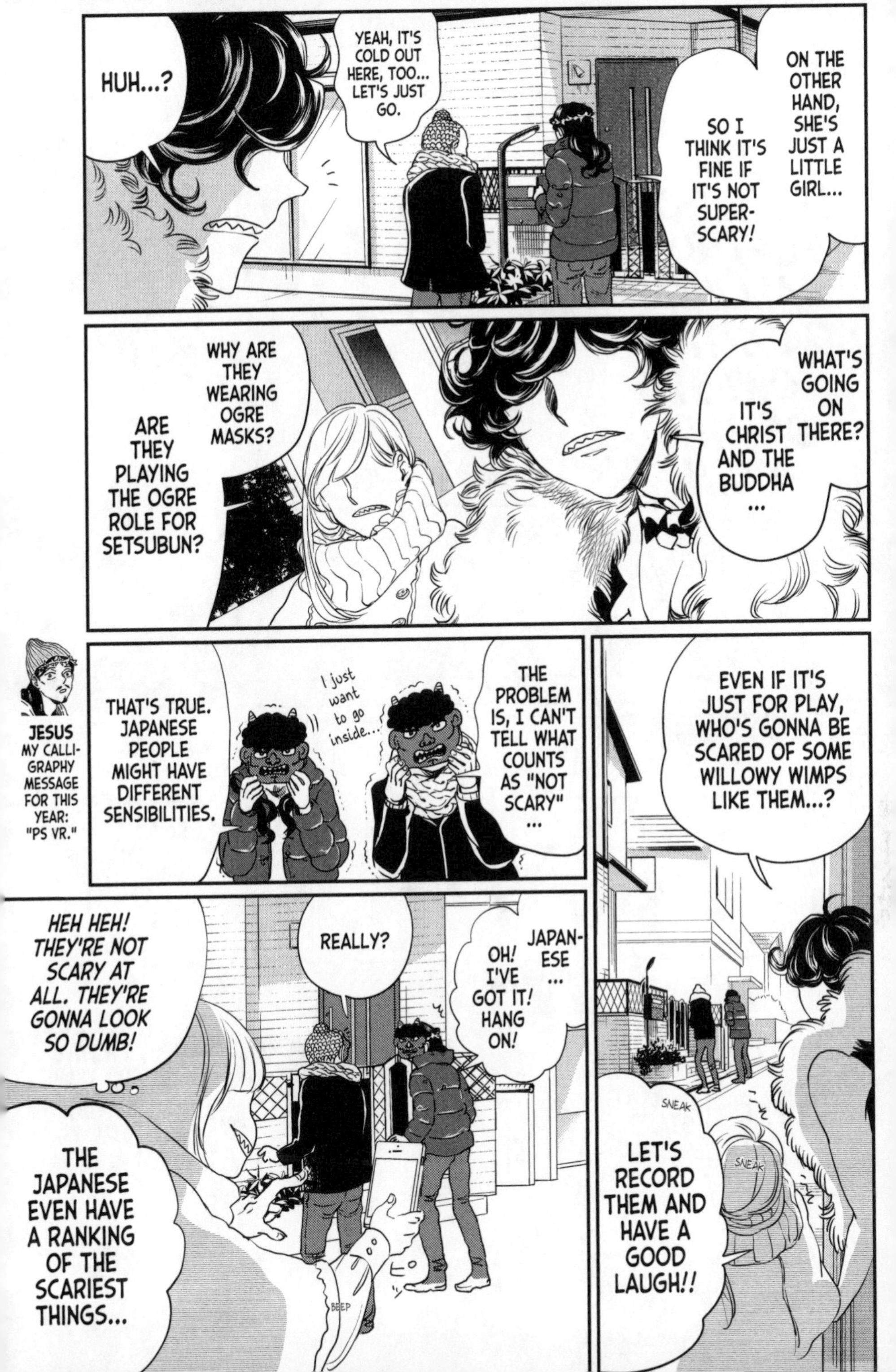
ON THE OTHER HAND, SHE'S JUST A LITTLE GIRL...
SO I THINK IT'S FINE IF IT'S NOT SUPER-SCARY!
YEAH, IT'S COLD OUT HERE, TOO... LET'S JUST GO.
HUH...?
WHAT'S GOING ON THERE?
IT'S CHRIST AND THE BUDDHA ...
WHY ARE THEY WEARING OGRE MASKS?
ARE THEY PLAYING THE OGRE ROLE FOR SETSUBUN?
EVEN IF IT'S JUST FOR PLAY, WHO'S GONNA BE SCARED OF SOME WILLOWY WIMPS LIKE THEM...?
SNEAK
SNEAK
LET'S RECORD THEM AND HAVE A GOOD LAUGH!!
THE PROBLEM IS, I CAN'T TELL WHAT COUNTS AS "NOT SCARY" ...
I just want to go inside...
THAT'S TRUE. JAPANESE PEOPLE MIGHT HAVE DIFFERENT SENSIBILITIES.
JAPANESE ...
OH! I'VE GOT IT! HANG ON!
REALLY?
HEH HEH! THEY'RE NOT SCARY AT ALL. THEY'RE GONNA LOOK SO DUMB!
THE JAPANESE EVEN HAVE A RANKING OF THE SCARIEST THINGS...
BEEP
JESUS
MY CALLIGRAPHY MESSAGE FOR THIS YEAR: "PS VR."

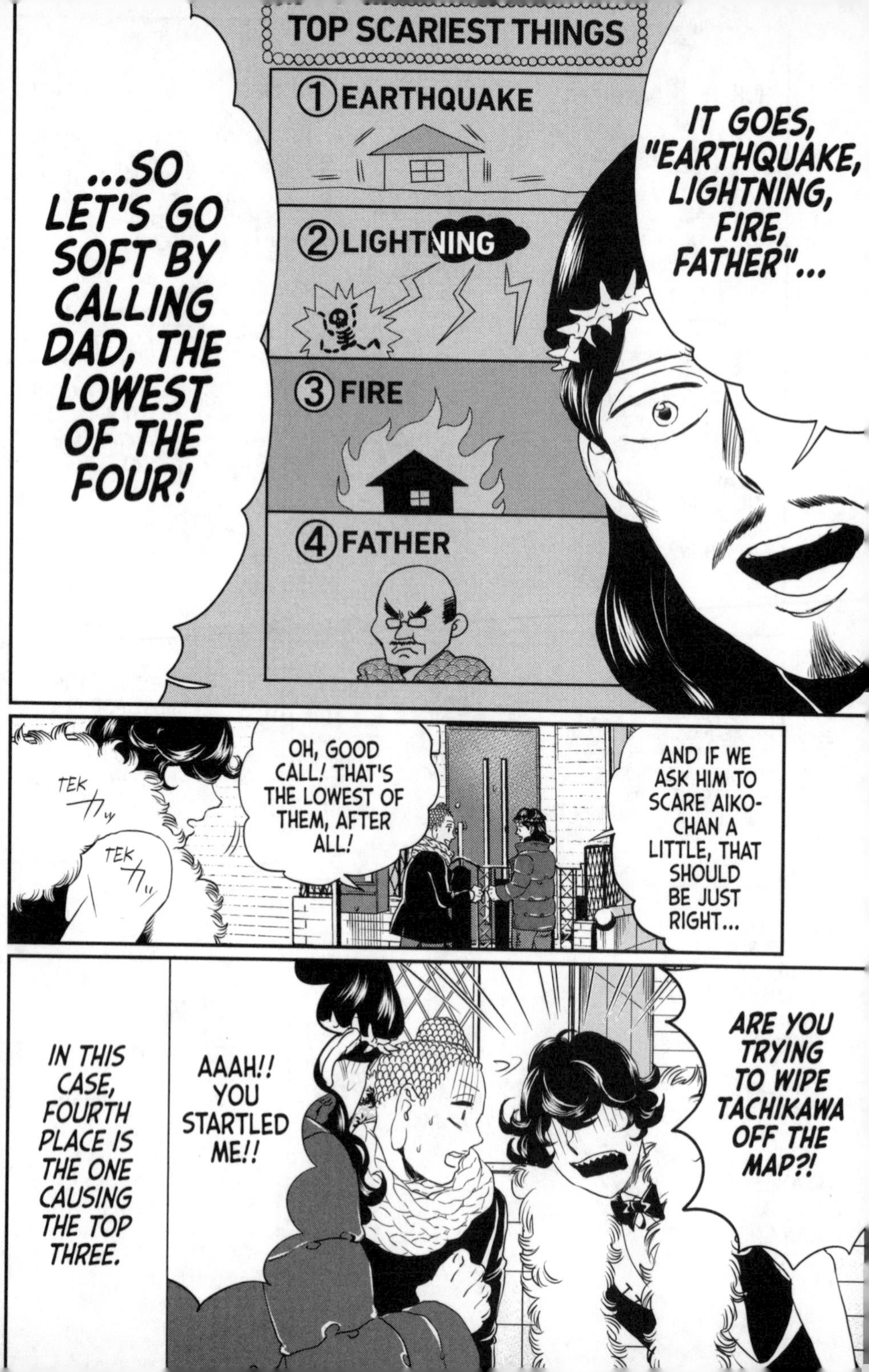
IT GOES, "EARTHQUAKE, LIGHTNING, FIRE, FATHER"...
TOP SCARIEST THINGS
①EARTHQUAKE
②LIGHTNING
③FIRE
④FATHER
...SO LET'S GO SOFT BY CALLING DAD, THE LOWEST OF THE FOUR!
AND IF WE ASK HIM TO SCARE AIKO-CHAN A LITTLE, THAT SHOULD BE JUST RIGHT...
OH, GOOD CALL! THAT'S THE LOWEST OF THEM, AFTER ALL!
TEK
TEK
ARE YOU TRYING TO WIPE TACHIKAWA OFF THE MAP?!
AAAH!! YOU STARTLED ME!!
IN THIS CASE, FOURTH PLACE IS THE ONE CAUSING THE TOP THREE.

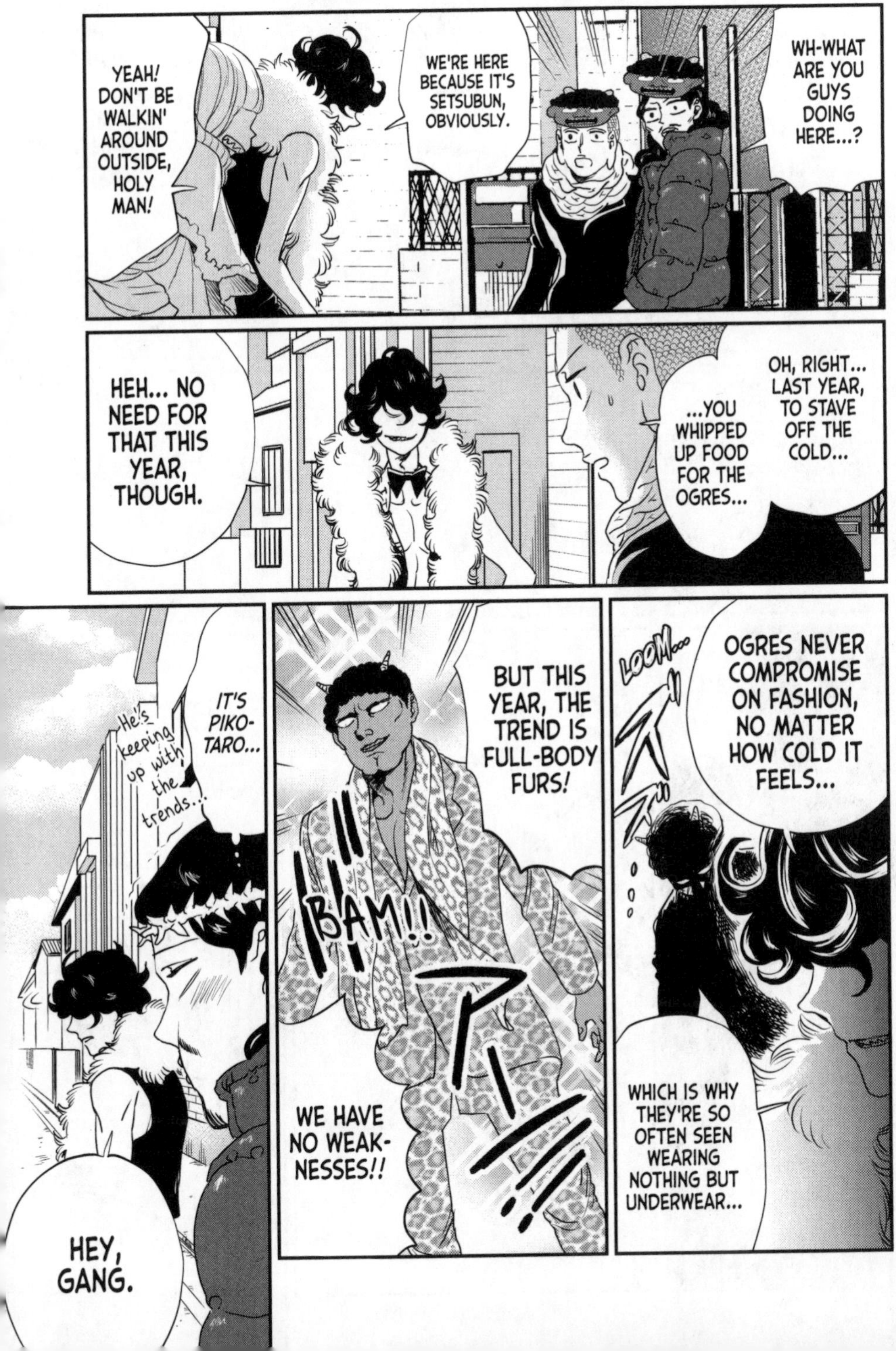
WH-WHAT ARE YOU GUYS DOING HERE...?
WE'RE HERE BECAUSE IT'S SETSUBUN, OBVIOUSLY.
YEAH! DON'T BE WALKIN' AROUND OUTSIDE, HOLY MAN!
OH, RIGHT... LAST YEAR, TO STAVE OFF THE COLD...
...YOU WHIPPED UP FOOD FOR THE OGRES...
HEH... NO NEED FOR THAT THIS YEAR, THOUGH.
LOOM...
OGRES NEVER COMPROMISE ON FASHION, NO MATTER HOW COLD IT FEELS...
WHICH IS WHY THEY'RE SO OFTEN SEEN WEARING NOTHING BUT UNDERWEAR...
BUT THIS YEAR, THE TREND IS FULL-BODY FURS!
BAM!!
WE HAVE NO WEAK-NESSES!!
IT'S PIKO-TARO...
He's keeping up with the trends...
HEY, GANG.

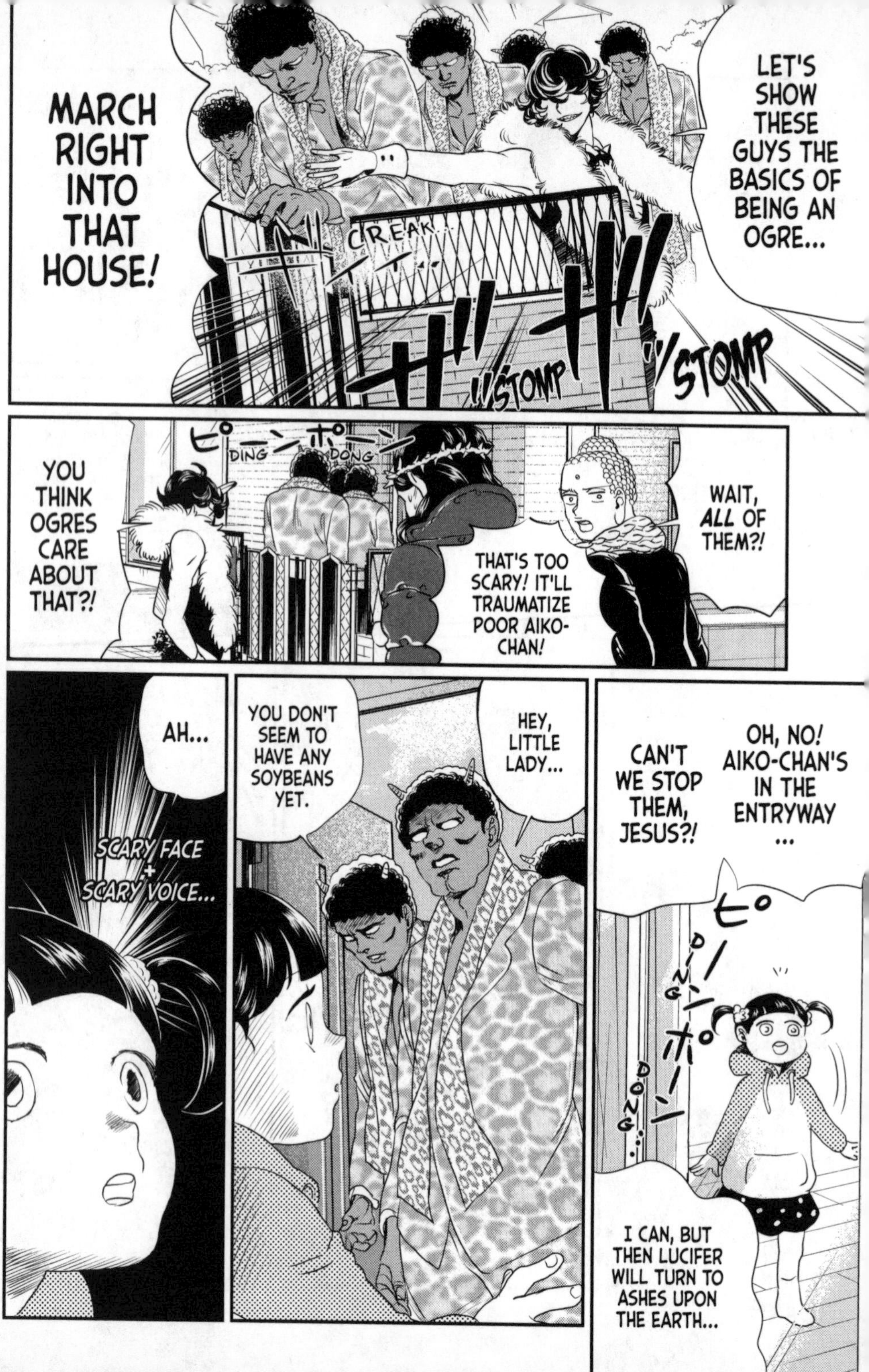
LET'S SHOW THESE GUYS THE BASICS OF BEING AN OGRE...
MARCH RIGHT INTO THAT HOUSE!
CREAK...
STOMP
STOMP
WAIT, ALL OF THEM?!
THAT'S TOO SCARY! IT'LL TRAUMATIZE POOR AIKO-CHAN!
ピーンポーン
DING DONG
YOU THINK OGRES CARE ABOUT THAT?!
OH, NO! AIKO-CHAN'S IN THE ENTRYWAY...
CAN'T WE STOP THEM, JESUS?!
DING DONG
I CAN, BUT THEN LUCIFER WILL TURN TO ASHES UPON THE EARTH...
HEY, LITTLE LADY...
YOU DON'T SEEM TO HAVE ANY SOYBEANS YET.
AH...
SCARY FACE + SCARY VOICE...

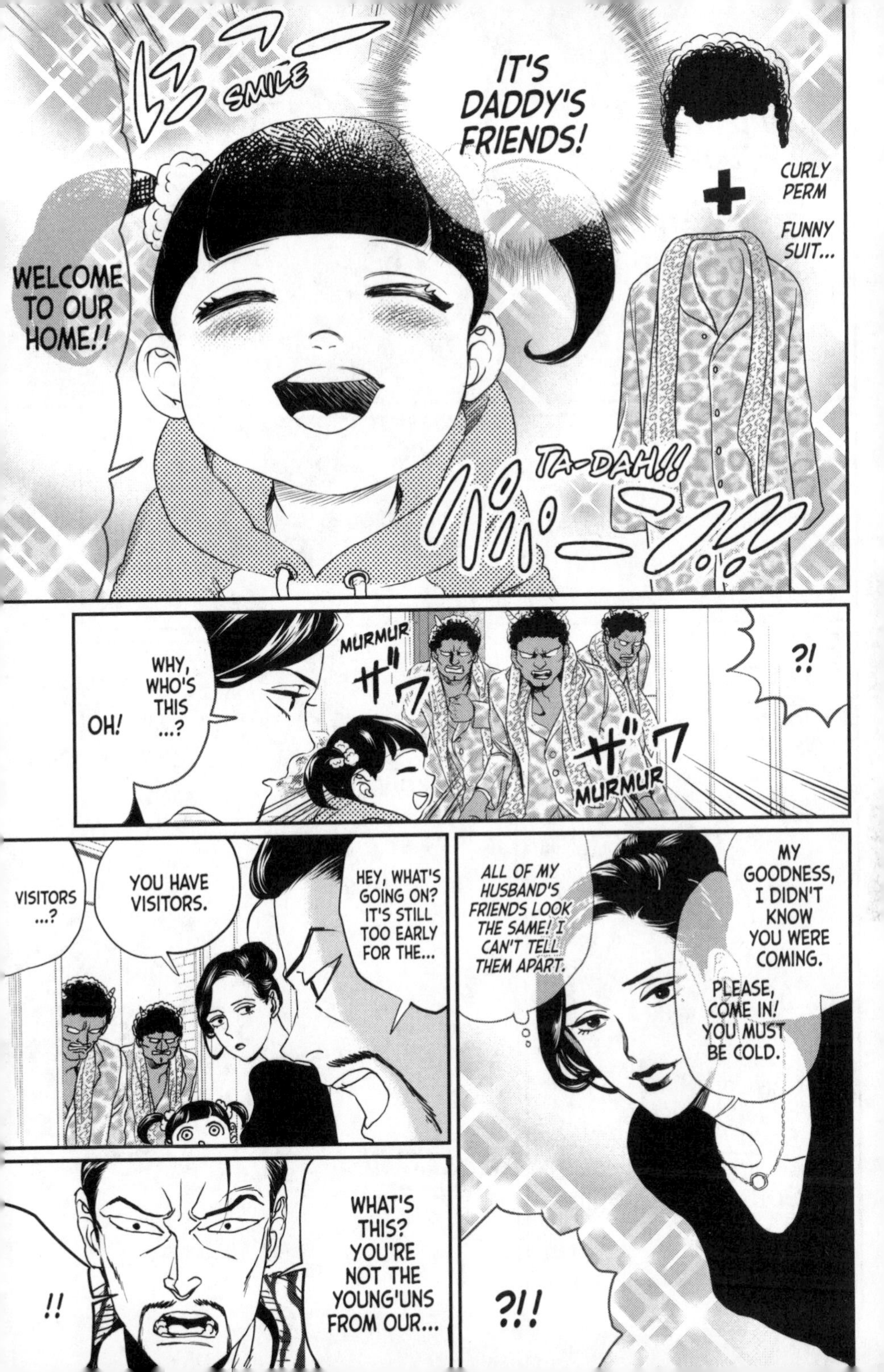
IT'S DADDY'S FRIENDS!
CURLY PERM
+
FUNNY SUIT...
TA-DAH!!
SMILE
WELCOME TO OUR HOME!!
?!
MURMUR
MURMUR
WHY, WHO'S THIS ...?
OH!
MY GOODNESS, I DIDN'T KNOW YOU WERE COMING.
PLEASE, COME IN! YOU MUST BE COLD.
ALL OF MY HUSBAND'S FRIENDS LOOK THE SAME! I CAN'T TELL THEM APART.
?!!
HEY, WHAT'S GOING ON? IT'S STILL TOO EARLY FOR THE...
YOU HAVE VISITORS.
VISITORS ...?
WHAT'S THIS? YOU'RE NOT THE YOUNG'UNS FROM OUR...
!!

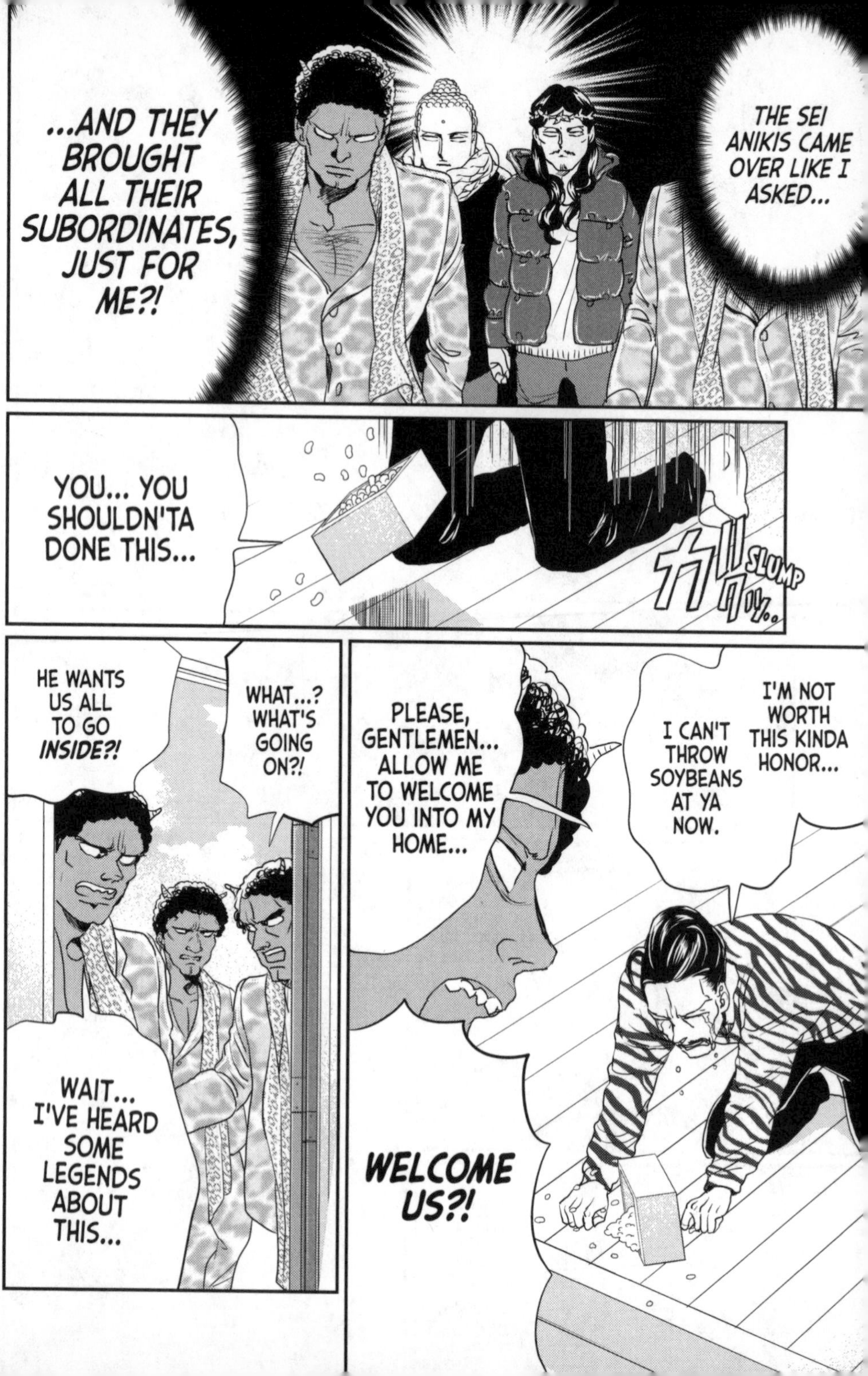
THE SEI ANIKIS CAME OVER LIKE I ASKED...
...AND THEY BROUGHT ALL THEIR SUBORDINATES, JUST FOR ME?!
YOU... YOU SHOULDN'TA DONE THIS...
SLUMP
I'M NOT WORTH THIS KINDA HONOR...
I CAN'T THROW SOYBEANS AT YA NOW.
PLEASE, GENTLEMEN... ALLOW ME TO WELCOME YOU INTO MY HOME...
WELCOME US?!
WHAT...? WHAT'S GOING ON?!
HE WANTS US ALL TO GO INSIDE?!
WAIT... I'VE HEARD SOME LEGENDS ABOUT THIS...

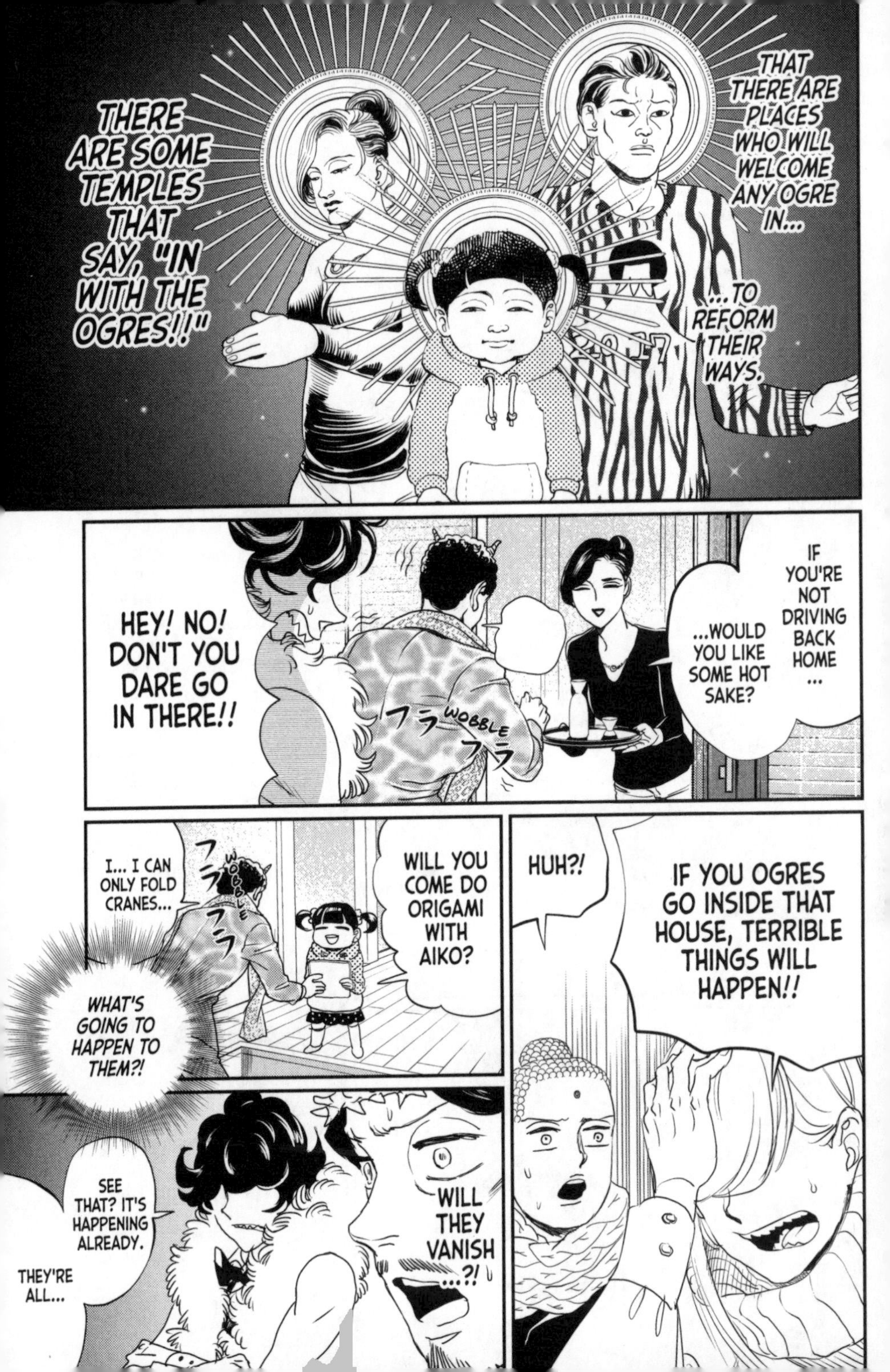

THAT THERE ARE PLACES WHO WILL WELCOME ANY OGRE IN...
...TO REFORM THEIR WAYS.
THERE ARE SOME TEMPLES THAT SAY, "IN WITH THE OGRES!!"
IF YOU'RE NOT DRIVING BACK HOME ...
...WOULD YOU LIKE SOME HOT SAKE?
HEY! NO! DON'T YOU DARE GO IN THERE!!
WOBBLE
IF YOU OGRES GO INSIDE THAT HOUSE, TERRIBLE THINGS WILL HAPPEN!!
HUH?!
WILL YOU COME DO ORIGAMI WITH AIKO?
I... I CAN ONLY FOLD CRANES...
WOBBLE
WHAT'S GOING TO HAPPEN TO THEM?!
WILL THEY VANISH ...?!
SEE THAT? IT'S HAPPENING ALREADY.
THEY'RE ALL...

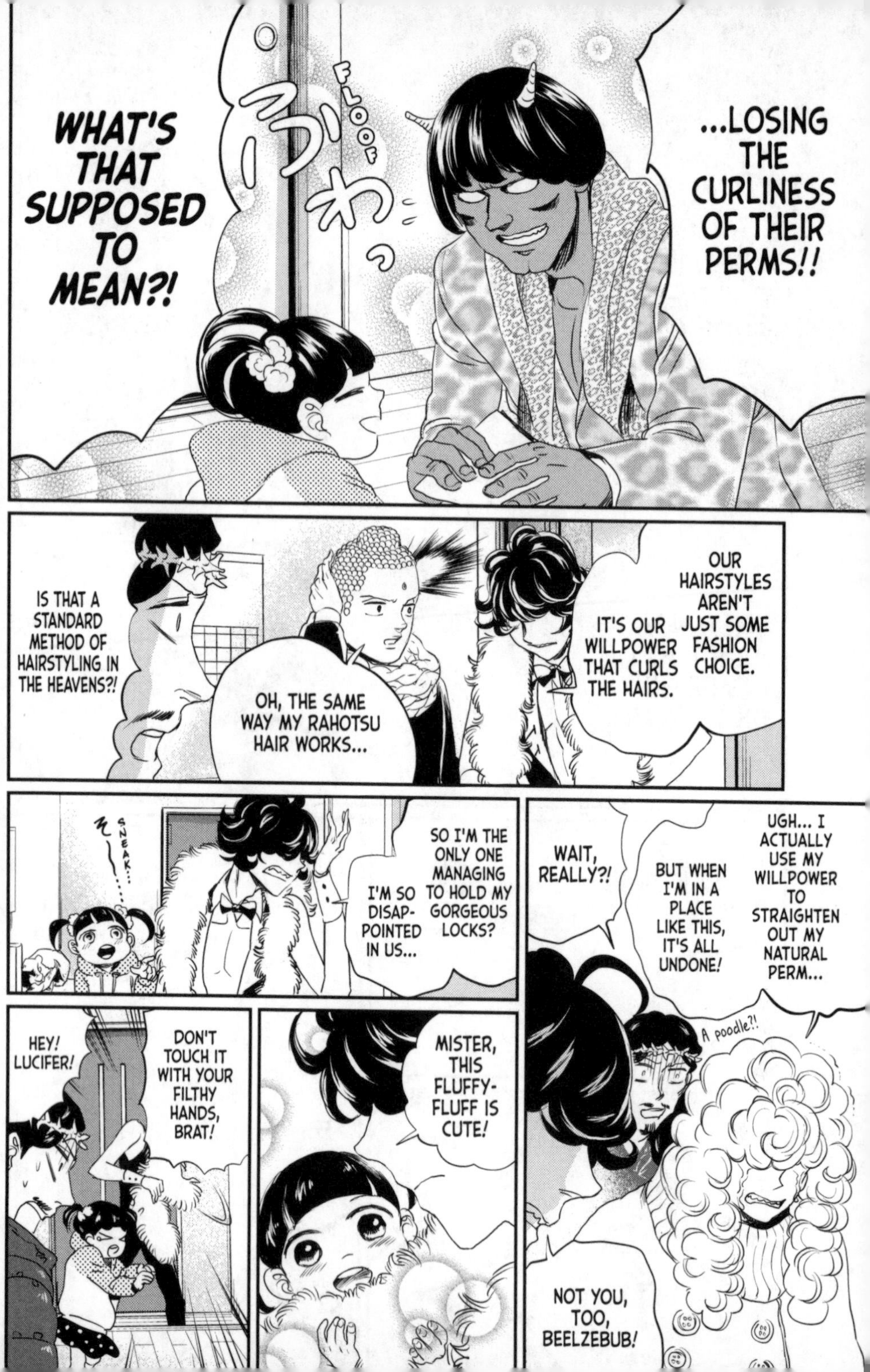
...LOSING THE CURLINESS OF THEIR PERMS!!
ふわっ
FLOOF
WHAT'S THAT SUPPOSED TO MEAN?!
OUR HAIRSTYLES AREN'T JUST SOME FASHION CHOICE.
IT'S OUR WILLPOWER THAT CURLS THE HAIRS.
OH, THE SAME WAY MY RAHOTSU HAIR WORKS...
IS THAT A STANDARD METHOD OF HAIRSTYLING IN THE HEAVENS?!
UGH... I ACTUALLY USE MY WILLPOWER TO STRAIGHTEN OUT MY NATURAL PERM...
BUT WHEN I'M IN A PLACE LIKE THIS, IT'S ALL UNDONE!
WAIT, REALLY?!
A poodle?!
NOT YOU, TOO, BEELZEBUB!
SO I'M THE ONLY ONE MANAGING TO HOLD MY GORGEOUS LOCKS?
I'M SO DISAPPOINTED IN US...
そ〜
SNEAK...
MISTER, THIS FLUFFY-FLUFF IS CUTE!
DON'T TOUCH IT WITH YOUR FILTHY HANDS, BRAT!
HEY! LUCIFER!

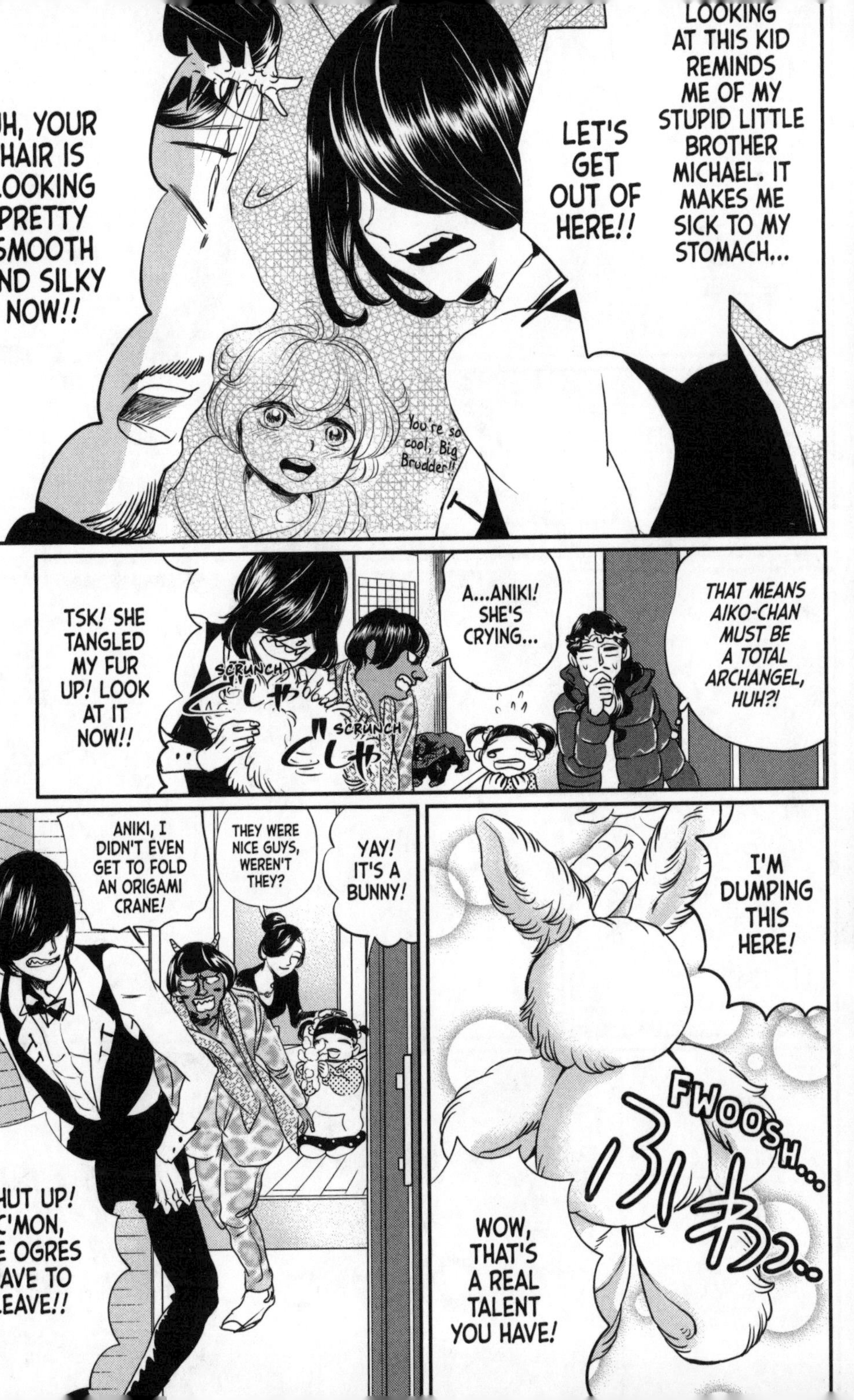
LOOKING AT THIS KID REMINDS ME OF MY STUPID LITTLE BROTHER MICHAEL. IT MAKES ME SICK TO MY STOMACH...
LET'S GET OUT OF HERE!!
UH, YOUR HAIR IS LOOKING PRETTY SMOOTH AND SILKY NOW!!
You're so cool, Big Brudder!!
THAT MEANS AIKO-CHAN MUST BE A TOTAL ARCHANGEL, HUH?!
A...ANIKI! SHE'S CRYING...
SCRUNCH
SCRUNCH
TSK! SHE TANGLED MY FUR UP! LOOK AT IT NOW!!
I'M DUMPING THIS HERE!
FWOOSH...
WOW, THAT'S A REAL TALENT YOU HAVE!
YAY! IT'S A BUNNY!
THEY WERE NICE GUYS, WEREN'T THEY?
ANIKI, I DIDN'T EVEN GET TO FOLD AN ORIGAMI CRANE!
SHUT UP! C'MON, WE OGRES HAVE TO LEAVE!!

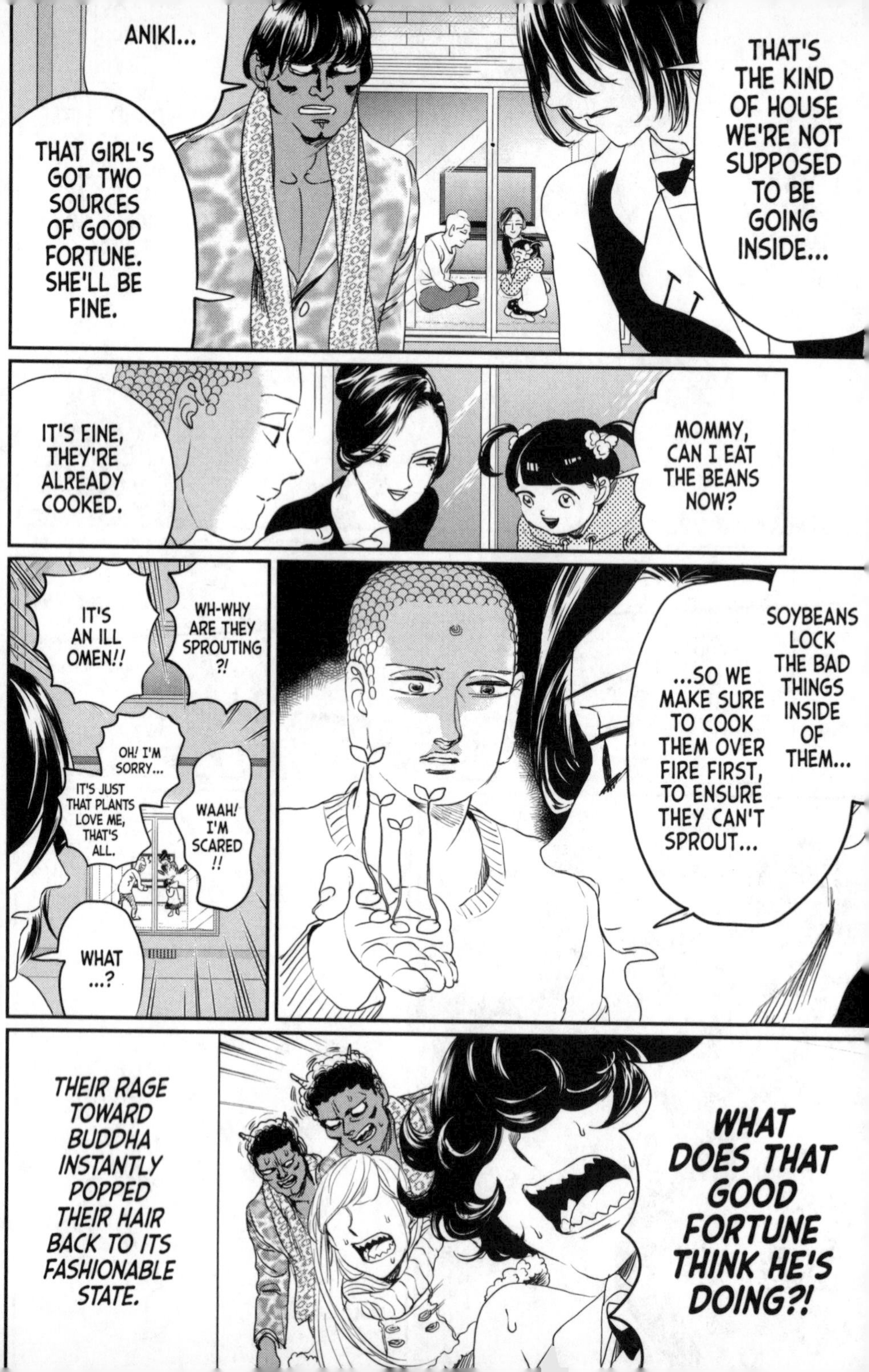
THAT'S THE KIND OF HOUSE WE'RE NOT SUPPOSED TO BE GOING INSIDE...
ANIKI...
THAT GIRL'S GOT TWO SOURCES OF GOOD FORTUNE. SHE'LL BE FINE.
MOMMY, CAN I EAT THE BEANS NOW?
IT'S FINE, THEY'RE ALREADY COOKED.
SOYBEANS LOCK THE BAD THINGS INSIDE OF THEM...
...SO WE MAKE SURE TO COOK THEM OVER FIRE FIRST, TO ENSURE THEY CAN'T SPROUT...
WH-WHY ARE THEY SPROUTING?!
IT'S AN ILL OMEN!!
WAAH! I'M SCARED!!
OH! I'M SORRY...
IT'S JUST THAT PLANTS LOVE ME, THAT'S ALL.
WHAT...?
WHAT DOES THAT GOOD FORTUNE THINK HE'S DOING?!
THEIR RAGE TOWARD BUDDHA INSTANTLY POPPED THEIR HAIR BACK TO ITS FASHIONABLE STATE.

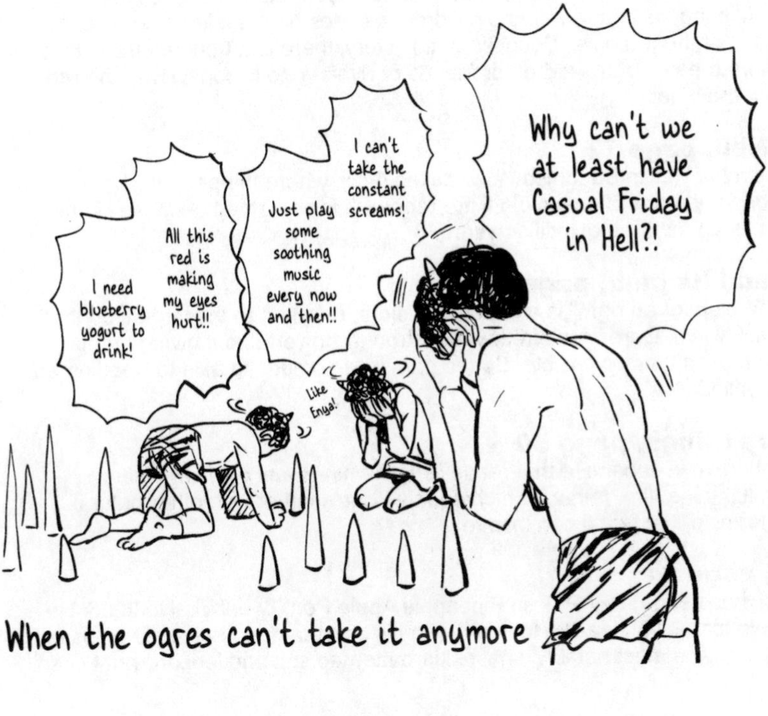
Why can't we at least have Casual Friday in Hell?!
I can't take the constant screams!
Just play some soothing music every now and then!!
Like Enya!
All this red is making my eyes hurt!!
I need blueberry yogurt to drink!
When the ogres can't take it anymore

SAINT☆YOUNG MEN

CHAPTER 101 TRANSLATION NOTES

Setsubun, page 73

The holiday of Setsubun happens in early spring, usually about the first week of February. In keeping with its proximity to the Lunar New Year, it represents new beginnings and a new year. The most notable custom associated with Setsubun is an enactment of driving out the ogre (*oni*) that represents bad luck or misfortune by throwing soybeans at someone wearing an ogre mask, while chanting the phrase, "Out with the ogre, in with good fortune!" from the doorway. See Chapter 60 for another Setsubun story!

Red & blue ogre, page 73

There is a famous folklore story about a red ogre and a blue ogre. Despite his fearsome appearance, the red ogre wishes to befriend the children of the village. So the blue ogre hatches a plan to frighten the children and allow the red ogre to "save" them, winning them to his side. The plan works, and the red ogre is beloved by all the children. But the blue ogre, realizing that he can never be friends with the red ogre without tainting his image with the children, decides he must leave forever, to the lamentation of the red ogre. Because of this story, there is a frequent trope that whenever there are two ogres--whether friends or rivals--one is considered the red and the other, the blue.

Endless Hell, page 77

The lowest level of Hell in Buddhism, also called Avici, where the people who committed the very worst offenses of all are reborn. It is so named because life here is said to last as long as three quintillion years.

An ogre and its club, page 78

The phrase "a club for an ogre" is a Japanese idiom, referring to the large club that ogres famously wield. Ogres are already monstrously powerful, but giving them their weapon makes them invincible. So the phrase is something akin to "feeding an 800-pound gorilla."

Four scary things, page 80

A famous aphorism in Japanese that reads *jishin kaminari kaji oyaji,* meaning "earthquake, lightning, fire, father," which equates one's father with other natural disasters in terms of the fear it can inspire.

Pikotaro, page 81

A comedian whose song "PPAP (Pen Pineapple Apple Pen)" went viral in 2016. He is recognizable for his yakuza-like fashion, with his short permed hair, tinted glasses, pencil mustache, and most notably, snakeskin-patterned suit and leopard-print scarf.

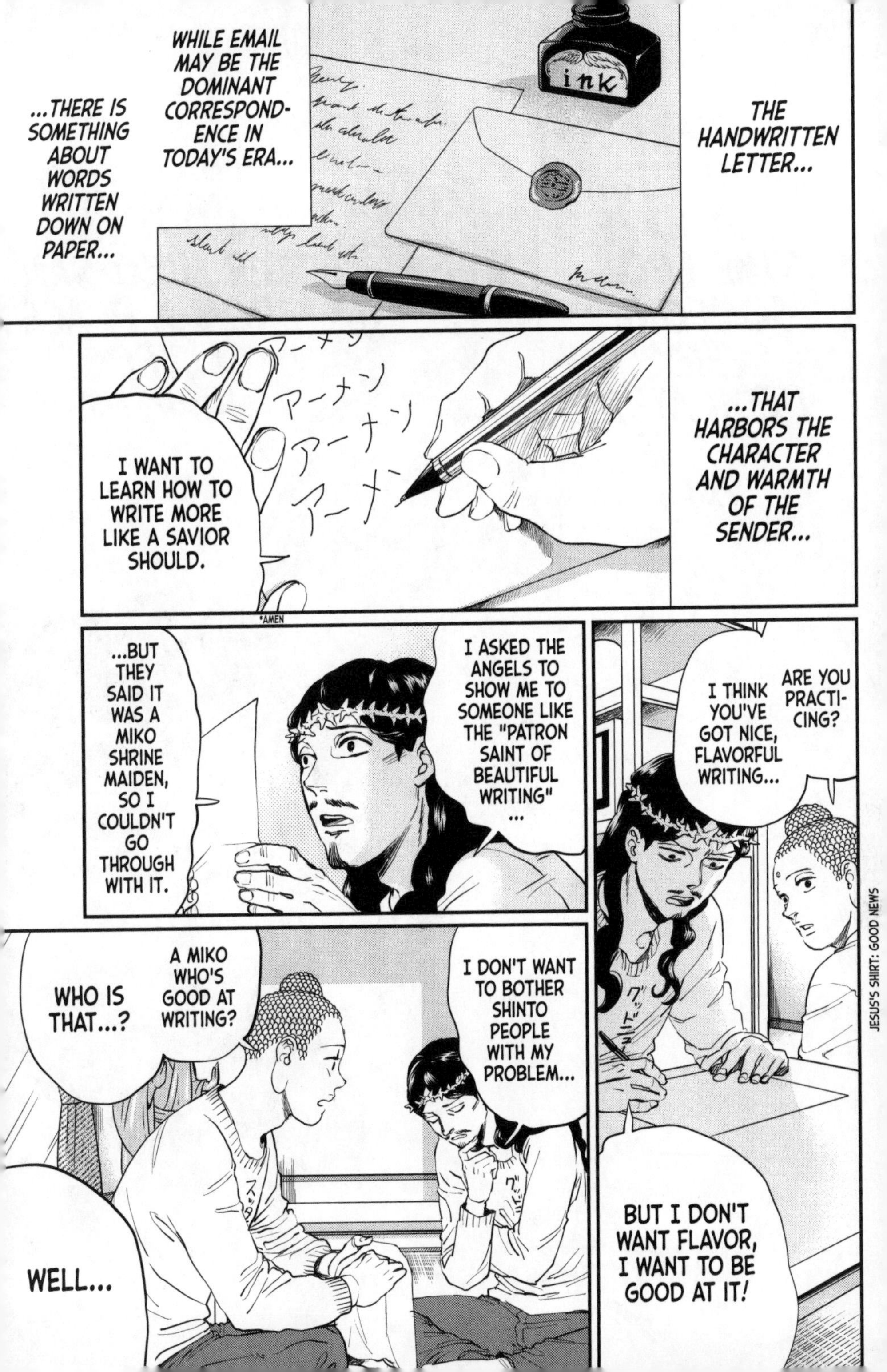
THE HANDWRITTEN LETTER...
WHILE EMAIL MAY BE THE DOMINANT CORRESPONDENCE IN TODAY'S ERA...
...THERE IS SOMETHING ABOUT WORDS WRITTEN DOWN ON PAPER...
ink
...THAT HARBORS THE CHARACTER AND WARMTH OF THE SENDER...
アーナン
アーナン
I WANT TO LEARN HOW TO WRITE MORE LIKE A SAVIOR SHOULD.
*AMEN
ARE YOU PRACTICING?
I THINK YOU'VE GOT NICE, FLAVORFUL WRITING...
BUT I DON'T WANT FLAVOR, I WANT TO BE GOOD AT IT!
I ASKED THE ANGELS TO SHOW ME TO SOMEONE LIKE THE "PATRON SAINT OF BEAUTIFUL WRITING"...
...BUT THEY SAID IT WAS A MIKO SHRINE MAIDEN, SO I COULDN'T GO THROUGH WITH IT.
I DON'T WANT TO BOTHER SHINTO PEOPLE WITH MY PROBLEM...
A MIKO WHO'S GOOD AT WRITING?
WHO IS THAT...?
WELL...
JESUS'S SHIRT: GOOD NEWS

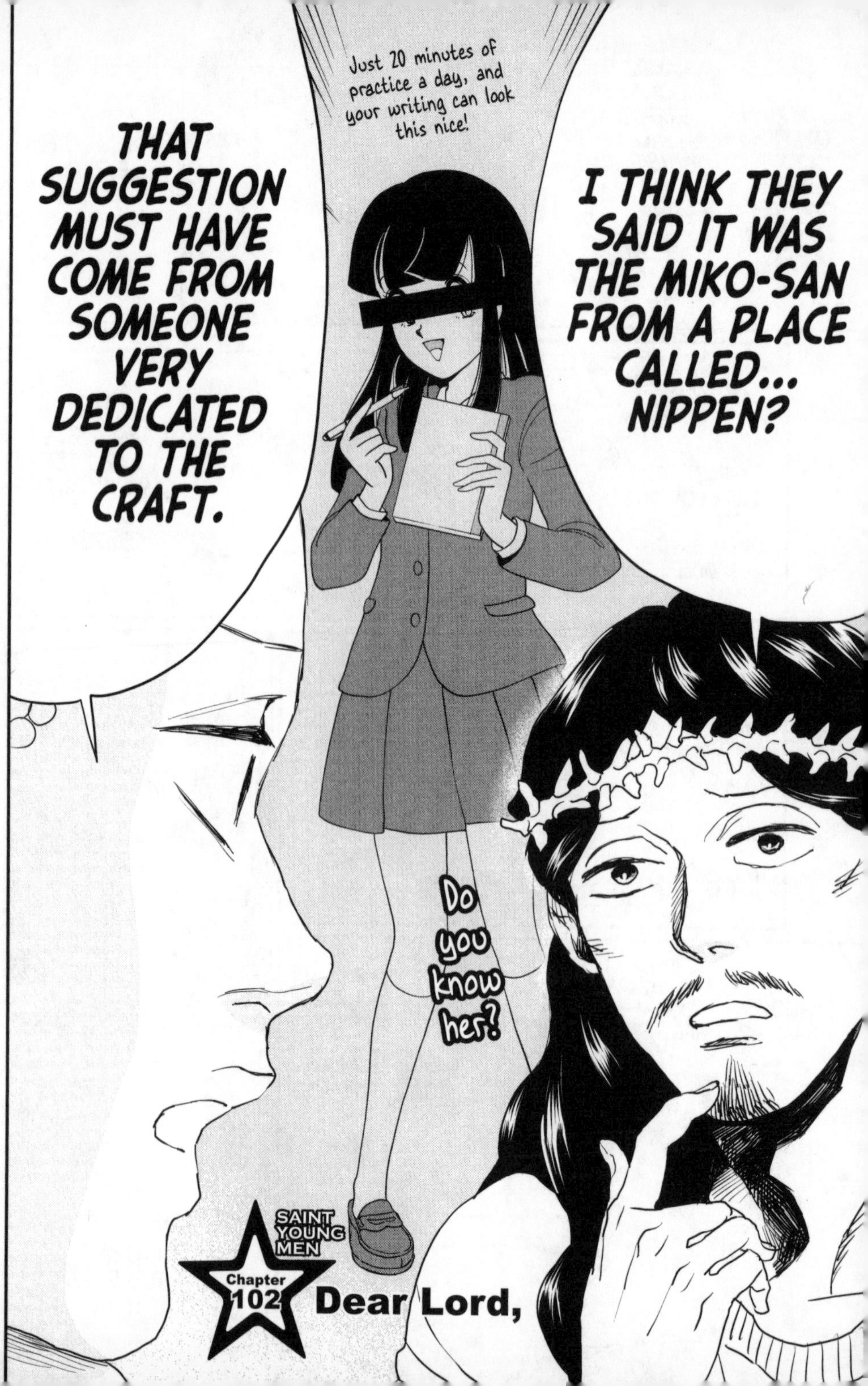
I THINK THEY SAID IT WAS THE MIKO-SAN FROM A PLACE CALLED... NIPPEN?
Just 20 minutes of practice a day, and your writing can look this nice!
THAT SUGGESTION MUST HAVE COME FROM SOMEONE VERY DEDICATED TO THE CRAFT.
Do you know her?
SAINT YOUNG MEN
Chapter 102
Dear Lord,

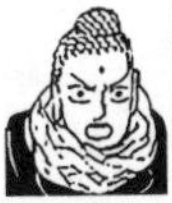

BUDDHA
WHAT IS AN APARTMENT BUILDING WITH DELIVERY LOCKERS? DOES IT MEAN THERE ARE MULTIPLE MATSUDA-SANS?!

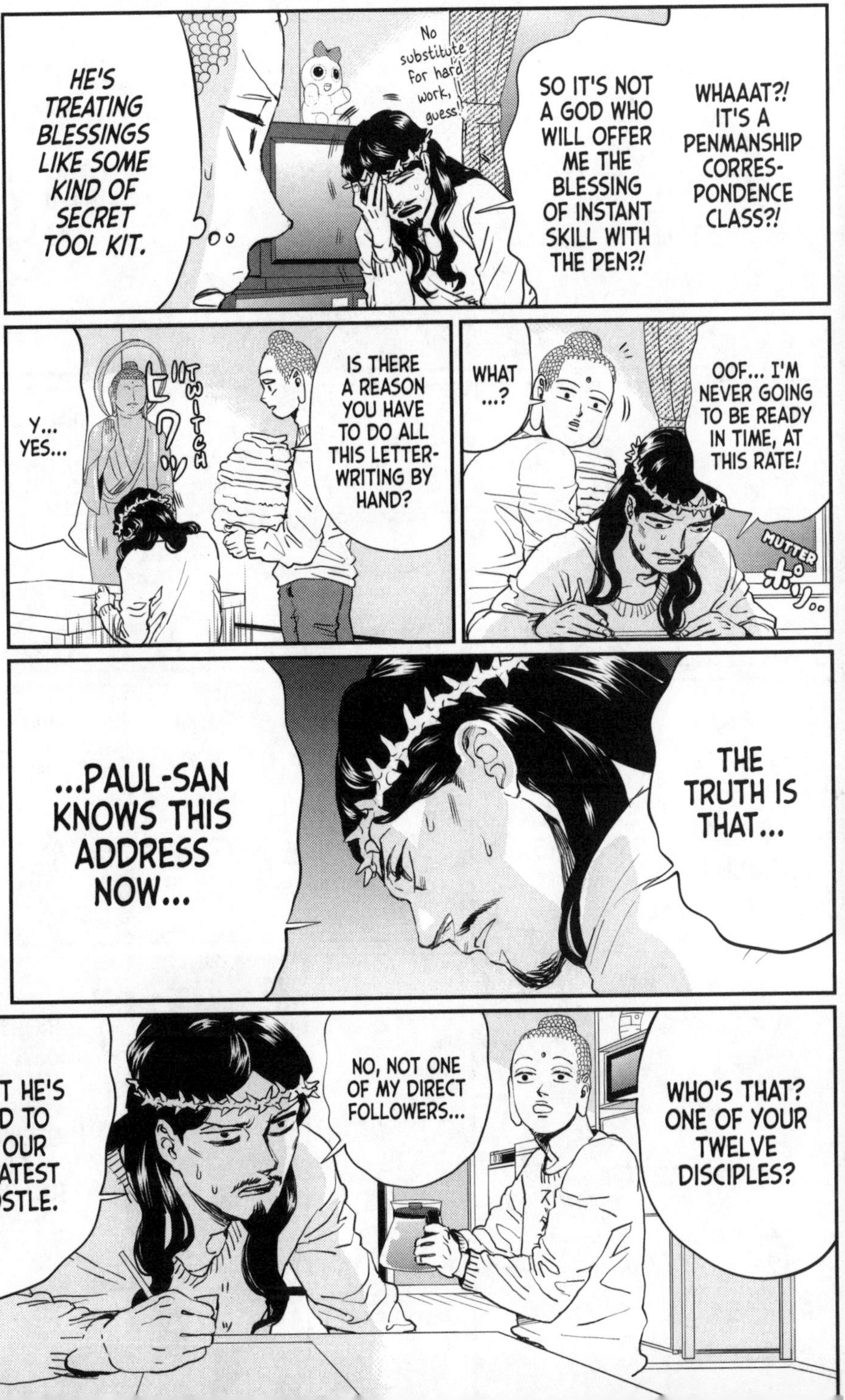
WHAAAT?! IT'S A PENMANSHIP CORRES-PONDENCE CLASS?!
SO IT'S NOT A GOD WHO WILL OFFER ME THE BLESSING OF INSTANT SKILL WITH THE PEN?!
No substitute for hard work, I guess!
HE'S TREATING BLESSINGS LIKE SOME KIND OF SECRET TOOL KIT.
OOF... I'M NEVER GOING TO BE READY IN TIME, AT THIS RATE!
MUTTER
WHAT ...?
IS THERE A REASON YOU HAVE TO DO ALL THIS LETTER-WRITING BY HAND?
TWITCH
Y... YES...
THE TRUTH IS THAT...
...PAUL-SAN KNOWS THIS ADDRESS NOW...
WHO'S THAT? ONE OF YOUR TWELVE DISCIPLES?
NO, NOT ONE OF MY DIRECT FOLLOWERS...
...BUT HE'S SAID TO BE OUR GREATEST APOSTLE.

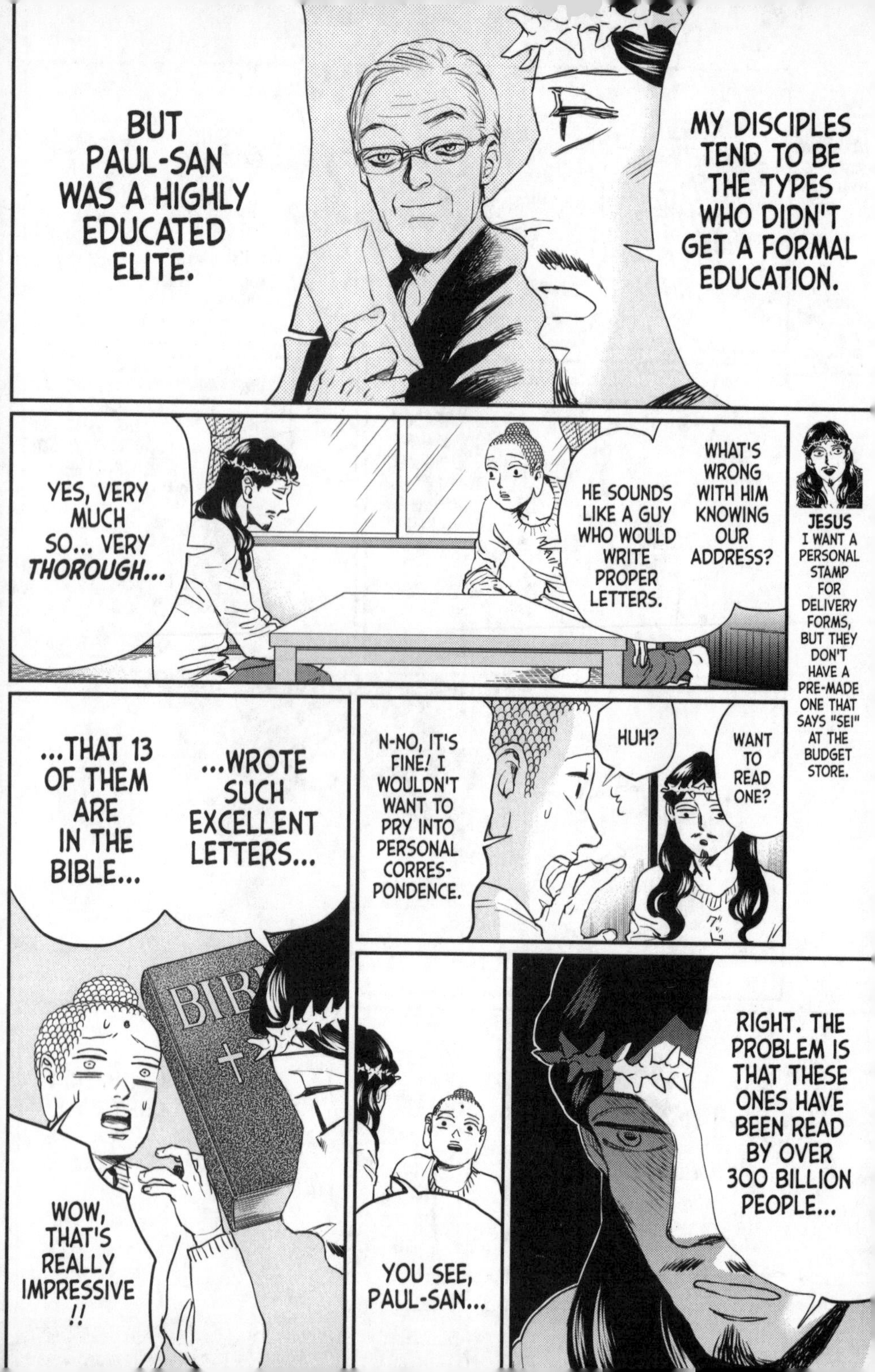
MY DISCIPLES TEND TO BE THE TYPES WHO DIDN'T GET A FORMAL EDUCATION.
BUT PAUL-SAN WAS A HIGHLY EDUCATED ELITE.
JESUS
I WANT A PERSONAL STAMP FOR DELIVERY FORMS, BUT THEY DON'T HAVE A PRE-MADE ONE THAT SAYS "SEI" AT THE BUDGET STORE.
WHAT'S WRONG WITH HIM KNOWING OUR ADDRESS?
HE SOUNDS LIKE A GUY WHO WOULD WRITE PROPER LETTERS.
YES, VERY MUCH SO... VERY *THOROUGH*...
WANT TO READ ONE?
HUH?
N-NO, IT'S FINE! I WOULDN'T WANT TO PRY INTO PERSONAL CORRES-PONDENCE.
YOU SEE, PAUL-SAN...
...WROTE SUCH EXCELLENT LETTERS...
...THAT 13 OF THEM ARE IN THE BIBLE...
WOW, THAT'S REALLY IMPRESSIVE!!
RIGHT. THE PROBLEM IS THAT THESE ONES HAVE BEEN READ BY OVER 300 BILLION PEOPLE...

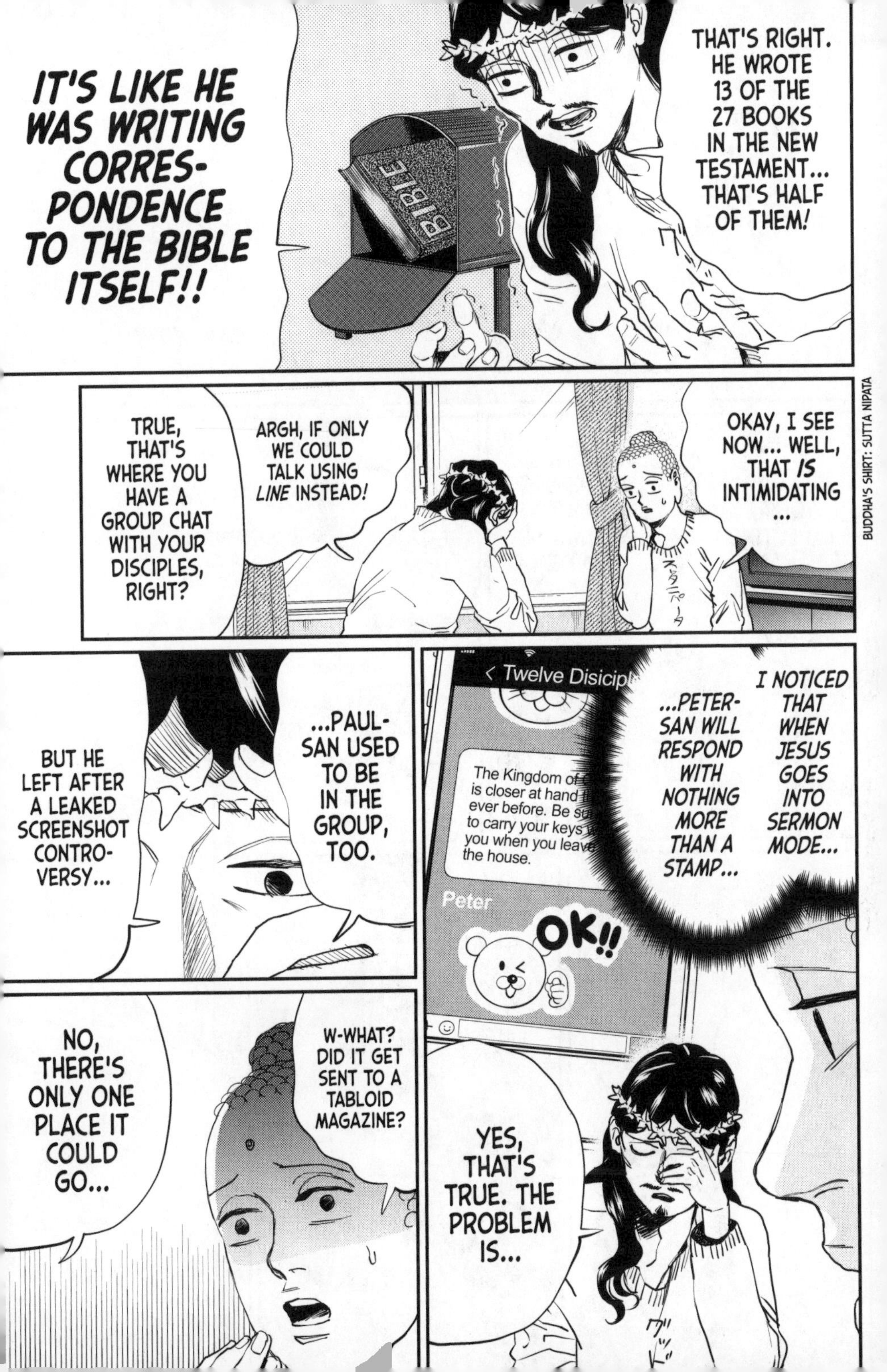

THAT'S RIGHT. HE WROTE 13 OF THE 27 BOOKS IN THE NEW TESTAMENT... THAT'S HALF OF THEM!
IT'S LIKE HE WAS WRITING CORRES-PONDENCE TO THE BIBLE ITSELF!!
BIBLE
OKAY, I SEE NOW... WELL, THAT *IS* INTIMIDATING...
ARGH, IF ONLY WE COULD TALK USING *LINE* INSTEAD!
TRUE, THAT'S WHERE YOU HAVE A GROUP CHAT WITH YOUR DISCIPLES, RIGHT?
BUDDHA'S SHIRT: SUTTA NIPATA
I NOTICED THAT WHEN JESUS GOES INTO SERMON MODE...
...PETER-SAN WILL RESPOND WITH NOTHING MORE THAN A STAMP...
< Twelve Discipl
The Kingdom of
is closer at hand
ever before. Be su
to carry your keys
you when you leave
the house.
Peter
OK!!
...PAUL-SAN USED TO BE IN THE GROUP, TOO.
BUT HE LEFT AFTER A LEAKED SCREENSHOT CONTRO-VERSY...
YES, THAT'S TRUE. THE PROBLEM IS...
W-WHAT? DID IT GET SENT TO A TABLOID MAGAZINE?
NO, THERE'S ONLY ONE PLACE IT COULD GO...

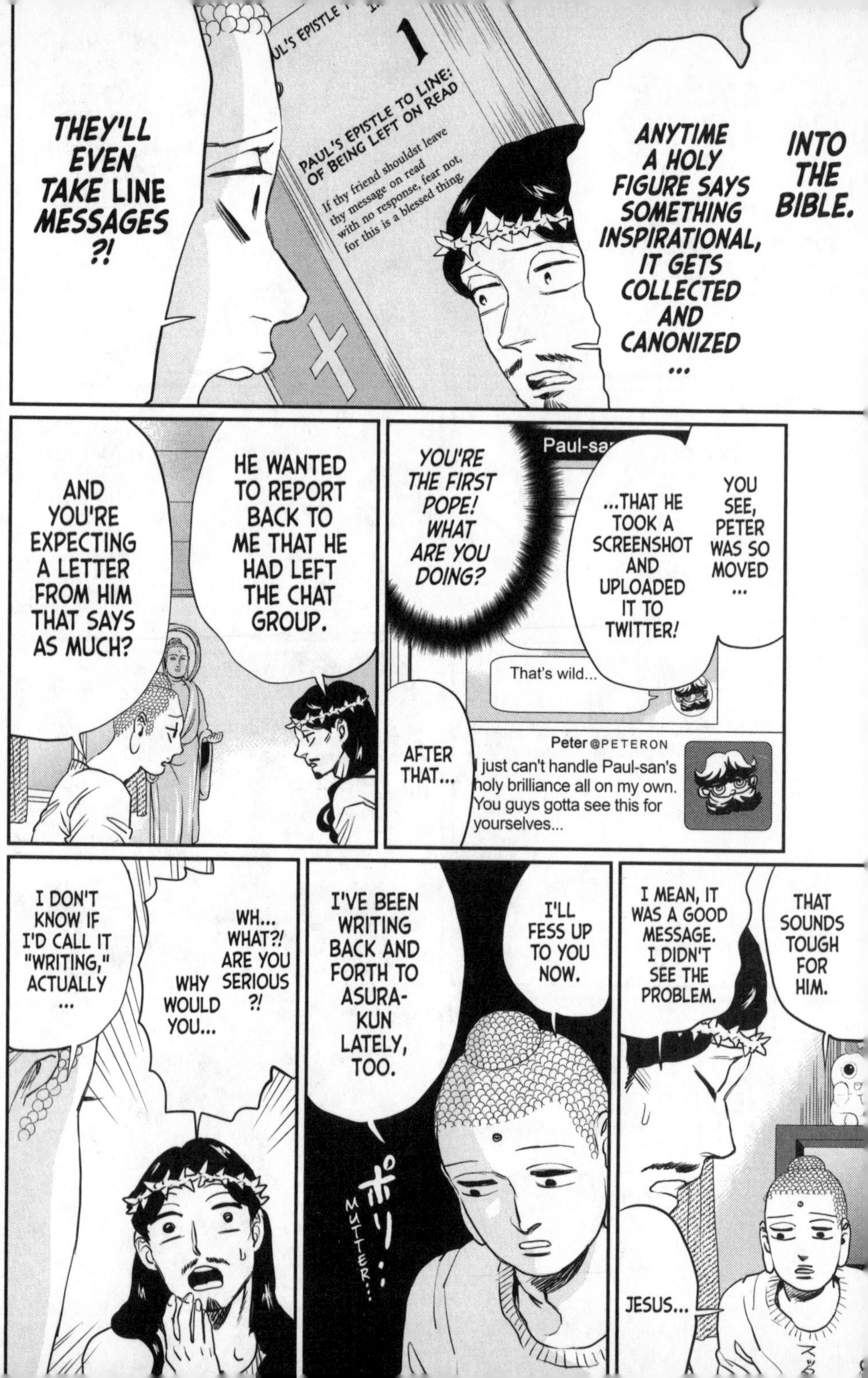
ANYTIME A HOLY FIGURE SAYS SOMETHING INSPIRATIONAL, IT GETS COLLECTED AND CANONIZED...
INTO THE BIBLE.
UL'S EPISTLE
1
PAUL'S EPISTLE TO LINE: OF BEING LEFT ON READ
If thy friend shouldst leave thy message on read with no response, fear not, for this is a blessed thing.
THEY'LL EVEN TAKE LINE MESSAGES?!
YOU SEE, PETER WAS SO MOVED...
...THAT HE TOOK A SCREENSHOT AND UPLOADED IT TO TWITTER!
Paul-san
YOU'RE THE FIRST POPE! WHAT ARE YOU DOING?
That's wild...
AFTER THAT...
Peter @PETERON
I just can't handle Paul-san's holy brilliance all on my own. You guys gotta see this for yourselves...
HE WANTED TO REPORT BACK TO ME THAT HE HAD LEFT THE CHAT GROUP.
AND YOU'RE EXPECTING A LETTER FROM HIM THAT SAYS AS MUCH?
THAT SOUNDS TOUGH FOR HIM.
I MEAN, IT WAS A GOOD MESSAGE. I DIDN'T SEE THE PROBLEM.
JESUS...
I'LL FESS UP TO YOU NOW.
I'VE BEEN WRITING BACK AND FORTH TO ASURA-KUN LATELY, TOO.
ポリ…
MUTTER...
WH... WHAT?! ARE YOU SERIOUS?!
WHY WOULD YOU...
I DON'T KNOW IF I'D CALL IT "WRITING," ACTUALLY...

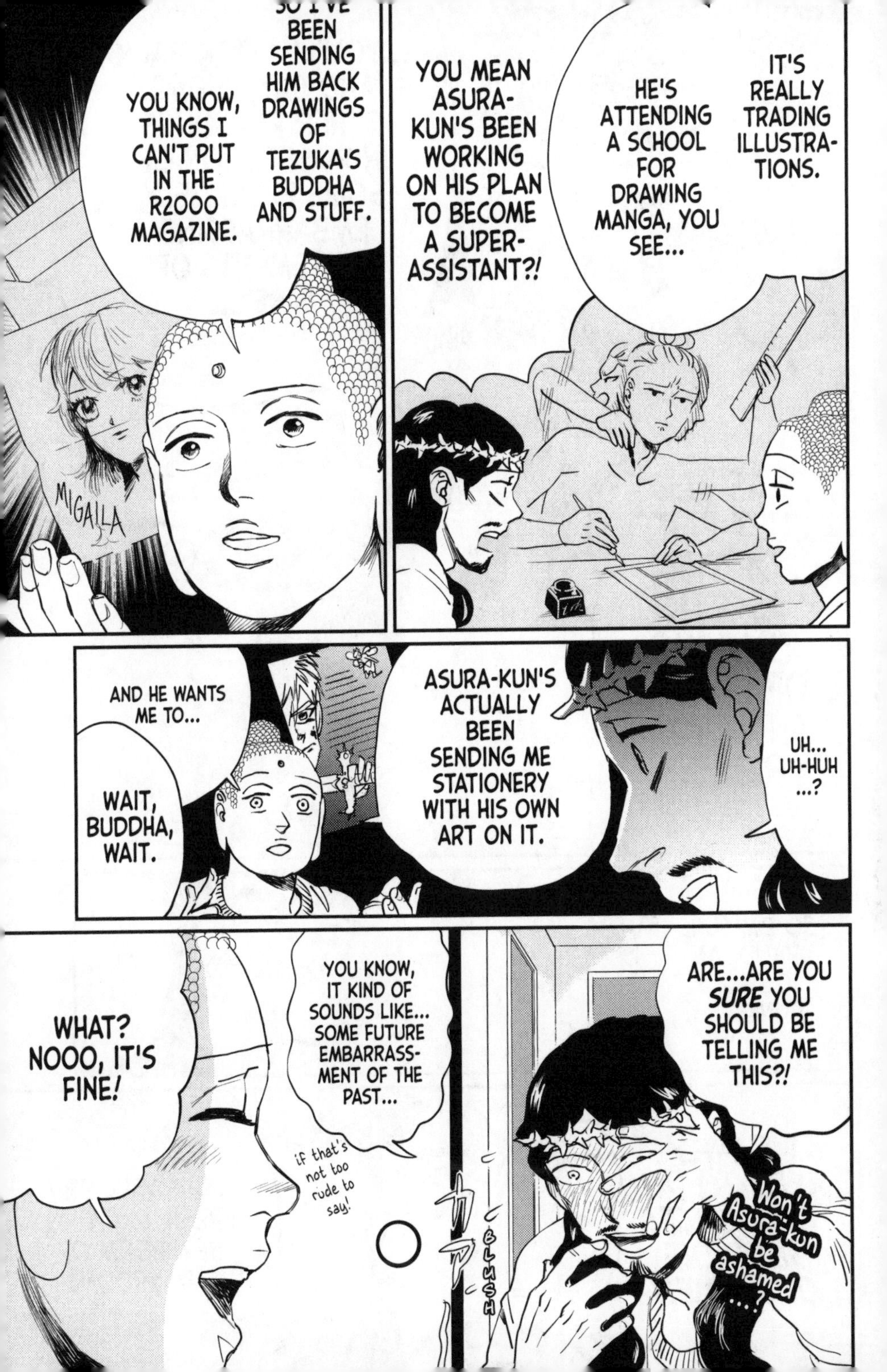
HE'S ATTENDING A SCHOOL FOR DRAWING MANGA, YOU SEE... IT'S REALLY TRADING ILLUSTRATIONS.
YOU MEAN ASURA-KUN'S BEEN WORKING ON HIS PLAN TO BECOME A SUPER-ASSISTANT?!
SO I'VE BEEN SENDING HIM BACK DRAWINGS OF TEZUKA'S BUDDHA AND STUFF.
YOU KNOW, THINGS I CAN'T PUT IN THE R2000 MAGAZINE.
MIGAILA
UH... UH-HUH ...?
ASURA-KUN'S ACTUALLY BEEN SENDING ME STATIONERY WITH HIS OWN ART ON IT.
AND HE WANTS ME TO...
WAIT, BUDDHA, WAIT.
ARE...ARE YOU SURE YOU SHOULD BE TELLING ME THIS?!
Won't Asura-kun be ashamed...?
BLUSH
YOU KNOW, IT KIND OF SOUNDS LIKE... SOME FUTURE EMBARRASSMENT OF THE PAST...
if that's not too rude to say!
WHAT? NOOO, IT'S FINE!

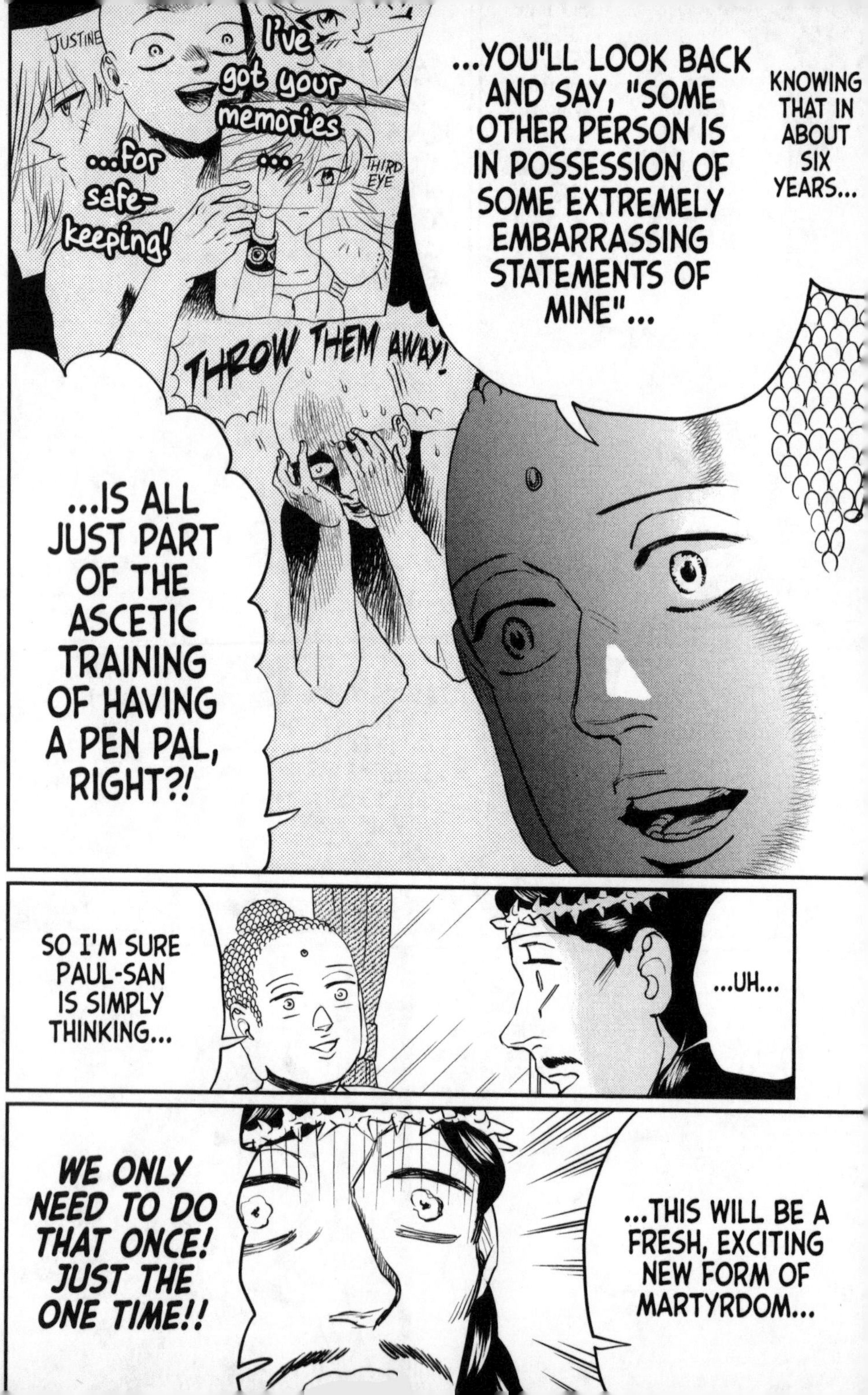
KNOWING THAT IN ABOUT SIX YEARS...
...YOU'LL LOOK BACK AND SAY, "SOME OTHER PERSON IS IN POSSESSION OF SOME EXTREMELY EMBARRASSING STATEMENTS OF MINE"...
I've got your memories...
...for safe-keeping!
JUSTINE
THIRD EYE
THROW THEM AWAY!
...IS ALL JUST PART OF THE ASCETIC TRAINING OF HAVING A PEN PAL, RIGHT?!
...UH...
SO I'M SURE PAUL-SAN IS SIMPLY THINKING...
...THIS WILL BE A FRESH, EXCITING NEW FORM OF MARTYRDOM...
WE ONLY NEED TO DO THAT ONCE! JUST THE ONE TIME!!

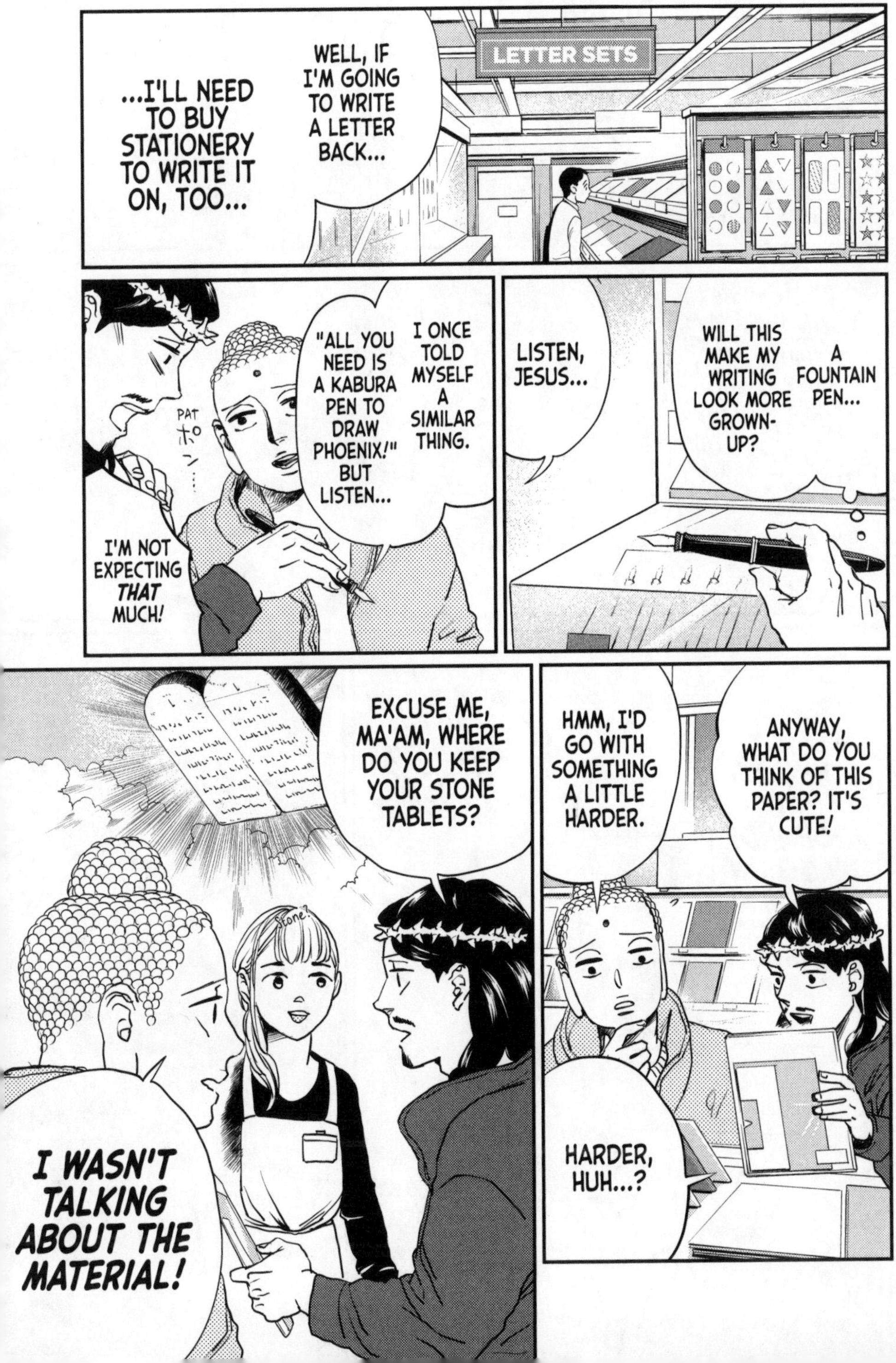
LETTER SETS
WELL, IF I'M GOING TO WRITE A LETTER BACK...
...I'LL NEED TO BUY STATIONERY TO WRITE IT ON, TOO...
A FOUNTAIN PEN...
WILL THIS MAKE MY WRITING LOOK MORE GROWN-UP?
LISTEN, JESUS...
I ONCE TOLD MYSELF A SIMILAR THING.
"ALL YOU NEED IS A KABURA PEN TO DRAW PHOENIX!" BUT LISTEN...
PAT
ポン…
I'M NOT EXPECTING *THAT* MUCH!
ANYWAY, WHAT DO YOU THINK OF THIS PAPER? IT'S CUTE!
HMM, I'D GO WITH SOMETHING A LITTLE HARDER.
HARDER, HUH...?
EXCUSE ME, MA'AM, WHERE DO YOU KEEP YOUR STONE TABLETS?
Stone?
I WASN'T TALKING ABOUT THE MATERIAL!

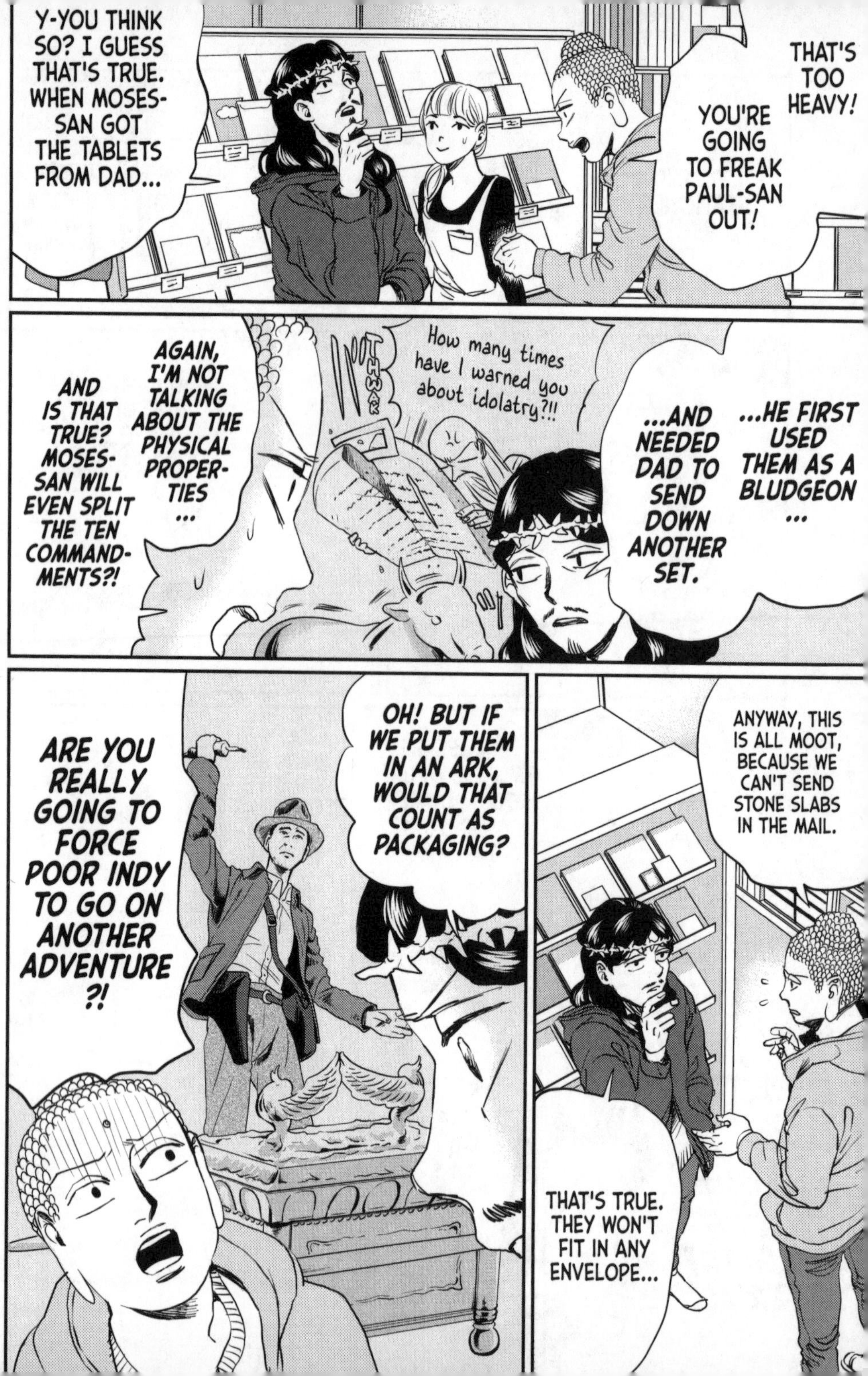
THAT'S TOO HEAVY!
YOU'RE GOING TO FREAK PAUL-SAN OUT!
Y-YOU THINK SO? I GUESS THAT'S TRUE. WHEN MOSES-SAN GOT THE TABLETS FROM DAD...
...HE FIRST USED THEM AS A BLUDGEON...
...AND NEEDED DAD TO SEND DOWN ANOTHER SET.
How many times have I warned you about idolatry?!!
THWAK
AGAIN, I'M NOT TALKING ABOUT THE PHYSICAL PROPERTIES...
AND IS THAT TRUE? MOSES-SAN WILL EVEN SPLIT THE TEN COMMANDMENTS?!
ANYWAY, THIS IS ALL MOOT, BECAUSE WE CAN'T SEND STONE SLABS IN THE MAIL.
THAT'S TRUE. THEY WON'T FIT IN ANY ENVELOPE...
OH! BUT IF WE PUT THEM IN AN ARK, WOULD THAT COUNT AS PACKAGING?
ARE YOU REALLY GOING TO FORCE POOR INDY TO GO ON ANOTHER ADVENTURE?!

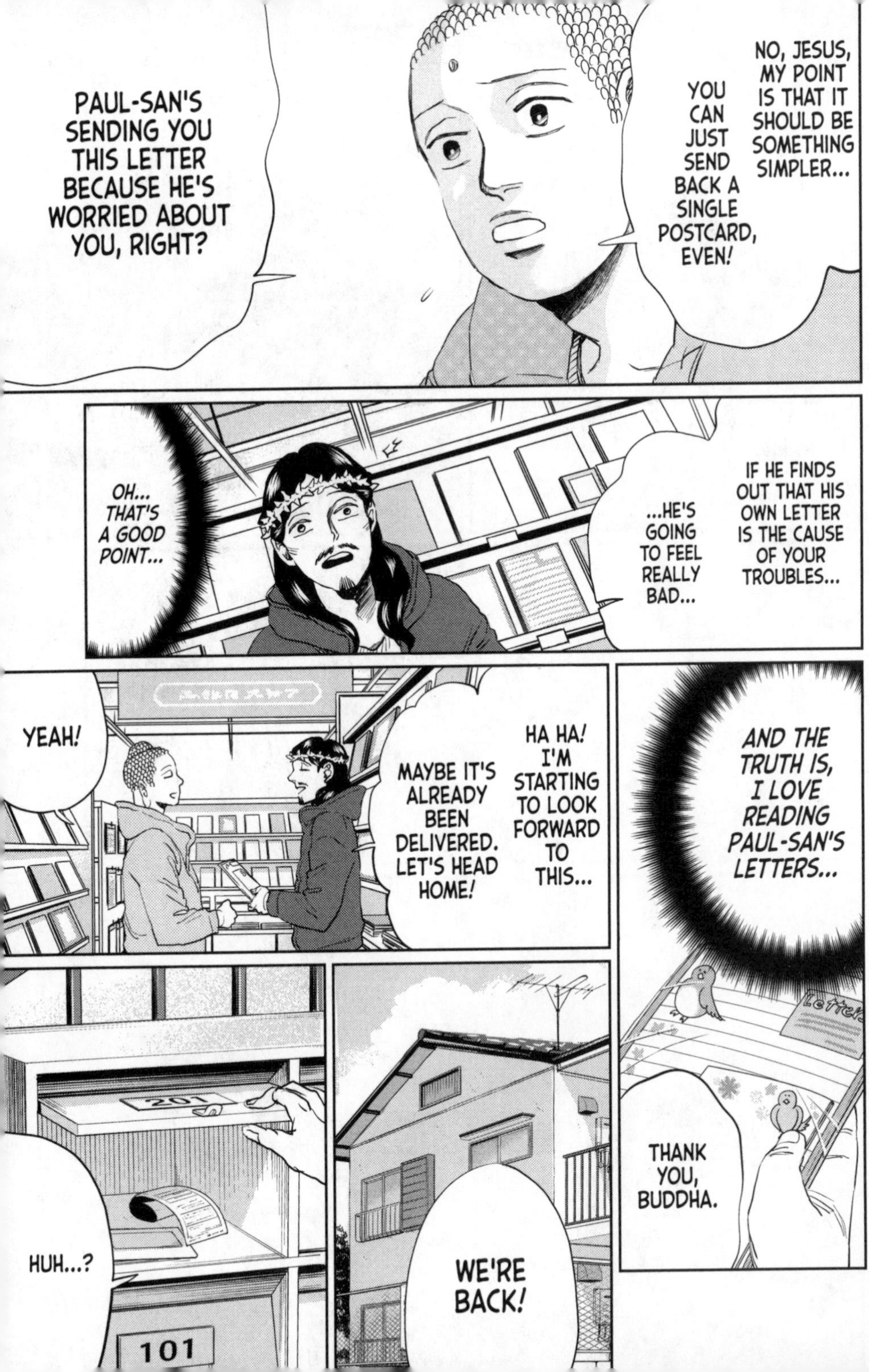
NO, JESUS, MY POINT IS THAT IT SHOULD BE SOMETHING SIMPLER...
YOU CAN JUST SEND BACK A SINGLE POSTCARD, EVEN!
PAUL-SAN'S SENDING YOU THIS LETTER BECAUSE HE'S WORRIED ABOUT YOU, RIGHT?
IF HE FINDS OUT THAT HIS OWN LETTER IS THE CAUSE OF YOUR TROUBLES...
...HE'S GOING TO FEEL REALLY BAD...
OH... THAT'S A GOOD POINT...
AND THE TRUTH IS, I LOVE READING PAUL-SAN'S LETTERS...
THANK YOU, BUDDHA.
HA HA! I'M STARTING TO LOOK FORWARD TO THIS...
MAYBE IT'S ALREADY BEEN DELIVERED. LET'S HEAD HOME!
YEAH!
WE'RE BACK!
201
HUH...?
101

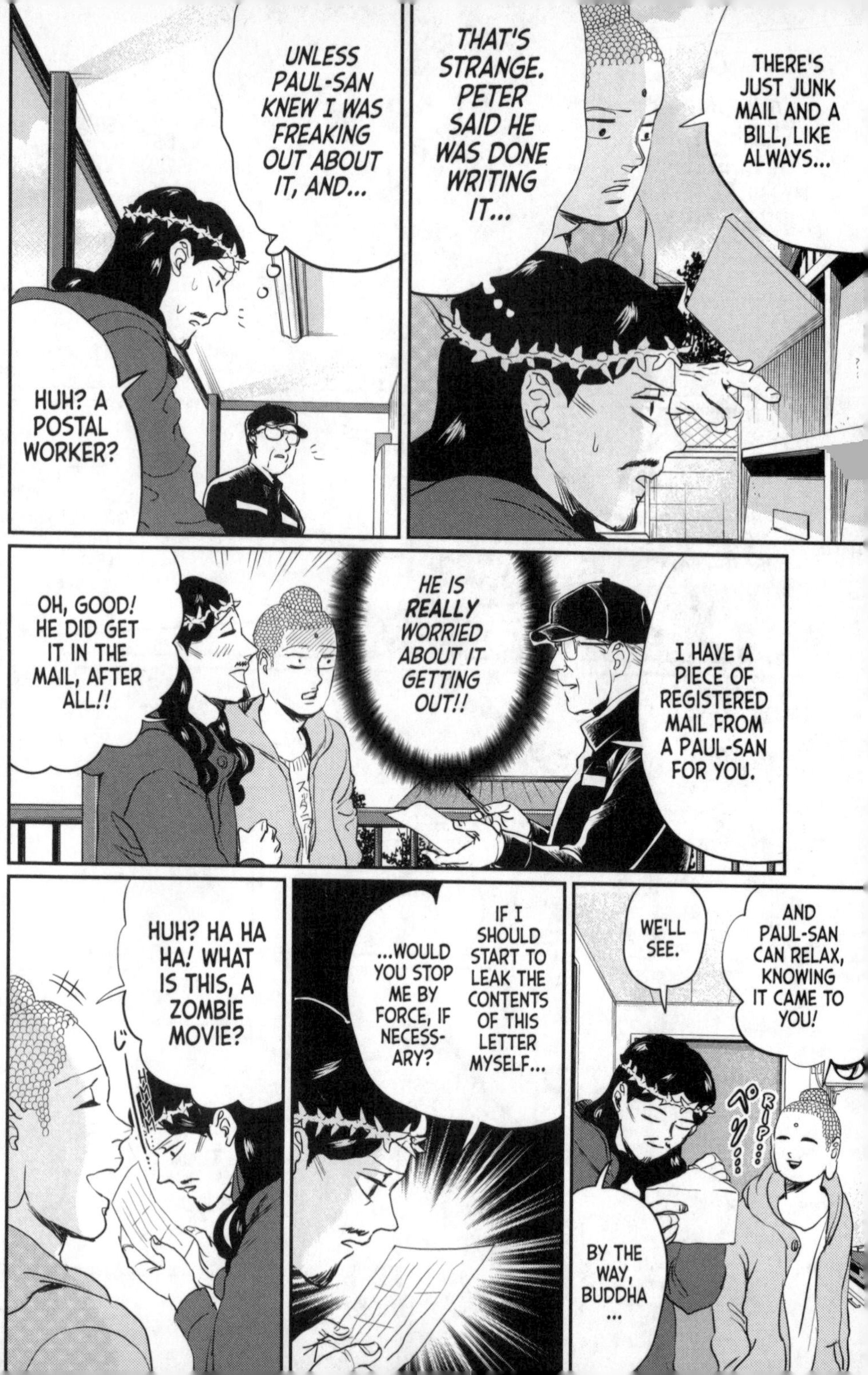
THERE'S JUST JUNK MAIL AND A BILL, LIKE ALWAYS...
THAT'S STRANGE. PETER SAID HE WAS DONE WRITING IT...
UNLESS PAUL-SAN KNEW I WAS FREAKING OUT ABOUT IT, AND...
HUH? A POSTAL WORKER?
I HAVE A PIECE OF REGISTERED MAIL FROM A PAUL-SAN FOR YOU.
HE IS **REALLY** WORRIED ABOUT IT GETTING OUT!!
OH, GOOD! HE DID GET IT IN THE MAIL, AFTER ALL!!
AND PAUL-SAN CAN RELAX, KNOWING IT CAME TO YOU!
WE'LL SEE.
RIP...
BY THE WAY, BUDDHA ...
IF I SHOULD START TO LEAK THE CONTENTS OF THIS LETTER MYSELF...
...WOULD YOU STOP ME BY FORCE, IF NECESSARY?
HUH? HA HA HA! WHAT IS THIS, A ZOMBIE MOVIE?

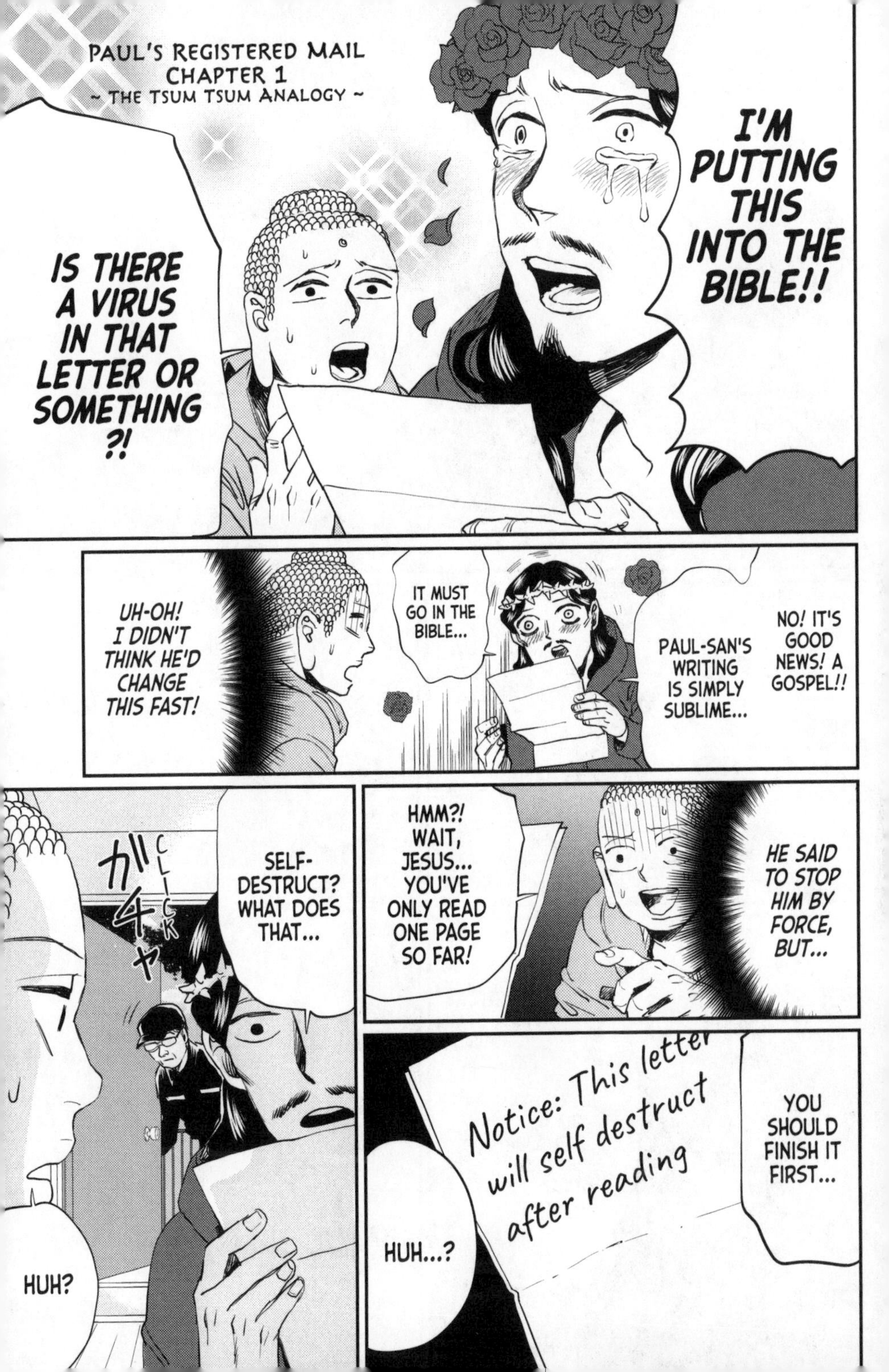
PAUL'S REGISTERED MAIL
CHAPTER 1
~ THE TSUM TSUM ANALOGY ~
I'M PUTTING THIS INTO THE BIBLE!!
IS THERE A VIRUS IN THAT LETTER OR SOMETHING?!
NO! IT'S GOOD NEWS! A GOSPEL!!
PAUL-SAN'S WRITING IS SIMPLY SUBLIME...
IT MUST GO IN THE BIBLE...
UH-OH! I DIDN'T THINK HE'D CHANGE THIS FAST!
HE SAID TO STOP HIM BY FORCE, BUT...
HMM?! WAIT, JESUS... YOU'VE ONLY READ ONE PAGE SO FAR!
YOU SHOULD FINISH IT FIRST...
Notice: This letter will self destruct after reading
HUH...?
SELF-DESTRUCT? WHAT DOES THAT...
ガチャ
CLICK
HUH?

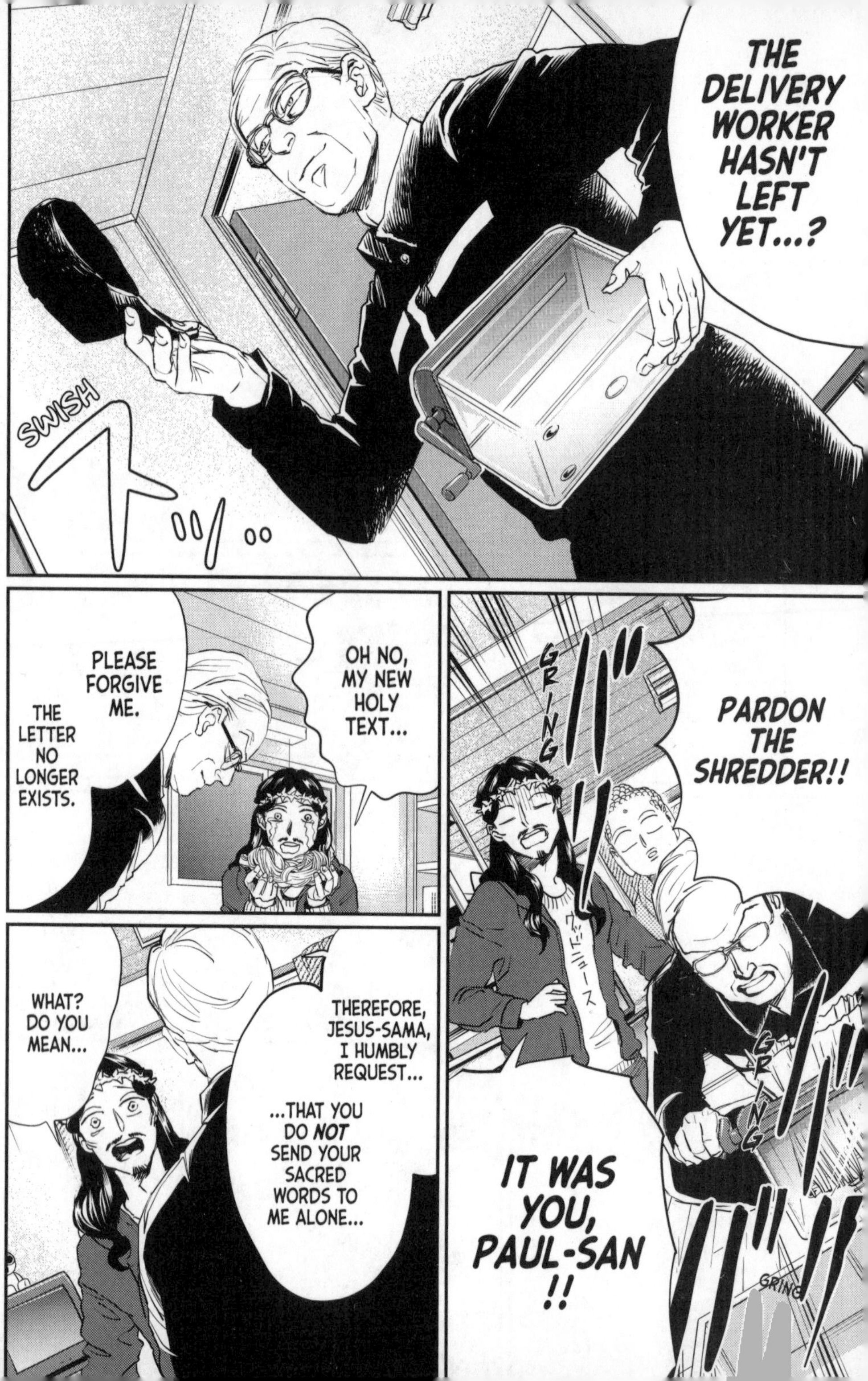
THE DELIVERY WORKER HASN'T LEFT YET...?
SWISH
PARDON THE SHREDDER!!
GRING
グッドニュース
GRING
IT WAS YOU, PAUL-SAN!!
GRING
OH NO, MY NEW HOLY TEXT...
PLEASE FORGIVE ME.
THE LETTER NO LONGER EXISTS.
THEREFORE, JESUS-SAMA, I HUMBLY REQUEST...
...THAT YOU DO ***NOT*** SEND YOUR SACRED WORDS TO ME ALONE...
WHAT? DO YOU MEAN...

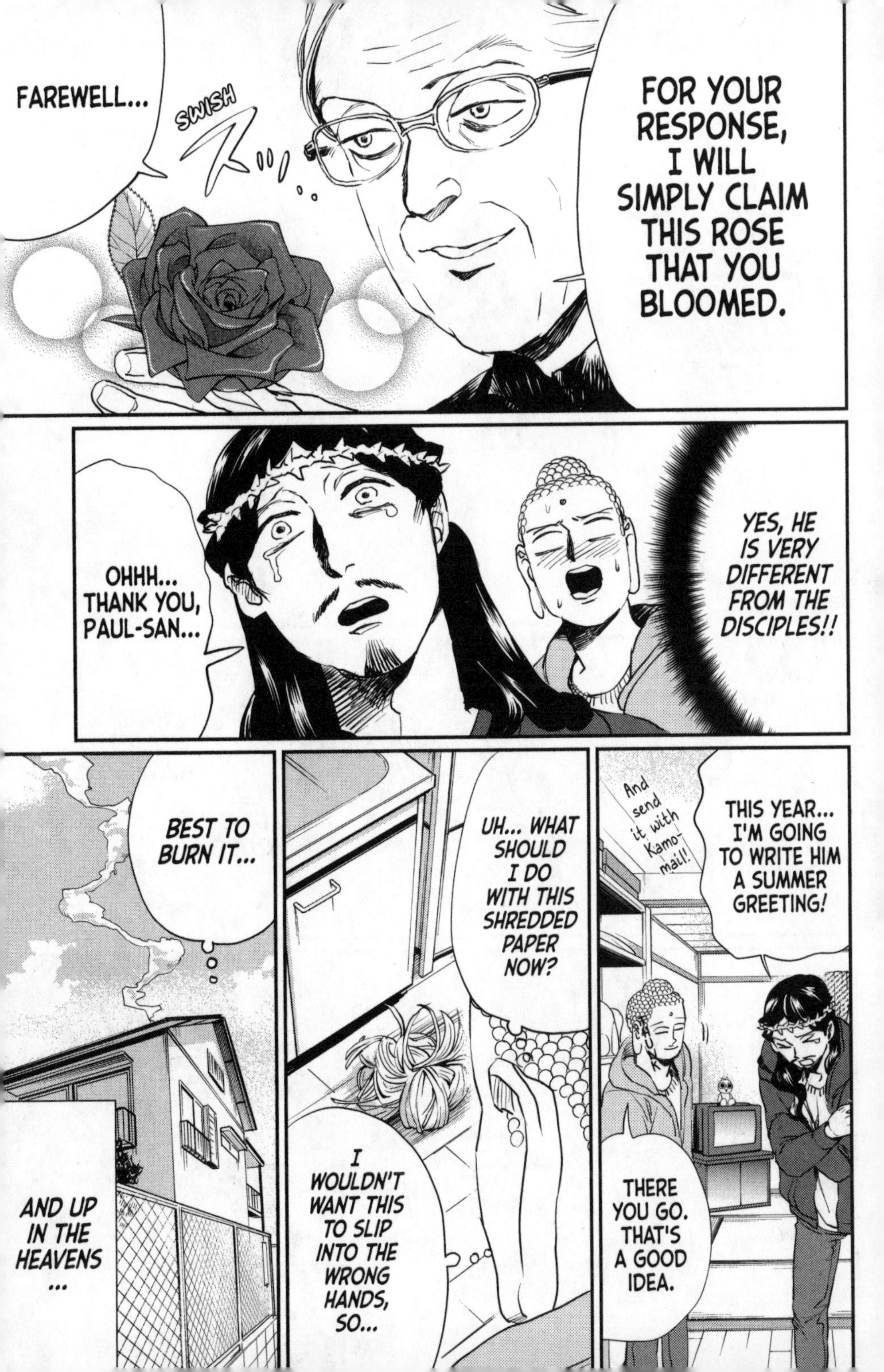
FOR YOUR RESPONSE, I WILL SIMPLY CLAIM THIS ROSE THAT YOU BLOOMED.
SWISH
FAREWELL...
YES, HE IS VERY DIFFERENT FROM THE DISCIPLES!!
OHHH... THANK YOU, PAUL-SAN...
THIS YEAR... I'M GOING TO WRITE HIM A SUMMER GREETING!
And send it with Kamo-mail!
THERE YOU GO. THAT'S A GOOD IDEA.
UH... WHAT SHOULD I DO WITH THIS SHREDDED PAPER NOW?
I WOULDN'T WANT THIS TO SLIP INTO THE WRONG HANDS, SO...
BEST TO BURN IT...
AND UP IN THE HEAVENS...

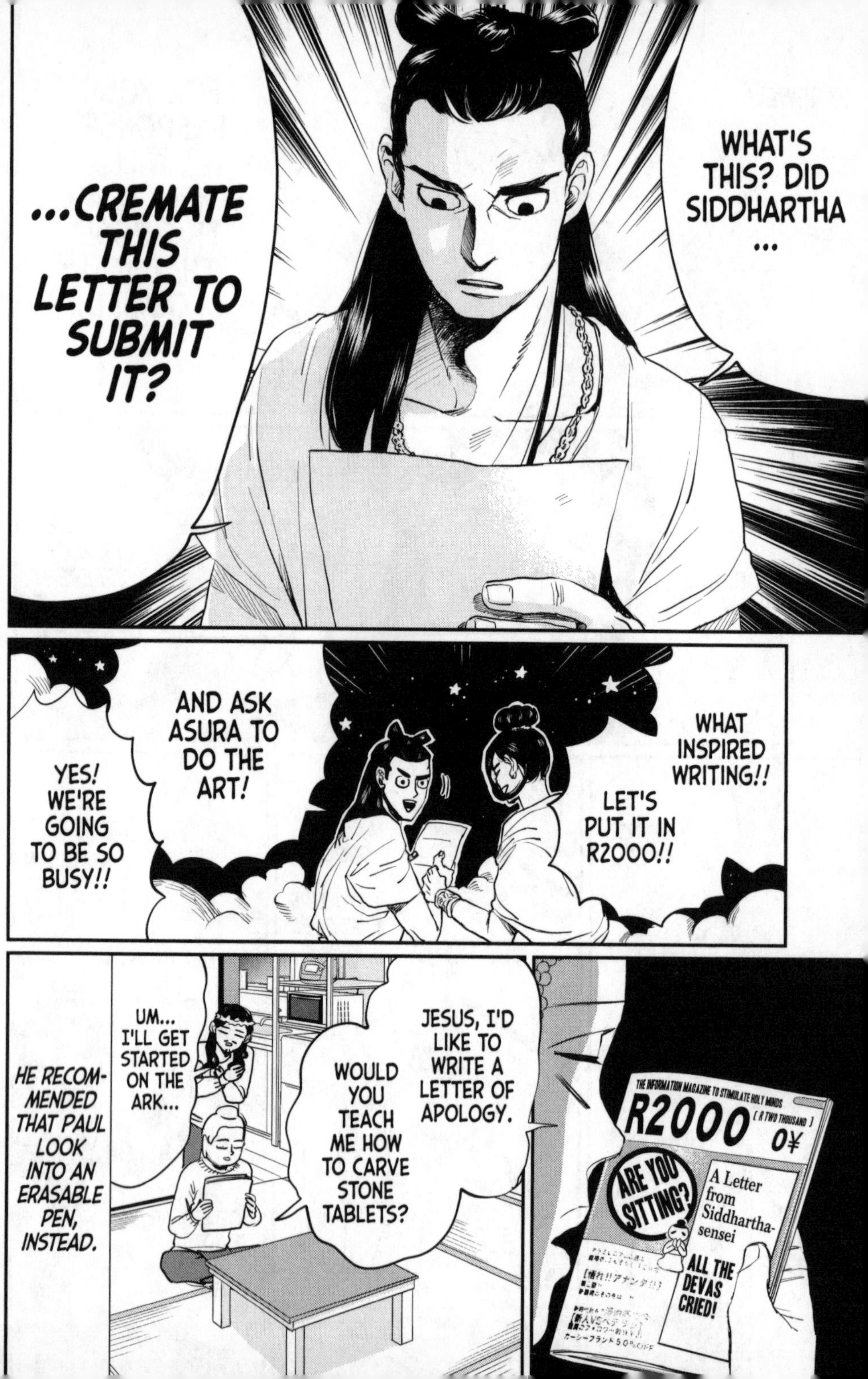
WHAT'S THIS? DID SIDDHARTHA ...
...CREMATE THIS LETTER TO SUBMIT IT?
WHAT INSPIRED WRITING!!
LET'S PUT IT IN R2000!!
AND ASK ASURA TO DO THE ART!
YES! WE'RE GOING TO BE SO BUSY!!
THE INFORMATION MAGAZINE TO STIMULATE HOLY MINDS
R2000 [R TWO THOUSAND]
0¥
ARE YOU SITTING?
A Letter from Siddhartha-sensei
ALL THE DEVAS CRIED!
JESUS, I'D LIKE TO WRITE A LETTER OF APOLOGY.
WOULD YOU TEACH ME HOW TO CARVE STONE TABLETS?
UM... I'LL GET STARTED ON THE ARK...
HE RECOMMENDED THAT PAUL LOOK INTO AN ERASABLE PEN, INSTEAD.

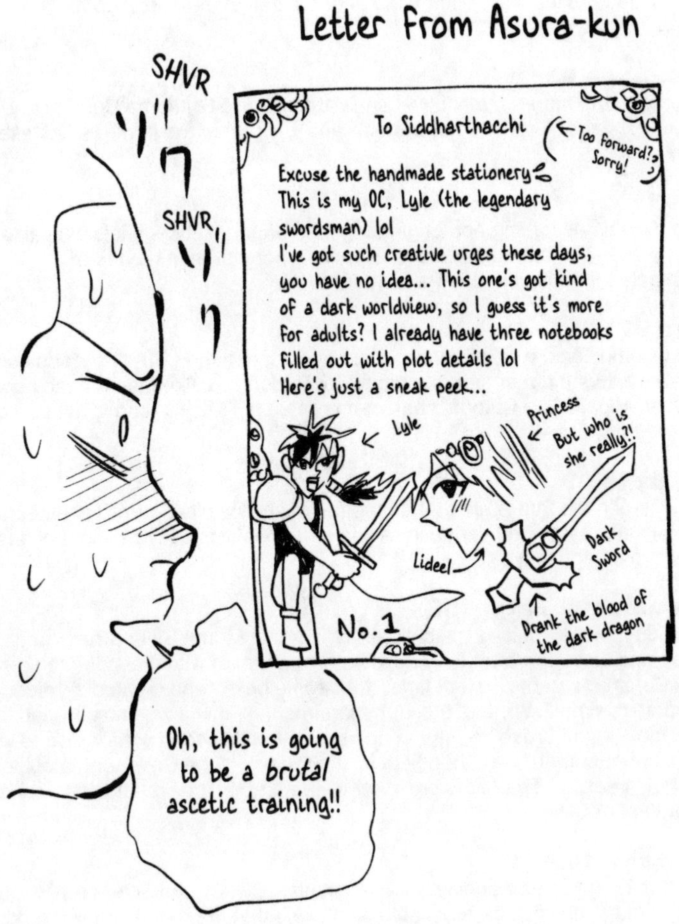
Letter from Asura-kun
To Siddharthacchi
Too forward!? Sorry!
Excuse the handmade stationery
This is my OC, Lyle (the legendary swordsman) lol
I've got such creative urges these days, you have no idea... This one's got kind of a dark worldview, so I guess it's more for adults? I already have three notebooks filled out with plot details lol
Here's just a sneak peek...
Lyle
Princess
But who is she really?!
Dark Sword
Lideel
Drank the blood of the dark dragon
No. 1
SHVR
SHVR
Oh, this is going to be a *brutal* ascetic training!!

CHAPTER 102 TRANSLATION NOTES

Nippen, page 92

The abbreviation of the Japan Penmanship Association, a group dedicated to lessons in handwritten Japanese. The group's mascot is named "Miko-chan," which is an unrelated homophone to the *miko* that is the shrine maiden at Shinto shrines.

Paul the Apostle, page 93

An apostle of Jesus, Paul was originally active in persecuting followers of Jesus before he eventually converted after the crucifixion, when he was visited by the ascended Jesus and fell blind for several days. Paul was one of the most influential figures in early Christianity following the end of Jesus's life, with authorship of about half of the books of the New Testament.

Sutta Nipata, page 95

A collection of some of the more advanced writings attributed to Gautama Buddha and his followers. The name means "Collection of Sutras," and it is part of the larger *Khuddaka Nikaya* collection.

LINE, page 95

The most popular social networking app originating from Japan, although it is available in other regions, as well. The stamp feature is especially popular as a means of communicating simple formalities in a fun and informal way.

Migaila, page 97

A character from Osamu Tezuka's *Buddha* story. She appears during Buddha's adolescent years and serves as a love interest and role model for Buddha. Unlike many of the people in *Buddha*, however, Migaila is a fictional character created by Tezuka, and is not part of the historical record.

Kabura pen, page 99

A type of all-purpose pen nib that is stiffer than the famously flexible G-pen. That means that while it is not as adaptable and varied in its line strengths, it is easier to control and have the lines remain steady in width.

Ten Commandments, page 100

In the Book of Exodus, Moses guides the children of Israel to Mount Sinai, where he ascends to the top and stays there for forty days before returning with the stone tablets featuring the Ten Commandments. In that time, the people below had created a golden idol of a calf to worship, violating one of the Commandments. Moses was so enraged that he cast down the tablets and broke them, and had to fashion a second set for God to write upon again. The Commandments are then kept inside the Ark of the Covenant, a golden chest carried by the Israelites. The Ark is prominently featured in the first Indiana Jones movie, *Raiders of the Lost Ark*.

Tsum Tsum, page 103

A Japanese brand of Disney merchandise, in which classic Disney characters are represented as ultra-cute minimalistic stackable plush toys that are meant to be arranged like a pyramid. The name is derived from *tsumu*, the verb for "to stack."

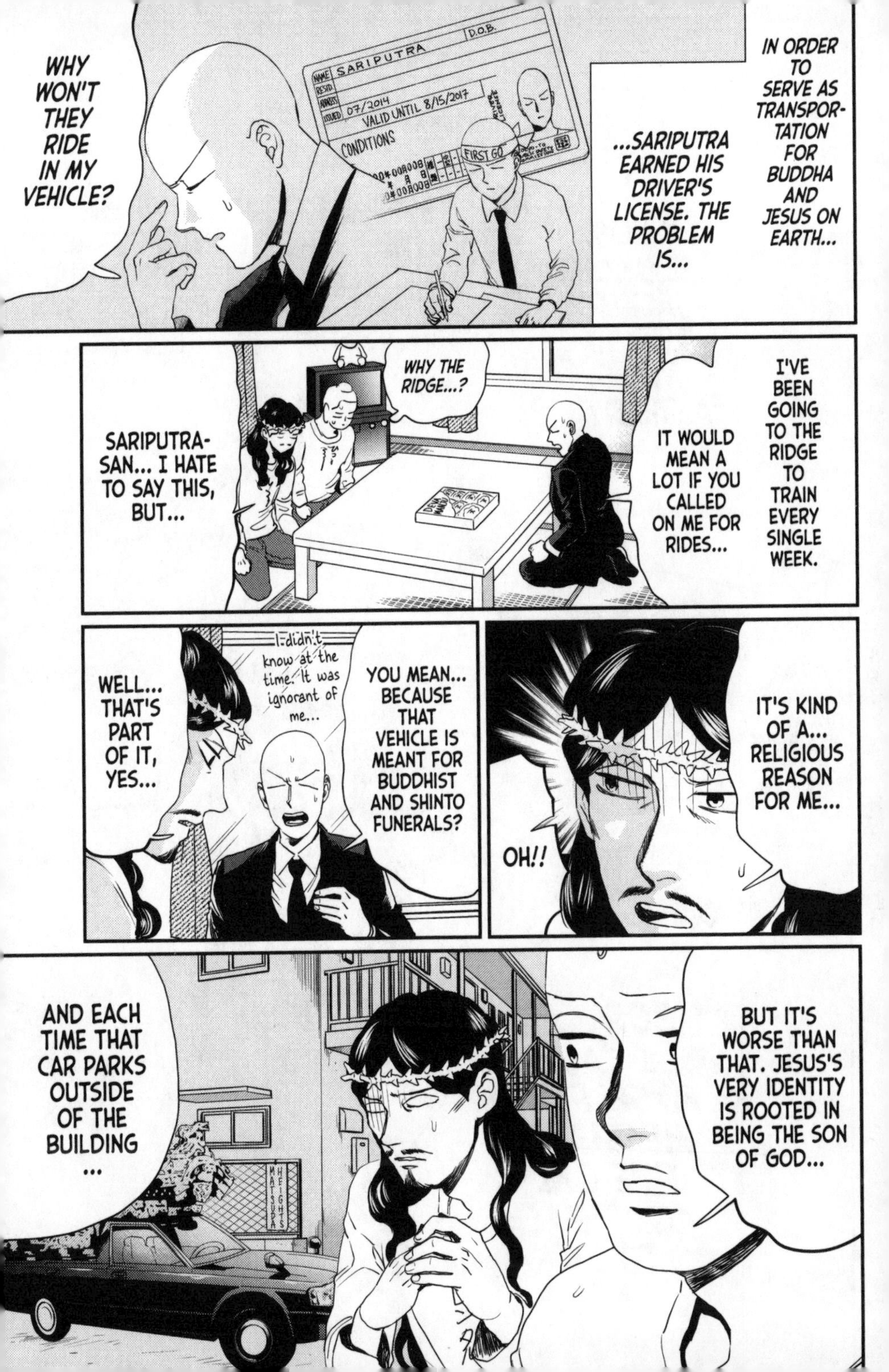

IN ORDER TO SERVE AS TRANSPORTATION FOR BUDDHA AND JESUS ON EARTH...
...SARIPUTRA EARNED HIS DRIVER'S LICENSE. THE PROBLEM IS...
D.O.B.
NAME SARIPUTRA
RESID
ADDRESS
ISSUED 07/2014
VALID UNTIL 8/15/2017
CONDITIONS
FIRST GO
WHY WON'T THEY RIDE IN MY VEHICLE?
I'VE BEEN GOING TO THE RIDGE TO TRAIN EVERY SINGLE WEEK.
IT WOULD MEAN A LOT IF YOU CALLED ON ME FOR RIDES...
WHY THE RIDGE...?
DEVA MANJU
SARIPUTRA-SAN... I HATE TO SAY THIS, BUT...
IT'S KIND OF A... RELIGIOUS REASON FOR ME...
OH!!
YOU MEAN... BECAUSE THAT VEHICLE IS MEANT FOR BUDDHIST AND SHINTO FUNERALS?
I didn't know at the time. It was ignorant of me...
WELL... THAT'S PART OF IT, YES...
BUT IT'S WORSE THAN THAT. JESUS'S VERY IDENTITY IS ROOTED IN BEING THE SON OF GOD...
AND EACH TIME THAT CAR PARKS OUTSIDE OF THE BUILDING...
MATSUDA HEIGHTS

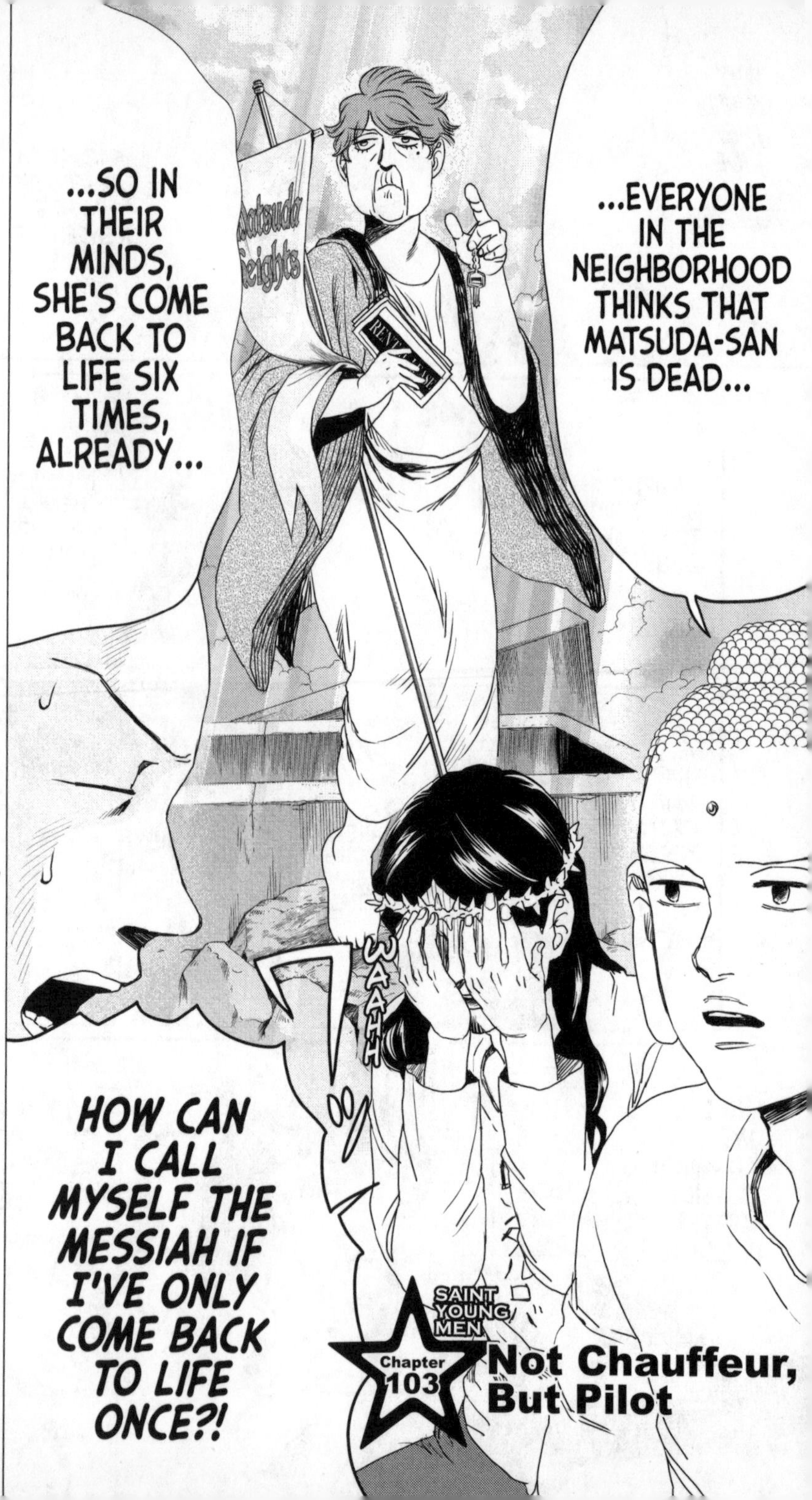
...EVERYONE IN THE NEIGHBORHOOD THINKS THAT MATSUDA-SAN IS DEAD...
...SO IN THEIR MINDS, SHE'S COME BACK TO LIFE SIX TIMES, ALREADY...
Matsuda Heights
WAAAHH
HOW CAN I CALL MYSELF THE MESSIAH IF I'VE ONLY COME BACK TO LIFE ONCE?!
SAINT YOUNG MEN
Chapter 103
Not Chauffeur, But Pilot
A THIRD MIRACLE-WORKER WAS BEING BORN IN TACHIKAWA.

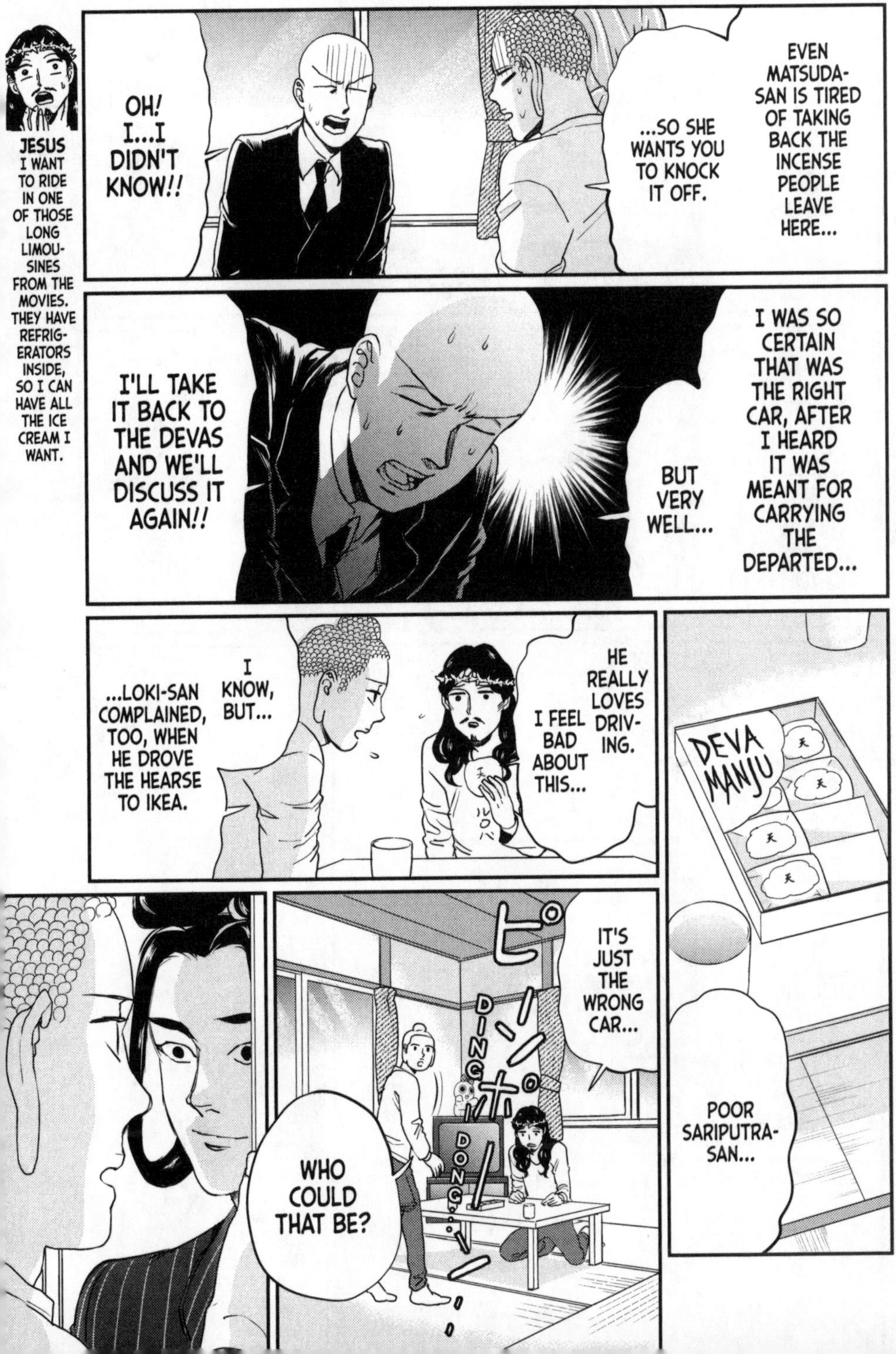
JESUS
I WANT TO RIDE IN ONE OF THOSE LONG LIMOUSINES FROM THE MOVIES. THEY HAVE REFRIGERATORS INSIDE, SO I CAN HAVE ALL THE ICE CREAM I WANT.
EVEN MATSUDA-SAN IS TIRED OF TAKING BACK THE INCENSE PEOPLE LEAVE HERE...
...SO SHE WANTS YOU TO KNOCK IT OFF.
OH! I...I DIDN'T KNOW!!
I WAS SO CERTAIN THAT WAS THE RIGHT CAR, AFTER I HEARD IT WAS MEANT FOR CARRYING THE DEPARTED...
BUT VERY WELL...
I'LL TAKE IT BACK TO THE DEVAS AND WE'LL DISCUSS IT AGAIN!!
DEVA MANJU
POOR SARIPUTRA-SAN...
HE REALLY LOVES DRIVING.
I FEEL BAD ABOUT THIS...
I KNOW, BUT...
...LOKI-SAN COMPLAINED, TOO, WHEN HE DROVE THE HEARSE TO IKEA.
IT'S JUST THE WRONG CAR...
ピンポーン
DING DONG
WHO COULD THAT BE?

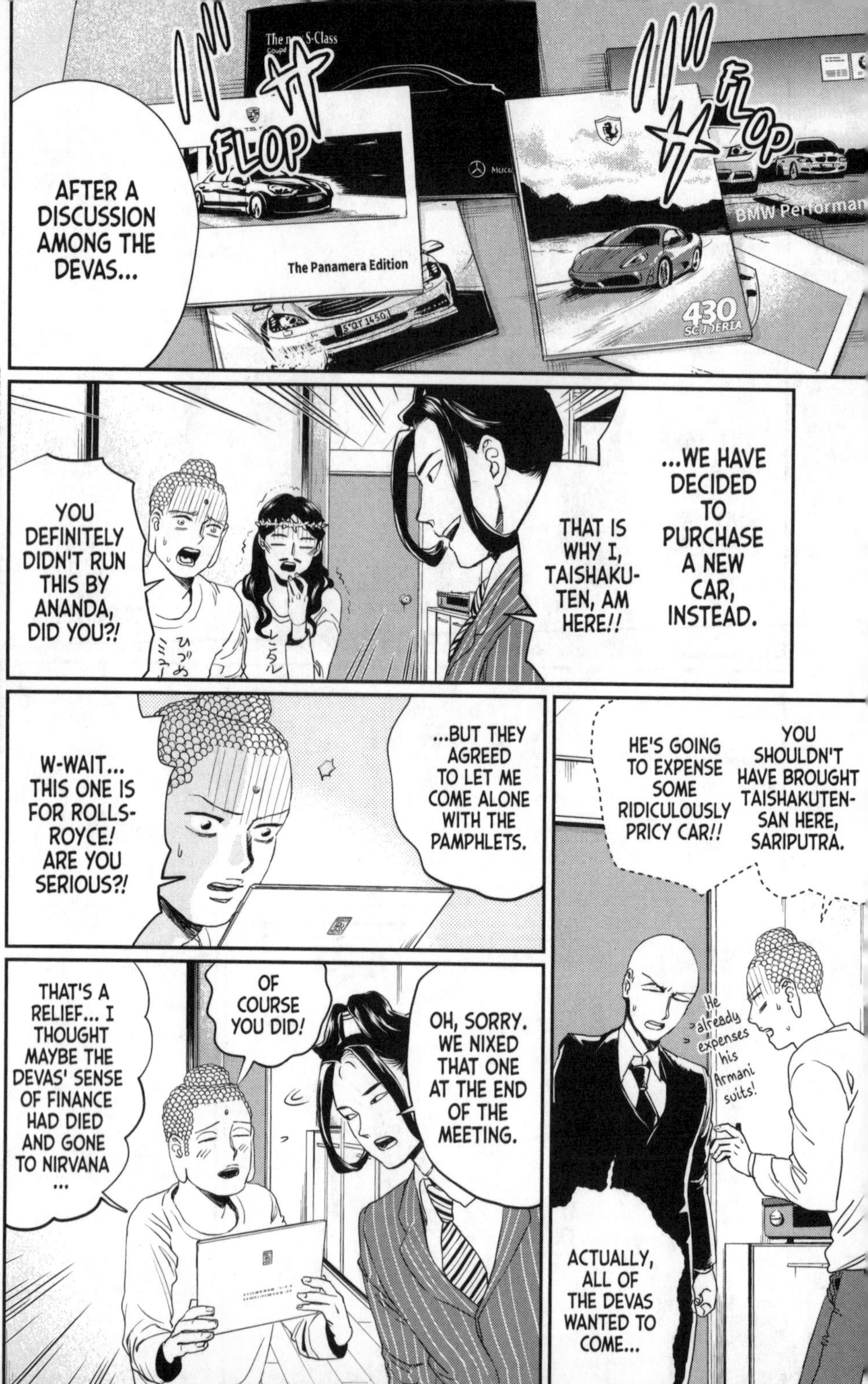
FLOP
FLOP
AFTER A DISCUSSION AMONG THE DEVAS...
The Panamera Edition
BMW Performan
...WE HAVE DECIDED TO PURCHASE A NEW CAR, INSTEAD.
THAT IS WHY I, TAISHAKU-TEN, AM HERE!!
YOU DEFINITELY DIDN'T RUN THIS BY ANANDA, DID YOU?!
YOU SHOULDN'T HAVE BROUGHT TAISHAKUTEN-SAN HERE, SARIPUTRA.
HE'S GOING TO EXPENSE SOME RIDICULOUSLY PRICY CAR!!
He already expenses his Armani suits!
ACTUALLY, ALL OF THE DEVAS WANTED TO COME...
...BUT THEY AGREED TO LET ME COME ALONE WITH THE PAMPHLETS.
W-WAIT... THIS ONE IS FOR ROLLS-ROYCE! ARE YOU SERIOUS?!
OH, SORRY. WE NIXED THAT ONE AT THE END OF THE MEETING.
OF COURSE YOU DID!
THAT'S A RELIEF... I THOUGHT MAYBE THE DEVAS' SENSE OF FINANCE HAD DIED AND GONE TO NIRVANA ...

BUDDHA'S SHIRT: MUTED HOOVES JESUS'S SHIRT: RENTAL MULE

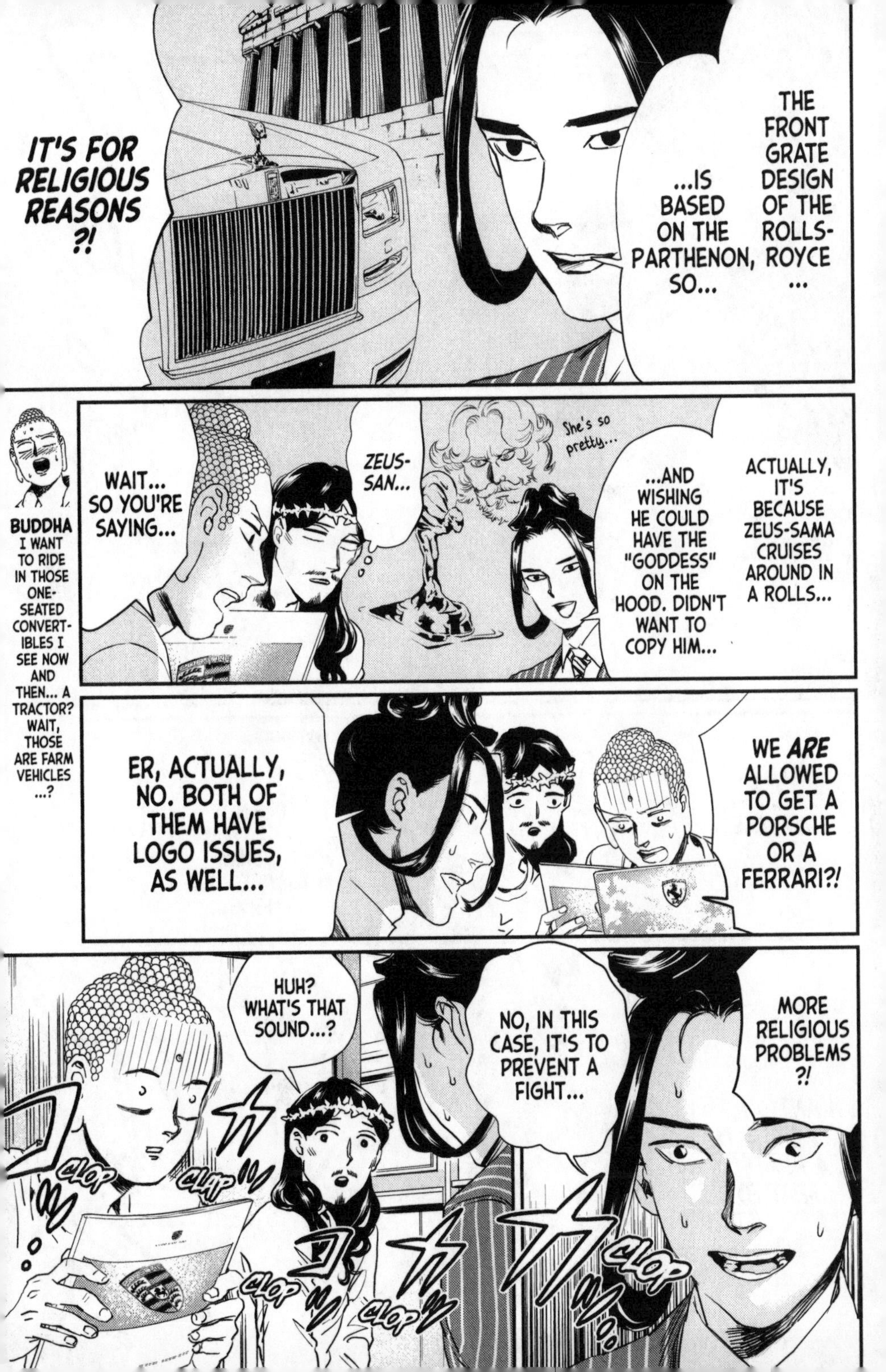
THE FRONT GRATE DESIGN OF THE ROLLS-ROYCE ...
...IS BASED ON THE PARTHENON, SO...
IT'S FOR RELIGIOUS REASONS ?!
ACTUALLY, IT'S BECAUSE ZEUS-SAMA CRUISES AROUND IN A ROLLS...
...AND WISHING HE COULD HAVE THE "GODDESS" ON THE HOOD. DIDN'T WANT TO COPY HIM...
She's so pretty...
ZEUS-SAN...
WAIT... SO YOU'RE SAYING...
WE *ARE* ALLOWED TO GET A PORSCHE OR A FERRARI?!
ER, ACTUALLY, NO. BOTH OF THEM HAVE LOGO ISSUES, AS WELL...
BUDDHA
I WANT TO RIDE IN THOSE ONE-SEATED CONVERTIBLES I SEE NOW AND THEN... A TRACTOR? WAIT, THOSE ARE FARM VEHICLES ...?
MORE RELIGIOUS PROBLEMS ?!
NO, IN THIS CASE, IT'S TO PREVENT A FIGHT...
HUH? WHAT'S THAT SOUND...?
CLOP
CLOP
CLOP
CLOP
CLOP
CLOP

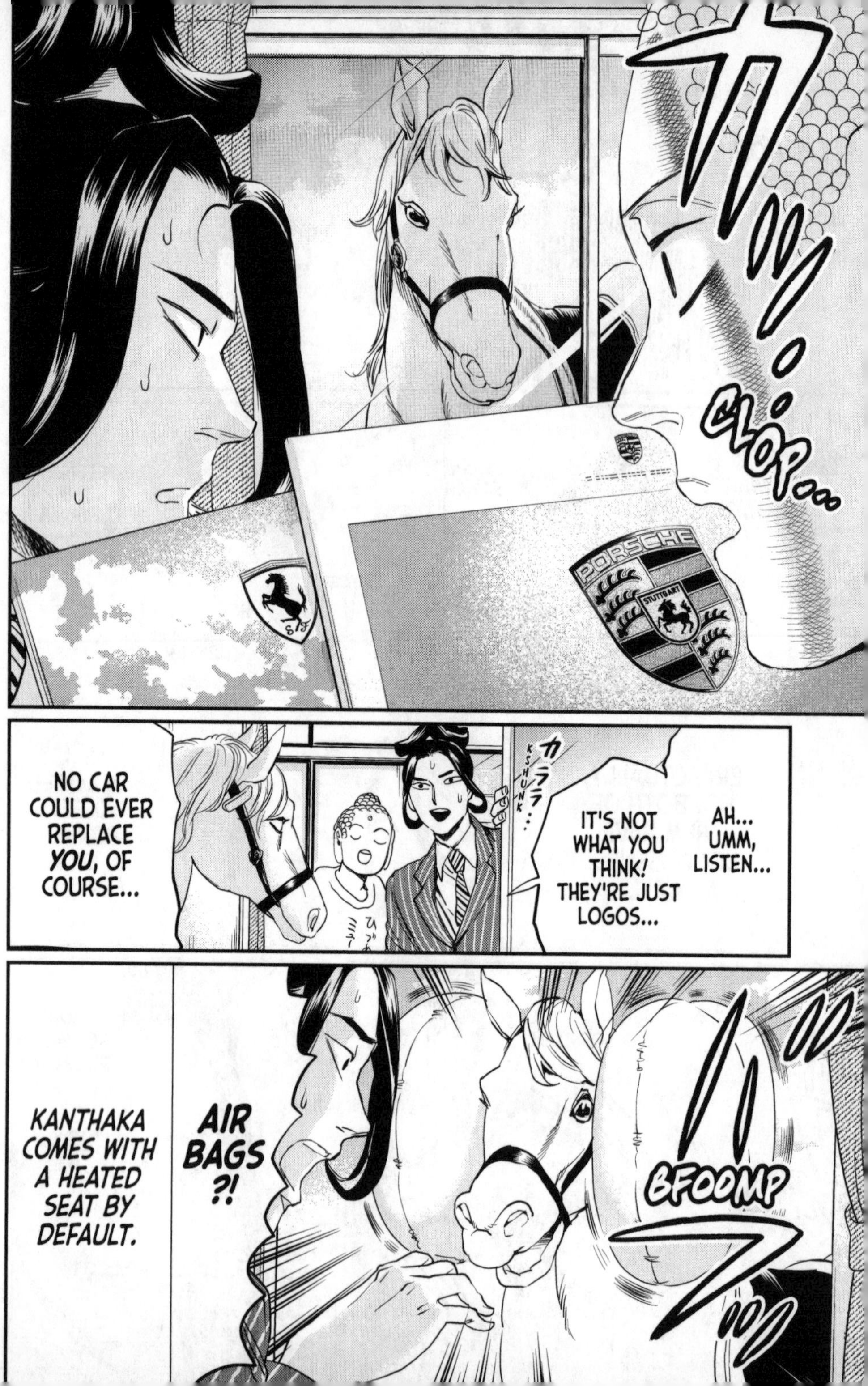
CLOP...
PORSCHE
STUTTGART
AH... UMM, LISTEN...
IT'S NOT WHAT YOU THINK! THEY'RE JUST LOGOS...
KSHUNK...
NO CAR COULD EVER REPLACE *YOU*, OF COURSE...
BFOOMP
AIR BAGS?!
KANTHAKA COMES WITH A HEATED SEAT BY DEFAULT.

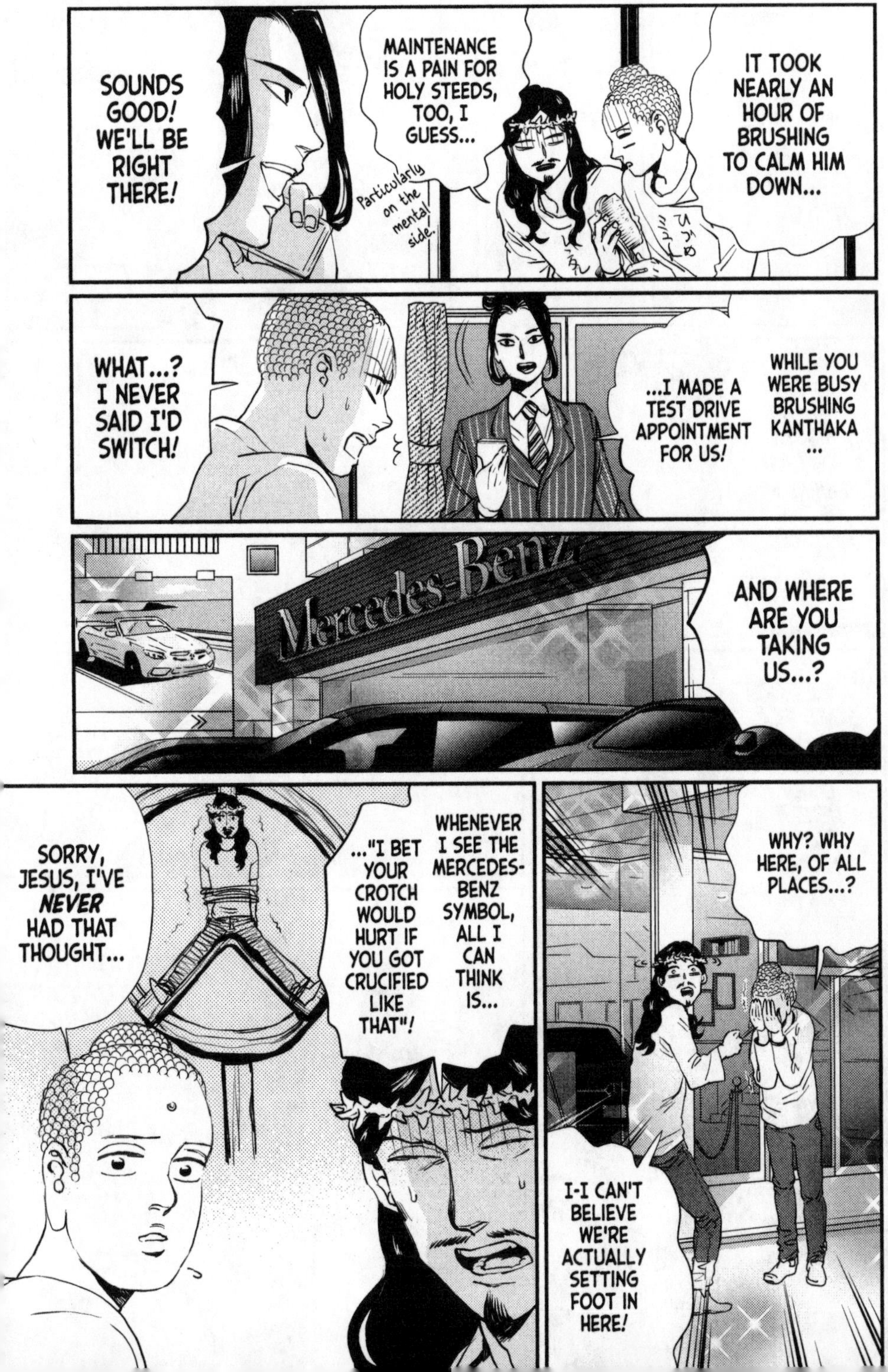
IT TOOK NEARLY AN HOUR OF BRUSHING TO CALM HIM DOWN...
MAINTENANCE IS A PAIN FOR HOLY STEEDS, TOO, I GUESS...
Particularly on the mental side.
SOUNDS GOOD! WE'LL BE RIGHT THERE!
WHILE YOU WERE BUSY BRUSHING KANTHAKA ...
...I MADE A TEST DRIVE APPOINTMENT FOR US!
WHAT...? I NEVER SAID I'D SWITCH!
Mercedes-Benz
AND WHERE ARE YOU TAKING US...?
WHY? WHY HERE, OF ALL PLACES...?
I-I CAN'T BELIEVE WE'RE ACTUALLY SETTING FOOT IN HERE!
WHENEVER I SEE THE MERCEDES-BENZ SYMBOL, ALL I CAN THINK IS...
..."I BET YOUR CROTCH WOULD HURT IF YOU GOT CRUCIFIED LIKE THAT"!
SORRY, JESUS, I'VE ***NEVER*** HAD THAT THOUGHT...

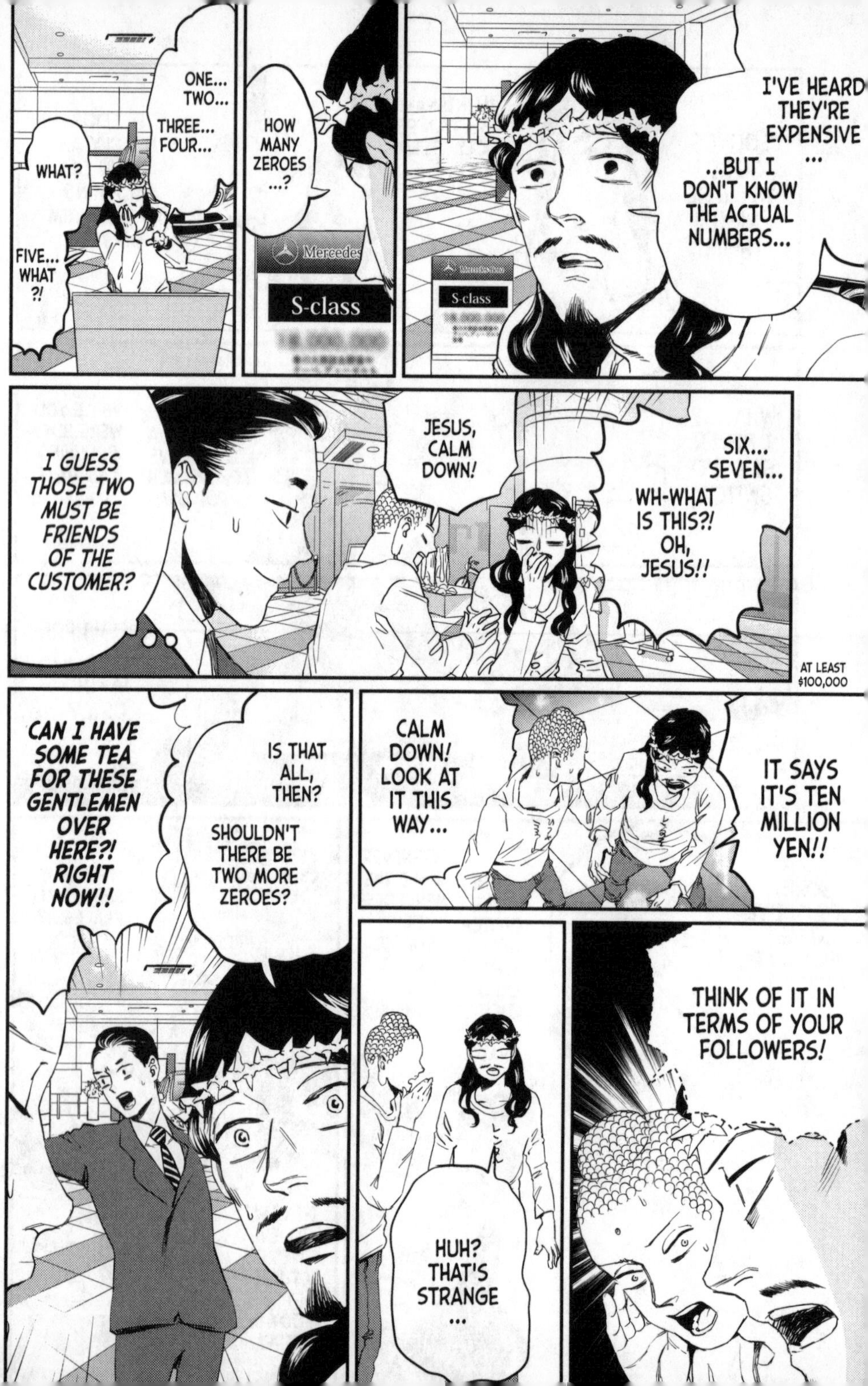
I'VE HEARD THEY'RE EXPENSIVE ...
...BUT I DON'T KNOW THE ACTUAL NUMBERS...
HOW MANY ZEROES ...?
Mercedes
S-class
S-class
ONE... TWO...
THREE... FOUR...
WHAT?
FIVE... WHAT ?!
SIX... SEVEN...
WH-WHAT IS THIS?! OH, JESUS!!
JESUS, CALM DOWN!
I GUESS THOSE TWO MUST BE FRIENDS OF THE CUSTOMER?
AT LEAST $100,000
IT SAYS IT'S TEN MILLION YEN!!
CALM DOWN! LOOK AT IT THIS WAY...
THINK OF IT IN TERMS OF YOUR FOLLOWERS!
HUH? THAT'S STRANGE ...
IS THAT ALL, THEN?
SHOULDN'T THERE BE TWO MORE ZEROES?
CAN I HAVE SOME TEA FOR THESE GENTLEMEN OVER HERE?! RIGHT NOW!!

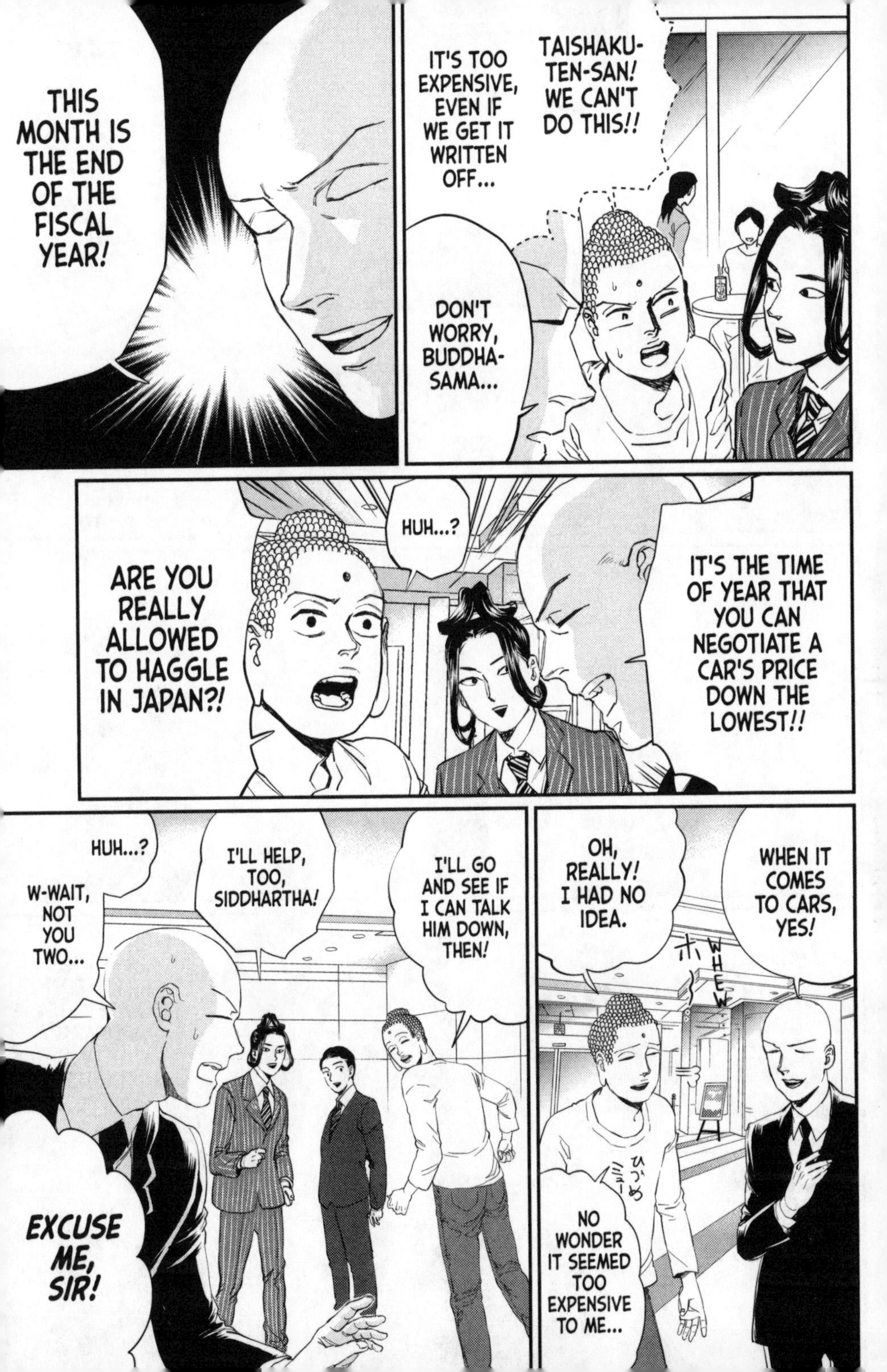
TAISHAKU-TEN-SAN! WE CAN'T DO THIS!!
IT'S TOO EXPENSIVE, EVEN IF WE GET IT WRITTEN OFF...
DON'T WORRY, BUDDHA-SAMA...
THIS MONTH IS THE END OF THE FISCAL YEAR!
IT'S THE TIME OF YEAR THAT YOU CAN NEGOTIATE A CAR'S PRICE DOWN THE LOWEST!!
HUH...?
ARE YOU REALLY ALLOWED TO HAGGLE IN JAPAN?!
WHEN IT COMES TO CARS, YES!
OH, REALLY! I HAD NO IDEA.
WHEW
NO WONDER IT SEEMED TOO EXPENSIVE TO ME...
I'LL GO AND SEE IF I CAN TALK HIM DOWN, THEN!
I'LL HELP, TOO, SIDDHARTHA!
HUH...?
W-WAIT, NOT YOU TWO...
EXCUSE ME, SIR!

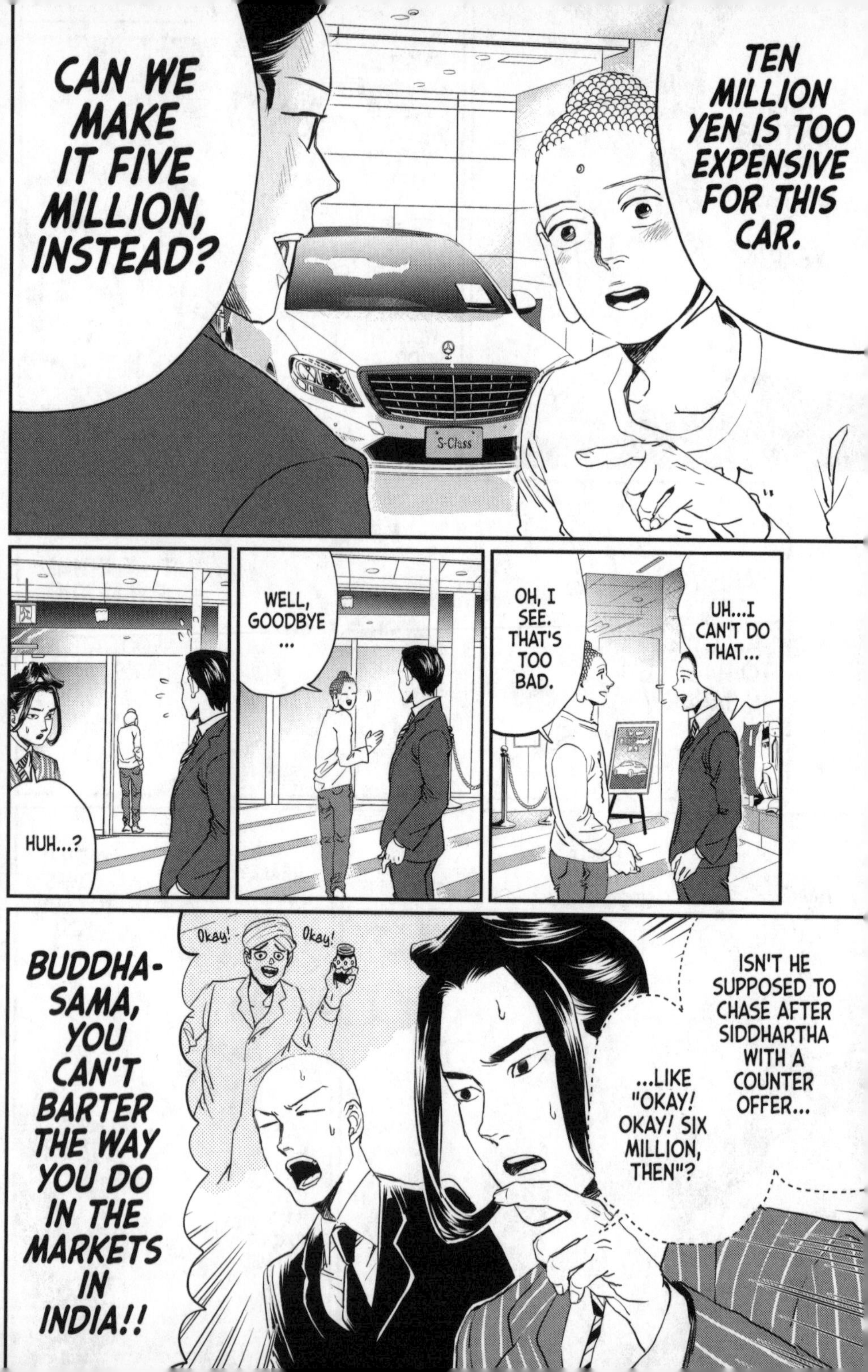
TEN MILLION YEN IS TOO EXPENSIVE FOR THIS CAR.
CAN WE MAKE IT FIVE MILLION, INSTEAD?
S-Class
UH...I CAN'T DO THAT...
OH, I SEE. THAT'S TOO BAD.
WELL, GOODBYE ...
HUH...?
ISN'T HE SUPPOSED TO CHASE AFTER SIDDHARTHA WITH A COUNTER OFFER...
...LIKE "OKAY! OKAY! SIX MILLION, THEN"?
Okay! Okay!
BUDDHA-SAMA, YOU CAN'T BARTER THE WAY YOU DO IN THE MARKETS IN INDIA!!

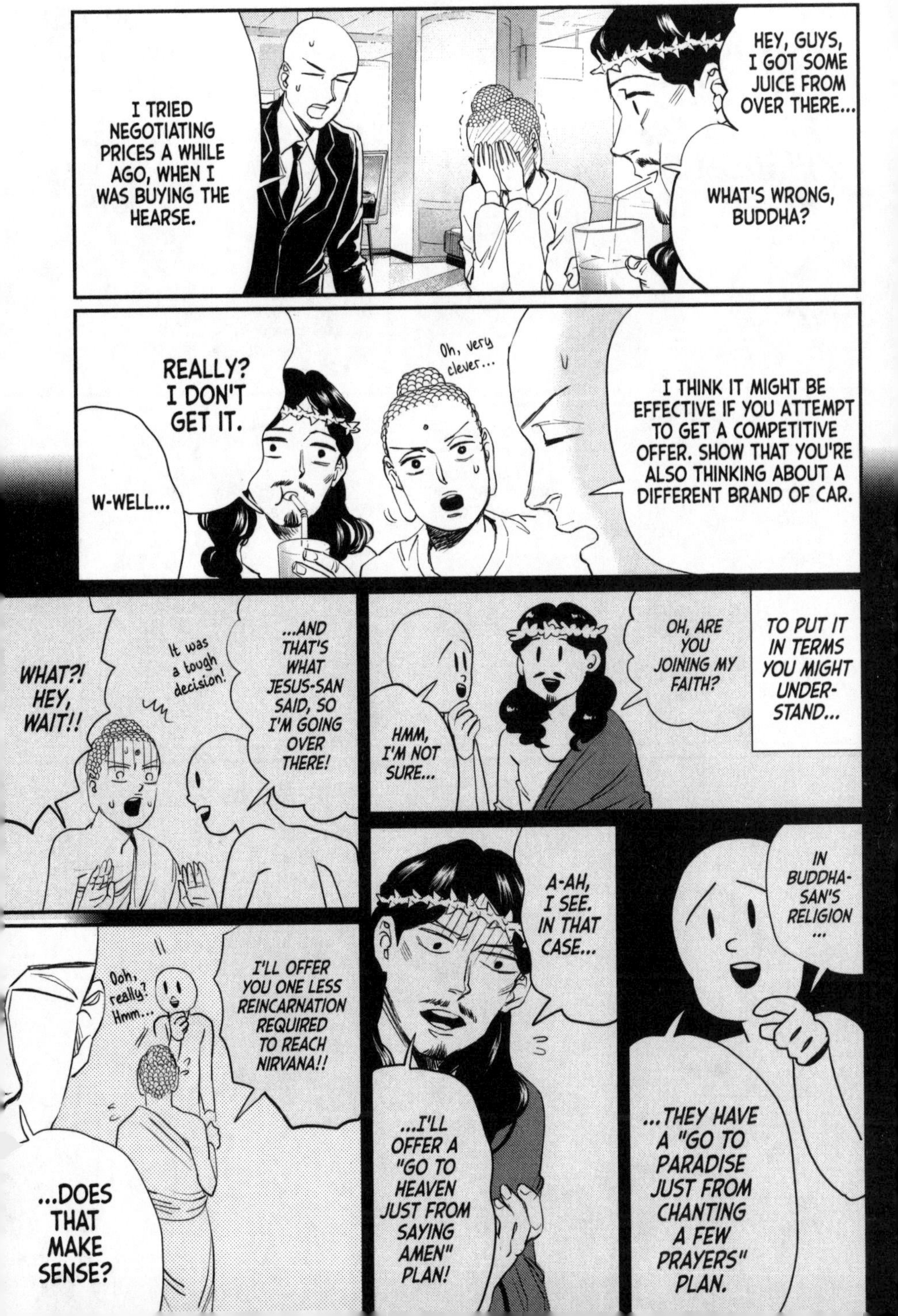
HEY, GUYS, I GOT SOME JUICE FROM OVER THERE...
WHAT'S WRONG, BUDDHA?
I TRIED NEGOTIATING PRICES A WHILE AGO, WHEN I WAS BUYING THE HEARSE.
I THINK IT MIGHT BE EFFECTIVE IF YOU ATTEMPT TO GET A COMPETITIVE OFFER. SHOW THAT YOU'RE ALSO THINKING ABOUT A DIFFERENT BRAND OF CAR.
Oh, very clever...
REALLY? I DON'T GET IT.
W-WELL...
TO PUT IT IN TERMS YOU MIGHT UNDER-STAND...
OH, ARE YOU JOINING MY FAITH?
HMM, I'M NOT SURE...
IN BUDDHA-SAN'S RELIGION...
...THEY HAVE A "GO TO PARADISE JUST FROM CHANTING A FEW PRAYERS" PLAN.
A-AH, I SEE. IN THAT CASE...
...I'LL OFFER A "GO TO HEAVEN JUST FROM SAYING AMEN" PLAN!
...AND THAT'S WHAT JESUS-SAN SAID, SO I'M GOING OVER THERE!
It was a tough decision!
WHAT?! HEY, WAIT!!
I'LL OFFER YOU ONE LESS REINCARNATION REQUIRED TO REACH NIRVANA!!
Ooh, really? Hmm...
...DOES THAT MAKE SENSE?

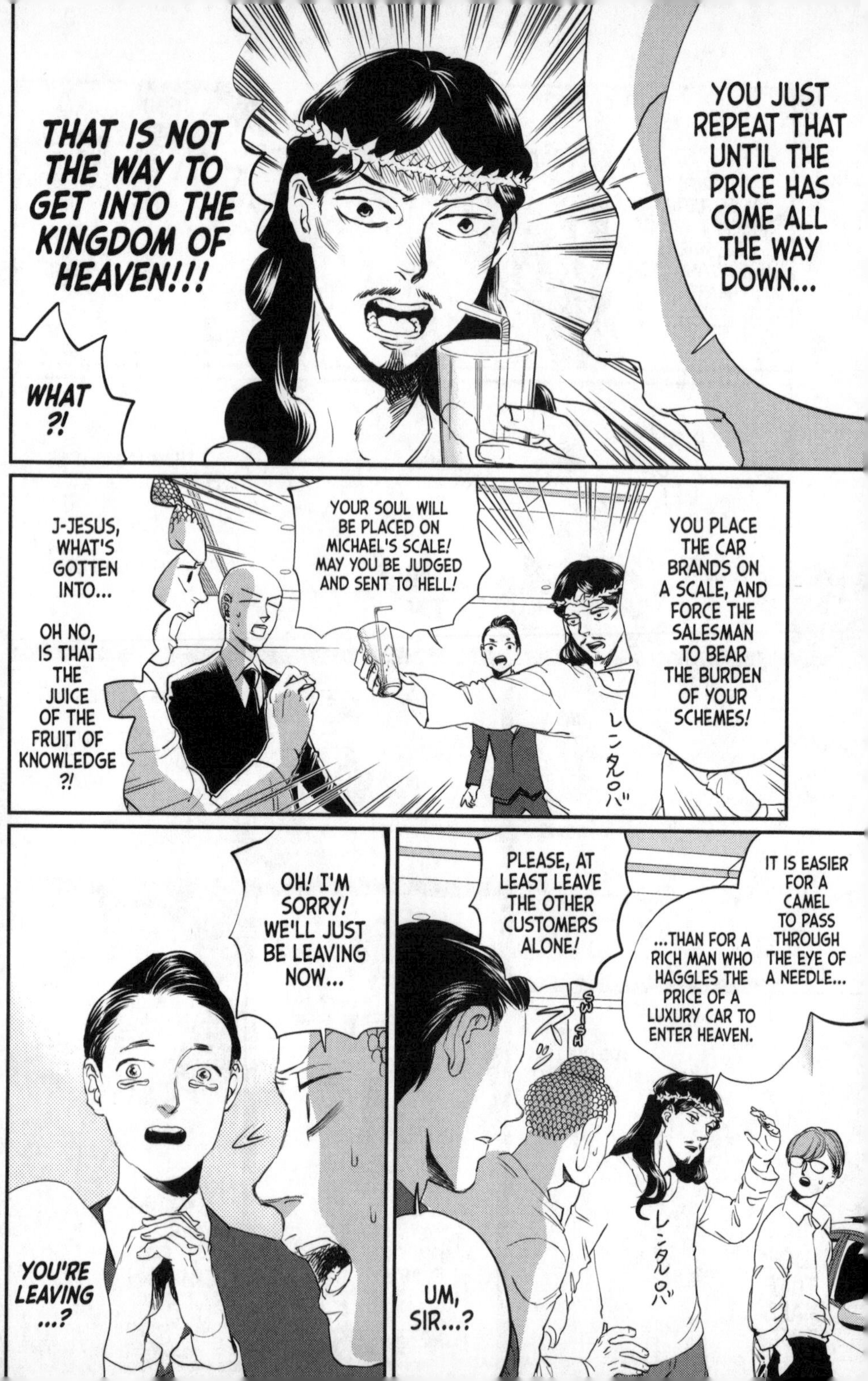
YOU JUST REPEAT THAT UNTIL THE PRICE HAS COME ALL THE WAY DOWN...
THAT IS NOT THE WAY TO GET INTO THE KINGDOM OF HEAVEN!!!
WHAT ?!
YOU PLACE THE CAR BRANDS ON A SCALE, AND FORCE THE SALESMAN TO BEAR THE BURDEN OF YOUR SCHEMES!
YOUR SOUL WILL BE PLACED ON MICHAEL'S SCALE! MAY YOU BE JUDGED AND SENT TO HELL!
J-JESUS, WHAT'S GOTTEN INTO...
OH NO, IS THAT THE JUICE OF THE FRUIT OF KNOWLEDGE ?!
IT IS EASIER FOR A CAMEL TO PASS THROUGH THE EYE OF A NEEDLE...
...THAN FOR A RICH MAN WHO HAGGLES THE PRICE OF A LUXURY CAR TO ENTER HEAVEN.
PLEASE, AT LEAST LEAVE THE OTHER CUSTOMERS ALONE!
SWISH
UM, SIR...?
OH! I'M SORRY! WE'LL JUST BE LEAVING NOW...
YOU'RE LEAVING ...?

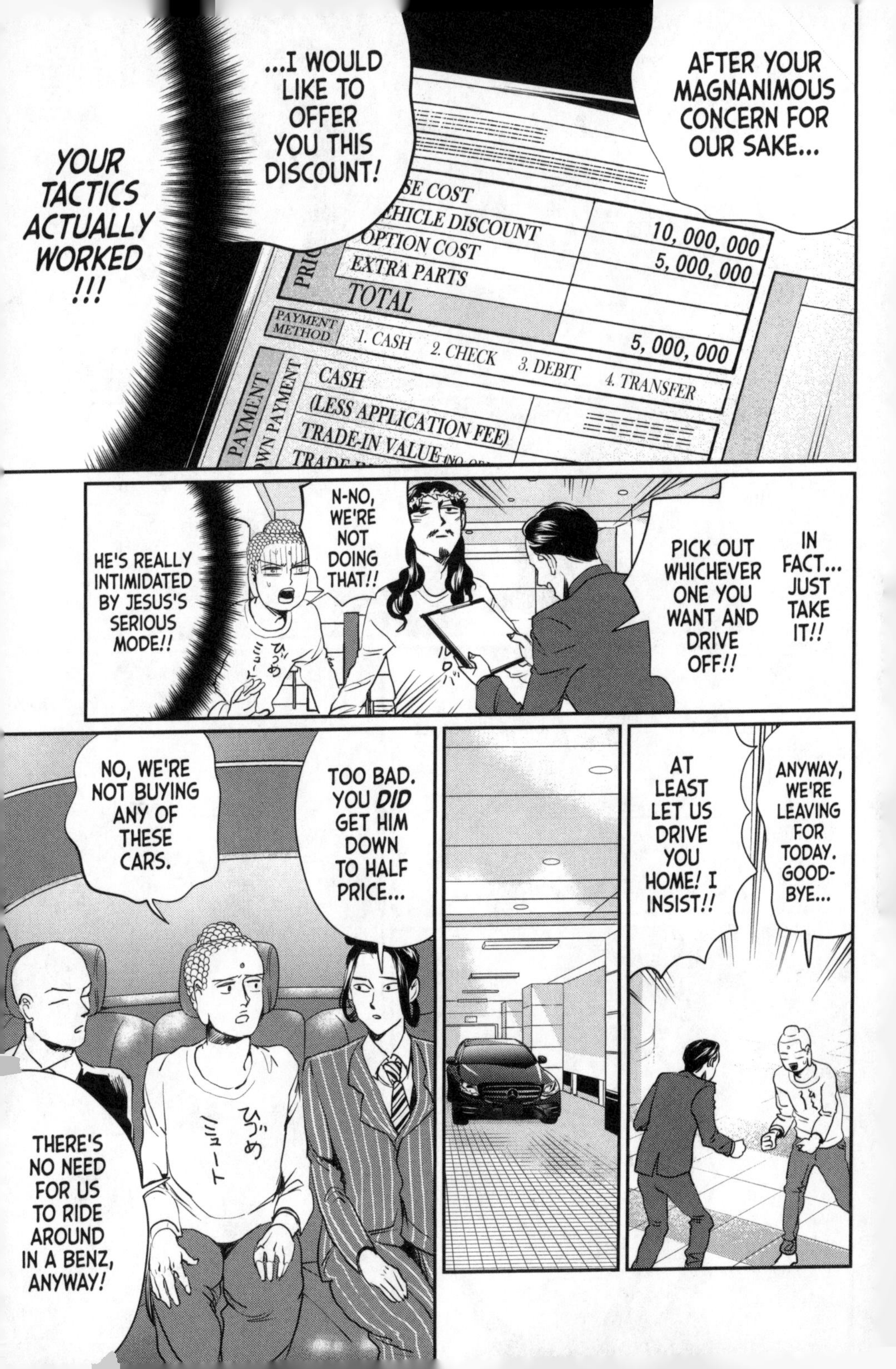
AFTER YOUR MAGNANIMOUS CONCERN FOR OUR SAKE...
...I WOULD LIKE TO OFFER YOU THIS DISCOUNT!
SE COST
EHICLE DISCOUNT 10, 000, 000
OPTION COST 5, 000, 000
EXTRA PARTS
TOTAL
PAYMENT METHOD 1. CASH 2. CHECK 3. DEBIT 4. TRANSFER
5, 000, 000
PAYMENT
CASH
(LESS APPLICATION FEE)
TRADE-IN VALUE
YOUR TACTICS ACTUALLY WORKED!!!
IN FACT... JUST TAKE IT!!
PICK OUT WHICHEVER ONE YOU WANT AND DRIVE OFF!!
N-NO, WE'RE NOT DOING THAT!!
HE'S REALLY INTIMIDATED BY JESUS'S SERIOUS MODE!!
ANYWAY, WE'RE LEAVING FOR TODAY. GOOD-BYE...
AT LEAST LET US DRIVE YOU HOME! I INSIST!!
TOO BAD. YOU *DID* GET HIM DOWN TO HALF PRICE...
NO, WE'RE NOT BUYING ANY OF THESE CARS.
THERE'S NO NEED FOR US TO RIDE AROUND IN A BENZ, ANYWAY!

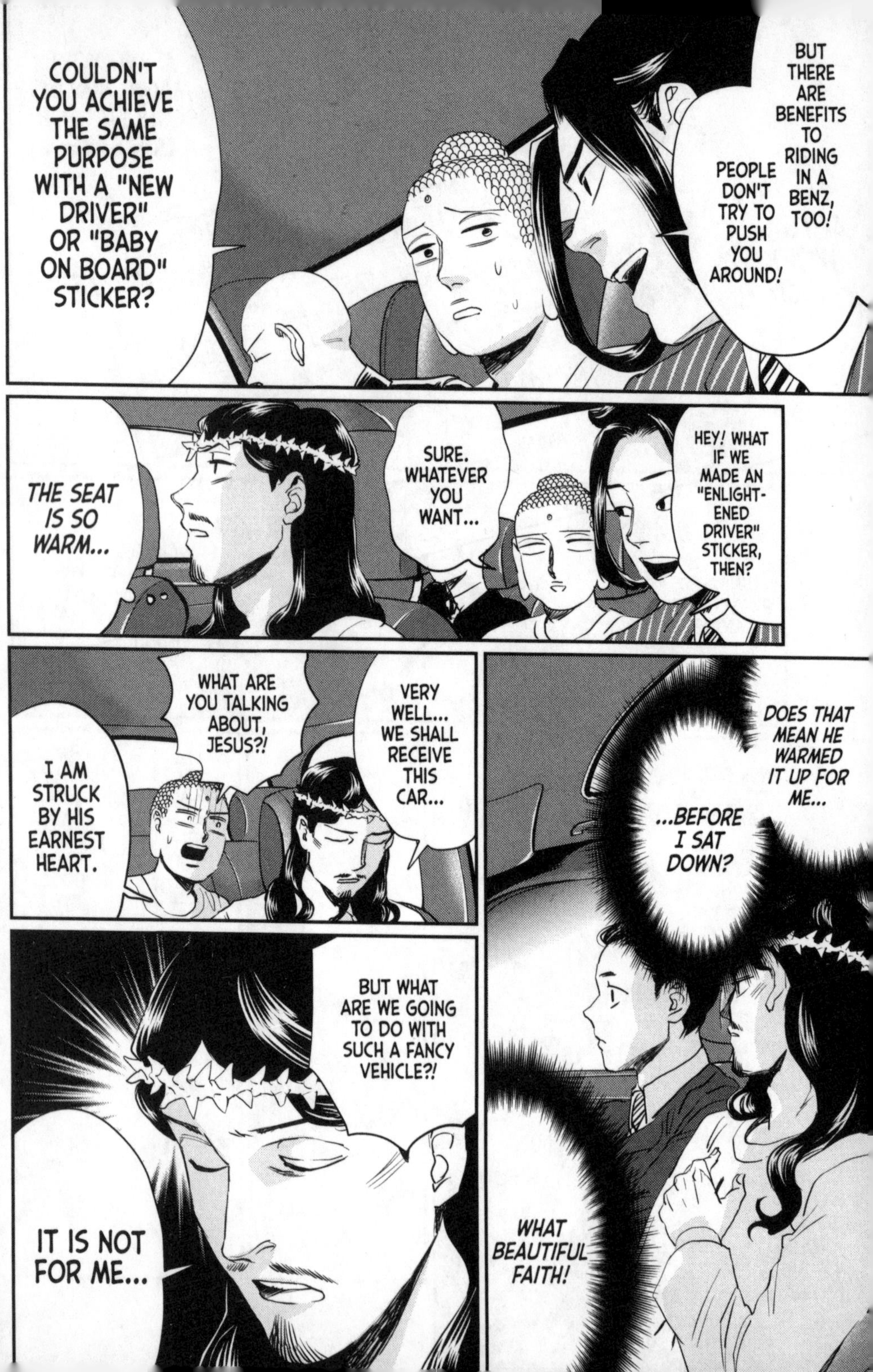
BUT THERE ARE BENEFITS TO RIDING IN A BENZ, TOO!
PEOPLE DON'T TRY TO PUSH YOU AROUND!
COULDN'T YOU ACHIEVE THE SAME PURPOSE WITH A "NEW DRIVER" OR "BABY ON BOARD" STICKER?
HEY! WHAT IF WE MADE AN "ENLIGHT-ENED DRIVER" STICKER, THEN?
SURE. WHATEVER YOU WANT...
THE SEAT IS SO WARM...
DOES THAT MEAN HE WARMED IT UP FOR ME...
...BEFORE I SAT DOWN?
WHAT BEAUTIFUL FAITH!
VERY WELL... WE SHALL RECEIVE THIS CAR...
WHAT ARE YOU TALKING ABOUT, JESUS?!
I AM STRUCK BY HIS EARNEST HEART.
BUT WHAT ARE WE GOING TO DO WITH SUCH A FANCY VEHICLE?!
IT IS NOT FOR ME...

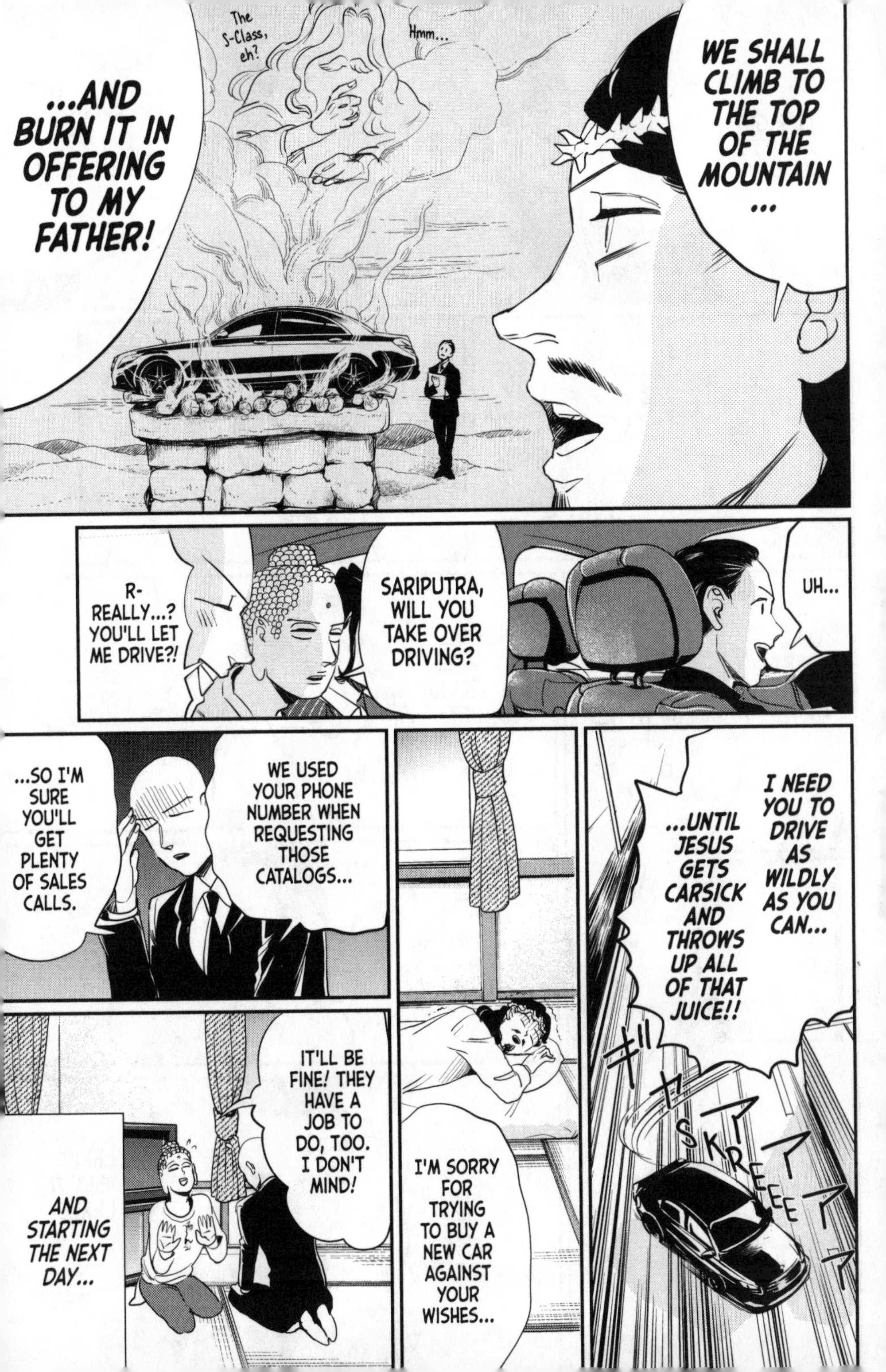
WE SHALL CLIMB TO THE TOP OF THE MOUNTAIN ...
...AND BURN IT IN OFFERING TO MY FATHER!
Hmm...
The S-Class, eh?
UH...
SARIPUTRA, WILL YOU TAKE OVER DRIVING?
R-REALLY...? YOU'LL LET ME DRIVE?!
I NEED YOU TO DRIVE AS WILDLY AS YOU CAN...
...UNTIL JESUS GETS CARSICK AND THROWS UP ALL OF THAT JUICE!!
SKREEEE
I'M SORRY FOR TRYING TO BUY A NEW CAR AGAINST YOUR WISHES...
WE USED YOUR PHONE NUMBER WHEN REQUESTING THOSE CATALOGS...
...SO I'M SURE YOU'LL GET PLENTY OF SALES CALLS.
IT'LL BE FINE! THEY HAVE A JOB TO DO, TOO. I DON'T MIND!
AND STARTING THE NEXT DAY...

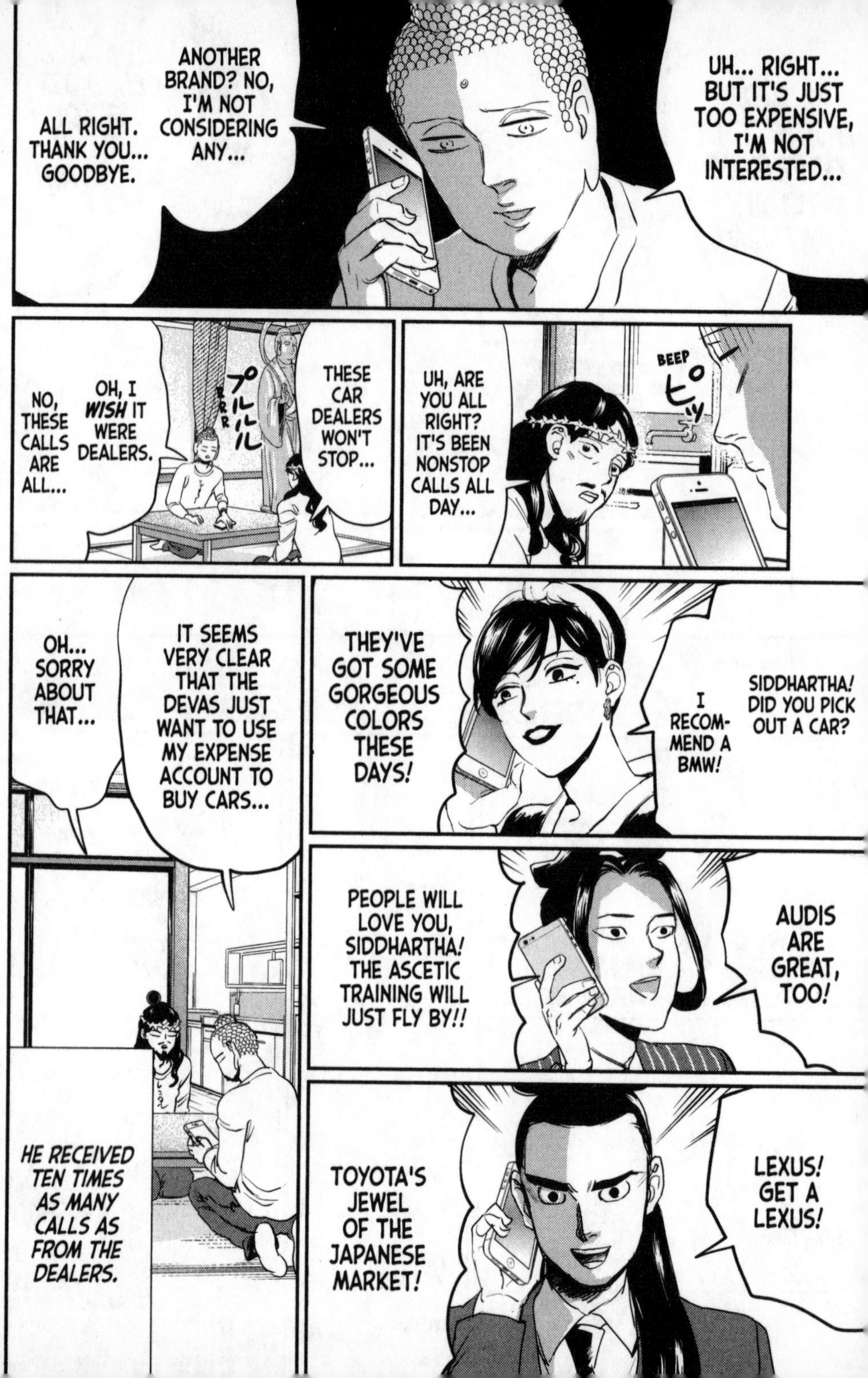

UH... RIGHT... BUT IT'S JUST TOO EXPENSIVE, I'M NOT INTERESTED...
ANOTHER BRAND? NO, I'M NOT CONSIDERING ANY...
ALL RIGHT. THANK YOU... GOODBYE.
BEEP
ピッ
UH, ARE YOU ALL RIGHT? IT'S BEEN NONSTOP CALLS ALL DAY...
THESE CAR DEALERS WON'T STOP...
プルルル
RRR
OH, I *WISH* IT WERE DEALERS.
NO, THESE CALLS ARE ALL...
SIDDHARTHA! DID YOU PICK OUT A CAR?
I RECOMMEND A BMW!
THEY'VE GOT SOME GORGEOUS COLORS THESE DAYS!
AUDIS ARE GREAT, TOO!
PEOPLE WILL LOVE YOU, SIDDHARTHA! THE ASCETIC TRAINING WILL JUST FLY BY!!
LEXUS! GET A LEXUS!
TOYOTA'S JEWEL OF THE JAPANESE MARKET!
IT SEEMS VERY CLEAR THAT THE DEVAS JUST WANT TO USE MY EXPENSE ACCOUNT TO BUY CARS...
OH... SORRY ABOUT THAT...
HE RECEIVED TEN TIMES AS MANY CALLS AS FROM THE DEALERS.

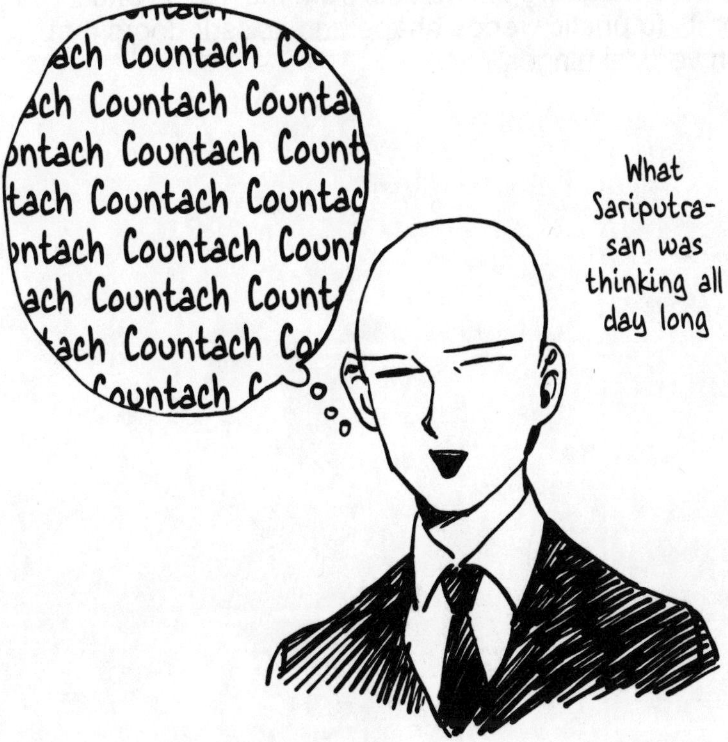
Countach
Countach
Countach
Countach
Countach
Countach
Countach
Countach
What Sariputra-san was thinking all day long

SAINT☆YOUNG MEN

CHAPTER 103 TRANSLATION NOTES

Muted hooves, page 112
One of the features of Buddha's horse Kanthaka is said to be two *yaksha* spirits that support his hooves, keeping them off of the ground and thus silent as he runs.

Countach, page 125
One of the signature Lamborghini models from the 1970s and '80s, famous for its futuristic wedge shape and scissor doors that open upward on vertical hinges.

CLAMP

1 Chobits

20TH ANNIVERSARY EDITION

Chobits © CLAMP·ShigatsuTsuitachi CO.,LTD./Kodansha Ltd.

Poor college student Hideki is down on his luck. All he wants is a
good job, a girlfriend, and his very own "persocom"—the latest
and greatest in humanoid computer technology. Hideki's luck
changes one night when he finds Chi—a persocom thrown out in
a pile of trash. But Hideki soon discovers that there's much more
to his cute new persocom than meets the eye.

KC
KODANSHA
COMICS

Young characters and steampunk setting, like *Howl's Moving Castle* and *Battle Angel Alita*

Beyond the Clouds © 2018 Nicke / Ki-oon

A boy with a talent for machines and a mysterious girl whose wings he's fixed will take you beyond the clouds! In the tradition of the high-flying, resonant adventure stories of Studio Ghibli comes a gorgeous tale about the longing of young hearts for adventure and friendship!

The boys are back, in 400-page hardcovers that are as pretty and badass as they are!

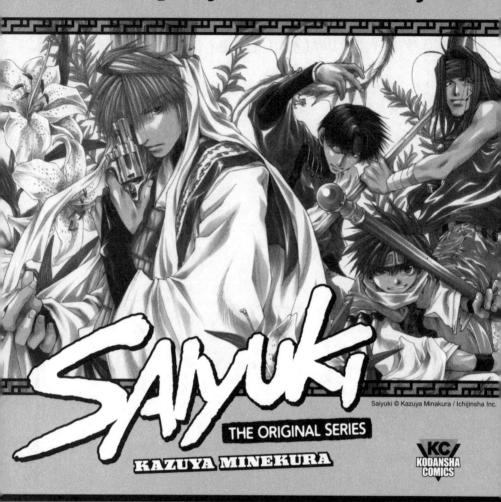

Saiyuki © Kazuya Minekura / Ichijinsha Inc.

THE ORIGINAL SERIES

KAZUYA MINEKURA

"AN EDGY COMIC LOOK AT AN ANCIENT CHINESE TALE." —YALSA

Genjo Sanzo is a Buddhist priest in the city of Togenkyo, which is being ravaged by yokai spirits that have fallen out of balance with the natural order. His superiors send him on a journey far to the west to discover why this is happening and how to stop it. His companions are three yokai with human souls. But this is no day trip — the four will encounter many discoveries and horrors on the way.

FEATURES NEW TRANSLATION, COLOR PAGES, AND BEAUTIFUL WRAPAROUND COVER ART!

PERFECT WORLD

Rie Aruga

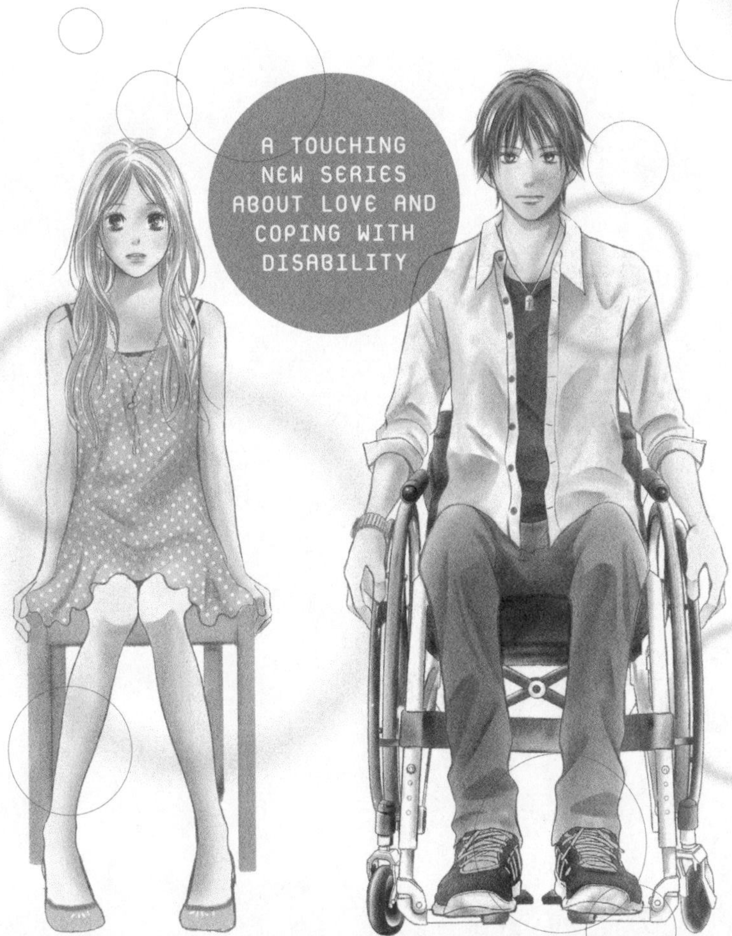
A TOUCHING NEW SERIES ABOUT LOVE AND COPING WITH DISABILITY

An office party reunites Tsugumi with her high school crush Itsuki. He's realized his dream of becoming an architect, but along the way, he experienced a spinal injury that put him in a wheelchair. Now Tsugumi's rekindled feelings will butt up against prejudices she never considered — and Itsuki will have to decide if he's ready to let someone into his heart...

"Depicts with great delicacy and courage the difficulties some with disabilities experience getting involved in romantic relationships... Rie Aruga refuses to romanticize, pushing her heroine to face the reality of disability. She invites her readers to the same tasks of empathy, knowledge and recognition."
—Slate.fr

"An important entry [in manga romance]... The emotional core of both plot and characters indicates thoughtfulness... [Aruga's] research is readily apparent in the text and artwork, making this feel like a real story."
—Anime News Network

KC KODANSHA COMICS

Saint Young Men 7 copyright © 2016-2017 Hikaru Nakamura
English translation copyright © 2021 Hikaru Nakamura

Published in the United States by Kodansha Comics, an imprint of Kodansha USA Publishing, LLC, New York.

Publication rights for this English edition arranged through Kodansha Ltd., Tokyo.

First published in Japan in 2016-2017 by Kodansha Ltd., Tokyo as *Seinto oniisan*, volumes 13 & 14.

ISBN 978-1-64651-231-7

Original cover design by Hiroshi Niigami (NARTI;S)

Printed in the United States of America.

www.kodansha.us

9 8 7 6 5 4 3 2 1
Translation: Stephen Paul
Lettering: E.K. Weaver
Editing: Nathaniel Gallant
Kodansha Comics edition cover design by Phil Balsman

Publisher: Kiichiro Sugawara

Director of publishing services: Ben Applegate
Associate director of operations: Stephen Pakula
Publishing services managing editors: Alanna Ruse, Madison Salters
Production managers: Emi Lotto, Angela Zurlo